MW00720161

DIRECTOR 7

DEMYSTIFIED

The Official Guide to Macromedia Director, Lingo, and Shockwave

JASON ROBERTS & PHIL GROSS

macromedia®
PRESS

Director 7 Demystified
The Official Guide to Macromedia Director, Lingo, and Shockwave
Jason Roberts & Phil Gross

 Published by Macromedia Press,
in association with Peachpit Press, a division of Addison Wesley Longman.

Macromedia Press
1249 Eighth Street
Berkeley, CA 94710

510/524-2178 • 800-283-9444
510/524-2221 (fax)

Find us on the World Wide Web at: **http://www.peachpit.com**
http://www.macromedia.com

Find the *Director 7 Demystified* Web site at: **http://www.demystified.com**

Editor: Lisa Theobald
Copy Editor: Judy Ziajka
Interior Design: Jason Roberts, Mimi Heft
Production Coordinators: Lisa Brazieal, Mimi Heft
Compositor: David Van Ness
Cover Design: Tolleson Design
Index: Steve Rath

ISBN 0-201-35445-4

9 8 7 6 5 4 3 2 1

Printed and bound in the United States of America

for
PATRICIA LOUISE
ma jolie

and

MARTHA KUHL
my constant companion

MEL AND SHEP HOUGHTON
ALEX GROSS
JOHN AND LYN KUHL
who made us who we are

ACKNOWLEDGMENTS

No project of this magnitude ever gets done by one or two people, even if we are the ones who get the credit. From the people who help us get through our daily lives and tolerate us as we struggle along, to the people who encourage us and coax us to let go of the next chapter, to those who provide us with all of the necessary information, this book has been the collaboration of some very talented and very special people.

At Peachpit Press: Thanks to the following people: Lisa Theobald, who kept the work flowing and everything in order with infinite patience and without resorting to the big stick; Marjorie Baer, who found the time to give personal attention, advice, and support whenever it was needed; Judy Ziajka, an excellent editor who asks all the right questions all the time; Carol Henry, whose proofreading skills polished the text into fine shape; Mimi Heft and Lisa Brazieal, production coordinators who kept the book on track and looking good; David Van Ness, the fastest and most excellent compositor in the world; and Victor Gavenda, whose technical expertise made the CD possible.

At Macromedia: Peri Cumali has read every word and offered many useful suggestions to keep us from straying. Thanks to Karen Tucker, Suzanne Porta, Buzz Kettles, Bud Colligan, and others at Macromedia, especially all of the engineers who answered everyone's questions during the beta-version development process.

Last, but not least, is Mike Gross, who took a great deal of time out of his life to help this book along. He's the one that gets the credit for ordering rewrites of ambiguous paragraphs, finding misstatements, and generally making sure that everything is included and accurate.

CONTENTS AT A GLANCE

TABLE OF CONTENTS

BOOK 1: DIRECTOR BASICS

Chapter 1: A Guided Tour of Director   3

Chapter 2: The Elements of Animation · 43

Project Profile 1: Oracle Screensaver · 79

Chapter 3: Making It Multimedia · 91

Chapter 4: Introducing Interactivity   121

Chapter 5: Introducing Shockwave 159

Chapter 6: Deeper into Graphics 189

Chapter 7: More Production Tools   251

BOOK 2: DIGGING DEEPER

Chapter 8: The Anatomy of Lingo — 283

Chapter 9: The Elements of Scripting — 311

Chapter 10: Building the Interactive Movie   359

Chapter 11: Deeper into Lingo   407

Project Profile 2: Levi's Screensaver   451

Chapter 12: Other Lingo Flavors   467

Chapter 13: Working with Multiple Movies and Casts   493

Chapter 14: Scripting with Net-Savvy Lingo 529

Chapter 15: Deeper into Shockwave 551

BOOK 3: SPECIAL TOPICS

Chapter 16: Lingo and Lists   589

Chapter 17: Debugging and Troubleshooting   607

Project Profile 3: Universal Import   641

Chapter 18: Parent/Child Lingo   651

Chapter 21: Extracurricular Lingo: Xtras 757

Chapter 22: Professional Topics and Techniques 787

REFERENCE

Appendix A: Director Resources on the Internet 809

INTRODUCTION

LIFE BEING VERY SHORT, AND THE QUIET HOURS OF IT FEW,
we ought to waste none of them in reading valueless books.

—John Ruskin (1819–1900)

ADVENTURES ON THE LEARNING CURVE

What you have in your hands is a book about Director 7, the authoring software created and marketed by Macromedia that enables you to develop multimedia and Web-based productions. That shiny round thing on the inside back cover is an interactive CD, packed with learning materials, samples, and resources for creativity. Together, the book and CD make up a multimedia approach to (ta da!) multimedia.

This is a cross-platform book, appropriate for both the Windows and Macintosh (MacOS) operating systems.

Director is marketed in versions for the Windows and Macintosh operating systems (MacOS). The two products are remarkably similar, with the commands, menus, and underlying principles practically identical for both platforms. Although the screenshots for this book were taken on a Windows system, all the information applies to Windows and MacOS alike. In the few instances where the platforms diverge, separate instructions are given for each.

In the pages to come (and on that shiny disk), we'll try to live up to the title of *Director 7 Demystified*. It's more than a nifty alliteration; it's a summation of the goals of this project. Both the interface and the concepts behind Director can be pretty intimidating, and all the hype about multimedia in general seems to breed a lot of confusion and muddled expectations.

Our task as co-authors is to slice through the abstractions and buzzwords and get down to business. Director may seem like a monolithic development platform, but ultimately it's just a tool, one that works as well in your hands as in anyone's.

What's new in this edition?

If you're familiar with previous editions of this book, you should know that this edition of *Demystified* represents a substantial revision and expansion with the release of Director 7. Even the appendixes alone, which include a *complete* lexicon of Director commands, functions, and properties, contains nearly 200 new elements.

This volume consists of three books plus a reference section:

- **Book One: Director Basics** focuses on mastery of the mechanics of Director, leading you to a working familiarity with all of its features and an understanding of how to build productions complete with animation, sound effects, and a degree of interactivity. If you've never used Director, you'll find this section invaluable. If you're an old Director hand, you'll still find it a worthwhile refresher; the interface in Director 7 departs significantly from that of earlier versions; you may find yourself not knowing your way around.

- **Book Two: Digging Deeper** eases you over the next hill on the learning curve: a firm understanding of Lingo, Director's powerful scripting language. Everything you need to gain proficiency in Lingo is here, from basic tutorials to advanced scripting exercises. And if you've never worked with a computer language before, you'll probably appreciate the in-depth discussion of the concepts behind programming.

- **Book Three: Special Topics** takes you deeper into Director by expanding on individual topics. Here you will find in-depth discussions of some specialized Lingo elements, such as lists, and the essentials of Director's built-in error-tracking and resolving capabilities, to help you debug your productions. You'll also find chapters to help you integrate sound and video into your productions. Information on Xtras will help you expand on Director's capabilities, and the final chapter will give you hints on how to avoid some common problems that plague productions, especially larger ones.

- The **Reference** section provides an assortment of useful appendices. Appendix C, "A Lingo Lexicon," is a book in itself. In it, Lingo terms are defined by type, with the various types thumbmarked for easy access. All Director commands, functions, and properties are described and shown with the appropriate syntax. Examples are given for each element to help you integrate the elements into your productions.

HOW TO USE THIS BOOK AND CD

The information and exercises in this book should take you from a raw beginner to someone able to author interactive CDs, Web pages, and other professional-level applications. The book is designed to have three lives: as a tutorial (with multiple exercises), as an inspiration (see the Project Profiles), and as a reference (hence, the substantial appendixes).

You could start with Chapter 1 and work your way through to Chapter 22, dipping into the CD only when directed to do so. But why opt for the boring linear approach to learning a nonlinear medium? Instead, we recommend taking the following steps:

- **Play**. Ignore the text at first. Just fire up the CD and play the arcade-style game Simple Invaders. Or experience the exploration-friendly interface of the Universal Import Demo. Each of the projects profiled were created with Director, so you'll be getting a feel for the software's creative potential—while having fun.

- **Peruse**. Skim the chapters, and don't bother with the exercises or even absorb the jargon. You'll get used to seeing the workings of Director in many manifestations, and you'll get a clearer picture of the conceptual terrain ahead.

- **Plow through**. Start at the beginning and work through the exercises chapter by chapter. As you progress, you may find that new levels of knowledge give you fresh ideas for real-world projects. You might want to have a notebook handy to write down your bright ideas, so you don't get sidetracked too long by the glittering potential unfolding before you.

What the symbols mean

Like most computer books nowadays, *Director 7 Demystified* employs a bit of custom iconography to guide the roving eye.

This indicates a helpful **suggestion**—not something that you necessarily have to pay attention to, but a bit of advice. It pertains not only to Director, but to other software as well.

This is the **Fast Forward** symbol, indicating a useful shortcut, such as a keystroke alternative to a menu command.

 This is the **key concept** icon, and it means Pay Attention. This Is Important Stuff to Remember.

 The check mark is a **reminder**, meant to head off possible problems. These sections usually point out common misconceptions or oversights, not potentially serious errors.

 The **see elsewhere** arrow points you to other sections in the book and CD. It often indicates where a topic is discussed more fully or where a file illustrating a principle can be found.

 The **explanation** icon indicates a curiosity-quenching passage—not a tip or a warning, but a bit of background.

 The **Try** icon denotes an optional activity that further illustrates a feature or principle.

 The **new feature** icon indicates that the action or function being discussed is either new or significantly revised in version 7. As some of the differences are substantial, those of you familiar with earlier versions (up to 6.0) should make a point of reading these sections.

  The **Windows** and **MacOS** icons call attention to information specific to each of those platforms.

 The **Yikes!** symbol pops up only when real caution is necessary—when a misstep or oversight could lead to data loss, massive time wasting, legal problems, or other hassles. Ignore these sections at your peril.

Most of the icons draw your eye to statements in the margin of the pages, but others point to **sidebars** like the one you're reading right now. The format distinction is primarily one of length.

In addition to the icons, *Director 7 Demystified* has a cast of characters… well, *one* character, to be exact.

MEET SWIFTY:
This energetic fellow is a character adapted from the pioneering photographs of Eadweard Muybridge.

This character is named **Swifty**, an apt appellation for someone as mobile and agile as he is. Swifty is the star of most of the tutorials, and we mention his name not to be cutesy, but because we'll be referring to him directly in the pages to come, saying "place Swifty on the Stage," rather than "place the animated sequence of the little walking man on the Stage."

Swifty is a collection of symbols of a human figure (walking, running, jumping, and so on) based on the historical work of Eadweard Muybridge (that's really how he spelled it). Muybridge was the nineteenth-century artist and inventor who first used a sequence of cameras to capture authentic motion, thus paving the way for the motion picture.

The CD component

Many of the contributors to the CD-ROM have not only created some pretty amazing stuff; they've graciously submitted their work in nonprotected form. That means you can muck about in their files and see not only what they did, but exactly how they went about doing it.

Although the contributors to the Gallery section of the CD have provided their projects in open form, they haven't given up the copyrights to their work. That means that you can browse through their files, learn from them, and copy them onto your hard drive—but please don't plunder them for your own projects.

The demystified.com Web site

As version 7 amply demonstrates, Director has become much more than an animation application. It's now a complete Web/Internet development environment, able to integrate media spread across a worldwide network as easily as it can coordinate files drawn from your hard drive. That's why we're maintaining a dedicated Web site at http://www.demystified.com.

This site serves a number of purposes:

- It's an online location for *networked media*. In the latter part of this book, you'll find exercises that download and manipulate media stored here. You can, of course, perform such snazzy Web tricks anywhere, but using the media provided simplifies the learning process for you.

- It's a *bulletin board* for late-breaking information on Macromedia Director (bug fixes, new versions, and so on) and its related technologies.

- It's a *forum* for corrections, clarifications, and enhancements to this book. If you're puzzled by something on these pages, check out the site: We may have something that clears up the matter. If we don't, drop us a line and let us know; you'll find contact information at the demystified.com Web site.

Comments? Suggestions?

If you have comments, questions, or reports of inconsistencies, or even suggestions of topics you would like to see placed on the Web site or in the next version of the book, you can contact me (Phil Gross) by e-mail. I can't guarantee an instantaneous response (I have a very busy vacation schedule that puts me out of the country and out of touch at times), but I'll do my best. You can contact me at pgross@jps.net

PRELUDE

THE DIRECTOR UNIVERSE

BEFORE YOU START GETTING UP TO YOUR ELBOWS IN TERMS AND techniques, let's take a few pages to put Director in perspective. In this prelude, we'll together trace the development of the software from modest animation tool to driving engine of the multimedia industry. We'll look at the features Director has added over the years and bluntly assess its strengths and weaknesses. Finally, we'll preview some of the many changes and new features that debuted with the latest version of Director.

DIRECTOR DEFINED

Macromedia Director belongs to a specialized genre: software used to create other software. As such, it's often referred to as an *authoring tool* or a *development platform*. Armed with only a copy of Director and your imagination, it's possible to create a fully self-contained, self-running program—and since Director is available in both MacOS- and Windows-compatible versions, it's relatively easy to produce work that runs on both Macintosh computers and PCs.

Since Director can incorporate sound as well as still and moving images, these productions are usually called *multimedia*. Furthermore, since they can include a high degree of user feedback, the double buzzword *interactive multimedia* is often applied. But interactivity isn't a given, and the term *multimedia* doesn't always apply; you could create a noninteractive work consisting of a single medium (such as a slide show of photographs), and Director would accommodate you nicely—so don't get hung up on buzzwords.

In the multimedia marketplace, Director has long been the standard authoring tool, used not just for developing CDs, but for creating special effects and for adding a whole new dimension to otherwise static pages on the World Wide Web. Some multimedia tools are useful only for disk-based production, but Macromedia has been aggressively retooling and upgrading Director to meet the growing need for Internet/intranet multimedia. As you'll discover for yourself, Director 7 has enough online features to make it an essential tool for Webmasters everywhere.

An authoring platform can be pretty nifty, but the real software power-houses are *computer languages* (such as C++, Pascal, and Java). Both can create free-standing software, but a language can more fully employ the raw number-crunching power of the computer. Still, the border between platforms and languages is starting to blur, especially in the case of Director, which includes Lingo, a built-in command syntax that, over the years, has evolved to qualify as a language of its own.

What's so special about Director?

Director may have a pioneering history as a multimedia tool, but history doesn't count for much with today's breakneck pace of software development and marketing. Plenty of competing authoring platforms have risen up to challenge it—and frankly, most of them, such as SuperCard, Apple Media Toolkit, and Quark/mFactory's mTropolis, haven't made much of a dent in Director's dominance. So why does Director remain king of the heap?

Superior animation

Director produces graphic motion with the same techniques as used by conventional animators: It places elements on individual layers and moves them through the scene one frame at a time. This can mean a laborious development process, but the end results are objects that move (and interact) in a believable fashion. Some authoring platforms don't use a frame-by-frame metaphor, opting instead for icons of specific screens (connected by linkages). That provides a faster way of developing an interactive infrastructure, but the finer elements of action are usually harder to control. With Director 7, the degree of control is even further refined, with new features that let you precisely synchronize sound and motion, twist and turn images, and include new image types. When it comes to setting images in motion, Director offers a clear advantage.

Royalty-free distribution

All files created with Director can be freely sold and distributed, without having to pay Macromedia a royalty for the privilege. That may be something you take for granted—after all, you don't pay Microsoft a royalty for a novel written with Microsoft Word—but some development platforms actually have licensing provisos that stipulate that you have to pay in order to market anything created with that product. Macromedia doesn't demand a piece of the action with Director-based works, but it does stipulate that a special "Made with Macromedia" logo be displayed on your work's packaging (the logo is included, in file form, on the CD that accompanies this book).

THE LABEL TO LOOK FOR: Rather than demanding a royalty on all products created with Director, Macromedia asks that this logo be incorporated into the product packaging.

Cross-system portability

As you probably know, not all software runs on all computers. There are different operating systems, and most software is designed to be compatible with just one of them. Some software products are "ported" from one system to another (usually Macintosh to Windows, or vice versa), but these new versions tend to be complete ground-up rewrites that bear only a surface resemblance to the original version. Such porting can be a very costly process.

Throughout this book, we'll use *MacOS* to refer to the operating system used by both Apple Macintosh models and third-party clones (such as Motorola and Power Computing), and *Windows* to refer to Windows 95, Windows 98, and Windows NT (as opposed to Windows CE or Windows 3.1), used by just about everyone else. Director no longer supports Window versions prior to Windows 95 or Macintosh systems prior to version 7.6.1.

When multimedia started to come into its own as an industry, developers were in a bit of a quandary. The Macintosh offered superior graphics capabilities, so it was the operating system of choice for designers and animators. But as target audiences go, the Macintosh-owning population is far outnumbered by those with Windows-compatible machines. Was it possible to combine the best of both worlds, by building multimedia on the Macintosh and then translating it into Windows-ready files?

Director made this possible, and with a minimum of headaches and hassles. Originally, a MacOS-based Director file could be ported to Windows with a special application called Player for Windows. Now there are two versions of Director (one for MacOS and one for Windows), and files created by one can be opened directly by the other and saved in a stand-alone form for either platform. The conversion process isn't completely seamless, but it's pretty close, and it sure beats rewriting the project from scratch. And when you store both versions on the same CD, you can market a single disk that plays on both Windows and MacOS machines.

How can Director provide such a smooth transition between the disparate worlds of these operating systems? The answer lies in the structure of its code, which includes an *Idealized Machine Layer* (IML). The IML is a sort of toolbox that maximizes portability by keeping the multimedia data isolated from the system-specific data (the Java language works on a similar principle, as does HTML). In its anticipation of the conversion process, the IML makes it possible to offer compatibility not only with Windows, but with a multitude of operating systems—including ones that don't yet exist. Apple and Microsoft are hard at work developing the next generation of their operating systems, and the IML approach makes it likely that no matter what new technical twists ensue, Director won't be left in the dust of obsolescence. So you can see why learning Director is worthwhile, despite the steep learning curve. It may not be the dominant development tool forever, but Director expertise isn't likely to be a dead-end street any time soon.

Shockwave: Director's Net result

For more information about Shockwave, see Chapters 5, 14, and 15.

Here's where Director's adaptability starts to get truly exciting: Director movies can now be ported to the platform where the *real* action is: the Internet, or more specifically, to the multimedia-hungry World Wide Web. With the advent of Shockwave technology, a Director movie can be seamlessly integrated into a Web page; anyone with a properly configured Web browser can interact with the movie while viewing the page. Converting Director movies with Shockwave is fast and easy and requires only a splash of specialized knowledge.

In the online interactivity field, Shockwave's primary competition is Sun Microsystems' Java scripting language. But Java requires multimedia to be remade from scratch (and has a steep learning curve), whereas Shockwave is essentially another porting process for Director. Most Director productions can be saved as Shockwave files, with only the limitations built into the browsers and the Internet to consider. Shockwave is probably the quickest way to turn multimedia into Internet content, and that's generating a lot of excitement and experimentation.

The X factor: Extensibility and external control

If you want to improve your hardware's performance, it's pretty easy to make incremental advances. You can just plug in a peripheral or add new memory or even speed up the CPU with an upgrade card. Usually, it's only after several years that the itch arises to chuck it all and start afresh.

Computer software tends to be a different story, however. Capabilities aren't added incrementally: They're clustered together in a new incarnation of the product (which instantly renders the old one obsolete). You can't take some of the neat new features of ThingMaker 7.5 and add them to your copy of ThingMaker 7.0—you have to throw out 7.0 to make way for 7.5.

For more information about Xtras, see Chapter 21: *Extracurricular Lingo: Xtras.*

Director isn't immune to these numbered-version incarnations, but it does offer the ability to employ special classes of software, called *Xtras*. Xtras are self-contained subapplications written specifically to extend or improve upon Director's features. Some are created by Macromedia, but many others are produced by third-party programmers. Once installed on your system, Xtras show up in Director's user interface, and working with them simply becomes part of working in Director. Using Xtras is kind of like adding extra blades to your Swiss Army Knife: Each one has a special purpose and can be whipped out when you need it.

It's in the script: The growth of Lingo

Why is English the dominant language of international commerce? Not because it's easy to learn (or even spell), but because of its massive and growing vocabulary. It's the same with Lingo: Director's unique scripting language may have started out as a close cousin to HyperTalk and SmallTalk, but it's definitely come into its own over the years.

Up until Director 7, while many new features have been added to Lingo with every update, the core syntax has remained very stable. Now, with Director 7, you have a whole new syntax at your disposal: *dot syntax*. This new syntax allows you to create scripts that are more like those created by object-oriented programming languages such as C++ and Java. The new dot syntax doesn't replace the older Lingo syntax; the two co-exist, and you can use either one or a combination of both—whatever feels more comfortable to you.

Nowadays, you'll find three distinct types of Lingo:

- **Core Lingo**, the scripting syntax and terminology that's built into Director itself—no extra ingredients are necessary.

- **NetLingo**, language developed to integrate Shockwave movies into the Internet environment. These terms tend to have a slightly different kind of syntax, as they're required to work in conformance with the file-serving standards prevalent on the Net.

- **Xtra Lingo**, which is simply additional language elements made comprehensible to Director thanks to an Xtra file. These elements aren't "official" Lingo—just custom vocabularies that are programmed to work in the context of scripting. Any adept programmer can write Xtras to provide new Xtra Lingo, and several already have. It's a means of customizing and extending Lingo, but the new terminology will work only so long as the correct Xtra is installed.

WHAT'S NEW IN DIRECTOR 7

With every release of Director, a number of new capabilities are added. The release of Director 7 is no different, except that even more new features were added this time than with most previous releases. As we go to press, more additions were made with the release of Director 7.0.2, including QuickTime 4 support and MPEG 3 sound streaming. If you have version 7.0, a free update is available from the Macromedia Web site at www.macromedia.com. It's well worth downloading for the fixes that have been made to 7.0 as well as for the new capabilities.

Here's a rundown of what's new:

- **Sprite skewing and rotation**. You can now set the rotation or skew of a sprite directly in the Score. If you set either or both for a sprite's keyframes, Director will automatically tween the value over the duration of the sprite segment. You can also rotate or skew a sprite at runtime using the rotation and skew properties.

- **More sprite channels and a higher frame rate**. You can now have up to 1,000 sprite channels, enabling you to create movies that are much more complex than movies you could create in previous versions. Using the Movie Properties dialog box, you can determine just how many channels you want to use, so Director doesn't need to check a large number of unused channels. Frame rates up to 999 frames per second can be specified in the tempo channel, although there is no guarantee that any given system will be able to support animation at that rate. You can also use the puppetTempo command to set frame rates up to a theoretical limit of 30,000 frames per second.

- **Preview in a browser**. Creating movies that will be played in a browser? Now you can use the Preview in Browser command (on the File menu) to quickly see how your movie will look or perform. No more having to create a Shockwave movie and the necessary HTML file before being able to inspect your movie; Director creates the necessary (temporary) files, including the HTML file, and invokes the browser for you.

- **Animated GIF and Flash movies**. You can now include animated GIF and Flash movies in your productions. They appear as cast members in the Cast and can be controlled through the Score or through Lingo.

- **Lingo changes**. Big changes have been made in the realm of Director's Lingo programming language. One of the biggest changes is the adoption of a new syntax called *dot property* or *dot syntax*. This new syntax allows you to write scripts that more closely resemble those of other object-oriented programming languages and that are more concise and easier to read. Add to that the use of the equals operator (=) for assignment of values and the use of square brackets for accessing lists, and anyone familiar with other programming languages will be right at home with Lingo. New Lingo elements (upward of 180 new elements since Director 6.0) provide improved network access, sprite rotation and skewing, and alpha channel support. Other new elements provide extended capabilities for existing operations such as the manipulation of QuickTime and Flash movies.

- **Library Palette**. On top of the improvements to Lingo, Macromedia has added a Library Palette to Director 7. Bring up the Library Palette window, and you have at your fingertips (or mouse click) a wealth of already-written behaviors for controlling the user interface, navigating through your movie, performing network operations, and executing other useful functions.

- **Text changes**. Text handling in Director continues to improve. Now you can have good-looking anti-aliased text fields that can be edited by the end user. The contents of a text field are limited by system memory rather than by any built-in Director limitation, so you can accommodate large amounts of text. And the text itself is stored in a form that is smaller than before, and it can include embedded fonts so you can be sure the font you designed for is available at runtime. In addition to previously supported Rich Text Format (RTF), Director now also supports many of the common tags used to format HTML documents.

- **Alpha channel support**. You can import 32-bit images from such applications as Photoshop or Fireworks and include an alpha channel along with the image. The alpha channel can be used to provide varying degrees of transparency for an image (like looking through a stained-glass window) or to determine which areas of an image detect mouse clicks.

- **New color support**. Director 7 allows you to specify colors using standard RGB values rather than limiting you to colors specified using a palette index. When a color is specified as an RGB color, it always will be displayed correctly if the color depth is 16 or 32 bits. On an 8-bit system, Director will map the RGB color to the closest available color on the current color palette.

- **Vector shapes**. Director has added vector shapes as a new type of image that can be used as an alternative to bitmaps. Vector shapes are anti-aliased, just like bitmaps, but they require a lot less memory and can be resized without the distortion normal to bitmaps. You can import vector shapes (from FreeHand, for example) or create them in Director's Vector Shape editor. You can modify vector shapes, or even create them from scratch, using the generous supply of Lingo elements provided to work with them.

- **JPEG and GIF compression**. JPEG and GIF images are now stored using their original compression, making them easier to download and store.

- **Web palette**. A new built-in palette, named Web 216, provides a set of colors for 8-bit display that are based on the palettes used by the major browsers. If you stick to the Web 216 palette, you can minimize any color problems that might otherwise occur when you play your movie over the Internet.

- **Multiuser applications**. The Multiuser Server Xtra allows you to create movies that can communicate with other movies being played on the Internet. It's now easy to create multiuser games, chat rooms, or other projects that can share information about what other users are doing. The Director Studio version even includes behaviors on the Library Palette just for this purpose.

BOOK 1:

DIRECTOR BASICS

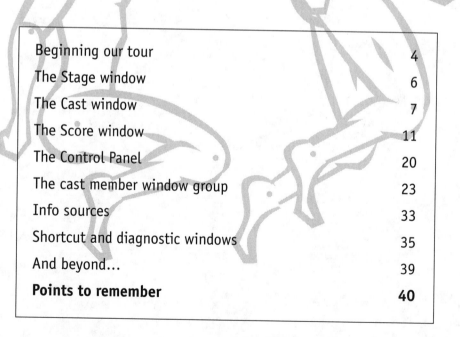

CHAPTER 1

A GUIDED TOUR OF DIRECTOR

NOW THAT WE'VE DEFINED DIRECTOR AND DELVED INTO ITS HISTORY, IT'S time to get comfortably acquainted with the software itself. We'll start experimenting with Director in Chapter 2, and we'll get down to work in Chapter 3—but in this chapter, we'll be exploring Director's onscreen presence. With a multitude of windows, menus, and menu choices, it takes a bit of orientation to navigate within Director with confidence.

We'll take an extended tour of the program, looking at its main elements to see how they work together. Along the way, you'll be introduced to the key concepts and principles behind a Director production.

BEGINNING OUR TOUR

This chapter is essentially a tour of a blank canvas: the one that's created whenever you open a brand-new Director file. Although Director has scads of windows, you'll be doing the bulk of your work with these four: the Score, the Stage, the Control Panel, and a Cast. But before you can start, you'll need to start Director.

> If you're the type that can't see a canvas without wanting to paint on it, you may find yourself growing restless after a few pages. If so, feel free to skip ahead to Chapter 2: *The Elements of Animation*, and refer back to this chapter when you feel the need. If you've worked with earlier versions of Director, this chapter is skimming material...so long as you're familiar with Director's multitudinous windows and dialog boxes and how they interrelate.

Starting up

If you've installed Director according to Macromedia's instructions, you should be able to launch the application simply by double-clicking its icon in the Director folder. If, however, your startup isn't successful, try the following:

- Double-check your application icon. Are you launching Director 7 or some earlier version?

- Check your hardware. Is enough RAM available to run the program? Check the software documentation for the required minimum configuration of hardware and operating software.

- Reinstall Director in a new folder. Director 7's installation procedure is fairly well automated. You should be able to designate a fresh directory as the target for a from-scratch installation and let the program do its work. If that does the trick, delete the folders of earlier installation attempts (but don't attempt to track down and eliminate the various support files that lurk on the system level unless you know what you're doing). It's usually okay to have earlier versions of Director on the same machine.

The four primary windows

There are, of course, minor interface "look and feel" differences between the Macintosh and Windows versions, but when Director is fully launched, your screen should look something like this:

THE SET-UP AT STARTUP:
Most of the action occurs in the Score, the Stage (that big empty space), the Control Panel, and the Cast windows.

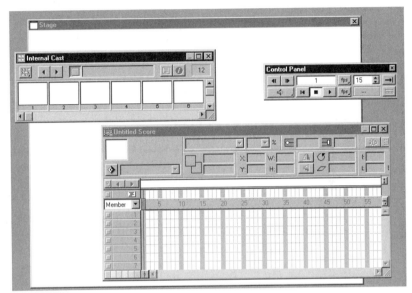

Four main windows should automatically be present upon startup (where they're placed depends on the size of your monitor). If your software isn't freshly installed, not all of these windows may appear—and additional ones may show up. For the purpose of our tour, you should close any extraneous windows and (if necessary) use the Windows menu to open the Stage, Control Panel, Cast, and Score windows.

OPEN A WINDOW:
Director's four main windows can be opened from the Window menu.

Not all Director windows go into hibernation when they're no longer active. Work that you do in the active window can affect changes in other windows as well, and sometimes a window that seems active isn't.

THE REAL PANE:
A minor change in one Director window can mean big changes in another, so tread carefully until you're aware of the full consequences of your actions.

As a rule of thumb, whenever it looks like your input (typing, mouse movements) isn't registering, take a quick survey of all open windows before proceeding. It may be that you're inadvertently making entries in an unintended location. Since Director 7 doesn't offer multiple layers of undo, I also highly recommend using the Save As function to make copies of your files whenever you're experimenting with variations.

THE STAGE WINDOW

That central void is the **Stage window**, where the end result of your work is displayed. It's the screen on which Director movies are projected; if you're creating a self-running piece of software, the Stage window is the universe in which that software will exist. Quite literally, this is where the action is.

What can you do to the Stage? You can change its color and size, and you can reconfigure it in a number of ways to suit the needs of a project. As a quick exploration, let's resize it right now.

RESETTING THE STAGE:
You can use the Movie Properties dialog box to modify the size and location of the Stage window (along with other program parameters).

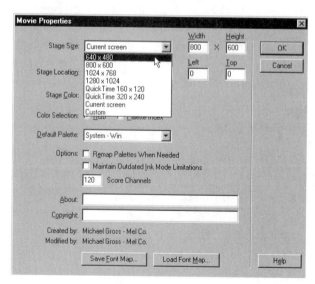

1. *From the Modify menu, select Movie and then Properties.*

2. *In the Movie Properties dialog box, note the current settings for the width and height of the Stage.*

3. *Click the pull-down menu in the Stage Size area.*

4. *Select a Stage size other than the current one.*

5. *Click OK.*

Your Stage should still be a blank screen but with different dimensions. It's possible (not practical, but possible) for a Stage to be larger than the monitor on which it's displayed: if you have a 16-inch screen and you build a 30-inch Stage, the monitor will display only a portion of the window.

6. *Return to the Movie Properties dialog box and restore the previous settings.*

You don't have to reset the Stage dimensions, but if you don't, any new Director files will open with the Stage at the current size. This won't affect existing Director movies (their Stages won't be resized), just those that you create using the New Movie command.

Don't forget to restore the Stage to its original dimensions (unless you prefer it as is).

You can change the Stage size of any movie at any time, but each movie can have only one Stage configuration. If you want your project to incorporate Stages of different shapes and sizes, you'll need to create several movies and link them in sequence—or invoke some programming tricks to create multiple Stages within a single movie (we'll cover those in chapters to come).

THE CAST WINDOW

CAST MEMBERS:
The individual elements that serve as the building blocks of a movie.

The theatrical metaphor that dubs Director's playback screen the Stage continues with the **Cast window** (Control-3 Windows; Command-3 Macintosh). Actually, it's here that the metaphor begins to break down: The Cast might more accurately be called the Cast/Scenery/Props/Musical Instrument Department. Essentially, everything that goes into a multimedia production can reside in the Cast:

- **Still graphics** (artwork or photo scans).

- **Sounds** (in digitized form).

- **Interface elements** (such as buttons and icons).

- **Text.** You can even use the Cast to manipulate text that doesn't yet exist, such as quiz answers the end user will eventually enter. A blank field (the empty container for future input) can be a full-fledged Text cast member. You should also know that there's more than one kind of text used in Director (we'll explore the different types in a bit).

- **Digital Video** (in the form of QuickTime and AVI movies).

- **Animation** (as PICS files or as Director film loops).

- **Palettes.** If you want to use a certain group of colors in your movie, you can designate that group as a palette, which is then saved as a single cast member.

- Director movies can even include **other Director movies** in the Cast. That means you can nest one multimedia production within another and then play back both at once.

- This strains the metaphor even further, but cast member status is also extended to commands themselves. These units are known as **scripts** (and sometimes **behaviors**). A command can be as small as a single word (such as "beep"), or as long as a run-on sentence. A script can incorporate lines and lines of commands in what seems like arcane code. These scripts are written in Lingo, the Director command language that we mentioned in the Prelude. You'll dive into the world of Lingo in Chapter 4: *Introducing Interactivity.*

Scared of scripting...or just in a hurry? Director 7 comes with ready-made scripts, called **behaviors**, that are fairly easy to use. Once you get your Lingo legs, you'll find these behaviors very useful, and later in the book you'll be properly introduced to them. For now, remember that all behaviors are scripts, although not all scripts are behaviors—it depends on how the script is used.

The Cast window, then, is Director's database of cast members: the visual, aural, and programming elements that you'll coordinate into a multimedia whole. You can add, subtract, and duplicate cast members at any time, and you can import and export them with ease. You don't have to use every cast member in your movie (although hordes of unused cast members can unnecessarily bloat file size).

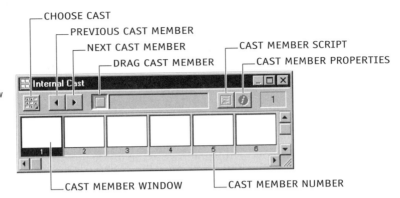

All cast members come into being in one of two ways: You can create them directly in Director, or you can import them from documents created by other applications. In either case, unless you specify otherwise, each is automatically assigned a location in the Cast database and given a cast member number (you can also give them names if you like). Director 7 initially provides 1000 blank slots for cast members, but you're free to add an unlimited amount—which is to say that the software won't provide population limits, but the functional aspects of your computer (processor, storage, and so on) probably will.

Once in the Cast, a cast member can be cut, copied, pasted, deleted, relocated, and modified. Any changes made to a cast member are automatically reflected in that cast member's appearance on the Stage. This means, for example, that if cast member 254 was originally a blue dot and you change it to a red one, all instances of the dot in the Director movie will be changed from blue to red.

If you change a cast member, you change all instances of that cast member on the Stage of your movie.

But the Cast stores more than the cast members. It also contains pertinent information about each cast member (which you can access via the Info or Cast Member Properties button). Another important feature is that the Cast allows you to attach a Lingo script to any cast member; whenever the cast member is clicked on the Stage, Director will automatically execute the script. This is especially useful for items such as buttons, which you want to perform the same functions wherever they're placed.

Okay, time to see if you've been paying attention. If you have, you'll probably note that this last statement contradicts my earlier one. *Wait a second*

THE UBIQUITOUS SCRIPT:
You'll find that Lingo scripts appear both as cast members and attached to cast members—and you'll find them in a number of other locations.

(I hope you're asking yourself)—*first he says that a script can be a cast member. Now he's saying that a script can be attached to a cast member. What gives?*

Well, both statements are correct, and they illustrate a key Director concept: *Lingo is everywhere.* Scripts can pertain to individual cast members, to specific frames in a movie, or to the movie as a whole, and they can reside in a number of nooks and crannies throughout the software. In fact, one of the keys to successful Director production is keeping track of exactly what scripts are in effect at any given time. When a script doesn't seem to work, oftentimes the reason is that somewhere there's another script canceling it out. You'll probably come to view troubleshooting scripts and behaviors as an integral part of the production process.

Embedding, linking, and sharing

Cast members can be **embedded** (physically residing in the Director file) or **linked** (pointing to an external file).

It's important that you understand the distinction between **embedded** cast members and **linked** ones. Since many of the cast members you'll be using will have been created in applications other than Director, such as Photoshop or SoundEdit, you will be importing them into the Cast of your movie. With most file types, you will have the option of importing them as embedded cast members or linked cast members. After a cast member is embedded into Director, the association between the cast member and the original file from which it was imported is destroyed. If you import a file as a linked cast member, on the other hand, only information about the cast member is stored in Director—and part of that stored information is the directions that tell Director where to find the file. In other words, a linked cast member still resides in its original file. When Director is instructed to display (or play) the linked cast member, it retrieves the file from your hard disk, the Internet, or wherever the file is located.

Why would you want to link rather than embed? If the file is quite large (let's say it's a sound file containing several minutes of music), linking will keep down your movie's file size. You can also link the same file to several different movies at the same time. And if you make changes to the source file, the link will automatically be updated the next time you open your movie (there's no need to reimport). The problem with linked files is that you have to keep the linkage intact. If you delete, rename, or just relocate the source file, the link may be lost and you'll have a dysfunctional cast member.

Since digital video files tend to be pretty hefty in both size and RAM requirements, Director automatically imports them as links; embedding is not an option.

Director has the ability to deal with multiple Casts in the context of a single movie and to share Casts between movies. The latter is useful when you have a project involving multiple movies. If the movies have a number of elements in common, you can store them in a single Cast file. Each movie can access those cast members independently.

THE SCORE WINDOW

The Stage may be where your project is manifested—and the Cast is where all the pieces reside—but the **Score window** (Control-4 Windows; Command-4 Macintosh) is where the project really takes shape. When Director runs a movie, all it's doing—for the most part—is interpreting the information in the Score and whisking elements on and off the Stage accordingly. I say "for the most part" because it's possible to create commands that overrule Score information (the "Lingo is everywhere" principle again). But the Score is really Production Central, where the different elements of the Cast are synthesized into that melange known as multimedia.

CHANNELS:
The rows of Score cells.

FRAMES:
The columns in the Score.

As you can see, the Score resembles a spreadsheet with lots of individual **cells** divided into rows and columns. The rows are called **channels**, and the columns are called **frames**. Each column has a number associated with it (they're marked off in shaded, five-column intervals), and each channel begins with either a number or a distinctive icon.

If the **Sprite toolbar** at the top of the Score window is not visible, you can display it by choosing Sprite Toolbar from the View menu.

WHAT'S THE SCORE:
The Score window is
the spreadsheet-like
environment that
Director "reads" while
playing a movie.

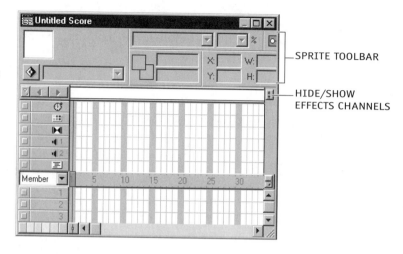

SPRITE TOOLBAR

HIDE/SHOW
EFFECTS CHANNELS

When you open Director, the Score may not display all of the effects
channels (the ones identified with distinctive icons). To bring these into
view, click the small Hide/Show Effects Channels arrows at the right
edge of the Score.

The timeline metaphor

Score information is organized in a strictly linear fashion, even when the
project is a nonlinear interactive movie. Each frame maps out a certain
instance of time during the planned playback; it's not a *specific* time but a
relative one. For instance, frame 15 isn't necessarily 15 seconds into your
movie (although it could be), and it doesn't necessarily represent 1 second of Stage time (although, once again, it could). In short, frame 15 is
simply a set of instructions for what Director should place on the Stage
before frame 16, but after frame 14.

The actual time occupied by the individual frame during playback can be
as little as a thousandth of a second, or as long as...well, forever. Since
you can direct Director to hold a single frame while waiting for user feedback, a frame can be onscreen indefinitely.

The playback head

Take another look at the Score window. Notice that reddish rectangle resting above the numbered channels, at frame 1? That's the **playback head**. The term comes from tape recorders, which have a physical playback head over which the tape passes. At any given moment, the segment of tape passing over the playback head is the segment being played.

THE BLOCK HEAD:
That red block at the top of the numbered channels is the playback head. It moves to indicate the currently active frame.

In Director, the process is a little different than a tape recorder: The information segments remain in place, and the playback head travels to move over them. When you play a Director movie, this block moves through the Score as each frame is placed on the Stage. If you want to know which frame is currently being displayed, look for the playback head.

Understanding channels

Director now allows up to 1000 channels in the Score; versions prior to Director 6 were limited to 256.

To make things happen on the Stage, things have to be placed in cells at various locations throughout the Score. But *what* gets placed, and *where*? That depends on the individual channel. There are six channel types, each designed to hold different types of data. Let's look at them in reverse sequence, from the bottom up.

Visual channels

The channels with no icons, just a number, are the visual channels; they're used to manipulate instances of graphic items. **Instances** is a key term here; the graphics themselves aren't literally pasted into the Score. Instead, they stay in the Cast all along.

What you place in a visual channel cell is a sort of pointer or link to the source graphic. When a movie is being played back, Director reads the visual channel cell and then goes to the Cast and places the appropriate graphic on the Stage, along with any modifications you have made for that particular instance.

You don't actually place a *cast member* in the Score; instead, you place an *individual instance* of that cast member in the Score.

Why the distinction between the cast member and the cast member instance? The pointer doesn't just identify the visual element; it also documents how you want it to appear on the Stage in this instance only. You can specify display size and location, along with a number of other parameters, without having to change the element itself. For example, you can have the same image in frames 20, 21, 22, 23, 24, and 25, each in the same location on the Stage but displayed in a slightly larger size. Then when the movie is played back, that image will seem to grow.

Behavior channel

The behavior channel *was* known as the script channel in prior versions. Long-time Director users will probably use the terms interchangeably for a while.

As you know, Lingo is everywhere. It even has its own Score channel, where scripts (behaviors) can be stored and executed frame by frame. In the **behavior channel**, you can place those scripts saved as cast members. You can also create new scripts directly in the behavior channel, but they too will become cast members (Director will automatically assign them a slot in the Cast database). Note that in previous versions of Director, this channel was called the *script channel*; changing the name to the behavior channel reflects Director 7's change in emphasis from custom scripts to prebuilt behaviors. You can still "roll your own" scripts just as easily in version 7 as in earlier incarnations, but using the off-the-shelf scripts is now even easier.

Sound channels

All audio cast members (embedded sounds and linked files) can be placed in either one of the two sound channels. There's no difference between the two, but unfortunately, there are only two (in contrast to the 1000 possible visual channels). The number of sounds you can have playing at one time is limited only by the resources of the user's system; however, if you want your movie to play more than two sounds at a time, you need to use Lingo. This isn't much of a limitation because if your movies are *that* complicated, you're probably already relying extensively on Lingo.

Transition channel

Not only is this channel a lot of fun, but it's one of the features that can make a Director movie seem impressively professional. With it, you can control how things change from frame to frame in your movie—the style in which elements arrive and depart. If you want one screen to dissolve smoothly into another, you can achieve this effect by using a simple transition channel command. If you want to make a cast member appear on the Stage as if it's floating down from the top of the screen, another transition command is all you need.

You don't place cast members in this channel; instead, you choose transition parameters from a pop-up menu. Let's take a look at how this works:

1. *Place the cursor on any cell in the transition channel.*

2. *Click once to select the cell.*

3. *Double-click the cell.*

This dialog box should put in an appearance:

IN TRANSITION:
Transition channel options are selected from this dialog box.

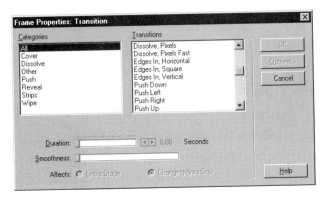

4. *Scroll up and down the list of transitions.*

You should find more than 50 different types of transitions, from wipes to reveals to zooms (Director groups them by category). Since you can customize most of them by specifying parameters such as transition time, there's a plethora of possibilities. Furthermore, you can choose whether the effect applies to what's already on the Stage in the current frame (the Stage Area check box) or to any cast members about to appear in the frame (the Changing Area Only check box).

5. *Click Cancel to close the dialog box.*

Palette channel

Although you probably won't end up using it as often as the transition channel, the palette channel can produce still more startling effects. As mentioned earlier, palettes are collections of colors used for display purposes. These collections can be saved and used as cast members in this channel.

Color display capabilities are often described in terms of **bit depth** (the amount of memory assigned to each pixel) An 8-bit display can show 256 colors at once; a 16-bit display, 32,768 colors; a 24-bit display, 16.7 million colors (32-bit is 24-bit with extra channels for special effects).

What's the point of palettes? Well, in the best of all possible worlds, we'd all be using systems that displayed nothing but 32-bit images and downloaded them instantly from the Internet. In the real world, however, you have no way of knowing to what color depth a user's system will be set and 32-bit images take four times longer to download than 8-bit images. So for now at least, it's best to design movies that will look good in all situations and that will download (if we are creating for the Web) in a reasonable amount of time. If we plan on passing around our project, we've got to design for all eventualities.

You can populate your movie with 32-bit graphics, but when they display on an 8-bit machine all of the colors will be remapped to the nearest of the 256 colors available, which is generally not the color you chose. Thus, you have two options: If size is not an issue, you can create multiple casts—one for each color depth—and your movie can switch casts depending on the color depth of the user's system. Otherwise, you can have your movie switch palettes when a primary image needs to access a different set of 256 colors. By allowing your movie to switch quickly from one palette to another, the palette channel provides some compensation for 8-bit color limitations. You can create your own palettes, import palettes when you import a graphic (they're saved as a new cast member), or use standard palettes. Standard palettes are available for Windows and Macintosh, and there's even a palette for Internet browsers.

Changing the palette of an image, without changing the image, can create some startling displays. Let's get a taste of the power of palettes in this respect. This experiment is most impressive if you have a colored desktop or some other image open in the background and Director doesn't cover the entire desktop:

1. *Use your computer's settings to change your monitor's display to a color depth of 8-bit (256 colors).*

2. *Double-click any cell in the palette channel.*

The following dialog box should make its debut.

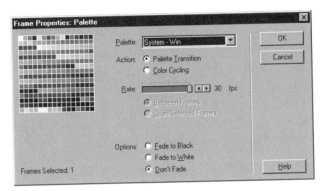

3. *Click the Palette pop-up menu.*

4. *Select Vivid from the list of choices.*

Notice how all the colors on your monitor suddenly change? If you have a multicolor Windows or Apple logo, you'll see that even it looks different. You can explore still further by selecting a few of the other palettes and watching how the colors are remapped to each.

It's interesting to note that the palettes affect all the colors on the display, not just the colors contained in the Director application itself. When you switch to another application, that application's palette takes over. But when Director and another application are both showing, and Director has the focus, Director determines the colors of the display.

5. *Select Cancel to close the dialog box.*

The colors displayed on your monitor should revert to their previous condition. If not, reopen the Palette window and select the default palette (System-Win for Windows or System-Mac for the Macintosh).

In Windows, when your system is set to 8-bit color depth and you use a palette other than System-Win, Director's user interface takes on a black-and-white look. This can be disconcerting while authoring, but it will not affect the look of the movie when it is played.

Director's palette channel has two main uses. It can be used to ensure more accurate representation of color graphics. If, for instance, you are incorporating digitized video into your movie, you might want to switch to the NTSC palette, which contains the standard colors used in broadcasting.

The second use of palettes is for flashy effects. By quickly swapping palettes, you can achieve a sense of animation even if nothing is actually moving. Let's say you are creating a game in which a spaceship explodes; you could take a single screen image of the explosion through several rapid palette changes, creating a dynamic kaleidoscopic effect (we'll be doing just that in Chapter 6: *Deeper into Graphics*). You can even instruct Director to spin through every color within a single palette in a process known as **color cycling**.

Palette effects work only when 8-bit color is enabled, because deeper color depths don't have palettes per se; their colors are numerous enough to become spectrums. Swapping around thousands or millions of colors at once would be overwhelmingly processor-intensive for most desktop computers.

Do not use palette changes in movies that are meant to play in a Web browser. The browser—not Director—controls the palette; the browser will ignore all palette changes. Also, for movies for the Web, map all of your 8-bit images to the Web216 palette supplied with Director. This is basically the same palette used by the major Web browsers.

Tempo channel

The final channel controls the time aspect of the Score timeline—in fact, it should probably be called the temporal channel rather than the tempo channel. You can use it to specify the rate at which Director zips through frames (that is, the tempo), but it's also the repository for more sophisticated pacing instructions. Let's check it out:

1. Double-click any cell in the tempo channel.

Here's what should appear:

As you can see, you have several options:

- You can set the playback tempo to any rate from 1 to 999 frames per second (fps).

- You can pause playback entirely, for a period of 1 to 60 seconds.

- You can make Director wait for a **user event**—in this case, a click of the mouse or a keystroke.

- You can make Director wait for a **cue point** in an audio or digital video cast member before continuing.

If a sound is playing in either of the Sound channels, or if a digital video movie is in progress in any of the graphic channels, you can use the Tempo channel to make sure that a specific point in playback is reached before the movie progresses to the next frame. Since a Director movie may perform at different speeds on different systems, this is a good means of ensuring that sounds and pictures stay synchronized.

By the way, the Wait for Mouse Click or Key Press command means just that: pause for *any* click or keystroke. If you want Director to respond to a specific user event (such as a click on one button among many or the typing of a particular word), you'll need more sophisticated control. And that means—you guessed it!—using behaviors or Lingo commands.

2. Click *Cancel* to return to the *Score*.

The tempo channel can be used to set a sort of speed limit on your movie. Without a specific tempo, a movie's playback speed would depend on the inherent speed of the computer on which it's running, which means that a sequence nicely paced on your machine might whiz by too fast on another.

However, a tempo setting is a maximum speed limit: If the tempo is, say, 30 fps, that doesn't guarantee playback at 30 fps. Director will try to achieve a playback rate as close to that as possible, but several factors (CPU and RAM limitations, the number of active cast members) can conspire to produce a slower playback speed. To determine the actual, rather than the optimum, tempo, you need to keep an eye on the final of our quartet of main windows: the Control Panel.

THE CONTROL PANEL

Actually, the Control Panel isn't strictly a window. It's a *windoid*: a window that can be moved but not resized. Nevertheless, the Control Panel not only offers you control (over the playback of your Director movie), but it also displays important information about your movie's performance.

To the new user, the Control Panel seems like a mix of the obvious and the arcane. If you've ever operated a cassette or videotape deck, the purpose of the main arrow buttons are clear. But what about the other items? Let's look into this windoid's anatomy.

A CONTROL STUDY:
The Control Panel lets you manipulate the playback head and keep tabs on your movie's performance.

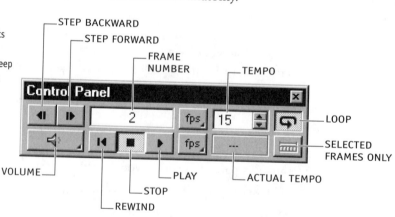

In brief, here's how each button functions:

Rewind moves the playback head all the way to the first frame of your movie.

Step Backward and **Step Forward** move the playback head by only one frame in their respective directions.

Stop halts playback entirely, and **Play** resumes it.

Volume lets you temporarily lower the volume or silence your movie while keeping your soundtracks intact. When you're fine-tuning a sequence (and thus continually playing it), this control can be a real sanity saver.

Loop On/Off dictates whether playback simply proceeds to the end of the Score and then stops or continuously repeats until further notice.

Selected Frames Only, when activated, limits playback to the frames highlighted in the Score window (as opposed to the entire Score). This control is useful when you're working on a single section of a larger movie—it can save you a lot of scrolling through the Score to find your place.

Frame Number displays the current location of the playback head in the Score. You can zip out to a specific frame number by typing that number in this field and then press Return (Macintosh) or Enter (Windows) on your main keyboard; the playback head will leap to the specified location.

This is probably a good place to mention the distinction between the Enter key on the Windows main keyboard and the Enter key on the numeric keypad. These two keys have two different functions within Director, so don't try to use the two interchangably. Throughout this book, when you're instructed to "hit Return (Macintosh) or Enter (Windows)," I'm referring to the Return or Enter key on the main portion of the keyboard, unless specifically stated otherwise.

Tempo mode displays the playback rate that Director is currently attempting to achieve. If you have specified a tempo in the Score's tempo channel it will be displayed here; otherwise, Director's default of 15 frames per second (fps) will be displayed. Click the fps symbol to reveal the seconds per frame (spf). The spf rate is a little more accurate, since it times a frame's duration right down to the millisecond, but unless you need the accuracy, the distinction is really a matter of taste. Click fps to reselect frames per second.

Tempo (actual) documents the *real* speed of playback. It's often enlightening to compare and contrast the number displayed here with the set tempo above it. You can also set this display to show three additional modes: Seconds Per Frame has already been discussed, Running Total calculates the total time elapsed since the beginning of your movie, and Estimated Total does the same thing but with a little more accuracy.

If you used Director prior to version 5, you may remember the Control Panel's color chip, which let you easily set the color of the Stage. Now the color chip is in the Movie Properties dialog box, which controls a number of playback particulars.

1. *From the Modify menu, select Movie and then Properties.*

2. *Click the mouse button over the square marked "Stage Color."*

What appears is the currently loaded palette (which is probably the default palette for your system).

A LITTLE LOCAL COLOR: This Movie Properties dialog box lets you set the color of the Stage window.

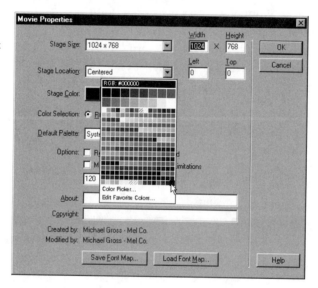

3. *Move the cursor to select a color. When you click a color, it will be selected. Click OK to apply your selection and close the dialog box.*

The Stage should now change to reflect your color choice. This is a nifty feature, but its utility is limited, since you can select only a single color for use throughout the entire movie (although you can switch it in mid-movie with Lingo). If you want to use a variety of backgrounds in your movie, one option is to create those backgrounds as cast members and then place them on the Stage via a Score location that makes sure they are displayed behind all other items.

THE CAST MEMBER WINDOW GROUP

You create cast members when you work in the Paint, Text, Tools, Color Palettes, Vector Shapes, or Script window.

It's possible to create a movie just by using the four main windows— Score, Stage, Cast, and Control Panel—but doing so would only scratch the surface of Director's capabilities. So let's round out our tour by making at least a cursory inspection of some of Director's other windows.

I've dubbed our next group the "cast member windows." This is because when you're working with them, you're modifying the Cast as well. If you use, say, the Paint window to create a graphical element, that element will automatically take up a slot in the Cast window as well. All of these windows can be accessed from Director's Window menu.

The Paint window

If you've ever worked with a color graphics application such as Photoshop, much of the Paint window (Control-5 Windows; Command-5 Macintosh) will probably seem familiar to you. There's a central canvas area where the artwork is created, bordered by a tool selection bar and a variety of pertinent controls.

The Paint window has some truly impressive features (such as an intelligent lasso and marvelous ink effects, which we'll discuss later), but in terms of sheer flexibility, it's not in the same league as standalone applications such as Photoshop or Painter. You can use it to create original artwork, but depending on your desired level of sophistication, you may find yourself choosing to create graphics elsewhere and then importing them.

The Paint window doesn't support multiple layers or levels of undo, but it does support the Photoshop plug-in standard. That means that if you have plug-in special effects that work in Photoshop, they'll probably work in Director as well. Just drag copies of them to your Xtras folder and then restart.

OL' PAINT:
Director's Paint window offers a pretty fair range of graphic-creation features.

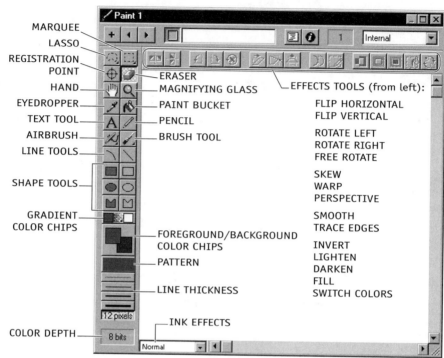

MARQUEE
LASSO
REGISTRATION POINT
HAND
EYEDROPPER
TEXT TOOL
AIRBRUSH
LINE TOOLS
SHAPE TOOLS
GRADIENT
COLOR CHIPS
COLOR DEPTH

ERASER
MAGNIFYING GLASS
PAINT BUCKET
PENCIL
BRUSH TOOL

FOREGROUND/BACKGROUND COLOR CHIPS
PATTERN
LINE THICKNESS
INK EFFECTS

EFFECTS TOOLS (from left):

FLIP HORIZONTAL
FLIP VERTICAL

ROTATE LEFT
ROTATE RIGHT
FREE ROTATE

SKEW
WARP
PERSPECTIVE

SMOOTH
TRACE EDGES

INVERT
LIGHTEN
DARKEN
FILL
SWITCH COLORS

Paint's stock in trade is the **bitmapped** graphic. That means that all elements of its artwork are stored and displayed as arrangements of pixels. This is in contrast to PostScript graphics (produced by Adobe Illustrator, Macromedia FreeHand, and the like), in which images are described in terms of individual lines and shadings. PostScript artwork can be converted to bitmapped art, but not by Director. If you have an Encapsulated PostScript (EPS) file that you want to incorporate into your movie, you'll need an intermediary program (such as Photoshop or DeBabelizer) to transform it into a PICT file.

You'll find that all bitmapped graphics—whether created in Director or imported from elsewhere—belong to the Paint hierarchy. This means that any imported image (even a scanned photo) can be found in the Paint window as well as in the Cast window.

One really convenient feature of Director is that it lets you specify an external application (such as Photoshop or SoundEdit 16 Pro) to edit a bitmap, digital video, or sound cast member. From the File menu, choose Preferences and then Editors to specify your choice for each cast member type.

When you double-click a cast member, the chosen program will automatically be launched (or made active if it is already open). When you close the file that you've been working on, Director automatically reimports the modified version of the cast member into the same slot—no muss, no fuss.

The Vector Shape window

The **internal vector shape creation tool** is a new feature of Director 7.

The Paint window handles bitmapped graphics, but those aren't the only graphic images in town. **Vector shapes** are similar to bitmaps, but instead of being a pixel-by-pixel representation of an image, a vector is a mathematical description of the shapes that add up to an image.

To understand the difference, imagine a simple line: You can either physically draw the line on a piece of paper, or you can jot down the coordinates of point A (the starting point) and point B (the ending point). Vectors take the latter approach, juggling the *mathematical representation* of a line rather than the line itself. Although the computer screen will display an actual line in either case, the vector format is a lot more versatile. Read on to learn why.

A vector's mathematical description isn't just length ("point A to point B") and shape ("a 30 degree arc"); it also includes the fill color and the thickness of the line. Although you can't include all of the detail with a vector shape that you can with a bitmap image, vector shapes have several distinct advantages. For one thing, you can resize them without introducing any distortion (such as jagged edges). For another, they can be controlled with Lingo while the movie is playing. (In fact, you can create vectors entirely with Lingo.) Most important, they require a lot less disk and memory space and will download and animate much faster when used on the Web. The Vector Shape window is new to Director 7, and it has been one of the most eagerly awaited of the version's new capabilities.

VECTOR SHAPES:
Director's Vector Shape window looks similar to a Paint window.

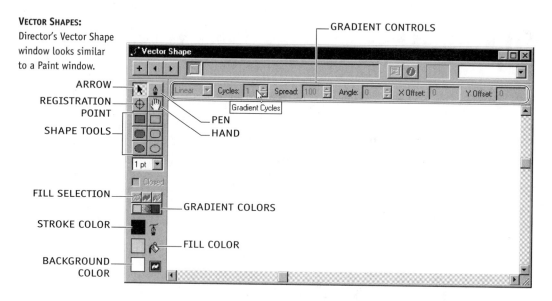

GRADIENT CONTROLS

ARROW

REGISTRATION POINT

SHAPE TOOLS

PEN

HAND

FILL SELECTION

GRADIENT COLORS

STROKE COLOR

FILL COLOR

BACKGROUND COLOR

The Text window

There used to be a lot of grumbling about Director's text-handling capabilities, but since version 5, Director has become a real text power-house. Along with specifying font, size, and style, you can set tabs, margins, leading (line spacing), and kerning (letter spacing) values. What's especially impressive is Director's ability to display text on the screen in anti-aliased form, which means the characters are smooth edged rather than jagged. And it's all done in the Text window (Control-6 Windows; Command-6 Macintosh).

JUST YOUR TYPE:
To create a text cast member, start typing in the Text window.

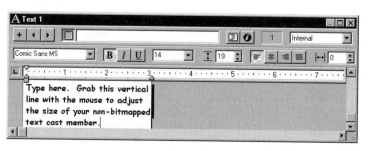

You can type directly in the Text window, or you can import files saved as plain text (ASCII files), saved in Rich Text Format (RTF), or (new to Director 7) saved as HTML documents. Rich Text Format is supported by many word processing applications and preserves some (but not all) formatting niceties. Director 7 recognizes most (but not all) HTML tags.

Director 7 allows text to be edited while a movie is playing and lets you control the text with Lingo. Fonts can now be embedded in a movie so that text will be displayed correctly on any system without concern for the fonts installed on a user's computer. Embedded fonts are compressed so that including a font generally adds only 14K to 25K to the size of a movie.

In addition, Director 7 no longer supports breaking up RTF files at page breaks. In previous versions, a separate cast member was created for each page of an imported RTF file. In Director 7 you need to have a separate RTF file for each cast member to be created.

The Field window

Text is handled slightly differently in the Field window (Control-8 Windows; Command-8 Macintosh). There are no tabs, paragraph formats, or typographic controls, and when placed on the Stage, a field cast member won't animate as quickly as a text cast member. The main advantage of fields is that they take up a lot less space (in terms of RAM and disk storage).

PLAYING THE FIELD: A field is similar to a text cast member, but it provides the smallest possible Cast size.

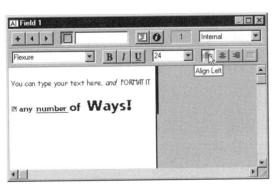

Text in context

You may have noticed that the Paint window has a Text tool as well. This illustrates the point that in Director, text can exist in three forms: as Text window text, as Field window text (requiring fonts installed in your computer's system for proper display), and as graphical representations of text (that is, bitmaps).

Each type of text has its own advantages and disadvantages. Bitmapped text (the Paint window type) will look the same no matter what machine is running your movie, but it takes up more disk space and RAM. System-derived text (the Field window type) is more compact and can be changed on the fly, but if the machine running your movie doesn't have a particular font installed, the text will be changed to a default font, potentially messing up your lovely designs. You will generally use fields for displaying large amounts of small text in standard fonts. Rich Text Formatted text (the Text window type) is sort of a middle path between the other two and is the best choice for large type that needs to look good. With a little experimentation, you'll probably find yourself using all three text types in your projects, according to your expectations and their limitations.

The Tool Palette

Unlike the Paint, Text, and Field windows, which have their own work areas, the Tool Palette (Control-7 Windows; Command-7 Macintosh) is designed to deposit its creations directly on the Stage. Of course, at the same time these creations will also take up residence in the Cast database. If you use the Tool Palette's Text tool (yes, yet another Text tool!), your subsequent typing will make an automatic entry in the Text window. Click the field tool, and the text will go into a Field window instead.

TOOLING AROUND: The Tool Palette also creates cast members, but they're placed directly on the Stage.

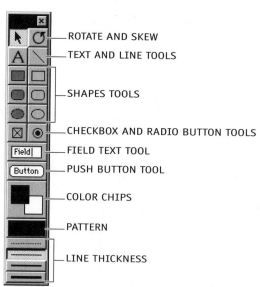

ROTATE AND SKEW

TEXT AND LINE TOOLS

SHAPES TOOLS

CHECKBOX AND RADIO BUTTON TOOLS

FIELD TEXT TOOL

PUSH BUTTON TOOL

COLOR CHIPS

PATTERN

LINE THICKNESS

Some of the tools in the Tool Palette look identical to those in the Paint window, but there's an important difference: lines and shapes (both filled and empty) created here are stored in a form that takes up less file space than bitmapped graphics, and they're easily modifiable at any point after their creation.

The Tool Palette's other strength is its button-creation function. If you want to create buttons with built-in animations that underscore their "button-ness," this is the source.

BUTTONS AT THE PUSH OF A BUTTON:
The Tool Palette automatically creates these standard button types.

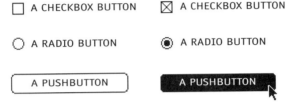

With Lingo, *any* physical element can be a button.

Nonetheless, it's useful to keep in mind that you don't need the Tool Palette to create buttons. In fact, anything residing on the Stage (even invisibly) can be turned into a button—it's just a matter of attaching a Lingo script to a sprite or cast member.

The Color Palettes window

You've already made the acquaintance of palettes. Well, the Color Palettes window (Control-Alt-7 Windows; Command-Option-7 Macintosh) is where you can create new palettes and modify existing ones. Each of the boxes in the central field represents one of the palette's 256 colors (don't forget; when we're dealing with palettes, we're operating in 8-bit color).

YOUR PALETTE PAL:
Use the Color Palettes window to create new custom palettes.

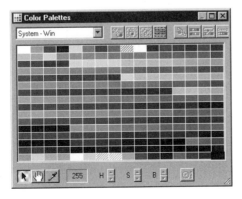

You can edit the colors of a palette in two ways. The first is by selecting the color (with a single mouse click) and then using the H (hue), S (saturation), and B (brightness) arrows to modify the color. This doesn't let you see the results of your actions, however, so here's a better method.

1. **Double-click any color. If you are modifying a built-in palette, Director creates a new palette (by copying the original) and prompts you to name the new palette.**

Here's what the Color dialog box looks like in Windows. You Mac OS users will see a somewhat different display, depending on your software and hardware configuration. This dialog box represents the full range of color choices. You build or modify a palette by deciding which of these colors goes into one of the 256 slots of color available in 8-bit mode.

SURFING THE SPECTRUM: You can use the Color dialog box to see all the colors available for your custom palette.

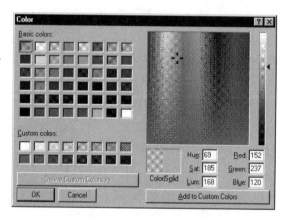

Color palettes are explored in detail in Chapter 6: *Deeper into Graphics*.

2. **Click anywhere in the large multicolored area.**

The selection cursor should move to your selected point in the spectrum, and the selection should show the new color you have chosen.

3. **Move the arrow at the far right to adjust the lightness.**

This scroll box controls overall lightness. If you scroll all the way to the bottom, any color you choose will turn black.

4. **Click OK to return to the Color Palettes window.**

The color you edited should reflect the color change you made.

5. **Close the Color Palettes window.**

6. *In the Cast window, find the new palette that was created with the name you gave it. Click the cast member to select it and then press the Delete key to remove it (for now, you don't need the complication of nonstandard palettes).*

If this seems like a tedious method of building palettes, it is. It's easier to import a piece of artwork with the color values you want to use. You can then import not only the artwork but its palette, which Director will display in the Color Palettes window.

The Digital Video window

For more about digital video, see Chapter 20: *Lingo and Digital Video.*

Before true digital video arrived for desktop computers, the only feasible way to create moving pictures was with animation programs such as Director. But the new technology didn't cancel out the utility of Director and its ilk—it just created standard formats for digital video files. Now Director movies can incorporate QuickTime movies and AVI movies, and (in a charming instance of reciprocity) you can even export a Director movie as a digital movie in either format.

When you import a digital video file into Director (as a linked file, not an embedded file, remember) it takes up residence in the Cast window and can be viewed in the QuickTime window (Control-9 Windows; Command-9 Macintosh) or, for AVI movies in Windows, in the AVI Video window. Note the standard playback controls. The logistics of playing a movie within a movie can get pretty thorny, especially since both can have independent (that is, conflicting) playback rates. We'll be dealing with those issues in chapters to come.

THE WINDOW SCREEN: QuickTime digital video cast members live in this window. Note the playback controls.

The Script window

At last, a glimpse of Lingo in its raw, natural form! At first glance, the Script window looks a lot like the Text or Field window. There's no column width handle, however, and the text is displayed in a different default font.

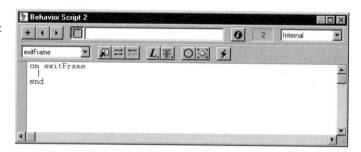

What you see when you open a Script window will depend on how you open the window and, therefore, the intended purpose of the script. If you open the Script window to create a frame behavior (double-click a cell in the Score's behavior channel), you'll see the text shown here. It's not a full-fledged script, but the beginning and ending of a script is supplied by Director as the most likely default script. The term on `exitFrame` refers to the event of the playback head leaving a single frame in the Score (there's also on `enterFrame`). The phrase end marks the conclusion of a Lingo script.

In this book, we'll indicate Lingo by using **this typeface** for the actual scripts. This represents what can be entered in the Script window and understood by Director.

One hallmark of Lingo is its unusual orthography. More than a few terms seem to be two or more words crammed together, starting out in lowercase but with at least one capital letter sprinkled in for good measure. You don't actually need to observe these conventions (Lingo isn't case sensitive, so you could type in ALL CAPS if you so desired), but it's one way of differentiating a Lingo term from an English word. Director 7 also adds the complication of dot-syntax, which means you have the option of writing Lingo in the older, more-or-less naturalistic form, or in the new dot syntax style which is closer to that used by other scripting languages such as Java.

The Library Palette

Director 7 allows you to choose behaviors from its new Library Palette.

Director 7 has several features designed to encourage you to use ready-made behaviors whenever possible, and one way this shows up in the interface is in the **Library Palette**, which lets you drag behaviors right onto your sprites or into a frame in the behavior channel. Director will walk you through the process of supplying any required extra information (*parameters*) for the behavior. You can now include some pretty impressive behaviors for creating animation, navigation, user interfaces—even an analog clock.

NO MUSS—NO FUSS: From the Library Palette, you can drag behaviors onto the Score or Stage.

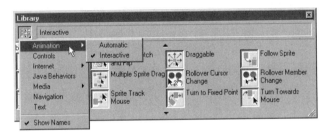

INFO SOURCES

The Properties dialog boxes

Once created or imported, every cast member is assigned its own dialog box, which contains information about its **properties** (various aspects of its manifestation and behavior). You can open that box by first selecting the cast member in the Cast window and then clicking the "i" (for Info) button. You'll also find this button in the individual windows for editing cast members (Paint, QuickTime, and so on), no matter what type they may be. The particulars of each Properties dialog box vary among cast types, but they do have several important elements in common.

Unload is covered in Chapter 22: *Professional Topics and Techniques.*

As you can see, each box contains the cast member's name, number, and size (the amount of space it takes up in the movie's file). Most Info boxes also have a pop-up menu for Unload: a feature that used to be called Purge Priority (it was renamed in version 5). Unload lets you maximize performance by determining when an individual cast member is flushed from RAM.

THE INSIDE INFO:
Each cast member
has an Info box of its
own. Their contents
vary according to cast
member type.

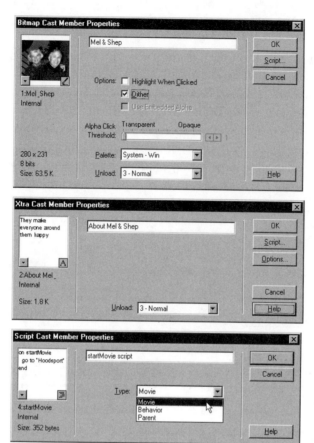

Director tries not to hog more RAM than absolutely necessary—otherwise, the sheer size of all the various multimedia elements would soon overwhelm most systems during playback. That's why you can tell it when each cast member should be dropped from memory. Once out of RAM, a cast member isn't deleted from your movie. It's just not ready for instant placement on the Stage.

Why doesn't the Script Properties box have an Unload setting? Because Lingo takes up very little RAM space, and there would be little to gain by having Director "forget" Lingo scripts. Usually, you'll want your Lingo scripts to be available to Director as long as your movie is running.

The Sprite Overlay

The Sprite Overlay is accessible from the View menu; choose Show Overlay and then Show Info to make this handy little information center appear on the Stage whenever a sprite is selected (you can use Show Overlay and Settings to specify when that information appears).

The overlay display gives you three important types of information about the sprite to which it's attached: the source cast member, the display parameters of the sprite itself, and the Lingo attached to the sprite. Clicking any of the three icons brings up an appropriate dialog box: Cast Properties, Sprite Properties, or Behavior Inspector (from top to bottom).

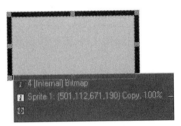

THE ROAD TO OVERLAY: With this useful tool for at-a-glance information, you can click any of the three icons to change important characteristics of the sprite or sprite segment.

SHORTCUT AND DIAGNOSTIC WINDOWS

In addition to the working windows covered earlier in this chapter, Director includes various shortcut and diagnostic windows that help make your work easier and more efficient.

The toolbar

The **toolbar** (from the Window menu, select Toolbar) isn't a window so much as a panel of shortcut controls you can have open when needed and closed when monitor real estate becomes an issue.

Each button on the toolbar is a shortcut to a commonly used command. Unlike similar features in other software, the toolbar can't be edited to remove commands, add new ones, or rearrange button order. However, the playback controls alone are valuable, since in most cases they can be used as a compact substitute for the Control Panel.

THE BAR IS OPEN:
If you can spare the screen space, the toolbar offers short-cuts in abundance.

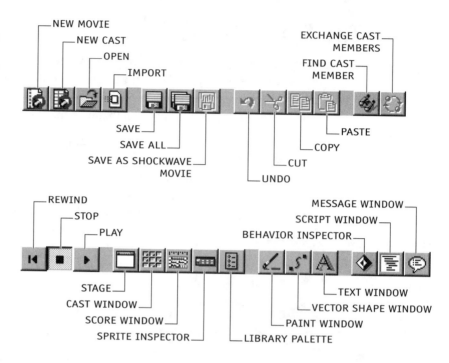

If you're unsure as to the meaning of icons in Director, open the General Preferences dialog box (on the File menu) and make sure the Show Tooltips box is checked. When Tooltips are active, a little descriptive label will appear every time your cursor lingers on an icon for more than a moment. Tooltips work throughout Director (not just in the toolbar), and the great thing about them is you can turn them off once you're familiar with the territory.

The Sprite Inspector

The Sprite Inspector (Control-Alt-S Windows; Option-Command-S Macintosh) is especially useful for users with smaller monitors. It essentially duplicates the information found at the top of the Score window but with a twist. By clicking the window's resizing box (on the Macintosh), you can make the information appear in a vertical format rather than in a horizontal bar. This way you don't have to extend your Score menu (and thereby dominate the monitor) to access and change particulars about your production. In Windows, the Sprite Inspector is always vertical. If you use the Sprite Inspector, you can turn off the sprite toolbar at the top of the Score window by selecting Sprite Toolbar from the View menu.

INSPECTION TIME:
Although you'll find this information at the top of the Score, it's more easily accessible here.

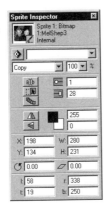

Help file access

Director has an extensive help file, which you can access through the Help menu (by clicking the ? on the Macintosh menu bar). Director Help takes you to the basic help system, where you can browse the help files or search for particular items. Lingo Dictionary will take you to specific information about Lingo elements. Web Links provides links to topics at the Macromedia Developer's Center on the Web.

HELP!
A sample of the Help files provided with Director.

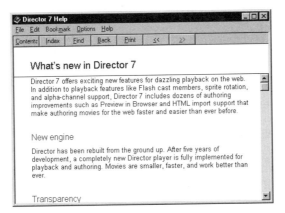

Director Help has greatly improved since the old days. It's now a separate application, so you can keep it open all the time without bogging down Director (although you will need to spare the extra RAM). Fortunately, the help files are extensive enough that you probably won't miss the context-sensitive help that was removed from Director 6.

> Since the help file is actually a separate application accessed from within Director, you'll need to make sure that the application and its required data file are properly installed on your system (otherwise, you'll get a "File cannot be opened" message). The Install program on your Director CD will do this automatically.

Memory Inspector

Unlike a conventional motion picture, a Director movie doesn't unfold at a constant rate of speed. It tries to match the playback settings you've specified, but the real determining factor in speed is the amount of RAM available for the task at hand. To keep your productions as zippy as possible, you'll want to keep an eye on your RAM resources. That's what the Memory Inspector window is for.

THANKS FOR THE MEMORY: Director's Memory Inspector window displays an accurate accounting of your current RAM use.

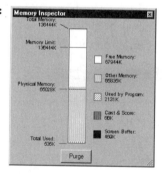

The Memory Inspector (accessed from the Window menu, by selecting Inspectors and then Memory) charts in detail how the RAM allocated to Director is being used. This may seem like unimportant data at first, but as your movies grow larger and more sophisticated, you'll find that memory management can be key to maximizing performance. You can refer to this display to pinpoint RAM bottlenecks and then fix them by adjusting the Unload settings of individual cast members.

Behavior Inspector

Not only can you attach Lingo to a cast member or sprite, but you can attach multiple scripts at both the cast member and sprite levels. Since all of these scripts are likely attempting to do different things, keeping track of scripts can quickly get confusing. That's where the **Behavior Inspector** comes in.

BEHAVE YOURSELF:
The Behavior Inspector window keeps track of the Lingo attached to specific sprites and cast members.

The Behavior Inspector serves as a sort of air traffic controller for Lingo, determining not only the nature of attached scripts but the order in which they're carried out.

The Behavior Inspector also makes it easy to connect (and disconnect) any number of off-the-shelf Lingo scripts, which means you don't have to become a Lingomeister to incorporate some nifty functions into your productions. We'll be working with the Behavior Inspector extensively in Chapter 4: *Introducing Interactivity.*

AND BEYOND...

There are many more windows, controls, and dialog boxes in Director, but these highlights should give you the basic overall picture. Before proceeding to the next chapter, feel free to explore on your own; as long as you keep clicking Cancel when exiting windows, you won't hurt anything. You'll be able to figure out the purpose of some things immediately, while others probably won't be clear until later. Point and click and experiment at will!

POINTS TO REMEMBER

Here are a few of the key concepts to be gleaned from what we've covered thus far:

- Director has four main windows: the **Stage**, the **Cast**, the **Score**, and the **Control Panel**.

- Director files are called **movies**.

- All action in a Director movie takes place in the Stage window.

- The action is *created*, however, in the Score window. The process of experiencing the action is known as **playback**; clicking the Play button on the Control Panel sends a cursor known as the **playback head** through the Score, which effectively runs your movie by sequentially processing the Score information.

- The elements of multimedia (graphics, sounds, digital video, even other Director movies) are stored and accessed in the Cast window. They are known as **cast members**. Some cast members are **embedded**, which means that they reside entirely in the Director movie. Others are **linked**, which means that the actual data remains in an external file.

- Each **column** (vertical row) in the Score represents a relative moment in time. Cast members placed in **cells** in a column will show up on the Stage at that given moment during playback.

- Each **channel** (horizontal row) in the Score represents a layer on the screen. There are specialized channels for sounds, transitions, tempos, and color palettes.

- Onscreen **text** can be created in three different ways: as formatted text (RTF), as a field (in the Field window), and as artwork (in the Paint window).

- **Lingo** is everywhere! The control language of Director can be attached to cast members and sprites, or it can be a cast member in its own right. It can also be placed in locations in the Score.

- Since multiple Lingo scripts can be attached to a single sprite, the **Behavior Inspector** provides a means of keeping track of them (and modifying the order in which they function). There's also a Sprite Inspector and a Memory Inspector to help you keep tabs on your productions.

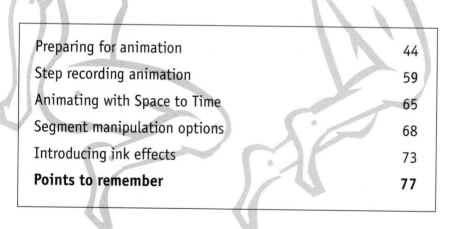

CHAPTER 2

THE ELEMENTS OF ANIMATION

OUR GRAND TOUR SHOWED US THE MAIN MECHANISMS AND PRINCIPLES of Director, and now it's time to set the gears spinning. In this chapter we'll start working in Director by producing a few basic onscreen elements (let's call them characters), which we'll then bring to life in some simple animations. Then we'll introduce and use a number of shortcut features to add a few more layers of sophistication. Get ready to get a move on!

PREPARING FOR ANIMATION

For our first experiment, we'll create a simple animation and then embellish it with some interesting extras. But first, let's configure Director to make it more user friendly for the task at hand.

Setting up

Start by setting up the Stage.

1.   *From the File menu, select New and then Movie.*

2.   *From the Modify menu, select Movie and then Properties.*

3.   *In the Movie Properties dialog box, set Stage Size to 640 x 480.*

4.   *Set Stage Location to Centered and Stage Color to White.*

5.   *Set Default Palette to System-Win (Windows) or System-Mac (Macintosh).*

6.   *Click OK to close the Movie Properties dialog box.*

7.   *From the File menu, select Preferences and then Cast.*

8.   *Select Number:Name for the label and then click OK.*

9.   *From the View menu, select Sprite Overlay and make sure that neither Show Info nor Show Paths is checked.*

10. *From the File menu, select Save and save the file as* **Gmetrics.dir.**

The Stage is set.

Adding cast members

Now let's create some cast members.

1.   *Open the Paint window; choose it from the Window menu or by pressing Control-5 (Windows) or Command-5 (Macintosh).*

2.   *Select the filled circle tool.*

As shown here, there are three pairs of geometric shapes: rectangles, ovals, and polygons. Clicking the members on the right side produces outline-only shapes, and clicking those on the left produces shapes filled with the foreground color chip (the default color is black).

TWO BUTTONS IN ONE:
The geometric shapes in the Paint window can create both outline and filled shapes.

3. ***Click anywhere in the canvas area. Then hold down the Shift key and drag the mouse.***

You want to create a black circle. Try to make it about the size of a quarter (if you want to be precise, select Rulers in the View menu). If you're unhappy with your result, you can clear the canvas by double-clicking the eraser tool and then trying again. If the color of the circle is not black, use the foreground color chip to set the foreground color to black.

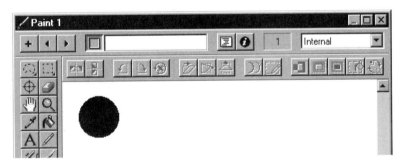

You'll notice that as you create in the Paint window, the first slot in the Cast window changes to reflect your work. The cast member number (1) also shows up in the Paint window, indicating that you are working on cast member 1.

PICON:
The miniature image of a cast member shown in the Cast window.

Our cast member shows up in the Cast as a smaller, thumbnail version of the actual artwork. This image is known as a **picon**, which is short for *picture icon*. All cast members—even nongraphic ones—are given picons when placed in the Cast database. In the case of visual cast members, the image is sized to fit the picon window, so large cast members may be harder to identify from their picons than smaller ones.

PICON AND ICON:
Each member of the Cast has its own picon on display, and a cast type icon appears in the lower-right corner of each picon.

If you take a close look, you'll see that the picon shows more than the little ball you just created; it also has a sort of subicon tucked into the lower-right corner. That icon identifies the **media type** of the cast member (in this case, it's a bitmapped graphic). Each type has its own distinctive icon.

ICONS BY CAST TYPE:
The icons that indicate cast type sometimes vary only subtly. Notice the minor difference between linked and embedded cast members.

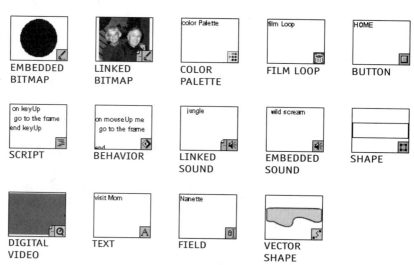

4. *In the Paint window, click the field just below the Paint 1 header. A cursor should appear.*

5. *Type* Marble *as the title. Then press Enter (Windows) or Return (Macintosh).*

Once again, the Cast window reflects the changes wrought in Paint. Notice that both the cast member number and the name "Marble" appear below the picon. This is because at the beginning of this lesson, when we set the cast preferences, we set Label to Number:Name. We could just as easily have set the label to just the name or just the number, but for now it's handy to see both.

NAME, PLEASE:
All cast members can
have both a name and
a number.

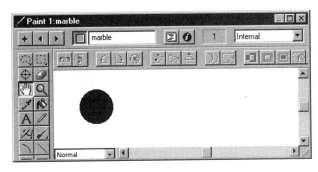

We now have two of the three elements we need to create a Director
movie: a Stage and a Cast. Now let's introduce one to the other, by way
of the third: the Score.

Building the first frame

We're ready to begin building our movie frame by frame in the Score
window.

1. *Close the Paint window.*

2. *Place your cursor over Marble's thumbnail in the Cast window.*

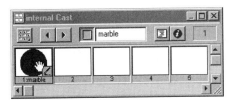

The cursor changes to an open hand icon. That's the **grabber** (well, that's
what I call it), and it indicates that Director is ready to place that cast
member in the Score.

3. *Drag the cursor over to the first cell of the first visual channel of
the Score.*

Remember that the visual channels are the numbered ones. The grabber
should change from an open hand to the arrow cursor, or **pointer**, and
once you're in the Score, the playback head should move to follow your
movements.

4. Release the mouse.

All at once, two things happen. First, a long bar appears in the Score itself; its length depends on certain settings in Director (the default is 28 frames). You'll note that it has a bullet on its left end and a handle on its right end. Also, the cast member's number and name are shown (remember that we set the label to Number:Name).

For the second event, look to the Stage. There's our cast creation—Marble—smack dab in the middle.

HOW TO BE IN THREE PLACES AT ONCE:
Once placed, the black circle you created resides in three places: in the Score (*top*), on the Stage (*middle*), and in the Cast (*bottom*).

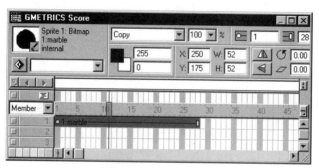

In Director versions prior to version 6, a cast member placed in the Score occupied a single cell (rather than multiple ones). Now, however, the default is a multiple-cell insertion. This is a logical refinement, since animated cast members tend to be placed over multiple frames. But at this stage, you'll find it useful to connect cast members conceptually with a single cell in the Score. We'll be taking that tack for the next few exercises. We'll begin by setting the default span duration.

Let's try a different approach.

1. *Go to the File menu and choose Preferences and then Sprite.*

2. *In the Span Duration box, type 1 and click OK.*

A SPAN-ISH LESSON:
Setting Span Duration to 1 changes the way Director places cast members in the Score.

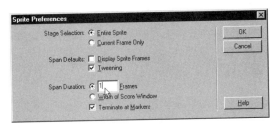

We've just changed the way Director displays the cast members placed in the Score. Now when we place a cast member in the Score (or directly on the Stage), things will be a little different.

3. *Select the long bar in the Score that represents Marble, and press the Delete key on the keyboard.*

4. *Position your cursor over Marble again in the Cast and drag this cast member to the first cell in the Score, just like last time.*

Things *are* a little different now, aren't they? Only one cell is occupied, instead of 28, and while the bullet is still there, the handle has disappeared. Check the Stage again, and you'll find that Marble is still there, within its bounding box.

SINGLE-CELL ORGANISM:
Our character now occupies only one cell of the Score.

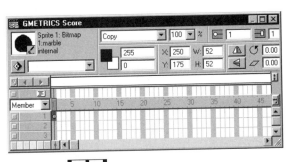

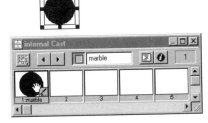

The whole thing seems a little convoluted, though—creating something in one window (Paint) so that it shows up in another (Cast), which we then drag to a third (Score) so that it shows up still elsewhere (Stage). Well, here's one more approach: We can cut one step out of the process by bypassing the Score.

1. *Position the cursor over Marble in the Cast. The grabber cursor reappears.*

2. *Drag the selection directly to the Stage; release the mouse.*

This time, it's the Score that's updated to reflect what's happening on the Stage. Note that another entry has been inserted into the cell directly below the previous one and that the new entry is selected.

3. *Click Marble's selection area and drag to place this cast member anywhere on the Stage.*

What's the difference between **indirect** and **direct placement** of cast members? When you place something on the Stage indirectly (by dragging a cast member to a Score cell), that element is placed in the dead center of the Stage. Our first Marble element is placed in the exact center of the Stage, demonstrating that automatic placement is useful for objects that need precise alignment, such as backdrops.

On the other hand, when you drag an element directly to the Stage, the element will be placed wherever you want it to be. However, no matter which method you use, you can adjust the position at any time. You can drag the element or use the arrow keys on your keyboard to move the selected object on the Stage by one pixel per keystroke.

If you have a small-screen monitor, cross-window operations like these can become a little awkward. Rather than dragging windows in and out of your view, you can have them share the same area and use keyboard shortcuts to make them visible in turn. These are the main window shortcuts (the Windows commands appear first, following by those for the Macintosh):

Stage	Ctrl-1/⌘-1		**Paint**	Ctrl-5/⌘-5
Control Panel	Ctrl-2/⌘-2		**Text**	Ctrl-6/⌘-5
Cast	Ctrl-3/⌘-3		**Field**	Ctrl-8/⌘-8
Score	Ctrl-4/⌘-4		**Script**	Ctrl-0/⌘-0

The concept of the sprite

Let's take stock for a moment. We have one frame in our movie thus far and one cast member. But in that single frame, we have *two* versions of our solitary cast member! You may recall that in the previous chapter we touched on the distinction between a cast member and the individual *instances* of that cast member displayed on the Stage. Well, here we have two instances at once, each with its own individual existence (as evidenced by separate Score channel entries).

1. *Click the Marble element in the center of the Stage. Its selection area should appear.*

2. *Click the handle in the lower-right corner. Hold down the Shift key while dragging.*

You're now resizing the first instance of Marble. Try to make this instance roughly twice the size of the other one.

TRY THIS ON FOR SIZE:
The two circles, though drawn from the same cast member, have separate identities. They can be individually resized and otherwise modified.

We could conceivably make dozens of different incarnations of Marble, each a different size, each with its own Score channel. These incarnations are called **sprites**, and they're the basic building blocks of Director animation. Understanding the role of sprites (and their potential) is a key step in working with Director.

Although Director will create multiple-cell sprites (remember our original, 28-cell Marble sprite?), for the purpose of this exercise you should think of a sprite as a single manifestation of a cast member—an entity that exists in exactly one cell in the Score, in one position on the Stage.

You'll create a sense of animation either by changing the sprite position from cell to cell or by switching one sprite for another. Sprites are usually referred to by the number of the channel they occupy. In our current movie, the small Marble instance is sprite 2 and the larger is sprite 1.

Changes to the sprite don't affect its source cast member, but changes made to that source cast member will be reflected in all sprites derived from it, as we'll now see. Marbles tend to be colorful, not flat black spheres, so let's add a little decoration.

1. Double-click Marble in the Cast window.

The Paint window should appear, with Marble right where we left it.

2. Click the foreground paint chip. In the Color Selection window, click on the square in the first column, tenth row.

The foreground paint chip is the black square overlapping the white square. Selecting the new color should change the foreground chip to a nice light blue.

FOREGROUND — COLOR CHIP

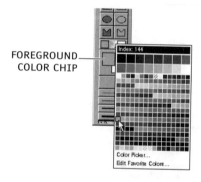

3. Select the filled rectangle tool; draw a square in the center of the circle.

LIKE SOURCE, LIKE
SPRITES:
By changing the appearance of the source cast member, we automatically change the appearance of every sprite derived from it.

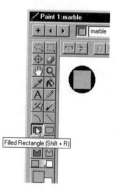

4. *Close the Paint window.*

Now check out the Stage. Both sprite 1 and sprite 2 have a new look; each retains its own location and size, but the modification we made to Marble (the source cast member) is reflected in them both.

Getting sprite info

Sprite 1 doesn't look as presentable as sprite 2—notice how jagged sprite 1's edges are? That's because we enlarged it by resizing it. Let's restore it to its original size and shape.

The shortcut for Sprite Properties is **Control-Shift-I** (Windows) or **Command-Shift-I** (Macintosh).

1. *Click sprite 1's cell in the Score (channel 1).*

On the Stage, the sprite's bounding box should appear, indicating that the sprite is selected and that it is able to be modified.

2. *From the Modify menu, select Sprite and then Properties.*

CUTTING IT DOWN TO SIZE: You can resize a sprite by editing its parameters in the Sprite Properties window.

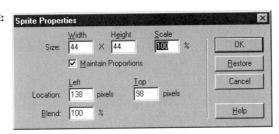

Here we have a set of controls that apply only to the selected sprite. We can resize the sprite by a percentage value or by entering desired dimensions. We can also relocate the sprite to exact screen coordinates.

3. *Click Restore. Then press Enter (Windows) or Return (Macintosh).*

Sprite 1 is now back to its original dimensions and is a veritable twin of sprite 2.

The registration point

When you place a sprite on the Stage by dragging a cast member to the Score, that sprite appears centered on the Stage. To achieve that nice balanced effect, Director has to calculate the physical center of the sprite as well as of the Stage. That's why every graphic cast member has a **registration point**, which you can see in the Paint window.

1. **Double-click the Marble cast member in the Cast to open the Paint window.**

2. **Click the registration point tool in Marble's Paint window.**

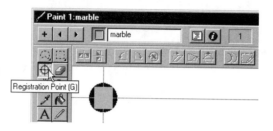

Crosshairs appear, intersecting at Marble's center. That's the default location of the registration point, but it can be moved.

3. **Drag the crosshairs until they're positioned at the lower-right edge of the circle.**

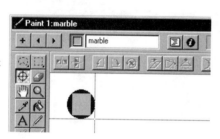

As soon as you release the crosshairs, you'll notice some action on the Stage; both sprites derived from Marble jump up and to the left. Director is redrawing them based on the new center you've assigned them. The fact that the "center" you've chosen is off center doesn't matter; the registration point can even be tucked way down in the corner of the canvas (try that and see what happens).

Since the registration point doesn't have to be in the exact center of the cast member, you can use it to make minor adjustments to the placement of sprites. But as always when you're working on the Cast level, keep in mind that your changes here affect all sprites.

4. **Double-click the registration point tool.**

Double-clicking the registration point tool sets the registration point to the center of the bitmap. The registration point should return to its original position, and so should both sprites.

Using Extend Sprite as a copying tool

Now we understand a bit more about what sprites are. But Director movies are rarely only one frame long. That's why Director by default gives us a 28-frame-long sprite (remember?). How are we going to make our sprites occupy more than one frame while retaining our preferred settings?

Well, if you select a single sprite along with any number of empty cells following it in the channel, the command Extend Sprite will fill those cells with copies of the original.

Extend Sprite is an extremely useful tool. It may become your most used command, and thus it's a good idea to learn the keyboard command for it: Control-B (Windows) or Command-B (Macintosh).

Extend Sprite is easy to use, and it's a good way to fill up channels with blocks of sprites. Let's use it to make sprite 2 take up 30 frames instead of 1 frame.

1. *In the Score, select sprite 2 (channel 2).*

2. *Shift-click in the Score on frame 30 in channel 2.*

A rectangular selection will flash momentarily in the Score to indicate that you've selected those cells.

3. *From the Modify menu, choose Extend Sprite.*

Lo and behold, we've extended the presence of the sprite in column 2 without dragging any more members from the Cast. If you look through the movie, you'll see that Marble's position in channel 2 remains consistent throughout.

4. *Repeat these steps for the sprite in channel 1 so that you have a movie 30 frames long with sprites in the first two channels.*

Playing back

Let's take a look at our movie.

1. **Click the Control Panel's Rewind button (◄◄).**

Even though the Stage hasn't changed visibly, a quick look at the Control Panel tells us we're back at frame 1.

2. **Click Play (►) on the Control Panel.**

Nothing happens, does it? Since the two sprites remain in the same position through all 30 frames, the Stage is unchanged even though we viewed 30 frames. We'll have to make this movie a bit more interesting.

> If you look carefully at the Score, you'll notice that the playback head always moves back to frame 1 after it reaches frame 30. This is because Director 7 enables **looping** by default. Looping can be useful, because it keeps us from having to press Rewind and Play repeatedly to see what happens on the Stage. If you'd like to turn looping off, simply toggle the Loop button (↺) on the Control Panel.
>
> You *can* keep looping running and make changes to a movie while it's playing; the changes will be incorporated into playback on the fly. But it's best to stop playback while making changes. That way, it's easier to keep track of exactly which frames you're working on.

Deleting sprites

We can achieve an interesting effect simply by selectively deleting sprites within a single channel. To do this, we'll use another Director feature: the ability to open and close sprites.

You've already found out that multiple-cell sprites are common in Director. Indeed, Director takes every opportunity to create them, as shown by its treatment of Marble just now. If there were no way to edit the individual frames within Marble's sprites, this feature would be more of a hindrance than a help. Fortunately, the folks at Macromedia have anticipated this and provided the means with which to open or close a multiple-cell sprite.

1. *Select sprite 1 in the Score by clicking somewhere within the sprite.*

2. *From the Edit menu, select Edit Sprite Frames.*

Whoa! Big difference, hey? Instead of being a long bar, sprite 1 is now made up of many small rectangles, each just one frame in size. You now see that sprite as its single-cell components, each of which can be edited separately; the sprite is considered open.

3. *Select sprite 1's cell at column 4.*

4. *Hold down the Shift key; click to select the next two cells in the channel, for a total of three.*

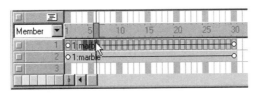

5. *Press the Delete or Backspace key to eliminate all three cells.*

Two things have happened here. Not only does a gap appear in channel 1, but you can see that Director now considers channel 1 to consist of two multiple-cell sprites.

6. *Repeat the process four cells later. Continue doing so until you reach the end of the sprite.*

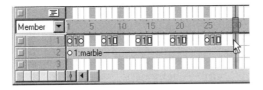

Channel 1 should now look decidedly gappy, with roughly the same number of deleted and remaining cells.

7. *Rewind the movie to the beginning.*

8. *Click Play on the Control Panel.*

Now, during playback, sprite 1 appears and disappears according to our deletions. But given the speed of playback, it seems to flash on and off!

Moving a sprite segment

Let's say we want to move sprite 2 lower on the Stage, just to see how it looks. Since we know how to open a sprite as a result of our foray into the world of the Edit Sprite Frames command, we could go through every single frame and move it down. The results would probably be unsatisfactory, though. Unless we take pains to move each frame *exactly* the same distance, we'll get a sprite that looks jittery during playback.

Fortunately, we can move all of sprite 2 at the same time, thus retaining frame-to-frame steadiness while changing the position relative to the other sprites.

1. **Click somewhere within channel 2.**

Because the sprite remains closed (by virtue of our not having opened it), the entire sprite is selected. By the way, if you click either the first or last frame of the sprite, the entire sprite will not be selected.

2. **Select sprite 2 on the Stage; move it to the upper-left corner.**

Now play back the movie. You'll see we've changed the sprite's position without introducing any motion.

The concept of sprite segments

SPRITE:
The individual instance of a cast member, which occupies a single cell in a single frame of the Score.

SPRITE SEGMENT:
A continuous sequence of a multiple-cell sprite in a single channel.

If things are getting a bit confusing at this point, don't blame your brainpower: it's because the sprite concept itself is so amorphous. In the past few exercises we've gone from a sprite's being one cell of one frame to examples where a sprite can be not only multiple cells long, but editable as single frames within that sprite. To clarify things, I'd like to introduce a term of my own: **sprite segments**.

Although it's not an official Director term, I think it's a necessary one, because a distinction does need to be made between the single-cell entity and the multiple-cell "greater whole" to which it might belong; since you can modify one and not disturb the other, there's a difference. So from now on, we'll refer to all multiple-cell sprites (open or closed) as sprite segments. Sprites considered on the single-frame level will, on the other hand, still be called just plain sprites.

You can move any sequence of sprite segments in the way just described (as long as they're all closed), not just a sequence in which the sprite stays still. In the case of our blinking sprite 1, you'd first need to close the individual sprite segments and then Shift-click the first sprite segment and then the last sprite segment that you want to move.

Closing an open sprite segment is easy (you may have figured this out already). Simply select any of the occupied frames within an open sprite segment and, from the Edit menu, choose Edit Entire Sprite.

STEP RECORDING ANIMATION

It's all well and good that we've made sprite 1 blink on and off and learned how to move sprite segment 2, but things could be more interesting, don't you think? Let's make sprite segment 2 move from its current position on the Stage using a method called **step recording**.

In step recording, you simply work on one frame until you're happy with it and then move on to the next. That might sound tedious, but you don't have to build the subsequent frames from scratch—you can copy the entire contents of one frame into the next and then make only the necessary adjustments.

Of course, even with cutting and pasting, it *still* sounds tedious. Luckily, Director can automate a hefty chunk of the process through a feature known as **in-betweening**, or **tweening**.

Drawing from Disney

In conventional hand-drawn cell animation (as practiced since the early days of Walt Disney), the making of moving figures is a two-part process. One artist sits down and designs the figures, drawing and painting essentially what is to be seen in the final version. But since animation is such a time-consuming process, these designers rarely produce every frame needed for every second of screen time.

Instead, they create what are known as **keyframes**: renditions of the crucial points—usually the beginning and ending frames of a specific action.

The result is then turned over to other animators (usually dozens of them) who work as "in-betweeners," creating the artwork needed to fill the gaps. Since the in-betweeners work in the style of the original designer, the end product looks like it flowed from a single pen.

In our case, Director is your in-betweener. You can create keyframes representing the beginning and ending of a motion, and Director will fill in the gaps almost instantly.

> In the context of Director, the "frame" in "keyframe" doesn't refer to frames in the Score (which can have several sprites) but rather to *individual* sprites. You can in-between a single channel, leaving the others untouched.

Streamlining with keyframing and auto-tweening

It won't be hard to make our sprite segment move across the Stage from left to right. We'll use two Director features to greatly ease the animation process: **keyframing** and **auto-tweening**.

Keyframing makes it easy to designate any point in a sprite segment as a keyframe. Auto-tweening enables Director to automatically "tween" (as in "in-between") the cells between keyframes to show any movement that should occur. In other words, with auto-tweening you can lengthen or shorten a sprite segment, and the motion of sprites within that segment will be compressed or extended accordingly. It used to be that every time you changed a segment's length, you needed to re-tween it yourself.

1. *Select the first cell of the sprite in channel 2 (the one with the bullet).*

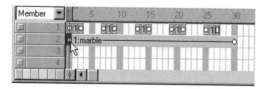

You'll notice that Director allows you to select just this one cell. If you tried to select any one of the middle 28 cells, Director would force the selection of the entire sprite segment. That's because Director recognizes both the first and last frames in any sprite segment as keyframes, and keyframes are selectable even in closed sprites.

2. *Press and hold down the Left Arrow key on your keyboard. Do not release the key.*

The Marble element should start to move left on the Stage.

3. *Keep pressing the Left Arrow key until the sprite disappears completely.*

That's right: You can place a cast member on the Stage and yet position it so that it's off the Stage—another Director idiosyncrasy.

4. *Click the last cell in the sprite segment in channel 2.*

5. *Repeat the procedure, only this time press the Right Arrow key.*

6. *Move the sprite until it disappears past the right edge of the Stage.*

Now play the movie and see what happens.

Pretty nifty, isn't it? Director took the information that was in the two keyframes (remember that Director recognizes the first and last cells in a sprite segment as keyframes) and produced a smooth animated sequence. That's auto-tweening in action.

If you hold the **Shift** key down when you press the **arrow** key, the sprite moves 10 times as fast.

Modifying sprite tweening

We just used auto-tweening to create a linear movement. If you want a little more sophistication in movement, you'll need to modify the sprite tweening characteristics.

You can use the Sprite Tweening dialog box to create a curved path for a cast member. To do that, you need at least three keyframes: the beginning, the nadir (a fancy word for the lowest point of a curve), and the end. As a demonstration, we'll replace the linear path of sprite 2 with a snazzy move: We'll make it seem as if this Marble element hits the bottom of the Stage and then bounces up toward the right edge of the Stage.

1. *Select frame 30 of the sprite segment in channel 2 and move it with your arrow key until it is flush against the right edge of the Stage.*

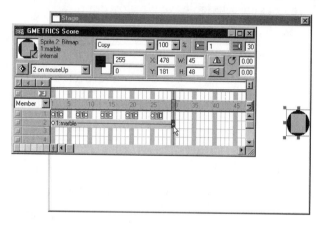

Now we'll set our nadir.

2. *Make sure that the sprite 2 segment is selected. Then select frame 15 within the playback head area.*

The playback head indicator should move to frame 15.

3. *From the Insert menu, select Keyframe.*

Congratulations! You've just used a very powerful tool for the first time. As you can see, Director has placed a keyframe (indicated by a bullet) within the sprite segment. That keyframe represents a point at which something changes within our sprite segment.

4. *Select frame 15 in the Score and then go to the Stage to drag the sprite to the bottom center of the Stage.*

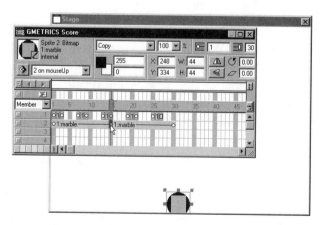

Now if you play the movie, you'll see that at this step, Marble's action is close to the desired result. Director has auto-tweened between the keyframes to bounce the Marble element off the bottom of the Stage and continue Marble's movement toward the final position. But since we now have three keyframes (frames 1, 15, and 30), we can modify the straight line Marble travels between the three points.

5. **Make sure that the entire segment is selected by clicking a non-keyframe cell within it.**

6. **From the Modify menu, select Sprite and then Tweening.**

This window appears:

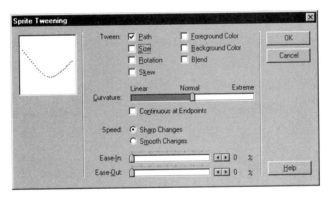

We're presented with a number of parameters we can use to adjust Marble's behavior. We can speed Marble up or slow it down, as well as change its size, color, or blend value as it's tweened.

For now, we'll use the sliding Curvature control, which lets us indicate how far inside or outside the curved path you want your sprites to be placed. The default setting puts the implied curve right through the center of your cast member, which is fine—but since we're experimenting here, feel free to move the slider back and forth. The path indicator shape (in the upper-left corner) changes to reflect the path your sprite will take.

7. **Move the slider to a motion path of your choice; then click the OK button. Play your movie.**

Tweening with the path

In the beginning of this chapter, we made sure that the Sprite Overlay selection Show Paths was turned off. Now let's flick that feature back on and see what we can do with it. First, though, let's get rid of everything in the Score (you're probably as tired of that flashing Marble as I am).

1. Delete all the sprite segments from the Score.

One easy way to do this is to drag over all of the occupied cells (start your drag operation in an empty cell). With all the cells selected, just press the Delete key. The Score and the Stage should now be devoid of sprites. But that doesn't mean we've lost our artwork—just its representations on the screen. The Cast window still has a solitary cast member: our Marble.

2. Drag the Marble cast member from the Cast window to the upper-left of the Stage.

3. From the View menu, select Sprite Overlay and then click Show Paths.

A dot, or **handle**, appears in the center of Marble on the Stage.

A SPRITE HANDLE:
The handle lets you drag the sprite to create a path.

4. As you did before, extend the sprite in the Score so that it extends through frame 30.

5. Click and hold the mouse on the dot in Marble and drag Marble to the upper-right side of the Stage.

A line appears on the Stage. The sprite segment is automatically tweened, and the tick marks on the line show the location of every frame. If we play the movie, Marble will follow the path determined by the line. Now let's make Marble bounce.

1. *Hold down Alt (Windows) or Option (Macintosh) and move the mouse over one of the tick marks near the center of the line.*

When the mouse is over a tick mark, the color of the mouse cursor changes.

2. *Drag the tick mark down to near the bottom of the Stage.*

As you drag the tick mark, the line changes to show the new path for Marble. We can repeat this process with other tick marks to make the path a different shape. We could also use the Sprite Tweening dialog box to modify the path as we did before. Notice that in the Score a keyframe has been inserted at the frame corresponding to the tick mark that we moved, and on the path line a hollow circle replaces the tick mark. Try adding more keyframes to change the path; then play the movie to see what it looks like.

3. *Go back and turn off Show Paths.*

ANIMATING WITH SPACE TO TIME

The two kinds of in-between commands are good for auto-animating straight lines, curved lines, and even circles—but what if we want a not-quite-so-generic motion? Director provides another technique, called **Space to Time**. With Space to Time, you place all the necessary sprites in a single Score frame, arranging them in the form of the action (it's kind of like a multiple-exposure photograph). Once you're satisfied with the flow of the sequence, a single command converts the arrangement into a segment suitable for playback.

Let's try this technique by making our Marble element seem to bounce. (Yes, bounce again, but this time let's see if we can make it look more realistic—did we mention that the marble is made of rubber?) We'll start by clearing the decks.

1. *Click anywhere in frame 1 of the Score window.*

2. *From the Edit menu, choose Select All.*

3. *Press the Delete or Backspace key.*

4. *In the Score, click frame 1 of channel 1 to set the start point.*

5. *Use the grabber cursor to drag a sprite of Marble directly to the Stage. Place this sprite near the upper-left corner.*

6. *Drag another sprite of Marble to the Stage, placing it just below the preceding one.*

7. *Continue the process with another 13 sprites of Marble, placing them in an order similar to the one illustrated below. We don't want the marble to bounce off the bottom of the Stage, though, so set the bounce point about halfway down and a third of the way over from the left.*

THE BIG BOUNCE:
With Space to Time, you can translate a succession of sprites into a linear motion.

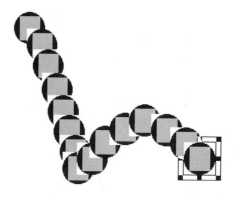

While you're doing this, check out the Score window. Director is entering each new sprite in a channel of its own, for a total of 15 channels, all in frame 1.

LAYERING:
Sprites in lower-numbered channels are displayed "behind" those in higher-numbered ones.

In this arrangement, some of the sprites are placed so that they're partially on top of their predecessors. This illustrates the principle of **layering** in Director: When two or more sprites overlap, the sprite in the highest-numbered channel is displayed.

Feel free to adjust the position and alignment of any of the sprites before proceeding. Just keep the sprites in chronological order of placement (that is, don't move the seventh sprite to the top of the arc before the first sprite, and so on).

8. *Shift-click to select all sprites in the Score (click down the column of frame 1).*

9. *From the Modify menu, select Space to Time.*

If the Stage suddenly seems to go blank, it may be because your selection includes one or more of the subsequent frames. Limit your selection to frame 1.

Director then asks us if we want to set any intervals of separation (that is, place extra frames) between the frames of these sprites.

SETTING THE GAP:
You can tell Director to add extra frames between sprites when using Space to Time.

We could stretch out our segment by using this dialog box to add a frame or two between each sprite. Director would then automatically tween through all of the frames. But we've placed 15 sprites because we want our bounce to last exactly a second (the tempo on the Control Panel is still set to 15 frames per second, or fps, right?), so we'll keep the segment as is, with each channel turning into a single frame.

10. Click OK.

The selected sprites swing up into the first channel. Turn off (deselect) looping on the Control Panel and then run the movie. Not a bad bounce for a marble, eh?

The Space to Time technique is even more useful when multiple cast members are involved. We used the same cast member for each element, but the cast members could just as easily have been different. If we were creating a path for a bird in flight, for instance, we could use cast members with the bird's wings in different positions. Or how about the marble's squashing when it hits the bottom of the stage (it is made of rubber, after all).

SEGMENT MANIPULATION OPTIONS

But nothing (not even the coolest marble in the world) bounces only once and then freezes in midair. To make our movie even passably realistic, we need to continue the motion. We could place more sprites on the last frame of our current segment and then perform another Space to Time operation, but why bother? Director has a few more tricks we can use instead.

Using Paste Relative

To demonstrate the power of the Paste Relative command, let's start by *not* using it. Let's perform a normal cut-and-paste operation instead.

1. *Shift-click to select the entire sprite segment.*

2. *Copy the segment (Control-C Windows; Command-C Macintosh).*

3. *Click to select the first vacant cell (frame 16).*

4. *Paste the segment (Control-V Windows; Command-V Macintosh).*

We've now doubled the size of the segment. But as playback will show (keep looping turned off), all we've done is reprise the action. Our marble bounces, freezes, and then disappears and reappears in its original position and goes through the motions again. What we want is a way to connect the two bounces smoothly, so let's clear the sprites we just pasted and start again.

1. *Click frame 16.*

2. *Shift-click frame 30 to select the remaining frames.*

3. *Select Cut Sprites from the Edit menu.*

4. *Click frame 16 to select it.*

5. *From the Edit menu, select Paste Special and then Relative.*

In the Score, the pasted sprites don't look any different than they did before—but playback demonstrates the difference.

This time, our bouncing action is repeated—but the starting point of the motion has been moved so that it links seamlessly with the earlier bounce. What Paste Relative has done is treat the last sprite in the old segment as a keyframe for the placement of your new sprites. Since we stopped the last bounce about halfway through the rebound arc, the marble now travels the same relative distance, only starting where we left off before. We now have a marble bouncing down the stairs.

If your marble still ends up on the Stage, you can add another Paste Relative operation, and you'll have a 45-frame animation in which the marble bounces all the way off the Stage.

6. *Click frame 31 of channel 1 to select it.*

7. *From the Edit menu, select Paste Special and Relative.*

The new action starts at a still lower point on the screen—once again, where the previous sprite left off.

Offsetting segments

Now we have one marble bouncing fairly realistically from the upper left until it drops out of sight on the lower right. If we decide we want to add another marble doing more or less the same thing, we can simply cut and paste this segment into a second channel.

1. *Select and copy the entire contents of channel 1.*

2. *Click cell 1 of channel 2 and then paste.*

Playback, however, demonstrates that there's a problem with this: The segments occupy different channels in the Score, but on the Stage they occupy exactly the same space and time. Since channel 2 is blocking out channel 1 entirely, what's the point? Cutting and pasting is only the first step in successful segment duplication. The next step is to massage the copies so that they take on identities of their own.

Offsetting in space

Our first recourse is to displace one of our two segments, so that both can show up on the Stage. And that's easy enough to do: If you select a number of sprites in the Score and then manipulate one of them on the Stage, then all the selected sprites will change accordingly.

1. *Click the last occupied cell in channel 2.*

2. *Shift-click cell 1 of channel 2 to select the entire sprite segment, and then move the playback head to the first frame.*

You could Shift-click to select the segments with the playback head in any frame, but since the Stage can display only one frame at a time, it displays the one in which the playback head is currently placed. We want to gauge our offsetting by the first position in our animation, so we've selected the first cell after selecting them all.

3. *On the Stage, move sprite 2 so that it's directly to the right of sprite 1.*

Now play back your movie. You should have two marbles bouncing: one next to the other.

Offsetting in time

One of our marbles is no longer eclipsing the other, but they're still performing in synchronized formation. This is good when we want a precision-choreographed look and feel, but our current task is to make two different marbles appear to be behaving naturally, so let's break the synchronization by making our next move a chronological one.

1. *Select all the sprite segments in channel 2.*

Since we're not eyeballing placement this time around, it doesn't matter on which cell the playback head is placed.

2. *From the Edit menu, select Cut Sprites.*

The sprites disappear.

3. *Select frame 25 in channel 2.*

4. From the Edit menu, select Paste Sprites.

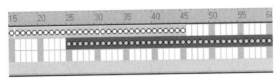

We haven't changed anything about the physical movement in the segment—just the time at which it happens. Play back the movie now to see the results. Interesting, isn't it, how the two bounces still look similar but not identical? By adjusting both space and time, we've added a lot of differences for the eye to interpret.

Reversing sequence

Now let's introduce even more disparity into the mix. The Reverse Sequence command will retain all of our sprite placement information but will simply flop the order within the segment.

1. Shift-click to select all of channel 2; from the Modify menu, select Join Sprites.

2. From the Modify menu, select Reverse Sequence.

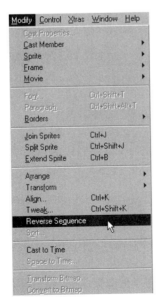

Now, on playback, sprite 2 seems to leap up rather than bounce down. Reverse Sequence is a good tool for orchestrating exits: You can animate a cast member's entrance onto the Stage, use In-Between to keep the cast member steady for any duration, and then paste the entrance animation and select Reverse Sequence to make the exit.

Switching cast members

There's one more way to make our second marble look still more different: by actually *making* it a different cast member. You can switch cast members corresponding to any sprite while retaining that sprite's placement information. Applying such a substitution to a segment of sprites effectively gives you the power to save the motion while changing the image.

To start, we'll need to add a second cast member.

1. *Open the Paint window.*

It should open with the graphic of cast member 1 (Marble) active. We need a new blank canvas, so we'll open a new slot in the Cast.

2. *Click the plus symbol in the upper left—that's the Paint window's New Cast Member button.*

3. *Use the Paint tools to create another filled black circle.*

4. *Decorate the inside of this sphere with colors of your choice.*

5. *Name this new cast member Marble 2. Close Paint.*

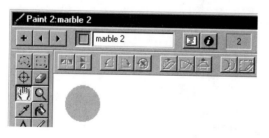

As you work in the Paint window, the Cast window will update to show your work. When you're done, Marble 2 should automatically be selected in the Cast. If it isn't, click it once to select it before proceeding.

6. Select all the sprites in channel 2.

An easy way to do this is to click the channel number. Just remember, though, that if the channel contains more than one sprite segment, all the segments will be selected.

7. Select Exchange Cast Members from the Edit menu (or the toolbar).

You'll find that throughout the channel, Marble 2 has replaced Marble.

The shortcut for Exchange Cast Members is **Control-E** (Windows) or **Command-E** (Macintosh).

Exchange Cast Members is an especially powerful tool, as it can allow you to build your movie first and then refine the graphic elements later. In chapters to come, we'll be making simple "sketch" graphics for cast members and then using the exchange method to drop in more sophisticated artwork later.

INTRODUCING INK EFFECTS

We're going to tackle one more quick-and-easy way to radically change a Stage presence: by using the variables known as **ink effects**.

We've already established that each sprite is an individual copy of a cast member. Well, ink effects can change the *nature* of that copy by dictating how it's drawn on the screen. The various "inks" are actually modes of display; some change the sprite's appearance radically, while others make subtle changes that show up only when one sprite interacts with another.

Ink effects open up an entire realm of possibilities, and we'll be discussing them more in later chapters. For now, let's introduce ink effects by way of a few experiments.

To start, we'll simplify our Score and add a black backdrop to our Gmetrics movie.

1. Delete all of the sprite segments in the Score.

2. As you did earlier, drag the Marble cast member to the left side of the Stage and then extend it through frame 30.

3. Use tweening to make the marble move across the Stage.

4. *From the Modify menu, select Movie and then Properties. Use the Stage Color chip to change the backdrop to some nice color, such as purple.*

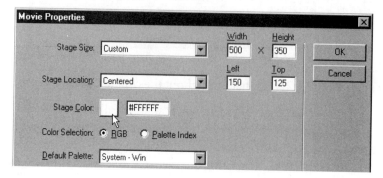

Run the movie. Notice how our marble now appears to have a white square around it? This is the **bounding box**, the quadrilateral area surrounding all cast members, even round ones. Since we had a white background previously, it wasn't especially apparent, though you may have glimpsed the bounding box when one sprite overlapped another.

Now direct your attention to the Score window. See the Ink menu? All the sprites placed thus far have had a single ink effect applied to them: Copy. Let's change that on one of our sprite segments.

5. *Select all the sprite segments in channel 1.*

6. *Click Copy in the Ink section of the Score window.*

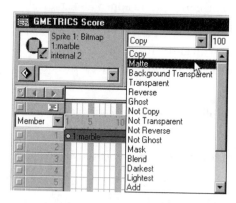

A pop-up menu appears with a total of 20 choices.

Score-level ink effects are explored in detail in Chapter 7: *More Production Tools.*

7. Select Matte from the pop-up menu.

Now run the movie. What happened to our marble? The bounding box is now invisible, and only the marble shows.

The Matte ink effect makes the sprite's bounding box transparent, allowing the background to show right up to the edges of the cast member. Try setting the ink to Background Transparent. Same thing, right? Actually, though, there is a difference between the two ink effects. If the sprite has a white area within it (which is our sprite's background color), it too would be transparent. Of the two ink effects, Background Transparent is preferred because it animates much faster. If parts of your sprite are the background color, however, you'll need to stick with Matte.

While we're at it, let's look at a related sprite property, Blend. Blend is used to make sprites transparent. It doesn't work with all inks, but it works fine with Matte and Background Transparent. In the Score, just to the right of the Ink pop-up menu is the Blend pop-up menu, in which Blend is set to 100% by default. You can use the pop-up menu or set specific values. Now let's set a blend and let Director tween it for us at the same time.

1. Click the last frame of the sprite in the Score. If the cell doesn't have a round circle (indicating a keyframe), select Keyframe from the Insert menu.

2. For this frame, set the Blend value to 10%.

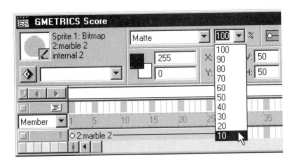

Now play the movie. Notice how the sprite fades as it crosses the screen? Not a bad way to make an exit or to make an animation fade off into the sunset. Speaking of which, try this one:

3. Select the end keyframe of the sprite again.

Just below and to the right of the Blend field are two fields labeled W and H (for width and height). These are the dimensions of the sprite's bounding box.

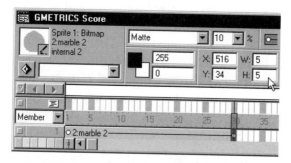

4. Set new values for the bounding box dimensions—about 5 x 5 should do.

Rewind and play the movie. Now the marble seems to fade off into the distance.

WHAT'S LINGO?
Lingo is Director's programming language. You'll start working with Lingo in Chapter 4: *Introducing Interactivity.*

The reason we used a simplified sprite for this demonstration is that Director's tweening occurs between keyframes. Because of the way we made it, our bouncing marble had a keyframe in every cell. We could still tween the blend and size for the sprite segment, but it wouldn't be automatic—we'd need to set individual values for each cell. That sounds like a tedious chore, but fortunately it can also be accomplished using Lingo.

Feel free to experiment with other ink effects—and any other animation aspects that strike your fancy—before moving on to the next chapter.

POINTS TO REMEMBER

In this chapter, we've touched upon the following:

- We discussed the basics of animation in Director: assembling a Cast, adding cast members to the Score (and thereby onto the Stage), and getting cast members to move around.

- We discussed the distinctions among **cast members**, **sprites**, and **sprite segments**. Cast members are media elements in a Cast database, sprites are their representations on the Stage, and sprite segments are those representations in sequence across the timeline of the Score.

- The **registration point** is what Director considers the physical center of a bitmap cast member. You can relocate the point in the Paint window to affect where the cast member appears on the Stage.

- Each physical element placed on the Stage has a **bounding box**, a square area that's as large as the outer perimeter of the object itself. It's always a rectangle, and it appears only when a sprite is selected. You can change the proportions of the box to change the appearance of a sprite, without changing the original cast member from which the sprite is derived.

- The main method of animation in Director is **step recording**. It involves placing the same cast member in multiple Score frames, in slightly different positions.

- Step recording is made somewhat less tedious with **auto-animation tools** such as Extend Sprite, Sprite Tweening, and Space to Time.

- Other ways to introduce a sense of animation are through the use of **ink effects** to vary modes of display for individual sprites, and by modifying the size of sprites.

IL'S KHMDL OMDG SDBBCSS

The Oracle Developer Programme

Oracle Screensaver:
Mascots in Motion

SCREENSAVERS USED TO BE INNOCUOUS BITS OF IMAGERY DESIGNED TO guard against monitor damage, but they're now well entrenched as a promotional tool. As this project demonstrates, they're also an effective format for making the most of Director-based animations.

Project background

When a computer isn't in active use, its monitor becomes a potential billboard. That reality wasn't lost on Katherine McBride, Media Production Manager for the Oracle Developer Program (ODP) in Redwood Shores, California. In planning for the annual ODP conference, she concluded that a customized screensaver could have two uses:

- As a means of underscoring ODP's identity on the dozens of displays installed at the conference, including a large-scale overhead projection.

- As a gift for conference attendees. They could install the screensaver on their systems and have an ongoing reminder of ODP as a resource for their software development efforts.

With this in mind, she approached us at Panmedia and laid out the parameters for the project. It had to be Windows 95 compatible and fit on a single floppy disk. It had to be easily installed and removed using the standard method for screensavers. It should have plenty of visual punch (to make people want to look at it), and the corporate identity aspect should be strong but not over-played. In other words, she wanted something with a bit more style than a simple logo floating in space.

The approach

Since a screensaver is designed to unfold automatically, with no interaction from the end user (in fact, it should quit when the user is ready to get to work), we decided to develop a linear, looping animation within Director. It was more than adequate for delivering interesting graphics in motion—but that was just the content. For the container, a fully functioning screensaver, we needed another software tool.

After some research, we settled upon CineMac ScreenSaver Factory from MacSourcery, a remarkably easy-to-use utility that converts Director projector files into fully self-contained screensaver files. Despite the company's name, the product is available for both the MacOS and Windows platforms. And aside from some special Lingo required to make the movie behave like a screensaver (which we'll get to), the CineMac approach required no special programming.

If you'd like to experiment with converting some of your Director-based animations into screensavers, trial versions of CineMac ScreenSaver Factory for both MacOS and Windows systems have been included on the CD that accompanies this book. You'll find them in the Demos section.

Our software quiver was rounded out with Adobe Photoshop and Illustrator. On the hardware side, we did as much of the animation as possible on the Macintosh (using a Wacom ArtPad II tablet to finesse the artwork) and then transferred the movie to a Windows system. Conversion to a projector, the projector's conversion to a screensaver, and testing were done in Windows.

THE AESTHETICS: ADDING INTEREST

To begin the project, McBride gave us a Director animation used in an earlier presentation, developed by In-Vision Communications. This short movie depicted all the elements of the ODP logo (two little men, two gears, and an enormous wrench)—but the animation itself was limited and the graphics were a flat black.

HARD BODIES:
In the original artwork, the elements were hard edged and geometrical, without showing color or dimensionality.

To add interest, we decided on three main aesthetic additions:

- *Color and depth in the logo elements.* This meant achieving a 3D look by adding drop shadows and administering colors that would seem to cycle through a range as the animation progressed. We also wanted to soften the artwork to make it seem more fluid and less geometric.

- *Dynamic entrances and exits.* Rather than beginning with all the elements in place, we decided that the logo should be assembled, set in motion, and then disassembled. Little flourishes would be added to give a sense of personality to the two characters, which we promptly named RG (for Running Guy) and WG (for Wrench Guy).

- *An unfolding code.* Even with the logo construction and deconstruction, we didn't feel that there was enough visual interest to command the attention of the casual viewer. We thought about the target audience—computer programmers—and realized that a bit of simulated code breaking might appeal to their hacker sensibilities. So instead of flatly displaying the ODP slogan ("It's about your success"), we displayed it as a cipher that gets solved as RG treads away on the gear mechanism.

CREATING THE CHARACTERS

We began by breaking up the elements of the original movie into graphic files for design manipulation. Since Director's export features don't extend to individual cast members, we used simple cutting and pasting: We opened a cast slot in the Paint window, used the selection tool with the Shrink setting enabled, and copied the artwork to the clipboard for transfer to Photoshop.

Manipulating the images

Once in Photoshop, we gave some of the elements a fluidity of line by intentionally blurring and then resharpening them. We applied the Gaussian Blur filter effect to diffuse the image and then adjusted the white, gray, and black points in the Levels dialog box (displayed by choosing Image and then Adjust) to flatten out the tonality until solid lines again appeared on the perimeters of the item. To keep the end result consistent, we saved our tweaking of Levels as an external Photoshop settings file and then reloaded it as needed.

NOT FADE AWAY:
To introduce more organic, rounded edges, artwork was blurred and then resolidified.

The next step was applying color. We wanted a sort of muted kaleidoscope effect, with the colors shifting during the motion of the final product. We compiled the multiple instances of each item (such as the five versions of the rotating main gear) into a single Photoshop file, selected them all, and applied a single gradient color from Kai's Power Tools Gradient Designer. Because the filter was applied to the colors in the gradient as a group, they show up in different locations on the images. When these are later set in motion in Director, the variance has the effect of a subtle, flowing color shift.

The final graphic step was adding the drop shadows. Although there are filters to achieve this automatically, we did it the old-fashioned way: by duplicating the artwork on another layer in Photoshop, adjusting the contrast until it became a flat black image, and then applying Gaussian Blur again. Placing that layer in the background and offsetting it slightly completed the effect.

One of the challenges of designing on one platform for delivery on another is the difference in display color. Windows systems tend to have a darker, denser display than the MacOS, which means that colors can shift several shades when ported. To eliminate the possibility of unpleasant surprises, it's a good idea to test your design choices on the target platform while the project is still in the preliminary stages. In this project, we adjusted the settings on our Macintosh monitors to more closely approximate Windows displays and stepped up both the brightness and contrast of all artwork.

Importing the elements

Then it was time to return to the Director environment. We used the Mode settings in Photoshop to desample every image down to Indexed (8-bit, diffusion dithered, and mapped to the System palette). Then we saved the files in the PICT format. These were imported easily into Director—but we made a mistake that's all too easy to do. Director doesn't save the new cast members at the color depths of their source files, but at the color depth set on the importing system's monitor. Since the import was performed on a monitor set to 16-bit color, all the elements were saved as 16-bit artwork, despite the fact that we had mapped them to 8-bit color in Photoshop. This didn't affect the quality of the resulting cast members, but it meant they were taking up more file space than necessary. Using the Transform Bitmap dialog box, available from the Modify menu, brought them back to the expected size.

PUTTING THE PIECES INTO PLACE

The initial animation was simple choreography: The gears roll in and come to a standstill against each other. Then RG dashes to the top of the works and awaits WG's entrance. WG applies his wrench, and they're off.

For preliminary blocking, we arranged the elements in their final positions and then applied tweening effects to single representative cast members. To get accurate alignment for the main tableau, we tweened the segments in reverse, applying the Reverse Sequence command. This got things moving, but it wasn't quite animation yet; since we were whisking in sprites derived from single cast members, they slid smoothly into place with no apparent internal motion. To set them rolling, running, and walking, we needed to swap new cast members into the sprite segments. We did that with the Exchange Cast Members command (on the File menu). We'd taken care to import the artwork in sequence, so the substitutions became a relatively straightforward assembly-line production.

A SLIDE SHOW:
Since rotary motion requires multiple cast members, the initial movements of the gears were made with single sprites, which slide into place via tweening commands. To change from sliding to rolling, we then swapped in a sequence of cast members.

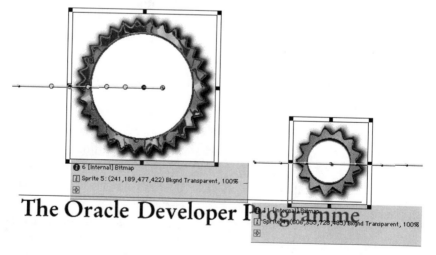

Setting registration points

Our animation still needed some tweaking. Switching cast members in the sprite segments created a plausible impression of movement, but with considerable jerkiness. The culprit? The registration points of the cast members: They varied slightly, causing the sprites to jump during playback.

The problem stemmed from the fact that when artwork is imported, Director sets its registration point at the exact center of the design. Since the dimensions of each piece of artwork were slightly different (even with the versions of the round gears), the registration shifted accordingly. It took painstaking adjustments to display the artwork consistently. Unfortunately, Director doesn't let you enter exact values for the registration point location; you have to eyeball it, shifting it in the Paint window while watching the results on the Stage.

The cipher effect

Getting the effect of code breaking in action was one of the most challenging aspects of the project.

In terms of animation, the effect was fairly simple to design: We created cast members of individual letters and laid them down on top of the "It's about your success" slogan, taking care to layer characters of the same approximate width (a "G" would be placed over an "O," a "J" over an "I," and so on). Once again, registration points and alignment had to be exact, to create the impression of rapid letter substitution.

KNOW THE CODE:
The cipher-cracking effect was achieved by superimposing selected letters (above) over the actual slogan (below).

The method by which the slogan is decoded, however, took some deliberation. When the random substitution solves a particular letter, all other instances of that letter have to be decoded as well. Thus, when one "S" is found, the other three in the phrase also must be revealed. It took several passes to get the animation to appear sufficiently random, yet unfold in a fashion that doesn't make the concealed slogan too obvious too soon.

POLISHING THE PRESENTATION

The next phase was a process of polishing and refining the action. A preliminary movie was shown to McBride, who made several recommendations relating to timing: RG should pause a little longer here, the gears should roll off there, and so on. Thanks to the Timing channel and the ease of reconfiguring sprite segments, none of her requests were difficult to implement. Then we were left to smooth down the edges and prepare for conversion to a screensaver.

Using ink effects

Since we had multiple elements coming into direct contact with one another, judicious use of Score-level ink effects was crucial. As you can see by examining the Score, a typical frame has five or six different inks operating at once, sometimes directly on top of one another. Using so many ink effects is usually what's called a performance hit—a significant burden on processing. If we'd been developing for a broader audience, this would have been a major point of concern, but the client assured us that the screensaver was intended for high-end systems with plenty of graphics-crunching power. We left the ink effects in place.

> When performance hits are a factor, one solution is to use a first Director movie (with ink effects) as a simple compositing medium and then take snapshots of the frames and import those snapshots into a second movie. It's an approach taken in Project Profile 2: *Levi's Screensaver.*

LINKS OF INKS:
We used a number of ink effects to keep the often overlapping elements displayed correctly.

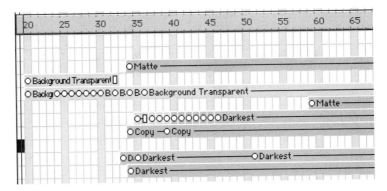

Since the filled centers of both gears remain stationary while the cogs are spinning, we gave each a Matte ink and applied Background Transparent to the gears themselves. In the case of RG, we applied the Darkest ink throughout, which worked because the only part of RG that overlapped other sprites was his shadow. The Background Transparent ink might seem to be a better choice, but the anti-aliased nature of the drop shadow gives it a thin light halo when that ink is applied (try it and see).

For WG, Darkest wasn't an effective choice, since his wrench has to pass over the darker small cog and yet remain opaque. Our solution was to keep him in Matte mode and manually whittle down a portion of the wrench's shadow— not the most elegant workaround, but since these sprites are seen for only a moment or two, it does the job.

Another nice ink effect comes toward the end, when the color elements make their exit from the Stage. They are left in their place is a burnt-in version of the logo, an effect achieved by lightly texturing a silhouette in Photoshop and then placing it in the movie with Not Copy applied.

Final animation tweaking

We rounded out the animation by playing with gravity. Instead of having WG float effortlessly down, we compressed some of the sprites to convey a sense of landing and recovery. And rather than reverse the entrance sequence, we opted for something different: The small gear now falls off the edge of the line underscoring "Oracle Developer Program," to be followed by WG taking the plunge. Again, we paid attention to sprite compression and elongation to add realism to the leap.

THE LONG AND SHORT OF IT:
The Wrench Guy character's leaps and landings are made more believable by momentary compressions and extensions of individual sprites.

This approach served us well when the client requested a last-minute text addition, to be tacked on after the animation. We cut and pasted the jumping sprite segment, which with minor modifications allowed WG to land on every line of the message. A quick transition effect made him appear to be taking a leap of faith each time, since each line waits until the last moment to appear. When we realized that the last line was a little short, we couldn't resist adding a humorous final flourish, making him miss the mark.

THE FALL GUY:
With a few modifications, the character's motion was adapted for last-minute additional appearances.

If you want to automatically receive the latest Oracle software and technical information before it hits the streets,

COMMENTS

- Once the animation was completed, conversion to final screensaver form took a bit of customized Lingo. To learn more about that process, see Project Profile 2: *Levi's Screensaver*.

- Notice how the shadows are slightly deeper on the little men than on the gears. When attempting a dimensional effect, careful application of shadows will go a long way toward underscoring the sense of layers.

- Note also that even though the small gear is "on top" of the larger gear in the hierarchy of the Score, it appears to be underneath. That's because it uses the Darkest ink effect, while the larger gear has Background Transparent applied.

- How could this project be improved? Well, you'll note that the gears have no interior shadows when they roll on and off the Stage. Also, the reason RG runs so swiftly up the side of the main gear is that we didn't draw him in a believable climbing motion. We copied a few of the images of him running and rotated them slightly. Take a look at the Score and you'll see that he bounds to the top in six quick frames. And why is it that he runs in and out on a different plane than the rest of the action? These are minor concerns, but ones we would have tackled had we had the time.

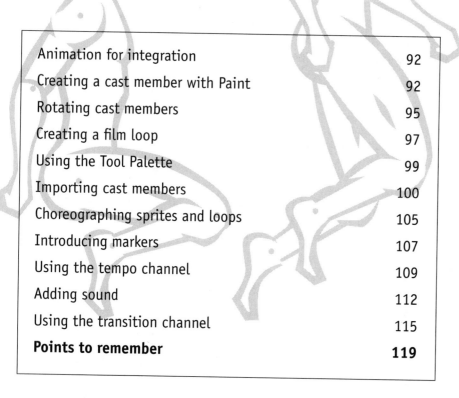

CHAPTER 3

MAKING IT MULTIMEDIA

ANIMATION IS ONLY ONE ASPECT OF DIRECTOR'S CAPABILITIES, AND THE visual medium is only one of the media in "multimedia." In this chapter we'll start placing the animation techniques that we've learned in a greater context, by beginning to take advantage of sound and tempo control parameters in our movies.

ANIMATION FOR INTEGRATION

This time we'll start by creating a slightly more complicated animation than the ones we worked with in the previous chapter. We'll be using in-betweening animation methods, plus a few new techniques—some new even to Director 7. In the process, we'll employ several of the effects channels and even add our first sound element.

1. *From the File menu, select New and then Movie.*

2. *From the Modify menu, select Movie and then Properties. Set the Stage Size to 640 x 480 and the Stage color to white.*

3. *From the File menu, select Preferences and then Sprite. Set Span Duration to 1.*

4. *Save this movie and name it Rolling.dir.*

CREATING A CAST MEMBER WITH PAINT

Make sure that the Ink Effect pop-up menu at the bottom of the Paint window is set to Normal before proceeding.

To create our first cast member, let's go a little deeper into the Paint window's graphic capabilities. The Marble cast member in Chapter 2 served us well for creating bouncing objects, but this time we want a cast member that can roll with a more visible motion. An eight ball should do the trick.

1. *In the Paint window, create a black circle about the size of a quarter.*

2. *Click the foreground paint chip (see the following illustration). Then select the first small square—the white one.*

3. *Create a smaller white circle within the upper-left quadrant of the black circle.*

A NICE ROUND FIGURE:
Use the tools in the
Paint window to
create a white circle
within the black
circle—the beginnings
of an eight ball.

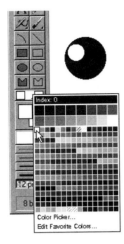

This is the little white circle that will contain the number 8. Try to set it well off center—that'll give it some dimension and make the rolling action more obvious. Remember that you can use the Undo command (Control-Z Windows; Command-Z Macintosh) to undo a mistake and try again.

Using Paint's Text tool

It wouldn't be an eight ball without the number 8, so let's add that. We'll create the 8 outside of the circle and then select it and move it to exactly where we want it to appear.

1. Select the Text tool (the tool with the letter A) in Paint.

2. Click anywhere outside of the two circles in the Paint window.

A blinking cursor appears.

Since Paint's text is bitmapped, you'll be able to apply formatting options only during creation. Once you deselect text you create in Paint, it becomes just another graphic element.

3. Type the number 8. (Don't panic if nothing seems to happen.)

Where is the 8 that you typed? Actually, even though you may not be able to see it, it's there. It just doesn't appear to be because we left the foreground paint chip set to white. Let's change it back to black:

4. Use the foreground paint chip to set the foreground color to black (the last square).

If you didn't inadvertently deselect the numeral by clicking elsewhere, it should now be black. As long as the type stays selected, you can employ a number of formatting options (even the Backspace and Delete keys).

Experiment with the font settings on the Modify menu until you've found a suitable 8 (I used 18-point New York, bold).

Using the Lasso tool

To move the numeral into its final position, we'll use the Lasso tool. You may have used a lasso in other applications such as Photoshop, but this one has an interesting twist.

1. **Select the Lasso tool.**

2. **Use the lasso to draw a circle around the 8.**

SELECT IT, COWPOKE:
The Lasso tool allows for messy selection since it can shrink to fit the object it surrounds.

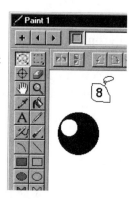

It doesn't matter how neat the selection is. Just surround the entire number 8, avoiding the black circle. The instant you lift your finger from the mouse button, the selection will disappear, and your 8 will start blinking (actually, it's more like a throbbing). That's the Lasso tool's Shrink feature in action: It identifies the actual graphic in the enclosed area (that is, the region with a color different from the background), and it adjusts the selection accordingly. Now you can slide the 8 into place.

If your lasso selection didn't shrink to the dimensions of the number, the lasso has probably been changed from its default setting. Click the Lasso tool's icon again (click *and* hold, on the Macintosh); a small pop-up menu should appear, from which you can select the Shrink mode: set it to Lasso.

3. **Move the lasso cursor over the selected area until it turns into an arrow.**

4. **Drag the selection to the center of the white circle.**

ROTATING CAST MEMBERS

Now that we have an eight ball, let's see if we can make it roll across the Stage. We've moved sprites across the Stage before and even made them shrink and fade. But the eight ball needs to look like it's actually turning as it rolls.

In earlier versions of Director, making the eight ball roll across the Stage required a separate cast member for each rotated position of the ball—as many cast members as you felt you needed to make the rotation look smooth. Now, using the new Director 7 **sprite rotation**, all you need is a single cast member and auto-tweening to rotate the sprite for you.

Another new feature is Director 7's ability to **skew** sprites—distorting their display without actually modifying the source image itself (this is especially handy for adding perspective and compression effects). As with rotation, you set the skew at a key point, and Director auto-tweens the frames in between. With previous versions of Director, you could skew only the source image itself.

1. *Close the Paint widow. Then drag the eight ball from the Cast to frame 1 in the Score.*

2. *Extend the sprite through frame 10.*

We've lengthened sprites before using Extend Sprite. Another quick way to do this is to hold down the Alt (Windows) or Option (Macintosh) key while dragging the sprite. For sprite segments, this isn't necessary—you just drag the sprite's end frame to extend a sprite. If you try that with a single-frame sprite, however, you will just move the sprite to a new location.

Use the **Alt** (Windows) or **Option** (Macintosh) key to extend a single-frame sprite by dragging.

3. *Click the last frame of the sprite. Only the last frame should be selected.*

4. *Open the Sprite Inspector (Control-Alt-S Windows; Command-Option-S Macintosh).*

Find the field next to the turning arrow (as shown on the following page). That's the **Rotation Angle control**. Right now it should be set to 0.00, meaning that there is no rotation.

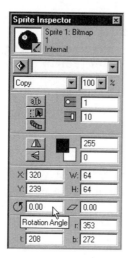

We want one full spin, so we'll set this angle control accordingly:

5. Set the rotation angle to 360—this value is in degrees.

The Rotation Angle control is also available on the sprite toolbar at the top of the Score window, as shown here (if you're keeping your Score window just big enough to see your work, you'll need to extend the Score window to find it).

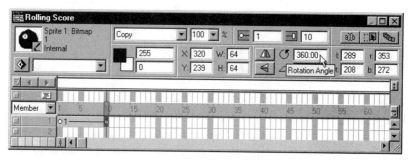

6. Play the movie to see how it looks.

Click the playback head and drag it right and left to see the action on the Stage. As you drag the playback head, the frames animate. (You don't need to run the entire movie to see the rotation.)

The rotation looks pretty good, although the eight ball just sits in one place and spins. Adding linear movement across the Stage will give us the real look of a rolling ball. Notice, though, that the ball spins *clockwise*. We plan on rolling the ball from right to left across the Stage, so we'll need the ball to spin in the opposite direction.

7. *Go back to the Rotation Angle control and set it to –360 degrees (minus 360). Make sure that only the last frame of the cast member is selected.*

8. *It's playback time!*

Now the eight ball rotates in the correct direction.

> When you set a rotation angle, Director uses the registration point (remember that?) of each cast member as the focal point, or axis, about which the sprite spins. By default, a Paint window bitmap's registration point is set at its center. You can try changing the registration point for your eight ball and watch how your ball spins. Loop-the-loop! Just make sure to reset the registration point by double-clicking the registration tool button when you're done playing.

CREATING A FILM LOOP

We now have a sprite segment that's 10 frames long, and it's created with just a single cast member. That sure helps keep down the size of your movie, and you can see how this technique can be used to create Web-friendly files that download quickly. But we're not done with squeezing the most animation out of a few kilobytes of file size.

The action within this segment's animation is interesting, but what if we want to extend it through more frames? Here's an experiment: Try tugging on the right keyframe to extend the segment for another 20 frames or so. Now play the movie (make sure looping is turned on in the Control Panel).

GET A GRIP:
Tugging on a sprite
segment's handle
extends that segment
for as long as you like.
The results, however,
may be different than
you'd expect.

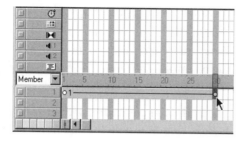

Well, that didn't quite work, did it? Instead of making the animation longer, it made it slower. That's because the rotation angle is still set to 360 degrees: Director extends the segment by adding more intermediate tweening. How, then, are we going to make the eight ball roll on?

FILM LOOP:
A cast member produced from a sequence of other cast members.

The answer is actually fairly simple. We can save this sprite segment as a single unit and then save that unit as a cast member itself. Such a cast member is called a **film loop**, and it's a key tool for managing action in Director. Return the sprite segment to its original length of 10 frames. Then let's get down to business.

1. *Select the entire sprite segment in channel 1.*

2. *Drag the segment to slot 2 in the Cast window.*

3. *A dialog box asks you to name the resulting loop. Name it* **eight ball.** *Then click OK.*

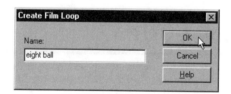

The film loop is now a full-fledged cast member. In the Cast database, it's represented by the title instead of a graphic image. Note the symbol in the lower-right corner of the cast member's picon.

Since we'll be working with this cast member rather than the one from which it was derived, let's clear the Score.

4. *With the Score window active (and the sprite segment still selected), choose Cut Sprites from the Edit menu (Control-X Windows; Command-X Macintosh).*

USING THE TOOL PALETTE

Now let's give our eight ball something to roll upon. We could use the line tool in Paint to make a simple horizontal line, but there is another method that takes up less memory. Instead of creating a bitmap, we'll use the Tool Palette to create a shape and draw the line directly on the Stage.

1. *Click the first cell of channel 1 (to move the playback head to the beginning).*

2. *Open the Tool Palette window.*

3. *Click the Line tool.*

The cursor changes to crosshairs. But if we draw a line right now, it will be an invisible one, since the default line thickness is None (represented by a dotted line). We need to set a thickness.

4. *Click the thickest (bottom) line in the line selection area.*

5. *Use the crosshairs to draw a short horizontal line on the Stage. Drag the new spite so that it is against the left edge of the Stage, approximately two-thirds of the way down from the top.*

6. *Use the sprite handles to extend the sprite over to the right edge of the Stage.*

Notice that as you draw the line, your actions were translated into entries in both the Score and the Cast. The cast member icon has its own unique subicon, too: a symbol for a shape cast member. This category also includes the filled or empty ovals and squares you can create with the Tool Palette.

One more task: The line exists only in the first frame, so we need to extend its presence in subsequent cells.

7. *Click to select the sprite in cell 1, frame 1.*

8. *Hold down the Shift key and click the channel in frame 50.*

9. *From the Modify menu, select Extend Sprite.*

The line is mass-duplicated. Since we used only one keyframe, tweening has no motion to extrapolate, so our "ground" stays put.

IMPORTING CAST MEMBERS

The shortcut for Import is **Control-R** (Windows) or **Command-R** (Macintosh).

Our Stage is set. But before we orchestrate any entrances and exits, let's round out our Cast. Instead of going to the Paint window and creating another cast member from scratch, this time we'll import the artwork from external files.

1. *From the File menu, select Import.*

The Import window appears.

2. *Make sure that the pop-up menu below the main window is set to Bitmap Image. In Windows, this menu is called Files of type; on the Mac, it's labeled Show.*

Since Director can import so many different types of cast members, it uses this menu to zero in on a specific file type. When Sound is selected on this menu, for example, only audio files will show up in the directory listing. In this case, we're looking for graphics files, so we set the file type to Bitmap Image.

Macromedia continues adding new import capabilities to Director. Director 7 can now import even more file types than earlier versions could. Now both Windows and Macintosh platforms can access BMP, GIF, JPEG, LRG, MacPaint, Photoshop 3.0, PICT (or PCT), PNG, and TIFF (or TIF) files. You can also import PICS files on the Macintosh, while Windows users can also choose from FLC, FLI, PCX, Photo CD, PostScript, and WMF files. And those are just graphics types. When you include other types of media, Director 7 can import just about every popular format you can think of.

A MESSAGE OF IMPORT:
In the Import window, you need to specify the type of file for which you're searching.

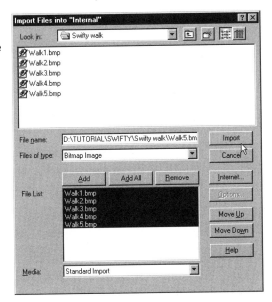

3. *Open the folder labeled Tutorials on the CD-ROM.*

4. *Open Swifty and then open Swifty Walk.*

A total of five files should appear, all with the .bmp suffix. This is the **file name extension**, a three-character code used to identify file types in the Windows operating system (it's not necessary on the Macintosh). In this case, the extension identifies graphic art files saved in the bitmap format.

FILE NAME EXTENSION:
The part of the file name used by Windows to identify the file type (.PCT, .BMP, and so on).

5. *Click the Add All button.*

6. *Click the Import button.*

The Image Options dialog box appears. Set Color Depth to Stage [8 bits] and set Palette to Remap to System-Win (or System-Mac, for Macintosh); then select the Same Settings for Remaining Images option.

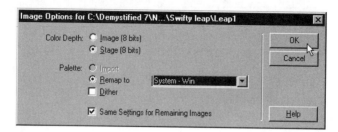

Each file is automatically placed in the Cast as a separate cast member. Files are placed in the order they are listed in the Import dialog box. Instead of using the Add All option, you can use the Add option to select one file at a time; cast members will then be created in the order that you choose. Since we started with three cast members (the eight ball, the film loop, and the line), the first imported file should become cast member 4. Notice how the names of the files become the names of the cast members (without any file name extension).

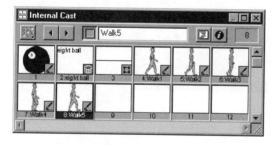

7. **Double-click cast member 4 to open the Paint window (if it's not already open).**

8. **Repeatedly click the Next arrow in the Paint window to display all five new cast members. (The Previous and Next arrows are at the upper left of the Paint window, next to the New Cast Member plus symbol.)**

Double-clicking a cast member is a fast way to open that cast member's editor.

What we have here are five silhouettes of Swifty walking. To bring him to life, we'll use another film loop. The first thing we need to do is get our cast members on the Stage.

Using Cast to Time

Now we will place our new cast members on the Stage. Just as Space to Time takes a group in the Score and places each member sequentially on the Stage, Cast to Time does the same for a group in the Cast.

1.   *Click channel 2, frame 1, in the Score.*

2.   *In the Cast window, Shift-click to select all five Swifty cast members.*

3.   *From the Modify menu, select Cast to Time.*

4.   *Turn off looping and then play back your movie.*

Cast to Time will import all selected cast members to the exact center of the Stage.

For a quick instant, Swifty appears to be walking and then disappears—the sequence is only five frames long, and the movie is 50 frames. Notice that the five Swifty cast members are combined into a single sprite segment in the Score. Prior to Director 6, using the Cast to Time command would have resulted in six individual sprites being placed in the Score in sequential frames.

5.   *As we did for the eight ball, create a film loop from the sprite segment by selecting it and dragging it to the first empty slot in the Cast. Name the resulting film loop* **Walking**.

6.   *Delete the Swifty sprite segment from the Score.*

Now that we have the film loop, we no longer need the sprite segment.

The mechanics of a film loop

Now that we have a film loop that does what the five Swifty cast members could do, do we need to keep the individual cast members? After all, the loop performs the action we want. Well, even if we never place the original cast members anywhere in the Score, we need to keep them in the Cast.

After creating a film loop, don't delete or modify the cast members from which the loop was created. Director needs them to re-create the animation you encapsulated in the loop. If the cast members that make up a film loop are deleted, there's no way to bring them back from the dead.

You may recall that in Chapter 1 we made the distinction between linked and embedded cast members. Well, a film loop is sort of a cross between the two—it's really just a set of pointers to the source artwork. If we were to delete any or all of cast members 4 through 8, the film loop wouldn't work correctly. Also, making changes to the source cast members will affect the appearance and performance of the film loop.

In versions of Director prior to version 6, even moving the cast members to different cast slots caused problems with film loops. Beginning with Director 6, you can move the film loop cast members around, but they must remain in the same Cast as the loop.

Film loops don't behave exactly like other cast members:

**FILM LOOPS
ARE DIFFERENT**
Film loops behave a little differently than other cast members.

- Remember how we used the playback head to step through an animation? That doesn't work with film loops. Film loops animate only when the movie is running.

- Making a film loop longer (or shorter) doesn't change the playback speed of the loop. It changes the number of cycles through which the film loop plays.

- If you want to use ink effects, you need to apply them to the original sprite. You can't apply ink affects to a film loop.

We deleted the sprite segment used to create the Walking film loop. However, if we need to modify it, to add ink effects for example, there is a way to get the sprite segment back. Highlight the film loop member in the Cast and copy it (Control-C Windows; Command-C Macintosh). Then select a cell in the Score and paste (Control-V Windows; Command-V Macintosh). The sprite segment from which the loop was derived should appear with all its frames intact.

CHOREOGRAPHING SPRITES AND LOOPS

We've established the length of our movie at 50 frames (that's as far as we extended the ground cast member). Let's start building our action by making our walking Swifty amble approximately halfway across the Stage, using some techniques that you already have experience with: keyframing and auto-tweening.

1. *Move the playback head to the first column by clicking the first cell of channel 2.*

2. *In the Cast window, select the Walking film loop cast member.*

3. *Drag Walking directly to the Stage and place it just above the ground line, near the left border (see the illustration).*

A WALK-ON PART:
When you use a loop, remember not to erase any of the cast members used to create it.

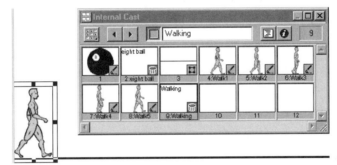

Since we're going to use Extend Sprite to complete this motion, our next step is to set the keyframe that ends Swifty's motion (for now). To make the walk take up half the movie, we'll place that keyframe midway through the film, at frame 25. Make sure the Score window remains active throughout this step.

4. *With the sprite in channel 2 still selected, Shift-click the cell in channel 2, frame 25.*

5. *From the Modify menu, choose Extend Sprite.*

Although we have extended the sprite, it has the same placement on the Stage throughout the frames, just like our Marble cast member in Chapter 2.

To finish our action, we'll nudge the ending sprite into position and let Director automatically tween the result.

6.   In the Score, select the sprite in channel 2, frame 25.

Remember that selecting one of the sprites in frames 2 through 24 selects the entire sprite. As we found in the last chapter, Director recognizes the starting and ending frames of a sprite segment as keyframes. You can select them individually.

7.   On the Stage, drag this sprite to a point approximately halfway across the length of the ground line.

8.   Rewind and play back the movie to see the result of auto-tweening.

Director has automatically reset the position of all the sprites between the starting and final frames of the segment, doing all the work for you. Swifty should walk halfway across the Stage and then disappear.

9.   Press Rewind and then use the Step Forward button in the Control Panel to view the movie frame by frame.

Notice that, unlike during playback, this time the Walking sprite doesn't change from one frame to the next; instead, Swifty remains frozen in the first portion of his stride.

A cast member substitution

One of the drawbacks of film loops is that each has only one representative image; it's hard to pinpoint exactly where you are in the cycle of an encapsulated animation. We want precise alignment of the sprites in frame 25, so we'll replace the final cell of this segment with a still cast member. Since we want to retain the Stage placement of the rest of the animation, the best way to do this is to use **cast member substitution**.

1.   In the Score, select the cell in channel 2, frame 25.

2.   In the Cast, click cast member 6 (the middle Swifty).

3.   From the Edit menu, select Exchange Cast Members (Control-E Windows; Command-E Macintosh).

Now we know Swifty's exact posture and position in that crucial frame.

Introducing the second film loop

Our protagonist needs an antagonist! The reason we've set him walking only halfway across the Stage is because that's where he's going to have a nasty encounter with our trusty eight ball. Let's roll it in from the right of the Stage:

1. *Drag the eight ball film loop from the Cast window to the cell at frame 10, channel 3.*

2. *Click the sprite on the Stage. Drag to position it on the ground line, halfway out of sight off the right side of the Stage.*

You can use your arrow keys to move a selected sprite one pixel at a time.

When you're satisfied with the position, place the second keyframe (which will be the end frame of this sprite segment) at the point of collision.

A ROLL PLAY:
We need only place the eight ball at the start and finish of its roll; In-Between will do the rest.

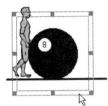

3. *Shift-click frame 25, channel 3.*

4. *Use Extend Sprite to fill in frames 11 through 25.*

5. *Select frame 25 and position the eight ball on the Stage so that it is in direct collision with Swifty.*

INTRODUCING MARKERS

We've already made three trips to frame 25. It's an easy enough number to locate on the frame counter, but as your movies become more complex, you'll find it hard to keep track of exactly what happens where. That's one reason why Director provides you with an unlimited supply of **markers**, good for both annotating and navigating within your Score (once you start using Lingo, you won't be able to live without markers).

Inserting markers

The marking system works much like the tab system in a word processing program: There's an area in which you can create as many markers as necessary. Unlike with tabs, however, you can also assign a label to each marker. Let's go to the area and designate markers for two key points in our movie.

1. *Place the cursor over the marker area in the Score window.*

2. *Click the area above frame 10. A fresh marker appears.*

This is where the eight ball makes its entrance, so let's title it as such. As soon as you place your marker, a text insertion box appears alongside. You should be able to enter your title just by typing, but if that doesn't work, click right next to the marker and try again.

3. *Type the words* **8 ball enters** *next to the marker.*

Make your mark: Place markers at key frames and use them as reference points.

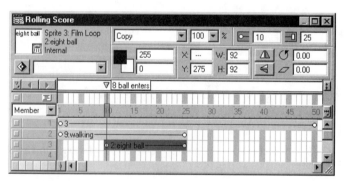

4. *Now repeat the steps to add another marker at frame 25. Name this one* **Collision**.

You can edit, relocate, and delete markers at any time. To remove a marker, just select it and drag outside of the marker area; the marker will disappear.

Navigating with the Markers window

Customized markers are good for clarity's sake, but they also serve a purpose beyond visual reference. Using the Markers window, you can jump automatically to any marked frame.

1. *From the Window menu, select Markers.*

If the marker title doesn't remain on its own line, new text will be incorporated into the title.

THE MARK OF A MARK: The Markers window lists all the markers in a movie and allows you to navigate among them.

Our two marked frames appear in the new window.

2. **Click once on "8 ball enters" in the left column.**

The playback head moves automatically to frame 10.

Why is the marker title repeated in the right column? That's an area in which you can enter still more information about the selected frame. Make sure to press the Enter or Return key after the title (to keep the title on its own line); then write whatever you like.

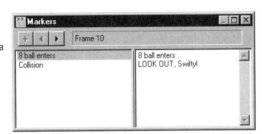

USING THE TEMPO CHANNEL

It's time to make our first foray outside the visual channels. We need to make the action stop briefly at the point of collision (frame 25), and for that we'll use the tempo channel.

1. **Navigate to the Collision marker.**

Since we are going to be working with the effects channels, we need to have them visible. If they aren't, click the Hide/Show Effects Channels arrows at the right of the marker area.

2. **Double-click the tempo channel in frame 25 to open the Frame Properties:Tempo dialog box.**

We can choose from among a number of options:

- We can reset the tempo, but in this case it wouldn't be effective (we want to pause in a single frame, not slow down several frames).

- The Wait for Mouse Click or Key Press option would bring things to a standstill, but it would introduce the element of interactivity.

- The Wait for Cue Point option is a possibility, as we will be introducing a sound effect. But as you'll see, it's not really appropriate for what we want to do.

- We can set a wait period of a specified number of seconds.

We will use the Wait option.

3. **Click the Wait radio button and then drag the selection lever until it reads 3 seconds.**

4. **Click OK.**

A SENSE OF RHYTHM:
The tempo channel can change the playback speed, pause for a specified number of seconds, or pause until an event occurs.

Examine the Score window. You'll find two changes: The tempo channel's Score cell at the point marked Collision now contains a letter (*W*), and the field at the top left of your Score contains descriptive text (*Delay 3 secs*). The *W* stands for Wait.

THERE'LL BE A SLIGHT DELAY:
When the playback head enters a frame with a tempo channel command, the field above the tempo channel displays a description.

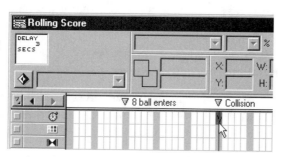

5. **Save the changes; then turn on looping and play your movie.**

Now when Swifty and the eight ball collide, you'll notice a portentous pause of 3 seconds before the movie proceeds. After observing the action, watch how the playback head pauses in the Score.

Setting the tempo playback speed

In the early days of Director, we used to struggle just to get playback fast enough to make animation look smooth; oftentimes we had to settle for a jerky flipbook-style motion. But with the advent of faster machines (and Director 7's new-and-improved playback technology), sometimes animation actually needs to be slowed down. I wouldn't be surprised if your Swifty currently seems to glide across the ground rather than saunter. The tempo channel has the cure.

1. *Double-click frame 1 in the tempo channel.*

2. *Click the Tempo radio button and set the frames per second (fps) to 8.*

3. *Click OK and play your movie.*

SPEED LIMIT
Since you don't know the inherent speeds of all computers on which your movie will be playing, it's a good idea always to set a tempo value in the first frame of your movie.

Experiment with different tempos. Remember that the tempo is a speed limit, not a guarantee that a movie will animate that fast. Using the tempo, you can ensure that a movie will not run too fast, but a slow machine (or animation on the Web) may animate the action at a slower-than-desired pace. You can set the tempo all the way up to 999 fps, but unless you have major processing power (and not much is happening on the Stage), it just ain't gonna happen. It's like those economy cars with speedometers that optimistically include up to 150 miles per hour.

Modifying a film loop

Let's take a look at our movie. The eight ball, which is positioned "over" the other channels (that is, it has a higher channel number), persists in showing its bounding box when it intersects both the ground and Swifty. Not too graceful, eh? Time to set the eight ball's ink effect so that the bounding box stays appropriately invisible. First let's recover the sprite segment.

1. *Delete the sprite segment of the eight ball film loop.*

2. *Select the eight ball film loop in the Cast and copy it (Control-C Windows; Command-C Macintosh).*

3. *Paste the film loop (Control-V Windows; Command-V Macintosh) into channel 3, frame 1, of the Score.*

The entire sprite segment is re-created in the Score. We've gotten back the spinning eight ball.

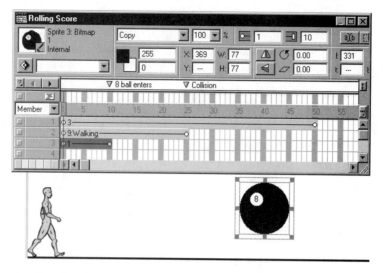

4. *Use the playback head to make sure that the segment works as expected. When you are satisfied, delete the existing eight ball film loop from the Cast.*

Now we'll create a new film loop.

5. *Select the entire eight ball sprite segment and change the ink effect to Background Transparent.*

6. *Drag the sprite segment to slot 2 in the Cast. Name the film loop* **eight ball** *again.*

7. *Re-create the rolling ball on the Stage as we did before, in frames 10 through 25.*

Now the bounding box of the eight ball no longer shows. That wasn't too much work—not as good as getting it right the first time, but at least re-creating the film loop was easier than starting from scratch.

ADDING SOUND

To make our moment of confrontation a little more realistic, let's introduce the element of sound. Up to now we've been working in a single medium: the visual one. By adding sound, you're now officially a multimedia creator. Congratulations!

Importing a sound cast member

In most cases, you'll probably want to import sound files from other sources, and this chapter supplies one. But when you want to insert a quick sound, a preliminary narration, or another "from scratch" sound, you can use whatever sound-recording capabilities are available on your system. The sound we are using is Ouch. If you want to create your own sound, keep the length to about a second or two so it works with the movie.

1. *From the File menu, choose Import.*

2. *In the Import dialog box, set the file type to Sound.*

3. *Open the folder labeled Tutorials on the CD-ROM.*

4. *Select the file Ouch.wav; then click Add.*

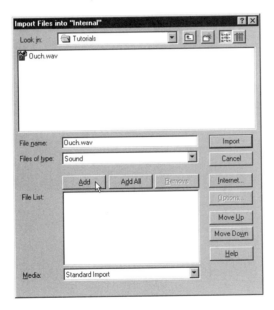

5. *Click Import.*

The sound file is imported and placed in the first available slot in the Cast window. Note that sounds, like other data types, have their own distinct subicon when they are displayed in the Cast.

Auditioning with the Properties window

You can preview graphic cast members simply by browsing through the Paint window, but you'll need a different tactic for sounds. To preview (or rather, audition) sounds before placing them in the Score, open their Properties windows.

1. *If necessary, click once to select Ouch in the Cast window.*

2. *Click the Info button (the lowercase i) in the Cast window.*

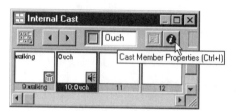

The Sound Cast Member Properties dialog box appears.

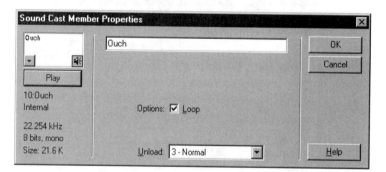

Every cast member—no matter what type—has a Properties box more or less like this one. But the sound Properties boxes have two unique features: the Loop check box (which we'll get to soon) and the Play button.

3. *Click Play to preview the sound.*

Note that Director doesn't retain a record of the length of a sound. (It does, however, record the amount of storage space a sound occupies.) If you're working with multiple sound files and require exact timings, you'll need to keep track of them with another application or with an old-fashioned stopwatch.

Placing a sound

No need to go into step-by-step instructions here—you're already familiar with the process of placing cast members in the Score. Drag Ouch into the sound channel 1 cell at frame 25. Now turn off looping in the Control Panel and play the movie.

Introducing sound looping

Here's a little twist you can add:

1. *Reopen the Info window for the Ouch cast member.*

2. *Place a check mark in the Loop check box.*

3. *Click OK.*

Much like selecting looping in the Control Panel, selecting this option makes the sound repeat as long as the playback head remains on the sound sprite. Since we set a wait of 3 seconds on frame 25 in the tempo channel, the sound will loop for 3 seconds.

USING THE TRANSITION CHANNEL

Thus far, we've created a character, manipulated him into a moment of crisis, and articulated his pain. Now we need to get him out of this fix. We could devise and execute an elaborate animation to do this, but there's an alternative that's elegant (and easier): using a transition effect to imply action. Transitions are generally used to control the flow of one screen into another, but they can also be used to choreograph the entrances and exits of individual sprites on the Stage.

Let's make the eight ball disappear, as if it were beamed away by an offscreen transporter. We won't need any additional in-betweening or cast wrangling—just a single invocation of the transition channel. First, we'll need to extend the presence of one element for one frame past the point of collision.

1. *Click to select the sprite in frame 25, channel 2.*

That's the Swifty in the frame where we performed the cast substitution.

2. *Copy the sprite (Control-C Windows; Command-C Macintosh) and select frame 26 in the same channel.*

3. *Paste the sprite (Control-V Windows; Command-V Macintosh) into frame 26.*

Now call up the transition choice, or the Frame Properties: Transition window.

4. *Double-click the transition channel in frame 26.*

MAKING TRANSITIONS:
You access the menu of frame-to-frame changes in the Frame Properties: Transition window.

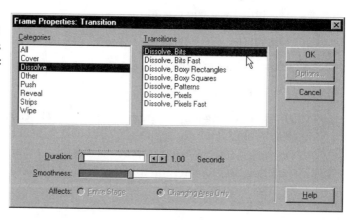

The field on the right side of this window displays an array of transition choices (on the Macintosh, each is accompanied by an icon that attempts to evoke the given effect). The field on the left lists the categories of transition types from which to choose (to make sure you don't miss one, you can select All).

5. *Scroll down and click to select Dissolve, Bits.*

The chosen effect is a dissolve: The item will break up into multiple units, which will then disappear. In this case, the units are *bits*, or small squares (not to be confused with the bits that constitute a byte of data).

The size of these bits is determined by the Smoothness slider, which creates a rougher effect as it approaches the right. (Note that there are also a couple of pixel dissolves, in which the transitioned object is broken into the tiniest bits possible: individual pixels.)

Smoothness is a consideration for two reasons: aesthetics and processor time. A dissolve with big bits might look less graceful, but smaller bits mean more number-crunching for Director to carry out, and that can mean slowed-down performance. (In Lingo, you will find this scale broken down into increments of 1 to 128, with 1 being smoothest.) For our purposes here, we'll choose the middle path.

6. Move the Smoothness slider to the center.

Now to the question of duration. Do we want a long, slow dissolve or a zippy one? Unlike in the tempo channel, time here is measured in units of five one hundredths (.05) of a second. Let's not make the eight ball linger too long:

7. Set the Duration slider to 1 (or use the arrows to move the slider to the left).

This should make the transition last 1 second. The key word is *should*, because duration can be affected by a number of factors: the complexity of the object being dissolved, the chunk size specified, the amount of available RAM, and so on. Also, remember that this duration overrules any you might set in the tempo channel: If you have a 1-second pause but a 2-second transition, the playback head will stay in that frame for 2 seconds.

The last parameter is the **changing area**. No, this isn't some sort of dressing room; it's how you designate what gets the transition effect applied to it. Look at it this way: A transition occurs when something is appearing or disappearing or changing on the Stage. Director doesn't link transitions to specific cast members—it just compares the sprites of the current frame with those of the preceding frame. If a sprite is new, modified, or freshly departed, then that sprite is considered part of the changing area. You will generally have the option of applying the transition to either those sprites that are changing or to the entire Stage. In this case, the option is not available—Changing Area Only is already selected. We want the dissolve applied only to the changing sprite (in this case, the eight ball), so Changing Area Only is just fine.

Note that there can be only one transition in a given frame, and that the transition is applied to *all* sprites that qualify as "changing" (that is, arriving or departing) in that frame. If you're updating the Stage status of multiple sprites but want to apply a transition only to one of them, you'll need to spread the activity over several frames.

8. *Play back your movie.*

You should now see the eight ball making an artsy exit. Transitions take effect upon entry to a frame—in this case, frame 26. The ground (channel 1) is the same in frames 25 and 26, and so is channel 2 (since we copied frame 26 from frame 25). Only channel 3 is changing, since frame 25 has the eight ball and frame 26 does not.

There's only one thing missing now in our movie: Swifty never completes his walk across the Stage. We'll fix that right now.

1. *Select frame 26, channel 3, and drag the Walking film loop from the Cast onto the Stage.*

2. *Use the Swifty sprite that's visible on the Stage (channel 2) in frame 26 as a guide, and position the loop directly on top of it.*

3. *Select and drag the loop that you've just positioned to channel 2, in frame 27.*

4. *Use Extend Sprite along with auto-tweening to complete Swifty's walk off the screen from frames 27 to frame 50.*

Perhaps when you were completing Swifty's walk, you forgot to hold down the Shift key to ensure that Swifty remained firmly on the ground. If you make a change to the Score that you're not happy with, you can easily undo it with the Undo Score option available from the Edit menu, and try again.

POINTS TO REMEMBER

Here are the conceptual highlights of this chapter (no, there will not be a pop quiz):

- Sprite sequences can be saved and reused as a unit, known as a **film loop**.

- For straight lines and shapes (as well as buttons), the **Tool Palette** is an alternative to the Paint window.

- When **importing new cast members** from external files, make sure the pop-up menu in the Import window is set to the type of file you're looking for. Otherwise, the file may not appear in the list.

- You can use a convenient shortcut to place cast members in a sequence on the Stage: the **Cast to Time** command.

- To swap in a new cast member while retaining the Stage placement of the old one, use the **Exchange Cast Members** command.

- **Markers** are useful tools for identifying and navigating the frames in your movie. Use 'em early and often.

- The **tempo** channel can be used to set playback speed, to pause for a defined period of time, to wait for a mouse click or keypress, or to wait until a cue point is reached in a digital video or sound member.

- **Sound** cast members can be made to repeat indefinitely by enabling the Loop option in the Info window.

- **Transitions** can apply either to the overall Stage or only to those elements that are different in the two frames straddled by the transition.

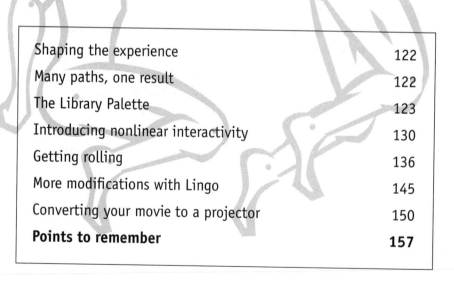

CHAPTER 4

INTRODUCING INTERACTIVITY

NOW THAT WE HAVE A FULL-FLEDGED MULTIMEDIA PROJECT UNDER OUR belt, it's time to start thinking about the end user. So far, everything you've done has been entirely passive as far as the audience is concerned: They're just watching Swifty's animated antics. Now it's time to pass on some degree of control by adding elements of interactivity.

In this chapter, we'll start with the easy approach, employing some out-of-the-box interactivity courtesy of the Library Palette's prebuilt behaviors. Then we'll take a look at the insides of those behaviors and even make a stab at writing them ourselves with Lingo. Then it's back to prefab behaviors, but with the added twists of looping and nonlinear navigation; we'll even provide feedback to the user. Finally, we'll use the Projector feature to convert a Director movie into a full-fledged self-running application.

SHAPING THE EXPERIENCE

Thus far, your Director movies have pretty much lived up to the metaphor behind their name. They may require a Control Panel rather than a film projector, but they're still streams of information played back at a fixed rate, designed to be passively viewed. For some of your needs, this may be perfectly adequate—you can certainly create some pretty impressive business presentations, for instance, using only what you've learned up to now.

INTERACTIVITY:
The ability of software to modify its performance in response to the actions of the end user.

But animation is only a part of what Director has to offer. Another big part is **interactivity**, the ability to provide the viewer with at least some measure of control. Don't be daunted by what may seem like a plunge from creativity into programming; interactivity can mean something as complex as an aircraft flight simulator, but it can also be as simple as a Quit button. You'll find that designing interactivity—shaping the experience—is as much a creative process as a technical one.

MANY PATHS, ONE RESULT

Interactivity, like many aspects of Director, can be accomplished in a number of ways. They all boil down to Lingo scripts; but for you, the author, there are several paths for creating scripts and several ways of viewing them. You have the Library Palette, which supplies drag-and-drop prebuilt behaviors. You have the Behavior Inspector, which lets you build behaviors a step at a time. You have the script editors, which let you write the scripts a line at a time.

What's a behavior?

So exactly what is a behavior? As mentioned in the last chapter, it's basically a Lingo script. And a Lingo script is a sequence of Lingo commands that are executed at (hopefully) appropriate times and that supply complexity to a movie that would not otherwise be possible.

Technically, a behavior is any script that is attached to a sprite or a frame in the behavior channel. That leaves cast scripts, which are attached to cast members, and movie scripts, which are cast members but not attached to anything. The distinction is a bit blurry since they're all scripts. You'll have to be a bit forgiving if we slip in a cast script when we seem to be talking about behaviors, or vice versa. Well, it's all about adding interactivity.

THE LIBRARY PALETTE

We're going to write a little Lingo in this chapter, but before we do, let's see what we can accomplish with behaviors that have already been written—behaviors provided by Director 7 in the Behavior Library Palette. We'll begin by learning to transfer elements from one movie to another. Then we'll work on a new movie. Finally, we'll take what we have learned and apply it to the Rolling.dir movie we created in the last chapter.

Copying a cast member

Let's see how easy it is to transfer elements from one Director movie to another. We are going to get a cast member (the eight ball) from the Rolling.dir movie and add it to our new movie. Even though it would be easy enough to re-create the eight ball, sometimes you'll want to copy large parts of a movie or a number of intricate cast members.

1. *Open the Rolling.dir movie you created in the previous chapter.*

2. *Select and copy (Control-C Windows; Command-C Macintosh) the eight ball cast member (the bitmap, not the film loop).*

3. *From the File menu, select New and then Movie.*

4. *Select slot 1 in the new Cast and paste (Control-V Windows; Command-V Macintosh) the eight ball bitmap.*

5. *Save the movie as FollowTheMouse.dir.*

Remember that although you can copy elements from movies (like the ones supplied on the CD that accompanies this book) that have the source intact, you will not be able to copy individual elements of movies that have been made into projectors or Shockwave movies.

We copied the cast member using only a single instance of Director. If you have a lot of elements, including Score elements, that you want to copy, this process can get pretty tiresome: open movie, copy; open second movie, paste; open first movie, copy; and so on. One of the handier capabilities added to Director some time ago is the ability to have more than one instance of Director running at the same time. If you're building a movie that has elements in common with another of your movies, you can have both open at the same time and copy elements from one to the other.

The number of formats in which a Director file can be saved can be a little confusing, so let's clarify some terminology. A **movie** is the raw master data file that can be opened by anyone with a copy of Director. A **protected movie** has the same functionality, but no one can "get under the hood" and tinker with the elements of the production. A **projector** runs by itself, whereas a **Shockwave movie** can be run only within the context of a Web browser such as Netscape Navigator. These last two types can't be modified either, which is why you always want to keep a copy of the original movie. Finally, there are supporting files such as **Xtras** and **external Casts**, which aren't movies but can be vital to your productions.

Adding a behavior

Before we add a behavior, let's add our eight ball to the Score:

1. *From the File menu, select Preferences and then Sprite. In the Sprite Preferences dialog box, ensure that Span Duration is set to 1 and then click OK.*

2. *Drag the eight ball from the Cast to the center of the Stage.*

3. *Use the Control Panel to make sure that looping is turned off.*

Because of the Span Duration preference we set for sprites, the eight ball sprite takes up only one frame in the Score. If we run the movie now, the movie is over almost before we can get the cursor off the Play button.

We're going to try building the movie in a single frame, so we need to keep the movie in frame 1 while still letting things happen. Let's see how:

1. *From the Window menu, select Library Palette.*

The Library Palette appears. In the upper left is the Library List button, which provides access to the various categories into which the library is divided. For now, we want the Navigation behaviors.

2. *Click the Library List button to display the list of categories; then choose Navigation.*

CHOOSE YOUR CATEGORIES:
Use the Library List button to select from the behavior categories, and then choose Navigation.

Each behavior is illustrated and, by default, has a name next to it. If you place the cursor over any of the behaviors, a Tooltip appears containing an explanation of the behavior and, sometimes, additional information. As you can see, the Navigation behaviors mainly have to do with going somewhere in the movie or playing something. If we place the cursor over the Hold on Current Frame behavior, for example, we learn that it is a frame behavior and that it keeps the playback head in the current frame.

TOOLTIP TIME:
If you place the cursor over a behavior button, a Tooltip serves up behavior information.

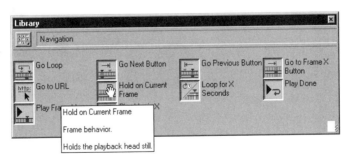

As we see, Hold on Current Frame is a frame behavior, so we know to apply it to a frame in the behavior channel rather than to a sprite segment.

PAUSE OBSOLETE:
Director will someday
stop supporting the
pause command—
don't use it.

Director users who have been around a while will remember that the
pause command was once a staple of programmers. It held the movie in
the frame where it was invoked until something else told it to get moving again. But as Director grew in complexity, too many questions came
up: While a movie is paused, does sound play? What happens to a film
loop? Director has tried to maintain some sort of backward compatibility, but it now specifies that pause not be used. In the next version,
who knows?—Director may pretend that pause never existed. The Hold
on Current Frame behavior (or its Lingo equivalent) replaces pause,
although its mechanism is entirely different.

3. Drag the Hold on Current Frame behavior from the Library Palette to the behavior channel at frame 1.

Note that the behavior shows up in several places: in the behavior channel, in the Cast (with its own distinctive picon), and in the Behavior List
pop-up menu of the Score. Play the movie now; you should discover that
the movie does, in fact, keep playing while the playback head remains in
frame 1. Congratulations! You've just added a behavior to your movie
without having to write a single line of Lingo.

HOLD ON THERE:
The Hold on Current
Frame behavior appears
in several places after
you drag it to the
behavior channel.

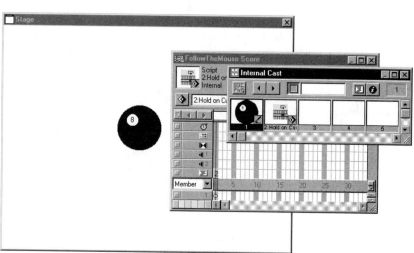

Interactive behaviors

Although the behavior you added is useful, it hardly seems interactive. So now let's play around a bit with our sprite and see if we can give the user something to do. This time we'll drag a behavior onto the eight ball sprite.

1. *Use the Library List button of the Library Palette to select Animation and then Interactive.*

2. *Find the Draggable behavior and drag it onto the eight ball sprite in the Score.*

This time we need to make a decision about whether or not the sprite can be dragged all the way off the Stage. This is known as **setting a parameter**. To make our lives easy, the behavior displays a dialog box in which we can answer the question (or set the parameter). We want the sprite to stay on the Stage:

3. *Make sure the Constrain to Stage check box is checked; then click OK.*

SET A PARAMETER:
To ensure that the sprite cannot be dragged off the stage, check this check box.

As you can see in the Cast window, another behavior is added to the Cast. Now go ahead and give the movie a try. While it's playing, click the eight ball and drag it around the Stage window. You can move it anywhere on the Stage, right up to the edge. Not bad for a simple click-and-drag operation!

Want to try another? Let's make the sprite rotate so that one side always faces the mouse cursor. This action is much more complicated from a programming standpoint, but with behaviors it's just as easy to implement.

1. *Find Turn Towards Mouse in the same group of interactive behaviors.*

If you don't find the Turn Towards Mouse behavior in your version of the Library Palette, don't dispair. Some Director packages don't include all behaviors, but you can use a version of this one included with the source files for this book. See the "Getting the Behavior" section in Chapter 18 for directions.

The behaviors are listed in alphabetic order; if you don't see the one you want, you can use the small arrow at the bottom of the window to scroll to it (or you can resize the window).

2. **Drag the Turn Towards Mouse behavior onto the sprite.**

> Here are a couple of handy facts about behaviors: You can attach more than one to a sprite, and you can arrange the order in which they are called. If one behavior is dependent on another, you can make sure that the correct one gets called first (we'll discuss linked behaviors more fully later in this book).

3. **For Turn, choose Away from Mouse and Always.**

In the Parameters dialog box that appears this time, we can set three parameters. In this case, the third parameter doesn't matter, since there is no "otherwise" to Always.

Go ahead and play with the movie. You'll see that the eight ball turns when you move the mouse around and that you can still click and drag the eight ball. Both behaviors are working on this single sprite. Now, that's interactivity!

Inspecting the Behavior Inspector

I happen to like the way the eight ball follows the mouse when the behavior is set to turn away from the mouse—it makes the 8 look like it's more or less following the cursor. But maybe you don't feel the same way about it; maybe you want the sprite to turn only when the mouse button is down. Wouldn't it be nice if there was an easy way to get back to the Parameters dialog box so you could make changes of this sort? Director has it covered, as we'll see.

But first, take a look at the sprite toolbar in the Score window (or the Sprite Inspector if you're using that instead). With the eight ball sprite selected, the eight ball picon appears in the upper-left corner of the Score. Just below that are the Behavior Inspector button and Behavior pop-up menu. Clicking the Behavior Inspector button will open the Behavior Inspector. The Behavior pop-up menu displays <Multiple> because we have attached more than one behavior to our sprite.

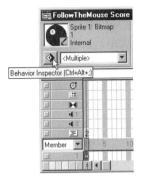

INSPECTOR QUICK:
Click the Behavior
Inspector button to
display the Behavior
Inspector.

1. *With the eight ball sprite selected, click the Behavior Inspector button.*

2. *If the windows of the Behavior Inspector don't look like the following picture, use the small triangular buttons on the left edge of the inspector to expand the windows.*

BEHAVIOR INSPECTION:
Behaviors are listed in
the order in which they
execute.

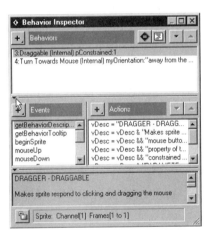

The upper window of the Behavior Inspector lists the two behaviors attached to the eight ball sprite. The two side-by-side windows in the middle list the **events** that occur and the **actions** that are taken for each event. Right now, that's probably more than you want to know. Later, when you learn how to work with Lingo, you'll find yourself becoming highly conversant with events. The window at the bottom of the Behavior Inspector contains a description of the behavior. In fact, if you want to view the description of a behavior, this is where you go to find it.

3. *Double-click the Turn Towards Mouse behavior in the upper window.*

A Parameters dialog box appears. You can now set the parameters to whatever settings you would like to try.

INTRODUCING NONLINEAR INTERACTIVITY

In our movie, a lot is happening on the Stage—but the playback head isn't going anywhere. In the last chapter's experiments, it didn't get around much either: it moved, but only to start at frame 1 and plow through until it reached the end. Our next few forays into behaviors will aim to boss around that playback head, to make it leap from one location in the Score to another.

Departing from the monorail track of the Score is one of the best ways to introduce true interactivity into your productions. A typical way to do this in Director is to have separate areas of the Score, each encapsulating a different function or element of a movie. Then you build centralized areas (such as a Main Menu screen) that let the user decide where to go next. The user makes a choice, and the playback head goes dancing off to that particular segment.

Ready to give it a try? We're going to approach this by having three distinct locations in the Score:

- A segment where nothing happens to the sprite

- A segment where the sprite is draggable

- A segment where the sprite turns to follow the mouse

Setting up

To begin, let's leave our sprite in the Score but detach the behaviors we attached to it earlier.

1. *In the Behavior pop-up menu (next to the Behavior Inspector button), choose Clear All Behaviors.*

Choosing Clear All Behaviors removes all behaviors currently attached to a sprite or sprite segment. This isn't strictly necessary for what we're going to do, but it will make the following steps a bit more streamlined.

CLEARING OUT:
Choose Clear All Behaviors to streamline your sprite.

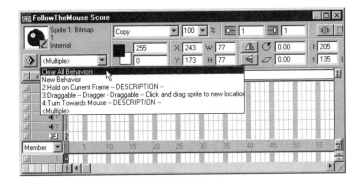

It's also a good habit to get into, because too many extraneous behaviors can make your movies harder to debug if something goes awry.

2. *Click frame 1 of the marker channel to create a new marker; name it* **Neither.**

3. *Add a marker at frame 10 named* **Follow** *and a marker at frame 20 named* **Drag.**

Since we're using only a single frame for each section of our movie, we could easily place the sections in frames 1, 2, and 3 of the Score. Why not do that? For readability's sake, that's why.

Although you might think that you'll remember everything about your movie, trust me: Once you set it aside for a while and come back to it (days or weeks later), you'll find the familiarity has evaporated, leaving you disoriented in your own Score. Separating disparate sections with empty spaces will make the movie easier to understand—both for you and for anyone else who needs to work with your movie. If that's not enough reason for you, do it simply because the extra space allows the marker labels to be visible and readable.

4. *In the Score, use the Shift-click technique to select and copy both the behavior in the behavior channel and the eight ball sprite together.*

5. Click the behavior channel in frame 10 and paste. Do this again at frame 20.

We now have three distinct sprite segments, each with an eight ball that does nothing, a marker, and a frame behavior that will hold the playback head at that frame (if it ever gets there). Your Score should look like this:

MAKING DISTINCTIONS:
After selecting and pasting the behavior and sprite, you'll have created three distinct sprite segments in the Score.

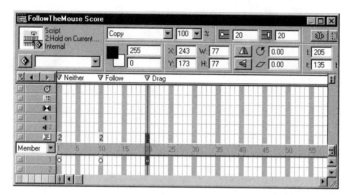

6. From the Cast, drag the Turn Towards Mouse behavior onto the eight ball sprite at frame 10 of the Score. Set the parameters as we did before or in a manner of your choosing.

Notice that when we detached (cleared) the behaviors from the sprite, we did not automatically delete them from the Cast.

7. Drag the Draggable behavior from the Cast to the sprite in frame 20.

Now we're set. The eight ball sprite at frame 10 will follow the mouse, and at frame 20 it will be draggable. All we need is a way to get from the place where the sprite does nothing to a place where the sprite does something.

Building the buttons

Okay, so we have some interactive behaviors attached to our sprites and a behavior in the behavior channel that prevents the playback head from moving. Now we need another interactive element (a button) that overrides that limiting behavior.

The physical button

We have to make a home for any behaviors that we'll use to navigate around our movie. We'll do that by creating buttons (cast members) and then attaching behaviors to them.

1. *Select frame 1, channel 3, of the Score. That's an unused cell.*

Just as we made the markers more readable by leaving some frames open, it's a good idea to group similar sprites together and leave open channels between them. This makes the Score much easier to decipher—which is especially useful now that Director 7 allows us up to 1000 channels.

2. *Open the Tool Palette.*

3. *Select the button tool.*

4. *Use the button tool to draw a box in the lower-left corner of the Stage.*

A cursor appears, flashing in the middle of the button box.

5. *Type* **Draggable** *inside the button.*

6. *Use the handles on the selection border to resize the box to suit your taste.*

Director automatically places the new sprite in the cell you selected. A new cast member is also placed in the Cast window, with an icon designating it as a button.

Time out now for a little test: Rewind and play the movie; then click the button. You'll find that while *something* happens (the button's color inverts when the button is selected), the button doesn't yet live up to its name. That's because we haven't told it what to do—we haven't attached a behavior to tell the button what job we want done.

The Jump to Marker behavior

Now that we have the button cast member and sprite, the next step is to add a behavior. We'll use another behavior from the Library Palette for this. Since we want the action of the button to be to jump to a new location in the movie, we will use the Jump to Marker Button behavior.

1. **On the Library Palette, click the Library List button to view the Controls group of behaviors.**

2. **Find the Jump to Marker Button behavior and drag it onto the button sprite on the Stage.**

You can drag a behavior onto a sprite on the Stage as well as onto a sprite in the Score.

A Parameters dialog box appears. The first parameter is On mouseUp, Jump to Marker. This parameter tells us that the action will take place when the mouse button is released on the sprite. We don't have any choice about whether the action takes place on a mouseUp or mouseDown event, but we can set the destination for the jump. In the pop-up list for that parameter, you should see several choices, including a list of all markers currently used in the Score.

JUMP TO DRAG:
In the pop-up list, you can tell the button to jump to the Drag marker when the mouse button is released.

3. **In the pop-up list for On mouseUp, Jump to Marker, select Drag. That's the marker we want to go to with this button.**

4. **For Jump Mode, select Go To.**

5. **Make sure that Remember Current Marker for Back Button? is not checked.**

Time for another test. Play the movie and click the Draggable button. The playback head should jump to frame 20 and stay there, and the eight ball should be draggable. Too bad we're stuck there. But we can fix that by adding some more buttons. First, stop the movie.

Copying and modifying the button

We have a Draggable button; now we need a Follow button and a Neither button. We could go back to the Tool Palette and draw another couple of buttons, but it's a good idea to make both new buttons the same size and shape, and the best way to guarantee that is by copying the original.

1. *Select the Draggable button's slot in the Cast window.*

2. *Copy the button.*

3. *Select a vacant slot in the Cast.*

4. *Paste the button.*

5. *Double-click the new cast member.*

The Text window appears. Notice that its column width is set to the width of the button. If you change this width, you'll automatically reconfigure the button as well.

6. *Change the text inside the new button from* Draggable *to* Follow the Mouse.

7. *Repeat steps 3 through 6 to create a third button, only this time, call the button* Neither.

8. *Click frame 1, channel 4, of the Score. Drag the two new buttons to the Stage so they line up vertically with the original Draggable button that already appears there.*

That takes care of the buttons' appearance. The buttons should be in channels 4 and 5 in frame 1 of the Score. Now we need to add behaviors to the two new buttons.

9. *Drag the Jump to Marker behavior from the Cast window to the Follow the Mouse button.*

That's right; we can drag the same behavior to a different sprite. A Parameters dialog box appears, and we can set parameters for this sprite that won't affect the parameters set for the other button. Director remembers the set of parameters for each use of a behavior.

10. *Set the parameters: Set the behavior to jump to the Follow marker, set Jump Mode to Go To, and make sure Remember Current Marker for Back Button? is not checked. Then click OK.*

11. *Drag the Jump to Marker behavior to the Neither button and set the parameters similarly, except make this button jump to the Neither marker when it's clicked.*

Now we've placed three buttons in frame 1. Clicking them will get us to the other sprite segments in the movie, but we still need to be able to change locations from those segments.

12. *Copy the three button sprite segments in the Score and paste them in frames 10 and 20.*

This gives us identical buttons in all three sprite segments.

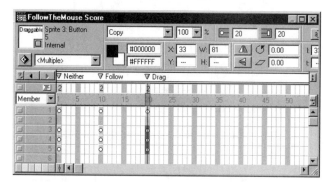

Now play the movie. You should be able to jump to any of the three sprite segments by clicking a button from any one of them. Of course, a user wouldn't know anything about there being three segments. That's all invisible to the user, to whom it would simply appear that clicking a button makes the eight ball draggable or makes it turn to follow the mouse.

We could still do a lot with our FollowTheMouse movie to make it fancier: we could add titles for each location or maybe add instructions. But let's move on and apply some of these techniques to the Rolling.dir movie we created in the previous chapter. While we're at it, we can expand our techniques to use Lingo as well as behaviors.

GETTING ROLLING

To start, let's give the Rolling.dir movie the most basic of interactive controls: let's give the user the ability to start the action.

PROJECTOR:
A Director movie that stands alone as its own application.

Now, you may well ask, "Isn't that what the Control Panel is for?" True, the Control Panel gives *us* that ability, but it's part of the Director application. Bear in mind that a movie can be converted into an application in its own right, which is called a **projector**. A projector doesn't need to invoke Director to operate—and thus the Control Panel (and any other Director window, for that matter) is absent. If you want to put controls in your projector, you need to put them directly on the Stage of your movie.

1. *Open your Rolling.dir movie (or the one supplied on the CD).*

2. *On the File menu, choose Save As to make a new copy of the movie. Name it* **Rbuttons.dir.**

Before we can begin to build our buttons, we need to make one more slight modification to the movie. When we create our projector, we'll want the action on the Stage to wait until the user clicks a Play button, so we need to instruct the Score to pause on the very first frame. We already know how to do that: we'll add a behavior.

3. *On the Library Palette, find the Navigation behaviors and drag the Hold on Current Frame behavior to frame 1 of the behavior channel.*

Now when you play the movie, the playback head remains in frame 1, and the movie does not proceed. Notice that the film loop of Swifty is playing just fine, although Swifty isn't getting anywhere. If you don't want him to be moving, you can replace the film loop in the first frame with one of the graphics of Swifty.

Adding a script to the Score

That's right—it's time to get your hands on Lingo. You'll find that, at least on the level of basic interactivity, Lingo is a lot like plain English. We can get an idea of what a Lingo script looks like by taking a look at the behavior we just created.

1. *Double-click the behavior in the first cell of the behavior channel.*

A Behavior Script window opens, displaying the Lingo script that makes up the behavior. There is much more here then we need to go into now; we are concerned with only the last three lines. However, in the upper lines, you should recognize the description of the behavior that appears in the Behavior Inspector and, below that, the description that appears as a Tooltip on the Library Palette.

In those final three lines, all the work is done to keep the playback head in one location. Just in case you don't believe it, we're going to get rid of this behavior and re-add it with a script we write ourselves.

2. *Close the Behavior Script window and then delete the behavior from the behavior channel.*

3. *Find the behavior in the Cast window (it should be cast member 12 and named Hold on Current Frame) and delete it, too.*

4. *Double-click (the now empty) frame 1 of the behavior channel.*

As with other types of channels, we're achieving two things with this double-click:

• We're creating a new cast member (number 12).

• We're placing that cast member in the selected channel within the selected frame.

In this case, the cast member's script window opens with much of the work already done for us and the cursor positioned at the point where we can enter our command.

When carrying out Lingo instructions in this book, type only the words shown in this typeface.

A FEW WORDS:
Many Lingo commands are simple, straight-forward English words such as go or end.

5. *Type* go to the frame

You've just completed your first Lingo script! The three lines that now appear in the window are almost identical to the three lines we saw in the behavior. Let's look at the script's anatomy.

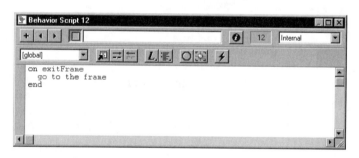

HANDLER:
A unit of Lingo code intended to be executed in correlation with a particular event.

The line on exitFrame is what's known as an **event handler**. It tells Director that there's something it has to carry out when a specific event occurs—in this case, the event occurs when the playback head leaves this frame (hence, exitFrame).

The line you wrote is a **command**. Director recognizes the phrase go to the frame as meaning "the frame you are going to next is this same frame"; the frame is a Director function that returns the frame number of the current frame (in our case, 1). So go to the frame is equivalent to "go to 1."

That may seem convoluted (why not just stay in one place?), but keeping the playback head in motion means more than one thing can be happening on the Stage, even in one frame.

The final line is the Lingo equivalent of a period. It contains the word end to tell Director that we're through giving orders for now. Since this line is needed to complete the script unit started by on exitFrame, it's also considered part of the event handler. Think of the words on and end as the bookends of every event handler.

Notice how the middle line is indented. Lingo (and other programming languages) use such indentations to keep the sense of multiple lines forming a single unit. You can look at a script as a sort of sandwich, with the command in the middle between layers of "when" and "that's all."

6. Close the Behavior Script window; then rewind and play the movie.

Nothing happens, right? Even though the Play button remains depressed on the Control Panel, the playback head in the Score stays on frame 1. That's Lingo in action. We created a behavior that acts just like the behavior we got from the Library Palette.

Don't be fooled here. Just because we created our behavior with three lines of Lingo (and had to write only one) doesn't mean that all Library Palette behaviors are so simple. Some of the behaviors require hundreds of lines of Lingo. Then again, once you have a good understanding of Lingo, you won't think twice about writing hundreds of lines of Lingo yourself.

Building the Play button

Having successfully written and placed a Lingo script that stops our movie in its tracks, we're now going to have to add a behavior that overrides the first script.

We have to make a home for this behavior before we write it, since it doesn't belong in the behavior channel.

1. Click frame 1, channel 4, of the Score. That's where our button will reside.

2. *Open the Tool Palette and use the button tool to draw a button box in the lower-left corner of the Stage.*

3. *Type the word* Play *in the button.*

4. *Use the handles on the selection border to resize the box to suit your taste.*

The button behavior

We could write this behavior using the script editor, but it's time to reintroduce the Behavior Inspector as a tool for creating behaviors rather than just inspecting them.

1. *With the Play button still selected, click the Behavior Inspector button in the Score window.*

2. *Click the Behavior button and select New Behavior.*

BEHAVE YOURSELF:
You can create behaviors as well as inspect them from the Behavior Inspector.

3. *In the Name Behavior dialog box, name the behavior* Start.

4. *Click the Events button.*

A BIG EVENT:
Events specify when something will occur, such as a mouse click or a key press; this behavior responds to the mouseUp event.

A wealth of event choices appear. The standard for buttons is for an action to take place when the mouse button is released, so choose Mouse Up.

5. Click the Action button and select Navigation and then Go to Frame.

TAKE ACTION:
Actions specify what will take place when an event occurs; in this case, the movie will jump to a frame when the Start button is clicked.

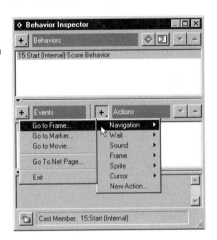

6. In the Specify Frame dialog box, enter 2; then click OK.

Now we have created a behavior that is attached to the button and responds to a mouse click. When the button is released (the event), the playback head goes to frame 2 (the action). Jumping to frame 2 will get us beyond the control of the frame behavior that's keeping us in frame 1.

Notice that the event handler for the behavior we just created responds to the release of the mouse button. The event (actually mouseUp) is the last half of a mouse click, when the mouse button returns to its original position (mouseDown, the first half, is considered a separate event). Director knows to execute this behavior when the user finishes a mouse click, and since the behavior belongs to a sprite (the Play button), Director runs the script only when the mouse is clicked on that sprite.

That's all we need to make the button work, so you can close the Behavior Inspector. The Play button is in frame 1 only, which is just fine; it wouldn't make sense to have it appear throughout the movie, since it provides no functionality.

Now play the movie. The playback head will remain in frame 1 (and so will the action) until you click the Play button.

Looping with a frame script

Just as we duplicated the Control Panel's Play function with a custom button, we will build the equivalent of the Looping feature into our movie, but because we'll leave looping permanently turned on, we won't need to create a button for it. Instead, we'll go to the very end of the Score and add a script that sends the playback head sailing back to the beginning of the action. Since such a behavior is particular to a specific frame, it's called a **frame behavior**. First, we need to add a marker to go to.

1. *Place a marker at frame 2 in the marker channel. Name it* **Replay.**

2. *Click the behavior channel cell in the last frame of the movie. Then click the Behavior Inspector button.*

The Behavior Inspector opens. Now we'll add a different behavior.

Keep in mind that "the last frame" means the last frame presently occupied by a sprite in your production, not the last available cell in the Score (that's a long way to travel).

3. *Click the Behavior button and select New Behavior. Name the new behavior* **Loop** *and then click OK.*

4. *Click the Events button and then select Exit Frame.*

This is the same event that we used to loop on frame 1 of the movie to hold the movie in one place. Now we'll use it to loop back to replay the movie.

5. *Click the Action button and select Navigation and then select Go to Marker.*

6. *In the Specify Marker dialog box, choose Replay. Then close the Behavior Inspector.*

MEET YOUR MARKER:
Select a marker from this menu to tell the playback head where to jump.

The Specify Marker pop-up menu lists the current markers in the movie as well as three relative jumps. Selecting a marker makes the playback head jump to that marker. Selecting one of the relative jumps moves the playback head to a marker determined by the marker's proximity to the current frame. If you choose Next in the pop-up menu, for example, the playback head would move to the first marker following the current frame.

Why loop back to frame 2 and not frame 1? Because we built a pause into frame 1, returning there wouldn't have the effect of looping, since the movie would simply pause at frame 1.

Now run the movie with looping turned off in the Control Panel. You should have continuous action.

Adding a nonlinear leap button

I don't know about you, but I can watch our little man get painfully frontswiped only so many times. Let's use nonlinear navigation to introduce another fate. We can add another button that makes the playback head leap past the moment of collision, avoiding the unpleasantness.

First we need to add a marker to jump to. It's difficult to add a marker so near to another existing marker, so we'll do things a little differently this time:

1. *Click frame 27 in the playback head area. Then, from the Insert menu, choose Marker. Name this marker* **8 Ball Gone.**

This is the first frame after the collision and the ball's subsequent dissolve, where the stroll resumes. This time, instead of using the Tool Palette to create our button, we'll use a shortcut approach built into Director.

2. *Select frame 2, channel 4, in the Score window.*

3. *From the Insert menu, choose Control; then choose Push Button.*

CONTROL FREAK, EH?
The Insert menu provides an alternative method of adding various types of buttons to your productions.

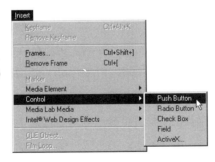

A familiar button appears on the Stage and occupies the highlighted frame in your movie.

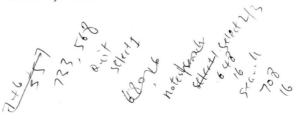

4. *Give the button the title* Avoid 8 Ball.

5. *Drag the new button to the lower-left area of the Stage.*

6. *Using the Extend Sprite command, extend this button through frame 24.*

Frame 25 is the moment of collision, so after frame 24 the button is superfluous.

7. *Click the Behavior Inspector button.*

8. *Click the Behavior button and select New Behavior. Name the new behavior* Avoid.

9. *For the event, choose Mouse Up.*

10. *For the action, choose Navigation and then Go to Marker.*

11. *In the Specify Marker dialog box, choose 8 Ball Gone; then click OK. Close the Behavior Inspector.*

You could also use a behavior to specify the frame number, as we did earlier, but citing the name of a marker allows you a little more flexibility. You can move the marker or add and subtract frames, and the script will still be valid.

Now run the movie and try out your handiwork. If you click the Avoid 8 Ball button in time, the playback skips the collision and goes right to frame 26. On the Stage, it seems as if Swifty just keeps walking, albeit with a bit of a lurch.

Since the looping from our frame script is in effect, you can forestall as many 8 Ball assaults as you like. See how close to the collision you can get before clicking the button. In effect, what you've created is a basic video game of the reflex-testing variety.

MORE MODIFICATIONS WITH LINGO

So far, all our scripts have been concerned with the playback head in one way or another. Either we've been pacing its progress or shuttling it about. But scripts can also be written that pay no heed to where the playback head is, instead affecting the general condition of the movie—in fact, we can write scripts that make changes not only to the movie but to Director itself. And that's exactly what we'll tackle next, with a few more sophisticated buttons that offer yet another level of interactivity.

Turning off sound with a toggling button

Let the movie run, and this time keep your mouse off the Avoid button. After a while, the sound of a voice going "Ouch" repeatedly may get a wee bit annoying. Wouldn't it be nice to build in the option of making our character a little more stoic?

We can do this by creating a button that affects the volume of the soundtrack. One approach would be to include two buttons—Sound On and Sound Off; but a more elegant solution is a single **toggling button**, one that turns the sound off when it's on, and on when it's off. This requires some new Lingo and a new button, but both are easy enough to create.

1. *Click frame 1, channel 5, of the Score.*

2. *Using the Tool Palette, create a new push button in the upper-left corner of the Stage. Name it* Sound.

3. *Extend the Sound button sprite through to the end of the movie.*

4. *Click the Behavior Inspector button to open the Behavior Inspector.*

5. *Select New Behavior from the Behavior pop-up menu and name the new behavior* Sound Control.

6. *Choose Mouse Up as the event.*

Now we need to add another arrow to our programming quiver. We want to turn sound on (or off), but the Behavior Inspector doesn't have a built-in action for that. We need to add some custom Lingo to do the job.

7. *Instead of using the Action button, click the Script button of the Behavior Inspector.*

LINGO AWAY:
Click the Script button of the Behavior Inspector to open the Script window and add your own Lingo script.

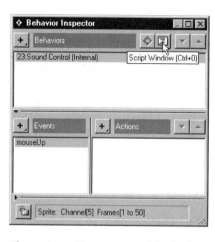

The script editor opens with the beginning and ending of a mouseUp event handler, the event we specified. Now we need to add the Lingo that is to be executed when the mouseUp event occurs on our Sound sprite.

8. *After the line* on mouseUp me, *type this line:*

```
set the soundEnabled to not (the soundEnabled)
```

Make sure to keep the text on a single line (you may have to scroll in the Script window) and include the parentheses and the unusual midCapitalization.

9. *Close the Script window.*

Let's take a look at that line of script. What we're doing here is actually turning off Director's ability to produce sound. We're not just suppressing the "Ouch" sound effect or turning down its volume; we're making the entire application temporarily mute. The condition of Director's sound is known in Lingo as the soundEnabled. When the soundEnabled is turned off (or set to FALSE), Director is hushed. When the soundEnabled is turned on (or set to TRUE), the program returns to its normal noise-ready state.

In this case, we've turned the soundEnabled neither on nor off. The set...to not construction means simply to change the condition to the opposite of what it currently is. Thus, the result of the button will change after each push, first turning the sound off and then on (the first click will turn off the sound because the default state of the soundEnabled is TRUE, or on).

Play your movie and try out the new button. You should be able to toggle the sound off and on.

Although we told you to place the previous Lingo command on a single line, you didn't actually have to. If you need to include a long command that you want to place on two lines, you can use the **continuation symbol** (¬) to break up the line and tell Director to read the command as if it were a single line. You create the ¬ character by pressing Alt-Enter (Windows) or Option-Return (Macintosh). So the last command we wrote could be written just as well as

```
set the soundEnabled to ¬
not (the soundEnabled)
```

We will use this continuation symbol throughout the book when we need to break long lines so they fit on a page. When you see it, you can enter the lines as shown or combine them onto a single line.

Displaying sound status

There's just one hitch, right? Since the button is called "Sound," after a few clicks it's easy to lose track of the sound status, and then the only way to tell if the sound is on or off is by waiting to hear (or not hear) the "Ouch." What's needed is a display on the Stage to indicate the sound status.

This is a good opportunity to demonstrate that the script of one cast member can be used to affect another cast member. We'll place a text field on the Stage and then add some Lingo to our Sound button that will actually change the contents of that field.

1. *From the Window menu, select Text to open the Text window.*

2. *Set the formatting by clicking the Bold button and the Align Center button.*

3. *Type the words* Sound On *in the text field.*

4. *Click the Cast Member Name field in the top center of the Text window. Type* Sound Status.

SOUND OFF (OR ON):
Use the text field to
enter text that will
be displayed in the
Sound Status field on
the Stage.

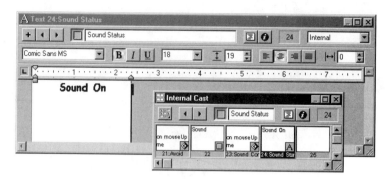

5. *Close the Text window.*

Look at the new cast member's slot in the Cast window. You should have
a cast member named Sound Status in slot 20 containing the words
"Sound On."

6. *Click frame 1, channel 6, of the Score. Then drag the new cast member*
   from the Cast to the Stage. Position it to the right of the Sound but-
   ton. Adjust the sprite's size so it approximates the size of the text.

7. *In the Score, use Extend Sprite to extend the sprite from frame 1 to*
   frame 50.

If you played your movie now, this text display would have only a 50 percent chance of being accurate at any given moment. We chose Sound On
because that's the default state of Director, but now we need to change
that text whenever the soundEnabled changes. We'll do that by changing
the script for the Sound Control behavior:

1. *Double-click the Sound Control behavior in the Cast. The Behavior*
   Inspector opens with the behavior displayed.

2. *Click the Script button to open the script editor.*

3. *Press Return before the* end *line to open up a new line.*

4. *Type the following:*

```
if the soundEnabled = TRUE then
    member ("Sound Status").text = "Sound On"
else
    member ("Sound Status").text = "Sound Off"
end if
```

Place a regular Return character (press Return [Mac] or Enter [Windows]) at the end of the lines. As you do so, you'll see that Director automatically indents the added lines to different points. The end result should be similar to the illustration shown here. If it isn't, don't try to insert the indentation yourself; clear what you've just typed and start again.

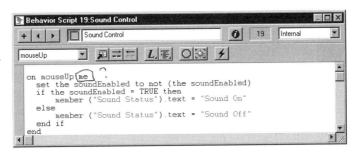

What we have here is a basic `if/then/else` statement: *if* a certain state of affairs exists (`the soundEnabled = TRUE`), *then* do something to (change the text of) some entity (cast member Sound Status). Otherwise (*else*), do something else. Note that this `if` statement requires its own ending (`end if`) before the end of the script as a whole.

The Lingo that we've added uses a syntax known as **dot syntax**. This is a feature that debuted with Director 7; it's a scripting dialect closer to the programming syntax used with other programming languages. In an earlier version of this book, you would have seen the same script segment looking like this:

```
if the soundEnabled = TRUE then
    set the text of member "Sound Status" to "Sound On"
else
    set the text of member "Sound Status" to "Sound Off"
end if
```

Both scripting styles will work in Director 7, although from here on in this book, we'll focus on the dot syntax. Why? Because the handwriting is on the wall for the old-style syntax: Don't count on Director's supporting it forever.

In the Director help files and documentation you'll find Lingo elements listed in both forms. If you already know Lingo from an earlier version of Director, feel free to use the old style—for now, at least. But if you're learning Lingo from scratch, I recommend opting for the dot syntax version; you'll be able to translate some of the key concepts more readily into other languages like Java and Perl.

Now play your movie. If it works as expected, the Sound Status text should be accurate 100 percent of the time, since it changes with each click of the Sound button.

Creating a Quit button

We have one last button to add before we turn this movie into a free-standing projector. Unless we *want* to induce frustration, we need to give the end user some means of exiting the program (remember that in the final product, Director's Quit menu choice won't be available).

1. *Create and place a button titled* **Quit** *on the Stage, below the Play button.*

2. *In the Score, extend the button's sprite to the length of the movie.*

3. *Use the Behavior Inspector to create a new behavior and name it* **Quit**.

4. *Choose Mouse Up as the behavior's event.*

5. *For the action, select Exit from the Navigation behaviors.*

If you look at the script for the behavior that we just created, you will see that the Lingo command used is halt. This command causes a projector to quit. When you are authoring in Director, though, it simply stops the movie, just as if you had clicked the Stop button on the Control Panel. Director also has a quit command that not only quits a projector but quits Director as well. You'll find the halt command to be much less frustrating.

CONVERTING YOUR MOVIE TO A PROJECTOR

This is a good time to take stock of your handiwork and pat yourself on the back. You've taken a simple piece of multimedia—an animation with a single sound and a special effect thrown in—and turned it into a highly interactive piece of software. Not only that, it's potentially self-contained; all the necessary controls are right up there on the Stage. Now all that's left is a gentle push out of the nest, in the form of a movie-to-projector conversion. Actually, "conversion" is a bit of a misnomer, since the original movie remains unchanged. The projector-making process is more of a translation, creating a new file that can actually encapsulate more than one movie. Projectors are the only way to make a Director production completely self-contained; saving a movie using Shockwave produces a more Web-friendly file, but it still requires the use of a browser application (such as Microsoft Internet Explorer or Netscape Navigator) for playback. We'll go into more detail about Shockwave in Chapter 5.

The Create Projector feature

If you're satisfied with the state of your Rbuttons.dir movie, let's make a projector. Save any changes you made to the file and then proceed.

1. *From the File menu, select Create Projector.*

The Create Projector dialog box appears (this one's the Windows version):

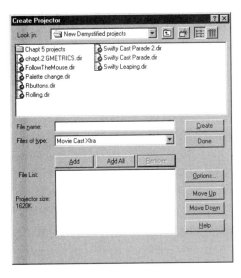

(The Create Projector dialog box looks different on the Macintosh; the windows appear side by side rather than one above the other.) The upper (or left on the Mac) pane is the Source Movies pane; use it to select the files you want to add to the projector (in this case, we have only one to add: the movie Rbuttons.dir). In your dialog box, you may need to navigate or at least scroll a bit to find Rbuttons.dir.

2. Select Rbuttons.dir in the Source Movies pane.

Note that the File of Type field shows Movie Cast Xtra, which means movies, casts, or Xtras, indicating that all three types will appear in the Source Movie pane.

3. Click the Add button.

The movie is listed in the File List field (the Playback Order field on the Mac). If we were bundling a number of movies into this projector, we could use the Move Up and Move Down buttons to create a particular play order (from top to bottom).

Notice the projector size indicator. On the Macintosh you see both the movie size and the projector size. When you select Rbuttons.dir, the movie size (shown on the left on the Macintosh), is fairly modest, while the projector size is significantly larger. That's because Director has to add a lot of resources to make the projector self-running, resources that thus far have been internal to the application and not the file. But as Director warns, "Actual projector size may be smaller because enclosed movies will be protected and compacted." In reality, the projected projector size is usually not significantly greater than that of the actual movie.

4. Click the Options button to open the Projector Options dialog box.

Options

In the Projector Options dialog box, we can further hone the playback and performance of our projector. The options available require a bit of explanation:

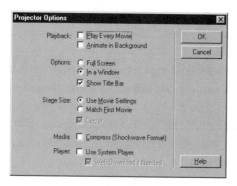

- **Play Every Movie** might seem a bit puzzling; if you didn't want to play a movie, why would you include it in the projector in the first place? Some movies, however, may actually be support files, designed not for display but to serve as repositories of resources for another movie. When Play Every Movie is not checked, the projector will play only the first movie listed—unless that movie includes Lingo that launches subsequent movies.

- **Animate in Background** doesn't refer to the background of the Stage, but to the times when the projector itself will be in the background—that is, when the user is running multiple applications and makes another application (such as the Finder on the Mac) active. When this option is left unchecked, the projector will essentially freeze when not active; if it is checked, the program will attempt to grab spare processor time to carry out any assigned tasks.

- **Full Screen** allows the movie to show over the entire screen, concealing any imposing windows from view. The alternative option, **In a Window**, runs the movie in a window and can have a title bar if you choose (and if you select **Show Title Bar**).

- **Stage Size** provides two alternatives and is useful when you're bundling two or more movies that use different Stage sizes. When **Use Movie Settings** is selected, the Stage of each movie will appear in the same dimensions as when the movie was created. If **Match First Movie** is selected, all subsequent movies will be placed on the same size Stage as the first one. This means that those movies originating on smaller Stages will have a border, and those originating on larger Stages will be cropped.

- **Center** keeps the Stage of the projector at the same location as it was in Director: smack dab in the middle of the screen. If this option is not checked, the Stage will instead be located in the upper-left corner of the screen. If you created a 12-inch movie on a 12-inch monitor, you wouldn't be able to tell the difference between a centered and noncentered Stage, since both would occupy the entirety of your screen real estate. But if you move the projector to a 20-inch screen, you would notice a difference. If you've designed a movie for playback on a wide variety of monitors, this is a good option to exercise.

- **Reset Monitor to Match Movie's Color Depth** (Macintosh only) does just that. If you've created a movie in which the graphics are no more complex than 8-bit color (256 colors), this option will check to see if the monitor of the system launching the projector is set to the same color depth. If it isn't—and if it's capable of 8-bit color—the projector will automatically reset the monitor. This is a useful option when you want to maximize performance, since a monitor set to a higher resolution than necessary will take up processor time needlessly.

- **Compress (Shockwave Format)** uses some of Shockwave's compression techniques to produce a projector with a smaller file size. A projector created with this option enabled will take up less storage space, but the tradeoff is that it'll probably take a little longer to get going when launched by the end user (it takes time to decompress). And even though this is billed as a Shockwave format, it doesn't turn the projector into a Shockwave movie; *that* Shockwave uses an entirely different file format.

- **Use System Player** allows the projector to use a Shockwave player instead of including a player as part of the projector. If a Shockwave player is not found on the user's system, the user can be prompted to download one (check **Web Download If Needed**).

- **Use System Temporary Memory** (Macintosh only) allows Director to tap available system memory when its own RAM allocation has been maxed out. When virtual memory is on, this option is disabled.

Let's get on with the making of our projector:

1. *Make sure the Center option is selected, and then click OK.*

Compiling

You've imported the movie and selected the options you desire. Now let's finish the job.

2. *Select Create.*

First you'll be confronted with a dialog box that asks you both where you want to place the projector and what you want to name it. The default name is Projector, which is good enough to use now.

3. Click Save.

Director will display a status box while it compiles the projector. When compilation is complete, you'll return to your movie.

The resulting projector

It's time to try out the projector. First, quit Director and return to the desktop in Windows or to the Finder on the Macintosh. There, in the location you specified, you will find a new file with its own icon. Macintosh users may need to change to View as Icons to see it.

Double-click the icon to launch the projector. The resulting program should be identical to your movie, except that Director's support windows and menu choices are absent. When you're ready, you can click the Quit button to return to the desktop (or Finder), but even if you hadn't built in a Quit button, the keystroke combination Alt-F4 (Windows) or Command-Q (Macintosh) would do the trick.

Projector information

You can inspect the projector's status by opening its Properties window (Windows) or Info window (Macintosh). In Windows, select the projector and then choose Properties from the File menu. On the Macintosh, select the projector and then select Get Info from the File menu (or press Command-I).

Here are a few points worth noting:

- The projector file is officially recognized as an application program rather than a document.

- The Version Info area contains not the version number of the projector, but that of the version of Director that created it. If you want to change that information, you'll need to use a resource editor such as ResEdit (Macintosh).

- The memory requirements (Macintosh only) are already set to both minimum and preferred RAM parameters. This is Director's best estimate of the projector's requirements; you can change either number by clicking it.

Projector considerations

In this case, the transition from movie to projector was fairly straightforward; we used only a single movie with only a few embedded cast members. But when you're converting a movie that incorporates linked files (such as sound or digital video cast members), you'll need to include those files with the projector.

Likewise, if you're using Xtras that are necessary for the projector to run (such as a transition Xtra), make sure to include them in the projector when you create it (from the Modify menu, select Movie and then Xtras). If your work will be distributed on both Windows and Macintosh operating systems, include properly named versions of Xtras for each platform. This ensures that any end user on any machine will have them available for use.

The Create Projector feature doesn't recognize movies that were made with a version of Director prior to 7. To make those movies accessible, you need to convert them with the Update Movies command in the Xtras menu.

Issues of cross-platform development with Director are discussed further in Chapter 22: *Professional Topics and Techniques.*

Keep in mind that although Director can be used to create cross-platform productions (Macintosh to Windows, or vice-versa), you can't generate projectors for one platform on the other. The Windows version will produce only Windows-compatible projectors, and the MacOS version only MacOS-compatible ones. So if you want to straddle platforms, you'll need to obtain both versions of Director (plus, of course, the necessary hardware), then port the file across platforms, and *then* generate the appropriate projectors.

Points to Remember

In this chapter, we've covered the following:

- **Behaviors** are actually Lingo scripts. They can be used prebuilt from the **Library Palette**, created step-by step with the **Behavior Inspector**, or created line-by-line with a script editor.

- Behaviors can be used to hold the playback head on a single frame.

- A **command** is that portion of a script that specifies an action.

- An **event** indicates when a script is to be executed (mouseDown, exitFrame, and so on). The Lingo line that specifies that occasion is called an **event handler** (on mouseDown, on exitFrame).

- With Director 7, the Lingo scripting language now has two dialects: the more naturalistic old-style syntax and the more modern dot-syntax (which more closely resembles the syntax used by other languages).

- Behaviors can be used to **move the playback head** off the linear progression of the Score (the Avoid 8 Ball button, the looping script in frame 50).

- A behavior can control an **overall condition** independent of the playback status (the Sound and Quit buttons).

- A script can **toggle** between two conditions, alternately executing one command and then another (the Sound button).

- The script of one cast member can affect another cast member (the Sound Status text field).

- **Conditionality** can be built into a script using the if/then/else construction (the script of the Sound button).

- Before a movie is converted into a stand-alone application, all necessary controls should be integrated into the movie, so that the movie is **self-contained**.

- The **Projector** feature creates a version of your movie that can be played as a self-running application file.

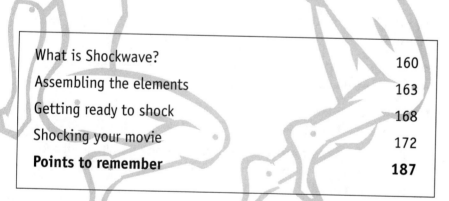

CHAPTER 5

INTRODUCING SHOCKWAVE

THE LONG TALKED ABOUT FUTURE OF THE INTERNET IS HERE...AND multimedia has arrived as a necessary and integral part. So many people now regularly surf the World Wide Web that no one can any longer doubt the Internet's influence on society. And Internet users aren't just looking for simple information—they expect to be entertained and amused in the process. The companies that maintain Web sites, who are maybe your current or potential employers, expect their sites to offer ever more diversion to entice people to visit them. With Director's new Internet capabilities, you can be part of that creation process.

In this chapter we'll look at Shockwave, Macromedia's technology for adding multimedia flash and functionality to the Web. You'll get to know all of its interlocking parts, and you'll learn how to use them for dazzling results. We'll wrap up by sharing tips on how to integrate your Shockwave productions into HTML pages and even take a look at what your work looks like when viewed through a browser.

What is Shockwave?

macromedia®
SHOCKWAVE

Because of the large quantity of data involved, multimedia presentations, until recently, meant delivering information on disk-based media, usually CD-ROMs. The Internet, on the other hand, struggled to achieve a compromise between boring text with a few graphics thrown in, which downloaded quickly, and glitzy sites that sent users out for coffee while the content was loaded onto their machines. Moving the data necessary to achieve multimedia dazzle through the bottleneck of modems and telephone lines once seemed a little like eating a seven-course meal through a straw.

Fortunately, this is no longer strictly the case. Although you still can't pull out your CD-ROM–based multimedia project and expect it to run over the Internet, you can expect to be able to provide interesting content over the Internet. During the last few years, phone technology has improved and the speed of the average modem used on the Internet has doubled. This means that an Internet site might load three or four times quicker now than it did several years ago. In addition, a number of companies have developed tools to make downloading multimedia much more efficient. These include Shockwave, Macromedia's offering, which has become one of the industry's standards.

Clearing up the confusion

So what exactly *is* Shockwave? There's a lot of talk (and hype) about what you can do or see using Shockwave, but good luck finding a definition that tells you what it really is. Actually, most people don't care. Most people hear about Shockwave only when they try to view a Web site and are told that they need to download it to view the Web page. People know it has something to do with the Internet, but things tend to get pretty murky from there. But you, as a potential developer, can't get away with that.

To understand what Shockwave is, first consider what a Web page is. What you see on the Web starts with a text file that's been embedded into an HTML (Hypertext Markup Language) file containing **HTML tags**, or commands, along with links to other accompanying media elements, such as graphics. The tags define how the Web page looks. When you arrive at a Web site, your browser reads in the HTML file, interprets the tags, and displays the page according to that interpretation. The commands defined by the tags are standardized, so all browsers (ideally) show the same page in the same way. The commands specify what appears where on the page and include the information necessary to incorporate any accompanying media.

So how does your browser know how to display everything specified in the HTML file? Well, most of the more common elements are built into the browser. But there are a lot of standards out there. You have various media (graphics, audio, and video, to name a few), various formats (JPEG, TIFF, QuickTime, MIDI, and more), and different compression systems. All in all, there are more types and combinations than we care to name, and more are appearing all the time. While it might be possible to create a browser with every possibility built in, it wouldn't be practical. So browsers, like many programs, allow their capabilities to be extended. Netscape introduced **plug-ins**. Microsoft added **ActiveX controls**. Here we'll call them all plug-ins, unless we specifically mean ActiveX controls. Most media formats that aren't displayed automatically by built-in browser functions have one or more plug-ins that allow them to be displayed. That's where Shockwave comes in.

One of the reasons Shockwave is so hard to define is because it is actually three things:

- A **standard** that defines a format for media that can be displayed using Shockwave

- An **extension** for browsers (plug-ins) that allows them to display Shockwave media

- The **tools** (such as Director and Flash) that enable the creation of Shockwave media

Shockwave lets you place multimedia in the context of HTML documents—which means that you can use it to put your Director productions out there on the World Wide Web, on corporate in-house intranets, and anywhere else HTML is used. In this chapter we'll use "the Web" to refer to all these environments, although they're not necessarily interconnected.

To get a better understanding of what all this means, it helps to think about what Shockwave *isn't*:

- *It isn't a product* like Director or FreeHand, at least not in the sense that you can buy it and put it on your shelf next to your other software. Some of it, that part required to create Shockwave media, is incorporated into Macromedia applications. The plug-ins used for displaying Shockwave media are given away free and can be downloaded from the Web.

- *It isn't a language,* like Java or HTML. There is some Shockwave-specific Lingo, but Shockwave itself doesn't require learning a new syntax or vocabulary. It's simply an enabling technology, one that extends the usefulness of what you already know.

- *It isn't a single piece of software.* It is the application you need to create Shockwave-compatible movies (Director, in our case), and it is the Shockwave plug-ins, which must be added to HTML browsers (such as Netscape Navigator or Microsoft Internet Explorer). In addition, the server software that places your HTML documents on the Net must be configured to recognize Shockwave.

- *It isn't exclusive to Director.* Right now, the bulk of Shockwave work is being done in Director, but other Macromedia products have their own Shockwave capabilities. Right now those include xRes, FreeHand, Authorware, and Flash; more may join the club later.

It's that last point that makes things a little more confusing. Although other Macromedia applications boast of Shockwave features, they won't all work with all Shockwave plug-ins. Although you'll see buttons on multitudes of Web pages exhorting you to "Get Shockwave," exactly which Shockwave should you get? At present, there are three flavors:

- *Shockwave* plays only Director and Flash files, and in earlier versions it played only Director. This is the most common version.

- *Shockwave Authorware* provides playback only for Authorware.

- *Shockwave Flash* supports only Flash.

When it comes to plug-ins, we're referring to the vanilla plug-in (for Director and Flash only) unless otherwise specified.

Clearly, Flash has the most plug-in support of all the Macromedia products. This is probably no accident, since Flash is probably the most Net-friendly of the line. Flash offers animation and interactivity similar to Director but in files that are, overall, significantly smaller.

Shockwave format

A Shockwave movie such as you might create with Director is a compressed version of data extracted from your original movie. All of the information in your original movie that Director considers necessary to allow editing is removed, as are elements necessary for playing the movie in Director. Unlike a projector, a Shockwave movie is not a stand-alone application. Also unlike a projector, the same Shockwave movie can be played over the Internet on either a Macintosh or Windows system. Shockwave movies can also be played by a projector, or they can be played as a movie in a window.

ASSEMBLING THE ELEMENTS

Having established that Shockwave exists in not one piece but several, our next task is to put those pieces together.

Shockwave plug-ins

Just as Photoshop developed a graphics plug-in standard that has now spread to other applications (including Director), Netscape Navigator's plug-in architecture has more or less become a standard and has been adopted by other browsers, most notably Microsoft Internet Explorer.

Before getting into the exercises in this chapter, you might want to download the most recent version of the Shockwave plug-in from Macromedia: *http://www.macromedia.com/shockwave/download/*. Follow the instructions on the page.

Which platform?

Although the Web is supposedly platform independent and browsers exist for a multitude of operating systems (including UNIX and OS/2), you're still as limited with Shockwave as you are with Director itself. At present, support is limited to MacOS and Windows.

On the Windows side, plug-ins are available for version 3.1, but the newest plug-in (Shockwave 7) requires Windows 95 or 98, or Windows

NT 4.0 or later. For MacOS, again there are plug-ins for older systems, but Shockwave 7 requires System 7.6.1 or later.

What are the hardware concerns? For the latest Shockwave on a Windows system, you will need a Pentium (or compatible) processor. For MacOS, you will need to be running a Power Macintosh.

If you have enough RAM to run the browser of your choice, you're pretty much set. If you have an older machine, you can run earlier versions of Shockwave. There is one issue to be aware of: Computers without hardware floating-point units (FPUs) won't be able to handle the streaming audio feature of Shockwave, known as SWA, which we'll be covering in Chapter 15. Shockwave movies that don't use this feature, however, will download and run on your system.

Which browser?

Your choices are also limited when it comes to browsers—although that's not much of a limitation, since the plug-in collection works on the browsers used by the vast majority of the online populace. For Windows, Macromedia claims support for Netscape Navigator, Microsoft Internet Explorer, and AOL, all version 3.0 or later. On the Macintosh, Macromedia claims support for Navigator 3.0 and later, Internet Explorer 4.01 and later, and AOL 4.0 and later.

Before you go searching for the right plug-in, check to see whether you even need one at all. Some browsers don't need plug-ins, since they already incorporate Shockwave technology. America Online's AOLBrowser integrates Shockwave, although at the time of this writing it supports only Shockwave derived from Director, and Microsoft's Internet Explorer can use either a plug-in or the Shockwave ActiveX control (also available from Macromedia). However, as of this writing the ActiveX version supports only Director and Flash versions of Shockwave.

Browser makers have acquired the habit of releasing "public beta" versions of their software, which means it's possible to have a copy of their supposedly latest edition. These beta versions can be less than completely stable and predictable. To minimize the likelihood of puzzling crashes and other blonkiness, it's a good idea to make sure you have the final release version.

Installation

Every browser seems to need a different set of installation instructions. Some, such as Internet Explorer on Windows, install automatically from the Web site. Others download the Shockwave software and an installer. The Macromedia Shockwave Download Center has instructions for various systems and browsers.

Whatever method you choose, it's a good idea to confirm the installation by checking from within the browser next time it's launched. For instance, Navigator has an item on its Help menu called About Plug-ins that identifies each plug-in and the browser's understanding of the data types it's supposed to hand off to that software assistant. You can also test your browser by viewing test Shockwave movies at the Macromedia Web site.

If you've had some previous exposure to Shockwave, you may have noticed the term *Afterburner* popping up frequently. Afterburner was the application Macromedia provided to convert Director movies into Shockwave files—you had to pass your productions through it before you could get them online. Afterburner is now obsolete for that purpose, since Director 7 handles all conversion directly.

Server side: Configuring MIME types

The final link in the Shockwave chain is the server software used by your Internet service provider (ISP) to place your HTML pages on the Web; it needs to be configured to recognize shocked movies as a data type. Nontext media is identified by MIME (Multipurpose Internet Mail Extension) type, and the Director/Shockwave MIME type is "application/x-director." When the server encounters files with Director's distinctive extension suffixes (.dir, .dxr, and .dcr), it knows to treat them as movie documents.

The actual steps for configuring a server to recognize a new MIME type depend on the hardware and software used, but unless you're the system administrator for your ISP, this isn't your department. Most ISPs are accustomed to changing their MIME files quite regularly, so chances are they've already made this accommodation. If, however, your Shockwave experiments aren't working (and you've eliminated any possible causes on your end), check with your ISP to see if it has adjusted for Shockwave. If it hasn't, direct your ISP to Macromedia's Web site.

Shockwave 7 and Director 7: What's new?

If you've used Shockwave with Director 6, be prepared to be pleasantly surprised. If you are coming from an even earlier version, be prepared to unthink any conclusions you may have come to about the limitations of the technology. In keeping with its determination to make Shockwave *the* multimedia standard for the Web, Macromedia has completely redesigned Shockwave so that it is faster and more stable than earlier versions and so that it will work more closely with various browsers. Here are some highlights of what you'll encounter with the version of Shockwave that coincides with the shipping of Director 7:

- **Minimal waiting period.** This feature is not new, but Shockwave 7 offers even better streaming capability than Shockwave 6. In earlier versions, Shockwave files needed to be downloaded in their entirety before they could start playing. But now Shockwave runs **asynchronously**, which is another way of saying that it's capable of input and output at the same time. With asynchronous Shockwave, movies are **streamed**—while each frame is being displayed, the software is busily downloading and decompressing the rest of the movie. Depending on how you structure your productions, this can mean that end users can start interacting with your work right away—no more thumb twiddling while waiting for the action.

- **Testing for media.** Using Lingo, you can check to see whether a specific cast member has been loaded or test to determine whether all of the media needed for a specified frame are ready. You can program your Shockwave movie to provide the user with menu options, for example, only when the media is available at the options' end-point.

- **Shockwave behaviors.** Director provides a number of behaviors to help with the creation of Shockwave movies. Examples include Loop until Media at Frame is Available, and Jump When Media at Marker is

Available. You also have progress-bar behaviors to show the status of downloading files or movies.

- **Shockwave auto-updating.** Users can select auto-updating, which means that if an out-of-date version of Shockwave is detected, the user will be informed that a newer version is available. If the user chooses to update, she will be automatically connected to the download site.

- **Preview in browser.** While you are authoring in Director, you can preview your movie in a browser (without converting to Shockwave first) to see how it will look. Director will create temporary Shockwave and HTML files and then launch your designated browser to play them.

- **HTML document creation.** When you create a Shockwave file from your movie, you can choose to have an HTML document created at the same time. The HTML document contains the HTML commands necessary to display your movie on the Web.

- **Aftershock.** Creation of a Shockwave movie is now performed from within Director, but you can use Director's Aftershock utility to create or update HTML files that display your Shockwave movies. Aftershock functions include detecting missing plug-ins, creating cookies, and generating indexes of text for use by search engines.

Shockwave limitations

Shockwave pulls off quite a feat, but this doesn't mean all your Director movies will find a new home on the Web. There are a few limitations to the technology, some quite intentional and some perhaps temporary.

Before they can go out onto the Web, Director movies need to be discreetly neutered. Director has a number of methods for manipulating external software and hardware (such as the FileIO Xtra's ability to create and write to text files, or the shutDown command's ability to turn off a computer). These capabilities are very handy, but they also hold the potential for abuse; how would you like it if you encountered a movie during your Net surfing that filled your hard drive with gibberish text and then shut down your system?

Rather than provide a framework for the equivalents of viruses and Trojan horses, Shockwave disables all features pertaining to the control of external files or devices. This means:

- **No custom palettes.** Shockwave movies play in the environment of a Web browser, and browsers have their own palettes (though the Netscape palette has pretty much become the standard, being now used by other browser makers). Palette switching and fades to black or white won't work.

- **No MCI control.** MCI stands for multimedia control interface; it's used by Windows to manage playback of digital video and other media types. Regular Director movies can control MCI by passing data to it via the Lingo command `mci`, but shocked movies can't.

- **No system-level Lingo.** If a command does something to anything other than the movie currently playing, it probably won't work under Shockwave. This goes for Lingo commands such as setting the `colorDepth` and `printFrom` and even open. The exception lets you use Lingo to write to a preferences (Prefs) file on the user's system. However, you can write to such a file only within the preferences folder.

Other Shockwave insufficiencies fall into another category: shortcomings that haven't been overcome—yet. One such shortcoming is that Shockwave doesn't support movies in a window (MIAWs). MIAWs are hard to achieve on the Windows platform and they're flat-out impossible for some browsers, so they're not part of Shockwave's vocabulary. The other main shortcoming is that the Lingo for installing and managing custom menus is not supported.

GETTING READY TO SHOCK

Shocking a movie is a relatively simple process, but preparing for Shockwave requires a measure of analysis and adaptation. Not all features of Director are functional in a shocked movie, and not all movies lend themselves to a Web environment. You'll want to familiarize yourself with the current limitations of a number of parameters: the evolving

Shockwave technology, the capabilities of your network server, and your audience's perception of what constitutes an acceptable demand on their browsers (and on their patience).

Should you shock your movie?

The real question should be, *Is a Shockwave movie the best way to achieve what I want to achieve?* You won't hear this from Macromedia, but sometimes Shockwave just isn't appropriate. Here are some questions you should ask and alternatives you might want to consider.

Is your movie linear or interactive?

Is your movie essentially a linear, noninteractive animation? If so, you can use the GIF89 format to display it as an embedded image in HTML. GIF89 is a display format that cycles through a number of images in sequence, so it can achieve the same results as playback of a straightforward Director animation. With a good GIF89 editor like GIFConvertor or WebImage, you can add looping, playback speed, and timing values as well.

This approach offers these advantages:

- **No special plug-in is needed** for Net surfers to view GIF89 animations; most browsers simply view them as standard images (which is what they are; they're just updated more often than regular still GIFs).

- Since the first image is displayed while the rest of the sequence is loaded into RAM, the effect is of a still picture coming to life. Streaming Shockwave can eliminate the wait in many cases, but in other instances the only thing users have to look at during the loading period is a rendition of the "Made with Macromedia" logo.

It also has these disadvantages:

- You won't be able to use **transition effects** or **sounds.**

- Creating your GIF movie may be a little tedious, since you'll have to export every frame of your movie to an individual graphics file. Those files must then be converted to GIF (Photoshop is good for this), and you'll have to make sure they're compiled into the final animation in the correct sequence. And if you want to modify the movie, you'll need to do everything all over again.

Do you want to reach out?

As we've already noted, Shockwave won't work with Lingo that reaches outside of the realm of the movie. This is an intentional limitation that cuts down on the possibility of abuse—but what if you want to produce something that persists after the interaction ends, such as a printout or a customized user preference file?

In that case, your best alternative is to create conventional projectors for your movie and then upload them and offer them for downloading from your Web page. How to do this depends upon the setup of your service provider, so check with your ISP to learn the particulars. And when preparing your project for distribution, keep these points in mind:

- **Offer multiple versions.** The Web is a platform-independent environment, but when your projector downloads, it's going to have to operate on a particular type of machine and operating system. If possible, offer both Windows and MacOS projectors and projectors optimized for variations within a platform (see the Options dialog box under the Make Projector command).

- **Keep it lean.** See the section "Creating for the Web" later in this chapter.

- **Tell users what they're going to get.** To help people decide whether they want to spend time downloading, try to describe the movie on the page that offers it. A screen shot and a bulleted list of features is always nice.

- **Virus check your projectors** and anything else you offer for downloading. This almost goes without saying, but sometimes people assume that if their system is functioning as expected, it's virus free. An executable downloaded application is a prime petri dish for viruses, so make sure yours is clean before sending it out to an unknown number of users.

Creating for the Web

Building Director movies specifically for Shockwave is a little like writing haiku: The constraints are severe, but they tend to encourage creativity rather than douse it. Getting the best possible ratio of bandwidth to performance requires tight planning and good discipline. Start by applying these principles:

- **Minimize the number of cast members.** Remove any that aren't used in the movie. Instead of using multiple versions of an image to indicate a change in color or size, use tweening, Lingo, ink effects, and sprite properties to modify the sprites of a single image.

- **Make images and sounds as low-res as is practical.** Does that 16-bit image have to stay at that bit depth, or can it be converted to 8-bit? Better yet, can it be replaced by a shape from the Tools window or the Vector Shape window? How about a tiled pattern derived from another cast member? Sounds should be short and sampled at no higher a rate than necessary; don't use high-resolution stereo sampling for a simple system beep, and so forth.

- **Use images that can be compressed.** Shockwave's compression capability can be pretty awesome. With experience, you will see that some images can be compressed more than others, depending on their complexity.

- **Simplify while streaming.** Animation and streaming both take up much of the processor's resources. Try to avoid having complex animation going on at the same time that the movie will be streaming in new data. One good way to do this is to use introductory scenes: Use a simple animation to hold the user's attention while other media is being loaded.

- **Test to see if media is loaded.** You can loop your simple animation until the media needed for more complex scenes is loaded. Use behaviors to test for the media before branching to the new scene.

- **Avoid long** `repeat...while` **loops.** These can cause the system not to respond to the user, making it appear that the system is hung.

- **Don't loop continuously.** A movie with a permanent playback loop will tie up RAM as long as its page is open. Free up that RAM by programming the movie to pause after a certain period, or give the viewer the ability to pause it.

Carry that wait...

There's a lot of talk about how cable modems and ISDN connections and the like will transform the World Wide Web into a veritable boulevard of bandwidth, but the reality is that the average Net surfer is still using a

28.8 modem, or even a 14.4 one. What's more, modem speed shouldn't be taken as the absolute measure of throughput; the Web population explosion is starting to cause Internet traffic jams as the servers for popular Web sites bog down under the burden. Even if your Web page is a modest affair that gets a few dozen hits a week, it can be slowed by traffic to other pages on the same server as yours or by the volume of activity at the viewer's service provider.

The upshot is that for now, you should err on the side of slowness and assume a download time of approximately 1 kilobyte of data per second. That means that a 60K movie will take a full minute before it starts playing, and that a 500K interactive extravaganza demands more than eight and a half minutes. In theory, you can offer up shocked movies of any size, and since Shockwave now offers streaming download, that size doesn't have to translate into a delay before the end user sees something happening. But streaming doesn't mean you can be blind to file size; you still have to take into consideration the fact that the larger the file, the more bytes you're trying to shove through your server connection. Big files can mean slowed or clogged servers—and just as important, they can cause browsers to crash because of overload.

SHOCKING YOUR MOVIE

Now that we have an idea of what to keep in mind when we create a Shocked movie, let's see if we can put that knowledge to the test. First we'll work on our old friend, Rbuttons.dir, and see if we can create a Web movie out of it. Just to make things easier, some simple changes have already been made to that movie, and it has been renamed ShockRbuttons.dir.

For the remainder of this lesson, we'll assume that you have a working Web browser, with the appropriate Shockwave plug-in installed and functioning, and a word processor to view or modify HTML files. The word processor can be a simple one (such as a text editor), so long as it's capable of saving files in plain text format.

Previewing in a browser

PREVIEW IN BROWSER:
You can now view
your movie in a
browser while you're
still working on it.

Another fine addition introduced in Director 7 is the ability to test your movie in Shockwave format without having to actually stop and create the necessary files. The Preview in a Browser function of Director 7 creates a temporary Shockwave file (in DCR format) and a temporary HTML file. Your browser is then called on to display the files—and there you are: Your movie is playing in a browser. Since testing your movie in a browser in this manner is quick and easy, you can use it to check the look or performance of your movie any time you have questions. Let's do it.

1. *Open the movie ShockRbuttons.dir in the Tutorials folder on the CD-ROM.*

If you want, you can also use the Rbuttons movie you created in Chapter 4. We started with the Rbuttons movie and made some changes to it so that it is more suitable to display in a browser. Here are the changes we made to Rbuttons.dir to create the Shocked version, ShockRbuttons.dir:

- It has been scrunched up at the top of the Stage, and the size of the Stage has been set to 640 by 200. The background color has been set to a pale blue. The size and Stage color changes were both made from the Modify menu by choosing Movie and then Properties.

- The Walking film loop of Swifty was changed so that its ink is Background Transparent, and the other Swifty sprites have been set to the same ink. As you remember, you can't set the ink effect for a film loop—you have to set the ink effects of the sprites from which the film loop is made.

- Two cast members have been added (a vector shape and a text member) that we will use for an introductory segment for the movie.

2. *From the File menu, select Save and Compact.*

SAVE AND COMPACT:
Your movie may not
play correctly in a
browser unless you first
use Save and Compact.

The Director movie you are working on may not stream correctly unless you first compact it. Save and Compact optimizes your movie by reordering elements of the movie, such as cast members, so that they more accurately reflect their order during playback. Save and Compact affects only Director's storage of the movie's information. It doesn't affect the way you see the cast members ordered in the Cast window, for example.

3. *From the File menu, choose Preferences and then Network.*

The Network Preferences dialog box is where you set up the way Director interacts with your browser. If the Preferred Browser field doesn't show the path to your browser, click the Browse button and select the path in the Select Browser dialog box. Make sure the option Launch When Needed is checked so that Director will open your browser when you use Preview in Browser.

We'll get back to Network Preferences and the other settings in Chapter 15, *Deeper into Shockwave*.

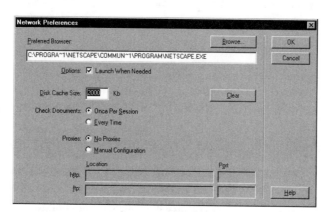

4. *From the File menu, choose Preview in Browser.*

Your browser should start. Then it should load and play the movie. Welcome to Shockwave!

Making modifications for Shockwave

Except for starting your browser, which takes some time, your movie loads and plays pretty fast. The movie is about 63K as a Director movie, but as a Shockwave movie, it would be reduced to under 20K. Still, if you figure 1 kilobyte of data downloaded per second, that's 20 seconds and a bit long for today's Web surfers to wait. Let's try taking our own advice by adding an introduction to the movie—one that will load quickly and play while other elements are downloading.

As we mentioned earlier, the ShockRbuttons.dir movie includes two new cast members just for this purpose. One is a vector shape, a kind of simple version of the eight ball. But because it's a vector shape, it requires less than 700 bytes, compared to over 7K for the eight-ball bitmap. Of course, both images will be compressed well below those figures in Shockwave, but you can see that the vector shape (we named this one Vector Eight) will load around 10 times faster that the bitmap would. By the way, without our adding an introduction, the Swifty film loop, Walking, would be one of the first elements to load. That would also require loading the five Swifty figures, for a total of more than 30K (before compression), before our little man could begin his walk. That's a lot of loading time.

So our objective here is to add an introductory scene to amuse the viewers while other loading takes place. Let's see how we can accomplish that.

Adding new frames

First we need to add some empty frames at the beginning of our movie.

1. *With the playback head at frame 1 in the Score, select Frames from the Insert menu. In the Insert Frames dialog box, set the number of frames to be added to 1; then click OK.*

Although we really want to add quite a number of frames, just adding one frame is the easiest way to begin. You will notice several things: A new frame is added; the new frame contains all the elements that were in the previous frame 1 (including elements in the effects channels); and all the other frames of the movie were shifted to the right (including the markers). We really want an empty frame, so let's get rid of the stuff in the new frame.

2. *Select and delete all the elements in the new frame 1, including the behavior and tempo settings.*

3. *Back in the Insert Frames dialog box, add 29 more frames.*

This is what we want: 30 blank frames. It turns out to be easier to add a single frame and clear it first, rather than clearing all the elements in the 30 frames right off the bat. It's important to note that by using Insert Frames to add frames, the relationship of the markers to the sprites was maintained. We could have selected all the sprites, moved them over, and then dragged the markers over by an equal amount, but in the process we might easily have lost or misplaced something and messed up our movie.

Adding the spites

Now we have more than enough room to work in our introduction. We want the vector shape to enter from the left of the Stage and travel to the right edge. Our text will enter from the right and travel left, dodging the other sprite in the process.

1. *Make sure the playback head is in frame 1; then drag the Vector Eight vector shape cast member (it's cast member 23) to the left side of the Stage. Position it just off the Stage and approximately vertically centered.*

2. *Extend the sprite from frame 1 through frame 25.*

3. *Click frame 25 of the new sprite and position the sprite just off the right side of the Stage. It will be automatically tweened to cross the Stage.*

4. *Select the entire sprite and set the ink effect to Background Transparent.*

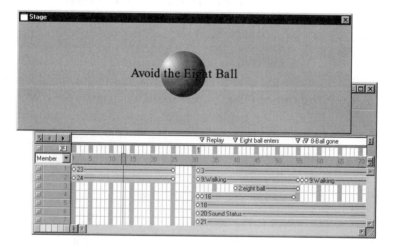

5. *In a similar manner, place the new text cast member (named Avoid Eight and in cast slot 24) in the Score so that it occupies frames 1 through 25; it should be tweened from the right side of the Stage to the left. Set its ink to Background Transparent.*

Now we'll modify the path of the Avoid Eight sprite so that it does not cross the path of the vector shape. We can do this by inserting a keyframe and moving the sprite at that location. Auto tweening will take care of the rest.

6. *Locate a frame just before the vector shape and the text would collide (about frame 10). Click the text sprite at that frame and then choose Keyframe from the Insert menu.*

7. Move the text sprite to a position on the Stage that's lower than the vector shape.

The path of the text sprite should pass under the vector shape as the movie plays. If the two sprites still collide, you can add another keyframe and make another adjustment. In fact, it's not a bad idea to do that just to make the animation more interesting.

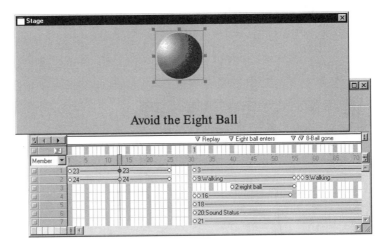

We decided a while back that eight frames per second was a good tempo for this movie. It still is, but now our tempo setting is in frame 31 because of the extra frames we added.

8. Find the tempo sprite in the Score and drag it back to frame 1.

Give your movie a test. The two sprites should cross the Stage without touching. Then nothing happens for a few frames. Then we get to the start of the old movie. Whoops! The Play button no longer works correctly. Adding the frames has messed with the way our behaviors function.

Behavior time

Actually, our behaviors work just fine—they do exactly what we told them to do. Unfortunately, what we told them to do is no longer what we want, and now the Play button isn't working like it used to. We just committed what many programmers consider a grave programming error. We told the behavior to jump to a specific frame number—which worked fine until we added new frames and messed with the frame numbering. Now you can see the advantage of using markers for jump locations.

The problem is easy to fix.

1. ***The Play button is in frame 31 of channel 4. Select it and then click the Behavior button in the Score.***

As you can see in the Behavior Inspector, the action is listed as go to Frame 2. But now we want to jump to frame 32. We could just change the number, but why not fix it a better way? Look at the Score, and you'll see that we already have a marker at frame 32 that we used for looping our Swifty. That marker is labeled Replay.

2. ***In the Behavior Inspector, click the*** go to Frame 2 ***action. Then press Delete to remove it.***

3. ***Use the Action pop-up button to add a new action. Under Navigation, select Go to Marker. In the Specify Marker dialog box, select Replay from the pull-down menu; then click OK.***

Close the Behavior Inspector; then rewind and play your movie. Everything should be in working order now. Also try viewing the movie in your browser (remember to use Save and Compact).

At eight frames per second, our animation gives the movie a little more than 3 seconds to load other media before our Swifty appears. For this small movie, that just might be enough. Or then again, it might not be. And anyway, we need to be able to deal with situations in which a fair amount of media will load. How about looping our intro animation until the media is loaded for the next segment. Did somebody say "behavior"?

Director provides a Loop Until Media in Marker Is Available behavior. We can set up this behavior just about as fast as you can read the name.

Before we create the behavior, though, we need to decide two things: where to loop to (a marker) if media is not available, and where to jump to (another marker) when it is ready. The second location is also where Director will look to see whether the media is loaded for that spot. The first decision is easy: back to frame 1.

1. *Place a marker at frame 1 and label it* **Intro Start.**

Frame 31 is where Swifty begins, and it's where we want to jump when the time is right to start the movie. This requires that we add a marker just next to the Replay maker, which may be tricky, but we did it once before.

2. *Click the playback head area at frame 31. From the Insert menu, select Marker. Label the marker* **Now Loaded.**

We have made our mark (so to speak) and are ready to add the behavior.

3. *Open the Library Palette. Use the Library List control to find the Streaming group of behaviors.*

4. *Find the Loop Until Media in Marker Is Available behavior icon and drag it to frame 25 of the behavior channel.*

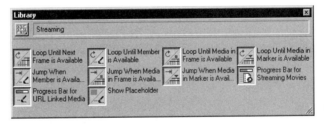

5. *In the Parameters dialog box that appears, set the Wait for Range of Media in Marker field to Now Loaded, the name of our marker.*

6. *Set the Loop Type field to LoopToSpecifiedMarker.*

7. *Set the Loop to Marker field to Intro Start.*

8. **Click OK. Since we are looping to a marker, the Loop to Frame field is not used.**

You could try choosing Preview in Browser from the File menu at this point, but you shouldn't expect to see a loop from our last behavior. The necessary media elements are going to load from your local drives too fast to ever require a second pass through the introductory animation. Unfortunately, Director doesn't have a Load at 1K per Second function for Preview in Browser. So let's move on to the creation of an actual Shockwave movie.

Shockwave for audio settings

Audio cast members can take up a substantial amount of disk space and RAM and make a Shockwave movie significantly larger and slower to download. One workaround for this is to keep sounds external to the movie in a compressed Shockwave for Audio (SWA) format, and then stream the sounds when they are required. SWA and streaming are covered extensively in Chapter 15: *Deeper into Shockwave.*

The drawback with dealing with sounds in this way is that because of the effort and time it takes to load the external sounds, this method makes sense only for large sound files, such as narrations and background music. For short sounds and frequently used sounds, such as a button click, it makes more sense to include the sound as an internal cast member. But even with internal cast members, we can still make use of Director's ability to apply Shockwave compression.

1. **From the Xtras menu, select Shockwave for Audio Settings. The Shockwave for Audio Settings dialog box appears.**

SHOCKWAVE COMPRESSION: The Shockwave for Audio Settings dialog box tells Director how you want to compress audio in your movie.

2. *Click the Enabled check box to tell Director to compress your movie's audio.*

The Bit Rate setting determines the level of compression that is applied—the lower the rate, the more the file is compressed. The more compression applied, the more information that is lost about the sound, with a higher probability of sound deterioration. Still, for most sounds, the lowest setting (highest compression) of 32KBits/second is probably still OK. For music, you would want to use less compression (or use an external SWA file). Unfortunately, this setting applies to all sounds in your movie—you can't choose to compress some and not others or use different settings for different cast members.

The Accuracy settings offer two choices for the quality of the compressed sound. I recommend always using the High option. You get better quality without a larger file size, and the few seconds more that compression takes is well worth the wait.

You select the Convert Stereo to Mono check box to convert stereo sounds to monaural sounds. For compression of 32KBits/second, this is done automatically. For other compression rates, you have a choice. If your sounds don't require stereo, you can convert them to mono and cut the size of your sound files in half.

Although you can set the Shockwave for Audio settings at any time, the shockwave compression occurs only when a Shockwave movie is created, when a projector is created (with the Compressed option enabled), or when the Update Movies command is used. You will need to test your audio (hopefully on a number of systems) to make sure that the compression you are using hasn't adversely affected the sound quality.

Shocking with Director 7

Once you've made your production as Web-friendly and bandwidth-lean as possible, it's time to do the Shockwave two-step: compressing it into Shockwave format (a DCR file) and embedding it in an HTML document.

1. *From the File menu, select Save as Shockwave Movie.*

The Save Shockwave Movie As dialog box appears. By default, the file you are working on is already selected, as is its current location.

2. *Click the Generate HTML check box to select it if it's not already checked. Then click Save.*

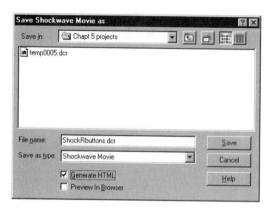

The "burning" process shouldn't take more than a few seconds, since the file is small. A new file will now appear in the same folder as the ShockRbuttons.dir movie, named ShockRbuttons.dcr (the extension stands for *Director compressed*). Notice that you don't need to use Save and Compress—Save as Shockwave takes care of any compressing that might be necessary.

3. *Quit Director and find the file ShockRbuttons.dcr. You should also see a ShockRbuttons.htm file nearby.*

That's it. You now have a Shocked version of your movie and an HTML file that can be displayed in a browser or over the Internet.

From the desktop, check out the size of the file. You'll find it's a fraction of the original; on my system, the 121K original burned down to a relatively tiny 20K. In contrast, producing a projector from the same file took up a whopping 1.3 megabytes. That's because a projector needs plenty of resources to stand on its own as a full-fledged application, whereas the Shockwave-built .dcr movie is simply in a new file format. The HTML file is only about 1K.

Prior to Director 7, you had to create your own HTML document from scratch, or in version 6.5 using Aftershock. Although the HTML file that was created with Director 7 won't win any design awards, it does contain everything you need to display the Shocked movie.

Our next step is to take a look at the HTML file and see what it contains. To do that, you can use any word processor or text editor.

Throughout the rest of the book, we'll use this typeface to indicate the terms that pertain to HTML.

Conversion to Shockwave is a one-way street: For compression purposes, Director discards much of the resources that a movie file needs. So unless you're absolutely sure you'll never want to modify your production (fat chance of that), hang on to the original unprotected movie as well as the .dcr file.

Placing the shocked movie in HTML

As computer languages go, HTML isn't too complicated; it's really little more than a set of formatting codes placed in a plain text file. The real pizzazz comes from the media that's linked to the text. HTML documents don't actually contain images, sounds, shocked movies, and the like; they just provide pointers to the source files for all that stuff. That's why HTML files can be quite small, and why we'll need nothing fancier than a basic word processor to create one.

If you've never looked at an HTML file, you can probably take a look at the work of others, using your browser. Most browsers allow you to view the source of the HTML file. For now, at least, there is usually no attempt to encrypt the files. Once you start creating your own Web site, looking at the existing work of others is a handy method of learning HTML.

Using your word processor or text editor, open the ShockRbuttons.htm file. Here's what you'll see:

```
<head>
<title>ShockRbuttons.dcr</title>
</head>
<body>
<center>
<h1>ShockRbuttons.dcr</h1>
```

```
<br> <object classid="clsid:166B1BCA-3F9C-11CF-8075-444553540000"
   codebase="http://download.macromedia.com/pub/shockwave/cabs/
   director/sw.cab#version=7,0,0,0" width="640" height="200">
<param name="src" value="ShockRbuttons.dcr">
<embed src="ShockRbuttons.dcr" pluginspage=
   "http://www.macromedia.com/shockwave/download/"
   width="640" height="200"></embed>
</object>
</center>
</body>
</html>
```

Some of the lines are shown wrapped because they are too long to be displayed on this printed page. When you are creating an HTML document, it doesn't matter what style or size of font you use; all such niceties are lost when the file is saved as plain text.

Embedding and setting parameters

As you may have already figured out, those pointy parentheses are the hallmarks of HTML. They enclose the commands that tell the browser what to do. Look at the first three lines, for example:

```
<head>
<title>ShockRbuttons.dcr</title>
</head>
```

These give the Shocked movie a title, ShockRbuttons.dcr, which will appear in the browser's title bar. The line

```
<h1>ShockRbuttons.dcr</h1>
```

will display a level-one head on the browser's page. You might have noticed both of these when you previewed your movie in a browser.

Shockwave movies are inserted into HTML with the <embed> command. This simple pass-through command informs the browser that a special media type follows and that it should be opened according to its type. The media to be opened is named with the src (source) parameter given in the same statement. The media type is indicated by the file name extension, .dcr.

The line (it really is a single line in the code)

```
<embed src="ShockRbuttons.dcr"
pluginspage="http://www.macromedia.com/shockwave/download/"
  width="640" height="200"></embed>
```

specifies the name of the Shockwave file to be displayed. It also specifies a
URL indicating the location on the Web for retrieving the Shockwave
plug-in, if necessary, as well as the width and height of the display.

- The `src` value points to the path name of our movie. So long as
  the file is in the same folder as our HTML document, that path
  name is synonymous with the file name, but it could also be something like this:
  `http://www.mydomain.com/Movies/ShockRbuttons.dcr`

- The `width` and `height` values are set to the dimensions that were
  set for the movie in Director. You can crop a movie in Shockwave by
  setting these values to form a window smaller than the movie's Stage.
  You can also make it larger, but that's pretty much just a waste of RAM.

The `<object>` tag is similar to the `<embed>` tag and provides essentially
the same information to the browser. The `<object>` tag is used by some
versions of the Microsoft browser and Director includes both tags for
compatability.

The major Web browsers out there offer full support for Shockwave plug-
ins, but not everyone uses those browsers—and among those who do, not
everyone wants to install the plug-in. To accommodate those folks, you
might want to provide an alternate still image, which you can do by
adding an entry adjacent to the **<embed>** command, following this syntax:

**<NOEMBED> <IMGSRC="[image pathname here]">
</NOEMBED>**

Whenever a non-Shockwave–enabled browser loads your page, the user
will see the image at the path name specified.

You can close your editor without saving, since we have made no changes.
If you do want to try making changes, such as changing the header, be
sure to save the file as plain text or text only or however your editor allows
you to save text without including formatting. Be sure to include the file
name extension .html or .htm, which is necessary for recognition of the
file by most browsers.

Viewing your shocked page

Your work is done! Now it's time to see the fruits of your labor. We'll use a Web browser to open the HTML document as a local file.

◆ *Launch your Web browser; then use the Open File, Open Page, or Open Local command (or equivalent) to open your ShockRbuttons.htm file.*

After a brief loading period, the introductory animation should appear. When the remaining necessary media is loaded, Swifty should appear walking in place. Use the buttons to interact with the movie as usual; it should behave just as it does in native Director mode.

> If you've committed to using Shockwave on your Web pages, you might consider using it for still images as well as movies. A single frame compressed with Shockwave can be more compact than the same image using JPEG compression or GIF encoding. Even motionless movies make demands on RAM, though, so don't plaster too many on a single page.

SHOCK TREATMENT:
The familiar Swifty is walking in the movie, brought to the Web courtesy of Shockwave.

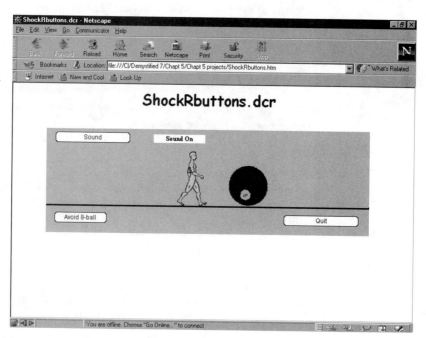

POINTS TO REMEMBER

We're just starting to scratch the surface of Shockwave. But carry these points with you as you continue your exploration and experimentation:

- Shockwave is an **enabling technology** for Director and other Macromedia products. It doesn't change your productions; it just makes them able to survive in the HTML-based environment of the Web.

- Without quitting Director, you can test your movies to see how they work when shocked by using **Preview in a Browser**.

- Before using Preview in a Browser, be sure to use **Save** and **Compact**.

- To view shocked movies, end users will need a **Web browser** capable of interpreting the Shockwave format. Most browsers need a special **plug-in** installed for this.

- You need to **design** your Shockwave movies so that they **play efficiently over the Internet** without requiring long download times.

- Director provides a number of **behaviors** designed specifically for Shockwave movies and other network operations.

- The most recent incarnation of Shockwave has far fewer limitations than earlier versions. Files can be **streamed**—that is, played back even before the downloading process is complete. **Audio compression** is more efficient, and **linked cast members** are allowed.

- You should use just about every trick in the book to try and keep your Shockwave movies as **small as possible**. Use Lingo to script animations (instead of using the Score), and keep careful tabs on the size and number of your cast members.

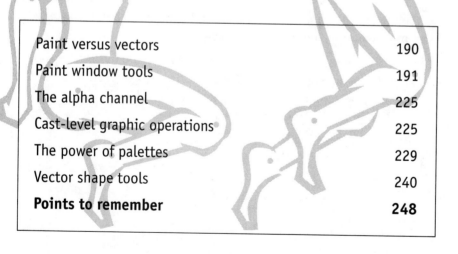

CHAPTER 6

DEEPER INTO GRAPHICS

LET'S TAKE A DEEPER LOOK AT WHAT'S ON THE SURFACE. IN THIS CHAPTER we'll be concerned solely with appearances—how you can create and modify the visual elements of your Director productions. You've already learned quite a bit about the possibilities of image manipulation and variation, but there's a lot more waiting to meet the eye.

We'll start by surveying the special effects available in the two main graphics windows: the bitmap-oriented Paint window and the vector-savvy Vector Shape window. Then it's on to tips for customizing your graphics tools, additional imaging options, and general graphics management issues. Finally, we'll look at techniques for building and deploying palettes, those collections of color that can produce dazzling (and disorienting) differences in display.

PAINT VERSUS VECTORS

Now that Director 7 has introduced the vector shape, you have two main forms of graphics to choose from: vectors and bitmaps. So how do you decide which is appropriate? Well, the decision is generally not that difficult: The areas of possible overlap are generally pretty small, and if you have a situation where either type will work, you'll probably choose the vector shape (if only for its smaller file sizes). To make a decision, keep these points in mind:

• Bitmaps are ideal when you're dealing with complex images. They allow you to control the image on a pixel-by-pixel basis.

• Vector shapes are ideal when you need a simple, smooth image with less detail than you find in bitmaps.

• Vector shapes can be resized without distortion, whereas bitmaps generally become jagged when resized.

• As pointed out earlier, bitmaps store information about each pixel, whereas vector shapes are a mathematical description of the shape. This allows vector shapes to use less RAM and disk space than an equivalent bitmap.

• Because they use less RAM, vector shapes load faster on the Web.

• Vector shapes can be controlled (and even created) by Lingo. You can write a script that manipulates a number of different parameters for each: size, shape, color, and so on.

• More tools are available, both within the Paint window and beyond, for creating bitmaps. It's easy to create and modify a bitmap in a high-powered application such as Photoshop and then pop it into the Cast; it'll automatically show up in the Paint window as well.

With these points in mind, let's take a more in-depth look at both, starting with the old standby—the Paint window—and ending with the newcomer—the Vector Shape window.

PAINT WINDOW TOOLS

Although it's not as feature-packed as a high-end graphics application like Painter or Photoshop, the Paint window in Director does place some powerful tools at your disposal. This section provides a rundown of some of them, along with tips on using them to your best advantage. We'll let you explore the most straightforward ones on your own and focus instead on those whose capabilities aren't immediately apparent.

One of the features introduced in Director 6 was the ability to specify that bitmap cast members are to be edited with an external program, such as Photoshop or xRes, rather than in the Paint window. You can override that preference: Simply hold down the Alt or Option key while double-clicking the cast member in question, and the Paint window will open instead of the external application.

There's something to be aware of, though. When Director imports a cast member that contains important information (such as layers in Photoshop), it retains that information only until the member is edited in the Paint window. In other words, once you do more than change a bitmap cast member's registration point, the external program ceases to recognize the member as its own creation and sees it as just another bitmap image.

Selection options

You can use two tools for selecting items in the Paint window's canvas area: the **Lasso** and the **Marquee**. The first allows you to select an irregular area by enclosing it within a line, and the second confines the selection to a field defined by right angles (unfortunately, there is no option for making round or elliptical selections). Both tools have several modes of selection. To access the modes, click and hold on the tool buttons. You'll see that each has a pull-down menu.

Interestingly, some modes act exactly the same for both tools. For example, the Marquee tool can act as the Lasso tool—or more precisely, as the Lasso tool does in Shrink mode. Let's take a look at the modes that apply to both tools.

Shrink mode

When you select Shrink mode, your selection is not defined by the actual area designated with the tool. Instead, the area collapses until it encounters pixels of a different color, resulting in a selection shrunk to the actual boundaries of an object. In the case of the Marquee tool, this selection is rectangular, as shown below; in the case of the Lasso, the selection fits the contours of the shape.

When selected with the lasso, an item in Shrink mode will throb around its edges.

No Shrink mode

Using No Shrink mode lets the tools behave more conventionally: The area you designate is the area that stays selected. The figure below shows a Lasso tool selection in No Shrink mode.

See Thru mode

Selecting in See Thru mode has essentially the same effect as selecting in Shrink mode with the Lasso tool, but with one difference: Not only is the item shrink-selected, but the Transparent ink is automatically applied to the selected area. This option is useful when you're creating assemblages of multiple items that will overlay another image or each other.

Once you have an item selected in your Paint window, you can apply a number of shortcuts:

Copy	Press Alt (Windows) or Option (Macintosh) while dragging.
Zoom (magnify)	Press Control (Windows) or Command (Macintosh) and click.
Constrain direction	Press Shift while dragging.
Delete	Press Backspace or Delete.
Proportional stretch	Press Control (Windows) or Command (Macintosh) and Shift while dragging.

The Palette toolbar

You'll notice that once you select an item, some buttons become active at the top of the Paint window. This is where you'll find most of your options for item manipulation. We'll start with the following image and will apply various options to it so that you can see the results.

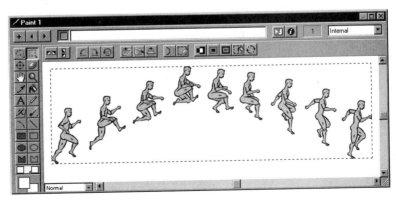

Flip Horizontal

Flip Horizontal turns the selected area on its horizontal axis. For this effect to work, you must use the marquee tool in Shrink or No Shrink mode.

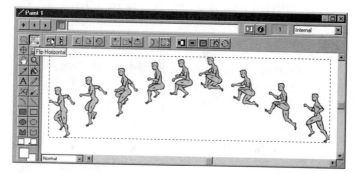

Flip Vertical

Flip Vertical turns the selected area on its vertical axis. Again, the effect works only on a rectangular selection, in Shrink or No Shrink mode.

Trace Edges

The Trace Edges effect is intriguing; it produces cookie-cutter versions of the selected items by deleting them and substituting a 1-point border around their former periphery. In place of the figure is an outline-like trace, slightly fatter than the original.

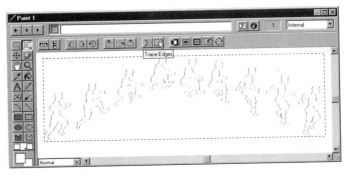

To get an interesting topographical effect, apply Trace Edges repeatedly. The edges will themselves be traced, adding another layer of edges. With enough applications of Trace Edges, your artwork will look like cross-sections of a surrealistic onion.

Invert Colors

The Invert Colors effect switches each color in the selection to the color opposite it on the color wheel—black becomes white, red becomes green—much like what you see in a photographic negative. The dark outlines on the illustration are the selection border.

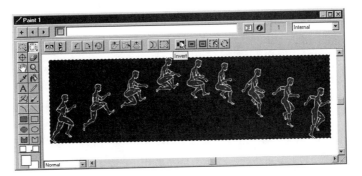

Darken

The Darken effect causes the selection to darken slightly. How slightly? In 8-bit color mode, the unit of change is approximately one-fifteenth the distance between absolute lightness and absolute darkness (that is, it takes 15 applications of Darken to turn a white item into a black one).

In the following illustration, the command has been applied five times, rendering the Swiftys black and the formerly blank background a hazy gray.

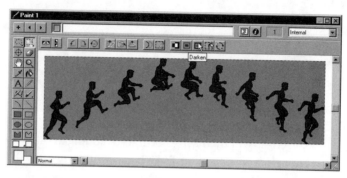

Lighten

Lighten is (you guessed it!) the opposite of Darken. The unit of change is the same, but everything shifts toward the bright end of the spectrum. With both Darken and Lighten, the Paint window remembers the selected artwork's original differentiation in detail—so if you go too far in one direction, you can backtrack by using the opposite command. Once you've dropped the selection, however, the Paint window no longer remembers the original shading.

> The behavior of Darken or Lighten will vary depending on the bit depth of the graphic you're working with. Both work fine on 32-bit graphics, but with 16-bit graphics they don't work at all, and the buttons will stay dimmed. You cannot use them with 2-bit or 1-bit images, either.

Fill

No need to illustrate this one. As you might imagine, the Fill command fills all of the selected area with a selected color.

But which color? It depends on what tool you use to make the selection before choosing Fill. If you use the Lasso—or the Marquee tool in a Lasso mode—it'll fill with the color in the foreground paint chip. If, however, you've used the Marquee tool (in non-Lasso mode—in either Shrink or No Shrink mode), the area will instead be filled with the current pattern in the pattern chip.

Switch Colors

Let's say you have an image of yellow ducks floating on a blue puddle; you want to make the ducks a lovely shade of purple, but you don't want the puddle to change color. The Switch Colors command can be used to substitute a single color in the selected area with another color of your choice. All other colors will remain unaffected.

Switch Colors uses the gradient color chips to determine the changing color (the left paint chip) and the color it's changing to (the right paint chip). If any pixel's color value matches the left chip, it'll be swapped for that of the right chip. This means you could select an image of a box of crayons and use Switch Colors to change the colors one crayon at a time.

Smooth

The Smooth command performs a version of anti-aliasing on the selected items, smoothing the transitions between one color and another by introducing intermediary pixel colorations. The result tends to be a blur effect. In the following illustration, Smooth has been applied in increasing amounts to each figure, from the second to the left (one time) to the rightmost (eight times).

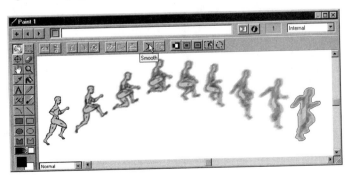

Rotate Left

Rotate Left is another command that works only with the Marquee tool (in non-Lasso mode). It spins the selection counterclockwise on its axis by precisely 90 degrees.

Rotate Right

Rotate Right is the twin of Rotate Left, only it spins the selection in the opposite direction. Again, the rotation occurs on the selection's axis. In the following illustration, Rotate Right was applied to the Swifty on the far right, and Rotate Left was applied to the Swifty on the far left.

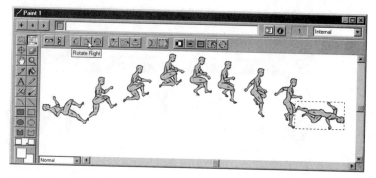

Free Rotate

When you choose Free Rotate, a special box appears around the selected area. Move the cursor to any of the corners and hold down the mouse button to spin the selection in any direction you choose, by any amount. Unfortunately, you can't set or determine the exact degrees of rotation; you'll just have to eyeball it.

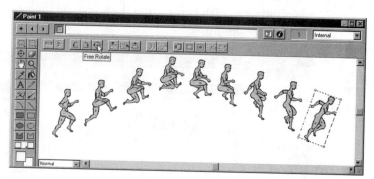

Free Rotate—and the other commands that follow—give you the option of making multiple adjustments to the selection before you freeze it in a single position. When you're ready to make the change permanent, click anywhere outside the selection area.

Skew

The same type of selection box appears with Skew as with Free Rotate, only this time you can move any combination of corners to create a variety of trapezoidal configurations. Skew simply slants things to the degree that you specify.

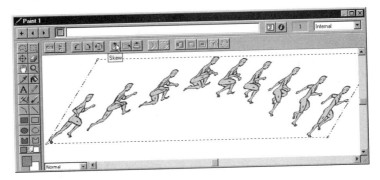

Warp

Warp allows you to distort the plane of the image to a different degree in all four corners of the selection. Although you can't truly twist the image, you can produce some pretty twisted results. For real distortion, try applying this effect several times.

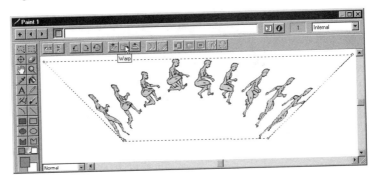

Perspective

Drag on any corner using the Perspective option to skew a graphic to your heart's content, creating a sense of planar depth.

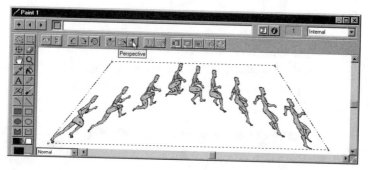

Auto Distort

DON'T DESELECT!
If the artwork is deselected, the information about its motions will be lost. Even moving or resizing the Paint window will cause the work to be deselected.

You can employ Auto Distort with any of the orientation effects (the three Rotates, Skew, Perspective, and Warp). First apply the effects; you can apply one or more in sequence. Next, from the Xtras menu, choose Auto Distort to open the Auto Distort dialog box. Then enter a number in the Generate: [n] New Cast Members field. Each cast member created will vary slightly from the one before it, until the last one reflects the degree of modification made to the selected original. To make the change more pronounced, lower the number of cast members created; to make it more subtle, increase the number. Remember to use only the allowable effects before generating the new cast members. Any other operation will result in a loss of the information regarding the changes.

Distortion effects and rotation work only on rectangular selections. You'll need to select your artwork with the Marquee tool (set to Shrink or No Shrink, not the Lasso mode).

Which effect is active?

There's a nice little Paint feature that often goes unnoticed. If you look closely, you'll see that each of the orientation effects uses selection handles in a distinct shape. Since it's easy to drop a selection and get stuck with the result, these symbols serve as a reminder of what's about to happen.

Using Photoshop-compatible plug-ins

One of the biggest enhancements to Director graphics came in version 5, when compatibility with standardized bitmap filters came into play. If you've ever used Photoshop, you've probably encountered some of these **plug-ins**, which appear on the Filters menu and usually perform a single specialized graphic operation: Distort, Blur, Twirl, and so forth. Some amazingly versatile graphics software is marketed as plug-ins, including Kai's Power Tools and Adobe Gallery Effects—and now you can add that versatility to Director's Paint window.

POWER PLUGS:
A sampling of typical Photoshop-compatible plugs-ins and their support files. The top middle widget is the standard icon, but variations abound.

KPT TE 3.0 Presets

Eraser Support

IPA Motion Blur 2.5.6

KPT3 Gradient Designer

GE Craquelure

KPT 2.1 Filter Hub

Plug-ins shouldn't be confused with Xtras; while both are modular external enhancements, plug-ins are written to different software standards. The likelihood of confusion is amplified by the fact that you treat plug-ins essentially the same as Xtras:

- **To install a plug-in,** drag a copy to the Xtras folder (the one at the same folder level as your Director application). Alternatively, if you want the plug-in to be accessible to other Macromedia applications, you can place it in a different Xtras folder: the one that's inside the Macromedia folder that should appear in either your Windows folder (in Windows) or your System folder (on the Macintosh).

- **To access a plug-in,** select any part of a Paint cast member (or click its slot to select it as a whole). Then from the Xtras window select Filter Bitmap. You'll see a dialog box from which you can choose a plug-in function.

FILTER FINDER:
Use the Filter Bitmap dialog box to pick and apply your plug-in effects.

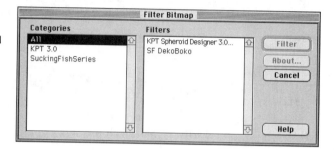

Plug-ins generally come in two forms: those that simply apply an effect straight out (such as Sharpen or Fragment), and those that require a few more parameters before they can get down to business. When you click the Filter button, you may encounter a dialog box customized for the plug-in, like the one for Naoto Arakawa's Deko-Boko filter shown here.

SUCKING FISH:
Deko-Boko, from Naoto Arakawa's Sucking Fish plug-in series, automatically places concave or convex beveled edges around a selection.

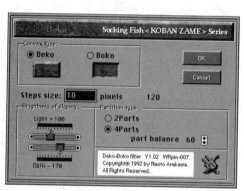

Incidentally, a couple of timesaving features are built in here: You can apply the same filter to multiple cast members simultaneously by selecting them as a group, and once applied, a filter appears on the Recent Filters menu for further quick access.

The Auto Filter feature

All plug-in effects can be applied to cast members in sequence, but some can even create new cast members, each an incarnation of the original but with the effect progressively applied. These filters show up not only in the Filter Bitmap dialog box but in Auto Filter as well. Like Auto Distort,

Auto Filter can extrapolate a number of versions of the original, given starting and ending values.

> Director supports the Photoshop plug-in standard, but that doesn't mean all plug-ins will run under your version of Director. Some plug-ins cut corners on standard conformity, and though they might work flawlessly in Photoshop, they may not perform as well elsewhere. Also, plug-ins vary in their memory requirements, and some of the more ambitious ones may demand more RAM than you can supply. You'll just have to experiment and remove plug-ins that you find troublesome.

Coloring options

Let's look at the various means available for creating and modifying color on the Paint window canvas.

Air brush textures

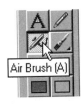

The Air Brush tool offers you a choice of five patterns, each of which you can modify with a number of parameters. To access these patterns, click and hold the downward triangle in the Air Brush icon's lower-right corner—a pop-up menu appears. The factory presets are multidot splatter effects, whose most important variable is size. The actual placement of the splatters is random.

A MATTER OF SPLATTERS: These are the five factory presets for the Air Brush tool (each splatter is a single click of the mouse).

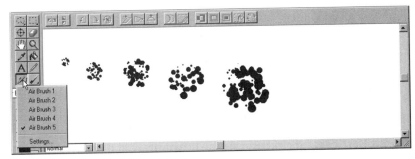

Click the arrow located in the lower right-hand corner of an icon to reveal a pop-up menu.

There is no revert function for air brush options. Once you modify one of the five air brush presets, it stays that way until you modify it again. The only way to restore it to its previous setting is by quitting without saving changes—or if it's too late for that, by reinstalling Director from its original discs.

To customize an air brush pattern, select the preset you wish to change. Then select Settings from the pop-up menu. You'll see this dialog box:

Use the Air Brush Settings option to make the air brush spray with the current paintbrush pattern.

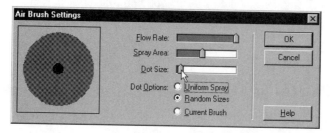

Choosing the Uniform Spray option changes the color coverage pattern to a consistent single stream. Choosing Current Brush will spray with a brush pattern that matches the current setting of the paintbrush tool. You can use this option to take advantage of the pattern editing capabilities of the paintbrush.

The Spray Area parameter refers to the overall area in which the tool will spray color—if you hold down the mouse without moving it, you'll see that while the splashes of color are laid down randomly, that randomness is limited to the area specified. Dot Size refers to the actual units that constitute each spray, and Flow Rate is a measure of how quickly the area being sprayed fills up with color.

Paintbrush strokes

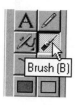

As with the Air Brush tool, five presets are available for the paintbrush (Brush tool) available through a pop-up menu. You can modify these, too, and (fortunately) you can revert to the original settings when you're done experimenting by simply changing the pop-up setting from Custom to Standard in the Brush Settings window.

BRUSH REGULARLY:
The Brush tool comes with five factory presets.

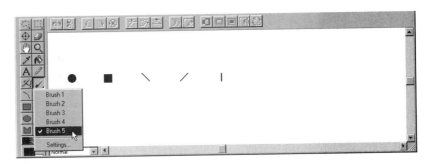

Again, you must select the Brush preset you want to modify. Then select Settings from the pop-up menu, or double-click the Brush tool icon. As you can see, you have considerably more options to choose from this time.

GETTING INTO SHAPE(S):
You can edit the individual brush shapes of the Brush tool.

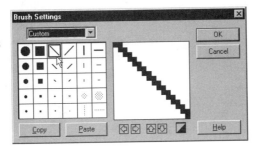

All brush shapes are straightforward groupings of pixels, but those group-ings can vary widely. To create a new one, click a target shape, and then

- Click white pixels to make them black (and vice-versa).

- Use the directional arrows to change the grouping's placement in the active area of the brush.

- Click the half-white/half-black box to invert the image (so that white becomes black, and so on).

You can use outside images as brush building blocks as well. If you click and drag the mouse anywhere outside the close-up portion of the Brush Settings dialog box, whatever you're dragging will appear in that box. Use this technique to turn text, icons, or other small objects into cus-tom brushes.

Using gradients

Gradients are two or more colors blended together. Since there's more than one way to achieve such a blend, there's more than one kind of gradient. You can start working with gradients by selecting two colors on the Color Gradient bar of the Paint window. The leftmost color chip displays the foreground, or **source**, color (the one the gradient starts from), and the rightmost chip displays the background, or **destination**, color (the one to which the gradient gradually proceeds).

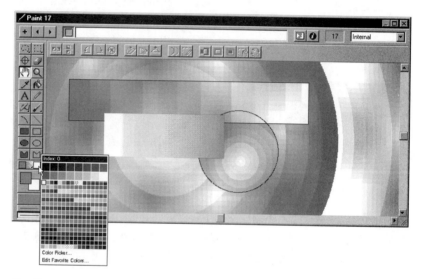

Gradients can be used with the Paint Bucket and Brush tools and with all filled shapes. To apply a gradient, select both the source and destination colors; then select the Gradient ink effect you desire and proceed. The path from source to destination color is not necessarily a straightforward one, however. You can introduce a variety of gradient effects by double-clicking the Paint Bucket tool or by choosing Gradient Settings from the Gradient Colors pop-up menu and working in the Gradient Settings dialog box.

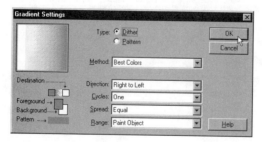

The Gradient Settings dialog box offers you another opportunity to set the two gradient colors, and it lets you set a pattern to be superimposed on the fill. But there are also five pop-up menus controlling five different parameters, with enough options for you to create hundreds of gradient variations.

Type

To create a gradient, Director has to fade one color into another. The formula it uses to achieve this fade can be set using Type, which has two paths: pattern methods, which overlay the chosen pattern, and dither methods, which use dithering to smooth the transition between the two colors. The Method pop-up menu in the Gradient Settings dialog box provides six different color combinations with which to implement these options.

Direction

The Direction menu determines the direction in which the gradient travels. There are seven options:

- **Top to Bottom, Bottom to Top, Left to Right,** and **Right to Left** do what their names imply.

- **Directional** is the only two-step effect, letting you set the direction from which the fill proceeds. A selection line appears; rotate it to indicate the angle.

- **Shape Burst** (Macintosh only) takes its cue from the shape of the item it's filling; if it's a rectangle, the fill will be a graded series of rectangles, and so forth.

- **Sun Burst** is similar to Shape Burst, but the shape grades out in a circular form.

Cycles

Use the Cycles option to set the number of times the gradient is applied to a given area. If more than one cycle is chosen, this option also determines how the gradients border each other: **Smooth** softens the borders and **Sharp** makes demarcation quite clear.

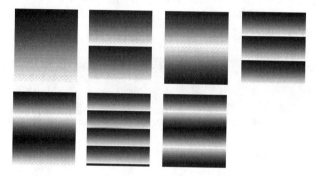

Spread

The Spread option setting determines the balance between the two colors of the gradient. There are four choices:

- **Equal** is the default. Both colors appear in equal proportions.

- **More Foreground** allows the foreground color to dominate.

- **More Middle** takes the middle point (the area in which the colors are in equal proportion) and gives it prominence.

- **More Destination** accents the destination color.

Range

The Range pop-up menu specifies the area over which the gradient is applied—not the area over which it's shown (it always appears only in the selected item), but the theoretical area over which the gradient is extended.

- **Paint Object** is the default. It assumes that the beginning point is one edge of the item, and the destination point is the opposite edge.

- **Cast Member** stretches the dimensions of the gradient to the overall area of all artwork on the Paint window canvas.

- **Window** draws its start and stop gradient points from the dimensions of the Paint window.

You can see the difference Range makes in the following illustration. The same black-to-white gradient is applied to each shape, but only in the left one does the square begin in black and end in white.

Paint ink effects

Ink effects are one of the biggest surprises you'll encounter in the Paint window. These tools create effects that would be hard to duplicate elsewhere, even in Photoshop.

Score-level ink effects are discussed in Chapter 7: *More Production Tools*.

Actually, ink effects are found in two realms: the Paint window and the Score window. Paint ink effects make permanent changes to the artwork of graphic cast members, and Score ink effects can be applied (and unapplied) to individual sprites—not just graphic sprites, but text, shape, and button sprites as well. In this section, we'll be looking only at Paint ink effects; for a rundown on the Score effects, see Chapter 7: *More Production Tools*.

It's a little difficult to convey the results of ink effects in black-and-white illustrations, and the best way to appreciate the effects is to put them to work, so you might want to open a Director movie and experiment as you leaf through this section. You'll find the ink effects pull-down menu at the bottom of the Paint window. The default setting is Normal, but if you click and hold the menu arrow, you'll see the array of effects that can be applied to your particular bitmap selection. The contents of the ink effects pull-down menu change in accordance with the Paint tool you have selected; the effects are specific to individual tools.

Transparent

Transparent ink causes the pixels of the selected artwork's background color to disappear. In this illustration, the leaping Swiftys were created in another cast slot and then selected and pasted over a grayscale graphic.

THE PAINT INK EFFECT set to Transparent.

Reverse

The Reverse effect compares the color values of both the selected artwork and the background, and reverses the background color in the areas in which it rests. Any white areas in the selection become transparent. Note how in the example here, the Swiftys outside of the background area are displayed normally. That's because they have no color area to react against.

THE PAINT INK EFFECT set to Reverse.

Ghost

Ghost is similar to Reverse but with an interesting twist: Color values are reversed, and Ghost also copies the saturation (degree of color intensity) of whatever color happens to be in the background.

THE PAINT INK EFFECT set to Ghost.

Thus, against a highly saturated backdrop such as dark blue or even black (black being the ultimate in saturation for all colors), Ghost will produce an equally vivid color. But the more unsaturated (that is, pale or washed-out) the background color, the more subtle the ink effect. And that's why this effect lives up to its name: When placed against a white background, the colors in Ghost will themselves become white. If the same color is in the sprite and the background, that color, too, will be displayed as white.

Gradient

Use the Gradient effect when you want to employ the current gradient parameters as a fill format. In this illustration, the Swiftys were filled using the Paint Bucket tool. Since the figures were mostly of a single color, the fill completely replaces that original single color with a variant of the gradient.

THE PAINT INK EFFECT
set to Gradient.

Reveal

Reveal works in conjunction with the graphical cast member in the slot immediately before the current cast member; the contents of the earlier image serve as a sort of fill or mask for the current image. In the following example, the Swiftys were filled with the Paint Bucket set to Reveal mode, so each one becomes a window to the contents of the slot before it.

THE PAINT INK EFFECT
set to Reveal.

If you want to create a quick mask of an object, Reveal is a good effect to use. Once you've applied the ink, you can rearrange the order of the Cast with no change to the artwork.

Cycle

Cycle is a **stroke effect**, which means that it works only with the Brush and Air Brush tools—tools that interpret mouse movements as strokes. In this case, the stroke is filled not with a single color but with a range of colors in the currently active palette. The size of the range depends on the colors in the foreground and background paint chips: The closer those are in the palette, the fewer intervening colors are included in the Cycle stroke. To use all colors in the palette, make the foreground color black and the background color white.

THE PAINT INK EFFECT set to Cycle.

Switch

A stroke effect similar to Switch Colors, the Switch ink will change only those pixels of a certain color (specified in the foreground paint chip), switching them for the color shown in the background paint chip. In this instance, the red of the Swiftys is replaced with green at the point where the brush stroke passes through them.

THE PAINT INK EFFECT
set to Switch.

Blend

A translucent effect, Blend mixes pasted and background objects, letting the former shade the latter with a variable degree of opacity. The default is 50% of the pasted item; the image shown here uses a 60% setting.

THE PAINT INK EFFECT
set to Blend.

You can vary the degree of opacity used by Blend when pasting one object on top of another. From the File menu, choose Preferences and then Paint. Then move the Blend Amount slider to the percentage you want. This value will be applied to the pasted object, while the background will remain opaque.

Darkest

The Darkest ink compares the pixels of both the pasted and the background items; of any two overlapping pixels, only the darkest is displayed.

THE PAINT INK EFFECT
set to Darkest.

Lightest

The opposite of Darkest, Lightest uses the same method of pixel comparison but displays the lightest pixels instead. In the figure below, the Lightest ink is applied only to a selected area, shown in white.

THE PAINT INK EFFECT
set to Lightest.

Darken

Not to be confused with Darkest, Darken is a stroke effect that adds no new colors per se, but lessens the brightness of the colors already present. In this example, a Darken brush has been passed over the image several times.

Lighten

The opposite of Darken, Lighten employs the same methods. Pixels are changed only by degree of brightness, to the maximum value allowed by the current palette. In the example here, multiple passes with a Lighten brush have reduced some of the gray pattern in the background to almost white, but the red of the Swiftys appears less washed out. That's because in the palette used (the default System palette), the progression of available reds is smaller than the progression from dark gray to white.

The degree of change for both Darken and Lighten can be set in the Paint Window Preferences dialog box (from the File menu, choose Preferences and then Paint). Just open the dialog box and adjust the Lighten/Darken slider bar.

Smooth

Like the Smooth selection command, the Smooth ink effect performs a version of anti-aliasing on the areas beneath the brush, smoothing the transitions between one color and another with the use of intermediate pixels. When applied often enough, this stroke effect creates pronounced blurring.

THE PAINT INK EFFECT set to Smooth.

Smear

Another stroke effect, using Smear is the equivalent of pushing a finger across a pastel drawing. The colors and images are pulled in the direction of the stroke, causing them to mush into one another. In the illustration here, Smear has been applied several times in left-to-right strokes.

THE PAINT INK EFFECT
set to Smear.

Smudge

Smudge is a more pronounced version of Smear. The color is carried from one area to another over a wider range, and the mushing is less subtle.

THE PAINT INK EFFECT
set to Smudge.

You can use Smudge as a means of mixing and blending colors, much as you would a painter's palette. Create filled areas of source colors, mush them around at will, and then use the color sampling tool, the eyedropper, to sample and select the result. Remember that no matter how artistic your mixing, the colors created won't fall outside the color range of the currently active palette.

Spread

Think of Spread as a means of loading a brush with a pattern and then using that pattern as a stroke. With Spread, anything under the brush when the mouse button goes down is the selected pattern; it's spread across the image for the remainder of the stroke.

THE **PAINT** INK EFFECT
set to Spread.

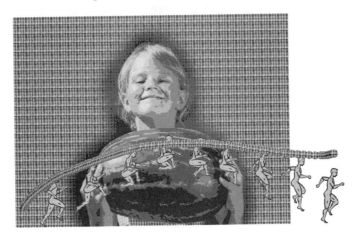

Clipboard

Like Spread, Clipboard takes a selection and drags it across the image in accordance with the stroke movement. But the stroke is drawn from whatever's currently on the system Clipboard. If the Clipboard selection is irregularly shaped, it'll be interpreted across the image within an opaque rectangle. In the illustration here, another graphic created in Paint was copied and then brushed across the Paint window.

THE **PAINT** INK EFFECT
set to Clipboard.

Using Paint Window Preferences

We've already touched upon the fact that you can use the Paint Window Preferences dialog box to customize the results of several ink effects. You can use it to do a lot more than that, as we'll now see.

PAINT CONSTRAINTS:
There's a lot to muck about with in the Paint Window Preferences dialog box.

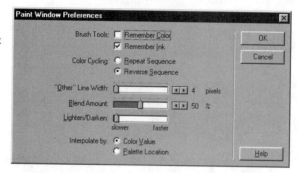

Brush Tools

The Brush Tools setting offers two options:

- When Remember Color is selected, the color chosen in the foreground paint chip will "stick" to that tool—that is, the color will be reselected every time you choose that tool, until you select another color.

- Remember Ink provides a similar form of "stickiness," only what stays associated with the tool in this case is the ink effect last chosen.

Color Cycling

The following two options determine the manner in which multiple colors are displayed in a Color Cycling ink effect:

- When you choose Repeat Sequence, color picking begins at the color chosen in the foreground paint chip and proceeds down the palette colors until you reach the color in the destination paint chip—then it skips back to the foreground color and the process begins anew.

- When you choose Reverse Sequence, cycling proceeds in a similar manner, except that when the cycle reaches the destination color, it reverses order until it returns to its starting point.

"Other" Line Width

See that 4 Pixels box at the bottom of the Paint window's line selection area? It indicates the default line thickness. You can use the "Other" Line Width slider to set the default thickness to any value from 1 to 64 pixels.

Blend Amount

Blend Amount performs a function similar to "Other" Line Width but it applies to the Blend ink effect, establishing the applied color's degree of opacity.

Lighten/Darken

The Lighten/Darken slider bar is used to set the degree to which the selected area changes with each application of a Lighten or Darken ink effect (yes, it's the same rate for both).

Interpolate By

The Interpolate By options provide another method by which Director interprets colors when performing a Smooth, Lighten, Darken, or Cycle ink effect.

- Color Value performs an end run around the order of colors in the current palette by ignoring their sequence when producing a blend between foreground and background colors. If your current palette stores colors with little regard to chromatic order, this effect can keep color blends from becoming too jarring.

- Selecting Palette Location ensures that all colors in the palette between the foreground and destination colors are used.

Working with patterns

Graphic areas in the Paint window can be filled with more than solid colors or gradients. Patterns, like brush tools, can be used in both preset and customized forms.

Preset patterns

To access the preset buttons, click the color area below the foreground and background paint chips. If you haven't clicked this area yet, it's probably a solid color.

DETECTING A PATTERN:
Use the Pattern pop-up menu in the Paint window to select a fill pattern.

This is the Standard set of patterns, one of four possible pattern groups. You can click to select any one of these patterns. Open the Pattern pop-up menu. Notice that while a few patterns appear in colors other than that of the foreground paint chip, the majority of patterns reflect the foreground color; if the foreground color is black, they'll be seen as shades of gray. These patterns don't have an inherent color—they're simply grids and blocks of the foreground color.

Pattern options

If you want more patterns to choose from, double-click the Pattern chip to open the Pattern Settings dialog box, which shows a grid of the same patterns you've already seen. However, these versions are ready for your modifications. That's why the pop-up menu above the grid shows Custom as an option.

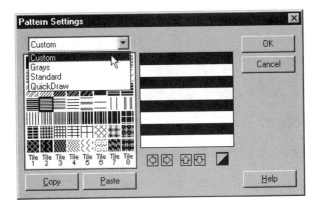

You can also choose one of three other options:

- **Grays** provides a grayscale palette.

- **Standard** is the default pattern group. You can use it to revert to the basics after modifying them in the Custom grouping.

- **QuickDraw** uses the patterns that are built into the operating system as part of its graphics display capabilities. If you have worked with MacPaint or other early graphics programs, you're probably familiar with these patterns.

If you want to edit or create your own patterns, first select Custom, and then select a pattern to change. The methods used here are essentially the same as those described for the Brush Settings dialog box (see "Paintbrush strokes" earlier in this chapter).

Working with tiles

TILES:
An extendable pattern created from all or part of a cast member.

Did you notice that extra row of colorful squares on the bottom of the pattern pop-up menu? Those are **tiles**. Although they can extend to fill an indefinite area, tiles aren't the same as patterns; they can contain up to 24-bit colors, and they can be derived from cast members rather than bitmapped squares.

There are eight slots for tiles in the Paint window. You can't edit them as you can patterns, but you can overwrite them by designating a portion of a graphic cast member to be tiled. Just select Tile Settings from the Pattern pop-up menu to access the Tile Settings dialog box.

VERY VERSA-TILE:
You can create custom tiles by designating the portion of a cast member you think bears repeating. Then apply the tiles to the Stage in a filled shape of any dimension.

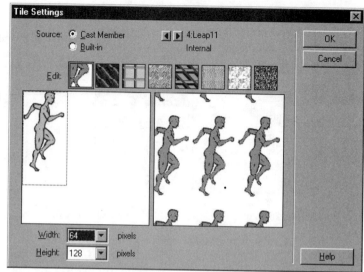

To create a custom tile, click the Cast Member radio button and then use the direction arrows to scroll through the Cast. Specify the area of the individual tile in the Width and Height fields and then drag the selection rectangle to the exact area you want. When the preview in the right-hand preview area suits you, click OK. The selected tile will be replaced by your design.

Custom tiles remain with the movie in which they're created; when you open a new movie, the tiling choices revert to normal. If you want to restore a custom tile to the default, simply select it in this dialog box and then click the Built-In radio button.

If you're developing a project for cross-platform or Web distribution, pay special attention to what happens to the patterns and tiles in the final product; you may find that their display changes somewhat in the porting. That's because the built-in tiles vary slightly between Director for Windows and Director for the Macintosh, and your choice may be automatically replaced by a substitute.

THE ALPHA CHANNEL

ALPHA AWAY!
Director's new alpha channel support means you can improve your graphics and create some outstanding effects.

For you Director users who are into the graphics side of creating movies, Director's new **alpha channel** support will be one of the most exciting new capabilities of Director 7. If you're into graphics, you've probably been using alpha channels all along in other graphics packages such as Photoshop or Freehand. For those of you who are new to alpha channels, it means there is an additional amount of information for each pixel of an image. This additional information defines the degree of transparency for the individual pixels. Previously, when you imported an image with an alpha channel, the information was lost on Director. Now you can include the alpha channel to improve your graphics and create some outstanding effects.

Consider creating clouds or fog, for example. Instead of the balloony looking clouds of a cartoon strip, with sharply defined edges, you can show the wispy effect of real clouds and fog. The transparency effects of the alpha channel allow the fog to blend with the background.

When you play with alpha channels, you'll see that talking only about transparency falls far short of the mark. You'll find yourself using alpha channels for softening and blending hard edges to make images look more realistic, creating glassy or watery effects, and implementing a host of other possibilities.

CAST-LEVEL GRAPHIC OPERATIONS

A number of modifications can be performed on graphic cast members not only in the Paint window but in the Cast window as well—and several of them can be applied to a number of cast members at once. These Cast-level graphic operations are good for enforcing consistency among your cast members and for making changes to cast member status.

Convert to Bitmap

We've already noted that text can be displayed on the Stage in three ways: as text, per se (text fields); as Rich Text Formatted (RTF) text, which is anti-aliased, formattable, and can use included fonts; and as bitmaps created with Paint. Text as text takes up the least space in memory but is dependent on installed fonts; RTF text is larger but looks better; text as artwork is the largest memory user, but it looks the same on all systems and is especially suited for large type.

You can't turn artwork into text, but you can turn text into artwork by way of the Convert to Bitmap command on the Modify menu.

Any field or text cast member can be converted to a bitmap graphic, at which point it will show up in the Paint window rather than the Field or Text window. Buttons can also be converted, although their behaviors will freeze; radio buttons and check boxes will no longer be selectable by the end user.

Director's text anti-aliasing feature offers a definite improvement over the jagged results seen in earlier versions of Director, but it doesn't always produce optimum results when the text is converted to bitmaps. For the smoothest possible images formed from text, you might want to use a high-end graphics program like Photoshop and then import the text as a bitmap file.

Even though the Cast menu allows you to apply Convert to Bitmap to lines and shapes created with the Tool Palette, this conversion has no effect on these objects.

Transform Bitmap

Choosing the Transform Bitmap command from the Modify menu opens a dialog box that can determine many aspects of a cast member: Size, shape, color depth, and associated palette can all be set here. If you have more than one cast member selected in the Cast window when you open the Transform Bitmap dialog box, any changes you make will be applied to them all.

CHANGING YOUR IMAGE:
Use the Transform
Bitmap dialog box to
change the scale,
shape, color depth, and
color palette of one or
more bitmapped cast
members.

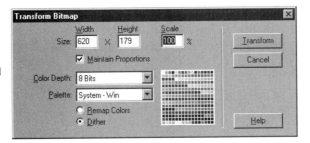

When working in the Transform Bitmap dialog box, remember that the changes you make will affect all sprites derived from the cast members you're changing. If all you really want to do is change the appearance of a single sprite segment, use the Sprite Properties dialog box (on the Modify menu) instead.

Changing cast member dimensions

In the Transform Bitmap dialog box, you can change the physical dimensions of a cast member in two ways: by setting the Scale value as a percentage of the cast member's current size, or by plugging in a new Width or Height value. Bear in mind that there is no Restore or Undo function here (you'd have to perform a movie-wide Revert operation), and that enlarged cast members will take up more memory than they did in their previous incarnations.

Changing cast member color attributes

The color commands can also effect two types of changes: The Color Depth pop-up menu can reset the number of colors used in the cast member, and the Palette pop-up menu can assign a new color palette—which is sort of like redrawing the picture, only with a different set of crayons.

Switching color depth is a little like changing the resolution of your printout on a laser printer; it determines how fine an image will be displayed, within limits. A plain black box will look equally black regardless of whether it uses 32-bit or 1-bit color depth—there's no room for nuance here.

Cast members with a lower color depth take up less storage space and consequently less space in RAM, making them easier for Director to whisk on and off the Stage. But there's a catch.

When a Director movie or projector plays in an 8-bit (256 colors) environment, the use of lower-bit-depth members can sometimes slow things down rather than speed them up. The reason is that Director must temporarily convert a 1-, 2-, or 4-bit cast member to an 8-bit image before it can be displayed. This takes time, and animation can slog along while the program performs the necessary calculations.

The bottom line? When authoring for an 8-bit environment, try to work with 8-bit images as often as is practical. The notable exception is Shockwave movies, where bandwidth issues make the smaller files worth the possible performance trade-off.

You should think of a color depth switch as a one-way trip down the scale. Once the extra color information is discarded, it can't be regained by changing the setting upward. And keep in mind that no matter what the color depth, the image quality's true top limit is your monitor's display capability. A 32-bit image will simply look like an 8-bit image on an 8-bit monitor, and it might even look a little worse than an image you've sampled down to 8 bits.

When changing to a new palette, you have a choice to make: What method should Director use to match the current colors with the ones in the new palette? There are a couple of options at the bottom of the Transform Bitmap dialog box:

- **Remap Colors** opts simply to find the color that most closely matches an old one, regardless of its position in the new palette. Depending on the two palettes in question, this could either produce no color change or a dramatic one. You might want to experiment, but remember that this kind of change can't be undone by clicking Revert, so work on a copy.

- **Dither** attempts to approximate the old colors in the new palette by finding the closest ones and then introducing black or white shading into the colored areas. Your eye mixes these shading pixels into the whole, creating an illusion of different color.

If you're developing projects for the Web via Shockwave, you should know that using dithering to approximate colors will result in larger file sizes for graphics. That's because the interposition of extra colors (even if it's just a few speckled dots) means the file has more information to encode.

THE POWER OF PALETTES

We experimented with color palettes back in Chapter 3, demonstrating how they can remap the monitor's display to match their collection of colors. But how are they really useful?

Look at it this way: Color is a resource. Like any resource, color needs to be managed to be put to best use. Although you could conceivably save every graphic cast member as a 32-bit element (with a palette containing all possible colors), it's unlikely that you'd want to—you'd be wasting RAM and clogging up processor time, invariably slowing down your movie. With color palettes, you can have only those colors you need read into RAM, which makes for optimum playback without compromising visual quality.

And why do you need different palettes? Consider a picture of a desert scene: The colors will be mostly shades of brown. Using the system palettes, there would not be enough shades of brown to display the image in the detail you want. Then you switch to an image of a snowy, winter day. Now you have mostly whites and blues. You can switch to a new palette when you switch images, to display each one just as you want.

Also, since you can switch rapidly from one palette to another, you can create arresting effects without too much hassle. In addition, some automated color-wrangling functions enable another level of animation, one in which colors move independently of the objects displayed on the Stage.

On the downside, using multiple palettes requires some careful planning. Since only one palette can be in effect at a time, all graphics (even the Stage color) need to use colors that are available in the current palette. If you have other graphics on the Stage, such as graphics used as buttons, the colors used by those graphics will change as you switch, for example, from the desert scene to the winter scene—unless you plan and integrate your palettes and sprites.

TIP

If you're developing projects for the Web, remember that Web browsers don't support palette changes. Director 7 includes a palette, Web 216, that very nearly matches the palette used by the most common browsers. When you're developing movies for Web-based delivery (for example, using Shockwave), you should consider remapping graphics to the Web 216 palette.

Importing palettes

Almost every time you import an external image file, you'll be asked if you want to import its palette as well. Unless the image is already mapped to one of Director's internal palettes, you'll encounter a dialog box like the one shown here.

YOUR PALETTE PAL:
If you're importing artwork that doesn't match the currently active palette, Director will offer to import the palette as well.

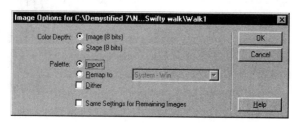

The Image Options dialog box provides a few helpful choices for importing a graphic that uses a palette different from the active palette. Import brings in the palette of the image as a cast member in itself. Once in the Cast, this palette can be applied to other cast members as well.

A LITTLE LOCAL COLOR:
Once installed in the Cast, a custom palette can be named, rearranged, and edited to suit your needs.

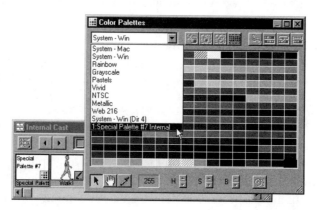

Every cast member has a palette associated with it. (You can identify it in the Palette pop-up menus of the cast member's Info window or in the Transform Bitmap dialog box.) But an individual frame can also have an assigned palette, which overrides the inherent palette of all sprites on the Stage during that frame. In the following illustration, two versions of the same image take on very different appearances, even though they're placed side by side on the Stage. The difference? The one on the right has an inherent palette matching the currently active palette and the one on the left does not. If you were to compare both images in the Paint window, you'd find them nearly identical, yet on the Stage they bear only a passing resemblance.

I GOT HUE, BABE:
Two versions of the same image, displayed under different active palettes.

You can't mix multiple palettes within a single frame. Only one is active at any given time, and that one is used to map all color in all images on the Stage, regardless of their inherent palettes.

Palettes in the Score

When a new Director movie is created, its default palette is either System-Win (on Windows systems) or System-Mac (on Macintosh systems). That palette will remain in effect during playback until another palette is placed in the palette channel of the Score. Once the movie encounters a new palette, that becomes the active palette, not only for the frame it occupies, but for all subsequent frames—which means that if you want the color to switch back to the default, you'll have to add a palette transition to make it do so.

Actually, you'll find two System palettes for Windows: One is the current default for that platform, and the other is a slightly different version that was a default in versions up to Director 4. If movies created with older versions of Director look strange when you import them into version 7, this palette difference may be the reason. You can switch back to the older palette by selecting System-Win (Dir 4) in the Movie Properties dialog box.

You can place a new palette in the palette channel directly; just drag the custom palette from the Cast or double-click the channel itself to bring up the dialog box. But when you place an image not using the currently active palette on the Stage, that image's palette is automatically added to the Score (since Director assumes you want the image displayed correctly). You can override this insertion, however, since switching palettes doesn't affect the inherent colors of the image.

TRUE COLORS: Information about the active palette is displayed in the Score's Info box.

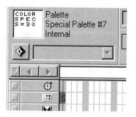

No matter how the palette appears in the Score, once it's there it's displayed in a consistent fashion. The display square in the upper-left corner provides an approximation of the palette's name and speed (expressed as S = *tempo*). The Score cell itself bears the cast number of the palette (if it's a custom one), or a number corresponding to the order of built-in palettes: System-Mac is 00, System-Win is 01, and so on. The order follows that of the palette options in a Properties dialog box.

That speed measure isn't the same as the speed setting in the tempo channel. Rather, it's a measure of how quickly palette effects unfold—a consideration that may take precedence over the tempo setting, depending on what's being deployed. This measure concerns two types of effects: **color cycling** and **palette transitions**.

Color cycling and palette transitions presently work only when your system's color depth is set to 8-bit (256 colors). That's because applying these effects to greater quantities of color requires number crunching that would slow your computer to a crawl. If your monitor isn't set to 8-bit, these effects will be ignored during playback.

Color cycling

Color cycling creates a temporary shift in the order of colors in the current palette, which gives the impression of a specialized rainbow spinning through its spectrum. The best way to understand it is to see it in action:

1. *Open the tutorial movie ClrPalet.dir.*

Because of the way that Windows and Director interact when you use a nonstandard palette in 8-bit mode, you will immediately notice a change to the Director interface when you open ClrPalet.dir. The interface seems to become black and white. Personally, I find this annoying and hard to work with, and you probably will, too. Remember, though, that this in no way affects the playing of a movie.

2. *Instead of playing the movie, click through each of its individual frames.*

There are five frames in this movie, and a different color palette is assigned to each. As you click through them, you'll see a distinctive jump from one palette to the next. Notice that there's a lag between frame 2 and frame 3; the color seems to change before the Stage does.

3. *Rewind and run the movie.*

Light show! Even though there's only one tempo command (a pause of three seconds in frame 2), the five-frame movie takes several seconds to play. That's because the frames with the Metallic and Vivid color palettes both have cycling effects enabled.

**A DAZZLING
PERFORMANCE:**
The Metallic palette
in midcycle.

Now let's look at one of these color cycles.

4. Double-click the palette cell of frame 4.

You've seen Frame Properties: Palette dialog boxes before, but this one is a little different. Some of the colors in the color table at the left have a slightly thicker border. Those are the ones selected for the range of colors to be cycled. In the case of 8-bit color, the number of colors involved in the cycling can vary from 2 to 256.

CYCLE-DELIC:
Selecting the range of
colors for a color
cycling effect in the
Frame Properties:
Palette dialog box.

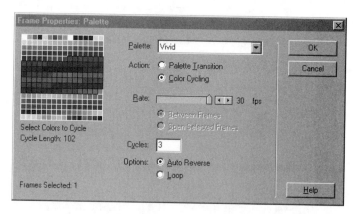

5. Make sure Color Cycling is selected; then click and drag to select all the colors in the color table.

The Cycle Length number should change to 256.

6. *Change the number in the Cycles field to* **1**. *Click Loop.*

The Cycles field sets the number of times the effect is applied, and when it's set to more than one cycle, the Options check boxes determine the manner of reprise: Auto Reverse will simply backstep to the beginning, and Loop will run through the colors again from the top.

7. *Click the OK button.*

8. *Rewind and replay the movie.*

This time the psychedelic effect is more pronounced, since more colors are used in the cycling. But it's also briefer, since only one cycle was chosen.

Palette transitions

Let's go back to that unusual transition between frames 2 and 3, where the colors change before the images do. That's the nature of palette switching in Director, and it can't be avoided. It can, however, be masked with palette transitions.

To keep the color shift from being too jarring, palette transitions will fade the screen to a solid white or black before making the switch. Unlike the transitions you'll find in the transition channel, these affect the entire screen; even the menu bar disappears.

Let's add a palette transition to the shift between the Grayscale and Metallic palettes. Since the palette channel in frame 3 is already occupied by a color cycle, we'll need to start by adding another frame to the Score.

1. *Position the playback head in frame 3 of the Score.*

2. *From the Insert menu, select Frames.*

3. *In the Insert Frame dialog box, set the Insert field to* **1** *and then click OK.*

The Insert Frame command duplicates the entire contents of the currently selected frame.

4. *Select and delete the contents of the palette cell in frame 3.*

Since the cycling palette is now spread across two cells, we need to delete the first palette cell before we can insert a new one.

5. *Double-click the now-blank palette cell in frame 3.*

6. *In the Frame Properties: Palette dialog box, click the Palette Transition button. Set the rest of the parameters to match those in the following illustration:*

ALL COLORS MUST FADE: Setting a full-screen fade to black in the Frame Properties: Palette dialog box.

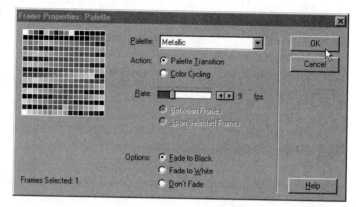

The current palette will be switched to the Metallic palette when the screen goes black; Rate sets the length of time the blackout will take. The fps measurement isn't meaningful in the context of a single frame, but you can think of the Rate setting like this: The lower the value, the slower the transition.

7. *Click the OK button.*

8. *Rewind and run the movie.*

Now the palette changes behind a veil of darkness. By the way, you can use palette transitions even when you're not switching palettes, but they'll affect the entire monitor screen whenever they're used.

Both palette transitions and color cycling can be set to take effect over multiple frames in the Score. Just select more than one frame in the palette channel and then open the Frame Properties: Palette dialog box and select the Span Selected Frames radio button.

Editing color palettes

The last frame of the Color Palettes movie contains a custom palette named Special Colors Internal. You can use it to experiment with switching, reordering, and otherwise modifying colors in a color table. You can open the palette by double-clicking its Cast slot or by opening the Palettes window and selecting the palette from the pop-up menu.

Changing a single color

If you like, you can modify a palette one color at a time. To identify exactly which colors are being used on the Stage, you can use the eyedropper tool in the Palette window. Click the eyedropper tool and then click any color in the Palette window. Without releasing the mouse button, move the cursor over the Stage. When you move the eyedropper over the Stage, the color that it's over will be selected in the color table. Release the button when the cursor is over the color you want to identify.

CATCHING A COLOR: Sampling to isolate an individual color in a custom palette.

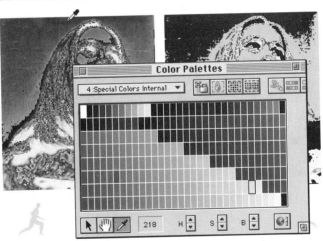

Once you've isolated a color, you can change it by clicking the HSB arrows. Each of these controls one color parameter: Hue, Saturation, or Brightness.

If you need a little more visual feedback when changing a color, double-click the color in the Palette window. You'll see one of the dialog boxes shown on the following page. This is one of the areas where the Windows and Macintosh versions have substantially different interfaces, but the same information is there for both.

COLOR IN A BOX:
Defining a new color for
the custom palette in
Windows.

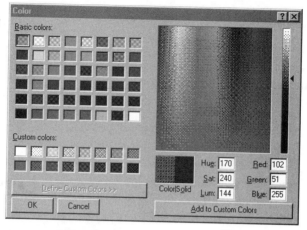

A SPIN ON THE WHEEL:
Defining a new color for
the custom palette on
the Macintosh.

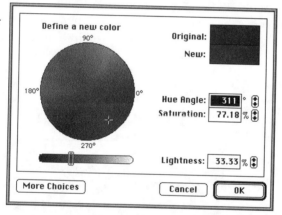

Under Windows, the colors you see may be affected by the black-and-white effect created by using palettes other than System-Win. You can achieve temporary relief by clicking an unused area of the Windows taskbar. It's not a very elegant solution, but anything that works is better than nothing.

You can select colors
by either HSB or RGB
values.

The Hue, Saturation, and Brightness settings are here, too (although Brightness is called Lightness or Luminosity), and you can click anywhere in the color box or color wheel to select a new color, which can be compared against the old one before you formalize your selection.

The problem with this click-to-pick approach is that HSB is only one method for quantifying color. If you've ever worked with Photoshop or other high-end color graphics applications, you may be familiar with the RGB method, in which all colors are considered in terms of how much red, green, and blue they contain. If you Macintosh owners want to work with RGB rather than HSB, click the More Choices button. The dialog box will expand to include a few more color choices; click Apple RGB and you'll be presented with a series of sliders, which you can use to set a new color mix. On Windows systems, the HSB and RGB dialog boxes are combined into one.

IN THE MIX:
Mixing a new color using Red, Green, and Blue proportions.

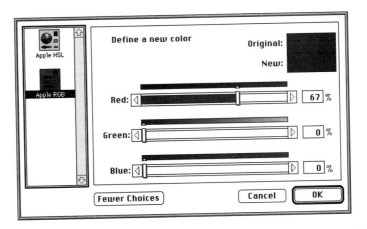

Palette customizing issues take on new importance once you start working seriously with digital video. That's because most video involves at least some images of human beings, and the standard 8-bit System palette doesn't have a lot of believable skin tones packed into its box of 256 colors. For more discussion of this topic, see Chapter 22: *Professional Topics and Techniques.*

Palette options

Whenever one or more colors are selected in the Palette window, a number of options become available on the Palette window toolbar. Here's a rundown of the options available there:

- **Reserve Selected Colors** can be used to keep selected colors from being used in color cycles. A reserved color also can't be used as a fill in the Paint window, and Director will avoid it when remapping a piece of artwork to your custom palette.

- **Select Reserved Colors** will highlight the colors in the current palette that have been reserved.

- **Select Used Colors** is good for isolating the colors needed to display a particular image or range of images. First select the cast member(s) in the Cast database; then invoke this command. All other colors (use Invert Selection to choose them) can be eliminated without affecting the display.

- **Invert Selection** doesn't modify any color values; it just changes the group of colors selected to the opposite of what you've chosen.

- **Sort Colors** rearranges the selected colors by order of Hue, Saturation, or Brightness value. You can select this command multiple times to sort by all three properties.

- **Reverse Sequence** shifts the order of selected colors in the opposite direction.

- **Cycle** moves every color in the selected range down one notch in the color table, with the last one scooting up to the first position. In other words, it does pretty much what a color cycling effect does, only on a permanent basis.

- **Blend** applies a sort of gradient effect to the range of selected colors, changing all colors between the first and last one for a smooth transition.

- Clicking the **Color Picker** (at the bottom of the window) is the equivalent of double-clicking an individual color, opening the color wheel dialog box. If more than one color is selected, any modifications will apply only to the first color in the selected range.

TRY

JUST CLICK IT:
If you want to see the effect a custom palette will have on the Stage, just click that palette (or a cast member mapped to that palette) in the Cast window. The entire monitor display will shift to that palette.

VECTOR SHAPE TOOLS

Vector shapes are a series of points with connecting lines. The shape or curve of the lines can be adjusted to create an image, and the image can be filled with color if desired. The Vector Shape window offers much less than the Paint window in terms of available tools. You have a Pen tool for freehand drawing and shape tools similar to those in the Paint window.

The rest of the Vector Shape window's arsenal is geared toward determining line and fill settings.

Creation tools

You can create new vector shapes using the Pen tool and shape tools. To edit vector shapes, use the Pen and Arrow tools.

Pen tool

Use the Pen tool to create lines and curves between points. To create a point, click the desired location. For a curve, click and drag. When you drag, you create handles that determine how the line will curve through your point. Extending the handles determines the length of the curve; rotating the handles determines the angle of the curve. Each point has two handles: One handle controls the curve of the line coming into the point, and the other handle controls the curve of the line going away. To add a new point, hold down the Alt (Windows) or Option (Macintosh) key and move the cursor over the line (the cursor will change colors); then click. Use the Shift key with the Pen tool to constrain a new point to a horizontal, vertical, or 45-degree position.

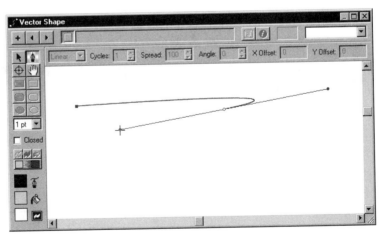

Shape tools

The shape tools are similar to those for Paint and include both filled and unfilled rectangles, rounded rectangles, and ellipses. Use the Shift key to create squares and circles. Try creating an unfilled circle or other shape to see how the handles relate to the shape.

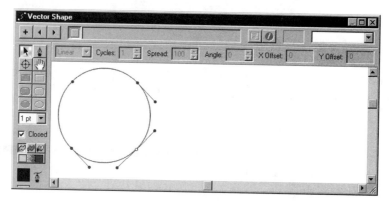

Notice how only the handles that relate to the selected point (where you release the mouse button) are visible.

Arrow tool

The Arrow tool is useful for editing your shape. When you click to select an existing point, you can drag the point to a new location or you can click and drag the handles to adjust the curve. The cursor changes colors when it is over a point or handle.

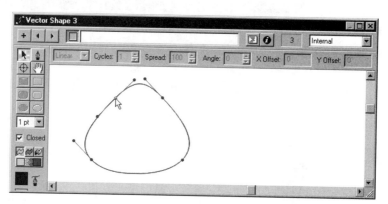

Line tools

Lines (strokes) connecting a vector shape's points define the image outline or border. The outline can be visible or invisible. If it is visible, you can select a color.

Stroke Width

Use the pop-up Stroke Width menu to set the width of the outline. Set the stroke width to 0 for no visible outline. Stroke widths are given in points.

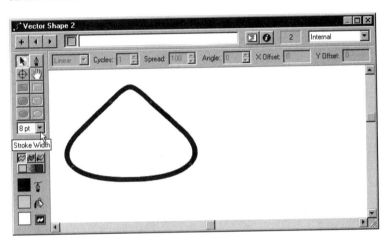

Stroke Color

The Stroke Color chip allows you to set the color for a shape's outline.

Closed

When you are drawing a freehand shape, you can select the Closed check box to automatically connect your last point to the first point. Closing a shape allows the fill options to be applied.

When you are creating with a shape tool, filled or unfilled, the Closed check box is selected by default, and the shape is, by definition, closed.

Fill tools

Once you have created a closed vector shape, you can determine how the inside of it looks. Shapes can be unfilled or filled with a solid or gradient color.

Fill type

There are three fill options to choose from: Unfilled, Solid Fill, and Gradient. Your choice determines which, if any, of the following controls are available.

Fill Color

The Fill Color chip is used to determine the color when you choose a Solid Fill type.

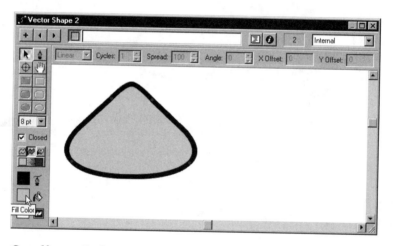

Gradient Colors

Two paint chips are available for Gradient Colors. The left chip sets the starting color of the gradient, and the right chip sets the ending color. Only when you have selected Gradient from the Fill type options does the Gradient tool bar become active.

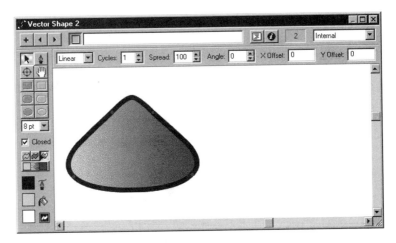

Background Color

In general, you'll get better performance by using a background color than by using an ink effect.

You can set a background color for a shape. In the Vector Shape window, the entire window background takes on the background color. When you place the shape on the Stage, though, the background is only as large as the bounding rectangle of the shape. Shapes with a background color will animate faster than they will if you rely on ink effects (such as Background Transparent ink).

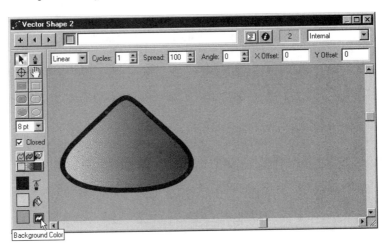

Linear/Radial

The Linear/Radial option is one of my personal favorites—so much power with so little effort! You can use it to switch between a linear gradient and a radial gradient. The terms refer to the pattern in which the spectrum of color values unfolds: A linear gradient moves in a straight line, and a radial gradient proceeds from a central point (which is why this effect looks kind of like a sunburst).

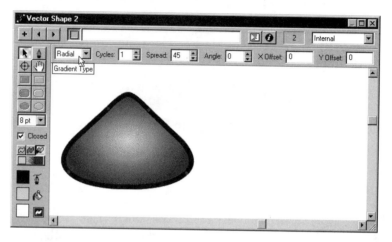

Gradient Cycles

The Gradient Cycles option determines the number of cycles that the start and end colors pass through while creating a gradient. With Gradient Cycles set to 1, the gradient blends only from the start color to the end color. With Gradient Cycles set to 2, it passes from start color to end color and then again from start color to end color.

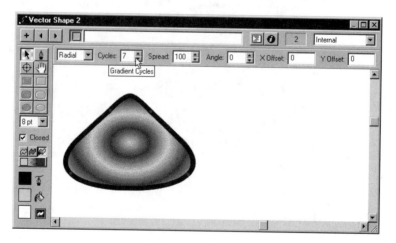

Gradient Spread

The Gradient Spread control determines the rate of the color change. The spread is given as a percentage, with 100% specifying that the colors blend over the entire area of the shape. A lower number makes the blend less gradual. A percentage higher than 100 creates the effect you would achieve if the blend extended over an area larger than that of the actual shape.

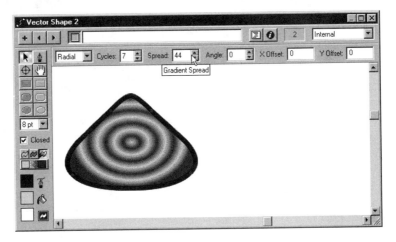

Gradient Angle

When used with a linear gradient, the Gradient Angle option tilts the angle of the blending, in degrees; for example, 0 degrees creates blending from left to right, 90 degrees creates blending from top to bottom.

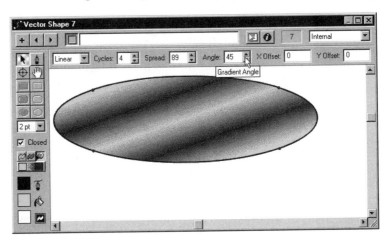

Gradient Offset

Use the X Offset (horizontal) and the Y Offset (vertical) to move the starting location of gradient effects. To see how this works, try using a radial gradient to simulate a sunset. By adjusting the offset, you can create the sense that the sun is below the horizon.

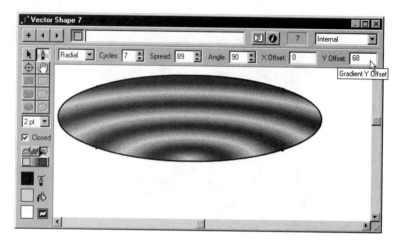

POINTS TO REMEMBER

When working with graphics in Director, here are a few things to keep in mind:

- **Vector shapes** are best for simple graphics; **bitmap** graphics are better for complex images.

- You can select artwork in the Paint window via four different methods: using **Shrink**, **No Shrink**, **Lasso**, and **See Thru** modes.

- You can apply a number of effects to selected artwork via the Paint window palette header. Director even supports **Photoshop-compatible plug-in effects.**

- You can create **custom stroke patterns** for the Air Brush and Brush tools.

- **Paint ink effects** are applied in the Paint window and are permanent. **Sprite ink effects** are applied in the Score and can be changed at any time.

- You can **convert text** to bitmapped artwork with the Convert to Bitmap command.

- To change the **color depth** of a graphic element, use the Transform Bitmap command.

- Seek the right level of color depth for your artwork. Don't bloat file size by saving graphics at a higher quality than your computer can display, but don't compromise quality by downsampling unnecessarily.

- You can create a **custom palette** by copying a current one or by importing a piece of artwork created in a nonstandard palette.

- **Palettes** can be associated with individual cast members as well as saved as cast members.

- Only one palette can be active at a time. Any artwork on the Stage not mapped to that palette will be inaccurately displayed. Sometimes that's a desired effect.

- **Color cycling** is a "light show" type of palette effect that spins through a range of color substitutions. It works only when the monitor's color depth is set to 8-bit (256 colors).

- **Shifts** in color palettes are processed before the Stage is visually updated, which can make for an abrupt transition. Use the **Palette Transition option** to mask that change by blacking or whiting out the monitor while the palettes shift.

- Use the **Pen tool** and **shape tools** to create vector shapes, and the **Pen** and **Arrow tools** to edit vector shapes.

- The points from which a vector shape is created have **handles** that you can use to adjust the curve of a connecting line.

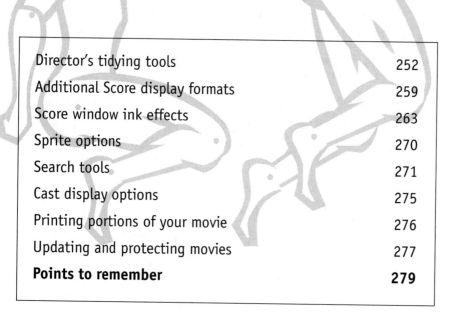

CHAPTER 7

MORE PRODUCTION TOOLS

AS YOUR PRODUCTIONS BECOME MORE AMBITIOUS, YOU'LL WANT TO TAKE advantage of some tools geared toward making your work easier. In this chapter we'll look at features in Director designed to give you more information about your productions and more control over your cast members.

We'll begin by examining Director's suite of tools that tidy up the Stage display and make animation more accurate. Next, we'll look at the several display modes offered by the Score window and Score-level ink effects. After that, we'll survey Director's primary search, organization, and documentation capabilities.

DIRECTOR'S TIDYING TOOLS

Director has a number of features that provide greater control over the display of graphic elements on the Stage. Since they all add up to a cleaner, more consistent look, I call them the "tidying tools."

The Grid submenu

If you've worked with page layout programs such as PageMaker or QuarkXPress, you're familiar with grids. They're a set of squares (usually invisible) that keep things tidy by exerting a sort of gravitational field: things near them tend to **snap to** their lines, thereby making items adhere to an underlying order.

SNAP TO IT:
With Snap to Grid Settings, all elements on the Stage can snap to a grid, even when the grid is invisible.

 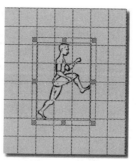

You can access Director 7's Grid tool from the View menu by pulling down the Grid submenu. You'll find three options there:

- **Show Grid** displays or hides the grid. You can toggle it on and off at any time (Control-Shift-Alt-G Windows; Command-Option-Shift-G Macintosh).

- **Snap to Grids** shifts sprites to the nearest grid line when you move them within a few pixels of that line. Unlike grid features in other applications, you can't set the grid proximity in pixels of this "snap-to" effect—that is, you can't designate how close the sprite is to a gridline before it snaps to the grid. You can, however, toggle it on or off (Control-Alt-G Windows; Command-Option-G Macintosh).

- **Grid Settings** brings up a dialog box that lets you set the specifics of grid display. You can change the proportions of the basic unit on which the grid is based and choose the grid color. You can even switch from lines to dotted coordinates, which are a little less intrusive.

GRID MAGIC:
The Grid Settings dialog box lets you customize the way your grid appears on the screen.

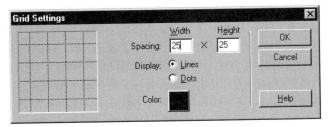

The Align windoid

There's another way to get your sprites to straighten up: by using the **Align** windoid, which you can either access from the Modify menu or toggle on and off (Control-K Windows; Command-K Macintosh). Align moves sprites not to absolute points on the Stage, but to positions relative to one another.

To use Align, select at least two sprites (Shift-click to make multiple selections). Then select from the windoid's pull-down menus to determine horizontal and vertical alignment; the rectangles displayed in Align's central window will change to suggest the general arrangement that your choices will produce. If you want to align on one plane only, select No Change from the menu for the other plane. When you're ready, click the Align button.

IN LINE, PLEASE:
Align lines up sprites on the horizontal and vertical axes.

Fortunately, Align can be used to standardize positioning on a single frame and across channels and frames. When doing its duty, Align uses for its reference point the "senior" sprite selected—either the sprite with the lowest channel number or the first in a sequence selected across frames.

Onion Skin

No, Director doesn't have a salad bar. The **Onion Skin** windoid is a tool for comparing Paint cast members without having to place them on the Stage. Since the Paint window stays open and active, you can create one sprite while referencing others. The term comes from onion skin paper, a thin, see-through paper used by conventional animators to quickly create overlays. To access the windoid, make sure the Paint window is open, and then from the View menu, select Onion Skin.

> Don't confuse Onion Skin with Director 7's Sprite Overlay feature (which we explored in Chapter 1). Overlay provides a shortcut to the various dialog boxes controlling the parameters associated with a single sprite, whereas Onion Skin lets you consider the arrangement and appearance of several sprites relative to each other.

The Onion Skin feature is especially useful when you want to tweak the precise physical relation of one object to another. For example, if you're animating a ball landing in a catcher's mitt, you'll want your mitt to have a shape that accurately fits the ball. With Onion Skin, you can achieve that effect by invoking an image of the ball, drawing the mitt around it, and then turning off the overlay when you're done.

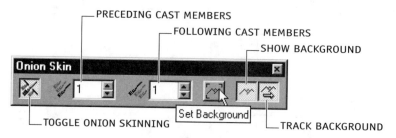

Here's a rundown of the controls as they appear from left to right in the Onion Skin windoid:

- **Toggle Onion Skinning** toggles the overlay display on or off.

- **Preceding Cast Members** places visuals of cast members in slots directly before the currently active cast member; you can set the number of members displayed by entering a value in the field (in the following illustration, the value is set to 3). How can you tell what belongs to the current window and what's just an image? Onion Skin fades the overlays in direct proportion to their distance from the cast member in the Cast, making the one farthest away the faintest.

- **Following Cast Members** functions in much the same way as Preceding Cast Members, except it overlays cast members in subsequent slots. The same dimness-to-distance ratio holds. You can set values for both the Preceding Cast Members and the Following Cast Members at the same time, to show cast members on both sides of the image you are editing.

- Viewing adjacent slots is all well and good, but what if you want to reference artwork parked halfway across the Cast? That's what **Set Background** is for. Navigate to the slot you want overlaid and then click the Set Background button to select it. Director will remember the selection and display the cast member in slightly shaded form when the **Show Background** button is selected.

- **Track Background** allows you to create a chain of overlaid images. If you toggle this on, when you create a new cast member (by clicking the plus symbol in the Paint window), the new canvas won't be blank; it'll have both the previous cast member and the one set as the background in Onion Skin mode.

The Text Inspector

There are a lot of places in Director where the written word is on display: the Text, Field, Paint, and even the Score window all have text that needs to be formatted in one way or another. Each window has its own internal text controls, but Director 7 also provides a single tool that'll do the job in any context: the **Text Inspector** (which you can access from the Window menu by choosing Inspector and then Text). The Text Inspector is a windoid you can toggle on or off (Control-T Windows; Command-T Macintosh).

INSPECTOR GADGET:
Use the Text Inspector to adjust formatting and display options just about anywhere text is found.

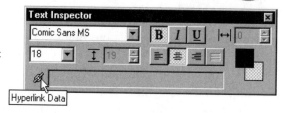

The Text Inspector offers a truncated version of the controls you'll find in the Text window, and it applies them whenever text is selected. You can even highlight a portion of text directly on the Stage (double-click to select a word, triple-click to select all) and then put the Text Inspector to work. If the selection is other than RTF text, the leading box (the up-and-down arrow) and the kerning box (the side-to-side arrow) will be disabled. To format a range of cast members, select them in their Cast and then apply the Text Inspector.

The lower-left field in the Text Inspector, the one with the label that looks like links of a chain (labeled Hyperlink Data in the image above), is used for creating **hyperlinks**. Hyperlinks are the underlined text you see at Web sites; when clicked, the links take you to a different location or Web site. With a section of text selected, you can enter a URL in the field. Director will automatically format the selected text so that it appears underlined and in blue. You can also enter a message in the field that will be sent to an on hyperlinkClicked handler if you have created one.

The Tweak windoid

Sometimes you need to make only minor adjustments to the placement of a sprite. You could drag it with the mouse, but then you'd have to eyeball the distance. You could open the Sprite Properties dialog box and plug in new location numbers, but then you'd have to calculate the coordinates. Fortunately, there's a middle path, the **Tweak windoid**, which lets you make an adjustment with the mouse *and* know the exact distances involved.

IS A NUDGE ENOUGH?
Use the Tweak windoid when you need to adjust a sprite's location by only a few pixels.

After you select Tweak from the Modify menu, you can access this windoid to set a distinct unit of movement and apply it to as many sprites as you want. Click and drag in the windoid's blank square; a black line will appear to trace your motion, and the horizontal and vertical arrows will appear. When you're happy with your sprite's position, select it (or them) and click the Tweak button to apply the movement. The value you've selected will be in effect until you change it or close the Tweak windoid.

Another tidying tool can be accessed from the Modify menu's Arrange submenu. It doesn't change a sprite's position on the Stage—just its position in the layering of sprites in the Score. Move Forward and Move Backward cause the sprite to ascend or descend by a single layer (moving it to the next open cell in the frame); Bring to Front and Send to Back move the sprite to the topmost or bottommost layer in the hierarchy.

Tweaking via the Score window

The Tweak windoid is good for making quick adjustments, but it doesn't offer very precise control over the location of sprites. For that, you'll want to use the coordinate controls in Director 7's Score window (or the same controls in the Sprite Inspector).

X & Y MARK THE SPOT: Ten coordinate control fields give you a convenient and precise way to adjust sprite position.

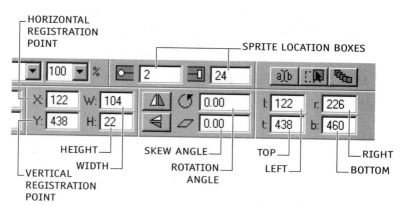

Among other fields at the top of the Score window are 12 editable data fields that allow you to set three different kinds of coordinates:

- The first coordinate group measures precise locations and sizes on the Stage. The X and Y coordinates tell you where the sprite's registration point is located, relative to the top-left corner of the Stage. The measurements are in pixels and reflect the distances across and down the screen. W and H are also pixel measurements, but they reflect the width and height of the selected sprite rather than its location. Typing new coordinates in these fields has the same effect as changing these values in the appropriate Properties dialog boxes.

- The two user-settable Sprite Location boxes (the middle controls—their labels look like start and end frames) tell you where a selected sprite segment begins and concludes in the Score. If you type new values in these fields, the sprite segment in question will move to the frames you specified. Be careful, because you don't want to unwittingly alter the length of an established segment while moving it to a new place in the Score. If the values you enter reflect a different length for the sprite segment, Director will automatically resize it accordingly.

- The lowercase group on the far right (l, t, r, and b) also establishes sprite location—but rather than measuring from the registration point (which isn't visible on the Stage anyway), they tell you how many pixels the selected sprite's left side, top, right side, and bottom are from a single point: the top-left corner of the Stage. These measurements are made from the bounding box (the rectangular area containing the sprite) rather than from the visible area.

ADDITIONAL SCORE DISPLAY FORMATS

We've seen only one face of the Score thus far—the Member view—but in fact there are others. Several different types of information about playback action can be extracted by altering the Score's display format. To access these other display modes, use the Display pop-up menu at the left side of the Score window (or see under the View menu). In each type of display mode, the cells-and-columns arrangement remains the same, but the contents of the cells vary widely.

Behavior

The Behavior mode shows which scripts are attached to which sprites by displaying the cast number of the script. If space is cramped in your Score view, only the first digit may show up. When you move the cursor over the sprite, the full number should show up in a Tooltip type box.

BEHAVE YOURSELF: The Behavior display mode reveals which sprites have Lingo scripts directly attached to them.

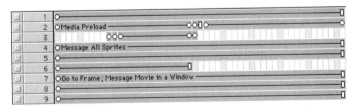

TIP

When you're viewing single-cell sprites, it's helpful to use the Zoom command (first mentioned in Chapter 1) to scale all that data down to a manageable size. The keyboard commands are Control-+ (Windows) or Command-+ (Macintosh) to zoom in, and Control--- (hyphen, Windows) Command--- (hyphen, Macintosh) to zoom out.

Location

The Location display mode is useful when you need to track the overall movements of sprites in a sprite segment. You'll see the X and Y locations displayed within the frames that make up the sprite.

A MOVING PICTURE:
The Location display mode tracks the direction of movement of individual sprites.

Ink

The Ink mode displays all sprites in terms of which ink effects are applied to them in the Score (as opposed to Paint ink effects).

For more information about these effects, see "Score window ink effects" later in this chapter.

Instead of the confusing number codes used in early versions of Director, the name of the ink appears within the multiple-cell sprite. If your sprite is too short to allow for the name of the ink, you'll see only the first letter or two.

THINK INK:
The Ink mode displays the Score-level ink effects applied to individual sprites.

Blend

The Blend display mode tracks one thing only: the degree to which the Blend effect has been applied to a sprite (we explored this kind of blending in Chapter 2). The rate of blend is displayed as a percentage, but a

BLEND INKS, NOT DRINKS:
The Blend mode displays the first blend applied to a sprite in the Score, but it won't display multiple blends applied to individual frames.

sprite that has had different blends applied to single-frame segments of the whole will display only the first percentage applied.

Extended

In Extended mode, the shaded area on the left side of the Score expands to identify the information shown in each cell. Each cell can show up to six lines, and each of those lines holds a different kind of data. The only problem is that this data can become impossible to read unless the sprite segment is long enough to display the text.

THE B-I-I-I-G PICTURE: The Extended mode displays an exhaustive amount of information about each Score cell.

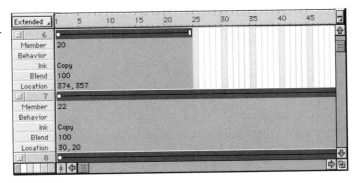

The format displayed here is the default for the Extended mode. If your view looks different, check out the options in the Score Window Preferences dialog box.

Going from top to bottom, let's take a stab at decoding the plethora of information available in this view. If some of these layers are missing from your Extended view, they may have been turned off in the Score Window Preferences window (from the File menu, select Preferences and then Score).

- **Member** identifies the number and name of the cast member being displayed.

- **Behavior** tells you which (if any) behaviors have been assigned to the sprite or sprite segment by number or name.

- **Ink** lets you know which ink effect has been applied (at a Score level) to the sprite (segment) in question.

- **Blend** indicates the percentage of the sprite's blend setting.

- **Location** describes the sprite's registration point relative to the top-left corner of the Stage. Whenever you're using Stage location coordinates, make sure you know where things are being measured *from*: the registration point or the physical perimeters of the sprite.

TIP

Although the Extended mode was available in earlier versions, beginning with Director 6 this feature has been brought to a friendly new level. There's always been (almost too much) detail here. That detail is now presented in an easily readable format that practically begs to be used as an editing and troubleshooting tool. From the File menu, choose Preferences and then Score to choose how much information should be shown in this format. A nice touch.

Viewing nonsprite info (in D5 mode)

The Extended display has no effect on the view of the elements in the effects channel. You can, however, view them in Extended view if you first set your Score display to the Director 5 style. The Score Preferences dialog box includes a check box for Director 5 Style Score Display. When the check box is checked, the Score (sprite channels, too) has the appearance that was the default for Director 5. It gives you a view that is particularly useful for keeping tabs on tempo channel commands and transitions.

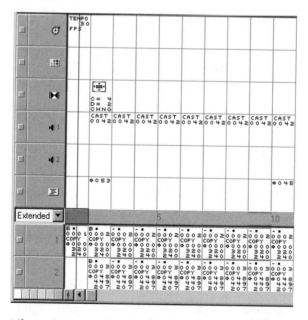

Like sprites, sounds and frame scripts are identified by the number of their Cast slots. But the tempo, palette, and transition channels show their full contents—the same information you'd normally access by double-clicking the cells:

- The tempo channel displays playback paces or instructions for delay—whatever you've chosen for those cells.

- The palette channel's cell provides a shorthand version of all the parameters in the Frame Properties: Palette dialog box.

- The transition channel displays little icons for the transition effects chosen. The other lines indicate the bit size of the chunks used (C), the duration of the effect (D), and whether the effect applies to the changing area (CHNG) or to the Stage (STGE).

SCORE WINDOW INK EFFECTS

We've already looked at the ink effects that can be applied to graphic cast members in the Paint window. Many of those effects also show up in the Score window, as do a few you won't find elsewhere.

For a discussion of Paint window ink effects, see Chapter 6.

The main distinction between Paint and Score ink effects is that the latter are temporary conditions; you can change the ink of a sprite at any time. Your choice of Score effect does not overwrite any inks permanently applied in the Paint window; rather, the two levels of effect work in conjunction. There are 20 Score ink effects and 18 inks in the Paint window, for a total of 360 possible permutations—and since several Score inks change in relationship to other elements on the Stage, the actual number of variations is practically unlimited. You'll find the Score ink effects in a pull-down menu at the top of the Score window.

> Black-and-white screenshots don't do these inks justice. That's why, in the Tutorials section of the *Director 7 Demystified* CD, there's a movie called Inkefect.dir. It was created as a tool to help you explore the interaction among the various Score-level inks. You can apply all inks to the sprites provided (in channels 2 and 3) or substitute your own sprites.

Copy

All sprites are copies of cast members, and those with the Copy ink selected are the most faithful representations of their source. The sprite is shown with an opaque white bounding box that extends to the outer limits of the artwork. Copy is the default ink and makes minimal demands on RAM. It's good for rectangular sprites, such as buttons and fields.

THE COPY INK.

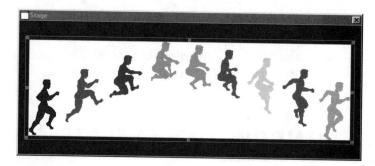

Matte

With Matte ink applied, the bounding box is no longer opaque; the shape of the sprite conforms to the perimeter of the artwork. However, any white or empty areas within that perimeter will be opaque, although they appeared transparent in the context of the Paint window. In the image shown here, the uncolored areas within each Swifty show up as white.

THE MATTE INK EFFECT applied against a black background.

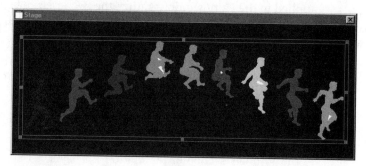

Background Transparent

The Background Transparent ink is similar to Matte except that all areas of background color (in the canvas of the Paint window) are treated as transparent. As you can see in the next illustration, this technique clears up "trapped" areas, creating the impression that the artwork is on a clear pane.

THE BACKGROUND
TRANSPARENT INK.

Transparent

Transparent ink makes the lighter colors of a sprite transparent, so that objects beneath them are visible. Darker colors are not affected.

Reverse

Like Background Transparent, Reverse also treats white pixels as if they're transparent. The values of color pixels are subtracted from the Stage background (either the Stage color or the color of another sprite), creating some interesting looks. If you're using palette color cycling, this ink will add to the overall kaleidoscopic effect.

THE REVERSE INK.

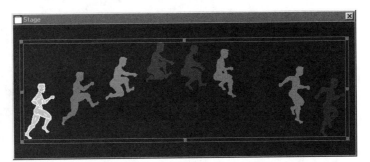

Ghost

Ghost works in terms of light and dark, operating more on the colors behind the sprite than on the sprite itself. Any black in the background becomes white, and anything white becomes transparent.

The Ghost ink against a black Stage and a light-colored rectangular sprite.

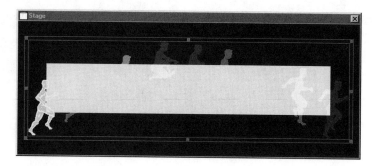

The "Not" inks

I've grouped these ink effects together because they each add exactly one twist to their non-"Not" equivalents: They reverse the foreground colors before performing their interpretations of the background color.

From top: **Not Copy, Not Transparent, Not Ghost, and Not Reverse.**

Director 7 allows for grayscale and 32-bit colored mask cast members.

Mask

If you've experimented with the Reveal ink in the Paint window, you're familiar with the principle of this ink. It introduces selective opacity by treating the rightmost adjacent cast member as a mask. The lighter an area is in a mask cast member, the more transparent the corresponding area will be in the sprite. Darker areas result in corresponding areas' being more opaque. Where earlier versions of Director allowed only for black-and-white masks, you can now use grayscale mask cast members (for 8-bit images) or even colored cast members (for 32-bit images). A 32-bit colored mask cast member will cause the colors in the mask to tint the sprite's colors.

THE MASK INK with a custom mask created in the Cast.

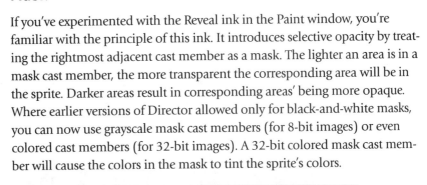

Blend

Blend has changed in Director 7; it's now essentially identical to Matte. In Director 6 it was used to determine the degree of the opacity and transparency of the sprite's color pixels in conjunction with a blend setting. Now the blend setting works with the Copy, Background Transparent, Matte, Mask, and Blend inks.

Darkest

The Darkest ink compares the pixel colors of the sprite to any background color and then displays only the darkest of the two.

THE DARKEST INK.

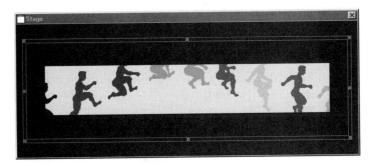

Lightest

This ink also compares the sprite and background color pixels, but in this case the lightest one wins out.

THE LIGHTEST INK.

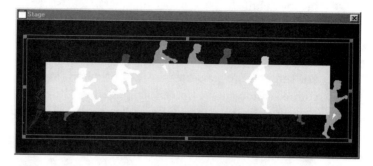

Add, Add Pin, Subtract, and Subtract Pin

The Add, Add Pin, Subtract, and Subtract Pin effects arrive at new colors by adding or subtracting the foreground color value from the background color value. Pins represent the maximum values in a color range; in the pin effects, the newly calculated color can't exceed that value. Since the results of these inks vary widely based on the colors involved, experiment with them to see what works for your production.

THE SUBTRACT PIN INK.

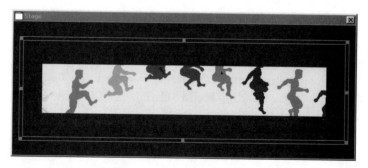

Darken and Lighten

Darken and Lighten both affect the way Director applies the foreground and background colors of a sprite. Darken ink causes the background color to be used as a color filter through which the sprite is seen on the Stage. Lighten makes the colors in a sprite lighter as the background color gets darker. For both Darken and Lighten, the sprite's foreground color is added to the image in varying degrees. For Darken or Lighten to have an effect, you must set the foreground and background colors of the sprite to different colors than the default black and white.

The more complicated the color calculations involved in an ink effect, the more processing time is required; some effects are so memory intensive that they can noticeably slow down animations and other Stage operations. If you use ink effects on sprites in a moving segment, you might want to experiment with a combination of inks to minimize RAM demands. For example, a sprite can use one ink when it's over blank areas of the Stage and then switch to another ink when it's over other sprites. In one simple test I made, Copy, Matte, and Background Transparent all took pretty near the same amount of time to animate. When I switched to Darkest or Lightest, animation took almost two-and-a-half times as long. When I used a Blend value (which I'll describe in a bit), animation took almost five times as long. In another test, Copy, Matte, Darkest, and Lightest all took about the same amount of time, and Background Transparent took 30 percent more time. So the point is, when animation starts to slow down, consider your inks as a possible cause or a possible solution.

The Blend field

The Blend field is just to the right of the Ink field in the top of the Score. As mentioned earlier, a blend value can be used with the Copy, Background Transparent, Matte, Mask, and Blend inks. The blend value can be used to make a sprite more or less transparent. A value of 100% makes the sprite totally opaque, and a value of 0% makes the sprite totally transparent. You can set the end points of a sprite to different blend values, and Director will tween the values in between, creating the effect that the sprite is fading in or out.

SPRITE OPTIONS

Next up are the three pushbuttons at the far upper-right of the Score. These can be used to modify the behavior of sprites on the Stage and, like ink effects, can be turned on and off from frame to frame.

Editable

The Editable option applies only to text sprites. When this option is selected, the text appears editable to the end user—a flashing cursor appears when the text is clicked, and its contents can be modified and deleted. It's the equivalent of selecting Editable in a cast member's Info window, but since it's in the Score, you can turn it on in one frame and off in the next. For example, you can place an editable field in one frame to receive the user's name and then lock that field once the entry has been made.

Moveable

Using the middle option, Moveable, is equivalent to setting the `moveableSprite of sprite` (which we have already used in the form of a behavior). When enabled for a sprite or sprite segment, Moveable ignores any motion commands in the Score, waiting instead for the user to click and drag the sprite.

Trails

The last button, Trails, works best in a multiframe context. When Trails is enabled for a segment of sprites, the Stage doesn't erase the old sprites as playback progresses through the frames. The result is an impression of a continuous string of sprites, a visible manifestation of motion.

HAPPY TRAILS:
When the Trails option is enabled, the previous versions of a sprite stick around as playback progresses through the Score.

Trails is a good tool to use for fine-tuning animations; turn it on in a sprite segment to pinpoint where motion needs slowing down, speeding up, or smoothing out. You can't click or move any of the trailed images, but you can step back in the Score until those sprites become selectable.

Each of these sprite options can also be set with Lingo, using these properties: **the editableText of sprite, the moveableSprite of sprite**, and **the trails of sprite.**

SEARCH TOOLS

As your productions grow more ambitious, it's likely that your movies will grow larger. After a while, you might find that you're spending less time creating and more time scrolling through a thicket of windows trying to find something you've already created. That's why Director has a variety of built-in search tools that you can use for both clarification and navigation.

Finding and Replacing text

Find Text will search only the type of cast member currently open.

Director's Find Text feature (Control-F Windows; Command-F Macintosh) is accessible only when a script, text, or field cast member's window is open and active. The type of cast member you open determines the nature of the search as well; if it's a text cast member, any searches will be limited to cast members of the same type. Likewise, opening a Script limits the search to scripts (although they can be both movie and score scripts).

WHAT A FIND:
Searching for (and replacing) text strings in the Cast database.

The Search Scripts choices determine the general direction of your quest, and the Options help you get more specific. The check box options are Wrap-Around (which extends the search to cast members before as well as after the currently open one) and Whole Words Only (which limits the search to words rather than a text string).

Searching for handlers

You can search for your scripts using the Find Text dialog box, but there's a more convenient approach: the Find Handler feature (available by choosing Find and then Handler from the Edit menu), which arranges all scripts for access according to their triggering event.

A REAL FIND:
Searching for handlers with the Find Handler feature.

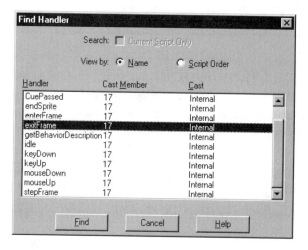

You can choose to view your handlers by name or by script order in the Cast database. Either way, they're displayed according to event (the on keyword is subtracted from the first line), with their Cast numbers following. If a cast member has also been given a name, it follows after a colon.

Since one script can contain many event handlers, Find Handler is a good means of identifying all executable modules without getting lost in a sea of script lines. Although you can't perform find-and-replace operations here, you can double-click any handler to go right to it.

Finding all cast members

If you want to locate and identify all cast members, not just text-based ones, from the Edit menu, select Find and then Cast Member. The Find Cast Member command is a database search engine, with plenty of options for narrowing or expanding your search.

CASTING CALL:
Locating cast members with the Find Cast Member dialog box.

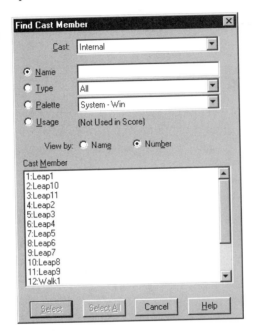

Cast members can be listed by name (which is helpful only when they've been given names) or by number (which includes names when given). The radio buttons let you select by type, by name, by palette used, or by actual appearance in the Score. You can also scroll through the central field and double-click any entry to choose that cast member.

This dialog box doesn't open the individual cast members; it just selects them in the Cast window. But once selected, you can rearrange them by dragging or, if you'd like, eliminate them by choosing the Clear Cast Members command on the Edit menu.

You can identify unused cast members by selecting that option in the Find Cast Member dialog box. Watch out; it selects all cast members without a direct presence in the Score, even though they may be called into action by Lingo. If you use Lingo to switch cast members (as in an animated button), the cast members called by Lingo will be identified as unused unless they also appear in the Score. Double-check before you delete a cast member.

Rearranging cast members

If you're the sort who likes all your ducks in a row, you might want to organize the contents of your Casts rather than keep them in the order of their creation. You can do that by selecting and dragging or by using the Sort command on the Modify menu.

AN ORDER, OF SORTS: Organizing the Cast from the Sort dialog box.

The first four arrangement options—Usage in Score, Media Type, Name, and Size—are pretty self-explanatory; the fifth one, Empty at End, keeps the current order of cast members, but eliminates any gaps in the Cast window by moving cast members forward to fill them.

Rearranging cast members won't affect the Score (all references are updated), but it can cause problems with Lingo scripts that refer to cast members by number. That's why it's best to name cast members and then refer to them by their names in your scripts.

CAST DISPLAY OPTIONS

You can change the way cast members are displayed in the Cast window by modifying the settings in the Cast Window Preferences dialog box (from the File menu, select Preferences and then Cast).

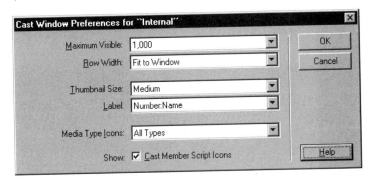

Here are the parameters that you can set:

- **Maximum Visible** determines the total number of slots shown in the Cast window. You can view from the minimum of 512 to the maximum of 32,000.

- **Row Width** is used to set the horizontal arrangement of cast members into a fixed block 8, 10, or 20 units wide. Since a smaller window causes some cast members to be hidden, you might want to leave this setting at the default of Fit to Window.

- **Thumbnail Size** chooses the scale of the picons displayed: Small, Medium, or Large.

- **Label** lets you choose the way cast members are identified in their thumbnail form: by number, name, or number and name.

- **Media Type Icons** establishes which cast members have subicons indicating their cast type: All Types, All but Text and Bitmaps, or None at All.

PRINTING PORTIONS OF YOUR MOVIE

Sometimes the best way to examine your movie is to drag yourself away from the screen and sit down instead with a pile of cold, hard printouts. Director's printout capabilities are quite versatile, allowing you to get black-and-white documentation of just about every aspect of your production. You can start by selecting Print from the File menu, which will summon this dialog box:

PAPER VIEW:
The Print dialog box can print just about any aspect of your Director movie.

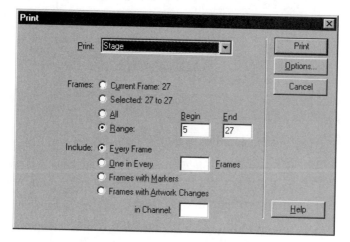

The Print pull-down menu allows you to select the elements of your movie that you want to print. You can use the Print dialog box (set to Stage) to select a range of snapshots of the Stage, specifying every frame, all frames with markers, and frames at designated intervals (the One in Every option). You can even limit yourself to those frames in which a change is registered in a specific visual channel—and a further level of customization opens when you click the Options button. You can also print the contents of the Score, all comments attached to markers, the picons in the Cast window, and the contents of cast members themselves. Just click the radio button of your choice.

As you progress in your multimedia work, it's a good idea to keep printouts of the scripts in your movies. They're a good reference and a resource for Lingo that you might want to adapt and recycle in future productions.

UPDATING AND PROTECTING MOVIES

Occasionally you may find yourself wanting to use or edit movies that were created in previous versions of Director. To do this, you'll have to update those movies from their original versions to Director 7. That's the primary reason for the Update Movies Options dialog box, which can be accessed from the Xtras menu.

CAREFULLY NOW: The Update Movies Options dialog box gives you a choice of backing up your old movie or deleting it entirely.

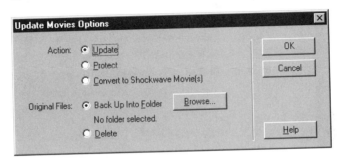

Open the dialog box and you'll see that the first Action listed is Update. By selecting this option and clicking OK, not only are you bringing the movie into a format that Director can understand (Director 7 format), but you're also optimizing that movie so that it performs as well as it can. (By the way, this compacting action is identical to the Save and Compact command on the File menu.)

The last thing to keep in mind is that Director 7 will update movies from Director versions 5 and 6 but not from earlier versions. If you have movies created in earlier versions, you'll have to use Director 5 or 6 to update them first. You'll then be able to use this dialog box to bring them into Director 7 format.

Converting older Director files to Director 7 format may result in some subtle changes that you don't expect. Some, including changes to ink effects, have workarounds; others may not. It's important that you keep backups of your original files until you are certain that you will never need to revert to them.

When Director 7 updates a version 5 movie, the single-cell sprites in the original movie are automatically transformed into multiple-frame sprite segments. If you're uncomfortable with this or simply prefer the older-style Score, you can choose Director 5 Style Score Display from the Score Preferences dialog box.

Protecting movies

On the *Director 7 Demystified* CD, all Director movies are provided in their normal, editable format. You're encouraged to browse through them and glean what you will. But movies in this format are the exception rather than the rule. Usually, you don't want strangers mucking about in your movies.

You can create a play-only version of a movie you have open in Director using the Update Movies Options dialog box. Select the Protect radio button and then click OK.

The new protected movie will use a different icon, but it'll still function just as it used to. The difference is that the resources containing the Lingo source code and Cast thumbnails will be stripped, so that even people with resource editors and other low-level file crackers won't be able to unlock its secrets.

Once your movie is protected, even you won't be able to open it from within Director. So be sure to protect a movie only when it's final, and make sure you have reliable backup copies of the original before proceeding.

POINTS TO REMEMBER

Time for another dose of the Big Picture:

- To take advantage of the greater control Director 7 gives you over the arrangement and appearance of sprites, use its **tidying tools**: the Grid, Align, Onion Skin, Tweak, and Text Inspector features.

- There are six different **display modes** for the Score window, each of which emphasizes a different grouping of information about the individual sprites and channel instructions. You can switch among these modes at any time.

- You can make the appearance and behavior of a sprite differ in a lot of ways from that of its source cast member. In addition to the Score-level ink effects, you can apply **trails** and make a sprite **moveable** or **editable**.

- Director has a whole bag of tricks for organizing and accessing portions of your production. You can search for, rearrange, and print just about every aspect of a movie.

BOOK 2:

DIGGING DEEPER

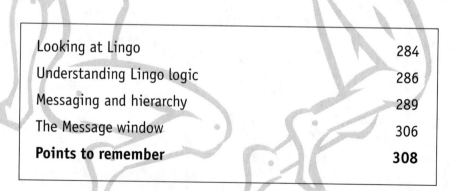

CHAPTER 8

THE ANATOMY OF LINGO

WE HAD A QUICK LOOK AT LINGO WHILE WE WERE EXPLORING BEHAVIORS and the Library Palette. But now it's time to get into the technical details. This is the chapter in which we'll start to study the conceptual underpinnings of Director: the logic by which it functions and the methods by which it goes about executing its tasks. That may sound intimidating, but it's really just a peek under the hood of your software.

A true understanding of these elements is crucial to anyone who really wants to put Lingo (and by extension, Director) through its paces, because these are the rules by which it plays. You can get a lot of multimedia work done with what you've learned thus far, but with Lingo the full potential of the software begins to come into focus.

LOOKING AT LINGO

Does the thought of learning a computer "language" like Lingo fill you with trepidation? Before you panic, think about this: Imagine having to learn a new language before going on your vacation or business trip—but the language has a total vocabulary of only a couple of hundred words, and no tenses, no conjugation, none of the other elements you should have remembered from sixth grade but have somehow forgotten. And best of all, no *i* before *e* rules that work only about half of the time, no irregular verbs, no past participles or future subjunctives. Just learn those couple hundred words—as many at a time as you wish, and in no particular order—and a new country (if not a new world) will open up to you.

When you put it that way, it's not so much of a sweat, is it?

Well, that's Lingo. Throw in a little syntax (without irregularities) and you'll have it mastered. Now, we aren't pretending that you'll become a Lingo expert from this chapter alone, but you *will* be able to pick up the essentials—to converse with the locals. Becoming a Lingomeister takes practice. So read this chapter and the next one—then go out and practice, practice, practice.

It's a curious thing, this entity called Lingo. It's one of Macromedia's most important products, yet you can't buy it in any store at any price. It grows and evolves and picks up new abilities while abandoning others, and yet it's never transformed into "Lingo++" or "LingoLite" or "Lingo Version 17.4." It's just Lingo: a set of rules by which media can be managed. And even though it has no incarnation outside of the boundaries of Director, it's a force to contend with in the realms of multimedia and the Internet.

As we said, Lingo is a language. You can't write poems or puns in it (although a few risqué double entendres are possible), but it does have a vocabulary, a syntax, and grammar. It uses text groupings that have consistent meanings, and these groupings are connected and interpreted in a consistent fashion. While it may not be as powerful as C, Pascal, or Java, some Lingo statements can replace what would take hundreds of lines of C code to replicate—and Lingo is a whole lot easier to learn.

If you're the type of person who's put off by the notion of learning another language (much less a computer one), take heart. In terms of simplicity and straightforwardness, if Lingo were a spoken language it would be somewhere between Pidgin English and Esperanto, which means three important things:

- **Improvisation is powerful.** If you arm yourself with a relatively small vocabulary and a handful of grammatical rules, you'll be able to make yourself understood in a surprising number of cases. A little Lingo can do a lot.

- **Understanding is incremental.** If you're learning French, you'll want to get fairly good at it before you go traipsing off to France. But you can deepen your knowledge of Lingo on a continuous (or fits-and-starts) basis over a period of time, as your projects get increasingly ambitious.

- **You can create, not compute.** You don't have to get too far into the jargony, number-crunching, detail-obsessed mode that other computer languages seem to require—a mode that sometimes works at cross-purposes with the free flow of ideas. Good programmers are probably some of the most creative people around; it's just that only other programmers are in a position to appreciate that creativity.

Keeping up with the changes in Lingo takes a bit of an effort and some measure of unlearning as well as learning. When a new version of Director debuts, it usually brings with it a raft of new Lingo elements (we've identified the Director 7 crop of new elements in *A Lingo Lexicon*, Appendix C). Some of this Lingo simply adds new capabilities, but some of it renders older Lingo obsolete. Usually there's a period in which both old and new can coexist, but eventually Director evolves to the point at which it can't acknowledge commands that used to be perfectly kosher. We've compiled these in Appendix B, *The Lingo Graveyard*.

UNDERSTANDING LINGO LOGIC

To get a solid grip on Lingo, we need to stop talking about it and start examining the logical assumptions upon which it's founded. Many of these assumptions drive not only Lingo but scripting languages in general, so the detour is worth taking.

So, before we get further into the nuts and bolts of practical applied scripting, let's look at the conceptual framework in which Lingo operates. What follows are some broad definitions of Lingo's main building blocks, coupled with a few demonstrative experiments. I promise not to wax too technical, but to get the big picture we need to take a plunge (albeit a shallow one) into the realm of computer science. You'll probably want to read this chapter straight through to pick up the general principles and then refer back to it for clarification as you progress in your Lingo adventures.

OOP: Introducing object orientation

Let's start by tackling an intimidating term with a goofy acronym: **object-oriented programming**, or OOP. This describes an approach to software construction, and languages that use this approach are of the OOP genus. C++, SmallTalk, MacApp, Java, and Lingo (among others) are OOP languages, but Pascal, BASIC, and FORTRAN are not.

What is the OOP approach? It consists of breaking down programming code into self-contained units, each of which performs a single function. When that function is needed, the application *calls* that unit by sending a stream of information through it. These units are called **objects**, and they are connected by a flow of **messages**.

Object may be a strange name for something that doesn't really have a physical existence, but it underscores the principle of self-containment. A convenient way of thinking about objects is to consider them black boxes, with an input hole and an output hole. Drop something in at one end and you'll get something out at the other, whether its the original item, a modified version of it, or something else entirely.

If objects were physical, they'd be the equivalent of simple machines; in a factory setting you can link simple machines to perform complex tasks.

Imagine you're running a factory that's contracted to produce gold coins. Here's an arrangement of black boxes that could do the trick:

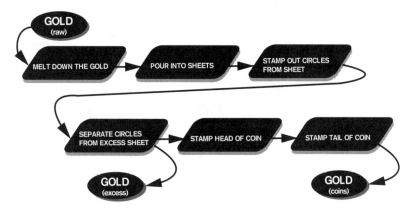

Each box takes the gold, performs a single function, and then passes along the result. Notice that even though each box does only one thing, there are two end products: coins and excess gold (which will presumably go back into the process). This is your basic production line, right?

Now imagine that you've taken on a second contract, this one to whip up a batch of festive cheddar cheese logs for the holiday season. It might be logical to set up a second production line, but did I mention that your factory is extremely small? Just about the only way to fit in new black boxes (or objects) is to squeeze them in between the existing ones. How can you do both jobs at once, without ending up with solid gold cheese logs or coins of cheddar? (For the sake of the metaphor, assume that sanitation is not a factor.)

The answer lies in modifying the objects so they can recognize whether the substance passing through them is gold or cheese. If it's gold and the object is designed to work on gold, then its function is carried out. If the substance is cheese, it passes through unmodified. The cheese-handling objects operate on the reverse criteria. The result is something like that shown on the following page.

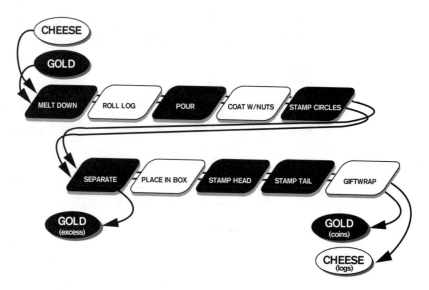

You still have a single assembly line, but two very different kinds of work are happening at the same time. Since the two types of objects affect only one material apiece (and act as a relay for the other), the functions don't conflict.

This is the essence of object-oriented programming—except that the material being processed is neither gold nor cheese but information. The material is the message. It's passed down the line, and a multitude of objects either act on it or ignore it (except to pass it on), according to their purpose.

What kind of information does a message contain? There are several kinds, but the one we'll concern ourselves with first is the most common kind of message: the event message.

Yeah? So what? (an aside)

But before we proceed, a word from your author. By now, you're probably asking yourself, "What does any of this OOPs and cheese log business have to do with making really great multimedia?"

Understanding the way Director gets things done—what it's really doing when it's doing what we tell it to do—can save you a lot of frustration and wasted effort. When you get past the basics of scripting, the bulk of your work in Lingo involves building intertwined production lines akin to the ones in our metaphor but designed to perform dozens of tasks at once.

Familiarity with Lingo-style object orientation will help you identify where to most effectively place your scripts and how to troubleshoot when something goes wrong. Later, when you want to move on to advanced Lingo functions (and the use of Xtras and Shockwave's NetLingo), your firm grasp of OOP principles will come in handy. Ultimately, OOP is worth understanding because object-orientation is the wave of the future: Most of the modern computer languages (and their various dialects) incorporate it to at least some degree.

MESSAGING AND HIERARCHY

OK, so maybe you speed read over a lot of the stuff in the beginning of this chapter. After all, who reads introductions? Now it's time to start really paying attention, though, because this part is important. Without understanding messages and how Director passes them (**message hierarchy**), you'll soon get lost and have to come back and read this chapter again.

In Chapter 4 we wrote scripts that functioned when something specific happened—the go to the frame script in the first frame is meant to execute only when the playback head leaves that frame, and the scripts attached to the buttons are supposed to run only when the respective buttons are clicked. These scripts (or **behaviors**) qualify as objects, and the kind of information they're concerned with is the news that an **event** has occurred in the course of playback. An event is Director's definition of something happening. That occurrence may be something as straightforward as a key being pressed, or it may be something quite esoteric (at least as far as the user is concerned).

We first encountered an event handler in Chapter 4: *Introducing Interactivity*.

What happens when an event occurs? First, Director sends a message throughout the software. ("Hey! The user just pushed down the mouse button!") The message then encounters **event handlers**—scripts intended to be triggered by that event. Since event handlers can reside in so many different places, the program always delivers the event message to those places in a certain order, or hierarchy. Usually, the dynamic is more of a relay than a delivery. When a Lingo location receives a message but has no related event handler, the message is passed on down the hierarchy. If Lingo does have a script to carry out, the message stops there (except in the case of primary event handlers).

Behaviors, as we pointed out in Chapter 4, are really scripts at heart. Whether you get them from the Library Palette, create them with the Behavior Inspector, or write them in a script editor, underneath there is a script. Don't spend too much time worrying about whether a script is a behavior or a behavior is a script; once you become fluent in Lingo, they're all just scripts to you.

The main events

Director recognizes surprisingly few events: 37 at last count, a marked increase over earlier versions (a few years ago there were only 10). Since events are the trigger points to which each script must be anchored, it's important to get to know them.

The following paragraphs offer a rundown of the most common events, loosely grouped by type. When reading them, keep these key points in mind:

- An event is an occurrence (such as a key press) that Director detects and to which it responds by sending a message.

- An event handler is a script (or a portion of one) that responds to a message. Handlers begin with on eventName and are terminated with end.

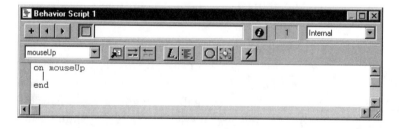

The Lingo events that debuted with version 7 of Director are **getBehaviorTooltip**, **hyperlinkClicked**, and **stepMovie**.

User feedback events

User feedback events, such as a keypress, are the events that first come to mind when someone is introduced to the concept of events. These events are conditional upon the end user and the various mouse and keyboard actions of an end user's session with your software. User feedback events are a bit more complex than you might at first expect, but after you give them a little thought, their complexity should make sense. A clicking of the mouse, for example, is not a single event: There is an event for the mouse button being pressed down and another event for the button being released. This complexity requires a little extra work by you, the programmer, but it gives you the ability to create the rich user interfaces that modern multimedia requires. So here are the most common user feedback events:

- keyDown is the depression of a keyboard button (as opposed to a mouse button). Not a specific key—any key. If you want something to happen only when a unique key is pressed, you have to write a script to determine whether the pressed key was the particular key in question.

- keyUp occurs when the keyboard button is no longer depressed (when the user's finger is lifted from it).

- mouseDown is the first half of a mouse click—when the mouse button is pressed down. There's also rightMouseDown, which occurs when the second button on a two-button mouse is pressed (in Windows) or when the Control key is held down while the button is pressed (on a Macintosh). The distinction is important when developing across platforms, since Windows recognizes the buttons as different whereas MacOS (built around the one-button mouse) usually treats them as identical.

- mouseUp is the second half of the mouse click—when the mouse button returns to its original state. There's also rightMouseUp.

- mouseEnter occurs when the mouse moves the cursor across the boundary area of a sprite on the Stage. This event was new in Director 6, and an eagerly welcomed feature. With it, you can write scripts that provide a level of passive user feedback, such as buttons that light up when the cursor rolls over them.

- mouseLeave is the "departure" corollary of mouseEnter.

- mouseWithin occurs when the cursor is within the bounds of a particular sprite. Unlike the other mouse events, which generate a single message, mouseWithin generates repeated messages as long as the mouse is over the sprite.

- mouseUpOutside is actually a move/click hybrid. It occurs when the user rolls out of a sprite's bounds and then releases the mouse button.

- hyperlinkClicked is a new event in Director 7. If you include text in your movie that you have designated as hyperlink text, a mouse click on that text generates a hyperlinkClicked message.

Playback events

Many events are related to the linear progress of a Director file. **Playback events** are what happens when the playback head moves to another frame, a movie is launched, a projector file is double-clicked, or a page containing a Shockwave movie is downloaded. Here are the most common playback events:

- prepareMovie and startMovie are the first event messages sent when Director opens a movie, projector, or Shockwave file. Scripts triggered by these events are attended to before any playback of the Score, so they are good events for housekeeping scripts (which perform tasks such as determining screen size or user preferences).

- stopMovie occurs when Director stops playing a movie. It's the last event sent and therefore an equally important trigger for scripts that ensure all data has been correctly disposed of or passed on to other files.

- enterFrame is the message sent when the playback head moves into a new frame in the movie. A frame may persist for a fraction of a second or for an eternity, but Lingo always breaks the display process into five parts: preparing the frame, entering the frame, hanging out, getting ready to leave, and then actually leaving.

- exitFrame occurs when the playback head leaves a frame. You might think that it would be simultaneous with the enterFrame event of the subsequent frame, but that overlooks the nonlinear possibilities of Lingo. With exitFrame, you can park scripts to be executed whenever the playback leaves the current frame to arrive at any destination (even a frame in another movie).

- prepareFrame is an event that makes an even finer distinction; it's sent not when Director enters a frame, but when it's getting ready to do so. Since you can now use Lingo to create and populate frames that didn't previously exist in the Score, this event provides a space in time to look (and build) before you leap.

- cuePassed is an important event for sound and digital video files. Some audio and video files (such as QuickTime and SoundEdit 16) have internal cue points that can be read by Director; when Director recognizes such a point, it sends the cuePassed event message. That makes it possible to write scripts that take effect at a certain playback point even though the Score is paused within a frame—a sort of Score within the Score.

- prepareSprite occurs when a sprite is first encountered. That is, if a sprite is in a frame, but wasn't in the previous frame, then the prepareSprite event occurs. Its counterpart is endSprite, which happens when the movie moves to a frame that doesn't contain a sprite that was in the previous frame. These are the only playback events concerned directly with sprites; with these events, you can associate an action with the entrance or exit of a sprite rather than with a specific frame, which means the script will execute even if you shorten, lengthen, or relocate the sprite segment.

Time events

Only two events don't look to Director, the operating system, or the end user for marching orders:

- idle is the catchall event; it occurs when Director has nothing else to do. It's a good event to use in scripts you want executed as often as possible, but beware—one of the easiest ways to slow down performance is to give Director too much busywork to do because of idle. Reserve this event for actions that need to occur both constantly and as near to instantly as possible.

- timeOut is the only user-variable event. It occurs after a specific period of time has passed in which nothing user related has happened, and you can vary that period to suit your needs. Setting a timeOut event is a way of interpreting lack of user feedback as a cue to trigger an action, such as a prompting sequence or a return to the main screen. The default duration of `timeOut` is 3 minutes.

Window events

MOVIE IN A WINDOW: Creating and manipulating more than one Director movie at a time is explained in Chapter 13: *Working with Multiple Movies and Casts.*

A number of events pertain to the times when multiple Director movies are running in multiple windows:

- `activateWindow` occurs when a window becomes active (either it's launched or the user clicks it after a period of inactivity). There's also a `deactivateWindow` event.

- `openWindow` is self-explanatory, as is `closeWindow`.

- `moveWindow` refers to the user's relocation of the window within the monitor configuration.

- `resizeWindow` occurs when the user has tinkered with the dimensions of the window itself by manipulating its variable resize box.

- `zoomWindow` occurs when the window in question is zoomed from one size to another. In Windows, this happens when the Maximize or Minimize command is transmitted; on the Macintosh, it happens when the upper-right corner zoom box is clicked.

Other events

These are most of Director's events. A few others, less commonly used, aren't included here. All of Director's events are listed in the Handler section of *A Lingo Lexicon* (Appendix C) of this book.

You'll notice some actions that seem like events aren't on the list, such as `halt` or `go to frame 1`. Those are commands, not events, and even though they change things on the Stage, they don't automatically execute scripts. **The presence of a verb in the Lingo doesn't necessarily imply an event.**

Just because a Lingo term describes an action, that action isn't necessarily an event.

Not all event messages are passed through all objects. It makes no sense, for example, to send a `keyDown` message to a bitmap sprite such as a button. The button does, however, receive `mouseDown` and `mouseUp` event messages, which it can then pass on—not to other buttons (they don't care; the click didn't happen to them), but to scripts placed elsewhere in the movie. This leads to flow scenarios like the one shown here:

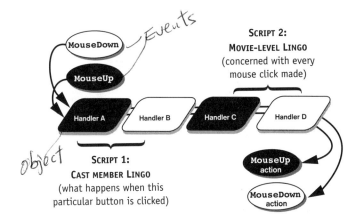

Remember that a script is any chunk of Lingo that resides in one location. It can contain multiple handlers. In the preceding illustration, both scripts have handlers for two different events, mouseDown and mouseUp. It's these handlers that qualify as objects, not the scripts or the cast members themselves.

If the explanation thus far seems less than crystalline, bear with me. It'll become clearer once we've more thoroughly surveyed scripting territory.

A trip down the object hierarchy

To understand how messages are passed around, let's take a quick look at message hierarchy in generalized terms. First of all, remember that there can be any number of handlers in a movie for the same event. For example, each and every frame can have an on exitFrame handler. So which one gets called? Logically, it's the handler attached to the frame that is being exited. Makes sense, and that is exactly what happens. What if both a button sprite and the sprite's cast member have on mouseUp handlers? Who then gets the message, or if they both do, who gets it first?

Director handles these situations by defining a specific order in which messages are sent to objects:

1. Messages first go to behaviors attached to the sprite in question— only a button sprite that was clicked, for example, and not to other sprites on the Stage.

2. Messages go to the cast member of the sprite in question.

3. The message is then sent to a behavior attached to the current frame.

4. Finally, movie scripts receive the message.

The first script found that contains a handler for the message gets executed. By default, other scripts in the message order do not get executed, though you can override this setting. Director ignores messages for which no handler is found.

Remember, now, that this is just a generalized order of the message hierarchy. There is some variation for some events, and you will need to check with the documentation until you are familiar with the use of each message. In particular, we have neglected to mention primary event handlers. They get the messages before anyone else, but they're a little different from other handlers (and there are only a few of them) so we left them out of the list. So now, let's follow the flow of event messages and travel down the object hierarchy, encountering each event handler much as a typical message would.

Primary event handlers

The first stop is the **primary event handler**. Since it's first, it's where you want to put scripts that are sure to be executed every single time. But primary event handlers don't exist for every event. In fact, you can write primary event handlers for only five messages: keyDown, keyUp, mouseDown, mouseUp, and timeOut.

As an example, let's say you want to keep track of exactly how many times the user clicks the mouse while running your program. You can write a primary event handler that keeps a running tally of mouse clicks. Think of this object as an interceptor point, since, unlike the other objects, it'll automatically pass on the message even when it does have a pertinent script. In the scenario described, a running tally script will run whenever the mouse is clicked—but if the mouse click is on a button with its own script, that script will be carried out as well.

Primary event handlers concatenate the word Script with the name of the event: for example, keydownScript or mouseUpScript. Primary event handlers do not follow the same structure that other handlers follow; they do not begin with on or end with end. Instead, you specify the entire contents of the handler within the command where the handler is set. Here's an example:

```
set the timeoutScript to "go to frame 354"
```

With this handler, anytime the timeOut event occurs, the playback head will jump to frame 354, a frame that could contain prompting information such as a help screen.

Sprite scripts (behaviors)

You're already familiar with behaviors that are attached to sprites. In Rbuttons.dir, for example, we attached a behavior to the Play button. Like all behaviors attached to sprites, the behavior for the Play button is also a cast member. In Rbuttons.dir, that was cast member 14. Here's what it looked like:

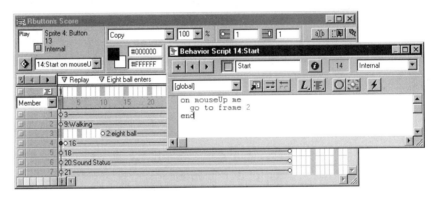

Sprite scripts are useful when you want an element on the Stage to have a consistent look but not a consistent function. For instance, a Go Back button may in some cases need a script meaning "go back one frame," while in other cases it may need a script meaning "return to the opening sequence." Assigning a script to sprites or sprite segments gives you that flexibility.

Sprite scripts are a little hard to keep track of, however. It's easy to access them directly (since they occupy their own slots in the Cast), but it can be difficult to tell whether a sprite has a script attached. You need to click the sprite and then see if the first line of a script appears in the Behavior field in the Score. If the Behavior field shows <Multiple>, you know that more than one behavior is attached to the sprite. Clicking the Behavior Inspector button will open the Behavior Inspector window, showing all the attached behaviors as well as their details.

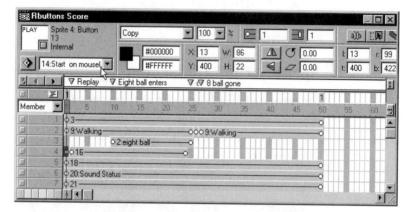

The Behavior field is actually a drop-down menu. All Score behaviors are added to this menu. To attach an existing behavior to a sprite, you can select the sprite and then select the behavior from the drop-down menu. To attach a new behavior, select New Behavior. You can delete all behaviors for a sprite by choosing Clear All Behaviors, but to remove an individual behavior from a sprite you need to use the Behavior Inspector.

Another way to view names of behaviors attached to sprites is with the Behavior display mode for the Score, described in Chapter 7: *More Production Tools*.

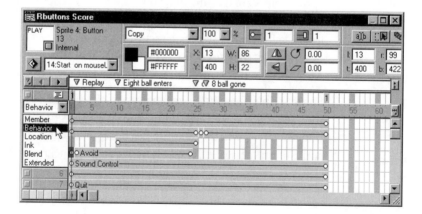

Cast member scripts

This is a new concept for you, but you've probably already figured out that cast members can have scripts attached to them. If you want a consistent function from every instance of a cast member, the best place for a script is attached to the cast member itself. But this raises a question: If it's possible to attach one script to a sprite and one also to the cast member from which that sprite is derived, what happens then?

Keep in mind the hierarchical order of event message processing. Since sprite scripts are higher in the hierarchy, they override cast member scripts. (More precisely, the cast member script will be ignored, since the message event won't be passed to its level.) Let's take the case of that hypothetical Go Back button. If in 90 percent of its incarnations on the Stage, one script would do (one that says "go back one frame"), it would be practical to place that script on the cast member level. For the remaining 10 percent, the second script (the one that says "return to the opening sequence") can be attached to the individual sprites. These sprites would technically have two conflicting associated scripts, but because of the hierarchy, only the sprite-level script would be executed.

Let's have a try at creating a cast member script.

1. *Open the movie Rbuttons.dir.*

2. *In the Cast, select the Walking film loop in slot 9.*

3. *Click the Script button.*

A script editor window opens with the title "Script of Cast Member 9:Walking." Notice that it already has the default beginning and end of a mouseUp handler created for you. This is the most common handler for a cast script, so it's nice of Director to provide the handler's framework. You don't have to use it, though, and you can change it to whatever event you desire. The mouseUp handler happens to be what we want, so we won't change what is already there. The editor's insertion point is right where we want it, so let's enter a simple command: beep. That's one of Director's built-in commands, and it makes the computer's speaker beep—well, actually it'll be the sound chosen in your Sounds Properties dialog box (Windows) or Sound control panel (Macintosh).

4. *Enter the* beep *command at the insertion point. Your script should look like this:*

5. *Close the script editor window and play the movie.*

6. *While the movie is looping on the first frame, click the figure of Swifty.*

When you click Swifty, you should hear the beep. If you click the Play button to start Swifty walking, you should still be able to hear a beep by clicking him as he moves across the Stage.

7. *Stop the movie and take a look at the Cast window.*

The picon for the Walking cast member should now have a second sub-icon in the lower-left corner, similar to the icon for the Script button. Any time you see a cast member with that icon, it means that a script is attached (actually, you can turn this display off in the Cast Window Preferences dialog box). Unlike behaviors, cast scripts don't appear as separate members of the Cast.

Cast members with attached scripts show a script icon in the lower-left corner, as shown in cast member 9.

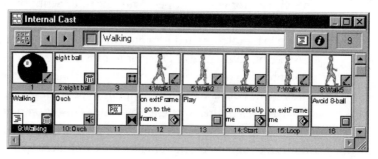

Frame scripts (behaviors)

Like sprite scripts, frame scripts are also behaviors. Generally, we associate frame scripts with the playback events relating to frames, such as on enterFrame and on exitFrame, although frame scripts can contain handlers for other events as well. We used frame behaviors twice in the movie Rbuttons.dir in Chapter 4: once for looping on frame 1 until the play button was clicked, and again for looping from the last frame of the Score back to the beginning.

Make sure you're working in the appropriate script window. Check the title. For frame scripts, it should read "Behavior Script," not "Movie Script" or "Script of Cast member."

Frame behaviors are always attached to cells in the behavior channel of the Score, and the behavior itself becomes a member of the Cast. Frame behaviors can be attached to the cell in a number of ways, including these: by dragging a behavior from the Library Palette or from the Cast to the cell in the behavior channel; by selecting the cell and then bringing up the Behavior Inspector (either by clicking the Behavior button or from the Behavior drop-down menu); or by double-clicking a cell of the behavior channel. The latter will open a behavior script editor window.

There are uses other than looping for frame behaviors. Imagine a scenario in which you are creating an interactive movie of Animal/Vegetable/Mineral. One particular frame is used to get answers from the user about whether an object shown is an animal, a vegetable, or a mineral, so you have some editable text fields on the Stage. When the fields are placed on the Stage, you want them to already have default contents. Maybe your field (named Answer) should contain the default text "Animal." In that case, you would write a handler for the on prepareFrame event in your frame behavior:

```
on prepareFrame
    member("Answer").text = "Animal"
end
```

The user has 1 minute to enter an answer (we can set that up using the tempo channel). At the end of that minute, we want to save the answer the user entered. We know that the playback head will move on at the end of that minute and the user can then make no more changes, so that's the time to save the response.

Since you can place handlers for other events in the same behavior, you can add another handler to save the information the user entered.

The on exitFrame handler is a good place to take care of such housekeeping at the frame level. Now your script might look like this:

```
on prepareFrame
    global saveAnswer
    member("Answer").text = "Animal"
end

on exitFrame
    saveAnswer = member("Answer").text
end
```

name assigned to textfield

When the playback head first gets to the frame, and before the sprites are drawn, the contents of the Answer field are changed to your default text. Then, when the playback head is leaving the frame, the user's answer is read and stored in a variable named saveAnswer. (Variables are elements in programming languages where you can put things until you need to use them again. We get into variables in detail in the next chapter, *The Elements of Scripting*.)

We can even make some decisions based on the user's answer within the on exitFrame handler:

```
on exitFrame
    global saveAnswer
    saveAnswer = member("Answer").text
    if saveAnswer = "Mineral" then
        go to frame "mMineral"
    else if saveAnswer = "Animal" then
        go to frame "mAnimal"
    else
        go to frame "mVegetable"
    end if
end
```

Now we not only save what the user enters, we also branch to a different location based on that answer.

Movie scripts

Movie scripts may be last in the message hierarchy, but they can be the most powerful scripts you write. The prepareMovie, startMovie, and stopMovie event handlers, if used, each need to be placed in a movie script. Use them to take care of your movie's initialization and house-cleaning. You can also place your own handlers in movie scripts—custom handlers you create to take care of custom messages you send from within other handlers. We'll cover the creation of custom handlers in detail in the next chapter, but for now, consider movie scripts as repositories for handlers that can be accessed from anywhere in the movie.

We can take a look at a movie script in action by writing a movie script that globally increases the sound volume of our Rbuttons movie.

1. **From the Window menu, select Script.**

A movie script editor window appears. Since most handlers that are placed in movie scripts are custom handlers, there is no default handler information placed in the script. We'll have to write this one from scratch. In this case, we are going to use an on startMovie handler:

2. **Enter the following Lingo:**

```
on startMovie
     set the volume of sound 1 to 256
end
```

volume sound

This changes the volume of all sound sprites placed in sound channel 1 to the level 256. Sound levels in Lingo are expressed in increments from –256 to 256, with all increments 0 or below being silent. Since we have one sound in this movie ("Ouch!"), we've effectively set it to maximum volume.

Run the movie and see the results for yourself; unless you already had your system sound turned to maximum, you should notice a difference in volume. If you want to change the sound level to some different value, you can reopen the script (double-click it in the Cast) and change 256 to another value. When you run your movie, notice that even though we've set a volume, the Sound button still works to turn the sound off—not because the script in the sound channel overrides the movie script, but because the two commands aren't mutually exclusive.

Look at the Cast and you will see a new cast member picon with a sub-icon of a script in the lower-right corner. This indicates that the cast member is a movie script. You don't "place" a movie script anywhere in the Score or Stage—you just write it, and it appears in the Cast.

Changing movie scripts to behaviors

So, what if you write a movie script and then decide that it really should be a behavior? One way to change from one to the other is to open the script and copy the contents and then open a behavior and paste the copied script into it. A simpler method is to use Cast Member Properties.

1. *With the movie script open in the editor window, click the Cast Member Properties button. If the script window isn't open, you can select the movie script in the Cast and click the Cast Member Properties button at the top of the Cast window.*

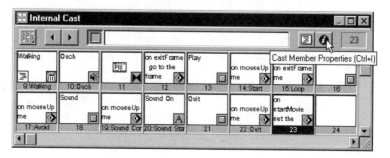

The script's Info window appears.

2. *Use the Type pull-down menu to change the script type from Movie to Behavior. Click OK to return to the Script window.*

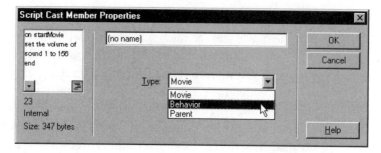

Notice that the Script window now is titled "Behavior Script." In this case, though, you'll probably want to change the script back to a movie script, since Director doesn't look for on startMovie handlers in behaviors and your script would never be executed.

As you may have noticed from the previous illustration, there's another type of script: the **parent script**. Parent scripts are tools for building powerful Lingo entities that exist entirely in RAM, thereby floating in a realm above that of the movie or the Score. Parent scripts can be made to respond to real-world goings-on, but they're not formally part of the message hierarchy and therefore not discussed here. For a real introduction to the subject of parent scripts, see Chapter 18: *Parent/Child Lingo*.

Passing events

We've already noted that the relay of messages down the object hierarchy comes to a halt at the first relevant script. If a mouseUp handler script is found on the cast member level, Director won't pass the mouseUp event on to frame scripts and movie scripts unless you tell it to do so. If that script includes the command pass on a separate line, the message will continue its travels after the rest of the script is carried out.

Passing along events is useful because it allows the execution of multiple scripts at the same time. For example, let's say you're creating an interactive multiple-choice quiz in which the user chooses from a group of buttons (each of which has its own cast member script). If you want to give the user some positive feedback without disrupting the action, you can add a script to the sprite of the "correct" button, which will display the message "Good Choice!" when the sprite is clicked. Normally a sprite script would disable the underlying cast member script, but if you add pass, then the text will be displayed and the button will perform its normal function.

What happens if the pass command is used to trigger two contradictory scripts? In the scenario of the Go Back button we explored earlier, including a pass command in the sprite script ("return to the opening sequence") would put it at odds with the cast member script ("go back one frame"). In such instances, the cast script wins out because it was executed last. But don't rely on that in every case. It's bad programming to include two scripts with contradictory commands.

The one object that doesn't need a pass command is the primary event handler. Its default policy on event passage is the opposite of the rest; it passes events on unless specifically instructed otherwise by the command stopEvent.

THE MESSAGE WINDOW

For an in-depth discussion of troubleshooting and debugging, see Chapter 17: *Debugging and Troubleshooting*.

Lingo may reside in a multiplicity of places, but there's only one place where you can see all of it in action. The Message window can offer a peek under the hood, so to speak, displaying everything that goes on in the background: every event message sent, every script executed. This window is a useful educational tool, and it's invaluable for troubleshooting.

1. **Open your movie RButtons.dir.**

2. **Open the Message window (from the Window menu, select Message).**

3. **Click the Trace button in the center of the window's toolbar.**

When the Trace option is enabled, all Lingo is reflected in the window's scrolling field.

4. **Click the Play button on the Control Panel, and then after a second or so click the Stop button.**

Even though starting the movie doesn't move the playback head (since we built in a loop at the beginning), there's activity to report:

```
-- Welcome to Director --
== Movie: E:\Demystified\Source\Rbuttons.dir Frame: 1 Script:
(member 12 of castLib 1) Handler: exitFrame
--> go to the frame
--> end
--> go to the frame
--> end
--> go to the frame
--> end
```

For information on working with path names, see Chapter 13: *Working with Multiple Movies and Casts*.

The second line shows the movie being run. Yours will look different and will reflect the location of the movie you are playing on your system. In any case, the text should consist of a string of words connected by colons or slashes. This is a **path name**, the actual address of the Rbuttons movie on your system. Path names are also used to access linked files, such as sounds and digital video.

When the Trace option is enabled, the Message window uses the following syntax:

- Events and other messages to be sent through the hierarchy are prefaced with a double equal sign: ==.

- Scripts are announced by their cast member number.

- The command lines contained in the script are prefaced with an arrow: -->.

The Rbuttons movie we wrote will continue to loop on frame 1 until you, the user, do something. So you'll see the lines

```
--> go to the frame
--> end
```

repeating over and over. That's what is going on; Director passes through frame 1, finds an on exitFrame handler, executes it, goes to frame 1, and so on.

To make what you see a little more interesting, rewind and restart the movie again, but this time also click the Play button on the Stage, and then the Sound button, and then the Quit button. Now you will see some additional lines in the Message window. Again, they reflect the Lingo side of what is going on in the running movie. Here's part of what you might see:

```
== Script: (member 14 of castLib 1) Handler: mouseUp
--> go to frame 2
== Frame: 2
--> end
== Frame: 10 Script: (member 19 of castLib 1) Handler: mouseUp
--> set the soundEnabled to not (the soundEnabled)
--> if the soundEnabled = TRUE then
--> member("Sound Status").text = "Sound Off"
--> end
== Frame: 19 Script: (member 22 of castLib 1) Handler: mouseUp
--> halt
```

Use **Control-A** (Windows) or **Command-A** (Macintosh) to select the contents of the Message window. Then you can press the Delete key to remove the text already there.

The frame numbers you see in your Message window will probably be different. In the example shown, the Sound button was clicked at frame 10, and the Quit button was clicked at frame 19. It may take some getting acquainted with this window to be able to readily decipher what is going on, but the more familiar Lingo becomes to you, the better you'll get at figuring out the trace information in the Message window.

Running a movie with the Trace option on will slow down performance times, since you're requiring Director to post reports on all activities, and many of those activities take more time to report than to perform. But whenever you're faced with a thorny scripting issue—something just doesn't work, or it works in an unexpected fashion—running a trace is usually the first step toward debugging.

POINTS TO REMEMBER

These are the main points I hope you've gleaned from the preceding pages:

- Lingo is a **living language**; its vocabulary is growing and changing. Each major revision of Director brings with it new terminology and sometimes the abandonment of outmoded Lingo.

- There are 37 distinct built-in occasions when Director looks for Lingo scripts to execute. These occasions are called **events**.

- When an event is detected, Director sends a **message** to that effect. This message is routed in a certain order to various Lingo locations.

- The scripts located in these various locations are classified as **objects**, and the order in which they receive the message is known as the **object hierarchy**.

- If an object contains a script pertaining to the event, the object will execute it. Such a script is called an **event handler**. If an object doesn't have a relevant event handler, it will pass the message further down the hierarchy.

- With one notable exception, the flow of a message usually stops at the first relevant event handler. But you can continue the message transmission down through the hierarchy by using the `pass` command, or you can stop the flow prematurely with `stopEvent`.

CHAPTER 9

THE ELEMENTS OF SCRIPTING

IN THE LAST CHAPTER, WE GOT AS CONCEPTUAL AS WE'RE GOING TO GET, exploring the logical structures implicit in Director's operation. Now we're going to begin the descent back into the nitty-gritty of Director-based production, and of Lingo script writing in particular.

In this chapter you'll encounter definitions and discussions of the elements involved in writing Lingo scripts: the special terms and syntax of this versatile scripting language. You'll also put your newfound knowledge to work immediately on tutorial projects that use Lingo to pack a lot of interactivity into single-frame Director movies. You should emerge from this chapter with a good grasp of the grammar of scripting, and at least a conversational command of the Lingo dialect.

TAKE THE MEGO TEST

Before we get down to the business of scripting in Lingo, let's tackle the conceptual building blocks upon which Lingo (and just about every other programming language, for that matter) is founded. Unless you're already comfortable with the terms and syntax of programming, these building blocks can all too easily become stumbling blocks or even crushing weights.

To know where you stand, try this simple test. Read the following paragraph; then honestly gauge your reaction.

> *Handlers can initiate an action or return a result. You can write handlers that take arguments or parameters and then either perform some action based on the parameters or return a result based on a calculation or expression that uses the parameters. Handlers that return a result are sometimes called function handlers, or just functions.*

That's a passage out of some official Macromedia documentation from a few years ago, and it's a good example of the kind of language you'll need to parse with impunity. Did it make sense? If so, good; consider yourself a programmer. Or did it instead have the My Eyes Glazed Over (MEGO) effect?

No sweat? If you already know your variables from your functions and your arguments from your parameters, you'll want to focus on the particulars of Lingo scripting rather than on the underlying concepts. But you might at least glance through the exercises, paying special attention to factors that you may not have encountered in other programming languages, such as the various types of properties available in Director.

Did your eyes glaze over? Take heart; the goal of this chapter is to keep that glazing at bay. By the time you're done here, you'll be revisiting that paragraph about handlers. I think you'll find that it not only makes sense, but it's really quite simple.

LINGO BITS: THE ELEMENTARY ELEMENTS

Let's start by defining the elements that are easiest to pin down, the little bits of Lingo that require only a modicum of conceptual thinking to grasp.

Commands

COMMAND:
A Lingo term that refers to a specific action to be carried out by Director.

We've already used the term **command** in the sense of a set of instructions to be carried out, but that definition could apply by extension to all of Lingo. From now on, we'll use the word command in the strictest sense: to refer to the specific word or word combination that implies an action. In this sense, commands are the verbs of Lingo.

Freestanding commands

Some commands are complete in themselves. As far as your computer is concerned, there's just no room for ambiguity in terms like these:

```
halt
quit
restart
```

(The restart command is a Macintosh-only command that shuts down the computer entirely; it's the equivalent of selecting Restart from the Special menu in the Finder.)

With these commands, there's no need for further clarification (`halt the movie`, `quit Director`, `restart this Macintosh`) because the context really doesn't permit differing interpretations.

Commands and arguments

Other commands, however, require further clarification. Sometimes the additional information needs to be placed right after the command, and sometimes it needs to be interwoven with the command:

```
go to [which frame?]
set [what?] to [what?]
puppetSound [which channel?], [which castmember]
```

ARGUMENT:
Additional information needed to give a command the correct context for action.

In the preceding listing, questions in brackets represent the information each command needs to have an effect. These bits of information are called **arguments**. When a command requires this sort of clarification, we say that it "takes an argument." Some commands take more than one argument, such as the `set...to` command in the listing; we must specify both the thing being set (such as the `soundEnabled`) and the thing it's being set to (such as TRUE). The italicized brackets (and their contents) are used in this book to indicate Lingo where you are required to place arguments. If you look at the commands in the appendix, you will see brackets being used constantly. When you use such a command, remember that your argument replaces *both* the brackets *and* their contents.

When a command takes more than one argument, watch out for **syntax** subtleties. The method of separating arguments varies, and it's not always logical. For instance, it might seem natural to use the `move member` command as follows:

```
move member 1 to member 20
```

But this wouldn't work; the culprit is the word `to`. The true syntax is

```
move member 1, member 20
```

To find the correct approach for a particular command, consult this book's *A Lingo Lexicon* (Appendix C) or Director's Lingo Dictionary, which you can reach from the Help menu.

Keywords

KEYWORD:
A Lingo term used to represent a fixed element or concept. Keywords are words defined in Lingo and reserved for specific purposes.

If commands are the verbs of Lingo, **keywords** are the nouns. You've already encountered several:

```
member
sprite
next
loop
field
the
```

The term *keyword* is used in most programming languages. Keywords, also known as *reserved words*, are words that are specifically defined in the programming language and can't be used for other purposes. If you try to use a keyword for a purpose for which it was not intended, you'll either be informed by Director of your error (the good news) or possibly will introduce some difficult-to-find bugs into your scripts (the bad news).

If you remember your basic language grammar, you're probably already questioning the "keywords as nouns" concept—you can accept `cast` and `sprite`, but `next` and `the`? It's a metaphor, and the metaphor holds because keywords represent fixed elements and concepts, which in the Lingo universe are the next best thing to being persons, places, or things. In Lingo, `next` isn't an adjective, it's short for "the next one of these." The isn't an article; it's short for "this particular thing called...."

Keywords usually exist in the context of other data. Some can function as arguments (`go next`, for instance), while others require arguments themselves (`member 1` or `member "Monster"`). What's interesting about keywords is that sometimes they're extraneous, while at other times they are vitally important. If you write the script `go frame "Otter"` rather than `go to the frame "Otter"`, Lingo will know what you mean. But if you write `set stageColor = 14` rather than `set the stageColor = 14`, confusion sets in. Rather than changing the property `the stageColor`, Lingo will assume you just created a new variable called `stageColor` with a value set to 14 (we'll explain variables and values shortly).

Statements and expressions

STATEMENT AND EXPRESSION:
A statement is a complete Lingo instruction. An expression is a logical part of a statement.

You will see both of these terms used quite frequently, so it's a good idea to understand just what they mean. A **statement** is a complete Lingo instruction that can be performed by Director. An **expression** is a part of a statement that makes a logical unit and can be evaluated, but it isn't necessarily an entire statement.

In common usage, then, a command and a statement are the same thing. Consider this statement:

```
go to the frame + 2
```

To be completely truthful, `go to` could be considered the command and the entire line a statement. The portion `the frame + 2` is an expression. The expression is evaluated as the frame "two frames to the right of whatever frame we are currently in."

Constants

CONSTANT:
A keyword that takes no argument but has a freestanding meaning of its own.

You can argue that **constants** are a subspecies of keywords, but it's easiest to think of them as symbols that you spell out—just as *zero* is a word spelling out the symbol 0, which itself represents the concept of emptiness. To make sure we treat constants as symbols rather than words, it's a tradition to spell them out in ALL CAPS:

BACKSPACE

EMPTY

FALSE

QUOTE

RETURN

TRUE

If you write the script `put EMPTY into member 1`, you've just blanked out any text that might happen to be in cast member 1. You could also write `put ""  into member 1`, using quotation marks with nothing in between, but using `EMPTY` makes your intentions obvious.

Operators

OPERATOR:
A symbol or term in Lingo used to perform a specific operation.

Operators aren't exactly keywords because they aren't exactly words. But they do have meanings that are specifically defined in Lingo. Probably the most common operator you will use is the equal (=) operator. For example, you might write `total = partA + partB`, where both the equal sign and the plus (+) sign are operators. Operators can be loosely grouped together by type:

- **arithmetic**, including plus (+), minus (-), multiplication (*), and division (/) operators

- **comparative**, including greater than (>), less than (<), equal to (=), and greater than or equal to (>=) operators

- **string**, including concatenate (&) and concatenate with a space between (&&) operators

- **logical**, including the terms and, not, and or

GETTING A HANDLE ON HANDLERS

We've bandied about the term **event handler** for a while now, and earlier we even wrote a few scripts that incorporated them. But our scripts so far all have a built-in limitation: They can spring to life only when the specified event occurs. And as you know from the previous chapter, Lingo acknowledges only a handful of occurrences as official events.

But event handlers aren't the only type of handlers on the block. You can write custom handlers that carry out any number of commands, and you can give them any names you wish. When you invoke these names in other handler scripts, those custom handlers will be triggered—the act of calling them sets them into motion. Since Lingo is event-based by its very structure, the chain of action must be set off by an event handler, but there's no limit to the degree to which handlers can be linked to other handlers.

When one Lingo element triggers another, it is said to **call** that element. A handler's calling another handler will carry out, or **execute**, that called handler's contents as well.

Writing a custom handler

Let's create a custom handler and then see how it works in conjunction with an event handler. We'll start by opening up a new movie file. Then we'll give it a name and colorize the Stage.

1. *Create a new movie in Director. Name it* **Bingo.dir**

2. *From the Modify menu, choose Movie Properties. Set the size of the Stage to whatever you like, and set the Stage color to black.*

This Director movie will be only a single frame long, so the next step is to set up a loop.

3. *In the behavior channel of frame 1, place the following script:*

```
on exitFrame
    go to the frame
end
```

Yes, you have seen this handler before, and no, it's not a custom handler. It is an event handler, but we need it to make our movie work the way we want. Of course, you could get the same effect by clicking the Loop button on the Control Panel, but remember that the Control Panel disappears when you spin off a movie into a projector or Shockwave file. You could also just drag a behavior from the Library Palette into the behavior channel and get the same handler. Once you get comfortable with Lingo scripts, we encourage you to do just that. For now, scripts are the way we want to go.

4. *In frame 1, use the Tool Palette to place a pushbutton in the upper-left quadrant of the Stage. For the text of the button, type* **Bingo!**

You can use the Font selection from the Modify menu to make the text in the button appear in any style you like.

5. *In the Tool Palette window, set the foreground color chip to a red of your choice. Then use the Filled Oval tool to draw a tall, thin oval directly on the Stage.*

The oval should appear filled with your chosen red. Make sure you're using the Tool window, not the Paint window.

6. *Check to make sure the oval occupies channel 2 in the Score and is in the same frame as your button.*

We're now ready to write a handler we'll call gadzooks. You can give any name to a handler, so long as it's only one word and contains only letters and/or numbers.

7. *Select the first empty slot in the Cast; open the Script window (Control-0 Windows; Command-0 Macintosh).*

Since you selected an empty cast slot, the Script window should open with the Movie Script heading.

8. *In the Movie Script window, enter the following:*

```
on gadzooks
    beep
    sprite (2).foreColor = random (255)
    updateStage
end
```

9. *Close the Movie Script window (a shortcut for closing a Script window is pressing the Enter key on the numeric keypad).*

We've specified that two things should happen when gadzooks is executed: The system beep should play, and the foreground color of the oval (sprite 2) should change to a random color. The random command picks any number, but the parenthetical statement (255) limits it to the numbers 1 through 255, which corresponds to the colors in the 8-bit System palette. The updateStage command tells Director to redraw the Stage, which makes the color change show up.

Normally, the Stage is redrawn whenever a new frame is reached (or the same frame is reached again), and for our simple movie that actually should be good enough. Whenever you have a lot of things going on, though, you may want to use updateStage to ensure that a user's action and the result are simultaneous, as in the button click and the resultant color change.

Working with custom handlers

Now we have a custom handler, but it's free-floating—nothing calls it just yet. Let's write a handler for the Bingo! button and call it from there.

1. *Open the Bingo! button's cast script (select its cast slot and then click the Script button).*

2. *In the line between* on mouseUp *and* end, *enter:*

gadzooks

3. *Close the Script window.*

Now run the movie and click the Bingo! button. All the commands encapsulated in the custom gadzooks handler should execute. The system beep should sound, and the oval sprite should change color.

If you've ever worked with macros in a word processing or spreadsheet application, you can see how custom handlers are similar to macros: complicated lines of typing are reduced to a single word—in this case, *gadzooks.* Also, by placing the Lingo in a single handler and calling it elsewhere, you make it easy to modify moviewide results by editing that handler. For example:

1. *Double-click the gadzooks slot in the Cast.*

2. *Change the line* beep *to* beep 3*; then close the Script window.*

> If you're having trouble getting your beeps to sound, it may not be your scripting; the command **beep** gets inconsistent results on some Windows machines. Try changing the sound on your system's Sound Properties control panel.

3. *Run the movie.*

The Bingo! button should now trigger three beeps instead of one. Imagine if we had an ambitious movie, with hundreds of sprites and dozens of buttons, all calling gadzooks. This simple modification would affect them all. That's the strength of scripting; with proper planning, you can make variations and improvements at any level, while retaining over-all consistency. The flip side of this, of course, is that it's all too easy to bollix up a project by messing with an oft-used handler (but you'll learn to proceed cautiously in that regard).

INSTANT LINGO: THE LINGO MENUS

Lingo may be a language, but it certainly isn't a spoken one. That means lots and lots of keystrokes to get your point across. If you easily tire of typing—or if simpel mistaeks have a way of creeping into your text—then you'll want to get acquainted with two of the timesaving tools in the Script window: the **Alphabetical Lingo** and the **Categorized Lingo** menus. Both permit you to draft scripts via menu choices rather than direct typing. All the standard Lingo elements are represented, and when you select one, it's automatically entered into the Script window at the current cursor position.

Alphabetical Lingo (found under that little *L* symbol in the Script window) groups the Lingo vocabulary into 26 categories, which don't correspond exactly to the alphabet. You'll find symbols such as =, +, and & under the Operators category at the top of the list.

FIND THE RIGHT WORD:
When writing scripts,
use the Lingo menu,
which lists common
elements in alphabeti-
cal order.

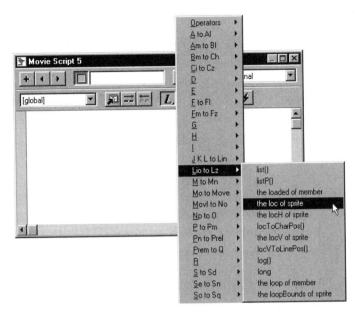

If you know what you want to do but don't know the Lingo to do it with, the Categorized Lingo button (directly to the right of that little *L* button) is a good place to start. It's where Macromedia has thoughtfully grouped all Lingo in loose categories of general use, from Navigation to Logic.

Both Lingo menus behave in the same way: You make a selection and it drops itself into the context of the currently open script. But that means more than a simple cut-and-paste job. When the syntax clearly calls for specifics, the menus place and select a variable, assuming that you'll then replace it with the real information. For instance, selecting `rollover` will actually get you `rollover(whichSprite)`, with `whichSprite` highlighted.

The Lingo elements typed in the Script window don't always exactly match the listing in the Lingo menu. For example, the menu item for **set...to** will produce **set variableOrProperty to expression**, with **variableOrProperty** highlighted. Unless you're familiar with the Lingo in question, it's easy to introduce redundant or incorrect scripting, so double-check before proceeding.

The Lingo menus come in handy when you don't want the hassle of repeatedly and flawlessly retyping a long command (such as `the pausedAtStart of member n`), but you may find the menus too circuitous for simple elements such as go to and halt. Remember that you can also cut and paste from other entries in the Script window.

> Since you don't want the names of your custom handlers to clash with official Lingo terms, it's a good idea to glance through the Lingo menu to see if your handler's prospective name is already taken.

Two syntaxes

Director 7 now allows the use of dot syntax for more concise scripting.

As mentioned before, Lingo is a language in perpetual transition that never sits back and rests on its laurels. That means new built-in events and commands are added to Lingo with every new version of Director… and one recent change in particular is pretty significant. Beginning with Director 7, a whole new syntax for Lingo came into being—the **dot syntax**, or dot property notation. It didn't replace the old syntax, but it can be used as an alternative syntax. So you will often see two ways of writing the same command. We used the dot syntax for the command

```
sprite(2).foreColor = random(255)
```

We could write that equivalently as

```
set the foreColor of sprite 2 = random(255)
```

The dot (it's actually a period) syntax is a bit more compact and follows the lead of other object-oriented languages. It's also more precise and has fewer exceptions. The other method (we'll call it "old Lingo") looks a lot more like English. Feel free to use whichever method makes you more comfortable, but expect to see a single statement written in any number of ways. The following statements are equivalent:

```
set the foreColor of sprite 2 = random(255)
set the foreColor of sprite 2 to random(255)
sprite(2).foreColor = random(255)
```

If you look in the *Lingo Lexicon* in Appendix C of this book, you'll see that the syntax of Lingo elements is presented in both ways wherever applicable. The same is true with the documentation supplied with Director Help. The Alphabetical Lingo and Categorized Lingo menus, as well, still provide the old-style syntax.

THEM CHANGES: CONDITIONS AND STATUS

One important abstraction in Lingo is that of the **condition**—setting and testing for conditions can be a significant part of your scripting. Simply put, a condition exists whenever there are two possible states for a Director element at any given moment; something is either present or it isn't. This is not to be confused with **conditionality**, which is the introduction of commands based on an `if/then` structure.

Conditions: Lingo's on/off switch

In Chapter 4, we wrote a script that turned the sound on and off by toggling the status of the soundEnabled condition. The exact Lingo we used was this:

```
set the soundEnabled to not (the soundEnabled)
```

This neither turned the sound on nor off; it just set it to the opposite of whatever it happened to be at the time a button was clicked. If we wanted specifically to turn on the soundEnabled, we would need to enter one of the following equivalent statements:

```
the soundEnabled = TRUE
set the soundEnabled = TRUE
set the soundEnabled to TRUE
set the soundEnabled = 1
set the soundEnabled to 1
the soundEnabled = 1
```

Replacing TRUE with FALSE, or 1 with 0, in the preceding statements will turn off the soundEnabled.

Since a condition has a binary existence (on or off), Director needs to have it declared either TRUE or FALSE, 1 or 0. Most conditions have a default setting; for instance, the soundEnabled is set to TRUE until you say otherwise.

In this usage, the equal sign (=) and the word to are equivalent whenever the keyword set is used. TRUE and FALSE do not have to be written in uppercase, although doing so is a Lingo convention.

See *Properties Made Plain* later in this chapter.

Keep in mind that the soundEnabled itself is not a condition; it is a *property*, and its current *status* is a condition (we'll be defining properties shortly). Here are some other properties that have conditions:

- the moveableSprite of sprite determines whether or not a sprite can be moved on the Stage by the end user.

- the loop of member indicates whether a digital video cast member is set to run on a continuous loop.

- the loaded of member specifies whether a cast member is currently loaded into memory. Like many conditions, this one can be tested for but not set (that is, you can determine whether the condition is TRUE or FALSE, but you can't set it to either state).

- the hilite of member is specific to checkboxes and radio buttons. When the button is selected, the condition is set to TRUE. This condition can be both tested for and set, which means you can use it to click buttons even when the user hasn't.

Notice that while the hilite of member can be both tested and set (changed), you can only check the current condition with the loaded of member. If you are trying without success to change a condition, check with the documentation to be sure that you really are allowed to change it.

Seeking (and using) status

In the realm of Lingo, **status** doesn't mean designer labels and luxury nameplates; it means the current state of affairs, as in "Status report, Mr. Sulu." The status of a condition is either on or off (or more precisely, TRUE or FALSE). But other elements can have a few more options to their status, and in your scripting adventures you'll want to take advantage of all the possibilities.

A good example of multiple status is the Lingo element known as the key. In a keystroke-related event handler (on keyDown or on keyUp), the key can be used to perform different operations depending on which key has just been pressed. Let's say we're creating an interactive quiz, and the user is prompted to type letters corresponding to the possible answers. We could write a handler like this:

```
on keyDown
    if the key = "a" then go "Wrong Answer"
    if the key = "b" then go "Right Answer"
    if the key = "c" then go "Wrong Answer"
    if the key = RETURN then alert "You must choose A, B, ¬
        or C."
end keyDown
```

We've just written script lines that test the keystroke status. If the status matches *a* or *c*, the playback head will then leap to the marker Wrong Answer. If the keystroke is *b*, it goes to *Right Answer*. And if it's the Return key, the playback head does no jumping at all; an alert box appears instead with a gentle reminder. We could assign a different action for each key if we wanted, but we've specified only four different status possibilities. If the keystroke is something else, this handler won't do anything.

When testing for the status of a keystroke using **the key**, the individual key's identity should be in quotation marks—**"a"** instead of a, **"2"** instead of 2, and so on. The exceptions to this rule are the so-called character constant keys, which should be written without quotation marks. These are **RETURN, ENTER, TAB, SPACE, QUOTE,** and **BACKSPACE.** As with all constants, the capitalization is a tradition rather than a requirement.

THE FORM OF FUNCTIONS

Just a few paragraphs ago I referred to the key as being a "Lingo element." That's true enough, but it's time to get down to specifics and identify the *kinds* of Lingo elements we'll be using in this book. In the case of the key, it's a **function**, one of dozens of functions available to you in Director.

Here we slip into the realm of the intangible; a function doesn't "do" anything—at least, nothing that shows up on the Stage. Functions are Lingo elements that return a value. They are the Lingo tools that help you determine the status and conditions of things. They're the probes and scanners, so to speak, used to retrieve data about the state of something at a given time. The function you use depends on what you want to know.

There's a bit of customized language associated with functions. When you write a script that requests a status report from a function, you're said to **call** that function. The answer the function provides is known as the **result**. Sometimes you'll encounter a statement along the lines of "function X returns Y." In such usage, **returns** refers to the result.

Testing functions in the Message window

To see the power of functions in action, it's not necessary to write and place elaborate scripts in a test movie. You can try out functions by typing directly into the Message window, without affecting the open movie.

1. *Open the Message window.*

2. *At the prompt, enter the following; then press Enter (Windows) or Return (Macintosh):*

```
put the time
```

In this line, put is the command, and it's used to call a function—in this case, the function the time. When you press the Enter or Return key, the results of the function call should be written on a following line—that *is* the time, isn't it? (If it's not, try resetting the system clock on your computer.) By the way, the put command places whatever is to its right in the statement, after evaluation, into the Message window. You can even use the put command in your handlers for a quick and easy means of checking some value.

Now try calling another function.

3. *Type the following; then press Enter or Return:*

```
put the long time
```

This time the time's a little different, isn't it? The extra digits express the time down to the second.

4. *Enter these lines:*

```
put the date
put the long date
```

Even though the information retrieved here is essentially the same, the date and the long date are two different functions, because they return the date in slightly different forms. There's also the abbreviated date (try it to see the difference).

GET THE MESSAGE:
The Message window can be used to check the status of various conditions.

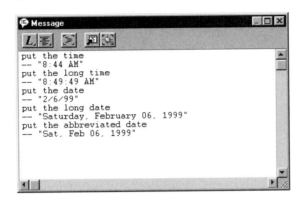

```
put the time
-- "8:44 AM"
put the long time
-- "8:49:49 AM"
put the date
-- "2/6/99"
put the long date
-- "Saturday, February 06, 1999"
put the abbreviated date
-- "Sat, Feb 06, 1999"
```

Here are a few other functions for you to try out in the Message window. Remember to use the put command with each.

- random([*someNumber*]) generates a random number in the range of 1 to [*someNumber*]. For example, random(3) will return a 1, 2, or 3. We already used random to generate numbers for colors assigned to the oval sprite in Bingo!

- the runMode returns words that identify the mode in which the movie is playing: Author, Projector, Plug-in (for Shockwave), or Java Applet. Since you are authoring in Director, this function will return Author. This function can be used to perform various actions depending on the runtime environment.

- the mouseH (or mouseV) returns the horizontal (or vertical) position of the mouse cursor at the time the function is called. The value is in pixels determined from the left (or top) of the Stage. Try placing the mouse at various locations on the Stage when you try out this function.

TICK:
Director's basic unit of time measurement. One tick is equivalent to one sixtieth of a second.

- the lastClick returns a number representing the time passed since the last time the mouse button was clicked. This duration is given in **ticks**, each of which is ¹⁄₆₀ of a second. Since a second is a long time to a microprocessor, Director uses ticks as its main unit of time measurement. To convert to seconds, divide by 60. Try this function with the movie running. Notice that Director counts only the clicks on the Stage, not clicks in the Message window.

Just to keep things straight, let's recap:

- **mouseDown** is an *event*.

- **on mouseDown** is the first line of an *event handler*.

- **the mouseDown** is a *function* that returns a condition.

- When **the mouseDown** event is occurring, the *condition* of **the mouseDown** is TRUE, or 1.

Now that you've tried out a few functions in the dry dock of the Message window, you can begin to see how useful they are. In a way, functions are at the core of interactivity—to handle all the changing conditions that *interactive* implies, we need a means of keeping tabs on those changes. That's what functions do.

PROPERTIES MADE PLAIN

PROPERTY:
An aspect or quality of an element that can be checked or set by Lingo.

On to our next important Lingo concept: the **property**. Once again, we're dealing with a potentially misleading word. *Property* in this case means some quality of an object, not something owned or possessed.

Perhaps a better term for property would be *aspect*, because that's what a property is: some aspect of a Director element. When a quality of something isn't necessarily constant—when it can, at least in theory, be altered—that quality is an aspect of the thing itself.

To understand this, hold up one of your hands and take a good look. Your hand has a number of properties:

- Number of fingers

- Color of skin

- Left hand or right hand

- Palm facing toward you or away from you

- Empty or holding something

- Number of rings on your fingers

- Webbed or unwebbed

- Color of nail polish

We could add more to the list, but you get the point: *A property is something that can be different, even if it isn't.* If you've never painted your nails in your life, the hypothetical property `colorOfNailPolish` still has a value (in this case, 0).

We've talked about conditions and status—the way things can change in the Director universe. Well, properties are the things those changes happen to. For example, in our Bingo! movie we changed the forecolor of a sprite. The generalized form of the statement for setting the `foreColor` property of a sprite is

`sprite([whichSprite]).property = [someValue]`

In the earlier command, we set the status of the sprite's `foreColor` property.

We can also check the status without changing it. In the Message window, we might enter something like this:

`put sprite([whichSprite]).property`

More typical would be making a decision based on the status of some property. Throughout Lingo scripts, you will see statements such as this:

`if [someProperty] = [someValue] then [doSomething]`

The value of properties

Why are properties important? By using Lingo to manipulate them, in essence you're getting a second crack at the creation process. Look at it this way: When you created the oval sprite that's the centerpiece of the Bingo! movie, you automatically set many of its properties:

- Size

- Color

- Position on the Stage

- Cast member from which it was derived

- Ink effect used to display it in the frame

Every one of these is a property that can be changed using Lingo. We've already used the property the foreColor of sprite to change the Bingo! oval sprite's color when the button is clicked. This means that properties give us the power of *contextuality*. The *inherent* color of the oval sprite is red and will remain so. But by manipulating properties, we can impart a contextual color to the sprite: It's blue when *this* happens, or periwinkle when *that* happens.

Properties are important even if you don't intend to change them. For example, let's say you're creating an interactive card game in which the sprites of cards appear on the Stage in succession. When a new card is dealt, it needs to overlap the previous one by a certain margin. One good way to achieve this is by writing a handler that determines the location properties of the previous card sprite. Then you can place the new card in a relative position.

Types of properties

Lingo recognizes dozens and dozens of properties, and these can be grouped according to the type of element they concern. It's useful to distinguish between these groups, since you don't want to waste time trying to manipulate a nonexistent property, such as the color of a sound or the volume of an image. But don't place too much emphasis on the somewhat arbitrary divisions. In fact, if there is any area where Director falls short, it's in the specification of property types. You may find that our idea (and probably yours) of what type a property should be doesn't necessarily conform to what is specified in the documentation. To further complicate matters, some properties apply to more than one type. The width property, for example, can be used with both sprites and cast members. Well, sometimes the distinction *is* arbitrary. Just remember that when it counts, the information is there. We may disagree on what is a system property and what is a movie property, but no one disagrees about what is a sound property or a digital video property.

To know or to control?

Properties are the aspects of existence in software. And just as in real life, there are two kinds of aspects: those you can change and those you can't. You can use Lingo to modify some properties and merely to report on others. It helps to know which is which.

Lingo tries to do at least one of two things to a property: *test* it or *set* it. If it can't do either, then as far as Lingo is concerned, the property doesn't exist.

If a property can be tested, that means a script can give you a status report on it. How much RAM does your computer have installed? What time is it? Lingo can find out.

A settable property is one that Lingo can change, if you know how to phrase the request. It can change the loudness of a sound as it plays or the color of a sprite as it displays. It can't, however, add more RAM to your computer or turn back the clock.

Like conditions, some properties are binary (either on or off, TRUE or FALSE) and others return information. You'll need to learn how to interpret this returned information to manipulate it. You've already seen this with the Bingo! exercise; ask Lingo to find a sprite's `foreColor` property, and you won't get the answer "robin's egg blue." Instead, you'll get a number that corresponds to the color's location in the currently active palette. Lingo will be throwing a lot of numbers at you, and they'll mean different things depending on the context.

System properties

Let's take a look at a few of the properties Lingo acknowledges on the system level. Lingo can actually learn quite a bit about both the hardware and software of the computer on which it happens to be running.

- The property the `multiSound` reports whether the host computer is capable of playing stereo or other multichannel sound (most Windows systems need a special card for this). If testing this property reveals that the user's computer cannot play that kind of sound, a lower-quality sound file can be substituted during playback.

- The property the `platform` is another practical property; it determines the general parameters of the operating system on the host computer (16-bit Windows, 32-bit Windows, Macintosh, or Power Mac).

With properties like these, you can essentially tell a Director movie to decide whether it wants to run on any given machine. Just give it a script that tests the host system and quits (or launches an alternate movie) if the optimum playback conditions aren't present.

Movie properties

Movie properties remain in effect as long as a particular movie is running. They can also be used in one movie to determine the performance of a movie that follows it in a playback session. Here's a sampling:

- When playback closes one movie and launches another, the the `updateMovieEnabled` property of the first movie determines whether any changes made by the user are automatically saved when closing.

- The property the `centerStage` establishes whether or not the Stage is centered on the computer screen when the movie is launched (the default is TRUE).

- The property the `stageColor` determines (of all things!) the color of the Stage. The default is 0 (white), but you can change this property at any time with a Lingo script that sets it to another digit corresponding to the active palette (0 to 15 for 4-bit color, 0 to 255 for 8-bit color). This is the equivalent of changing the Stage color via the pull-down paint chip in the Movie Properties dialog box—but the great thing is that you can do it automatically, hundreds or thousands of times within the same movie.

- The property the `fixStageSize`, when set to TRUE, locks the Stage to its current size. This means that when you open subsequent movies, Director will set their Stages to the current Stage size, even if they were created in a larger or smaller size.

- The property the `emulateMultiButtonMouse` determines whether Director looks for different kinds of mouse clicks (which are common with the two-button kind of mouse often used with Windows), or whether it treats all mouse clicks the same (as is appropriate for the Macintosh, which assumes a single-button mouse). It also demonstrates just how unwieldy a Lingo term can become.

Sprite properties

Probably the greatest number of recognized properties are sprite related. That's good, because the more you can manipulate sprites from Lingo, the less time you'll have to spend building frame-by-frame animations. For instance:

- The properties the `width of sprite` and the `height of sprite` control the physical size of the sprite. When you first place a sprite on the Stage, it has the same dimensions as the cast member from which it is derived; you can resize it by resetting these properties either directly on the Stage or through Lingo.

- The property the memberNum of sprite is an especially useful property; it lets you change the source cast member from which a sprite is derived. Switching cast members on a sprite can give you a lot of animation effects—if you want a button that lights up when pressed, you can create two versions (lighted and unlighted) in the Cast and then write an on mouseDown event handler that changes the cast member number of the button sprite when it is clicked.

Cast member properties

Next to sprite properties, cast member properties are probably the most common. That's partially because many of the things that can be done to a sprite can also be done to the cast member it was created from (making changes to cast members also makes changes to the derived sprites displayed on the Stage), and partially because there are so many types of cast members. Here are a couple of properties that relate to cast members in general:

- the number specifies the slot number, within a particular Cast window, of a cast member whose Cast name is known.

- the size specifies the amount of memory required for a specified cast member.

Sound properties

These properties control the overall sound-making capabilities of the movie:

- You've already encountered the property the soundEnabled. It turns the system's sound entirely on or off.

- the soundLevel sets the playback volume level. Using it is equivalent to modifying the volume setting in the Control Panel.

And these sound properties relate to specific sounds:

- the percentPlayed indicates the percentage of the specified Shockwave audio file that has actually played.

- The property the loop of member specifies whether a sound will continue playing (looping) after it reaches the end.

Digital video properties

Since a digital video file can contain both sounds and images, you can use a number of properties to bring those elements in line with the rest of the Director movie in which the digital video is placed:

- the `loop of member` determines whether the digital video is set in a repeating loop.

- the `sound of member` determines whether a digital video's sound is enabled. The default is TRUE, which is enabled.

- the `mostRecentCuePoint` indicates the number of the cue point most recently passed. This property is particularly useful for synchronizing animation to video.

Networking properties

With the advent of Shockwave, Director needed to expand beyond the confines of the host computer and into the twin realms of the Internet and intranets. Here are a few pertinent properties you'll find in Lingo:

- the `URL of member` is a settable property and therefore a means of indicating the URL (universal resource locator) of a Shockwave audio (SWA) cast member. With it, it's possible not to name a cast member, but simply to state the address at which it can be found.

- the `preLoadTime of member` is another settable property pertaining to Shockwave audio cast members. Use it to set how many seconds of audio are loaded into the movie's RAM before the sound begins to play.

Other property types

We have only begun to touch on the types of properties in Director. Among the various cast member types are properties specific to text, fields, bitmaps, and other objects, including menu properties, frame properties, and window properties. The properties we've discussed give you a general idea of what's available within Director. Almost anything you can think of as a possible property exists in one form or another. I recommend opening up *A Lingo Lexicon* (Appendix C) every once in a while and just browsing. You'll be surprised at how many times you'll see something there and say, "I didn't know I could do that!"

The blur-blend of properties and functions

Thus far, you may have detected a certain fuzziness in the distinction between properties and functions. It's a distinction that blurs for many a Lingo-head. If both properties and functions can be said to return a result, then what's the difference?

Here's the short, blunt response: A function is an answer, and a property is a result of existence. Consider, for example, that a clock on the wall has the function of telling you the time. It can also have the properties of being decorative, of making a tick-tock noise, and of covering up that crack in the plaster, but those are probably not the reasons you picked it up at the store.

As a rule of thumb, consider a property something that just *is*, and a function something that is *done*; don't worry too much about the distinction.

When properties function as functions

Not to complicate matters, but it's worth pointing out that you can sometimes "functionalize" a property—that is, you can extract information from a property as if it were a function. To demonstrate this, let's open Bingo! and make some modifications to the script that changes the color of the oval sprite. This time we are going to check the value of a property and use the value in an `if...then` statement. And we are going to do so without using a function to retrieve the value.

1. *In the Bingo! movie, click the Tool Palette's Field button and place a blank text box on the Stage, to the right of the oval.*

This text box should automatically occupy the main Cast's slot 5. If it doesn't, move it there. There's no need to place any text in it, since you'll be using Lingo to enter and update its contents.

2. *In the Cast, name this field* ColorResult.

3. ***Double-click to open the gadzooks handler movie script. If you are running Windows, change the script to read as follows:***

```
on gadzooks
  sprite(2).foreColor = random(5)
  if sprite(2).foreColor = 1 then member(5).text = "Light blue"
  if sprite(2).foreColor = 2 then member(5).text = "Magenta"
  if sprite(2).foreColor = 3 then member(5).text = "Dark blue"
  if sprite(2).foreColor = 4 then member(5).text = "Yellow"
  if sprite(2).foreColor = 5 then member(5).text = "Lime Green"
  updateStage
end
```

If you are working on a Macintosh, change the script to read as follows:

```
on gadzooks
  sprite(2).foreColor = random(5)
  if sprite(2).foreColor = 1 then member(5).text = "Yellow 1"
  if sprite(2).foreColor = 2 then member(5).text = "Yellow 2"
  if sprite(2).foreColor = 3 then member(5).text = "Yellow 3"
  if sprite(2).foreColor = 4 then member(5).text = "Yellow 4"
  if sprite(2).foreColor = 5 then member(5).text = "Yellow 5"
  updateStage
end
```

Director ignores the blank lines in the revised handler script.

Notice that the beep line is eliminated (it *does* get annoying, doesn't it?), and that the number following random has been changed from 255 to 5. This limits the randomization to a choice of five colors.

Since only five status possibilities are available for the color of the oval sprite (the foreColor), we can write an if...then statement for each. On the Windows System palette, the colors 1 through 5 are all different colors, so we list a color for each possible number. On the Macintosh System palette, colors 1 through 5 are various shades of yellow, so we know that the random choice will always be one of these.

TEXT STRING:
A grouping of text (words and spaces) that can be manipulated with Lingo.

As we did long ago in Chapter 4, we're again using the text property to set the contents of the text field. Back in Chapter 4 we didn't even know what a property was. Now we do, and we even know that text is a text cast member property. What exactly are we placing in the text field? It's known as a **text string**, or sometimes just a string. The text string is usually whatever's included within the quotation marks (it can include numbers and special characters as well as text).

4. Close the Script window and run the movie.

Now, whenever you click the Bingo! button, the sprite of ColorResult should update to indicate the current color of the oval.

THE COLOR OF BINGO:
The two parts of the script work together to choose a random color, apply that color to a sprite, and then let the user know the name of the color.

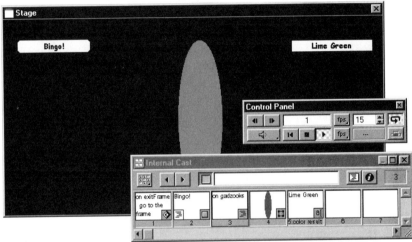

We've likened functions to probes or scanners, yet it's interesting to note that here we're manipulating a property (the foreColor) without first launching a function to get its current condition. That's because when a property can be quantified, Director usually keeps track of that quantification in the background—and if you know the form of the quantification, you can invoke that information without a specific function. In this case, we know that all colors have numbers assigned to them based on their locations in the loaded palette, so we can use integers to refer to the colors.

You can try this for yourself in the Message window:

1. Rewind the Bingo! movie and then open the Message window.

2. Type the following, pressing Enter (Windows) or Return (Macintosh) at the end of each line:

```
put sprite (2).foreColor
put sprite (2).right
put sprite (2).memberNum
put the platform
```

Your results should be pretty similar to the following (although I'd be surprised if they were identical):

PUT-PUTTING:

Using the put command in the Message window.

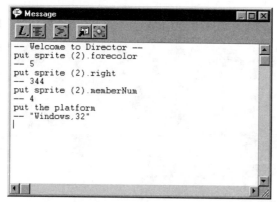

```
-- Welcome to Director --
put sprite (2).forecolor
-- 5
put sprite (2).right
-- 344
put sprite (2).memberNum
-- 4
put the platform
-- "Windows,32"
```

In each of these cases, the number that is returned reflects a different form of quantification:

- The 5 corresponds to the current color of the oval, as mapped on the 256-unit, 8-bit active palette (System-Win or System-Mac). The number you get depends on the tone you originally chose when creating the cast member. In this case, the highest possible number is 255, a solid black.

- The 344 is a count of the number of pixels between the *right* edge of the widest point of the sprite and the *left* edge of the screen. Even though the property concerns the right edge, the measurement is made from the left of the Stage, because all Stage coordinates are expressed as pixel counts out and down from the upper-left corner (which is 0,0). In this case, the highest possible number is the pixel width of the Stage (640 for my version of Bingo!).

- The 4 is the cast slot number of the cast member from which the sprite was derived. If we moved the cast member within the Cast, this value would change (Director would automatically update the link between the cast member and sprite). In this case, the highest possible value returned would be 32,000, the maximum number of cast member slots available for a Cast in Director.

- The string "`Windows,32`" or "`Macintosh,PowerPC`" indicates the platform on which the movie is running. Those are the only two possible values (though that may change in the future).

Remember that although all properties can be *tested* in Lingo (that is, their current values can be retrieved), not all can be *set* (that is, not all have values that can be changed). Changing the `forecolor` sprite property will change the color, but attempting to change the `platform` system property will not change your Windows machine into a Macintosh (wouldn't that be nice!). Instead, you'll get an error message like this one:

The *Lingo Lexicon* (Appendix C) has entries for all official properties and indicates which properties can be set as well as tested.

While we're thinking about the `the platform` property, let's look at a way to use it to combine the two scripts we used before (one for Windows and one for the Macintosh):

```
on gadzooks
  sprite(2).foreColor = random(5)

  if the platform contains "Windows" then
    if sprite(2).foreColor = 1 then member(5).text = "Light blue"
    if sprite(2).foreColor = 2 then member(5).text = "Magenta"
    if sprite(2).foreColor = 3 then member(5).text = "Dark blue"
    if sprite(2).foreColor = 4 then member(5).text = "Yellow"
    if sprite(2).foreColor = 5 then member(5).text = "Lime Green"

  else
    if sprite(2).foreColor = 1 then member(5).text = "Yellow 1"
    if sprite(2).foreColor = 2 then member(5).text = "Yellow 2"
```

```
      if sprite(2).foreColor = 3 then member(5).text = "Yellow 3"
      if sprite(2).foreColor = 4 then member(5).text = "Yellow 4"
      if sprite(2).foreColor = 5 then member(5).text = "Yellow 5"
   end if
   updateStage
end
```

Here we're checking to see if the string returned by the platform contains "Windows". If it does, the code designed for Windows machines is executed. If it doesn't, the code for a Macintosh machine is executed. The keyword contains is actually an operator, something like plus (+) or minus (−), except contains is designed for strings rather than numbers.

VARIABLES: THE DATA DEPOSITORIES

VARIABLE:

A container for data generated by Lingo, existing within the context of the runtime of the Director movie.

I've saved one of the most powerful programming concepts for last: the **variable**. A variable is an item that exists not in the Cast, the Score, or any other window, but in Director's equivalent of virtual reality: RAM itself. Unlike a property, which is data that reflects something else, a variable is a quantification that has its own independent existence. The data a variable contains is known as its **value**, and that value can change throughout the running of the movie. In a sense, variables are locations that have no location, data storehouses that exist only in Lingospace—and even then they exist only when the movie is running. The values disappear whenever they're no longer needed, or when the movie stops and RAM is flushed.

What's the use of such an ephemeral entity? You can employ variables as depositories and processing centers for data created while the end user runs the movie you're creating: test scores, user preferences, system characteristics, and the like. How many times has the user tried to get the right answer? Keep track in a variable. How far have you moved a sprite across the Stage? Keep track in a variable. Once you start writing complex Lingo scripts, you'll find yourself storing almost everything that has a value in a variable.

Creating variables

To get a feel for variables, let's go back to the Message window. Remember that the Message window can be used not only to track the running of

Lingo in a movie, but also as a dry-run area in which we can test code before actually placing it in a movie.

1. **With the Bingo! movie open but not running, open the Message window. Click the Trace icon to enable this function.**

2. **On a fresh line, type:**

Nanette = 10

3. **Press Enter (Windows) or Return (Macintosh). Your Message window should look something like this:**

HERE, HOLD THIS:
You can create a variable and put it to work at the same time by naming it and giving it a value to contain.

```
-- Welcome to Director --
Nanette = 10
== Movie: C:\Demystified 7\New Demystified
projects\myBingo.dir Frame: 1 Script: (member
26320 of castLib 123) Handler:
--> Nanette = 10
== Nanette = 10
```

Depending on whether you've run the movie, opened a new movie, or whatever, Director may feel compelled to give out some additional information about the movie. We're interested in only two of the lines: the one beginning with --> and the one beginning with ==. For -->, read "this is the command we are executing." For ==, read "this is what happened." Since what was executed and what happened are the same, the lines look the same. We'll see the difference between them pretty quickly, though.

What we've done is create a variable named Nanette and assigned it a value. That's all it takes—no formal declaration or fancy parameter elaborations like what many programming languages require. If you assign a value to a name that's unfamiliar to Lingo, it assumes that you're creating a new variable.

You can give a variable any one-word name you like—including a name already used by another Lingo element. Not that you'd want to, but it's possible to write a handler that uses both a custom handler called beep and the official command beep. In such a case, Director won't get confused, but you might. It's best to stick to unique names, preferably those that have some bearing on the task at hand (I'm using whimsical names here to illustrate the customizability of variables).

4. **On a fresh line of the Message window, type** Nanette = 10 + 1 **and then press Enter (Windows) or Return (Macintosh).**

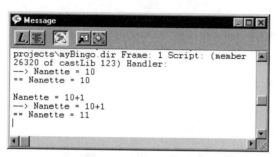

```
projects\myBingo.dir Frame: 1 Script: (member
26320 of castLib 123) Handler:
--> Nanette = 10
== Nanette = 10

Nanette = 10+1
--> Nanette = 10+1
== Nanette = 11
```

Now there are two lines that are slightly different, and you can see the difference between the command being executed and the "what happened." The "what happened" is that the value of Nanette is shown as 11.

The value we assigned to the variable Nanette is a *whole number*, or *integer*. But variables can also store a myriad of other types of values. In fact, any type of value that Director understands can be stored in a variable. Director keeps track of the variable's value and the type of the value. Let's look at some other types.

5. **In the Message window, type the following lines (press Enter or Return after each):**

```
myString = "Shephard"
myColor = sprite(2).Color
myPoint = sprite(2).loc
myRect = sprite(2).rect
```

Your Message window should look similar to this:

SO MANY TYPES, SO LITTLE TIME
Director can store values of any type that it recognizes in a variable.

```
myString = "Sheppard"
--> myString = "Sheppard"
== myString = "Sheppard"

myColor = sprite (2). Color
--> myColor = sprite (2). Color
== myColor = paletteIndex( 5 )

myPoint = sprite (2). loc
--> myPoint = sprite (2). loc
== myPoint = point(275, 35)

myRect = sprite (2). rect
--> myRect = sprite (2). rect
== myRect = rect(275, 35, 344, 275)
```

We've created four new variables and assigned them four new (to us) value types. The variable myString is assigned a value of type string. The color system property is used to assign a value of type color to myColor, the foreground color of the sprite. The loc (short for *location*) sprite property is used to assign a value of type point to myPoint. The rect property is used to assign a rect (short for rectangle) value to myRect.

Note that Director's idea of a variable's type is a little different than just described. It is actually possible to check a variable's (or object's) type in Director, and if you do, you will see types given as **#string**, **#point**, and so on. The pound sign (#) is used to specify symbols in Director. To see the actual type of an object, use the **ilk** function. For example, in the Message window enter the command **put ilk(myPoint)**, and you will get the return line **== myPoint = #point.**

So far, we've been using the equal operator (=) to assign a value to a variable. Some programmers think that using the optional set command makes statements more readable. For example, we could write this:

```
set Nanette = 11
```

An older style, but still in use, uses the to keyword instead of the equal operator. If you use to, then the set command is no longer optional:

```
set Nanette to 11
```

An even older style used the form put...into, as in

```
put 11 into Nanette
```

Using the put command to assign values to variables is now officially discouraged, although it still seems to work.

Using variables

Variables wouldn't be of much use if we could only put things into them and never get that value back out again. Actually, you generally don't need to get the value out again; that is, you don't get the value and then use the value. Instead, you just use the variable; anywhere you might want the value, you can place the variable instead.

In the Message window, type these lines, pressing Enter (Windows) or Return (Macintosh) after each one:

```
Mike = Nanette * 253.76
Mel = Nanette - Mike
Shephard = integer(Mel)
```

In each case, a result will be returned:

TAG-TEAM TALLYING:
You can use variables to perform calculations in the Message window.

```
Message
Mike = Nanette * 253.76
--> Mike = Nanette * 253.76
== Mike = 2791.3600

Mel = Nanette - Mike
--> Mel = Nanette - Mike
== Mel = -2780.3600

Shepard = integer (Mel)
--> Shepard = integer (Mel)
== Shepard = -2780
```

The Mike variable's initial value is presented as a multiplication of Nanette times the decimal number 253.76 (using the arithmetical operator *). Since Nanette is currently equivalent to 11, the resulting value is 2791.36. That value is then used to create yet another variable (Mel) by subtracting it from the first value, resulting in the negative number –2780.36. Finally, we massage the numbers just a bit by dumping them into yet another variable (Shephard); this one uses the integer function, which rounds off a decimal value to the nearest whole number (–2780).

TIP

The fact that Director keeps track of value types has advantages and disadvantages. It certainly makes creating variables (and assigning values) easy, but it also can lead to bugs that are difficult to track down. Director doesn't care if you assign a string to a variable that previously contained an integer. But what happens if you then multiply that variable by another integer? The result will probably not be what you expect or want. The upshot is that you need to keep track of your variable types and use them only for their intended purposes. Many programmers use identifying letters for their variables; for instance, they write **intMike** to identify an integer variable and **strMike** to identify a string.

Kinds of variables

Lingo has two kinds of variables. A **local variable** exists only in the context of the handler that uses it. The local variable contains no value before the handler is called, and it returns to oblivion after the handler is executed. A **global variable** can be kept in memory as long as the movie is running; it contains information that can be accessed by any number of handlers and even by several scripts at once.

Why not just have global variables? Why not have all variables accessible from everywhere? One of the main reasons has to do with large projects. As soon as you have more than a dozen or so handlers, you can easily lose track of what variables are being used. Remember that you may not be the only programmer working on a project. By using local variables within handlers, you know that only your handler is using them and that they won't conflict with variables of the same name in someone else's handler.

Local variables in action

Thus far we've seen variables at work only in the petri dish of the Message window. The next step is to allow them a useful task in a practical context, so let's create a single-frame movie that uses local variables to convert any given number into a Fahrenheit or centigrade temperature reading.

1. *Open the movie ConvTemp.dir in the Tutorials folder on the CD.*

2. *Double-click the picon of cast member 1 to open the Movie Script window.*

3. *After the end of the* on startMovie *handler, enter a blank line and the following two new handlers:*

```
on convertFahr
  Var1 = member("EnterTemp").text
  Var2 = Var1 -32
  member("TempDone").text = string(Var2 * 0.5555556)
end

on convertCent
  Var1 = member("EnterTemp").text
  Var2 = Var1 * 1.8
  member("TempDone").text = string(Var2 + 32)
end
```

You've just written two custom handlers: one named `convertFahr` and the other `convertCent`. Each uses two variables (`Var1` and `Var2`) to extract the entered number (the `text of member "EnterTemp"`) and then to perform the necessary calculations.

The first handler subtracts 32 from `Var1` and then places the result in `Var2`, which is in turn multiplied by a decimalized fraction once again, with the `*` operator. The ultimate result is converted to a string using the `string` function and is placed not into a third variable (although that's an option) but instead piped directly into the cast member TempDone.

The second handler performs the same value extraction and insertion, but it performs different calculations in the interim. Notice that we can use the same variable names without conflict; we're dealing with local variables here, and they're disposed of as soon as the handler is executed.

4. Close the Script window and run the movie.

I've already written `on mouseUp` scripts for both buttons, each triggering the appropriate new calculation handler. If you get an error message when clicking either button, check to see if the names you've given the handlers match those in the button scripts.

A MATTER OF DEGREES: Use local variables to perform temperature calculations.

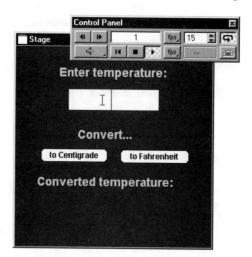

5. At the insertion point, enter 32.

6. Click the To Centigrade button.

The result, displayed in the lower part of the Stage, should be 0. Now try the other button:

7. In the Enter Temperature field, enter 37.

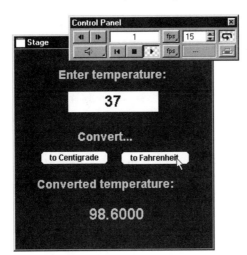

8. Click the To Fahrenheit button.

The answer should be the Fahrenheit reading for normal body temperature: 98.6.

Troubleshooting local variables

Keeping track of the work that variables carry out can be tricky, since the work is done without visible manifestation. If you need to troubleshoot a variable or a sequence of variables, use the Message window with the Trace option enabled. As each variable is declared and occupied, the window displays the current contents as an equation. If you're getting incorrect results from your variables, put them through their paces in a running movie and then scroll back through the traced entries in the Message window and scrutinize them.

TRACE ELEMENTS:
You can troubleshoot scripting with the Trace option enabled.

```
mouseUp
--> convertCent
== Script: (member 1 of castLib 1) Handler:
convertCent
--> Var1 = member("EnterTemp").text
== Var1 = "37"
--> Var2 = Var1 * 1.8
== Var2 = 66.6000
--> member("TempDone").text = string(Var2 + 32)
--> end
== Script: (member 7 of castLib 1) Handler:
mouseUp
.== Script: (member 3 of castLib 1) Handler:
exitFrame
```

Global variables

The problem with local variables is that they disappear once the context in which they were created disappears. Sometimes you need data to persist, however. For example, you might want to get the name of your end user early on in your production and then use it to personalize feedback thereafter. The best solution to such needs is the global variable, which can be accessed and changed by just about any script.

GLOBAL VARIABLE:
A variable designed to be accessible by Lingo in more than one script.

To make a variable global, just declare it as such with the `global` keyword. Whenever you want to invoke that global variable, you'll need to reprise the keyword statement; otherwise, Director assumes you're working with a local variable that happens to have the same name as a global one. The syntax of a typical script looks like this:

```
on mouseUp
    global gUserName
    put gUserName into field "Feedback"
    go to frame "New Game"
end mouseUp
```

Global variables are often indicated by names that begin with g (as in gUserName).

You'll notice that the global variable begins with a lowercase g. This isn't strictly necessary (globals can be named anything, so long as it's a single word) but many Lingo scripters use this convention so they can discern at a glance which variables are global.

We can't demonstrate global variables in the Message window because it doesn't interpret multiline scripting. So let's look at a movie designed to put the power of globals to work:

1. *Open (but do not run) the movie Globals.dir in the Tutorials folder.*

There's a text field on the Stage, where you're prompted to enter your first name. This is the text we're going to capture and place in a global variable. Now take a look at the script behind the Done button.

2. *Open the Script window of the button cast member Done.*

You'll find not one but three globals in the script:

```
on mouseUp
  global gName
  gName = member("Name").text
  global gResult
  gResult = "Hello," && gName & "!"
  global gNameNumber
  gNameNumber = the number of chars in gName
  go to the frame +1
end
```

This script does a few things. First it creates a global variable called gName, which contains whatever's entered in the Name field. Then it adds a few more words to that variable, using special symbols that place text before and after the user entry (this process is called **concatenation**). The completed string of text is then placed in another global variable (gResult). That done, the characters in gName are counted (using the function the number of chars), and the result is placed in yet another global variable (gNameNumber). Finally, the command go to sends the playback head to the following frame.

Remember that a global declaration is necessary in every handler where you use a global variable. Globals don't, however, need to be placed in the same location in the script (as they were here in the Done button script). Equally effective would be to place them at the start of a script, as in the following:

```
on mouseUp
  global gName, gResult, gNameNumber
  gName = member("Name").text
  gResult = "Hello," && gName & "!"
  gNameNumber = the number of chars in gName
  go to the frame +1
end
```

3. Run the movie. Enter your first name and then click the Done button.

GOING GLOBAL:
Text placed in this field will also be placed in a global variable.

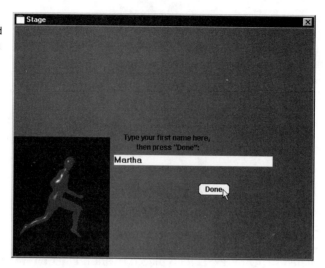

Two things happen: First, your name is displayed in a colorful welcoming statement, and second, an important statistic is displayed. Both of these events make use of the global variables we created.

Let's look under the hood again.

4. **Stop the movie and double-click frame 3 of the behavior channel.**

The script reads:

```
on prepareFrame
  global gResult
  member("Result").text = gResult
end
```

The most important thing to note is that even though the global variable isn't changed in this script, it's still declared with the global keyword. Note also that we used a prepareFrame handler for this script. Since the prepareFrame event occurs before any spite is drawn, we can be sure that the correct text is in the field when the field is displayed.

In any handler where a global variable is used, the variable must first be declared with a **global** statement. This is true even when the value of the variable isn't being modified.

5. Open the behavior script of frame 5.

Here we have another concatenation script employing our two other global variables:

```
on exitFrame
  global gName, gNameNumber
  member("Name Count").text = "Did you know that you have" && ¬
  gNameNumber && "letters in your name," && gName & "?"
end
```

A BANG-UP WELCOME:
The global variable transfers text to this field later in the Director movie.

Using globals in the background

Global variables are more than storehouses for user input. They're also good for keeping track of conditions entirely in the background, as you can see for yourself:

1. Run and use the Globals.dir movie again.

2. Click the New Name button twice, to enter a total of three names.

The movie will interrupt you on the third try, with an indignant admonition.

COUNTING ON YOU:
A background global variable keeps track of how many times a button is clicked during a session.

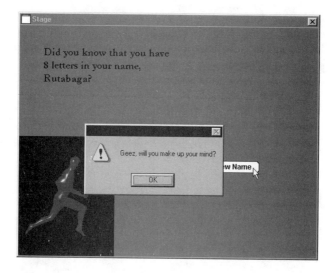

This alert message is the product of a global variable called gTries. You'll find it in the startMovie script in the first cast slot, and in the button script for New Name, which reads:

```
on mouseUp
  global gTries
  gTries = gTries + 1
  member("Name").text = EMPTY
  if gTries = 3 then
    alert "Geez, will you make up your mind?"
    set gTries = 1
  end if
  go "input"
end
```

CUSTOM FUNCTIONS AND PARAMETERS

One final twist, to round out our understanding of the powers of scripting: Many official functions are hard-coded into Lingo, and you can create custom functions when the need arises. If you write a handler that does nothing but retrieve a particular kind of data when called, that handler can be said to be a function as well.

Try it for yourself. Let's say you find yourself frequently calculating the cubic volume of spaces. You know the formula is width times length times height, but there's no Lingo volume function to crunch the numbers for you. So you roll your own.

1. ***Click an unused Cast slot and open the Script window. It doesn't matter what movie you are working in, but make sure that you are opening a movie script, not a Score or parent script. Write a handler that reads***

```
on calcVolume iwidth, ilength, iheight
  return iwidth * ilength * iheight
end
```

You've just created a handler called calc.volume and told it exactly what to do. When invoked by other Lingo, this handler responds with a calculation of width times length times height. The keyword return is what makes it work as a function, since it sends back (returns) an answer.

But volume needs to know not just what it's supposed to do; it needs to be supplied with raw materials—in this case, the numbers to crunch. That's what those words right after the handler name are all about. They're the designated placeholders for the arguments that will be provided when this function is used. They're called **parameters** because they provide the basic shape of the calculation to be performed. For every argument used, a parameter has to be provided.

2. ***Open the Message window and enter the following:***

```
myBox = calcVolume (10,40,225)
```

3. ***Press Enter (Windows) or Return (Macintosh).***

There should be no feedback in the Message window (unless Trace is turned on). But you've done three things: You've called your custom function, provided it with arguments (the raw data) to match its parameters, and told it to report the result by dumping it into a local variable called myBox.

4. ***In the Message window, enter:***

```
put myBox
```

The window should return the result: -- 90000

The potential of custom functions is pretty impressive. As you progress, you'll find plenty of occasions when you need to massage certain types of data (the parameters) in certain ways (the return formula).

> Don't confuse the keyword **return** with the constant **RETURN**. The former behaves in the way just shown, while the latter refers to the Enter (Windows) or Return (Macintosh) key on the keyboard. Lingo won't confuse the two no matter how you capitalize them, but you might, and that's a good reason to use consistent capitalization when writing scripts.

You may be wondering why we gave elements in the calcVolume handler the names we did (including the handler name). Why not these, instead?

```
on Volume width, length, height
  return width * length * height
end
```

Well, it turns out that volume, width, length, and height are all used by Lingo. In this case, it wouldn't matter; the handler would work just fine. But it's not a good idea to take chances like that. So I added i, for integer, to each variable name (p for parameter would be useful, too). One easy way to tell whether a word already has a meaning in Lingo is by its text color in the Script window. You've probably already noticed that the words in your scripts are of different colors. To see how the colors are set up, check out the Script Window Preferences dialog box (from the File menu, choose Preferences and then Script).

THE COLOR OF KEYWORDS: The Script window can show keywords in a color different than that of other text.

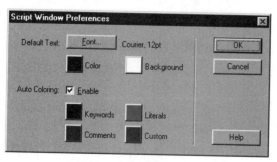

THE MEGO TEST REVISITED

Now let's take another look at that techno-jargony paragraph cited at the beginning of this chapter. If it didn't make sense before, it should now (at least with a little paraphrasing to underscore the concepts in this chapter):

> *Handlers* [the basic unit of scripts] *can initiate an action* [do stuff] *or return a result* [get info]. *You can write handlers that take arguments* [require additional info to work] *or parameters* [the holders for that additional info] *and either perform some action based on the parameters* [do stuff], *or return a result based on a calculation or expression that uses the parameters* [get info]. *Handlers that return a result are sometimes called function handlers, or just functions.*

Simple once you get the hang of it, isn't it?

POINTS TO REMEMBER

We've covered a lot of ground in this chapter, but here are the most important things to remember:

- **Commands** are a class of Lingo elements that imply an action to be taken. They can be self-contained or require additional information (arguments).

- **Keywords** are the nouns of Lingo; they are concrete elements.

- **Handlers** are executed when an event occurs, but you can write handlers for custom events (like gadzooks in Bingo!) and then write other scripts that trigger those handlers.

- **Prefab Lingo** is available in the Script window, with elements grouped both alphabetically and by type of use.

- A **function** is a sort of information-retrieval device that returns a report on the current status of something. You can use off-the-shelf Lingo functions or create your own.

- **Arguments** are the additional data that a Lingo element needs to operate. For instance, the command add needs the arguments of at least two numbers to work. If you build a custom function you need to provide **parameters**, placeholders for the arguments that will be provided.

- A **property** is an aspect of a Director element. It's something that can (in theory) be changed, even if it isn't. Some properties you can **set** using Lingo; other properties you can only **test**.

- **Variables** are RAM-based storehouses for data. There are two types: **local variables** (which exist only in a single handler) and **global variables** (which can be shared by handlers throughout your movie).

- Global variables must always be **declared** with the global keyword before they are used.

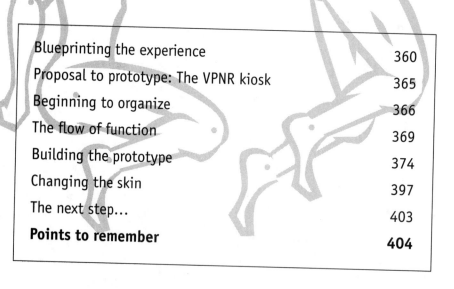

CHAPTER 10

BUILDING THE
INTERACTIVE MOVIE

THIS CHAPTER COMBINES BOTH BIG-PICTURE ISSUES AND ROLL-UP-YOUR-sleeves exercises, as we review the thinking and organization that go into the process of multimedia planning and production.

We'll begin by considering the general aesthetic and practical issues that should be tackled even before Director is launched. Then we'll fire up the application and start on the basics of building a prototype to meet our considerations. In the process, you might learn a thing or two about programming for consistency and clarity and perhaps acquire some habits that'll save you hassles further down the line.

BLUEPRINTING THE EXPERIENCE

Director movies are software, and software is a tool; its quality is linked to its utility. Yet many people undertake projects with only a fuzzy notion of the project's purpose. Such vagueness is further complicated by the temptation to hide it with the bells and whistles of multimedia, compensating for poor planning and inadequate content by smothering the project with cool but irrelevant graphics, extraneous sounds, and other gewgaws. These tactics may have worked in the early days of multimedia when such elements had the sheer force of novelty, but as users grow accustomed to interactivity, their impatience with gimmicks grows as well.

Whether your goals are direct and utilitarian or artistic and abstract, they're still goals—and the success of your multimedia work will be judged by how well those goals are met. So before you start creating the software, take time to visualize the *experience* you want to create. When you have a clear vision, the structure, organization, and technical requirements will follow.

Consider the context

Consider the context in which the end product will exist. Ask yourself these questions:

Who's the typical user?

The clearer your picture of the intended audience, the better. But all too often, having such a picture breeds stereotypic approaches: marble-and-pinstripe styles for a business presentation, primary colors and loud noises for children's software, and so on. A sense of the typical user gives you insight into users' expectations—some of which you may want *not* to meet.

Conversely, when there *is* no typical profile, you want to stay away from anything that suggests otherwise. A museum exhibition, for example, might need to strike a note of maximum accessibility, with a tone, content, and interface that are not too simplistic for adults nor too complicated for kids. Making something neutral without rendering it boring is one of the challenges of multimedia design.

Do you have to earn attention?

With interactivity, there's an economy at work—the economy of attention. Attention is like money: People will pay it, but only if you earn it. The question is, how hard does your project need to work to get and keep the attention of its intended audience?

An interactive kiosk in a trade show exhibit may need a considerable amount of flash, since it competes with a multitude of other presentations for the interest of the trade show attendee. Pulling out all stops for visual and sonic impact probably makes good sense. If your movie is a Shockwave tidbit at a Web site, it might be nothing but flash—something to attract the eye and induce users to click it.

But what if your project is a reference CD, say a database of replacement parts? You don't need to seduce users into paying attention—their need to know already motivates them to do that. The fancy animations and sound effects that worked in the trade show kiosk might be inappropriate here, especially if the CD is accessed several times a day. Even the most impressive fripperies can get very old, very quickly—and if they slow down the information-retrieval process, they'll be resented. Similarly, if your Shockwave movie slows a Web page to a crawl, those Web surfers will be unlikely to come back for a second look.

The trick is to inject entertainment value where it's most needed and to aim for clarity and consistency elsewhere. If you're creating a foreign language tutorial, for instance, you might want to use multimedia tricks to make tasks like vocabulary drills less tedious. But elsewhere, excessive animation and special effects could detract from the subject.

What's the frequency of use?

Is the interaction a one-shot deal, a matter of multiple exposure, or an ongoing thing? If you're using multimedia to make a business proposal, you may intend it to run exactly once. If you produce a promotional piece, you may expect most recipients to review it a time or two. A CD designed to help cram for the SATs may be used intensively for a month or so but rarely afterward.

The anticipated frequency of use can help dictate the intensity of communication and the style you use to convey it. With the hypothetical one-shot business presentation, you might want to make sure the salient points are repeated several times, especially at the conclusion. The interactive brochure might not need to be so insistent, but it's a good idea to give the user the option of printing an information sheet for future reference (you can't expect users to boot up your movie just to get your phone number). The SAT trainer project might benefit from a stepped structure, with progressive levels of drill and review as the test date approaches.

How deep is the content?

No, not deep in the sense of being serious or profound, but how many nested levels and layers and directories and so forth will your project require? It's an important consideration, for two reasons:

- **Convenience.** When there are dozens of levels and a myriad of screens to plow through, it's usually appropriate to offer at least a few shortcuts, such as a Skip Animation button or a Go Recent command (to jump to locations accessed previously in the session). One pet peeve of mine is browsing through screens on one level, only to find that the only way to return to the previous level is to click back through the screens, retracing my steps exactly. An Up One Level or Return to Main button is welcome in such cases. Another interface nicety is navigational markers that change during the session, letting you know when you've already been to one section or another.

- **Confusion.** The more the levels multiply, the easier it is for users to lose a sense of their current location in the matrix of data. The risk isn't really one of users getting lost so much as it is of losing their interest. If all levels look alike, there's little sense of progression, surprise, or exploration. Usually it's a good idea to standardize the important interface elements and then introduce some stylistic variations, just enough to differentiate each level as new territory.

How much customization is needed?

Can your movie perform in the same way for all users, or is a degree of customization required? Perhaps you want to incorporate references to the user's name in various screens or modify sequences based on the user's age level. In such cases, you need to build in the customizing capability from the very beginning.

Incorporating such features is a two-step process. First you need to build the mechanisms that process the personalization, such as the Lingo script that interprets the name and stores it as a variable. Then you have to design your movie to accommodate that information, with screens that have blank text fields for name placement and so forth.

Is anything produced from use?

Most movies have an intangible end product, be it entertainment, education, or enlightenment. But some also have a tangible one: A kiosk might prompt users to register for a contest and then write their responses to a text file for use in a mailing list database. Or a teaching drill game might offer a printout of all of the player's wrong answers for further study.

You want to decide on such elements as early in the design process as possible, because they introduce new variables that'll require extra time for streamlining and debugging.

The usage profile

It's usually a good idea not only to answer the preceding questions, but to commit those answers to writing. Such a document, commonly called a **usage profile**, serves as a charter of sorts for the ensuing project. This profile is especially important when other people are involved, whether they are supervisors, clients, collaborators, or subcontractors—you can't count on everyone to automatically share your vision of the project.

A usage profile can and should be revised when the need arises; it's an important tool for keeping production on track by keeping expectations realistic. Here's a sample profile (modified from an actual project) that's brief and to the point. In this case, I've cited a movie that has a Shockwave file as its final disposition, but the principles apply to just about every type of production.

Usage profile: See-U-Later Calculator

Product configuration: Shockwave movie, possible second use as downloadable projector file.

Project goal: To underscore the extreme reliability of our client's computer peripheral products by letting end users estimate how many more years of trouble-free service they can expect. The secondary goal is to promote quality, by estimating the current resale value of the product line (going back three years).

Creative considerations: This movie should look and feel more like an application than an animation. However, its projected placement on a number of "cool" sites means that it should have a certain amount of visual appeal. Suggest an interface within the interface of a Web browser, with a metallic 3D look or another factor that says "click me!"

Technical considerations: Final version for placement in HTML should be no larger than 65K. Color palette should cause no surprises in browsers on either Windows or Macintosh systems. No soundtrack, but (if space permits) a few blips and bleeps might underscore the calculator concept.

Since See-U-Later calculations are based on the current market value of used peripherals, the Shockwave movie should draw from an external data file (in HTML or text format, but online). That way, we can keep the results valid by updating the data rather than reengineering the movie itself.

Target audience: We're targeting MIS managers and the tech-savvy executives of corporations and service organizations. We're giving them a tool to generate statistics that support their decision to use the client's products, so the results need to invoke positive budgeting buzzwords such as "Return on investment" and "Persistence of value rate."

Frequency of use: We expect most of the target audience to use it twice: once when they encounter it for the first time (at which point they're motivated by novelty value) and again when they realize an actual need for the data (such as when they're preparing a report for their superiors). Because of this, ease of use is important; the entire help screen should consist of three, one-sentence instructions.

Attention factor: This will be supported by a banner ad campaign that draws people to the site, so the eye-catching factor is distributed elsewhere. However, the team for that project has suggested that some of the Lingo for this application might be adaptable to Shockwave banners. This is optional, but if anything seems portable, let them know.

Customization: No particular customization is necessary, although the result fields should be large enough for the user to easily cut and paste the results into a word processing program or spreadsheet.

Proposal to prototype:
The VPNR kiosk

Now that we've established the conceptual parameters of undertaking an interactive project, let's get down to where the rubber meets the road. For the rest of this chapter, we're going to build a Director production that incorporates many of the aspects you'll typically find in professional projects. We'll take it through only the first rough prototype here, but you'll be using the concepts developed in this chapter in later chapters and in your own projects.

We're going to build an interactive kiosk for a hypothetical real estate company called Very Pleasant Neighbor Realtors. Let's sketch out a quick usage profile:

Project configuration: Freestanding kiosk in local mall.

Project goal: To enlighten passers-by as to the current property listings of Very Pleasant Neighbor Realty (VPNR).

Creative considerations: Must be eye catching yet confidence inspiring. The goal is not only to sell homes, but to attract new listings and build name recognition for VPNR.

Technical considerations: Kiosk should be powered by a standard Pentium processor in a high-traffic enclosure. Mouse will be a centrally mounted trackball. There will be no printout capability or Web link.

Target audience: Current and potential homeowners in the age range 21 to 54. Keep in mind that most are in the mall to run errands or shop recreationally.

Frequency of use: We want to discourage repeat visits. If people aren't serious about searching for a property, we don't want them tying up the kiosk. If they are serious, they should be hooking up with a broker as soon as possible.

Attention factor: We're talking a mall here! Can't be so flashy (or noisy) that it annoys/distracts nearby merchants, but neither should people mistake it for the cash machine.

Customization: Users should be able to narrow their search by price range, geographical area, and type of desired housing.

BEGINNING TO ORGANIZE

SCENES:
A discrete unit of function or information in an interactive movie.

Once we've defined the project in terms of its ultimate use, the next step is to break up the work required into discrete segments. Just as plays are broken into acts and novels into chapters, interactive works also have their experiential units—let's call them **scenes**.

Unlike scenes in linear works, an interactive scene doesn't necessarily have a beginning, middle, and end. It's more analogous to a "singles bar scene" or "coffeehouse scene"—that is, it's a site where you can expect certain types of activity to take place.

Don't confuse *scene* with *sequence* (a unit of animation) or *segment* (a sprite's motion and placement path).

A scene can consist of a single screen or several screens. It can have multiple points of entry and exit, and it can incorporate plenty of user feedback or none at all. To define it at all, you'd have to say a scene is any portion of your movie that, when you leave it, makes you feel like you're going somewhere else.

You can start by simply making a labeled box for each scene you foresee building. Don't worry about connecting them in any particular order just yet. Here's a sample preliminary scene list for our Very Pleasant Neighbor Realty project:

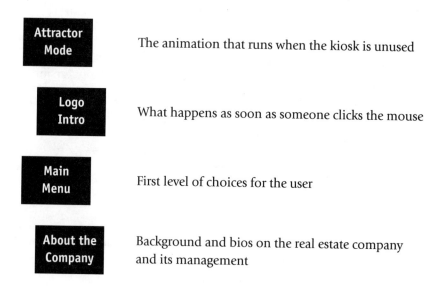

Attractor Mode — The animation that runs when the kiosk is unused

Logo Intro — What happens as soon as someone clicks the mouse

Main Menu — First level of choices for the user

About the Company — Background and bios on the real estate company and its management

Choose by Location	A clickable area map to define geographic regions for searching
Choose by Type	Narrows the search to the categories of condominiums, townhouses, duplexes, and single-family houses
Choose by Price Range	Another search-limitation criteria
Retrieval Wait Mode	Music and animation designed to hold the user's interest while the database is searched for criteria matches
Result Display	Shows a tally of listings that match the search criteria
Result Browser	Lets the user look through individual screens for each property in the search match
Follow-up Info	Lets the user leave a name and number for further contact
Help	A step-by-step explanation of how to use the kiosk
New/Quit	Allows the user to begin a new search or to end use of the kiosk
Goodbye	The animated company logo, accompanied by a "Thank You" message

That's a total of 14 scenes for an interaction intended to last approximately 2 minutes per user. We could probably design a kiosk that performs essentially the same function with fewer scenes, but the result might be confusing (or worse, boring) for the end user.

Once the building blocks of scenes have been identified, further contextual analysis can pinpoint the special needs that arise for many of them:

- The Attractor Mode probably requires the flashiest animation to catch the eyes of passers-by. Some music is appropriate, too, although it should be subtle enough that it won't annoy others in the vicinity. Remember that this is the scene that will likely run the most often.

- The Logo Intro should be impressive but not too elaborate or long. Otherwise, users may feel as if they're watching a commercial and wander away.

- The Main Menu should offer access to several scenes (Help, About the Company) but emphasize the database search as the main option.

- The data-gathering scenes (Choose by Location, Type, and Price Range) need to direct the user clearly but swiftly—the meat of the interaction is the result of the database search.

- The Retrieval Wait Animation has to keep the user engaged while the search is compiled. It should be clear that something is happening, or the user may misinterpret the delay as a malfunction.

- The individual housing listings need to be in a consistent interface, so they can be browsed in any order yet appear as part of a whole.

There are also global considerations intrinsic to the nature of the project and the context in which it will operate:

- Since there is no "typical user," the overall look and feel should be friendly and accessible—nothing too high tech-looking, which might scare away the technophobic.

- Not everyone can be expected to formally end their use of a kiosk by clicking the Quit button. Handler scripts for the `timeOut` event will be needed to reset the presentation when users walk away. Perhaps a special message can prompt for action after a preset period; if there's no response, the movie can return to the Attractor Mode.

See how useful a scene-by-scene breakdown can be? We haven't designed a single screen yet (or even fired up Director), but the project is already taking shape.

THE FLOW OF FUNCTION

Now that we've named and cataloged the pieces, the next step is to figure out how they go together. We'll do that by building a **flowchart**, a document that graphically displays the possible pathways through the scenes.

You'll find that the connections of even a modest interactive project can be a tricky business to map out on paper. That's because such diagrams are inherently linear interpretations of a nonlinear process, and accuracy and clarity can quickly clash—if a flowchart is comprehensive, it's often incomprehensible. But just as an artist can sketch a two-dimensional representation of a three-dimensional object, a good multimedia maker can graph the general flow of functionality in at least enough detail for evaluation and editing.

Step one: The primary flow

Using our hypothetical real estate kiosk as an example, let's start by flowcharting the user's primary intended movement through the interaction. For the moment, we'll disregard side trips such as the Help scene and timeout messages.

Although the database it accesses might be vast, the kiosk itself requires a relatively straightforward interface. There's really only one point at which the user is required to make a decision: whether to quit or begin a new search session.

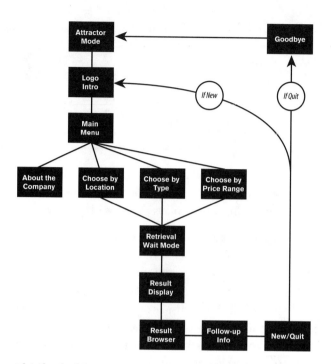

This looks like a clear, concise organization, right? Should we launch Director and get started?

Not so fast. This arrangement would clearly work in terms of sheer functionality and lack of confusion—but does it create the optimum experience? Let's look at it with a critical eye:

- This setup allows the user to choose only one of three criteria (location, type, or price range) for the database search. Wouldn't it be better to offer all three criteria, each one further narrowing the search specifications?

- The Follow-up Info scene pops up only after the user has browsed through the individual screens in the Result Browser. Wouldn't it be better to let users request more information as soon as they encounter a listing that interests them?

- Does the decision to start a new session really need to lead to a redux of the Logo Intro? Wouldn't it be better to launch directly into a new search?

The second draft of the flowchart attempts to address these criticisms.

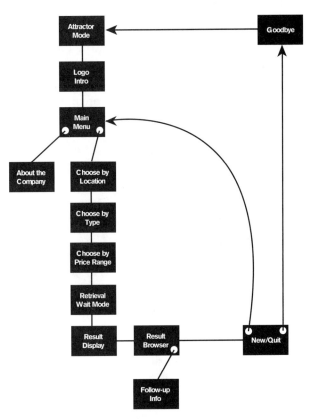

Note the new symbol: The white circle indicates a button, and the line proceeding from it is the navigational choice made when that button is clicked. This way, we can distinguish between direct progressions (a fixed scene order) and conditional progressions (a scene that can be accessed at any point from within another scene). The number of screens in the Result Browser may be variable (depending on the results of the search), but each of those screens will have a Follow-up button linking it to Follow-up Info.

Before proceeding, take a further look at the flowchart and see if you can second-guess any of the structural decisions. For example, why does the button requesting a new session lead to the Main Menu and not directly to Choose by Location? I decided to do it that way to give users a chance to digress—they may not have taken a look at About the Company the first time through.

Step two: Quantifying Lingo work

We've defined and arranged our scenes. Now it's time to address what's going to go on *behind* the scenes: the work that Director, and Lingo in particular, have to do to make the interaction a meaningful one. Like air-conditioning ducts and plumbing pipes, these features are things the user will never see, but they are part of the architecture nonetheless.

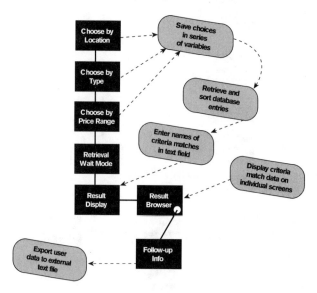

Let's look at the flowchart in light of the Lingo scripting that it implies. Many of the scenes require no specialized Lingo; here, our focus will be on those that do. The gray areas in the illustration are functional units, tasks that might ultimately be performed by a number of different scripting strategies. And then there's the global Lingo to consider, such as setting the `timeOut` to a specific period of inactivity and writing on `timeOut` event handlers to return to the Attractor Mode.

A button inventory

Having gotten a fix on the big-ticket Lingo work ahead of us, the next step is to account for the smaller interface elements we'll need. It's no big deal to add a button at any point in the development process, but there are two reasons for creating an anticipated inventory right at the start:

- **Convenience.** When you identify elements that will be present in multiple locations, you'll be able to construct them (and their scripts) to make them functional in all their contexts, not just in a single scene.

- **Consistency.** In this case, it makes sense to keep the interface as clear as possible, and that means keeping things consistent: Buttons should always have the same look and function from screen to screen. So when the time comes to create each button, we'll want a design that meshes comfortably with all of the screens it will occupy.

The next flowchart shows a button inventory for our project.

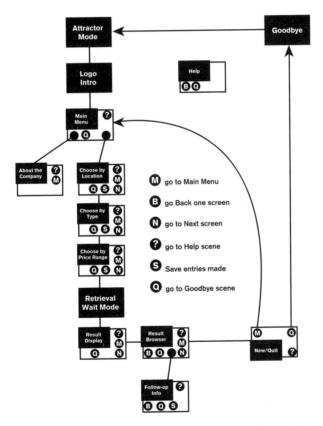

This button inventory isn't exhaustive—we'll probably end up using buttons to make selections in the "Choose by" scenes as well. But we've identified six buttons that make up the controls of the interface, and we can design and script them accordingly.

BUILDING THE PROTOTYPE

At last! It's time to stop planning and start building. Actually, were this a professional production, at this point you might want to divide the work into two streams: *design* (honing the aesthetics of the screens and scenes) and *prototyping* (programming the structure without concern for content). Since the former is a matter of personal taste, we'll focus on the latter for now.

In conventional manufacturing, the **prototype** is a preliminary version of the eventual product, to be discarded when the real thing is finalized. But with Director you can build a prototype and then refine and augment it until it *becomes* the final product. The original work becomes the armature on which all else rests—which illustrates why sound planning is important before laying the foundation.

We won't be prototyping the entire production, since full functionality would involve Lingo principles we haven't covered yet. But we can do enough to get a general feel for the process.

Marking out the scenes

Start by opening and saving a new movie file in Director (with a screen size and background color of your choosing). Name it *Kiosk.dir*. We have 14 separate scenes mapped out (13 in our flowcharts, plus Help), so let's use markers to specify 14 locations.

1. *Go to the marker well and place a fresh marker at frame 10 and then at every 10-frame interval to frame 140.*

2. *Label each marker with the name of a scene. Follow the order in which the scenes were first listed under "Beginning to Organize," earlier in this chapter.*

You can abbreviate the scene names: About the Company can be just About, and the Choose by scenes can become Location, Type, and Price Range. In fact, it's a good idea to keep scene names concise, since you'll be referring to them in scripts. Simpler names mean less chance of typing errors.

How long (in terms of frames occupied) will each scene be? We have no way of knowing at this point, so we'll allocate one frame to each of them for starters. The nine empty frames on either side won't affect playback, since we can set up scene-to-scene jumps that ignore them completely. When the time comes to fill up the actual frames used by the scenes, we can add or subtract from this buffer zone as needed.

Next we'll need a means of telling one scene from another. We could discern a current location during playback by monitoring the markers in the Score, but it's easier to place labels on the Stage, on the scene screens themselves.

3. Use the Text window to create 14 cast members, each one the name of a scene.

Use the full name of each scene in these labels. You can make the labels any font or point size you want. You don't even need to make them all alike, since a little variety can make the prototype more fun to work with. If you want even more variety, you can use the Paint window to make colorful labels.

4. Place each label in the appropriate scene, in channel 1 of the Score.

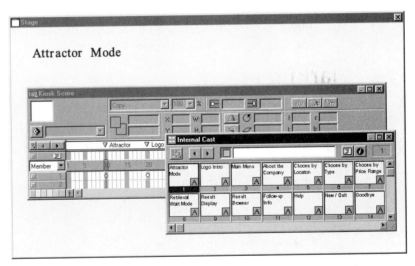

Writing and applying a frame script

To keep the playback head from plowing through all our scenes in a few seconds, we need to insert a script at each relevant frame. We'll write a behavior for the Attractor Mode and then use the Behavior pop-up menu to apply it to the other scenes.

1. *Double-click the behavior channel in frame 10.*

2. *In the* on exitFrame *handler, enter this line:*

go to the frame

3. *Click the Behavior Script window's close box.*

The simple script now shows up in four places: in the behavior channel, in the Score's Behavior pop-up menu, as a new cast member, and in the display area above the Behavior pop-up menu.

4. *Click to select the behavior channel in frame 20.*

5. *From the Score's Behavior pop-up menu, select the behavior we just created.*

Behaviors are added to the pop-up menu in order of their cast numbers.

6. *Repeat steps 4 and 5 for each of the remaining scene frames.*

Because this is a temporary command (we'll eventually want many scenes to play through several frames), using a single frame behavior gives us the advantage of later eliminating its function in one fell swoop, just by opening the script and changing the line go to the frame.

Building "scratch" buttons

In the film and video world, a **scratch** is an interim element in the pre-production process. A film editor might use a scratch soundtrack (made up of sound borrowed from other movies) as a guide for visual pacing, while the composer is busy creating the real score. Most documentaries use scratch voice-overs until the final stages, as the narration usually goes through several revisions to reflect the changing flow of images.

Scratching is a useful concept in multimedia, too. We've just built scratch screens for the kiosk, and now we'll whip up some scratch buttons. Like the prototype as a whole, a scratch element can be transformed into the final form rather than replaced. Usually you'll scrap the content (such as the graphics themselves) but keep the functionality and placement in the context of the movie.

For this kiosk, we'll move beyond the standard buttons created with the Tools window, opting instead for something with a bit more impact. Let's make the buttons graphic cast members and then introduce a level of user feedback by writing a custom handler.

1. *Single-click to select a vacant slot in the Cast window. Open the Paint window if it's currently closed.*

2. *In the Paint window, use the Filled Circle tool to draw a circle approximately the size of a dime.*

That's our scratch button template. Now we'll make some quick copies. We could use the Lasso or Marquee Selection tools, but there's a faster way.

3. *Single-click the new cast member's slot to make the Cast window active.*

4. *From the Edit menu, choose Copy Cast Members, or press Control-C (Windows) or Command-C (Macintosh).*

5. *Click to select the next vacant Cast slot.*

6. *From the Edit menu, choose Paste Bitmap, or press Control-V (Windows) or Command-V (Macintosh).*

7. *Repeat steps 5 and 6 four more times, to create a total of six button cast members.*

There's a subtle but important difference between copying and pasting wholesale (as you've just done) and using the selection tools: This method transfers not just the image, but any attached information as well (scripts, names, Info window options, and so on).

8. *Open each of the buttons in turn. Use the Text tool in the Paint window to add a symbol to each (see the illustration).*

9. *Give each button a name in the Cast, as shown in the illustration.*

NAMING NAMES:
You can add names not only to the buttons themselves, but to their slots in the Cast.

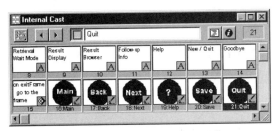

Writing a button handler

We want all our buttons to behave consistently, right? They perform different functions, but they should still be similar in terms of user feedback. So let's encapsulate the common aspects of their behavior in a custom handler, which we can then call from individual button scripts.

In this case, let's write a Lingo script that does the following:

- Moves the button slightly when depressed, to simulate a sense of its being pushed

- Automatically reverses the color of the button

- Plays a clicking sound

- Restores the button when the mouse is released

We'll put all this action into a single handler called buttonclick.

1. **Select an empty slot in the Cast and then open the Script window from the Window menu.**

The Script window opens to a blank entry field.

2. **Type** on buttonclick **in the first line.**

This declares the handler. To call the handler anywhere else in Lingo, we'll only need to include the command buttonclick.

These, of course, are not the only things we can make buttons do. With some of the event messages introduced in Director 6 (**mouseEnter**, **mouseWithin**, **mouseLeave**, and **mouseUpOutside**), it's easy to attach specific behaviors not just to the act of mouse clicking but even to the passive act of the cursor's idly cruising over the button's sprite. Changing the button when the cursor passes over it tells users that this is something they can click.

Defining and filling a variable

Now we'll define and fill the variable.

variable name

3. **After the first line, type**

thisOne = the clickOn

This uses the property the clickOn, which defines the sprite over which the mouse was last clicked. If the sprite of a button is placed in channel 9, then the clickOn will return 9, and so forth (note that the number refers to the channel placement, not the sprite's cast member number). So this line takes the result of the clickOn and puts it in a custom variable, which I've named thisOne. You can use another name if you like, but remember that all custom names, whether for handlers or variables, must start with a letter, must use *only* letters and numbers, and can have no spaces.

> When naming an element of custom scripting, check first to make sure the name is not one already in use by standard Lingo. Using an identical term can disable the function of the original and lead to offbeat results. (Advanced programmers sometimes intentionally augment or overrule Lingo features by writing scripts with the same name.)

Can you see the purpose of creating such a variable? Since the mouse click will be over the sprite of a button, the `clickOn` will give us that sprite's channel number (this being a sprite we want to manipulate throughout the rest of this script). Putting the result into `thisOne` frees us from having to laboriously apply our Lingo to individual sprites or to confine the placement of buttons to particular channels.

Lingo to move a sprite

The usefulness of the variable `thisOne` will become clearer as we use it to write a few script lines that change the placement of the sprite on the Stage.

4. Type the following:

```
sprite(thisOne).locH = sprite(thisOne).locH +5
sprite(thisOne).locV = sprite(thisOne).locV +5
updateStage
```

We're invoking two properties here: `locH` is a sprite property that specifies the sprite's horizontal location on the Stage (measured from its registration point, which will be dead center for all our buttons). `locV` is the equivalent measurement of the sprite's vertical position. By setting these properties to different values, we are in effect moving the sprite relative to the Stage's coordinates. We change the value by taking the current value and adding to it—hence, set [property] to [property] + 5. This moves the sprite by 5 pixels in each of the specified directions.

> Location coordinates begin from the upper-left corner of the Stage, so adding pixels to `locV` and `locH` will move the sprite down and to the right.

Since we created the variable thisOne, we can refer to sprite (thisOne) rather than naming a specific sprite channel. Any sprite whose source cast member's script invokes the buttonclick handler will have its channel number inserted at the appropriate points in these lines (replacing thisOne).

The updateStage command

We added a third line, consisting of updateStage. This is a command you'll frequently find useful as you get more ambitious with scripting.

As you may recall, the Stage is usually updated only when the playback head enters a new frame. Since we are looping on the current frame, this happens fairly regularly—but in this case, not before our entire buttonclick handler has finished executing. As you will see, we intend to stay in this handler until the mouse button is released and we restore the button to its original state. That's much too late for showing the button's depressed state. The updateStage command is the solution here: Director will redraw the Stage as soon as it encounters this command, whether playback is paused or not.

The updateStage command is useful not just for quick screen revisions but for anything that needs to happen right away. When a sound is associated with a script (such as the click we'll be placing in this one), an updateStage command is needed to make that sound coincide with the mouse click.

Repeat, the stillDown, and nothing

Consider the action of a real-world button:

- It moves down when you push it.

- It stays down as long as your finger presses on it.

- It moves back up when you take your finger away.

Thus far in the script, we've made the button move down by changing locV and locH. Now we need to keep it in the new position while the mouse button is down.

5. *Still in our* buttonclick *handler, type the following:*

```
repeat while the stillDown = TRUE
    nothing
end repeat
```

The repeat while keyword (remember that keywords don't have to be just one word long) will execute a command statement if a particular condition is valid. In this case, the condition is the stillDown = TRUE, which is to say the mouse button is still depressed. the stillDown is a system property that reflects the condition of the mouse button; as long as the button is down, the stillDown is TRUE. When the user releases it, the stillDown is set to FALSE.

So what is the command that's repeatedly carried out while the mouse button stays down? Nothing—or more precisely, nothing. That's an official Lingo command, and it comes in handy often. Look at it this way: We're trying to mimic the movement of a physical button. We've already written Lingo that moves the button down, and we'll have to write more that moves it back up again. If we didn't have an interim action, the entire handler would be executed in the blink of an eye, and both the down and up movements would add up to a flicker on the Stage. Hence the importance of nothing.

You should also know that repeat while is one of a group of repeat keywords that also includes variations on repeat with. Whenever a repeat is invoked, the command lines it pertains to must be followed by the line end repeat.

TIP

A lot of scripting requires applying Lingo to a number of elements, and using **repeat with** is a good way of automating that process. For instance, if you had to move the sprites in channels 5 through 25, you could write 21 lines of script—or you could write

```
repeat with mycount = 5 to 25
sprite(mycount).locH = sprite(mycount).locH +5
sprite(mycount).locV = sprite(mycount).locV +5
end repeat
```

Not only is this approach easier, but it gives you the option of expanding, shrinking, or transposing the block of sprites being moved; just change the range of values that equal **mycount.**

Restoring the button position

Time for the final step of the three-step process: moving the button back to its original location. This time, instead of adding 5 to locV and locH, we'll simply subtract 5.

6. *Enter the following into the script:*

```
sprite(thisOne).locH = sprite(thisOne).locH -5
sprite(thisOne).locV = sprite(thisOne).locV -5
updateStage
```

> The standard copy and paste functions work in the Script window. You can save yourself some typing time by copying the lines from earlier in the script and then changing the plus sign (+) to a minus (–).

Subtracting 5 from the horizontal and vertical locations has the effect of canceling out the original movement. And since we're using relative values, the action will be the same no matter where the button is located on the Stage. Don't forget the second updateStage command, by the way.

Closing the handler

Your custom buttonclick handler can do more than make buttons move. You can add Lingo to change their color and add sound, too. But by now you're probably eager to see your buttons in action, so let's close the handler and start placing them. Besides, a pause in the Lingo action will demonstrate one of the big advantages of custom scripting: You can augment and edit the function of handlers at any time, even when sprites calling that handler are sprinkled throughout the Score.

7. *Add this final line to the script:*

```
end buttonclick
```

**8. *Use the Name field in the Script window to name the script*
*buttonclick.***

The complete entry in the Script window should now look like this:

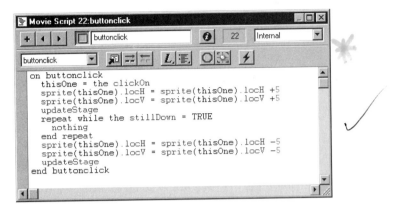

```
on buttonclick
  thisOne = the clickOn
  sprite(thisOne).locH = sprite(thisOne).locH +5
  sprite(thisOne).locV = sprite(thisOne).locV +5
  updateStage
  repeat while the stillDown = TRUE
    nothing
  end repeat
  sprite(thisOne).locH = sprite(thisOne).locH -5
  sprite(thisOne).locV = sprite(thisOne).locV -5
  updateStage
end buttonclick
```

Strictly speaking, the statement **end** would work just as well as **end buttonclick.** That is, while the name of a handler is required on the handler's opening line, it is not required on the closing line. Many people, however, follow the custom of closing the **end** statement with the handler's name so it's easy to tell at just which handler's **end** you're looking. This makes particular sense when you have many handlers in a movie script, each one of which might have hundreds of lines.

In this exercise, we're scripting a good deal of the control over the buttons. If we weren't so interested in learning Lingo, we would probably have started out by using a button behavior from the Library Palette. The Library Palette's button behavior already includes the necessary commands for changing the button's appearance for **rollOver**, **mouseDown**, and **mouseUp** events—and even for cases when the button is clicked and then the mouse is moved off the button before the mouse button is released. You can then add whatever custom commands to the handler you want for your particular situation. If you look around on some of the Web sites pertaining to Director, you'll probably find button behaviors that can make your buttons perform in just about any way you can imagine.

Writing the cast member scripts

To put our custom handler to work, we need to attach it to our button cast members. While we're at it, let's add the navigational Lingo to make them fully functional.

1. **Select the Main button in the Cast; then open its script (click the Script button in the Cast).**

The script entry opens up with the cursor underneath an on mouseUp event handler. We want to use that mouseUp event (the end of a mouse click), but first we need to add a mouseDown command:

2. **Above the first line in the Script window, add the following:**

```
on mouseDown
    buttonclick
end
```

This calls our custom handler.

3. **In the blank line beneath on mouseUp, enter**

```
go "Main Menu"
```

Use quotation marks and to write the name of the scene exactly as you did on the frame marker. The final script should look like this:

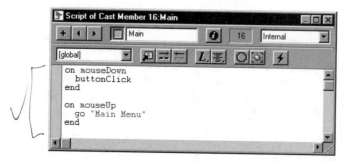

By the way, the terms go, go to, and go to the frame are interchangeable. If followed by a frame number or the name of a marker, they all will move the playback head to that location.

4. **Repeat steps 1 and 2 for the remaining buttons (skipping the Save button). Then repeat step 3, substituting the following script lines:**

- For the Back button, write go to the frame -1

- For the Next button, write go to the frame +1

- For the Help button, write `play "Help"`
- For the Quit button, write `go to "Goodbye"`

> You can speed up this process by copying the first button script from within the Script window and then pasting it in the successive Script windows. Just be sure the pasted script replaces the default script lines entirely—that it's not just inserted into the existing script. Otherwise, you may end up with multiple **on mouseUp** entries and other confusing duplications.

We'll skip placing a script in the Save button because that function will involve more complex scripting. And why don't we put a `quit` command in the Quit button's script? Because this is a kiosk; we don't want to shut down Director, but rather start the playback cycle all over again. When you're done, the total population of your Cast window should look something like this (cast member order doesn't matter):

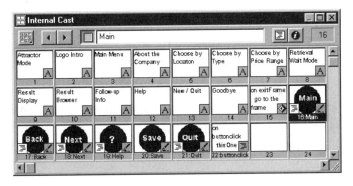

> If you used abbreviations for the scene names while creating frame markers, make sure the navigational commands match the marker names. Director isn't concerned with capitalization (_goodbye_ will get you to a frame marked _Goodbye_), but extra words and additional characters will prevent the script from working.

The go to the frame command and relative navigation

Just as our buttonclick handler used locV and locH to introduce movement relative to the current location of a sprite, our cast scripts for the Back and Next buttons use go to the frame for relative navigation within the Score. The term the frame refers to the frame currently displayed on the Stage, and you can specify any frame relative to it by adding a plus (+) or a minus (–) and any integer.

> Lingo has **go next** and **go previous** commands, but they pertain to frame markers, not to individual frames. For instance, in the current kiosk a **go previous** command in the Main Menu scene would move the playback head to the Logo Intro scene, and a **go next** command would move it to About the Company.

The play versus go to commands

You'll notice that the statement for the Help button uses the command play rather than go to. Both move the playback head to the designated sequence—but unlike go to, play also instructs Director to remember the frame from which the playback head departed. When a play done command is issued, the playback head returns to that location.

Most scenes in this kiosk are meant to be experienced as a logical progression, but the Help scene is a brief side trip that can be made at any time. The user needs to be able to pop into it and back at a moment's notice; hence the utility of play rather than go to.

Positioning the buttons in the scenes

Now that they've been created and scripted, let's put our primary buttons to work. Placing them in the movie is a two-part process: first positioning them on a representative screen, and then copying and pasting *both* the buttons and their positions onto other screens. That way their location remains consistent throughout all screens, which keeps them from jumping when a transition occurs from one scene to another.

1. *In the Score, go to the Main Menu screen (frame 30).*

Take a moment to consult the button inventory we compiled a few pages ago and you'll see a list of the buttons required for each scene. We're starting work on our movie with Main Menu because it requires the two most-used buttons: Help and Quit.

2. *Click in the Score to select channel 2 of the frame.*

3. *Drag the Help cast member from the Cast to the Stage. Then repeat this step with the Quit cast member.*

4. *Position the buttons in the upper-right corner of the Stage.*

5. *Shift-click to select both button sprites in the Score (channels 2 and 3).*

6. *Set the ink of both sprites to Matte.*

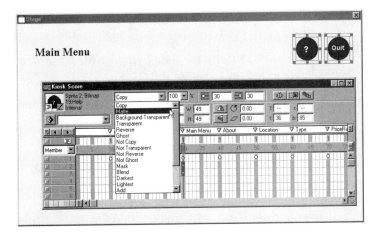

If you want to make sure two or more sprites are aligned on the Stage, Director allows you a number of ways to do so. One way is to place both sprites directly adjacent to each other, match up their bounding boxes, and then use the arrow keys to move them (1 pixel per keystroke) into their final positions. Holding down the Shift key while pressing the arrow keys moves sprites 10 pixels per keystroke. You can also use the Align window. Shift-click to select all the sprites you want to align (in the Score or on the Stage) and then use the Align window (accessible from the Modify menu) to align the sprites. The Align window is discussed in Chapter 7: *More Production Tools.* Yet another method is to show grids (available from the View menu) on the Stage, which make eyeballing pretty accurate.

When you're happy with the placement of both buttons, it's time to apply them to the other scenes where they are needed.

7. *With both sprites still selected, choose Copy Cells from the Edit menu, or press Control-C (Windows) or Command-C (Macintosh).*

8. *Click to select channel 2 of the frame in Choose by Location.*

9. *From the Edit menu, choose Paste Cells (Control-V Windows; Command-V Macintosh).*

Notice that even though you selected only one cell, both of the copied sprites are pasted in subsequent cells. You don't need to select a full range of cells to paste information into them, but you should take care to paste the sprites consistently: the Help button in channel 2, Quit in channel 3, and so on. Keeping the same objects in the same channels makes it easier to deal with common elements throughout the movie.

10. *Place a sprite of the Main button to the left of the two existing buttons and set its ink to Matte.*

These three buttons now need to be applied as a group to a number of other scenes. Refer to the button inventory on page 373 of this chapter to see exactly what goes where.

11. *Shift-click to select all three button sprites. Copy them.*

12. *Paste the three buttons in all relevant scenes.*

By pasting in the Score rather than on the Stage, you keep the positions constant. And feel free to paste all three buttons on a screen where only a few apply; you can then delete the unnecessary ones—such as in the About the Company scene, where I chose to leave out the Quit button. (I thought that by compelling people to return to the Main Menu first, we'd have one more opportunity to tempt them into a database search.) Eliminating that button may leave an empty cell in channel 3, but that's all right; resist the temptation to move the Main button in channel 4 up a notch. We have plenty of other channels, and it's better to keep the Main button in channel 4 throughout. Don't worry about placing the Save button in the scenes, since we won't use it for this demonstration program.

13. *Using the same technique you used earlier, place, copy, and paste all remaining buttons in accordance with the button inventory on page 373. Don't worry about the unlabeled buttons (such as the one going from Main Menu to About the Company); we'll get to those later.*

It's a matter of taste, but when building interfaces I usually prefer to separate high-use buttons (such as Back and Next) from occasional-use buttons (one hopes that Quit will be used only once). This approach reduces the risk of accidental click-ons, and it results in smaller clusters of buttons (which usually seem less intimidating). Hence, I grouped the buttons in opposite corners, as shown in the following illustration:

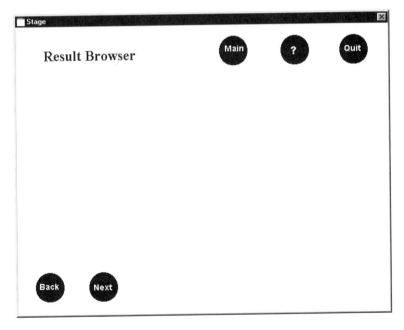

Taking stock

Let's stop and think for a minute about what we have done so far. Sometimes, if you are following along with all the steps, you can get lost in the details without seeing the overall picture. Here's a recap:

- We decided what the major scenes for the movie would be and then created markers and an illustrative text for each scene. This gives us the overall body of the movie.

- We decided what the common navigational elements would be for the movie and created buttons for them. Since these buttons appear throughout the movie and have the same function everywhere, we created a moviewide `buttonclick` handler and used cast scripts for each button's actions.

What we *don't* have is a way to travel from one scene to another. If you were to play the movie now, the movie would reach the Attractor Mode scene and sit there. Our next couple of steps will be to simulate the passage through scenes where there is no user interaction and provide some navigational controls where there is user interaction. Let's start with the former.

Modifying the nonmodal scenes

There's one more step before we can start pointing and clicking within a running movie: We need to make adjustments to the scenes that have no buttons—in this case, the Attractor Mode, Logo Intro, Retrieval Wait Mode, and Goodbye scenes.

Since these scenes offer no mode of choice to the user—they just unfold on the screen—they're called **nonmodal**. The distinction applies to any interface element: If a dialog box offers you any choice (even if only an opportunity to click OK), it's modal. An example of a nonmodal dialog box is the one that often pops up after the Print command, which declares only that pages are being spooled to disk.

As it stands, our nonmodal scenes are dead ends. Each nonmodal scene has a frame behavior that loops on its frame. Let's remove that behavior and then add a few transitions and tempo delays so these scratch scenes will have some discernible presence as they flash past.

Let's start with the Attractor Mode. Then we'll apply the same steps to the other three nonmodal scenes.

1. *Click the behavior channel of the Attractor Mode scene (frame 10).*

2. *Select Clear All Behaviors from the pop-up Behavior menu in the Score.*

Clear All Behaviors is Director-speak for applying no script to the frame; you can achieve the same result by pressing the Delete key on your keyboard when the behavior is selected. Remember that the goal is to detach the go to the frame script from these frames, *not* to remove or modify the script itself.

3. *Double-click the cell of the tempo channel in the same frame.*

This brings up the by-now-familiar Tempo dialog box.

4. *Click Wait; then move the slider to enter a delay of 3 seconds. Click OK to close the dialog box.*

5. *Double-click the transition cell in the same frame.*

You're free to choose any transition you like, but for the present I recommend the no-frills Dissolve, Bits Fast. Set the Smoothness lever near the left of the scale for a fine dissolve, and make sure the transition applies to the changing area only, not the Stage.

6. *Choose your desired transition. Then click OK to close the dialog box.*

These parameters (transition and tempo delay) can be cut and pasted from frame to frame, much as the buttons were. Rather than go through the preceding steps for the remaining nonmodal scenes, do the following:

1. *Click to select the transition cell; then Shift-click to select the tempo cell as well. Copy the cells.*

Shift-clicking between two nonadjacent cells in the Score selects not only those cells, but all cells in between. In this case, the palette cell is also selected, but since it's empty, that's not much of a concern.

2. *Click to select the tempo cell of the next nonmodal scene. Paste the tempo and transition into it.*

As we go to press, Director 7 seems to have a problem with copying the tempo channel along with other channels. This is the kind of problem that is often addressed in post-release incremental builds, so it may disappear in your version. If you follow the preceding instruction, check to make sure that the Tempo sprite is correct (it has a Wait). If it isn't, you'll have to do things the hard way and copy the tempo channel and transition channel separately.

3. *Repeat the paste operation for the other two nonmodal scenes.*

When pasting sprites in the Score, you need to pay attention to where you place the insertion point. If you choose an insertion point of a different type, Director will quietly paste nothing—offering no warning that you've just mixed your apples and oranges. If you're pasting combinations of different types of sprites (as we just did), there's also the danger of a partial paste: Had you mistakenly clicked the palette channel rather than the tempo channel, the result would be a correct pasting into the transition cell (because it's below the palette cell), and no pasting into the tempo cell.

When pasting sprites, make sure the receiving cell is of the same channel type as the source cell. Otherwise, pasting will have either no results or a partial result.

4. *Rewind and play the movie.*

The movie plays throughout the Attractor Mode and Logo Intro scenes and then sits at the Main Menu scene. Now we need some user controls to get us to some of the other scenes.

More navigation

From the Main Menu scene, we should be able to go to four scenes: Choose by Location, About the Company, Help, and Quit. We already have buttons placed for Help and Quit, so let's continue by creating two more buttons for the other two scenes. Just to make our lives easier, we're going to create a generic button called Move On that we can use in a number of locations. We can use Move On to get from the Main scene to Choose by Location, from Choose by Location to Choose by Type, and so on. Then, if we later want to replace the button with one supplied by our graphics department, we can simply switch cast members.

By the way, since these buttons are not meant to have the same action everywhere they are placed (like the buttons we've already created), we will use sprite behaviors instead of cast scripts to define their actions. Sprite behaviors allow us to use the same cast member, but still have unique actions for each use of a button.

1. *Open the Paint window and create a solid filled rectangle about $3/4$ inch high by 2 inches wide. Use Paint's Text tool to place a label on it with the text Move On.*

2. *As with the other buttons, make a copy of the Move On cast member and change the label to About.*

3. *Place these two new cast members, one above the other, near the center of the Stage on the Main scene. Place the Move On button in channel 7 and the About button in channel 8.*

The About button gets placed only on the Main scene, but we will use the Move On button in a number of locations.

4. *In the Score, select and copy the Move On button in the Main scene. Then paste it into channel 7 of the scenes About, Location, Type, Price, Display, and Help.*

Now we have all of the buttons that we are going to use for this demonstration program. Time to add some behaviors to make the buttons work.

The play and play done commands

We'll start with the About button. The About scene is one of our locations, similar to the Help scene, where we want users to go and then return to where they started. So instead of using a go to command, we'll use a play command. We can then place a play done command in the destination scene that will return the user to the Main scene.

1. *Select the About button in the Score. In the Score's Behavior drop-down menu, choose New Behavior.*

2. *A Behavior script window opens. Modify the default script shell so that you have the following two handlers:*

```
on mouseUp
  play "About"
end
on mouseDown
  buttonclick
end
```

The buttonclick command in the mouseDown handler is the same command we used in our other buttons to provide the "tactile" feedback when the button is clicked. The play "About" command in the mouseUp handler will send the movie to the About scene when the mouse button is released. Now let's do something about getting back from the About scene.

3. *In the Score, find the About scene and then select the Move On button there. In the Score's Behavior drop-down menu, choose New Behavior.*

4. *Modify the default script shell so that you have the following two handlers:*

```
on mouseUp
  play done
end

on mouseDown
  buttonclick
end
```

The play done command tells Director that it's time to go back to the location where the play command was executed. Although it's not required, and Director never checks, it's important to include a play done command for every play command used. One reason is that Director is required to set aside memory to remember the return location. Numerous play commands without matching play done commands will increase the memory requirements of your movie. It's just a good habit: If you start getting sloppy with matching play and play done commands, eventually you will find yourself issuing a play done command without anywhere to return to—with unexpected results.

5. *Rewind and play the movie. At the Main scene, click the About button.*

The About button should branch the movie to the About scene. At the About scene, you can click the Move On button and return to the Main scene.

Moving on

Now let's set up the Move On button in the Main scene. If we wanted to take the time to create more buttons, we could have labeled this button something like Listing Search. Its function will be to take us to the first of the three scenes used to specify the limits of the search. Since Choose by Location is the first of those three scenes, that's where we want to go.

1. *In the Score, select the Move On button in channel 7 of the Main scene.*

2. *In the Score's Behavior drop-down menu, choose New Behavior.*

3. *Modify the default script shell so that you have the following two handlers:*

```
on mouseUp
  go to "Location"
end

on mouseDown
  buttonclick
end
```

Since going to the Location scene is a one-way street, we use the go to command rather than the play command.

4. *Before you close the Behavior Script window, select and copy the entire contents. We can use almost identical contents in the next behaviors we create. Then close the Script window.*

5. *Repeat steps 1 through 3 for the Move On buttons in the Location, Type, Price, and Display scenes. As you create each set of handlers, modify the* go to *command in the* mouseUp *handler so that Location goes to Type, Type goes to Price, Price goes to Retrieval, and Display goes to Browser.*

Notice that for each of the behaviors we have been creating, a behavior cast member is created in the Cast window. These behaviors also show up in the Behavior drop-down menu in the Score. If we have occasion to use a behavior identical to one that already exists, we can apply it from the Behavior menu rather than create a new behavior. We used a behavior that included play done to return from the About scene, and we can use that same behavior to return from the Help scene.

6. *In the Score, select the Move On button in channel 7 of the Help scene.*

7. *In the Behavior drop-down menu, find and select the behavior with the* play done *command.*

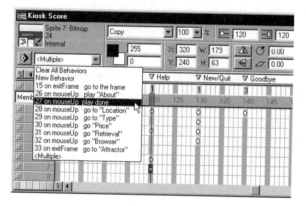

A couple more steps and we'll have a working prototype. Right now, when the movie reaches the Goodbye scene, the movie stops. Since this movie is designed as a kiosk and should continue playing even when someone quits, the Goodbye scene should return to the Attractor scene. Also, the Attractor scene should remain in Attractor Mode until someone steps up to the kiosk and makes himself or herself known. Both of these scenarios are quick and easy to produce.

1. *Double-click the behavior channel at the Goodbye scene.*

2. *In the* on exitFrame *handler, add this line:*

```
go to "Attractor"
```

3. *Go to the Attractor scene in the Score. Use the Tool Palette's Text tool to create a text sprite that says* Click the Mouse to Continue.

4. *Open the tempo sprite for the Attractor scene and change the tempo setting to Wait for Mouse Click or Key Press.*

Play-through and debugging

Our prototype doesn't work yet in the sense of performing its ultimate function (selling real estate), but it is beginning to operate as a cohesive whole. Play the movie and play *with* it: Is everything working as intended? Are there any "look and feel" issues you want to reconsider? Most multimedia producers take a two-step approach to testing:

- **Experiential testing.** Look at the flow of animation and information and how it all fits together.

- **Destructive testing.** Try to intentionally make bugs surface by doing things you wouldn't normally expect the end user to do—important because end users have a way of not knowing what's expected of them. Repeated button clicks and illogical actions are some of the hallmarks of destructive testing.

At this stage of the game, both types of testing are still pretty much intertwined in the same process. But as your hypothetical production nears completion, you'll probably separate the two tasks.

CHANGING THE SKIN

Now that the basic functionality is in place, let's give the movie a new skin. The beauty of the cast metaphor is that it's easy to give a Director movie a whole new look: Just substitute one cast member for another (while taking care to preserve the Lingo functionality of each).

If you skipped some of the steps in the earlier parts of this chapter, or if you want to check how your work compares to ours, you can take a look at the movie Kiosk.dir in the Tutorials folder of the CD. That movie contains all the work we have done so far.

In the case of the VPNR project, let's imagine that an interface designer has been hard at work while you've been building the scratch demo. Because you had a comprehensive button inventory, the designer was able to do some serious aesthetic crafting while you wrangled with handlers and such. Now the design elements await importing:

1. *From within Director, select Import from the File menu.*

2. *In the Import Files dialog box, find the folder named KioskArt in the Tutorials folder on the CD, and import the entire contents of the folder.*

You Windows users will probably want to remap the imported images to the System-Win palette. The images were created with System-Mac. If you don't remap the images, assuming you have been using System-Win all along, you will find palette changes taking place in your movie. Also, some of the graphics that you created will change colors because of the mismatched palettes.

You should now have the art in your Cast, but to place the elements on the Stage you're going to have to perform a blend of cast substitution and brute cutting and pasting.

Cast substitution

When there's no Lingo to be lost—or when you're switching one data type for another—cast substitution is the way to go. It's done in the Score rather than the Cast window.

Take a look a the new artwork you just imported; you'll notice that there are a number of full-screen backgrounds that can replace the simple text tags you've been using for demarcation. You could substitute one for the other using the Exchange Cast Members command (Control-E Windows; Command-E Macintosh), but that would insert the new art at the same location as the old, making things generally askew. Because they're full-screen backgrounds, the new art should be fully centered on the Stage, and the best way to do that is to drag the cast members directly to the Score (remember that all cast members dragged directly to the Score are automatically centered on the Stage).

1. *In the Score, select channel 1 of the Attractor scene and then press the Delete key to remove the sprite that's there (the text sprite).*

2. *Click the Cast window to make it active.*

3. *Drag the cast member named Attractor to the recently vacated cell in the Score.*

All of our sprite segments in this demonstration movie are only one frame long. If we were working with longer sprite segments, we would be selecting the entire sprite segment and deleting it. We would then need to place the new cast member and extend it to cover the same frames that were covered previously.

4. *Repeat this process for the remainder of the text tags. Some of our new cast members are used in several locations, so use the following list as a guide:*

    • Place cast member Attractor in the Attractor scene.

    • Place cast member Logo in the Logo Intro scene.

    • Place cast member Main in the Main, About, Retrieve, Followup, New/Quit, and Goodbye scenes.

    • Place cast member Location in the Location scene.

    • Place cast member Type in the Type scene.

    • Place cast member Price in the Price scene.

    • Place cast member Listing in the Display and Browser scenes.

    • Place cast member HelpMe in the Help scene.

Switching images only

The buttons are another matter. We want to maintain their general positions on the Stage—and more important, we want to keep their scripts attached. Substituting cast members would lose both the sprite and cast-level scripts. A cut-and-paste job in the Cast window would preserve sprite scripts, but not those attached to cast members. So the logical step is to switch only the images, which you do from within the Paint window.

To change images only, cut and paste from within Paint. To affect cast-level scripting, make changes in the Cast window. To affect sprite-level scripts, make changes in the Score.

1. *In the Cast, click the new button cast member, Main, to open it in the Paint window.*

2. *Use the selection tool (Lasso or Marquee) to select the button; then copy it.*

3. *Open the Paint window of our original corresponding scratch button Main; double-click the Eraser tool to blank the entire contents.*

4. *Paste the copied image of the new design.*

Check out the results on the Stage. Every instance of the original Main cast member should have been replaced with the new image. Now look in the Cast and notice that the Cast script attached to the Main button is still in place; it should retain that little scripting symbol in the lower-left corner, indicating that Lingo is still attached.

5. *Repeat the process for the buttons Back, Next, Help, and Quit (we don't use the Save button).*

Tidy time

You should now have two identical sets of button graphics: the ones you just imported, and the originals you pasted them into. It's a good idea to delete the former now, since they're cluttering up the Cast and could cause confusion later.

Now browse through your movie. You'll probably find that the button placement needs a good deal of tweaking because the button dimensions aren't the same as those of the originals. Go ahead and adjust until you're satisfied, but keep in mind that consistency is a primary virtue of interface design; when a button appears, it should always appear in the same place on the screen, right down to the exact pixel. For maximum conformity, you can adjust the exact coordinates in each sprite's Properties dialog box.

Here are some other quick improvements we can make:

1. *In the Attractor scene, we no longer need the text we placed there to tell the user to click the mouse. That's the sprite in channel 2, so delete that sprite and delete the cast member as well.*

2. *When the movie passes from the Attractor scene to the Logo Intro scene, it passes through the blank and unused frames. Create a frame behavior in the behavior channel in the Attractor scene that jumps straight to the Logo Intro scene:*

```
on exitFrame
  go to "Logo Intro"
end
```

3. *Create a similar frame behavior in the Logo Intro scene that jumps to the Main Menu scene.*

Sound and sight

We promised a long time ago that our buttons would make a sound and change colors when they were clicked. Since all of our buttons use a single handler, buttonclick, it's easy to add that functionality. You may have noticed that one of the files you imported was a sound named "click." We'll use that sound to make a clicking noise when the button is selected.

1. *Double-click the movie script cast member containing* buttonclick. *Add the lines shown here in bold:*

```
on buttonclick
  thisOne = the clickOn
  sprite(thisOne).locH = sprite(thisOne).locH +5
  sprite(thisOne).locV = sprite(thisOne).locV +5
  sprite(thisOne).ink = 2       ⇒ reverse
  puppetSound "click"
  updateStage
  repeat while the stillDown = TRUE
    nothing
  end repeat
  sprite(thisOne).locH = sprite(thisOne).locH -5
  sprite(thisOne).locV = sprite(thisOne).locV -5
  sprite(thisOne).ink = 8       ⇒ Matte
  puppetSound 0
  updateStage
end buttonclick
```

When we placed the buttons on the Stage, we set the ink to Matte. Using the ink sprite property, we can use Lingo to change the ink effect while the movie is running. Look at ink in *A Lingo Lexicon* (Appendix C) and you will see a list of numbers for the various inks. For the state when the mouse button is depressed, we set the ink effect to 2, which is the Reverse ink. For the state when the mouse button is released again, we set the ink effect to 8, which is Matte.

Back again

Hey, what about those Next and Back buttons? We never really got around to implementing them. Their main uses would be in the Browser scene, where the user should be able to go back and forth through the various choices of listings. Once we start displaying the listing, we can implement these buttons as well. We can also, however, use the Back button in our About and Help scenes. Instead of using our Move On buttons to return to the calling scene, let's implement this functionality with the Back button. The Help scene already has a Back button in place, so let's start there.

1. *In the Score, find the Help scene and then select the Back button.*

2. *Using the Behavior drop-down menu of the Score, attach the behavior that contains the* play done *command.*

If you have trouble finding the behavior, remember that the Help scene has a Move On button with that same behavior attached. You can select the Move On button and check the Behavior menu to see which behavior is used for that sprite.

3. *Delete the Move On button's sprite from the Help scene.*

4. *Copy the Help scene's Back button sprite.*

5. *Paste the copied sprite in channel 6 of the About scene; then delete the Move On button in that same scene.*

When you copy and paste a sprite that has a behavior attached, the behavior is copied along with other information about the sprite.

THE NEXT STEP...

Starting to look like a real production now, isn't it? When properly managed, the transition from scratch to full-dress prototype is one of the most enjoyable steps in development.

This prototype is still a ways from being a finished product, but it's served to demonstrate the important points:

- Defining the flow of information

- Identifying the scripting elements

- Applying those elements uniformly

If you like, you can keep working on your prototype, adding features and functions as you learn them in the rest of this book. Or you might like to browse through FullKiosk.dir on the *Director 7 Demystified* CD. Look for it in the Vpnkiosk folder in the Movies folder. That version has a few more bells and whistles, but underneath it lie the bones of this prototype.

If you choose to flesh out your prototype on your own, here are some questions to keep in mind:

- What kind of tricks can you use to make the Attractor Mode visually stimulating?

- How can you access the various listings in the bare-bones "database," and how can you display them?

- How can you retrieve and store information from the end user?

- If this were developed for online delivery (i.e., a Shockwave format), how would you approach things differently?

- Are there more efficient ways to handle the Lingo coding, particularly if scalability is an issue? If the kiosk were expected to grow tenfold in each subsequent build, how would you approach scripting?

The tools and techniques you'll need to answer each of these questions are contained in the chapters to come.

POINTS TO REMEMBER

The main points of this chapter are these:

- Before you begin programming, consider sketching out a **usage profile** that describes exactly how you anticipate the production will be used and what should be gained from its use.

- Begin by identifying the **individual scenes** your production will require. Try to define those scenes as fully as possible.

- Draft a **flowchart diagram**, tracing the general flow of the interactive experience.

- Identify the **interface elements** common to all scenes and place handlers for those elements in movie scripts to ensure consistent action and operation.

- Create a **prototype** that connects the scenes in a logical fashion, using scratch design elements.

- Test both **experientially** (with an aesthetic mindset) and **destructively** (trying to break the program).

- When a prototype is functionally complete, replace the **scratch elements** with final designs.

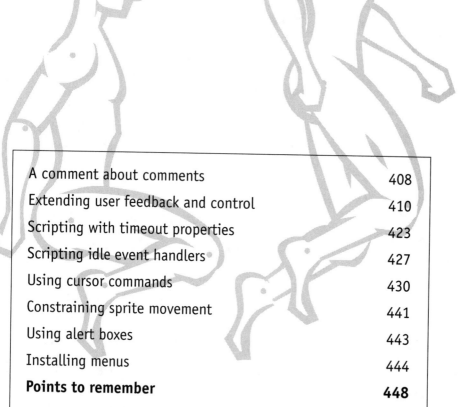

CHAPTER 11

DEEPER INTO LINGO

TIME TO EXPAND YOUR BAG OF LINGO TRICKS. BY NOW YOU HAVE A GOOD understanding of the Lingo basics (writing scripts, creating handlers, and so forth), so the next step is to expand that understanding and ground it more firmly in practical experience. The more you work with Lingo, the more you'll appreciate the easily tapped power of this scripting language.

In this chapter we'll get you started with an introduction to some of the elements that can make your scripts more readable and that improve decision-making in your handlers. Then you'll put these elements to use, extending the degree of feedback and control available to the end users of your productions. Finally, we'll show you a number of Lingo-based techniques that provide an additional gloss of professionalism, making use of such nifty features as custom animated cursors, custom menus, and official-looking alert boxes.

A COMMENT ABOUT COMMENTS

In the scripts we created in the previous chapters, nearly every word of every statement has been written with the intent that it would be read and acted on by Director. That's okay for short handlers and small projects— especially if we don't expect those projects to be around much past the next chapter. However, once you get into *writing* Lingo, as opposed to *learning* Lingo, you're going to find that brevity pretty limiting.

Typically what happens is something like this: You're working on a project and realize that you need to create a new handler. You stop what you're doing and pop open a script editor and, in a flash of insight, see a concise, interesting, and elegant way to achieve the results you want. You quickly write the 100 or so lines of Lingo that you need, give it a quick test (sure enough, it works), and go back to what you were doing before. Three weeks later, your boss and client inform you that what they really want is a cloaking device rather than the shirt-of-invisibility you had discussed previously. You need to modify the handler, so you open it up to make the changes. You stare at the code, and all you can do is wonder who the heck wrote this thing. Whatever bit of cognitive leap that inspired the handler in the first place is missing today (someone changed the brand of coffee in the cafeteria). You can't even figure out what those cryptic variable names are supposed to be referencing.

That the preceding story is fiction doesn't matter; it's close enough to the truth. Ask any programmer who has been around for a few years, and you'll hear similar tales. Most will recall the time they were asked to modify some program, written by someone no longer with the company, that was 5,000 lines long with not a word of explanation.

COMMENTING:
Adding noncommand lines to Lingo code (preceded by a double hyphen).

Fortunately, Director has the solution well in hand. As with all real programming languages, Director allows for the use of **comments** in your scripts. Any time Director sees two hyphens together (--), it reads them as a command to "ignore everything that follows on this line."

Commenting has two primary roles:

- You can use comments to add notations and communications, either to yourself or to other people who may encounter your scripting. It's often a good idea to add a few comment lines at the start of each handler describing the handler's purpose, what input is required, and what output is expected. Add comments throughout your scripts to describe what is going on.

COMMENT CONCEPTS:
You can write a comment, reminder, or instruction in any script by preceding it with double hyphens.

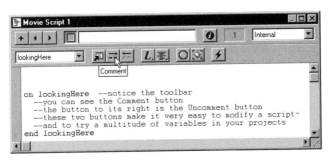

```
Movie Script 8
on beamUp
    sprite (9).memberNum = 5  -- No bitmap at all
    puppetTransition 04  -- Wipe up transition makes it fade
    updateStage  -- do it now
end beamUp

on moveAround  -- make the sprite moveable by the user
    sprite (10).moveableSprite = TRUE
    --sprite (10).cursor = 3
    --sprite (10).cursor = [17,18]
    --global hand
    --sprite (10).cursor = hand
end moveAround
```

- If you want to turn off a bit of scripting, you don't have to delete and retype it. Instead, you can "comment it out" by inserting double hyphens before each line. Director's script editors include buttons that allow you to comment out (and uncomment) blocks of selected text.

DASH IT ALL:
Select a block of text in a script editor window and then use the Comment and Uncomment buttons.

```
Movie Script 1
lookingHere           Comment
on lookingHere  --notice the toolbar
    --you can see the Comment button
    --the button to its right is the Uncomment button
    --these two buttons make it very easy to modify a script
    --and to try a multitude of variables in your projects
end lookingHere
```

Let's give comments a try in the Message window.

1. *Open the Message window and type the following line, ending with Enter (Windows) or Return (Macintosh):*

```
Alex = 28  -- Alex's current age
```

Director accepts the assignment to the variable Alex without any complaint about the comment. So what happens if you try to enter a comment without the double hyphens?

2. *Enter the following in the Message window:*

```
Alex = 28  Alex's current age
```

What you will get is a message, often cryptic, from Director, complaining about your script.

WHAT'S THE WORD?
Any time Director doesn't understand elements in a script, it displays an alert box.

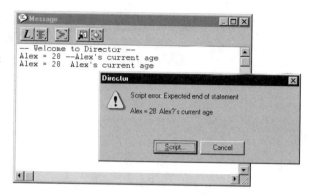

If you want to turn off a handler that's called by other handlers, you can comment out the command lines within it (so that the handler does nothing) rather than commenting out the handler as a whole. Otherwise, the handlers that call that handler won't work, since they'll be hung up looking for a script that (in the eyes of Lingo) no longer exists.

It may seem that we've spent a lot of time talking here about two hyphens, but it's hard to overemphasize the need for comments. If you have a comment line for every line of Lingo you write, you will be well on your way to becoming a professional-level programmer.

EXTENDING USER FEEDBACK AND CONTROL

The exercises in the remainder of this chapter all have the same goal: to explore the ways in which your production can interact with the end user. By now you should be confident about the basics of clickable buttons and nonlinear navigations, so it's time to tackle new interface tools.

Middle-ground interactivity

Let's start by experimenting with a level of feedback and control that's somewhere in the middle ground between active and passive. Usually, a click of the mouse represents a decision on the part of the user—but before making that decision, people often idly move the mouse around the screen. By interpreting those movements, you can write scripts that subtly reinforce the principles of the interface.

For instance, if your interface includes buttons that don't look like buttons (in the stereotypical "push me" sense), you might underscore their clickability by having the cursor change shape whenever the mouse rolls over them. You could also unleash a warning beep when the cursor strays out of bounds, or even pop up occasional reminders that a choice needs to be made.

When scripting for this sort of middle-ground action, your main Lingo tools are the events mouseEnter, mouseLeave, and mouseWithin, and the function the rollOver. The mouse events let you associate scripts with the passage of a cursor over a sprite (and they're no more difficult to use than the familiar click-based mouseDown and mouseUp), but they're meant to be attached to individual sprites or cast members. You can't write a movie-level or frame-level script that dictates the mouseEnter actions of multiple sprites.

The function the rollOver is a little more difficult to script with, but it gives us the advantage of centralization: One script can dictate the behavior of sprites in every single channel. The disadvantage is that it's a function, not an event, and therefore needs to be tied to an event that sets it in motion. The idle event works well for this purpose, but it's also a bit of overkill—idle can happen several times between the time a movie enters a frame and leaves again. Asking Lingo to do something almost continually will affect the amount of processing power involved. A compromise is to use the enterFrame event, which we'll use as the basis of our rollOver-based approach.

In the next exercise, we're going to write scripts that demonstrate some of the different effects that can be achieved using the rollOver. In the process, we'll be using more sophisticated Lingo: nested conditionality, repeat statements, and the like. This time you won't have to start from scratch—I've assembled the non-Lingo elements in a movie called Sitting.dir, which you'll find in the Tutorials folder on this book's companion CD.

Viewing the frame script

We are going to be working with a movie in a single frame this time. I've already written a script that keeps playback in a loop and executes a handler we'll want refreshed every time the loop repeats.

1. Open the movie Sitting.dir.

Our animated Swifty character appears in five incarnations, each seated on what will soon look like a chair. We're going to give each Swifty a different kind of action associated with the rollOver.

ROLL OVER, SWIFTY:
The mouse position on the screen can call an action with the rollOver function.

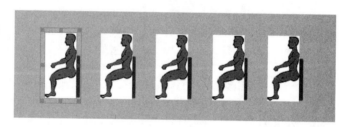

2. In the Cast, select the behavior in cast member slot 7 and open it using the Script button.

The script reads:

```
on enterFrame
    action   -- call our custom handler
end

on exitFrame
    go to the frame   -- loop on this frame
end
```

TWO HANDLERS, ONE SCRIPT:
A script cast member can contain multiple event handlers.

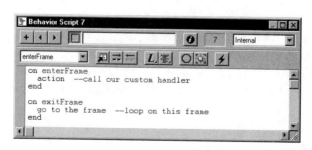

I've added two handlers in this Score script. The word *action* is the name of a custom handler we'll be writing shortly.

3. **Close the script; then double-click the behavior channel of frame 1 of the Score.**

Same script; the behavior is already attached to the appropriate frame.

Repeating with repeat

You may have noticed in the Sitting.dir movie that all of the sprites have their bounding boxes showing because their ink effects are set to Copy. You could select the sprites and change the ink, but we'd rather show you how it can be done in a simple repeat with statement. We already used a repeat while statement in a previous exercise; repeat with is a little different. This is the general format:

```
repeat with [countVariable] = [first] to [last]
  [statement(s)]
end
```

Any number of statements can be included in the repeat construct. The first time through, the *countVariable* value is set to *first* (an integer). On successive loops, the *countVariable* value is incremented until, on the final pass, *countVariable* is set to *last*. It's easy to see how this works with a simple script that adds all the numbers from 1 to 100.

```
total = 0  -- initialize to zero
repeat with thisNumber = 1 to 100
  total = total + thisNumber
  -- add the current number to the total
end repeat
put total  -- display the total in the Message window
```

One thing to notice is that *countVariable* (thisNumber in our script) is a real variable and can be used in the statements in the repeat construct.

Since we want to change the ink before the user ever sees the sprites, we'll place our repeat statement in a startMovie handler.

1. *Click cast slot 8 and open a movie script.*

2. *Enter the following* `startMovie` *handler:*

```
on startMovie
  -- set the ink of all the sprites
  repeat with channel = 1 to 10
    sprite(channel).ink = 8 -- matte ink effect
  end repeat
end startMovie
```

Rather than writing 10 individual lines to set the ink of each sprite, you've used one `repeat` command to do it all. The `repeat with` construct can be used to apply instructions to any number of scriptable elements. But don't forget to turn it off explicitly right after it's called, with an `end repeat` line.

All indentations in Lingo scripts should be made by Director (which automatically reformats as you type) rather than by yourself. If a script doesn't work, your first step should be to check the text: Only the first and last lines of each handler (the **on** and **end** lines) should be flush left. Statements inside of constructs such as **repeat** should also be indented.

We can't test the `startMovie` handler just yet because we have a call to the `action` handler in the frame behavior, and that handler hasn't been written. If you want, you can open the script for the behavior channel and comment out the `action` command. Then run the movie.

Director increments the variable used for counting in a **repeat** construct by 1 automatically each time though. Unlike some other programming languages, you don't have to set this value explicitly. On the other hand, you can't change the amount by which the counting variable is increased with each pass. There is, however, a **repeat with...down to** construct that decrements the counting variable with each pass.

Scripting with the rollOver function

The function the `rollOver` tracks the current location of the mouse cursor on the screen. When that location coincides with the coordinates of a sprite on the Stage, the `rollOver` returns the number of that sprite. It's a value that can be tested but not set, which means that you can know where the cursor is, but you can't move it to a different location.

Remember that **the rollOver** is a function, not an event. Scripts with constructions like **on rollOver** will not work. The syntax for **the rollOver** function comes in two flavors: **the rollOver** returns the channel number of the sprite the cursor is over; and **rollOver (x)**, with **x** being an integer expressing the channel number of a sprite, returns TRUE or FALSE, depending on whether the cursor is over the specified sprite. To attach a **rollOver**-like action to a single sprite or cast member, use the events **mouseEnter**, **mouseExit**, and/or **mouseWithin**.

If the ink effect of a sprite is Matte, the `rollOver` considers the mouse to be over the sprite only if the cursor is over the visible sprite. For the other ink effects, the `rollOver` uses the entire bounding box of the sprite. So if you have an irregular shaped sprite and want to exclude the invisible areas of the bounding box, use the Matte ink rather than Background Transparent.

Writing the movie scripts

We've already started our movie script with the `startMovie` handler. Our next step is to write some more handlers what will be called while the movie is playing. We'll need the following:

- A handler that specifies actions for a range of the `rollOver` functions. We've already established that this handler will be called `action`.

- A housekeeping handler that undoes the `rollOver` actions by restoring the sprites to their original dispositions. Without this handler, the consequences of the `action` script would remain even when the `rollOver` function is no longer valid.

Since both of these handlers need to be continually accessible to handlers anywhere in the movie, we will give them a home in a movie script.

Using multiple nested If and Else statements

The first thing we're going to do is write the action handler. Since we want to script a different response for each of the Swifty sprites, this handler needs to anticipate six rollOver values: one for each of the five characters, and one for when a rollover occurs anywhere else. We'll do this by making calls to individual sprite handlers and by using the if...then...else construction to create six degrees of conditionality. As you'll see, a lot of automatic indentation occurs.

1. *In the Cast, double-click the movie script in slot 8 to open the Movie Script editor window.*

2. *Below the end of the* startMovie *script, type the following:*

```
on action  -- called from enterFrame
  if rollOver (6) then sprite (6).memberNum = 2
  else
    if rollOver (7) then changeColor
    else
      if rollOver (8) then fallDown
      else
        if rollOver (9) then beamUp
        else
          if rollOver (10) then moveAround
          else
            cleanUp
          end if
        end if
      end if
    end if
  end if
end action
```

Notice the number of end if statements. If they don't balance out the number of if statements, Director can't figure out the handler.

Note also that in all but one case, we've resorted to calling more handlers (changeColor, fallDown, beamUp, moveAround, and cleanUp). This prevents the handler script from getting too long, and it keeps things modular: We can tinker with each action individually.

The convenience of case and otherwise

Indenting the script every time another if is introduced gets pretty awkward after a while. That's why Lingo provides an alternative construct: using case and otherwise.

Nested if...then statements can now be replaced by the Lingo keywords case and otherwise.

These keywords make it possible to spell out instructions for conditionality without having to worry about balancing if and end if statements. Instead, you declare a case statement, link it to a particular value (in this case, the value returned by rollOver), and then list possible values and their specific actions. The general syntax is as follows:

```
case [some Expression] of
  [some Value]:[some statement]
  [another Value]:
                    [many statements]
  otherwise:[some statement]
end case
```

The expression on the case line is evaluated, and that value is compared to the values (which can also be expressions to be evaluated) on the succeeding lines. If a match is found, then the statement(s) associated with the match are executed. Other possible matches are ignored. If no match is found, then the statements associated with the otherwise keyword are executed.

We can rewrite the action handler using a case statement:

1. **Open the movie script and select the entire** if...end if **construct you just created.**

2. **Use the Comment button of the script editor to comment out the entire construct.**

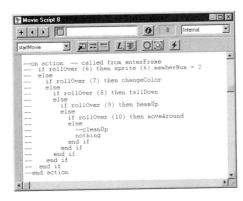

3. *Type the following* action *handler, which uses the* case *statement:*

```
on action   -- called from enterFrame
    case the rollOver of
        6: sprite(6).memberNum = 2
        7: changeColor
        8: fallDown
        9: beamUp
        10: moveAround
        otherwise cleanUp
    end case
end action
```

What's nice about this approach is that additional conditional state-ments can be added *ad infinitum*, so long as they're inserted before the otherwise instruction line. The nested nature of conditionality isn't too clear with case, though, so I wanted you to do at least a little scripting in the old-fashioned syntax. In the future, feel free to use either approach.

Writing the individual action handlers

The next step is to script those sprite-specific handlers. I've chosen ones that illustrate the broad range of Lingo-based controls that can be triggered by a rollover. These handlers can all reside in the same movie script, too.

4. *In the Movie Script window, add the following handlers:*

```
on changeColor
   sprite (2).foreColor = random (255)  -- new color for chair
   the stageColor = random (255)  -- new color for the stage, too
end changeColor

on fallDown
   sprite (3).blend = 0  -- make chair transparent
   sprite (8).memberNum = 3  -- use fallen cast member
end fallDown

on beamUp
   sprite (9).memberNum = 5  -- no bitmap at all
   puppetTransition 04  -- Wipe Up transition makes it fade
   updateStage  -- do it now
end beamUp
```

[handwritten annotations: so und field ✓ end 10, Bold Select 242 214 254 5 ∠8 38]

```
on moveAround  -- make the sprite moveable by the user
  sprite (10).moveableSprite = TRUE
end moveAround
```

> Just as you don't really need to follow the capitalization conventions of Lingo, you don't need to conclude each handler with a recapitulation of the handler name: **end** will work just as well as **end beamUp**. But it's a good convention to follow, if only for clarity's sake.

Writing the cleanup handler

[handwritten annotation: sound in Recipes ⟵ 76, 91]

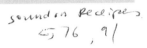

The action handler is structured so that if the rollOver doesn't return any of the sprite numbers, a cleanUp handler is called. This will restore all of the sprites to their original positions.

5. ***In the Script window, add the following:***

```
on cleanUp  -- restore defaults when cursor is over no sprite
  the stageColor = 245  -- stage back to gray
  -- replace sprite's cast that may have changed
  sprite (6).memberNum = 1
  sprite (8).memberNum = 1
  sprite (9).memberNum = 1
  sprite (3).blend = 100  -- back to visible
  sprite (2).foreColor = 69  -- original chair color
  sprite (10).moveableSprite = FALSE  -- user can't move sprite
end cleanUp
```

6. ***Close the Script window and run the movie.***

If nothing is happening, did you comment out the action command in the frame behavior to test your movie earlier? If you did, uncomment that statement now and try again.

7. ***Move the cursor from left to right across the seated characters.***

As you roll the cursor over each sitting Swifty, various antics should ensue:

- The leftmost Swifty should spring in and out of his chair, the illusion of motion created by a simple cast member (memberNum) substitution.

- The next handler (changeColor) should trigger a riot of colors, both in the background and in the chair. Notice how this Swifty changes continually—actually, all handlers are updated every time the playback head loops, but this one has a variable result due to the two random functions. This handler also illustrates that `rollOver`-based scripting doesn't have to manipulate solely the sprite in question.

- Like the first Swifty's handler, the third one (`fallDown`) uses a `memberNum` substitution for an animated effect. It also gets the chair out of the way not by actually removing it, but by making it invisible: `sprite (3).blend = 0` changes the blend for the chair, effectively making it transparent (100% is totally opaque).

- The fourth handler (`beamUp`) should cause the next Swifty to dematerialize, foot first, from his chair. The disappearance results from the substitution of the source cast member with an empty cast slot (remember how we kept slot 5 vacant?). The style of departure is created by using a transition: `puppetTransition 04` applies the Wipe Up effect. Since the sprite is the only changing area on the Stage, the transition applies only to it. The `updateStage` command makes the transition immediate. Without that, the transition would be lost when the playback head loops back to frame 1.

When using **puppetTransition** to apply transitions within a frame, keep in mind that it will apply only to the changing area unless you specify otherwise. If you want the transition to occur over the Stage as a whole, you need to turn off the default action by setting it to **FALSE**. Hence, **puppetTransition 04, FALSE** will apply the Wipe Up effect to the whole works.

- The final Swifty shouldn't do anything when you roll over it. The `moveAround` handler simply sets to TRUE the sprite property `moveableSprite`. Hold down the mouse button, and you can drag the rightmost Swifty around the screen.

MOVING FREELY:
The moveableSprite property allows the user to drag a sprite on the Stage.

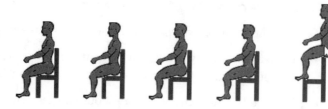

Did you figure out why the Swiftys repeat their actions instead of just performing them once? Take the falling Swifty, for example. The new cast member for the Swifty is in a different location on the Stage, and the mouse is no longer over the sprite. When the mouse is not over any Swifty sprite, the cleanUp handler gets called, and the original cast member is switched back in. Suddenly, the mouse is over the sprite again, and again, and….

Here are some more questions for you. What happens when the mouse is over two sprites at the same time? Why are there two syntaxes for rollOver? Why are these two questions related? To look into the answers to these questions, let's play with the moveable sprite on the far right.

8. **With the movie running, hold down the mouse button on the rightmost Swifty and drag the character about the screen. Make sure to pass over the other Swiftys.**

Nothing in particular happens when two Swiftys are over each other. If something is happening, make sure that you are using the action handler created with the case statement.

Now let's try a little experiment:

9. **Carefully drag the moveable Swifty on top of the leftmost Swifty and release the mouse button.**

Both Swiftys should stay where they are. The cleanUp handler isn't being called because the mouse is still over a Swifty.

10. **Being careful not to move the mouse, open the Message window using the keyboard: Control-M for Windows, or Command-M for Macintosh.**

11. **Type the following and then press Enter (Windows) or Return (Macintosh); don't move the mouse.**

```
put the rollOver
```

This is the syntax for the rollOver that we used in the case statement. The function the rollOver returns a single number (10), even though the mouse is over two sprites. The number returned is the channel number of the sprite that is in the forefront—the sprite with the highest channel number.

ROLLOVER ONCE:
When used as the rollOver, only the topmost sprite is reported.

12. *Type two more lines, following each by pressing Enter or Return (don't move that mouse!):*

```
put rollOver(6)
put rollOver(10)
```

The function the rollOver returns 1, or TRUE, in both instances. So Director knows that the mouse is over both sprites; it's just that the the rollOver form of the function can return only a single channel number. Since we use the rollOver in our case statement, only the forefront sprite that the mouse is over is acted on. We could, if we wanted, rewrite our action handler to check each sprite individually using the rollOver(x) syntax and act on each and every sprite underneath the mouse.

ROLLOVER TWICE:
The rollOver(x) function knows about every sprite under the mouse.

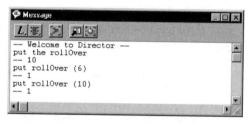

Don't confuse the two **rollOver** syntaxes. If you are testing whether a *specific* sprite is under the mouse, use the form with the parentheses: **rollover(x)**. If you are testing to see whether *any* sprite is under the mouse, use the form **the rollOver**, with no parentheses allowed.

Since it's easy to comment and uncomment blocks of commands in the script editor, try using the **if...else** construct for the **action** handler instead of the **case** construct. Just select each of the handlers and comment or uncomment them as you desire.

SCRIPTING WITH TIMEOUT PROPERTIES

We noted that using the rollOver provides a middle ground of user interaction, somewhere between active and passive. We'll now venture into the realm of the entirely passive: scripts that do something only when the user does nothing. We'll do that by manipulating some of the properties associated with the timeOut event.

A timeOut event occurs after a time has passed (a time we determine) in which no user action takes place (we determine which user actions count). For example, if we are interested only in mouse clicks, we can use the timeOut event to say, "If the user hasn't clicked the mouse in 3 minutes, then do the following." Director keeps a running count of the amount of time that has elapsed. If the user clicks the mouse, Director's timer is set back to zero.

Working with timeOut events is a slightly more involved process than we've encountered thus far. This event is the only one that has a variable value (timeoutLength), and we first need to set that value to a specific amount of time. Another complication is that there are two methods we can use to handle a timeOut event: We can write an on timeOut handler, or we can use the property the timeoutScript.

There are a number of properties related to the timeOut event, all of which can be tested and set:

- the timeoutLength is the property used to establish the amount of time passed before a timeout is declared. The default length is 10,800 ticks, or 3 minutes.

- the timeoutLapsed is the property that reflects the time passed since the property was last reset. This is Director's timeOut counter value. When the properties the timeoutLength and the timeoutLapsed have the same value, the timeOut event is sent through the messaging hierarchy.

- the timeoutScript specifies the Lingo to be executed when the timeOut event occurs. This property does not contain those handlers; rather, it points to them. The distinction is useful in instances when you want specific timeout scenarios in specific portions of your movie; you can set this property to point to a new handler as the need arises.

- the `timeoutKeyDown`, when set to FALSE, will keep `keyDown` events from resetting the `timeoutLapsed` to zero. In other words, this property determines whether keystrokes count as user activity, at least as far as the `timeOut` event is concerned.

- the `timeoutMouse` does the same thing for `mouseDown` events. When set to FALSE, mouse clicks won't keep the `timeOut` event from occurring.

There is no property related to mere movement of the mouse. However, if you want to, you can write a **rollOver** script that resets **the timeoutLapsed** to zero and then attach that script to various sprites (or to one big sprite with Transparent ink in the background).

When Lingo was created, the folks at Macromind (now Macromedia) tried to keep the language as Englishlike as possible. This makes it more user friendly, but the flip side of that friendliness is the possibility of creeping confusion. In this case, Macromedia seems to be as confused as anyone. The Director documentation says things like "since the last timeout." What this really means is "since the last time **the timeoutLapsed** was set to zero"—which is to say, since the last time you reset **the timeoutLength**, or since a **timeOut** event or an allowable user event occurred.

With two ways to determine how a `timeOut` event is handled, how do we decide which method to use? If we write an on `timeOut` handler (in a movie script), that handler will be called whenever a `timeOut` event occurs anywhere in the movie. That's the way to go if you want the same action throughout your movie. On the other hand, the `timeoutScript` allows you to determine, on the fly, what actions should take place—you can change the handlers called or call no handler at all.

We could use either method for the next exercise, but the `timeoutScript` is so different from our previous treatment of events that we want to give it a try. We'll use the timeout properties to change the way our Sitting.dir movie works. Rather than restoring the conditions of each of the characters immediately after the cursor has passed them, we'll buy a little time to savor their antics by changing the circumstances under which the cleanUp handler is called. Instead of calling cleanUp when the mouse is no longer over a sprite, we'll call it after a timeOut event occurs.

1. ***Open the movie script (cast slot 8) of the movie.***

2. ***In the*** startMovie ***script, insert the following statements after the*** end repeat ***statement and before the*** end startMovie ***statement:***

```
the timeoutLength = 6 * 60
the timeoutScript = "cleanUp"
the timeoutKeyDown = FALSE
cleanUp
```

I've chosen to express the property the timeoutLength as an arithmetical operation: * is the operator for multiplication, so the value is 6 times 60, or 360 ticks. The integer 360 would work just as well, but by expressing this property in multiples of 60, you can tell at a glance how many seconds are involved (in this case, 6).

Notice that in designating the timeoutScript, the handler invoked is named in double quotation marks ("cleanUp"). This syntax is important; otherwise, all you'll get is another error message:

THE ERROR OF YOUR WAYS: Don't forget quotation marks when you're naming a handler.

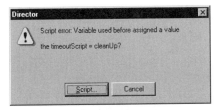

The quotation marks are necessary because you're *naming* the handler, not *calling* it. Since you're assigning a value (as shown by the equals operator), Director assumes that cleanUp is some sort of variable containing that value—and it can't find any such variable.

The fourth new line is a simple invocation of the cleanUp handler. Since you'll be stopping and starting the movie repeatedly over the next few exercises, it makes sense to ensure that the Stage returns to its original configuration whenever you start the movie.

Nothing to the rescue

Before we can run the movie, we have a problem to surmount: Our timeoutScript calls the cleanUp handler, but so does the action handler.

We'll have to take that call out of action. In the case construct, that's as simple as commenting out this line:

otherwise cleanUp

If we are using an if...then construct for cleanup, the process is a bit more complicated. Because the if and else statements are nested, excising this line

else cleanUp

would throw off the balance of if...end if nesting and render the handler unexecutable.

In either case, however, we can use the nothing command as an elegant solution.

3. In the action handler, substitute the term nothing **for the term** cleanUp.

A CASE OF NOTHING:
Using otherwise nothing makes the script more readable.

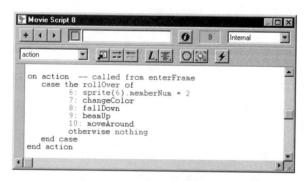

```
on action  -- called from enterFrame
    case the rollOver of
        6: sprite(6).memberNum = 2
        7: changeColor
        8: fallDown
        9: beamUp
        10: moveAround
        otherwise nothing
    end case
end action
```

NOTHING MATTERS:
In if...else statements the balance of if, else, and end if statements must be maintained, sometimes by telling Director to do nothing.

```
end startMovie

on action  -- called from enterFrame
    if rollOver (6) then sprite (6).memberNum = 2
    else
        if rollOver (7) then changeColor
        else
            if rollOver (8) then fallDown
            else
                if rollOver (9) then beamUp
                else
                    if rollOver (10) then moveAround
                    else
                        nothing
                    end if
                end if
            end if
        end if
    end if
end action
```

This is another demonstration of the true utility of nothing. We don't need to rewrite our script to compensate for the loss of a command; instead, we plug a nonproductive command in its place.

4. *Save and run the movie.*

Now when you initiate the various rollOver actions, their results should stay in place for a total of 6 seconds after the mouse is no longer over a sprite, and then the sprites should revert to their original dispositions. Try parking the mouse and then pressing one or more keys while waiting for the timeout. Since we turned off the property the timeoutKeyDown, the keystrokes should have no effect.

> One of the problems with the **timeOut** event is that there is only one. Sometimes you will find yourself needing to track the elapsed time for a number of occurrences. Director also has a timer system property (**the timer**) that can be used to track the amount of time elapsed. More commonly, if you need to keep track of the time for a number of occurrences, you will use the system property **the ticks.** This property returns the number of ticks since the computer was started. You can get and save the value when you want to start your timer and then regularly check the current value to see if your time has elapsed. Any number of handlers can use **the ticks** because it is never reset while the movie is running.

SCRIPTING IDLE EVENT HANDLERS

We've set up scripting that returns the sprites to their original positions every 6 seconds—but is there any way for the end user to know that? Since we're currently exploring the possibilities of user feedback, let's look into providing some sort of countdown, an onscreen visual representation of the time remaining until the cleanUp handler is executed.

To do this, we'll write a handler that uses the idle event, our guarantee that the handler will be executed as often as possible (that is, whenever Director isn't doing something else). We'll put that idle handler in a frame behavior script; it would work just as well in a movie script, but then it would also apply to frames we might later add to the movie. Unless you're absolutely sure that your movie will remain a single-frame production, it's a good idea to keep frame-specific scripts out of the movie script.

1. *Click to select cast slot 9; open the Field window using Control-8 (Windows) or Command-8 (Macintosh).*

2. *Type the digit 1 in the text area.*

This single digit will be used to indicate the time remaining until cleanUp is called. In my version of this movie, I used the Field menu to make it big (36 points) and bold, but you can make it any size and style you'd like. The actual digit used doesn't really matter, since the number displayed will soon be a function of Lingo rather than of your present handiwork.

3. *Name this cast member Countdown and then close the Field window.*

4. *Drag the Countdown cast member from the Cast to the upper-right corner of the Stage.*

This should automatically insert the sprite of Countdown into channel 11 of frame 1 of the Score.

5. *Select sprite 11 in the Score; use the pull-down Ink menu to set the sprite's ink to Reverse.*

The digit should now show up black on white.

6. *In the Score, double-click the behavior channel sprite.*

The behavior script appears. We're going to use the case and otherwise approach again to keep our Lingo from becoming incomprehensibly entangled in if statements.

7. *In the space between the enterFrame and exitFrame handlers, type the following:*

```
on idle
    put the timeoutLapsed / 60 into myTime
    case (myTime) of
        5: set the text of member "Countdown" to "1"
        4: set the text of member "Countdown" to "2"
        3: set the text of member "Countdown" to "3"
        2: set the text of member "Countdown" to "4"
        1: set the text of member "Countdown" to "5"
        otherwise set the text of member "Countdown" to " "
    end case
end idle
```

Let's take a look at the lines in this script. The line

```
put the timeoutLapsed / 60 into myTime
```

does three things:

- It retrieves the property the `timeoutLapsed`.

- It uses an arithmetic operator (/) to divide that property value by 60, thereby converting the time measurement from ticks to seconds.

- It puts the new value into a custom variable called `myTime`.

The subsequent `case` statement evaluates this `myTime` variable and then compares its value with a series of fixed numbers. When `myTime` equals 5, the text of Countdown is changed to read 1, and so forth.

When it comes to changing properties, sometimes you need to address the source cast member of a sprite rather than the sprite itself. For instance, the text of a sprite can be changed by one of two methods: changing the text of the cast member (as we just did) or switching source cast members with a **sprite([*which sprite*]).memberNum** command.

Notice that when `myTime` equals zero, the Countdown cast member is set to contain an empty text string. This makes the Countdown cast member effectively disappear at that point. Since the timeout duration is set to 6 seconds, the value of `myTime` is presumably returned to zero at that point. It will also return to zero any time a bona fide `mouseDown` event occurs.

Our **on idle** handler doesn't include an **updateStage** command, because it isn't necessary; we're looping through this frame several times a second, and the Stage is updated automatically every time **the enterFrame** is executed. But if you're writing an **idle** script for placement in a nonlooping frame, you'll probably need an **updateStage** command to ensure that the Stage reflects the changes in the handler as soon as they're made.

8. *Save and then play the movie.*

Countdown, sitdown:
By adjusting the idle
time and displaying its
status, you can keep
users well informed.

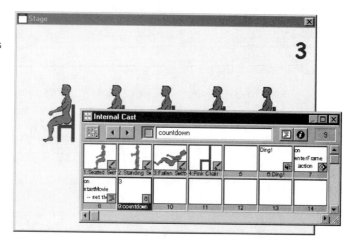

As you experiment with the movie, you'll find that the countdown progresses every 6 seconds, whether or not the mouse is over any of the sprites. If you click the mouse button at any location, the countdown number immediately is reset to zero. On the other hand, any keystrokes you type won't impede the countdown.

Using cursor commands

Another tool in your bag of tricks is the **cursor**. Not only can you tap into the standard cursor set of the computer, but you can design (or procure) and use custom cursors for that extra-professional look. Furthermore, you can associate specific cursors with individual sprites (which is a good way to prompt the user for specific actions). You can even hide the cursor, for those occasions when you want the user to do nothing.

Calling all cursors...

Six cursors are built into both the Windows and Macintosh operating systems. That means their designs are part of the system software used to start the computer—since the system is always running, the icons are always available. Each of these cursors has a distinctive ID number; to use a cursor, you must invoke its ID number in a line of Lingo script.

CURSOR CAST:
Windows and Macintosh have six standard cursors, each with an ID number.

CURSOR	ID NUMBER
[no cursor set]	0
![arrow cursor]	-1
![I-beam cursor]	1
![crosshair cursor]	2
![plus cursor]	3
![watch cursor] (Mac)	4
![hourglass cursor] (Win)	4
[blank cursor]	200

What's the difference between cursor 0 (no cursor) and cursor 200 (blank cursor)? The first indicates that no special cursor is needed, in effect passing cursor control back to the operating system. The latter sets a specific cursor; it just happens to be a blank one. Use 0 when you're done with cursor manipulation, and use 200 when you want the cursor to disappear.

Changing the overall cursor

To change the overall cursor (the one that appears whenever the mouse is over the Stage) to a standard cursor, simply use the cursor command in conjunction with an ID number. Let's change the overall cursor in our current movie to crosshairs:

1. ***In the movie script of the movie, add the following line to the*** on startMovie *handler:*

cursor 2

A CURSORY SUBSTITUTION:
All the standard cursors can be called using their ID numbers.

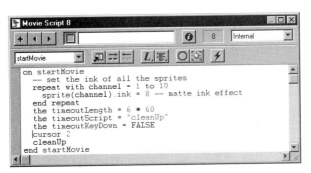

```
on startMovie
  -- set the ink of all the sprites
  repeat with channel = 1 to 10
    sprite(channel).ink = 8 -- matte ink effect
  end repeat
  the timeoutLength = 6 * 60
  the timeoutScript = "cleanUp"
  the timeoutKeyDown = FALSE
  cursor 2
  cleanUp
end startMovie
```

Remember to insert the command after existing script lines, but before the end statement. By the way, you can set the overall cursor in frame scripts as well as movie scripts—whatever location works best in the context of your project.

2. Close the Script window and run the movie.

Now the cursor used throughout should be the crosshairs (+). If you like, experiment by changing the cursor ID number designated in the movie script. You can also use the Message window (while the movie is running) to issue cursor commands.

Setting a sprite cursor

Take a look at our five sitting Swiftys. In four cases, the rollOver action is obvious—it happens automatically. But the rightmost Swifty doesn't change appearance when the cursor is over it; that Swifty becomes a draggable sprite, but how is the user supposed to know that?

One way to indicate that a sprite is different is by changing the cursor when it rolls over that sprite. We could do this with the cursor command, but instead we'll do it by designating the cursor sprite property that sets the cursor for a specific sprite. Let's use it to give the fifth Swifty a cursor of his own:

1. Open the movie script; scroll to the moveAround **handler.**

2. Add the following to the handler:

```
sprite(10).cursor = 3
```

We're placing this line in a handler called by another, rollOver-based handler, but it would work equally well placed in the startMovie handler or in a frame script. There's no need to associate it explicitly with rollOver.

3. Close the window; then run the movie.

Now when the cursor is over sprite 10, it changes to a meatier crossbar. Notice that everywhere else on the Stage, the default cursor remains the crosshairs.

CURSORS IN CONTEXT:
You can make the cursor change appearance when it passes over a certain sprite.

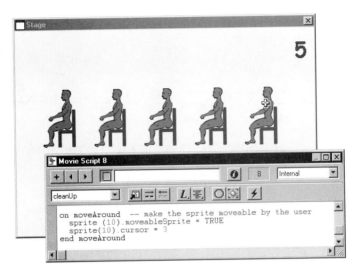

Using a bitmap cursor

Using a sprite-specific cursor is all well and good, but having only six cursors to choose from is a bit limiting. Take the exercise just completed: The cursor changes from a thin cross to a thick one—but just what does that convey to the user? It's hard to infer that the sprite character in question is moveable.

Fortunately, Director lets you add and use an unlimited number of custom cursors. The process is a bit tricky but worth mastering. Any bitmapped graphic cast member can be designated as a cursor, but unless it meets certain criteria, the custom cursor will be ignored and the default cursor substituted.

To work as a cursor, a cast member must

- Be a 1-bit graphic (black or white pixels only).

- Conform to a square of 16 pixels by 16 pixels. If it is larger, Director removes the lower and rightmost portions of the graphic. Smaller images will work fine.

Checking the bitmap

In my completed version of this movie (Sitdone.dir), you'll find that I've already created two cast members that seem suitable as cursors.

1. *Open the movie Sitdone.dir in the Tutorials folder on the CD.*

2. *Select and copy cast members 17 and 18.*

3. *Paste these into the same cast slots in your version of Sitting.dir.*

FROM HAND TO MOUSE: Bitmaps used for cursors must be black and white and 16 x 16 pixels in size.

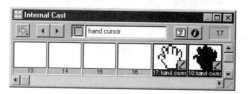

The first image looks like it'll do as a cursor. But we'll have to check to make sure.

4. *Select cast member 17 in the Cast window.*

5. *From the Modify menu, select Transform Bitmap.*

The width, height, and color depth are correct. If you're not sure of these parameters, you're bound to be frustrated when you work with custom cursors.

A LITTLE BIT COUNTRY: Bitmaps for cursors must be stored in 1-bit form in order to work on the Stage.

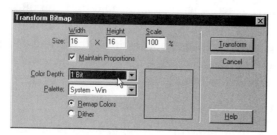

Since 1-bit color is, in this case, no color at all (just black and/or white pixels), it doesn't matter which palette is chosen, or whether the conversion method is Dither or Remap. The result will be the same.

6. *Click Cancel to close the Transform Bitmap dialog box.*

It's hard to get precise measurements of graphics in Director's Paint window, but you want to make sure that your cursor occupies a square area of 16 x 16 pixels. One way to ensure that is to create the cursor in a bitmapped graphics program (such as Adobe Photoshop) and then import it into Director. Use the application's document setup options to create a canvas 16 pixels square, and then draw right up to the edges.

Using the bitmap

Let's see this cursor in action:

1. **Open the movie script. Scroll to the** moveAround **handler.**

2. **Change the current** cursor **command line to this:**

```
sprite(10).cursor = [17]
```

The square brackets [ ] surrounding the number are important; they indicate that the integer refers to the cast member number, not a resource ID number. Even if you've given the cursor a name in the Cast database, you must refer to it by cast member number.

Refer to custom cursors by their cast member numbers surrounded by square brackets [ ].

3. **Save your changes. Then run the movie.**

The hand cursor should appear whenever the mouse is over sprite 10—but the effect leaves a little something to be desired. The cursor consists only of an outline of a hand, and it all but disappears against the background.

AN ODD HAT:
Without a mask,
the cursor appears
transparent.

MASK:
A second cursor image used to designate white areas in the resulting cursor.

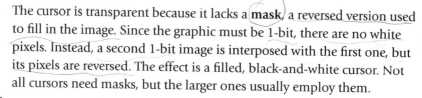

The cursor is transparent because it lacks a mask, a reversed version used to fill in the image. Since the graphic must be 1-bit, there are no white pixels. Instead, a second 1-bit image is interposed with the first one, but its pixels are reversed. The effect is a filled, black-and-white cursor. Not all cursors need masks, but the larger ones usually employ them.

Using a mask

As you can see by its name—Hand Cursor Mask—cast member 18 is intended to serve as a mask for our hand cursor. It's already set to the correct size and color depth, so all you need to do is incorporate it into the Lingo.

1. *Open the movie script; scroll to the* moveAround *handler.*

To designate a cursor mask, add a comma and the mask's cast member number to the bracketed statement.

2. *Change the current* cursor *command line to*

```
sprite (10).cursor = [17, 18]
```

Adding a comma and the cast member number to the bracketed statement designates which cast member is to be used as the mask (the space after the comma is optional).

3. *Save changes; then run the movie.*

This time, the custom cursor should fill in nicely.

THE MASKED MAN:
A cursor mask is frequently used for larger cursors, to ensure that the user can always distinguish it clearly.

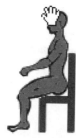

Rather than repeat the bracketed statement every time a custom cursor is invoked, you can give that cursor a name by setting a global variable in the **startMovie** handler. For example, **hand = [17, 18]** would designate that particular cursor and mask combination as **hand**. Thereafter, a functional syntax would be **sprite (10).cursor = hand.**

Creating a custom cursor

Director 6.5 introduced true system-level animated bitmap cursors. Now you can use a series of 8-bit colored cast members to create a cursor that actually can change shape and color. We can't use the cursor sprite property with an animated cursor, so we'll use the cursor command and a mouseEnter handler to set the cursor for the moveable Swifty.

Building the cursor

Once you have artwork for your cursor, there are only a few steps you need to take to actually create an animated cursor. Just as in the previous exercise, I have already created some art for you.

1. *Open the movie Sitdone.dir in the Tutorials folder on the CD.*

2. *Select and copy cast members 19 and 20.*

3. *Paste these into slots 19 and 20 in your version of Sitting.dir.*

ALL HANDS ON DECK: You can use a number of bitmaps to create an animated cursor.

Once again, we want to check to make sure that our cast members fit the requirements, but now we are concerned only that the cast members have an 8-bit color depth. If a cast member is larger than our desired cursor size, Director will scale the bitmaps to the appropriate size. Note that this is different from when you use the cursor sprite property, where the bitmap will be cropped if it is larger than 16 x 16 pixels.

4. *Use the Cast Member Properties button in the Cast window to make sure that your cast members are 8-bit. If they are not, use Transform Bitmap on the Modify menu to convert them to 8-bit.*

5. *Select the empty cast slot 21.*

6. *From the Insert menu, select Media Element and then select Cursor.*

The Cursor Properties Editor window appears. With the controls of this window, we can choose which bitmaps to include and make adjustments to the way the cursor is displayed and behaves.

7. **In the Cast Member area of the Cursor Properties Editor window, use the arrows to find cast member 19.**

An image of the selected bitmap appears in the windoid above the arrows.

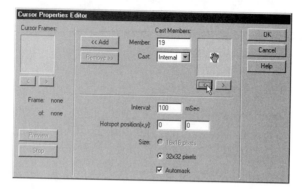

8. **Click the Add button.**

9. **Use the arrows again to find cast member 20 and then click Add again.**

10. **In the Interval field, set the interval to 300 milliseconds.**

The Interval is the amount of time between each changing of the bitmaps in the animation. If this setting is too fast, you won't be able to see the changes.

11. **Choose a cursor size from the options available.**

The Size options available to you depend on the system you are using. Macintosh systems support only 16 x 16-pixel cursors. Windows systems may support 16 x 16 or 32 x 32 pixels, depending on the display card installed. If an option in not available to you, it will be dimmed.

12. **Set the Hotspot Position fields. If you are using a 16 x 16-pixel cursor, set each field to 8; if you are using a 32 x 32-pixel cursor, set each field to 16.**

The Hotspot Position fields allow you to select the actual spot on the cursor that indicates the exact point of a mouse click. You sometimes have to use your imagination for this one. With the standard arrow cursor, the obvious choice is the tip of the arrow. For a round cursor, you'd probably choose the center. We'll use the center for our hand cursor.

13. **Make sure that the Automask check box is selected.**

The area on the left side of the Cursor Properties Editor window allows you to inspect your cursor. Use the arrow keys there to view each of the bitmaps used by the cursor. You can also see a preview of what your cursor will look like when it's animated.

14. Click the Preview button. When you're through previewing, click the Stop button.

CURSORY CHECK:
You can preview what a cursor will look like.

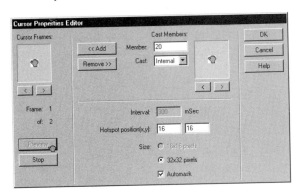

15. Click OK to close the Cursor Properties Editor window.

Notice that you have a new cast member in the Cast window. It displays a picon of the cursor and an arrow cursor for the subicon.

16. Name this new cast member **Close Hand.**

Using the cursor

As mentioned earlier, the cursor sprite property can't be used with animated cursors. That puts a bit of a crimp in our style, since that sprite property automatically applies a cursor when the mouse is over the sprite. Fortunately, the mouseEnter and mouseLeave events are just as easy to use. We can use the cursor command in those behaviors and apply our animated cursor only when we want it. First, though, we need to remove our other cursor command so there isn't a conflict.

1. Open the movie script and find the moveAround *handler.*

2. Comment out the statement we used to set the cursor for sprite 10. Close the movie script.

The mouseEnter and mouseLeave handlers we are going to write need to be in a behavior attached to the moveable sprite, which is in channel 10.

3. Select the sprite in channel 10 of the Score. Use the Behavior drop-down menu to select New Behavior.

4. *Delete the default* mouseUp *handler and replace it with the following two handlers:*

```
on mouseEnter  -- set the cursor for the sprite
  cursor (member "Close Hand")
end

on mouseLeave  -- use the system cursor
  cursor 0
end
```

When the mouse moves over the sprite, it triggers a mouseEnter event. That event is passed to the on mouseEnter handler where we set the cursor. Notice that to use the animated cursor, we use the member keyword to specify the cursor cast member. When the mouse moves off of the sprite, the mouseLeave handler sets the cursor back to the system default.

5. *Close the Script window; then play the movie.*

When you position the mouse over the moveable Swifty, the cursor changes to an opening and closing hand.

If your cursor doesn't seem to be animating, try closing the Cast or Score window. That may sound strange, but some systems on which I tested this movie seemed to have trouble keeping up with everything, and our animated cursor was losing out. Closing the windows removes some of the elements that Director is updating every time the **on idle** handler is called. This illustrates the care you should give to deciding when (or if) to use an **idle** handler. Since **idle** events occur so often, placing too much work in them can quickly bog down your movie. When the movie is converted to a projector, Director no longer needs to update the authoring level windows. The cursor should work fine in a projector.

You may notice that after moving off the moveable Swifty, the cursor changes back to the system arrow, even though we set it to the wide cross at the beginning of the movie. There is no command for "go back to the previous cursor." Although we don't do it here, if you change cursors like this in a movie, you should use a global variable to keep track of the preceding cursor every time the cursor changes. Then you can use your global variable to switch the cursor back again.

CONSTRAINING SPRITE MOVEMENT

We've made our rightmost figure moveable by the user, and we've added a custom cursor to underscore that point. Presumably, the user could figure out the possible interaction and would have some fun dragging the character hither and yon.

But what if we want to limit the area of movement? Right now, the mouse can be used to move the sprite not only anywhere on the Stage but completely off it (how far off depends on the size of your monitor). Let's fence in our wandering Swifty.

1. *Click to select an empty cast slot (but not slot 5—that should remain empty).*

2. *Select channel 12, frame 1 of your movie.*

3. *Select the Unfilled Rectangle tool from the Tool Palette. Make sure the line thickness is set to No Line (the dotted line).*

4. *Draw a rectangle on the Stage, well within the margin of the Stage edges.*

CONSTRAINING SPRITES:
A moveable sprite can be kept within the boundaries of another cast member.

5. *Open the movie script and insert one more line into the* startMovie *handler:*

```
sprite (10).constraint = 12
```

6. *Save and then run the movie.*

Whoops! Nothing happens. In fact, none of the Swiftys are reacting anymore. Well, this is a bit like a programmer's real life—you fix one thing only to break another. The culprit here is the way we use `rollOver` in the case statement. Remember? the `rollOver` only gives us the number of the topmost sprite. That sprite is now our invisible sprite. Fortunately, the `if...else...end if` construct we used for one version of the `action` handler uses the `rollOver(x)` syntax. (You did save that, commented out, didn't you?)

7. **Open the movie script again and uncomment the** action **handler using the** `if...else...end if` **construct. Then comment out the other** action **handler.**

8. **Make sure that the** `else cleanUp` **statement is changed to** `else nothing`**, just as in the** case **statement.**

Now run the movie again.

The invisible sprite serves only one purpose: to act as a constraining area for sprite 10. As you move the latter around this time, you'll note that the movement isn't limited to the physical borders of the Swifty but to its registration point instead.

Any graphic or shape sprite can be used to constrain another sprite; it doesn't matter which one is "on top" in the layering of the Score. If you want to free a sprite from its boundaries, use the statement `sprite [number].constraint = 0`. Since there is no sprite channel 0, there's nothing to hold it back.

In the interest of keeping the focus on the concepts at hand, I've been unabashedly resorting to shortcuts—some of which should be acknowledged as less than elegant. For example, we've been "hard coding" the channel number in most of our scripts; in real-world scripting, however, I'd almost never recommend using an explicit channel number. Instead, set global variables in a central place (generally a movie script) and use those variables in the commands. I mention this because, in regard to our just-solved problem with the invisible sprite, another solution would be to rearrange the sprites so that the invisible sprite is in a lower channel. Using global variables, you could rearrange the sprite order and then, in one location only, change the value of the globals. Everything else in the movie would still work.

USING ALERT BOXES

Anyone who's used a Windows or Macintosh system for a while is familiar with alert boxes: the messages the system presents when it needs your immediate attention. Unlike other dialog boxes, an alert box usually appears to the accompaniment of a system beep and includes only one button (which you're supposed to click after you've read the message). No other operations can be performed until you click OK.

It's easy to add these official-looking boxes to your own productions. When you create a self-running file (with a projector), using alert boxes helps provide the standardized look and feel of a regular application.

Adding an alert message is a single-line process:

1. *Open the Script window of cast member 4, Pink Chair. Add this script:*

```
on mouseUp
    alert "Hey! Don't mess with my chair!"
end
```

Since this script is attached to the cast member, it'll apply to all sprites derived from that cast member.

2. *Save and run the movie. Click any of the chairs on the Stage.*

You should get a system beep (or whatever warning sound you have selected for your system) and the message shown in the illustration here:

STAYING ALERT:
It's relatively simple to create your own official-looking alert box.

Hey! Don't mess with my chair!

OK

INSTALLING MENUS

Another way to make your movie's interface reassuringly official-looking is to install pull-down menus for the end user. The process is a little more complicated than triggering alert boxes, but it's worth learning. Professionalism aside, menus often make sense: They unclutter the Stage (by eliminating a thicket of choice buttons), and it's easy to add key-equivalent shortcuts, too.

To install menus, you

- Create a field cast member with the menu information in a specially encoded form.

- Add a command on the movie script level that tells Director to read from that cast member when creating menus.

The menu text

We'll begin by writing the text that becomes menu commands, using a special symbol that tells Director not to interpret the passage as text. Fortunately, that symbol is now the same for both platforms. On the Macintosh, it used to be a sort of double tilde, but now it's the pipe, or vertical dash (|) for both Windows and Macintosh platforms.

1. *Create a field cast member for cast slot 11. In it, enter this:*

```
Menu: Swifty Choices
Change Color | changeColor
Fall Down | fallDown
Beam Up | beamUp
Reset | cleanUp
```

2. *Name the new field* sitMenu.

On the Macintosh, custom menus used to require a special double-tilde symbol (Option-X). But now the pipe (or vertical dash) is recognized by both Macintosh and Windows, which means there's no need to modify the code when authoring across platforms.

In this text, the term `Menu:` designates the name of the menu itself, which will show up in the menu bar when the movie is playing. Each line following corresponds to an item in that menu; the text before the | is the name of that item, and the text after the | is the script to be executed when the item is selected. Here, we're invoking the handlers we've already written.

> Each item can have a script attached to it (on the right side of the vertical dash), but that script must be only one line long. If you want to invoke a multiline script (as in step 1), use this line to name the handler you want executed instead and place that handler in a movie script.

Only one field cast member can be the menu source at any one time, but in that text you can place as many menus as will fit on the screen. Just make sure to declare each new one with a `Menu: [name]` line.

The installMenu command

The next step is to point to this text as the menu source, using the command `installMenu`. You can place this command in any kind of script, but we'll put it in the `startMovie` handler:

3. *In the* `startMovie` *handler in the movie script, insert this line:*

```
installMenu "sitMenu"
```

4. *Save and then run the movie.*

That's all it takes. Now the normal array of Director menu choices disappears when the movie is running, replaced by the custom Swifty Choices menu. If you're using a Macintosh, you'll notice that even the ubiquitous Apple menu is conspicuously absent.

WHAT'S ON THE MENU?
It's easy to create pop-up menus in Director.

Shortcuts and other menu options

With the knowledge of just a few more codes, you can make your custom menus look and function just like standard Windows or Macintosh menus, complete with special formatting and keystroke shortcut equivalents.

1. Reopen the text in cast slot 11. Modify it to read as follows:

```
Menu: Swifty Choices
Change Color/C | changeColor
Fall Down/F | fallDown
Beam Up/B | beamUp
(-
Reset/R | cleanUp
```

Adding the forward shash character / after each item name indicates a Control key (Windows) or Command key (Macintosh) shortcut, and the character that follows is the one associated with that shortcut. The new line (- places a disabled line on the menu; it's useful for setting off sections of commands.

2. Save and then run the movie.

This time, the menu should look a little different.

You can go ahead and try all of the Control- or Command-key shortcuts. And if you like, you can also experiment with some of the other formatting options (they're case sensitive, so type them accurately).

The following are available on the Macintosh only:

@	Adds the little Apple logo to the menu bar.
!√menuItem	Adds a check mark before the item. (Use Option-V to get the check mark symbol.)
menuItem <B	Displays the item in **boldface**.
menuItem <I	Displays the item in *italic*.

`menuItem <U`	Displays the item in <u>underlined</u> style.
`menuItem <S`	Displays the item in shadowed style.
`menuItem <O`	Displays the item in outlined style.

The Disable Item option is available on both Windows and Macintosh:

`menuItem(`	Dims or disables the item.

You can find a finished version of this movie saved as Sitdone.dir both on the CD and at the Demystified Web site (**www.demystified.com**). You might want to compare and contrast your version and mine.

If you dip into Macromedia's Lingo Dictionary or *A Lingo Lexicon* (Appendix C) of this book, you'll find an abundance of other scripting elements that you'll want to try out in the laboratory of the Sitting.dir movie. For instance, you can

- Make an onscreen announcement of which sprite is being clicked, using the property **member([*whichMember*]).text**.

- Disable menu items, with the property **the enabled of menuItem**.

- Bypass menu commands entirely and enter commands with direct keystrokes and key combinations, using the functions **the key** and **the commandDown**.

POINTS TO REMEMBER

Here are some of the key concepts we covered in this chapter:

- Use **double hyphens** before lines of Lingo to disable their execution or to include commentary in your scripts. In the Script window are buttons that add and remove these hyphens automatically.

- To trigger actions when the mouse rolls over a specific sprite, you can use the rollOver function or the event messages mouseEnter, mouseWithin, and mouseLeave. The function can be used to group behaviors for multiple elements on the Stage, but the events must be attached to individual cast members or sprites.

- Any custom handlers contained in a movie script can be invoked by Lingo in **score** scripts (on the frame or sprite level), in **cast member** scripts, and in **movie** scripts.

- Use the repeat with... construction to apply Lingo to several sprites in sequence.

- You can introduce layers of **conditionality** in scripting with the if...then...else construction, but take care to balance each if with an end if; a tidier approach is to use the keywords case and otherwise. Use the command nothing when you need to even out levels of instruction.

- Properties pertaining to the timeOut **event** can be used to trigger actions after a certain period of time has passed without specific activity on the part of the end user.

- To change the appearance of a sprite on the Stage, try switching its **source cast member** by resetting its memberNum property.

- You can **change the cursor** to another standard cursor, to a bitmap for use as a cursor, or to a series of cast members designated as an animated cursor. Custom cursors can be applied overall or associated with specific sprites.

- To limit the area in which a **moveable sprite** can be moved, use the constraint sprite property to give it boundaries inside another cast member (which can be invisible to the end user).

- Official **warning-type dialog boxes** can be created with the `alert` command.

- You can install **custom menus** in your movie with the `installMenu` command. Special characters can even specify shortcuts and simulate display effects (check marks, boldfacing, dimming of unavailable commands, and so on).

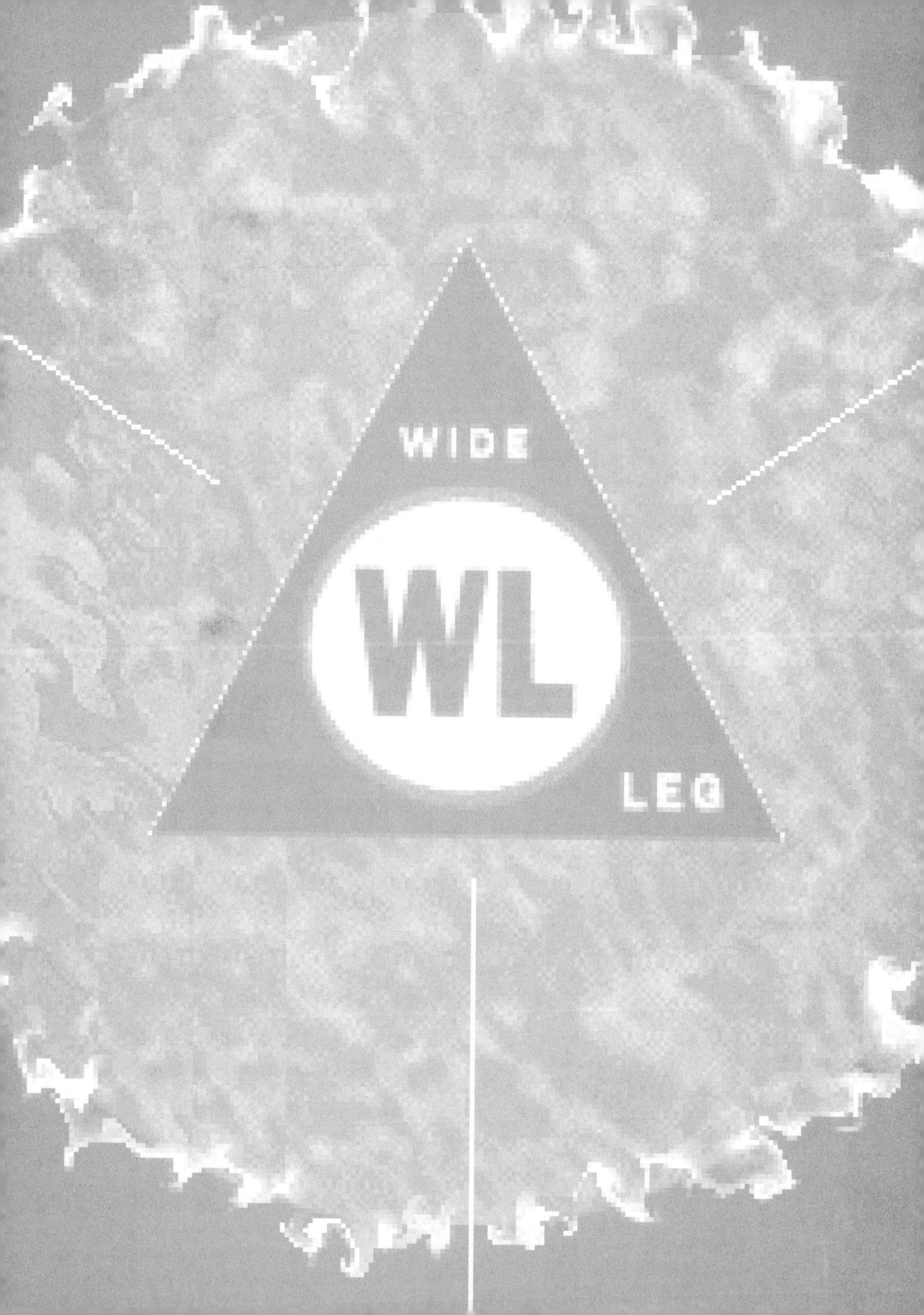
WIDE
WL
LEG

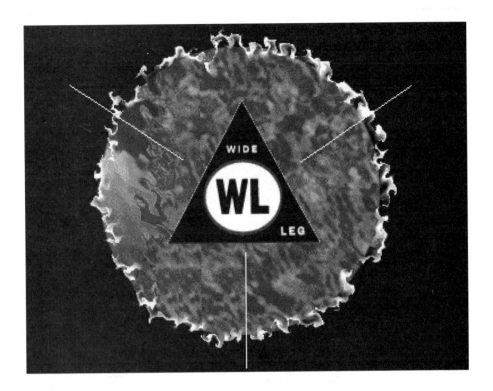

Levi's Screensaver:
Wide Open Spaces

A SCREENSAVER CAN BE MORE THAN A SIMPLE ANIMATION; IT CAN contain sophisticated Lingo to make the movie more lively and to make it behave in a consistent manner, no matter what the configuration of the end user's system. As this project demonstrates, sometimes the best approach is to create several Director movies, each serving as a means to an end.

PROJECT BACKGROUND

A Web audience is a perpetually hungry one, as the powers behind the Levi Strauss & Co. Web site (http://www.levi.com) can attest. In keeping with the company's reputation for cutting-edge marketing, the site goes far beyond the typical corporate content of mission statements and photos of managers. It's a site with practical applications (you can use it to locate a Levi's-selling store near you), but the real goal is attitudinal: to underscore the clothing maker's position as a keystone of fashion and hipness. At any given moment, Levi.com might contain an interview with Tokyo street punks, a "customer lounge" complete with images of occupied dressing rooms, and a search for the oldest Levi's denim jacket in the United States.

THE LOWDOWN BEFORE DOWNLOADING:
The Levi.com Web site dispenses the Wide Leg screensaver for free—but not before the visitor fills out some background information.

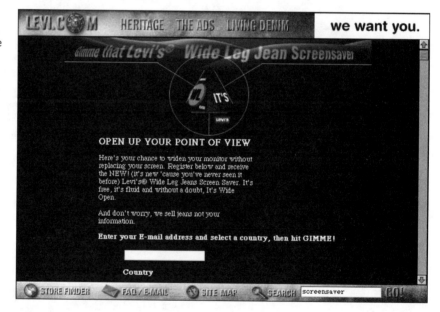

As part of that programming, True North Technologies (a sister company of Foot, Cone & Belding, the advertising agency then responsible for Levi's Web presence) approached Panmedia to provide what they termed a toy: a giveaway promotional screensaver that people could download and enjoy. It needed to tie in with their new Levi's Wide Leg Jeans television and print campaign. And because it served as a reward for providing demographic information (with users required to fill out a questionnaire before being allowed to download the file), it had to seem worth the hassle on the part of the end user.

THE APPROACH

When Todd Moritz, a senior producer at True North Technologies, began working with us on the project, he brought a number of aesthetic elements from both print and broadcast components of the Wide Leg campaign. Two of these seemed ripe for adaptation to a screensaver:

- *A shiny black pyramid, rotating to reveal the logo and the slogan "It's wide open."* It was used as a subtle visual note in the TV spots, but it seemed like a good centerpiece for our purposes.

- *Numerous images invoking the wide-open spaces of nature.* By combining images of the desert, a wind storm, water, fire, and even outer space, we pieced together an interesting tableau.

In keeping with Levi's style-is-attitude aesthetic, we were instructed to develop something that didn't feel too blatantly like an ad, something that people would want on their computer screens simply because it looked cool and that had enough visual interest to keep them from getting bored with it after a few days or weeks. We were told that the Levi's logo should remain small and discreet, and at no time did anyone suggest that we include an image of the actual product being promoted.

Unlike the Oracle screensaver completed a few weeks earlier (see Project Profile 1: *Oracle Screensaver*), this one would be operating on a broad variety of MacOS and Windows computers, so we had to make sure it would run swiftly and stably on machines with average RAM and processor configurations. And since the target audience wasn't computer professionals but 18-to-24 year-olds, we needed to make downloading and installation as easy as possible.

CRAFTING THE ANIMATION

To set the elements in motion, we actually used Director in two different modes:

- First, as an *animation studio*. As with the Oracle screensaver, we assembled the components on the Stage, using Director's suite of ink effects to blend them together and the Score display to tweak individual frame-by-frame motions.

- Next, as a *playback platform*. All those ink effects and multiple layers were pretty, but this time we couldn't afford their impact on processing time. Our workaround was this: Once we had our Director movie with the animation just as we wanted it, we took a screenshot of each frame. From these we created a second movie, importing the screenshots into new frames. This made a sort of flipbook of the earlier movie, one that looked the same but had a smaller cast, a movie that was far less memory intensive because all layers and effects had been flattened into single images. The process was time consuming, but worth it.

The seamless backdrop

Our first challenge was to create the impression of smooth, continuous motion in the background; the tableau needed to play like a closed circle, with no discernible beginning or end. We started by looping a **go to** script for continuous playback, but the effect needed to be seamless. How do you make a sprite segment seem like it goes on forever?

We achieved an "endlessness" effect by using two segments in two channels. We used tweening to move the tableau cast member (a rather long 1,429 pixels) from right to left across the Stage—starting and ending with the image half on and half off the visible area. We then copied the resulting sprite segment, placed it in a new channel above the previous one, and chopped it down into two chunks: one to fill the gap when the main segment is entering the Stage, and one to cover the gap when the main segment exits. In the illustration here, the two are deliberately offset so you can see where they're actually joined.

THE BIG SPIN:
To create the impression of an endless backdrop, sprites derived from the same cast member have carefully choreographed entrances and exits.

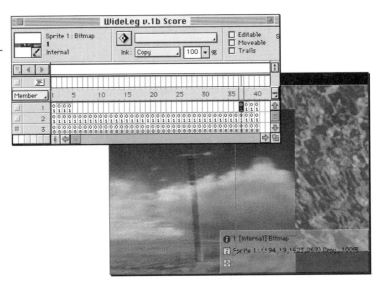

That done, we decided to blur the demarcation even more by softening the borders between the images within the tableau. We tried a number of tacks, but we liked the organic squiggle effect we got by selecting each border region in Photoshop, feathering the selection by a factor of 8, and applying the Swirl plug-in from the Black Box collection (from Alien Skin Software).

The knothole effect

Still, it wasn't enough to have the artwork zoom by like a succession of billboards; we wanted to focus the action on the center of the screen, in the area where the pyramid would eventually float. After some experimentation, we hit upon the idea of limiting the background motion to a circular area. Placed against a black field, it gave the impression of viewing the action through a knothole.

To get this effect, we created a black field and then filled a circle in the center with white. This then went into its own channel, on a layer above the backdrop image. When the Darkest ink effect was applied, the field turned into a functional mask, blocking out anything except what appeared in the white circle, since nothing was darker than the black and everything was darker than the white.

The ring-of-flame effect

The knothole was nice, but once again we found ourselves not completely satisfied. The hard, geometric edges seemed counter to the organic flow of the images behind it, so we set about softening it up. We tried adding a white, diffused glow (like the corona of the sun during an eclipse of the moon), and although the effect was interesting, it was a little too subtle. On 16-bit or better monitors, the gradients of color from light to dark were believable, but on 8-bit monitors, the display broke down into simple, boring banding.

We decided to evoke flames instead. This involved a number of contortions in Photoshop. Starting with a white ring about 10 percent larger than the circle used for the keyhole, we repeatedly applied Motion Blur and then Twirl. After adjusting the Brightness and Contrast values to play up the wispiness, we again resorted to Alien Skin's Swirl plug-in, upping the complexity of the swirling until a realistic flame emerged.

THAT BURNING SENSATION: To get the flickering effect, the nimbus of white flame was copied and rotated in the Paint window.

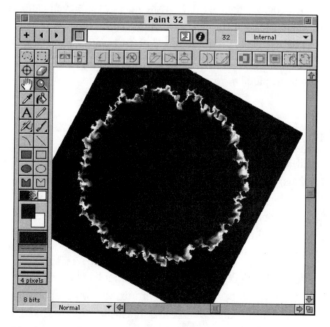

We then imported the circular flame into Director as an 8-bit graphic and placed it over the knothole with the Lightest ink effect applied. To get a flickering effect, we simply duplicated the cast member, rotated the subsequent versions, and then applied random cast substitutions to the sprites in the segment. Thus, the flame is actually a single image, with the flickers popping up in different locations from frame to frame.

The 3D pyramid

For the first working version of the screensaver, we built our own 3D model in Macromedia Extreme3D. It was functional but didn't exactly match the version used in the TV spots, so Moritz tracked down a copy of the original, which had been created in Strata StudioPro. We modified it slightly and then rendered it in 144-dpi resolution in 12 different positions.

A PYRAMID SCHEME: It took only 12 renderings of the Wide Leg pyramid to create the sensation of continuous rotation.

We brought the renderings into Photoshop, where we resized and desampled them down to 72 dpi (the standard monitor screen resolution). It might seem as though we could have saved a step by creating the original rendering at 72 dpi, but in most cases, you get noticeably better detail if you render at twice the target resolution and then sample down.

What happens when you import a graphic at a higher resolution than the standard 72 dpi? If you have a graphic application that supports higher resolutions, you can try it yourself. Save an image at 144 dpi and then import it. You'll find that Director converts it to 72 dpi—not by ignoring half of the pixels, but by making the cast member twice as large as the original artwork.

It was easy to import the resulting cast members and to string them together in an animation (you'll note that we moved the registration point of each to the very peak of the pyramid). But up against the backdrop of the tableau, the fuzziness of the edges showed, displaying a persistent white fringe even when the Matte ink was applied.

These fringes have been the bane of Director productions for years; they result from the anti-aliasing methods that render the rest of the artwork nice and smooth. The smoothness is achieved by subtly blending contrasting color values when they're juxtaposed. This leaves some off-white pixels on the perimeter and prevents the edges from being sharp and crisp. Director 7's rewritten-from-scratch animation engine does quite a good job of minimizing the "white fuzzies" on items created within the Paint window, but you'll still encounter the effect on images imported from other applications—unless you import the image's alpha channel as well.

There are a number of ways to fight this fringing. If you're working with type, you can usually just turn off anti-aliasing. Graphic designs, especially those with numerous curves, are a little trickier. One common technique is to select the image in Photoshop, use the Shrink option to tighten the selection by a pixel or so, and then select Inverse and delete the peripheral pixels. Another approach is to select using the Border option and then adjust the Contrast setting. Yet another method is to tinker with the Replace Color settings to eliminate the washed-out colors on the fringe. The success rate for each technique varies widely.

In our case, none of these techniques worked very well. Fortunately, the pyramid was made up of straight lines, so we finally eliminated the dicey fringe pixels by simply laying down a thick white line on each edge. The result was a series of pyramids that look like "stair-steppy" in closeup and downright chunky when viewed in the Paint window—but place them on the Stage, and they stand out smoothly against the background.

STRAIGHT TO THE EDGE: The top image (both dithered and anti-aliased) looks smoother against a white back-drop, but the bottom one (no dithering or anti-aliasing) looks better when placed in the layers of Director.

One of the great things about Director 7 is that it supports **alpha channels**: the extra layer of information that graphics programs like Photoshop and DeBabelizer use to track the intended transparency of visual elements. With alpha channels intact, not only are unwanted edge pixels eliminated, but sprites can be created with just about any degree of translucence or opacity. What's more, Director 7's dynamic alpha channels let you change the degree of translucence or opacity on the fly, using Lingo. We couldn't use this feature for two reasons: This project predates version 7, and we were working with non–alpha-channel renderings from the 3D program. But if we were developing this project now, we'd definitely take advantage of this feature, perhaps to make the pyramid cast a subtle shadow or to throw in see-through light effects.

FROM COMPOSITE MOVIE TO FINAL PRODUCTION

Once the animation was complete and approved, we stepped through the movie, made screenshots of each frame, and then imported those into the flat, 40-frame version. Then we encapsulated *that* movie into a film loop and imported it into a third movie. We ended up with a single sprite in a single channel of a single-frame movie.

Why go to the trouble of creating that third movie? Because projectors don't always handle the looping of a multiple-frame movie smoothly; sometimes the playback head pauses noticeably before returning to the beginning. By crunching the multiframe animation into a single frame, we made the playback head's trip as short as possible, which smoothes out the process.

Preparing to program

Our animation was done, but the client wanted more than simple onscreen motion—the movie itself should move. Specific rules were established for this motion:

- The Stage of the movie should always be sized to occupy the entire monitor (or multiple monitors, since many users, especially on the MacOS side, have more than one).

- The animation within the movie should start centered on the screen and then appear and disappear at random locations.

- However, this randomness couldn't be truly random. At no point should the image move to a location where the Levi's logo is obscured.

These requirements posed a few scripting challenges. It is easy to black out the screen (by selecting the Full Screen option when creating a projector), but that does nothing to address the animation's movement on the screen. The action is, by necessity, confined to the Stage—and the Stage can't be resized and repositioned with Lingo. We could have made the Stage big enough to fit even the largest monitor, but that would be an unnecessary drag on RAM. Besides, the action had to be confined to a visible area; if we had a 20-inch Stage but someone was running the movie on a 9-inch monitor, much of the action wouldn't be seen.

The Stage can't be resized or moved around, but Movies in a Window (MIAW) can. The key was to work with not one movie but two.

- The first movie (dubbed 2Launch.dir) would actually have a very tiny Stage and no graphic cast members at all. Its job would be to blank out the rest of the screen and then launch the second movie as an MIAW.

- The second movie (named 2Play.dir) contained the animation as a film loop. Since it opened in a borderless window, it would blend seamlessly into the black backdrop established by the first movie. Since it was an MIAW, Lingo scripts could be written to shuttle it about to appropriate locations on the screen.

This may sound like a roundabout approach, but it worked quite well. The two-movie tactic didn't complicate the end product, as both could be easily incorporated into a single projector.

Building the 2Launch.dir movie

If you open up the 2Launch.dir movie on the *Director 7 Demystified* CD, you won't find much. The Stage, in fact, seems to be missing entirely.

It's not gone, though; check out the Movie Properties dialog box and you'll see that it's been made both tiny (16 pixels by 1 pixel) and remote (located off the visual area of all but the largest monitors). That's because Director places a 1-pixel border around the Stages of its root movies, which can be distracting when you're trying to blend several elements together into a visual whole. Thus, the Stage is rendered the next best thing to invisible.

The movie's real power is in the handler in cast slot:

```
on startmovie
    cursor 200        → makes the cursor disappears
    set the windowtype of window "2play.dir" to 2
    set the rect of window "2play.dir" ¬
    to getLast (the desktopRectList)
    open window "2play.dir"
end
```

gets the last item value in a list

The line **cursor 200** makes the cursor disappear, an appropriate indicator that a screensaver is in action. But the rest of the script achieves the following:

1. It sets a borderless window type (code **2**) for the second movie.

2. It sets the size of the MIAW to a rectangle equivalent the size of the current monitor. That's because the **rect** coordinates of all monitors are stored in the property **the DesktopRectList** (try typing **put the DesktopRectList** in the Message window and see what's returned). Since the property is actually a list, if more than one monitor is present, **the DesktopRectList** will have more than one entry. That's what the **getLast** command is for: to retrieve only the last entry if multiple entries exist. Without this, the presence of more than one monitor would render the script meaningless.

Lists are special multipart variables, and **getLast** is one of many specialized Lingo elements designed to work with them. For more information about lists, check out Chapter 16: *Lingo and Lists.*

3. With the proper coordinates now established, the script opens the MIAW and launches 2Play.dir. Now the active area of the second movie always exactly matches the available area of at least one monitor on the end user's system.

Building the 2Play.dir movie

The second movie contains the animation, but it has more than simple playback as its goal. It also has to keep track of the time the animation spends in any given location and to find suitable locations for its continuous relocation. These tasks called for more custom scripting.

Adding Lingo for self-centeredness

Like its companion, the 2Play.dir movie contains a single movie script. Within that script is a handler named **pickaspot**:

```
on pickaspot
    global goodLocH, goodLocV
    put random (the stageright - (the width of ¬
sprite 1 + 100)) into bucket
    if bucket > (the width of sprite 1) then
        put bucket into goodLocH
    else nothing
    put random (the stagebottom - (the height of ¬
sprite 1 + 100)) into otherbucket
    if otherbucket > (the height of sprite 1) then
        put otherbucket into goodLocV
    else nothing
end
```

This is a little more convoluted than the MIAW-launching script, but it's not really more complicated. Here's what's happening:

1. Two global variables are established (**goodLocH** and **goodLocV**). These will contain the horizontal and vertical coordinates of a location that meets the specified criteria.

2. The **put random** line chooses a random number, but the randomness is limited to the number in parentheses directly following the command. That statement in the nested parentheses is actually a number: It's the width of the stage in pixels (the property **the stageright**) with the width of the

animation sprite (plus an extra 100 pixels) subtracted. The resulting random number will therefore be random, but it'll always represent a location on the Stage that's at least 100 pixels less than the width of the image. Once generated, the number is placed in a local variable called **bucket**. This is our potential horizontal location.

3. Because we've limited the maximum range of our hypothetical location, we know it won't place our artwork too far to the right. But what if the number chosen is too small? The previous line could, in theory, produce numbers like 14, 110, or even 1—which, as horizontal coordinates, would place the image at least partially off the screen. So the next line tests the contents of **bucket** to see if the random number is acceptable in terms of our minimum as well as our maximum by checking to see if it's at least as wide as the sprite itself. If it is, **bucket** is dumped into the global variable **goodLocH**; if it isn't, then nothing is done, and the global variable keeps its old contents.

4. The process is then repeated in slightly different form, only this time using the property **the stagebottom** to pick a suitable random value for the vertical coordinate. If this number passes its test, it'll be handed over to the global variable **goodLocV**.

Triggering the movement

To get this movement handler rolling, we needed to trigger it at intervals, so we added a few lines to the movie script: *default timeout value is 3min*

```
set the timeoutLength to 10 * 60   ← sets it to 10 seconds
set the timeoutscript to "scoot"
```

Once again, properties to the rescue! The property **the timeoutlength** lets us specify the amount of time before a timeout occurs, and **the timeoutscript** designates the handler to be executed whenever a timeout is declared.

Now all that remained was to write **scoot**:

```
on scoot
    global goodLocH, goodLocV
    pickaspot
    set the locH of sprite 1 to goodLocH
    set the locV of sprite 1 to goodLocV
end
```

Since the **scoot** script is triggered every 10 seconds (10 times 60 ticks) and it in turn triggers **pickaspot**, you might conclude that the sprite containing the animation changes every 10 seconds. Actually, the movement is randomly timed, since **pickaspot** updates the global values only when the numbers in **bucket** and **otherbucket** pass their respective tests. If they don't, Director waits another 10 seconds before trying again.

COMMENTS

- We've provided not only the final movies for your perusal, but some of the interim versions as well. If you look in Version2.dir, you'll see that the knothole mask is in 8-bit color. Why didn't we cut down on file size by using a 1-bit image instead? Because we knew we would collapsing all layers into a single image in the end, and that that image would be in 8-bit color. Nothing would have been gained.

- How could this project be improved? If you look closely, you'll see a slight bobble during playback: One of the white lines leading into the spinning pyramids moves during a single frame. Also, a fine, white residue of the flame effect appears some distance from the flames themselves; that should probably have been tidied up. From a Lingo standpoint, it would be nice to figure out how to extend the movement across multiple monitors, rather than confining the action to one and blanking out others. Also, the resulting projector tends to take a little too long to quit when the mouse is moved (we suspect it's because the MIAW isn't expressly closed—instead, Director is simply directed to quit).

- Since there's very little Lingo in this project, we left it in "old style" form—that is, in the more literal, pre–dot-syntax form. Did you find it easier or harder to follow?

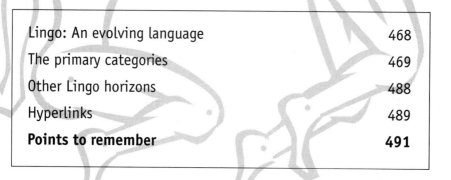

CHAPTER 12

OTHER LINGO FLAVORS

YOU'VE LEARNED THE CENTRAL CONCEPTS OF SCRIPTING AND THE MAIN rules for Lingo's syntax. You've also had lots of practice using Lingo and writing handlers. In fact, you're probably surprised at just how much you can do with what you already know. Let's round out your education by introducing some new Lingo vocabulary.

In this chapter, we'll build upon your current knowledge by showing you some of the many variations of special-purpose Lingo (I like to call these "flavors"). When you expand your knowledge of the available terminology, you'll find yourself contemplating an ever-broadening panorama of programming possibilities.

As a reward, after we finish discussing text-handling with Lingo, we'll take a stab at creating a movie that uses hyperlinks.

LINGO: AN EVOLVING LANGUAGE

Programming languages are like human languages: some are "dead" (like Sanskrit), and some are vibrantly alive. Lingo falls into the latter category, growing significantly with every revision of Director. What was once a simple playback-control dialect (similar to SmallTalk and HyperCard) continues to take on breadth and complexity every year— but surprisingly, a lot of Lingo's capabilities often remain unexploited. Even professionals using Director on a daily basis tend to stick to a tried-and-true core of scripts. In many cases, Lingo isn't used for much more than making buttons behave like buttons or for making the playback head leap around.

Going beyond the basics requires some mastery of more sophisticated programming concepts, but primarily it's a matter of expanding your vocabulary. In the following pages, I'll try to spur just such an expansion by touching on at least some of the more intriguing varieties of Lingo, sometimes by giving examples, and sometimes by just mentioning them in passing. You'll find more details in Appendix C: *A Lingo Lexicon*.

Most appendices are dry, boring stuff designed for only occasional reference, but I'd suggest treating Appendix C as required reading. In it you'll find detailed definitions of the full spectrum of Lingo, complete with sample scripts and cross-references. When faced with a programming task that just seems too onerous, try roaming through the *Lexicon*. You just might discover a bit of Lingo that does the job admirably.

THE PRIMARY CATEGORIES

Macromedia has classified Lingo into a number of categories, defined by usage; you can even access shortcut Lingo from an open Script window via a Categorized Lingo pull-down menu. At last count, there were 33 categories.

THE PRACTICAL SORT:
In addition to an alphabetical listing, you can find the Lingo vocabulary grouped by usage type in the Script pull-down menu.

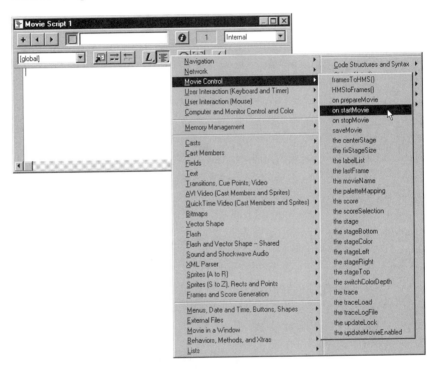

Some of the Lingo categories are already covered in previous chapters. Others are important enough to warrant their own chapters. What follows is a look at several of the primary kinds of Lingo that will come in handy in probably every project you undertake. I'll give the broad definition for each type and then show some examples. The mentions are more illustrative than exhaustive, so jump to the appendices at the back of this book when you want to know more about a particular category. In some cases, I'll go a little deeper into terms I've already mentioned to reinforce some concepts that I consider particularly important.

You can test a number of the elements discussed here quickly and easily in the Message window. You can use the simple movie Flavors.dir, included on the CD, for testing. Before you go on:

1. **Start Director, and then open Flavors.dir.**

2. **Open the Message window.**

Cast member Lingo

Let's start with the Lingo for the individual contents of cast slots. Many of these bits of Lingo are distinguished by use of the keyword member, as in member(3).name. You'll find many of the terms self-explanatory, although there are a few surprises.

Cast members can be identified by various means. Two of the more common member properties are number and name. Although a cast member's name and slot number may seem obvious to you as you're looking at the Cast, there are many times when this information will come in handy as you're writing Lingo code. Often you will know the cast number and you'll need to find out its name. Following are the steps for doing this.

1. **In the Message window, enter the following line:**

put member(5).name   *property*

This returns the name assigned to the cast member—*if* the slot in question has been given a name. If the cast member has no name, or if the slot is empty, you'll get a set of empty quotation marks in reply.

CAST NAME:
Use the name cast member property to retrieve a name when you know a cast member's number.

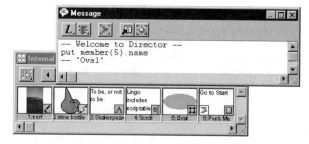

Now suppose you know that for some cast members you have both a regular version and a highlighted version. You also know that the highlighted version has the word *High* at the end of its name. You can use the name property to retrieve the name of the unhighlighted cast member. You can then build the new name and reference the highlighted cast member with that new name.

2. Enter the following lines in the Message window:

```
newName = member(5).name && "High"
put member(newName).number
```

We use the && operator to concatenate the member's name with the word "High", adding a space in the process (more on && later in the chapter). Check in the Cast window and, sure enough, you'll see a cast member in slot 7 named Oval High. You could use this method to change a sprite's cast member when the sprite is clicked. Notice that we used the number cast member property to get the number of the new cast member.

CAST NUMBER:
Use the number cast member property to retrieve a number when you know a cast member's name.

A similar-sounding but different bit of Lingo is the fileName property, which actually provides the location (path name or online address) of the source file from which a linked cast member (such as an audio or digital video file) is derived. Here's how you can find the location of a cast member's source file.

3. Enter this line:

```
put member(9).filename
```

Cast slot 9 is a QuickTime cast member and, by default, it's linked to an external file. Your result will be slightly different from the one shown here, depending on the location of the QuickTime movie on your system.

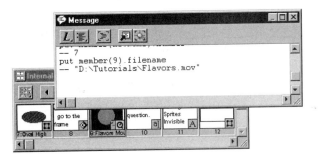

A related property is the URL cast member property, which pertains exclusively to online files accessible via a universal resource locator (URL) address.

Want to know more about a cast member? You can use Lingo to determine and modify the appearance or content of cast members. Many of the more common Lingo scripts are used to get or set the physical attributes of a graphic cast member. Check out some of these in the Message window:

4. Enter these lines:

```
put member("surf").type
put member("surf").depth  -- the color depth
put member("surf").palette  -- see appendix for values
put member("surf").height  -- of original cast, not the sprite
put member("surf").width
put member("surf").rect  -- the rectangle coordinates
put member("surf").regPoint  -- registration point
```

THE PROPERTIES OF SURF:
Most cast member types have properties that can be tested or set.

```
put member(9).filename
-- "D:\Tutorials\Flavors.mov"
put member("surf").type
-- #bitmap
put member("surf").depth  -- the color depth
-- 16
put member("surf").palette  -- see appendix for values
-- -102
put member("surf").height  -- of original cast, not the sprite
-- 439
put member("surf").width
-- 298
put member("surf").rect  -- the rectangle coordinates
-- rect(0, 0, 298, 439)
put member("surf").regPoint -- registration point
-- point(149, 219)
```

As you'll recall, the registration point is the center of a graphic cast member—it's automatically placed in the visual center but is moveable via the Registration Point tool in the Paint window. You can also change it using the regPoint property, which provides another way to create simple motion on the Stage. If you want something to shift position but don't want to tinker with a particular sprite, try using this property to move the registration point. To create an apparent upward motion, move the registration point down (or to create a downward motion, move it up). Remember that the registration point remains fixed on the Stage, and the sprite moves relative to that point.

The values returned by the **rect** and **regPoint** properties are based on coordinates. Rectangle values are of the form (left, top, right, bottom). Point coordinates are of the form (**horizontal, vertical**). For cast members, the coordinates are given from the upper-left of the cast member's bounding box. When you use points and rectangles with sprites, the coordinates are given from the upper-left of the Stage, which is point (**0,0**).

A number of powerful commands for cast member Lingo are also at your disposal, such as erase member (which clears out the slot entirely), duplicate member (which creates a quick clone that can be modified without affecting the original), and importFileInto (which zings a new element, such as an external file, directly into a specific cast slot). And if you've forgotten whether or not you've made any changes to a cast slot since you last saved your production, you can check the modified property, which keeps track of such things.

One shortcut to learning a lot of Lingo is to scrutinize the Properties dialog boxes of sprites, cast members, and movies; many of the properties set in these boxes have Lingo equivalents. For instance, you can set the color of the Stage by clicking the Color Palette in the Movie Properties dialog box, or you can achieve the same end by using the Lingo property **the stageColor.** The advantage of the Lingo route is that the property can be changed multiple times without requiring action from the end user.

set the ⑤⑦ stageColor = 249
deep
green

Cast Lingo

Cast Lingo consists of elements that manage Cast files (opening and closing them, maintaining links, and so forth). Cast issues have become increasingly complicated in recent revisions of Director: Now you can work with multiple Casts, save them under different names, and even switch one for another. Most Cast properties (as opposed to cast member properties) are based on the castLib keyword. We'll get into using multiple Casts in Chapter 13, *Working with Multiple Movies and Casts*, but following are some examples.

- Note that the name of a Cast and the name of the window containing it aren't necessarily the same; that's why there are name properties (castLib(*x*).name) and filename properties (castLib(*x*).filename). The former gives the window a name (it can be switched without changing the source file), and the latter is used to identify the file of origin. (If the Cast is internal, this property is empty. So far, we have been dealing with internal Casts only.)

- To find an open slot in a Cast database, use the function findEmpty in conjunction with a specified cast member. This function returns the number of the next available slot following the specified cast member's slot (although it works only on the currently active Cast).

- Need information on quantities? The property the number of members of castLib will give a complete population count, and the number of castLibs will tell you how many Casts are in the current movie.

- Other Cast-related Lingo includes save castLib, which lets you write changes to an external Cast, and the selection of castLib, which determines which slots in the specified Cast are selected.

Sprite Lingo

Director's categorized Lingo lists more than 50 elements designed to help you tinker with sprites. We used a number of sprite properties when we wrote handlers to change sprites or make sprites moveable. In addition to elements, two events are also associated with sprites, beginSprite and endSprite. A beginSprite handler is called before the sprite is actually drawn so you have a chance to take some action as the sprite appears. An endSprite handler is good for performing cleanup after a sprite disappears from the Stage.

When working with sprite properties, you'll always use the sprite keyword to specify the sprite's channel number. One of the more common properties you'll use is memberNum, which identifies the cast member used for the sprite. Here's how you use it:

1. **In the Message window, enter the following line:**

```
put sprite(3).memberNum
```

The number returned is the cast slot of the sprite's cast member. A similar property is member, which returns the cast number as well as the cast library, as shown here:

2. Enter this line:

```
put sprite(3).member
```

WHICH CAST MEMBER?
Use the memberNum sprite property when you need to know the associated cast member.

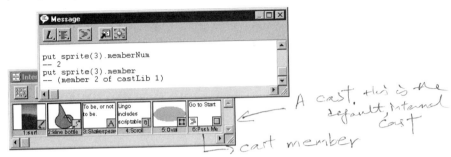

A cast, this is the default, internal cast

cast member

Since the memberNum property can be both tested and set (like most sprite properties), we can even use it to change the cast member associated with a sprite. Before we try that, though, let's look at the location and rectangle of the sprite. It's interesting to see how these properties change (or stay the same) when a sprite's cast member is swapped for another one. For the location of a sprite, we use the loc property.

3. Enter the following line in the Message window:

```
put sprite(3).loc
```

The value returned is of type point and is of the form point(horizontal, vertical), where horizontal is the distance (in pixels) of the sprite from the left edge of the Stage and vertical is the distance from the top of the Stage. Both are measured to the sprite's registration point. Two related properties are locH and locV (for horizontal and vertical), which return integer values, as shown next.

4. Type these two lines in the Message window:

```
put sprite(3).locH
put sprite(3).locV
```

WHAT'S THE POINT?
Find the location of a sprite's registration point on the Stage.

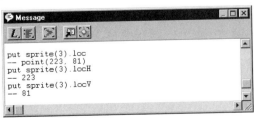

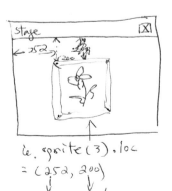

i.e. sprite(3).loc = (252, 200)

locH   locV

At first, points may seem more difficult to work with than integers, but using them is actually very simple. Here's how you'd use points to move a sprite down 5 pixels and over 1 to the right:

```
sprite(3).loc = sprite(3).loc + point(1,5)
updateStage
```

Now take a look at the rectangle of a sprite. The `rect` property returns a value of type `rect` of the form `rect(left, top, right, bottom)`. Once again, the return value represents the number of pixels from the upper-left of the Stage. This time, though, it's not the sprite's registration point but the sprite's bounding rectangle that is being specified.

5. Type the following in the Message window:

```
put sprite(3).rect
```

As you can with elements of type `point`, you can add and subtract values of type `rect` to modify a sprite's size. Now let's change the cast member of sprite 3 and see how it affects the sprite's bounding rectangle.

6. Enter the following lines in the Message window:

```
sprite(3).memberNum = 1  -- change to the Surf cast member
updateStage
put sprite(3).rect
put sprite(3).loc
```

RECT IS A RECTANGLE: The rect property indicates the bounding rectangle of a sprite.

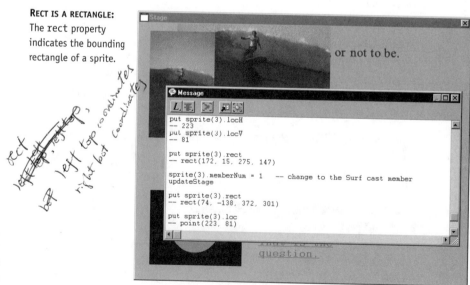

You hardly need to check the sprite's new bounding rectangle to see that it has changed. That's pretty obvious. On the other hand, the registration point for the sprite is exactly the same as it was before cast members were swapped. Now let's try changing the sprite's bounding box.

7.   Type the following:

```
sprite(3).rect = rect(172, 15, 275, 147)
updateStage
```

That puts the sprite back to its original size and location, and the bitmap is scaled to fit into the bounding box.

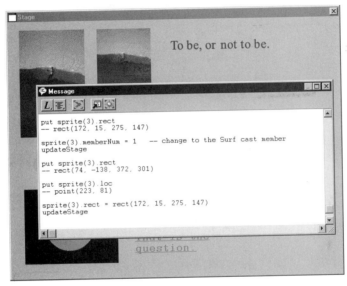

We've already experimented with Lingo-based changes to the ink effect applied to graphic sprites, but there are other ways to radically alter our sprites' appearance. For example, the paletteRef property links each sprite to the palette used to display the sprite (the default palette being the one used by the source cast member). You can change this property without modifying the cast member. You can also set the blend property (blending being roughly equivalent to the sprite's degree of transparency). This property works only with the Copy, Background Transparent, Matte, Mask, and Blend inks.

Setting the blend value to 0% will make a sprite effectively disappear, but an easier way is simply to switch off visibility with the visible property. Setting this property to FALSE (or 0) has the same effect as disabling the channel in which the sprite resides. In fact, this property does more than make the sprite invisible: It essentially removes the sprite from the Stage without disturbing the Score.

> The **visible** property is something of a misnomer; it should probably be called "the playable of channel" or some such, because it really applies to the channel. When using **visible**, keep in mind that it totally disables the channel. When the property is turned off, clicking the area of the hidden sprite won't trigger any sprite scripts. And if you don't explicitly turn the property back on when you leave the current frame, you will find that all subsequent sprites in that channel have disappeared as well.

Just as you can switch the appearance of a sprite by swapping in a new source cast member, you can also change its behavior script by using the scriptNum property to assign an entirely different behavior to the sprite.

You already know the cool trick of using the moveableSprite property to make sprites moveable by the end user. To keep the interaction more manageable, it's often useful to limit the movement of that sprite to a specific area of the Stage. We did that in Chapter 11, using another sprite to define the bounding area and applying the constraint property.

You can create another interesting effect by using the trails property with a moveable sprite. Here's how:

1. *Start the movie Flavors.dir.*

2. *While the movie is running, enter the following lines in the Message window:*

```
sprite(3).moveableSprite = TRUE
sprite(3).trails = TRUE
```

3. *Now move the sprite around on the Stage.*

HAPPY TRAILS:
Moveable sprites with trails set to TRUE produce interesting effects.

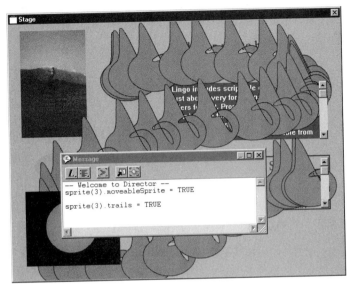

Frame Lingo

In addition to the events for frames that we have been using throughout our Lingo forays (prepareFrame, enterFrame, exitFrame) are some other frame elements that you will find useful at times. Some of these have to do with the effects channels. They are a bit different from other properties we've been using: Although there is a command for checking the value, that command can't be used to set the value. Some frame elements have a different command for setting the property, and some can't be set at all.

- frameLabel lets you determine the label of a marker for the current frame. The marker function is used to determine the frame labels of frames other than the current frame. There is no way to set a label for a frame while a movie is playing. *put the frameLabel*

- frameTempo identifies the tempo assigned to the current frame. To set the tempo with Lingo, use the puppetTempo command.

- framePalette identifies the cast member of the current palette being used in the movie. To change the palette using Lingo, use the puppetPalette command.

- `frameTransition` identifies the number of the transition cast member for the current frame. To set a transition, use the `puppetTransition` command.

- `frameSound1` and `frameSound2` identify the numbers of the sounds assigned to the current frame in sound channels 1 and 2. To set a sound, you can use the `puppetSound` command.

ie set the frameSound1 = the number of member "Jazz"

Number-crunching Lingo

OPERATORS:
The symbols that perform arithmetic or comparison operations between two numbers.

It's not exactly a calculation-loving language like FORTRAN, but Lingo does have some number-crunching functions. These are typically called **operators**, because they perform a single operation and produce a result. These operators include the usual suspects: * for multiplication, / for division, + for addition, and so forth.

Closely related are the **comparison operators**, which pronounce a TRUE or FALSE (1 or 0) verdict on the implied comparison between two expressions:

- Greater than: >
- Less than: <
- Less than or equal to: <=
- Greater than or equal to: >=
- Not equal to: <>

Although the symbology of > and < is pretty obvious, a surprising number of scripts go awry because the wrong comparison operator is used. To keep them clear in my head, I remember the principle I was taught in the third grade: *The bigger one gets to ride in the rocket.* Works every time.

Other Lingo represents mathematical concepts, like `sin` (the sine of a given angle) and `pi` (the ratio of a circle's circumference to its diameter). The `pi` function gives us an opportunity to explore a useful property, the `floatPrecision`. Try this simple exercise:

1. In the Message window, enter this:

`put pi`

The number returned should be 3.1416, or pi to the fourth decimal place.

2. ***Now enter this:***

```
the floatPrecision = 14
put pi
```

GIVE OR TAKE:
Setting the
system property
the floatPrecision
determines just how
accurately floating-
point numbers are
displayed.

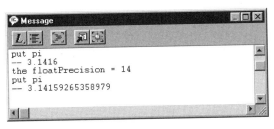

By setting the floatPrecision, you're establishing how accurate you want Director to be when displaying **floating-point numbers** (that is, numbers with values below the decimal point). The maximum number of decimal places that can be displayed is 14. The floatPrecision value doesn't affect Director's internal storage of a floating-point number; that number always remains the same. So calculations aren't affected by the floatPrecision setting, only their display. The floatPrecision value is handy for making sure that floating-point numbers will fit into a field with a fixed size.

3. ***Now enter these lines in the Message window:***

```
the floatPrecision = 0
put pi
```

THE VALUE REMAINS:
Even though only some
decimal digits are dis-
played, Director still
knows the full value.

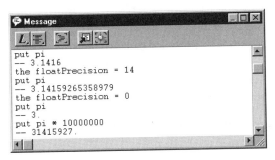

When Director adjusts a number to display fewer digits, it rounds off the number. To round off a number to an integer, use the integer function, which rounds values of a specific number (rather than globally). You can also test a number to determine whether it's of the floating-point variety with the function floatP or an integer with integerP. Both of these return 1 (or TRUE) if it is, and 0 (or FALSE) if it isn't.

String Lingo

The written word is the preoccupation of two distinct but related types of Lingo. String Lingo is used to manipulate actual strings themselves. You can set a string, compare strings, concatenate strings, and perform a host of other operations on strings. Text Lingo deals with manipulation of the containers in which strings are placed: fields and text sprites and cast members. We'll get to text Lingo in a minute.

If you are imparting information in your movie, you are sure to be using a lot of Lingo to manipulate strings. String Lingo focuses not on macramé but on **strings** of text (that is, the spaces and characters that fit between quotation marks). Since you don't always want to fetch the whole thing, Director provides a number of ways to gain partial access in a number of contexts. These are called, picturesquely enough, **chunk expressions**. That's because they focus on "chunks" within the string. This terminology always reminds me of dental floss, but that's the lingo of Lingo.

Chunks explained

What is a chunk? Well, that depends on the Lingo in question. In the case of word...of (as in put word 4 of myText), it's a chunk of words—or more precisely, any group of characters punctuated before and after by a space. If I said to you, "I *fjlkew* you very much," you wouldn't recognize *fjlkew* as a word, but Director would. By looking for spaces as the starting and stopping points of word chunks, Lingo is using them as **delimiters**. The chunk expression item...of uses commas as delimiters instead; an element is an item if it's preceded by commas, no matter how many words are used. Then again, char...of uses no delimiters at all, simply counting the characters (blank spaces and all) in a given string. The following screenshot of the Message window shows all three of these expressions in action.

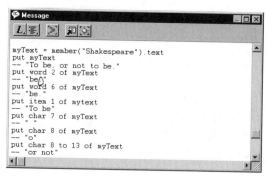

We can write the same commands using dot syntax, as shown in the following screenshot:

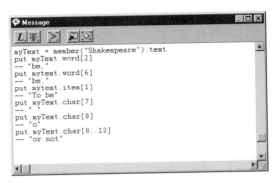

```
myText = member("Shakespeare").text
put myText.word[2]
-- "be,"
put mytext.word[6]
-- "be,"
put mytext.item[1]
-- "To be"
put myText.char[7]
-- " "
put myText.char[8]
-- "o"
put myText.char[8..13]
-- "or not"
```

I'm sure that by now you have noticed several methods of writing the same command in Lingo. We have focused on the dot syntax because it more closely relates to other programming languages and emphasizes the object-oriented nature of the language. It's also more concise and exact. But I do know several people who balk at switching when it comes to chunk expressions. The old style of **put word 2 to 5 of myText** is just so much more meaningful than **put mytext.word[2..5]**. You can decide for yourself which to use.

[handwritten annotations: word 2 to 5 / —be, or not to / 2 3 4 5 / word]

Counting with chunks

Some chunk expressions aren't concerned with capturing so much as they are with counting, and these operate on the same delimiting principles: the number of words in, the number of chars in, and the number of items in. It's important to note that these expressions all return their counts not as text strings but as numbers (the values are not surrounded by quotation marks when they're returned in the Message window). This means you can add them to number-crunching scripts, perhaps to keep track of total word counts. Again, two syntaxes can be used, with the count function providing the alternative syntax.

1. *In the Message window enter the following lines:*

```
myText = member("Shakespeare").text
put the number of words in myText
put myText.words.count
```

[handwritten annotations: can be ommited / put mytext.word.count]

WORDS COUNT:
The count function and the number of words both return the same value.

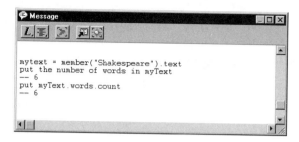

```
mytext = member("Shakespeare").text
put the number of words in myText
-- 6
put myText.words.count
-- 6
```

One of the more common actions performed with strings is determining the last word. You can calculate the last word using the count function, or you can use the last function that Director conveniently provides.

2.   *Type the following in the Message window:*

```
put the last word of myText
```

Manipulating chunks

Not only can you look at chunks, but you can also change them. The syntax for inserting chunks into a string requires the put command in one of its various forms.

To replace a word, use the put...into command.

1.   *Enter the following in the Message window:*

```
put "surf," into myText.word[2]
put myText
```

You can also try the put...before and put...after commands.

2.   *In the Message window, enter:*

```
put "or to swim," after myText.word[2]
put myText
```

SWIM AFTER EATING:
You can put new chunks into, before, or after other chunks in a string.

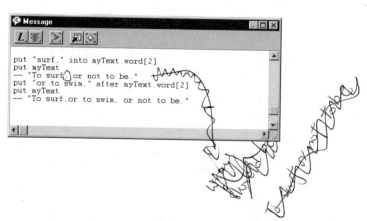

```
put "surf," into myText.word[2]
put myText
-- "To surf, or not to be."
put "or to swim," after myText.word[2]
put myText
-- "To surf, or to swim, or not to be."
```

Or you can change the entire text of a string of a cast member. Change the cast member's text with the following:

3. In the Message window, type:

```
member("Shakespeare").text = "To surf, or not to surf."
put member("Shakespeare").text
```

Not only does the member's text change show up in the Message window, but it also shows up on the Stage.

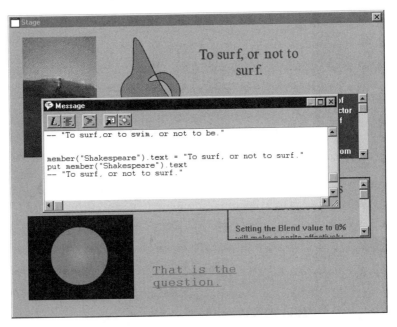

The characters & and && are the concatenation operators. The & operator is used to put two strings together; && is the same but places a space between the two strings.

4. You can test the concatenation operators in the Message window:

```
put "Mike" & "Gross"
put "Mike" && "Gross"
```

There are some elements that you can't put directly into a string by typing—a quotation mark, for example. Director supplies constants for such cases.

5. *Type these lines in the Message window:*

```
put "His name is" && QUOTE & "Mike" & QUOTE && "to friends."
put "Line 1" & RETURN & "Line 2"
```

QUOTE ME:
Use constants such as QUOTE to insert elements you can't type into a string.

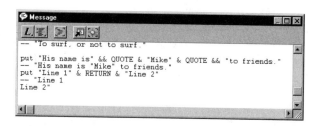

Other constants that you can use are BACKSPACE, ENTER, RETURN, SPACE, and TAB. Although not required, using uppercase for constants is considered standard programming practice.

Sometimes you need to convert a string to a number or a number to a string. If you ask the user to type his or her age in a field, for example, that age will be returned as a string. To work with the string as a number, you may first need to convert it. Lingo provides the value function to convert strings to numbers and the string function to convert numbers to strings. Now try converting some numbers and strings.

6. *Type this:*

```
put string(1234)
put value("12345")
```

Testing chunks

When you get user input, you will frequently be performing some sort of comparison or test on that input. You can use the comparison operators listed in the section "Number-crunching Lingo" with strings as well as with numbers. You can also use the contains operator, which is especially useful and returns TRUE if the second string is found in the first string. Neither the contains operator nor the equals (=) operator is case sensitive. The other operators, greater than (>) and so on, *are* case sensitive. Now try testing a string.

Type the following lines in the Message window.

```
theAnswer = "Mel Houghton"
put theAnswer contains "Mel"
put theAnswer contains "mel"
put theAnswer = "mel houghton"
put theAnswer = "Mel Hoghton"
put "M" > "m"
put "m" > "M"
```

ANYBODY IN THERE?
The contains operator is extremely useful for finding a chunk in a string.

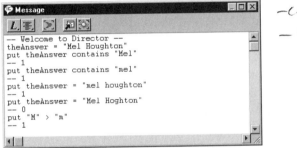

— contains
— offset

good for sorting words

One powerful but often overlooked function is **offset**, which seeks out the first instance in which one text string occurs inside another text string. Let's say you have a field called Shopping List, and you know that the text "buy prunes" is in there somewhere. A statement like **put offset ("buy prunes", field "shopping list")** will return the number of the first character of the match. Don't forget to include the parentheses, or Director will parse the multiple arguments incorrectly.

Text Lingo

Text Lingo is the second type of textual Lingo. It concerns itself with the containers for strings, namely field and text cast members in which text can be entered or displayed. The chunk expressions just discussed in the last sections will work on text and fields, as will line...of, which uses return symbols (that is, Return keypresses) as delimiters to locate individual lines of text. There's also a counting counterpart, the expression the number of lines in.

Other text- and field-related Lingo includes the following:

- Scriptable equivalents of just about every formatting option Director offers for text. Properties like the `font of member`, the `fontSize of member`, the `fontStyle of member`, and the `height of member` can all be tested and set from the Script window or Message window. You can even set the `alignment of member` or produce an especially funky effect with the `dropShadow of member` (field members only).

- If you want to give special emphasis to a chunk within a text string within a field, use a chunk expression in conjunction with the command `hilite`. A statement like `hilite word 7 of field "shopping list"` will make that word appear highlighted as if it had been selected with the cursor. If you want to specify the selection area more precisely, use the field properties `SelStart` and `SelEnd`; these designate the beginning and end characters of a selection and thus allow you to select as little as a single character or as much as the entire text.

OTHER LINGO HORIZONS

As you continue to bound up the learning curve, several more flavors of Lingo await your discovery. Here's an advance notice of pending encounters:

- **List Lingo** and **parent script Lingo** are topics for chapters to come (Chapters 16 and 18, to be exact). They're both concerned with entities residing entirely in RAM, which can have multiple components and characteristics when necessary.

- **Shockwave** and **Shockwave audio Lingo** pertain to playback and media manipulation within the context of Shockwave movies and the networked environment (Internet, intranets, and so on). Since they often have to interact with other applications (such as Web browsers), other languages (such as HTML), and other operating systems (such as UNIX), such Lingo can be tricky to puzzle out and sometimes employs a syntax not seen in other Lingo. We'll examine this type starting in Chapter 15: *Deeper into Shockwave*.

HYPERLINKS

HYPERLINKS:
Hyperlinks are text that can be clicked to perform some action.

As promised, here's a more in-depth look at the **hyperlink** capabilities of Director 7, complete with some extracurricular practice. The idea behind hyperlinks is to provide text that not only can be read, but from which additional information can be gained. Everyone familiar with Net surfing is familiar with hyperlinks—those sections of underlined text in a different color that we can click to jump to somewhere else.

In Director, we can designate a chunk of a text cast member as a hyperlink. When the user clicks the hyperlink text, an event message is sent containing information we supply. We catch that message with a handler that performs our actions. Often that means switching to another Web page, downloading a file, or branching to another location in our movie.

To create a hyperlink in Director, we need three elements:

- A text cast member containing text

- The link information to be sent when the text is clicked

- An on `hyperlinkClicked` handler to catch the event message

Let's start with the text cast member. I have a text cast member already included in Flavors.dir, so we'll start with that.

1. *Find the cast member Text for Link in the Cast window, and double-click it to open the Text window.*

2. *Find and select the string `"visible property"`.*

3. *With the text still selected, open the Text Inspector (from the Window menu, choose Inspectors).*

The lower area of the Text Inspector is a the Hyperlink Data field, where you can enter the text of a message. This text is sent, along with the `hyperlinkClicked` message, to the `hyperlinkClicked` handler. In this example, we are going to jump to a new frame when the hyperlink is clicked, so the text we enter will be the label for the destination frame: visibleLink.

4. In the Hyperlink Data field, enter the text visibleLink.

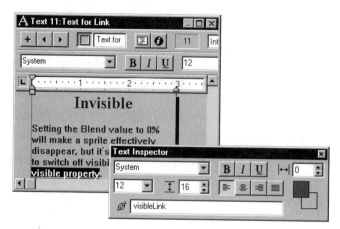

5. Close the Text Inspector and the text editor window.

Now we need to create the on hyperlinkClicked handler. The most logical place for this handler is either in a cast script for the text cast member or in a behavior for the text sprite. Let's go with the latter.

6. Select the text sprite (channel 10) and then choose New Behavior from the Behavior drop-down menu.

7. Delete the default mouseUp handler and type the following hyperlinkClicked handler:

```
on hyperlinkClicked me, whereTo
  go to whereTo
end
```

The declaration of the hyperlinkClicked handler contains two parameters: me and whereTo. The me parameter is automatically passed to behaviors and can be used by them to identify the current object. We don't use the me parameter, but we need to include it so that the number of parameters is kept in order (actually, the name me is just a convention and could easily be called something else). The whereTo parameter is the message you entered in the Hyperlink Data field of the Text Inspector, visibleLink, which is the label to which we are jumping.

8. Close the behavior editor and play the movie.

9. *Scroll down in the Text field to find the hyperlink; then click it.*

The hyperlink text is shown in a dark blue and is underlined. Also, when you move the mouse over the hyperlink, the cursor changes to a hand. These attributes are provided automatically by Director.

That's it—you've created hypertext. You can create a number of different hyperlinks in one or more text fields. You can give each one a different message or the same message. If you are working on a Shockwave movie, you can use a URL as the Hyperlink Data message and branch to another Web page when the user clicks the hyperlink.

POINTS TO REMEMBER

I hope this chapter has whetted your appetite for expanding your Lingo vocabulary. What are its key takeaways?

- Many features that can be set in Properties dialog boxes can also be set in **scripts**. Check out *A Lingo Lexicon* (Appendix C) for Lingo equivalents.

- Turning off the property **the visible of sprite** represents a total disabling of the channel. Think of this property as "the playable of channel" and make sure to turn it back on when you're through.

- When it comes to keeping track of **comparison operators** (the ones using < and >), remember: The bigger one gets to ride in the rocket.

- **Text strings** are any grouping of text characters. **Chunks** are specific units within those strings. **Delimiters** are the characters that help Director identify chunks: spaces define words, commas define items, and Return keypresses define lines.

- **Hyperlinks** are text chunks that can be clicked by the user to perform some action, such as branching to another Web page.

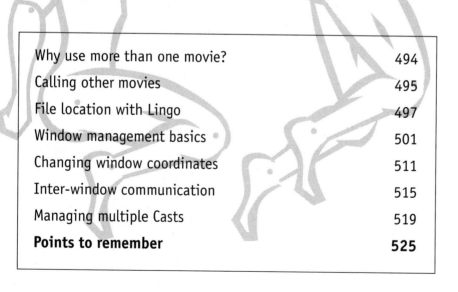

CHAPTER 13

WORKING WITH
MULTIPLE MOVIES AND CASTS

YOU CAN CREATE AMAZING MULTIMEDIA PROJECTS WORKING WITH A single movie and/or using only a single cast for all your movie's elements. If you never branch out into multiple movies and casts, however, you'll miss out on a whole territory of Director development that extends your ability to organize projects and allows you to expand your interactivity by displaying more than one movie at a time. In this chapter, you'll learn how to use Director in both of these ways.

To start, we'll use simple linkages—launching one movie from another and even returning to the original movie again. Then we'll look into Movies in a Window (MIAWs), in which one movie can have multiple movies open in subwindows, all running at the same time (and even communicating with each other). Finally, we'll see how media resources can be shared or swapped using multiple internal and external cast files.

WHY USE MORE THAN ONE MOVIE?

In the previous chapters, we treated the Director movie as an entity unto itself. We explored interactivity and nonlinear navigation, but only in the context of leaping from one section of a movie to another. It's theoretically possible to get just about everything done within the confines of a single movie, but there are times when it's a better idea to jump out of one movie and into another—or to have several movies running at once. It's a relatively straightforward way of producing some surprisingly sophisticated results.

When are multiple movies called for? Give them a try when the following considerations are important to you:

- **RAM demands.** The bigger the movie, the more RAM it occupies when loaded into memory. Although we mention several tricks and techniques for managing RAM in this book, it's still all too easy to make a movie so big that the computer bogs down just loading the cast members. The solution is to identify sequences that work as individual units, spin them off into their own movies, and then link them together. When done correctly, the result is transparent to the end user—there's no indication where one movie ends and the other begins.

- **Layered movies.** In addition to playing more than one movie in sequence, you can also play movies as MIAWs: multiple movies that appear as windows in the current movie. Not only can you retain full interactivity on all levels, but all movies can communicate, passing Lingo instructions back and forth. MIAWs are pretty impressive, but they have one drawback—they aren't supported by Shockwave yet (but we hope they will be soon).

- **Ease of organization.** When you take the multiple-movie approach to your multimedia productions, you also have the challenge of making all the movies look consistent, part of an overall interface design. This could become a major headache, but fortunately you can save the common design and scripting elements and share them among all movies. Much as style sheets affect text in a word processor, any changes to an original movie element will automatically be reflected in all instances of that element in all the movies.

- **Modularity.** With a multiple-movie structure, you can pull out and plug in new elements without having to put the whole production into dry dock. Let's say you have an information kiosk that lets the user browse through your client's entire product line. Rather than reconfigure the works when the client rolls out a new widget, you can have a smaller Widgets movie that's called by the larger, underlying Kiosk application. You can then just update the Widgets movie, slip it on a CD, overwrite the old file on the kiosk's hard drive, and you're back in business.

Calling Other Movies

The easiest way to coordinate multiple movies is in a linear fashion: Just include a command in movie A that opens and runs movie B, and include a command in movie B that jumps to movie C (or perhaps back to movie A). You already know the necessary Lingo: the go to and play commands. They work just as well across movies as they do across movie sections.

Basic inter-movie navigation

Let's use the go to and play commands to link two movies.

1. *Find the Multiples folder (inside the Tutorials folder) on the CD and copy the entire folder to your hard drive.*

2. *Open the movie JumpDemo.dir in the Multiples folder.*

You'll find a modest movie with two buttons, both of which have scripts attached to them. Go ahead and run the movie; then click the movie's Play button. Swifty performs a quick jump, and the movie loops back to its beginning.

3. *Open the Script window of the Walking button cast member.*

Do this by selecting the cast member in the Cast window and then clicking the Cast window's Script button. The script should read

```
on mouseUp
    go to movie "WalkDemo"
end
```

4. Close the Script window. Save the movie.

We save because opening a script makes Director think you've made
changes to the movie. If you don't save the movie now, before running it,
you'll be prompted with a Save? dialog box as soon as Director tries to
leap into the next movie. And remember that elements called by a movie
must be in the same folder as that movie: If you save JumpDemo.dir
to a different location, you must also move WalkDemo.dir. (unless you
specify a complete path name within the calling script). Likewise, if
you rename an element, you must change the name within the scripts
that call it or Director won't be able to find it. We'll examine this process
in detail shortly.

WHERE DO WE GO?
These two movies have
buttons that launch
each other in turn,
using the go to movie
command.

5. Run the movie; click the Walking button.

Pretty easy, eh? The Stage should have switched from the JumpDemo
movie to the WalkDemo one without a hitch. And the movie is still running. Go ahead and click the movie's Play button to see Swifty walk.

Now let's inspect the button script that gets the user back to the Jumping
movie. This time we've used a slightly different syntax.

6. Open the Script window of the Jumping button. It should read

```
on mouseUp
     go to frame 2 of movie "JumpDemo"
end
```

7. Run the movie. Click the Jumping button.

This script jumps us to the second frame of Jumping, so it skips the looping on the first frame and jumps right into the animation. Most of the

navigation commands you've learned thus far can be applied across movies as well as within them: You can specify a frame number or marker name, you can use the play command instead of go to, and you can use a play done command (when it follows play) to return the playback head to the location from which it entered the second movie. Let's take a look at the play command.

8. **Stop the movie while JumpDemo.dir is running. Open the cast script for the Walking button.**

9. **Change the script to use the play _command:_**

```
on mouseUp
  play frame 2 of movie "WalkDemo"
end
```

10. **Save the movie and open WalkDemo.dir.**

11. **Double-click the Score cell in the behavior channel at frame 14 of the movie and change the script as follows:**

```
on exitFrame
  play done
end
```

Now we have a play command in JumpDemo that jumps right into the animation of WalkDemo. When WalkDemo reaches the end of the movie, the frame behavior issues a play done command, and the movie returns to JumpDemo at the frame from which it left. You really don't need the Jumping button in WalkDemo any more, since the movie is so short. If the movie were longer, maybe with branching of its own, you could put in a Back or Return button that also issues a play done command.

FILE LOCATION WITH LINGO

Straightforward go to and play commands work fine on all movies residing in the same folder of the same volume of the host system. But if you try to open a movie that's not in the immediate vicinity, you'll get a dialog box like the one shown here.

A QUEST REQUEST:
You may receive this prompt when a script calls for a movie that's not in the same folder as the one currently running.

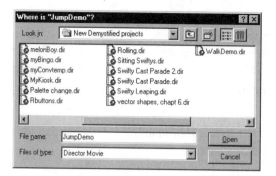

To open movies that reside in different locations, you need to refer to them by their full names. The name that shows up on the desktop is only part of a file's name as far as the computer is concerned— the full name includes specific information about the file's location in the storage hierarchy. For example, on a Windows system, the full name of the JumpDemo movie on the CD is this (where D is the drive letter of the CD-ROM):

```
D:\Tutorials\Multiples\JumpDemo.dir
```

On the Macintosh, the full name is this:

```
DD CD-ROM:Tutorials:Multiples:JumpDemo.dir
```

The file would have a different full name if you copied it to another drive, but you get the gist: The full name of a file is its address—the path you take to get to the file. For that reason, it's called the **path name**.

Although the term *path name* refers to the full address of a file, the Lingo function the moviePath returns only the path name minus the current file name.

You'll note that in the path name for the Macintosh, all the elements are separated by colons (:) *without* spaces. That's because the colon is a special character to the MacOS, indicating another notch down the file hierarchy. In Windows, the backslash (\) serves a similar function. This is why your computer won't let you use colons (or backslashes) when naming files. A name like Jump:Demo would cause your system to look fruitlessly for a nested folder named Jump that probably doesn't exist.

Although the MacOS uses colons rather than backslashes as level indicators in path names, Director 7 can automatically interpret backslashes as colons or colons as backslashes on the respective platforms. This means, if you're developing for cross-platform distribution, you can use backslashes instead of colons and be assured that your path name instructions will be understood.

Invoking a path name

The path name of a file, as returned by the `moviePath`, always begins with the name of the volume—the hard drive, floppy disk, CD-ROM, or other storage medium that can be named and treated as a separate unit. The path name ends not with the name of the currently open file, but with the folder in which the file resides.

Although you can do so, it's generally a bad idea to specify a movie you want to play using the full path name. You can never be sure where users will place files on their systems. One can, hopefully, assume that they will keep files in the same relative locations. A **relative path name** is a path name that begins with the location of some other folder—your currently running movie's folder, for example. Your movie can say, "I don't care where I am, but I know what folder I'm in, so look in my folder for another folder named *somefolder* and play the file I want out of there." All this is made simple with the `moviePath` movie property. We can test this out by first looking at what happens when your movie can't find the file.

1. *On your hard drive, find the folder where you placed JumpDemo.dir.*

2. *Create a new folder there called* **New Home.**

3. *Move the WalkDemo.dir file into the New Home folder. Make sure that you move, not copy, the file.*

4. *Open and run JumpDemo.*

When you click the Walking button, Director won't find your WalkDemo movie. It tries to be friendly by giving you, the user, a chance to search for the movie by displaying a Browse dialog box. But users shouldn't have to search for a file every time a movie switches, even if they know what they're looking for. The proper method is to set up the movie so Director knows where to look.

THE @ OPERATOR:
Use the @ operator when navigating between Director movies.

We can use the `moviePath` property to retrieve the current movie's path and then tack on the relative path of the new movie, but there is a better way that uses the @ operator. The @ operator specifies the path to the current movie and has the additional advantage of working just as well on the Macintosh as it works in Windows. Here's how you can set the path to the WalkDemo movie:

5. *Stop the movie and open the cast script of the Walking button in JumpDemo.*

6. *Change the* play *command as follows:*

```
play frame 2 of movie "@\New Home\WalkDemo"
```

You can use a colon (:) instead of the backslash if you prefer; Director doesn't care. For that matter, even the forward slash (/) will work just fine. Note that the only space used in the path we created is between the word *New* and the word *Home*. Spaces anywhere else can cause the movie not to be found.

> The @ operator is a pretty handy tool for specifying path names. You can even specify a folder above the current folder. For example, @\\myMovie is in the folder one level up, and @\\\myMovie is in the folder two levels up.

7. **Run the movie. Then click the Walking button.**

The JumpDemo movie should play the WalkDemo movie and then return to JumpDemo. We don't need to specify the path name to return to JumpDemo because Director keeps track of the return location. If we used the go to command instead of play, however, we would need to set the path name both going and returning.

> If you're ever unsure of the complete path name of a movie, open that movie in Director and then open the Message window and type **put the moviePath**. This will return the path name in quotation marks. You can also use this property in your scripts. You should also check out the *Lingo Lexicon* entries for **the applicationPath** and **the searchPath** (see Appendix C).

The path name concept applies to online movies as well. If you're developing for the Shockwave environment, you can write scripts that open and close shocked movies at various online locations. In such instances, the path name doesn't include a root volume address (such as C\:) but instead includes the universal resource locator (the URL, such as http://www.demystified.com/~exercises). Keep in mind that no matter what medium you're navigating, opening movies via Lingo is a two-step process: First you establish the path name that guides Director to the file's front door, and then you issue the play command.

WINDOW MANAGEMENT BASICS

Leaping from one movie to the next is all very well and good, but the real power of multiple movie management comes when you have several movies open at once—**MIAW**.

With MIAW, one movie remains open at all times; we'll call it the **root movie**. Other movies (or more correctly, the windows containing other movies) can be opened and closed using Lingo commands; we'll call these the **window movies**. Each window movie can be completely interactive, which means you can click buttons in the window and the movie will respond. What's more, instructions and other information can be passed from one movie to another; what happens in a window movie can affect the root movie, and vice versa.

Creating MIAWs is a multistep process. Typically, the process is something like this:

1. Define the window and specify the movie to play in the window.

2. Set the window's properties.

3. Open the window and play the movie.

4. Close or delete the window.

We'll call the first three items on our list "creating the window," and we'll call the final item "removing the window." Surprisingly enough, removing an MIAW can be just about as important as creating one, as you will see.

Creating windows

Over the next few exercises, we're going to use MIAW to build a multiwindow extravaganza, with no less than four movies running at once. Let's begin at the beginning.

1. ***Open the Multiplex.dir movie in the MultiWins folder (inside the Multiples folder you copied to your hard drive).***

Multiplex is the root movie. You'll see that I've already set the Stage and added some cast members. Let's add a script that opens the first movie.

2. ***Click to select the sprite of the leftmost Open button.***

3. Select New Behavior from the Behavior pop-up menu in the Score window.

The Behavior Script window should open. We're attaching the script to the sprite, and not to the cast member, because we have three sets of Open and Close buttons on the Stage. This way, we can use the same two cast members for all of the buttons.

4. Enter this script:

```
on mouseUp
  global wRunning  -- so we can reference elsewhere
  wRunning = window ("Running")
    -- define the window and specify the movie
  wRunning.visible = true  -- set the window's properties
  open wRunning  -- open the window
end
```

5. Save and run the movie. Click the Open button for which we just created the behavior.

A new window should appear in the root movie. As you can tell from the new movie's title bar, it's the movie Running (another simple loop animation). The size of the window is the size of the Stage in the Running movie: a modest 160 x 120 pixels.

NOW PLAYING:
An example of the basic Movie in a Window (MIAW), running superimposed over the Stage of the root movie.

You're already familiar with windows like this one; they show up in almost every application. You can click and drag the title area to relocate it anywhere on your monitor screen, and you can close the window by clicking the MIAW's close box. But now let's look at something interesting.

6. Click the Stop button on Director's toolbar (or on the Control Panel).

You've stopped the root movie, but the MIAW keeps on running and is still visible. You can even close the window the MIAW is running in, and the MIAW will still be running, although you can't see it. Don't believe me? Try this:

7. Open the Message window and click the Trace button.

The messages in the Message window show that the MIAW is still running, even though the root movie is stopped. Without an explicit closing command, the MIAW would still be running even if you closed the root movie and opened another movie. So we need to provide a housekeeping script that closes the window. But first, let's shut it down manually.

8. In the Message window, click the Trace button again to turn off the Message window's messages.

9. Enter the following line in the Message window and then press Enter (Windows) or Return (Macintosh):

```
forget wRunning
```

The MIAW should disappear, and, if you try clicking Trace again, you will find nothing happening.

A global aside

Why did we use a global variable to define the window? Again, it's good programming practice. We could just as well have used these commands:

```
window("running").visible = TRUE
open window "running"
```

We could then use the command

```
forget window "running"
```

to shut down the Running movie. In fact, that command would have worked just as well as the one we entered in the Message window—
`forget wRunning`.

To see why this is so, enter the following line in the Message window:

```
put wRunning
```

The result is (window "running"), so forget window "running" really is the same as forget wRunning. What we gain by using a global variable is the ability to change the movie. In your own working project, on a professional level, you'd define the window and the movie to be played in a movie script using global variables. Then you could change the name of the movie that is to be played in a single location in the movie. The rest of the movie would take care of itself.

Closing windows

Okay, so we can't have the user closing MIAWs for us. Let's do it the right way with Lingo. You can use two commands to close an MIAW: close window and forget window. The distinction is one of memory management: close will make the window disappear, but the movie playing in it will remain in RAM (though not running); forget will shut down the window and flush the movie from memory. You'll want to use the former when dealing with an MIAW you expect to reappear sooner rather than later; forget will use less RAM, but it takes longer for the window to reopen if you need it again.

1. *Open a Behavior script for the sprite of the leftmost Close button and enter the following handler:*

```
on mouseUp
  global wRunning  -- the name of the "running" movie
  close wRunning  -- but leave it in memory
end
```

Just to be sure, and to make authoring easier, we can also create a stopMovie handler that uses forget to stop the MIAW.

2. **Select an empty slot in the Cast window and open a movie Script.**

3. **Enter the following** stopMovie **handler:**

```
on stopMovie
  global wRunning
  forget wRunning
end
```

Now even if you decide to stop the movie while the MIAW is still running, both movies will be stopped when the root movie is stopped. Note the use of forget rather than close. That's because you want the window (and the movie running in it) to be flushed from RAM as well as banished from the end user's screen. Director is a RAM-intensive application to begin with, and keeping unnecessary objects in memory is a quick way to bog things down.

4. **Run the movie and try playing and stopping the Running movie.**

Now experiment with the window movie a bit. Move it to a new position on your screen and drag in the lower-right corner to resize it (yes, the window of a movie can be larger than that movie's Stage). Now when you close and reopen the Running movie (without stopping the root movie), the root movie remembers the window's size and location. Had you used forget window rather than close window, the window would revert to its original disposition every time the movie was closed and reopened.

You can also make an MIAW disappear without closing or "forgetting" its window. When the **visible** window property is set to FALSE, the window won't show up on the monitor. Since this property affects the display of the window rather than the window itself, it's good for tasks such as quickly toggling the view with a mouse click.

Setting the window name

If you experimented with making the window of the Running movie larger than its Stage size of 160 x 120 pixels, you saw an important fact demonstrated: *A window has an identity of its own,* distinct from the movie that's running in it. It's like a screen in a movie theater—you can set it up at a particular size and location and then project any number of movies onto it.

Since the movie and window are separate entities, you can even give the window a name. Right now, the name of the window and the name of the movie that runs in the window are the same, Running, even though we refer to the movie with a global variable. We can create a window, give it a name, and then use the fileName property to assign a movie to the window.

1. **Modify the Open button's behavior to read**

```
on mouseUp
  -- define the window and set the movie to run
  window ("runSwifty").filename = "Running"
  -- set the window's properties
  window("runSwifty").visible = true
  open window "runSwifty"
end
```

Now we have a window named runSwifty and a movie set to run in the window named Running. Although we aren't using a global variable now to reference the window, we could do that as well. The window's name, though, works just as well and can be used throughout the root movie. Notice how, now that we aren't using a variable, we need to use the window keyword as well as the window's name.

Before we run the movie again, let's make sure we can close the window, too. We need to adapt our Close button behavior and the stopMovie handler to use the new window name.

2. **Modify the Close button's behavior to read**

```
on mouseUp
  close window "runSwifty"  -- but leave it in memory
end
```

3. **Modify the** stopMovie **handler as follows:**

```
on stopMovie
  forget window "runSwifty"
end
```

4. **Close the Script window and run the movie.**

The script that sets attributes of a window (such as its name) doesn't have to be in the same handler as the command that opens the window. Instead, you might want to place the script in a **startMovie** handler so it executes on startup. If a handler doesn't have to define a window but simply open it, it'll execute more quickly, thus minimizing appearances of the hourglass or wristwatch. Another trick is to use the **preLoadMovie** command, which loads enough of the movie to start displaying the first frame. Without **preLoadMovie**, the movie isn't actually loaded into RAM until the window is opened.

Types of windows

At least seven different styles of windows are common to both the Windows and MacOS platforms. Each has a numeric code, which you can assign to a window using the windowType property.

The **standard document window** is the default; it's the window type you've already seen. It has a close box and a title bar, and the window can be resized. The code that identifies this type is 0.

**THE STANDARD
DOCUMENT WINDOW:**
ID code 0.

The **alert box style window** is the type of window used for system alert messages. It has a double border but no title or close box; it can't be resized or moved. Its ID code is 1.

The **plain box style window** is just that: a version of the window movie's Stage without identifying features. It's good to use when you want to mask the MIAW, making it blend into the backdrop of the root movie. Its ID code is 2.

The **document window without size box** looks like the standard window you've already encountered, but it cannot be resized. Its ID code is 4.

The **modal document window without size box** looks like the standard window you've already encountered, but again, it cannot be resized. Its ID code is 5.

The **document window with zoom box and variable resize box** also looks like the standard window, but the title bar includes a zoom button. Its ID code is 8.

THE DOCUMENT WINDOW WITH ZOOM BOX:
ID code 8.

The **document window with the variable resize box disabled** is the same as window type 8 but without the window resizing capability. Its ID code is 12.

THE NONRESIZEABLE DOCUMENT WINDOW WITH ZOOM BOX:
ID code 12.

Three other window options are available for Macintosh users: ID 3 is the same as ID 2, but it has a small drop shadow that makes the image "pop" nicely; ID 16 is similar to ID 4, but it has rounded corners; and ID 49 is a stationary window.

The most important thing to remember when you're developing for cross-platform playback is to use a type of window that's available in both platforms, or set the type depending on the system (as determined by the **platform** property).

Setting the window type

You can designate the type of a window by setting its windowType property:

1. *In the Open button's behavior script, add the following line before the command to open the window:*

```
window("runSwifty").windowType = 2
```

2.   Save and run the movie.

The movie in the window opens in style type 2.

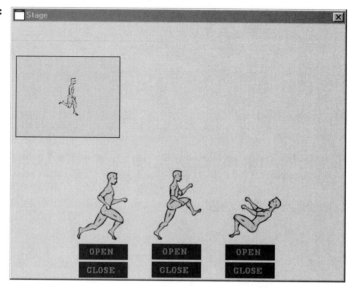

3.   Change the Open button's behavior to set the window type to 8:

```
window("runSwifty").windowType = 8
```

4.   Save and run the movie.

Now the MIAW has a title bar and buttons.

Opening multiple windows

Having multiple windows open can be a simple matter of issuing several
"open window" commands.

1.   Attach this script to the middle Open button:

```
on mouseUp
  window ("jumpSwifty").filename = "Jumping"
  -- set the window's properties
  window("jumpSwifty").visible = true
  window("jumpSwifty").windowType = 8
  open window "jumpSwifty"
end
```

*2. **Attach this script to the middle Close button:***

```
on mouseUp
  close window "jumpSwifty"  -- but leave it in memory
end
```

*3. **Attach the same scripts to the rightmost Open and Close buttons, this time substituting** flipSwifty *for* jumpSwifty.*

*4. **In the Movie script, add the following lines to the** stopMovie **handler:***

```
forget window "jumpSwifty"
forget window "flipSwifty"
```

*5. **Save and play the movie.***

Now you can open any of three movies, in any order you choose. But there's just one problem: We haven't specified where each movie will be placed; each of the movies may open up in the same location at the same time, so only one can been seen at a time. You can move the movie windows, but that isn't the effect we want. To see what to do next, we'll explore the whys and wherefores of window size and position.

Now that you're working with multiple windows, you should know about the Lingo property **the windowList**. It returns a complete listing of all MIAW windows currently opened in memory, even if they're not currently visible—try entering **put the windowList** in the Message window the next time you have multiple MIAWs. Since it's easy to overload RAM (and the end user's attention span) with too many windows, you can use this property to limit additional launchings or to quietly close windows when they're no longer needed. We'll get into the use of lists in Lingo in Chapter 16: *Lingo and Lists*.

CHANGING WINDOW COORDINATES

When you want to depart from the default display of a window, the first thing to understand is that window size and location are inextricably linked: You can't set one and not the other. What you have to do is stake off a certain rectangular area on the screen where the window belongs.

In describing that area, you set both dimensions and position. This is done by setting the `rect` window property.

The rect

The simple word *rect* can have multiple meanings and uses in a Director movie. The keyword `rect` can refer to a data type, a function, a sprite property, a cast member property, or a window property, depending on how it is used. Don't let that get you nervous, though. Once you understand what a `rect` data type is, the rest falls into place and is automatic.

The simplest way to understand the `rect` data type is to think of it as the coordinates of all four corners in relative terms; and there's the complication—relative to what? For sprites, it's relative to the Stage. And that makes sense—a sprite is always on top of the Stage. But for an MIAW, you get more flexibility; you can place the MIAW anywhere you want on the entire screen, so the `rect` of a window is relative to the monitor.

We've mentioned this in a previous chapter, but we'll show the `rect` syntax here again (what the heck, you'll probably have to look it up the first 20 or so times you use it):

```
rect(rleft, rtop, rright, rbottom)
```

The `rleft` coordinate is the distance from the left edge of the monitor (for a window) to the left edge of the window. The `rtop` coordinate is the distance from the top of the monitor to the top of the window. The `rright` coordinate is the distance from the left of the monitor to the right of the window. The `rbottom` coordinate is the distance from the top of the monitor to the bottom of the window.

For an MIAW, the **rect** property defines the location (and size) of a window relative to the monitor. For a sprite, the location and size are relative to the Stage. When you are authoring, an MIAW's **rect** location will appear to be relative to the viewable area of the Director window, but if you create a projector, you will see that the window is relative to the monitor.

Scripting with rect

Let's give each of our three MIAWs a little breathing room of its own. Insert these commands right before the open window command in each Open button behavior script:

1. *Add this line to the script of the Open button for Running:*

```
window("runSwifty").rect = rect(100, 100, 260, 220)
```

2. *Add this line to the script of the Open button for Jumping:*

```
window("jumpSwifty").rect = rect(300, 100, 460, 220)
```

3. *Add this line to the script of the Open button for Flipping:*

```
window("flipSwifty").rect = rect(500, 100, 660, 220)
```

4. *Save and run the movie.*

A TRIPLE FEATURE:
The Multiplex.dir movie with all three MIAWs opened in their respective locations, set with the property the rect.

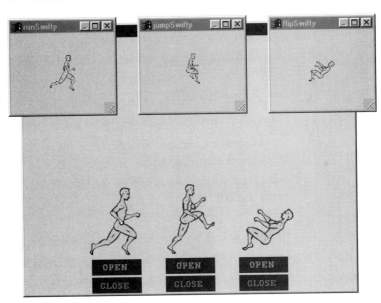

Now, when you click the Open buttons, each MIAW opens in a different area; it's easy to see all three at once. If you analyze the coordinates we set by subtracting the first value from the third, and the second value from the fourth, you'll see that they all match the Stage size used to create the three movies (Flipping, Jumping, and Running): 160 x 120 pixels.

Placing windows relative to the Stage

Absolute monitor coordinates are fine when a movie is destined to play only on the current monitor—but what happens when it plays on other monitors with varying shapes and sizes? A hundred pixels to the right or down from the top corner of a 9-inch screen is a different location than the same coordinate on a 20-inch screen.

That's why it's usually best to set the rect in terms that are relative to the Stage size of the root movie. Fortunately, a set of helpful functions are handy:

- the stageLeft returns a measurement in pixels of the distance from the left edge of the root movie's Stage to the left edge of the monitor screen.

- the stageRight returns a measurement from the left edge of the monitor screen to the right edge of the root movie's Stage. Note that it doesn't measure the *right* screen margin; instead, it gauges distance from the same starting point as the stageLeft. You can calculate the width of the Stage by subtracting the stageLeft from the stageRight.

- the stageTop is equal to the distance from the top of the screen to the top of the Stage.

- the stageBottom starts from the same measuring point as the stageTop but returns the distance to the bottom of the Stage. To calculate the height of the Stage, subtract the stageTop from the stageBottom.

Scripting with positional functions

The trick to setting windows relative to the Stage is to create custom variables that add or subtract from the positional functions and then plug those variables into a rect statement. Let's modify the script of the Open button for the Running window to illustrate this:

1. *Open the behavior script of the Open button for the Running window, and replace the command line that sets the window's* rect *coordinates with the following lines:*

```
runTop = (the stageTop + 10)
runLeft = (the stageLeft + 10)
runRight = (the stageLeft + 170)
```

```
runBot = (the stageTop + 130)
window("runSwifty").rect = rect(runLeft, runTop, ¬
runRight, runBot)
```

2. **Save and run the movie.**

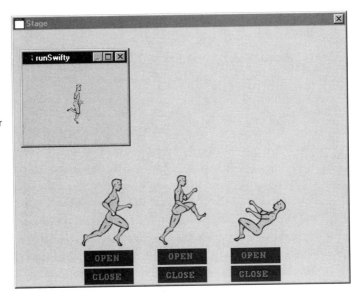

GOTCHA CORNERED:
Now the coordinates of the Running movie are set relative to the edges of the root movie's Stage. The movie will show up in that location no matter what size monitor the end user has.

Now the MIAW runs at a set location relative to the Stage, 10 pixels in from the left and top edges. No matter what monitor you use to play this movie (or a projector made from it), it'll always show up there. The other windows can be set up similarly.

INTER-WINDOW COMMUNICATION

Now that we have all four movies in view and running at the same time, let's explore how information can be passed from one to another.

The tell command

When you want something to happen in a MIAW, you simply tell it to do so, using the tell command. To demonstrate, let's change the Swiftys on the Multiplex Stage into buttons themselves: Click one, and the respective MIAW will be transformed.

1. Select sprite 1 (the leftmost Swifty) in the Multiplex.dir movie.

2. Select New Behavior from the Score window's Behavior pop-up menu. Enter the following script:

```
on mouseUp
  tell window "runSwifty" to set the stageColor = random (255)
end
```

3. Repeat steps 1 and 2 to add scripts to sprites 2 and 3, substituting "jumpSwifty" and then "flipSwifty" for the window name "runSwifty".

4. Save and run the movie.

These scripts change the background color of each of the window movie's Stages to a random color (within the standard 8-bit palette range of 256 colors) whenever a button is clicked. Try using these buttons when the windows are open. Then close the windows, click the buttons, and open the windows again; you'll find that the command (to change the color) is carried out even when the windows are closed—that's because we used close window (which keeps the movie in memory) rather than forget window (which doesn't).

The stage property

The tell command works in the other direction as well: Scripts can be passed from a window movie to the root movie. But since Director needs to know which command is intended for which movie, the property the stage is used. Commands sent to the stage are passed on to the root movie, whatever that movie happens to be. This way, several movies can open the window movie, all with the same results.

So let's turn the animated Swiftys into buttons as well; clicking them will now change the condition of the root movie.

1. Open the movie Running.dir.

Not much here; just a simple loop.

2. Select all sprites in channel 1.

3. Select New Behavior from the Score window's Behavior pop-up menu. Enter the following two handlers:

```
on mouseDown
    tell the stage to put "I'm Running!" into member "Report"
end

on mouseUp
    tell the stage to put " " into member "Report"
end
```

The empty quotation marks are necessary because they're not really empty; there's a space between them, and this space will replace whatever text is currently in the Report cast member. This script passes one message to the root movie when the mouse button is clicked on the animation sprites, and it passes another message when the button is released.

4. **Save and close the movie.**

5. **Repeat steps 1 through 4 to add the same scripts to the Jumping and Flipping movies, changing the word Running to an appropriate verb.**

6. **Reopen and run the Multiplex movie.**

The cast member Report is a text area I've placed in the middle of the movie, unseen thus far because it's remained empty. But now when you click the moving figures in any of the three MIAWs, their actions are enthusiastically announced. Notice that the playback of other movies comes to a halt as long as you keep the mouse button down over the scripted sprites.

RUN, MOVIE, RUN: MIAWs can be fully interactive and pass information to the root movie. Here, the Flipping movie announces itself by placing a message in a field in Multiplex when clicked.

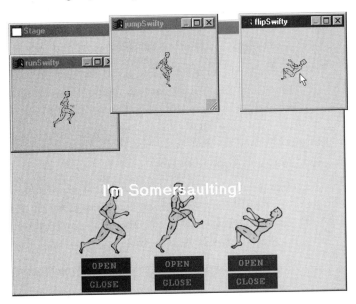

You can use the **tell** command to communicate between any existing windows, not just back and forth between the root movie and other windows. In our example movie, the window **runSwifty** can send messages directly to the movie **jumpSwifty**. Also, if you need to send a number of commands instead of a single message, you can use a **tell...end tell** construct and place the statements to be executed in between. For example:

```
tell window "whichWindow"
    member(12).text = "Hello there."
    -- more statements
end tell
```

Blocking communication

Sometimes you want to turn off the flow of information from the root movie to a window movie. When that's the case, use the modal window property the `modal of window`:

1. **In the Multiplex.dir movie, open the script of the leftmost Open button and add this line before the** open window **command:**

```
window ("runSwifty").modal = TRUE
```

2. **Close the Script window, run the movie, and click the button.**

When this property is set to TRUE, the movie running in the window can't receive input from outside sources. Not only will it ignore the background color-change script for the Swifty button, but the Close button will not have any effect either. However, when you click the animation sprites in the window movie, you'll see that the message "I'm Running!" still passes to the root movie.

When an MIAW is running with its modal property turned on, it won't stop running until it encounters a command turning the modal property off. That's why if you try to stop the movie by clicking elsewhere—even on the Stop button in the Control Panel—nothing happens.

3. **Press Control-Alt-period (Windows) or Command-period (Macintosh) to stop the movie.**

4. *Revert to the previously saved version of the movie, or remove the command line that set the window's modal property.*

Since it takes precedence and effectively shuts down control, the modal window property is best used only in those circumstances when you want all resources to be focused on a single window—such as when a processor-intensive animation is unfolding and you don't want the end user to slow things down with idle mouse clicks elsewhere.

When you're building a multiple-movie production, don't neglect one important scripting tool: global variables. After they're declared in the root movie, they can be accessed by all movies that open during that session (the period in which Director or the resulting projector or Shockwave file is running).

MANAGING MULTIPLE CASTS

Coordinating playback isn't the only way multiple Director movies can work together. It's also possible to share anything that can be placed in a cast slot: scripts, graphics, video, palettes, and so on. When your multi-movie multimedia production starts getting ambitious, you'll want to take advantage of this capability.

Why share cast resources? Here are three main reasons:

- **Consistency.** If the same resources are used in all movies, it's easy to maintain a consistent look and feel.

- **Performance.** All cast members from a movie's internal Cast are flushed from RAM whenever a movie closes. If common elements are stored in an external Cast file, they can stay in memory. That means that the loading and startup time of the next movie can be cut to a minimum.

- **File size.** Why make individual movies any bigger than you have to? If you identify the common elements and isolate them in a separate shared file, you'll use less overall storage space.

Multiple Casts might even make sense for a single-movie production. For instance, let's say you're building a "dress-up doll" application. You could script the movie so that the user chooses wardrobe items—and then multiply the possibilities by creating multiple wardrobes, each with its own Cast. It's easy with Director 7, which lets you open, modify, and close as many Cast databases as you like.

Internal or external?

In Director, Casts can be either **internal** or **external**. Internal Casts (like the default one that opens with every movie) are saved as integral parts of a movie. External Casts are saved as files in their own right (in Windows, their file names bear the extension *.cst*). Both types have their advantages and disadvantages:

- Internal Casts can't be shared by more than one movie, but they free you from the hassle of having to keep track of linkages. They do add to the size of the movie file, so you may want to use internal Casts only when they are specifically called for. Remember that the good ol' default Cast can hold up to 32,000 cast members.

- External Casts can make guest appearances in as many movies as you'd like, but you'll have to maintain the link. Also, keep in mind that shared Casts have to be modified with care, as the changes wrought for the sake of one movie could wreak havoc with another.

Creating new Casts

Internal or external, the process of Cast Creation is the same. In the top-left corner of the Cast window, you'll see an icon that's somewhat evocative of a tic-tac-toe board—that's the **Choose Cast button**. Let's use this button to create a new cast.

1. **Click the Choose Cast button and choose New Cast.**

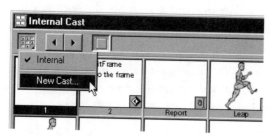

You can now name the new Cast (you don't need to, though) and choose the internal or external format. If you opt for an external format, the Use in Current Movie check box also becomes available. When this is enabled, the Cast will be opened each time your movie's opened. Let's skip that option for now.

2. *Name your Cast* **Characters;** *choose the External option.*

A new Cast window appears.

3. *In the Paint window, use the tools of your choice to create a few cast members in Characters.*

It doesn't matter what you put in this Cast. Just fill it with something unique, so you can identify it later.

4. *Close the External Cast window.*

You'll be asked to save the Cast somewhere on your system. The pathname issue will rear its ugly head again, so try to put the Cast in a logical place where it can stay put. A moved or renamed external Cast file will prompt Director to ask you to hunt for the file.

When you're placing sprites on the Stage or in the Score, you can draw them from cast members of any Cast that happens to be open and active. Don't worry if the members have identical cast numbers (or even names); Director will be able to tell the difference.

If you have the opportunity to examine older Director productions, you may find movies named Shared.dir popping up with regularity. That was the extent of Cast sharing in earlier versions of Director: If a file by that name was placed in the same folder as another movie, the application would integrate both movies' Cast information into a single Cast window. It was a means of sharing resources, albeit a cumbersome one, because you had to make sure that no cast members in either movie had the same cast number, or they'd be overwritten. For that reason, the elements in Shared.dir movies are usually placed very low in the Cast, usually starting at slot 500 or thereabouts.

Adding and subtracting linked Casts

When you go to the Modify menu and choose Movie and then Casts, you'll see a dialog box that lets you both forge and break your movie's links to internal and external Casts.

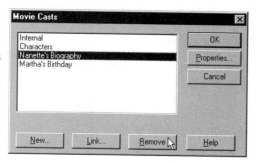

To dispose of an internal Cast, simply select it in the dialog box and click the Remove button. Doing the same with an external Cast won't delete it, however; it will just remove the link. The Link button displays a dialog box that lets you navigate to (and designate) a new candidate for linkage. You can also use this dialog box to update the connection to a file that's been moved.

You can set the **preloading point** (the moment of reading into RAM) for both internal and external Casts. Just select a Cast and then choose Cast Properties from the Modify menu. You'll see a dialog box that lets you choose from the three standard preload options: Before Frame One, After Frame One, and When Needed.

Cast-related Lingo

You can do a fair amount of Cast wrangling via scripts as well. Although you can't open and close Casts with Lingo, you can write scripts that modify their contents and even rename them. Here's a sampling of some Cast-specific Lingo; you'll find in-depth descriptions of them in *A Lingo Lexicon* (Appendix C).

- The keyword `castLib` is your handle for designating specific Casts when accessing cast members in Casts that are open or linked to the current movie. For instance, scripting a change to a text string in slot 7 of the Cast we've named Characters would use either of the following two syntaxes:

```
set the text of member 7 of castLib "Characters" ¬
to "new text"
```

```
member (7, "Characters").text = "new text"
```

Remember that setting text in this fashion works only if the cast member is already of the text or field type. Notice that many Director elements that take cast member numbers as parameters (such as member) allow the Cast to be specified. You can specify a Cast either by using its name (as just shown) or by referring to its number.

TIP

Although both syntaxes shown will work, one syntax that used to work in earlier versions of Director will now cause a script error:

```
set the text of member (7) of castLib "Characters" ¬
to "new text"
```

- What *is* a Cast's number? The property `the number of castLib` will yield the answer. Casts are assigned numbers based on the order they're read into Director in the context of the current movie, so an external Cast may be `castLib 4` in one movie and `castLib 3` in another (the default internal cast is always `castLib 1`). For that reason, it's usually prudent to name your Casts and refer to them by their names.

- The one exception is the powerful `castLibNum` sprite property—which, as the name implies, must refer to the `castLib` number. Fortunately, you can get around having to know that number by using syntax like this:

```
set the castLibNum of sprite 1 to the number ¬
of castLib "Characters"
```

This will keep the script accurate no matter what number is assigned to that Cast. This property is important because it lets you switch the Cast from which a sprite is derived, which can entirely change your movie's appearance and behavior. If a sprite was derived from slot 8 in Cast A, it'll subsequently be derived from slot 8 in Cast B. You have to watch for consistent media types, however—if slot 8 is occupied by a graphic in Cast A and a Lingo script in Cast B, the former will simply disappear without so much as a warning dialog box. Also keep in mind that this property can map only to Casts as a whole. If you want to change the sprite's derivation to a cast member in a different slot, you have to modify both the `castLibNum` property and the `member of sprite` property.

To get a taste of the power of the **`castLibNum of sprite`** property, open a movie with multiple Casts and use it in the Message window to experiment with the changing of sprites' parent Casts. Don't forget to add **`updateStage`** command lines to see the results.

- Need to extract information about a Cast? The property `number of members of castLib` will give you a count of how many slots are currently occupied, and the `fileName of castLib` will let you track down the source of the Cast. For internal files, the `fileName of castLib` returns the name of the current movie; for external files, it displays the path name to the linked file. One of the nifty aspects of this property is that it lets you swap in an entirely new Cast via Lingo; by changing the link to the file from which an external Cast is derived, you're essentially changing the Cast itself. So if you have a Cast named OtherOne (presumably linked to a file by the same name), you can use a statement like this:

```
set the filename of castLib "OtherOne" to ¬
the pathname & "YetAnother"
```

This will cause the Cast window that displays OtherOne to display the contents of a file named YetAnother instead, although the window will still bear the name OtherOne (remember that you're not opening a new Cast, just changing the link). As you can imagine, careless use of this property can cause a lot of confusion. You could think you're working with Cast A when you're really messing with Cast B, so tread cautiously.

If you place an external Cast file in your Xtras folder, you'll find it available from the Xtras menu whenever you launch Director. This is a handy location to store handler scripts and other Lingo that you reuse regularly—but copy and paste the scripts into conventionally connected Casts before you place them in the Score.

POINTS TO REMEMBER

Here's a summing up of the salient points of this chapter:

- To play **associated movies** in a linear fashion, use the go to movie or play movie command.

- To direct Director to the location of a movie, it helps to be familiar with the concept of the **path name**—the list of storage volume levels that add up to a file's address.

- To open a movie outside the location of the current movie, you need to name the movie using its **full path name**.

- To play a **Movie in a Window (MIAW)** in its default configuration, use the command open window "[*movie name*]".

- There are two commands you can use to **close a MIAW**: close window (which hides the window but keeps the movie in memory) and forget window (which closes the window and flushes the movie from RAM).

- A window is a **separate entity** from the movie that plays in it. The window can have its own name and a size and position that differ from the Stage parameters of the window movie. There are several other Lingo properties specific to windows.

- Use the windowType of window property to designate **types of windows.**

- You can have **multiple MIAWs** open at once, but each one places real demands on processing time and RAM resources. Too many MIAWs will slow the performance of your production.

- You can't change *just* the size or *just* the location of an MIAW. You change *both* from their defaults by setting the **rect property** of the window. The `rect` value is a group of four coordinates describing the dimensions of the window rectangle relative to the dimensions of the monitor.

- Window dimensions can be set in **absolute** terms (as locations on the monitor screen of the host system) or in **relative** terms (relative to the Stage of the root movie).

- The **root movie** and **window movies** can control one another, using the `tell` command to communicate Lingo scripts. If you want one window movie to control another, you'll need to pass commands through the root movie.

- If you don't want commands to pass among movies, use the `modal of window` property to turn off communication.

- Use the `windowList` property to keep track of **how many MIAWs are active**.

- **Multiple Casts** can be used by a single Director movie, and a single Cast can be shared by several movies.

- There are two kinds of Cast: **external Casts** (saved as individual files) and **internal Casts** (saved as part of the Director movie). Only external Casts can be shared.

- You can **add or subtract from the inventory of Casts** (both internal and external) connected with a movie by going to the Modify menu and choosing Movie and then Casts.

- You can **change a source cast member** (from which a sprite is derived) by switching the Cast as a whole with the property `the castLibNum of sprite`. To **change the Cast** displayed in a Cast window, use the property `the filename of castLib`.

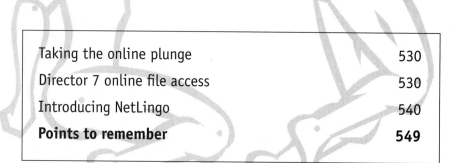

CHAPTER 14

SCRIPTING WITH NET-SAVVY LINGO

ALL THE WAY BACK IN CHAPTER 5 WE INTRODUCED SHOCKWAVE, but Shockwave is only one of the means Director 7 provides to take advantage of online access. In this chapter, we'll look into the capabilities provided to help you use elements stored in remote locations while you are authoring. You or others working on your project can store media to be used in a movie on a remote site and then access that media as you need it in your movie. Even the movie itself can be stored at a remote location and opened by Director running on your system. We'll also take a look at how to use Lingo to download or preload media from a remote site while your movie is running.

TAKING THE ONLINE PLUNGE

Chapter 5: *Introducing Shockwave*, contained exercises concerned with developing a Shockwave movie that could play back in a Web browser—but in truth, we didn't get anywhere near the World Wide Web. Everything happened in the dry dock of your own system.

Ladies and gentlemen, fire up your modems (or turn on your direct-access T1 lines—whatever). This time around, we're going to get thoroughly networked without resorting to Shockwave—or even to a browser. Director 7 has a hefty toolbox of features that let you turn the online world into an extension of your hard drive, and it's high time you got acquainted with them.

In these pages, I'm going to use the word *network* to refer to all systems in which documents can be located by means of URLs (universal resource locators). Don't confuse this network with local networks or with any other uses of this overused term. I mean it to indicate pages on the World Wide Web or on intranets, extranets, splinternets, and any other entities that are essentially manifestations of the same technology. And when I say *online*, I mean placed on one of these systems rather than on a locally accessible volume (such as the hard drive on your machine).

Most of the exercises that follow assume that you have access to the World Wide Web and that your connection is up and running. When we need to be fetching various media from a networked location, we'll be doing it from `www.demystified.com`, the Web site created especially for this book. Have your Web browser open as you read; use it to surf to the home page (at the URL just mentioned). Make sure both your connection and our file server are online before proceeding.

DIRECTOR 7 ONLINE FILE ACCESS

Our first example of Director 7's net savvy isn't the province of Lingo or even of Shockwave. It's that feature first noted way back in Chapter 1, when I pointed out the extra button marked "Internet" in the standard

Open dialog box. Simply put, some file-related operations are almost as easy to undertake online as they are on your local system. You don't need a browser or file transfer software or any other tools. About the only complicating factor is that you need to know the exact URL of the files in question, because Director 7 doesn't let you browse through the directories and subdirectories of HTTP- and FTP-configured servers. But that's a minor matter, considering that Director is one of the first multimedia tools to integrate online file retrieval into its very core.

Opening Director files from the Net

A Director movie, cast file, or media element can "live" in an online server, without being converted to the Shockwave format. It can't be played back in a Web browser, but it can be opened just like any other file of its type. Here's quick proof (make sure you're online before proceeding):

1. *From the File menu, select Open.*

2. *In the Open dialog box, click the Internet button.*

3. *When the Open URL dialog box appears, click OK after entering the following:*

```
http://www.demystified.com/AUTODONE.DIR
```

Keep in mind that unlike Lingo, many servers are case-sensitive, so pay close attention to capitalization when entering URLs.

THE URLY FEATURE: Locating Director movies and casts online is a simple matter of supplying the correct universal resource locator.

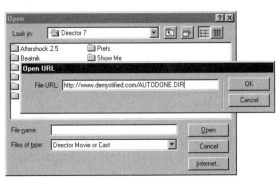

Before too long, a new movie should show up within Director. To open a cast file, follow the same procedure—with no compression, no decoding, no rigmarole. You can now play the movie, look at the cast (and change it), or do just about anything else you can do with a Director movie (except save it).

If you try to save this movie, you'll notice that the Save selection of the File menu is disabled. That's one difference in the way Director 7 treats movies and casts from an online source: Saving isn't automatic. If you want to save this movie, you'll have to save it to a local hard drive, and you'll have to use Save As instead of Save. And if you want to save it back online, you'll need to take the Save As version and upload it separately, using a file utility developed for that purpose. Of course, you'll also need upload-level access to the targeted server location. (If you don't have access and you think you should, contact the server's administrator.)

> The ease of opening online versions of Director files is a feature to take advantage of, even if your finished production isn't going to have an online component. Director's online access makes it easy to collaborate with other folks, no matter where they're located. And if you're doing cross-platform development for Windows and MacOS, parking the files online will give you equal access from both platforms.

Importing other file types

Not only can Director 7 open movies from the network; it can also crawl around online to find files in a broad range of media and then import them into an open movie. You wouldn't want to do this with data types that are automatically linked rather than wholly imported (such as digital video files) without an extremely fast connection. But for text files, bitmap images, and the like, the process is fast and simple:

1. *From the File menu, select Import.*

2. *In the Open dialog box, click the Internet button.*

3. *When the Open URL dialog box appears, click OK after entering this URL:*

`http://www.demystified.com/text1.txt`

The file name isn't all uppercase this time, and you can tell from the .txt extension that we're going after a text file (such extensions aren't necessary for Director, but the server may require them). Director 7 actually parses the URL and discerns the name of the file itself; you'll notice that text1.txt is added to the to-be-imported list. You can gang up several files, in any number of locations (both online and local), in a single import session.

4. *Click the Import button in the Import Files dialog box.*

The new cast member bears the same name as the original file. Notice that text is imported as text-type text rather than as field-type text.

INTERNAL AFFAIRS:
An online file can be imported into the internal Cast just like any other media type. Even its name will be retained.

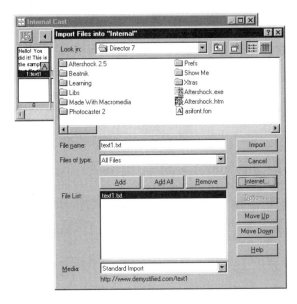

Importing through Lingo scripting

Director 7's online search skills are shared by several Lingo elements, making the action of importing media a scriptable one. With the command importFileInto, you can not only import a file from the network, but you can specify which slot you want it to occupy.

In the Message window, enter this:

```
importFileInto (member 16, ¬
"http://www.demystified.com/pic1.gif")
```

In the first line above, I added a continuation operator (¬), but you may have noticed that this operator is not available in the Message window. I used the continuation operator here because the entire line is too long to fit across the page of this book. The Message window (unlike script editor windows) will wrap long lines for you, so even though a command may appear to reside on several lines, Director will correctly interpret the command after you press Enter (Windows) or Return (Macintosh).

Note that the URL is given as a text string within quotation marks. You need to identify the slot by name or number and then type a comma and the address of the source file. As soon as you're done, Director attempts to fetch the file and deposit it as specified. If it can't find the URL, you'll encounter an error message like one of these:

FEELING DISCONNECTED?
You'll see a variation of these alert boxes if Director can't locate the given URL.

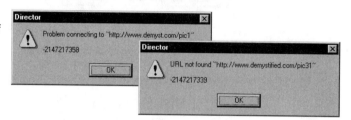

The actual alert messages you see may be more-or-less arcane, depending upon the exact problem. The "URL not found" message generally indicates a problem with the specific file. The "Problem connecting to" message generally indicates a problem finding the site from which you are trying to download the file; either you incorrectly listed the URL or there is a problem with the site's server. In either case, check to make sure that you have specified the exact site and file correctly.

If you get tired of entering tediously long URLs, you can simplify the process by using a global variable or even taking advantage of the net-savvy aspects of another familiar bit of Lingo: the property the searchPaths. Use a script line like this:

```
the searchPaths = ["http://www.demystified.com"]
```

Then you can refer to files within that directory by name only. A script statement along the lines of this will then work just fine.

```
importFileInto member 16, "pic1.gif"
```

Note the use of square brackets when setting the searchPaths. The square brackets indicate that enclosed elements constitute a list, and the list could actually contain a number of comma-separated sites. We cover lists in detail in Chapter 16: *Lingo and Lists*.

Although it does work, Macromedia recommends against using URLs with the searchPaths. If you set the searchPaths to include locations both on and off of your local system, the inclusion of remote sites can severely slow down the search for files that might otherwise be found and loaded quickly from your local system. An alternative is to specify the remote site with a variable:

```
mySite = "http://www.demystified.com/"
```

Then you can use the variable in your commands:

```
importFileInto(member 3, mySite & "pic1.gif")
```

> If you use **importFileInto** to place a cast member in a slot that's already occupied, the current contents will be overwritten. To avoid that, use the function **findEmpty** to locate the nearest empty slot following a given cast member. For instance, if slots 1 through 22 are filled, the instruction (in the Message window) **put findEmpty (member 1)** will return 23.

Playing online MIAW movies

Now that we know how to open movies that are stored on the Web, let's see if we can integrate some of what we learned in the last chapter with our new knowledge. For a good example, let's try opening an MIAW (Movie in a Window). The twist this time is that the movie we will play in the window resides online.

1. *From Director's File menu, select New and then Movie.*

We're going to write a behavior to play the MIAW, so the first thing we need is a sprite to hang the behavior on. We can use a shape or any other graphical element—just something to serve as a simple button that we can click to play the MIAW.

2. *Use the Tool Palette to create a button labeled* **Play MIAW** *on the Stage.*

3. *Select the empty cast slot 2 in the Cast window, and then open the Movie script editor. Enter the following two handlers:*

```
on startMovie
  global dym
  dym = "http://www.demystified.com/"
  global theWindow
  theWindow = window ("Playing Online")
end
```

```
on stopMovie
  global theWindow
  forget theWindow
end
```

In the `startMovie` handler, we define a variable to contain the location of our remote site. That will allow us to use the variable `dym` anywhere in our movie scripts, rather than having to retype the location and possibly make a mistake. We also define our window and keep track of it with the global variable `theWindow` (although we don't yet say much about the window itself). The `stopMovie` handler contains the command to remove the MIAW from memory using the `theWindow` global variable. As in the last chapter, we use this handler to simplify the authoring process. Defining the window in `startMovie` is also for our convenience. If you try to forget a window that hasn't been defined yet, the `forget` command will cause a script error. With the `startMovie` and `stopMovie` handlers set up as they are, we should be able to start and stop our movie, even if we never play the MIAW.

Now we need to create a behavior for our button that will use both global variables.

4. Select the button's sprite in the Score window; then, from the Behavior pull-down menu, select New Behavior.

5. In the behavior script editor, enter the following `mouseUp` handler:

```
on mouseUp
  global dym, theWindow
  --set window's properties
  theWindow.filename = dym & "AUTODONE.DIR"
  runTop = (the stageTop + 10)
  runLeft = (the stageLeft + 2)
  runRight = (the stageLeft + 600)
  runBot = (the stageTop + 300)
  theWindow.rect = rect(runLeft, runTop, runRight, runBot)
  theWindow.visible = true
  open theWindow
end
```

6. *Turn on looping; then run the movie and click the button.*

Shortly after the specified event (mouseUp) occurs, the MIAW should open. But keep in mind that this isn't streaming media *à la* Shockwave; the movie needs to download fully into RAM before the action begins.

7. *Stop the movie and save it as netMIAW.dir.*

Director's network cache

Just how long it takes for the MIAW to open depends on what you have done before. If you just opened Director and created this new movie, it should take several seconds before the new window appears. If you have followed everything in this chapter without closing Director, then the MIAW should appear immediately. So what's the difference? Once a file is downloaded from the Web, it is placed in Director's **network cache**. When Director needs to reuse the file, it first checks the cache; if the file is there, Director knows it doesn't need to download the file again. Let's try an experiment with the cache.

1. *Stop and then restart the movie, and click the Play MIAW button.*

This time, there should be no delay between the button click and the appearance of the MIAW.

2. *Stop the movie again. In the Message window, enter*

```
clearCache
```

3. *Play the movie again and click the button.*

Now Director needs to go to the Web to find and load the file, since it's no longer in the cache. If you really don't trust me on this, try dropping your network connection and then play the movie again. Your movie should play just fine, and so should the MIAW. But if you clear the cache and try to play the MIAW, Director will make an attempt to get to the file on the Web.

Note that Director's network cache applies only when you're working in Director and playing projectors. For Shockwave movies, the browser supplies the cache, not Director, and Director's cache commands aren't valid. If you're curious, try entering the following command in the Message window:

```
put cacheSize()
```

Director will return the number of kilobytes being used for its network cache.

THE CACHESIZE()
FUNCTION:
The cacheSize() func-
tion returns the number
of kilobytes used for
the network cache.

Setting network preferences

While we are on the subject of Director's cache, let's take another peek under the hood to see where the cache size is set, along with some other interesting Director attributes.

From the File menu, select Preferences and then Network. You'll see a dialog box with options pertaining to Director's behavior in the network environment.

NETWORKING CENTRAL:
Settings in the Network
Preferences dialog box
dictate several aspects
of online operation.

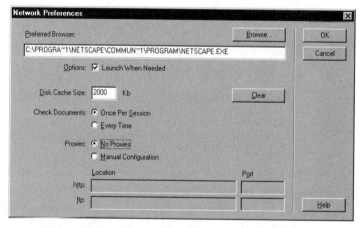

- **Preferred Browser** is the field that lets you designate which Web browser you want to work with while using Director. If you check the Launch When Needed option, your choice will automatically open anytime you execute a script that calls for a browser. But the choice you make for Preferred Browser doesn't affect only your authoring environment; it's also a cue for any projector files you might make that involve network operations. For that reason, you might want to consider modifying this setting before you create projectors. If you check the box but don't enter a path name, any resulting projectors will automatically launch whatever browser has been established as the default on the end user's system. If neither the check box nor the path name are specified, a dialog box will ask end users to navigate to the browser of their choice.

- **Cache Size** determines the size of a support file that speeds up operations by storing downloaded data. Your browser has a similar file—it saves the most recently viewed images and text, which is why it often takes much less time to reload a page you've visited recently. Don't confuse the two caches: Director movies and projectors will use this Cache Size setting, but Shockwave movies run off the browser's cache setting.

- **Check Documents** has two possible settings. Once Per Session tells Director (or the projector) to get a file from the network once and to thereafter use the file from the cache. Every Time tells Director to always get a new version from the network whenever the same URL is referenced.

- The **Proxies** section pertains to the firewall security measures most intranets use to limit access to the network from the greater outside Internet. Since users often need to jump over the firewall (in either direction), an appropriately configured proxy server can provide the necessary temporary access. If you're working within an intranet, your system administrator can probably give you the information you need to enter here. If security and limited access are issues, you definitely want to take Proxies into consideration when creating projectors.

The **cacheDocVerify** function provides you with a Lingo equivalent of the Check Documents setting in the Network Preferences dialog box. Used as **cacheDocVerify()**, it returns the current setting: either **#always** or **#once**. To change the current setting, use **cacheDocVerify #once** to get subsequent requests from the cache, or use **cacheDocVerify #always** to always attempt to retrieve a new version from the network.

INTRODUCING NETLINGO

It's great that lots of Lingo is now network fluent, but Director 7 has yet another tier of scripting capabilities to offer. There's a whole genre of Lingo developed specifically for the online environment, called **NetLingo**. In the early days of Shockwave (Director 5), some of these elements were called *Lingo network extensions*, and they were presented as not strictly Lingo. Today these commands, keywords, and functions are official parts of the Lingo vocabulary, although their syntax often differs from that of non-network Lingo.

The differences are inevitable, since NetLingo needs to shuttle back and forth between two worlds: that of the end user's host operating system (Windows or MacOS) and that of the server's system (more often UNIX or Windows NT). It's a good idea to approach NetLingo as a distinct dialect; pay special attention to deviations from what you've come to expect in scripting. This is especially important because error messages don't always bridge the gap between the realms. If something goes wrong, you may be left with no clues as to the culprit.

For NetLingo functions to remain valid, the NetLingo Xtra must remain installed in your Director 7 setup. If you use NetLingo in a production, that Xtra should be automatically bundled with your movie or projector. If it seems only NetLingo operations are going awry, however, check on the presence and soundness of the NetLingo Xtra. While authoring, you can check to see that the NetLingo Xtra is included with your movie by looking in the Movie Xtras dialog box—from the Modify menu, select Movie and then Xtras. If you don't see the NetLingo Xtra, click the Add Network button in the Movie Xtras dialog box.

You can also add script lines that test for the property **the netPresent**, which returns 0 or FALSE if this Xtra is unavailable. Note that this property has changed since Director 6, which used the syntax **netPresent()**. The **netPresent()** syntax will cause a script error if the network Xtra is not available.

The concept of net events

The primary difference between NetLingo and standard-issue Lingo is that instead of setting out to do a task (and doing nothing else until it's done), NetLingo elements get started on a process and then free up RAM for other chores (such as redrawing the Stage). This ability to perform a network operation while other operations are taking place is often called **background loading.** You can even have more than one network operation happening at the same time. Since the speed of network transfer depends on many factors, this **asynchronous** approach keeps movie playback consistent, no matter what else is going on.

Opening a file on the Web, downloading a new cast member, and surfing to a new URL are all **net events** (ones you've already undertaken, by the way). From a scripting standpoint, net events take a little getting used to. Events are no longer near-instantaneous happenings—they're a process, with a beginning, middle, and end. You can even check in from time to time to see how a particular event is progressing. Think of a juggler who tosses most balls to shoulder-height and then suddenly lobs one about three stories overhead. It takes a different kind of attention to track the longer arc of the far-traveling ball and at the same time keep those other balls moving.

Performing network operations with Lingo is basically a four-step procedure. You shouldn't have too much trouble if you keep these steps in mind:

1. Start a network operation and save the value returned by the network command.

2. Test to make sure the operation is complete.

3. Check for errors.

4. Make use of the network operation results.

The netID

With regular Lingo, Director simply processes events as they happen, on a first-in, first-out basis. But given the asynchronous nature of net events, the event that started first may not be the one that finishes first. Needless to say, there's a lot of room for confusion in such circumstances. To enable a movie to keep track of each network operation, every network command that obtains information from the network also returns a unique identifier commonly called the **netID**. When you start a network operation, you must save this netID in a variable. Later, using your variable and Director's netDone and netError functions, you can check the status of your network operation.

To see what a netID looks like, we can add some commands to the startUp handler we wrote for the movie netMIAW.dir.

1. *If it's not already open, open netMIAW.dir. Then open the movie script that contains the* startUp *handler.*

2. *Add the following commands to the* startUp *handler, just before the* end *command:*

   ```
   myNetID = preloadNetThing (dym & "AUTODONE.DIR")
   -- show the netID in the Message Window
   put "The netID is" && myNetID
   ```

3. *Close the movie script and play the movie.*

You don't need to play the MIAW; everything we are looking at here happens when the movie starts. Open the Message window and you will see a line such as The netID is 1, although your number may be different. In fact, if you stop and start the movie again, the number will be different the second time, the third time, and so on. The actual number is of no importance to us. What's important is that the number is unique and that we can use it with other Lingo commands.

If you worked with NetLingo prior to Director 6, you may have become accustomed to using **getLatestNetID** to find the netID of a network operation. That function still worked in Director 6, for backward compatibility, but it has disappeared from Director 7 documentation. To be truthful, it still seems to work, but there is no telling when it will cease to function. It's best to get used to using the netID returned by Lingo network functions.

The thing commands

The `preloadNetThing` command that we introduced in the last exercise is a keystone of network-based file wrangling. With that command, you can download a file from a network server into the cache of your end user's machine. That makes the downloaded element ready for immediate use when your movie needs it. The "thing" being preloaded can be an HTML document, a text file, a Shockwave movie, an image, or just about anything else that can be stored online. The cache used depends on your movie. For a Director movie or projector, it is Director's cache; for a Shockwave movie, the preloaded element is placed in the cache of the user's browser.

The script line that we used in the preceding exercise

```
myNetID = preloadNetThing (dym & "AUTODONE.DIR")
```

fetches the AUTODONE movie that we play as an MIAW. Just that one line is a major improvement on our netMIAW movie. By the time the user takes a look at the screen and decides to click the button, the AUTODONE movie is likely to be already available and ready to be displayed.

> Remember the **importFileInto** command we used at the beginning of this chapter? Well, it turns out to be much more efficient to use **preloadNetThing** first to bring the file into RAM and then issue the **importFileInto** command. If you are creating a Shockwave movie, this sequence is not only more efficient; it is required. For Shockwave movies, the network operation that preloads the file must be completed before the **importFileInto** command is executed.

Similar to `preloadNetThing` is the `downloadNetThing` command. Instead of loading the element into the cache, however, the file is loaded onto the user's drive. You can specify where on the end user's system the file should go, and you can even specify the name the file should have once it's downloaded. The following script line (yes, it's *one* line) fetches a file called Swiftytext from the given URL address and stores it on the host computer in a file of the same name:

```
downLoadNetThing ¬
"http://www.demystified.com/movies/Swiftytext", ¬
the pathName&"Swiftytext"
```

One big limitation of downLoadNetThing is that it's disabled in Shockwave movies. Why? Because it works in the background, without notification to the end user. You might want to use it to quietly download useful support files, but some less scrupulous souls might take advantage of this command's unobtrusiveness and use it to introduce viruses or other bits of nastiness. You can use it in Director movies and net-aware projector files, but not in Shockwave.

Even though it's been disabled in Shockwave, you could still do some damage with **downLoadNetThing** from a projector if you used it to download the wrong kind of file to the wrong location. Keep in mind that system configurations vary greatly, and any attempt to make changes to them (no matter how innocent) can do more harm than good. For instance, you might think it's a good idea to download a file called Vital Info—but what if you accidentally overwrite someone's novel that just happens to have the same name? Before your projector downloads a file, you should notify the end user and supply the option of canceling the operation. And always make sure to download files only from sites that can be trusted to be free of viruses.

Determining the done status

Of the four procedures we listed (earlier in this section) for you to keep in mind when using Lingo for network operations, so far we have discussed only the first. Now it's time to take a look at rule 2: determining when a network operation is finished.

Since net-related events tend to take some time to occur, we need a means of keeping an eye on their progress and of adjusting the timing of other script elements to suit. For instance, let's say you used NetLingo to preload a cast member, and then you used author-level Lingo to generate an animated sequence starring that cast member. If the latter operation got underway before the former one was finished, you'd have a script that was theoretically correct yet couldn't work. Timing is everything.

It's no trouble to delay the execution of a script, so long as you have a way to track the status of a net event. For that purpose, we have the netDone function. If a network operation (that is, anything worthy of receiving a netID) has been successfully completed, the function netDone will return 1 or TRUE. If the process has started but isn't finished yet, it'll return 0 or FALSE. That means you can write a delaying feature into your scripts, like this:

```
if netDone (myVar) = TRUE then   -- if it's done
   doThatThing
   else go to the frame   -- not done, try later
```

Here are a couple more rules to follow when using netDone:

- Don't test the status of a network operation in the same handler from which the network operation was started. Director doesn't guarantee the value returned by netDone until the handler in which the operation was initiated has finished.

- Don't test netDone in a repeat loop. The repeat loop can monopolize the processor and make the system appear unresponsive while a network operation takes place. Basically, you are defeating the purpose of background loading. Instead, you can test netDone in an on idle handler in a frame behavior.

Let's see how we can incorporate the netDone command into our netMIAW movie. What we are going to do is start preloading the MIAW movie and then loop on a frame without the Play MIAW button until the movie is loaded. When the MIAW movie is loaded, we will switch to a frame that contains the button so the user can click it.

1. **Open the movie script and modify the** startMovie **handler as shown here in bold:**

```
on startMovie
  global dym
  dym = "http://www.demystified.com/"
  global theWindow
  theWindow = window ("Playing Online")
  global myNetID
  myNetID = preloadNetThing (dym & "AUTODONE.DIR")
end
```

Here we have made the variable myNetID a global variable so we can use it in other handlers. We also got rid of the commands that displayed the value of the netID in the Message window, although you could leave those lines if you wanted to.

2. *Select frame 1 of the Score. From the Insert menu, select Frames and add a single frame.*

3. *In the new frame 1, delete the button sprite.*

Now we need a frame behavior at frame 1 to continue looping on that frame until the MIAW movie is loaded. We'll use an `exitFrame` handler for that and perform the testing in an `if/end if` construct.

4. *In the Score, select the behavior channel. From the Behavior pull-down menu, select New Behavior and modify the* `exitFrame` *handler in the following way:*

```
on exitFrame
  global myNetID
  if netDone(myNetID) = FALSE then
    go to the frame  -- loop until loaded
  end if
end
```

We can't use Director's looping anymore, so we need to add a frame behavior at frame 2 to loop on that frame.

5. *Add the following* `exitFrame` *handler to a frame behavior in frame 2:*

```
on exitFrame
  go to the frame
end
```

6. *Save your movie, and then play it.*

When the movie plays, you will see a blank screen until the MIAW movie is ready; then the Play MIAW button will appear. When you click the button, the MIAW should immediately start. Of course, in a final product you would never display a blank screen, but you get the idea.

Determining the error status

There's one fly in the ointment: If the `preloadNetThing` operation ended not because its task was completed but because of some error, the netDone function will *also* return 1 or TRUE. That's where `netError` comes in handy. It reports on whether the operation's conclusion was intentional or otherwise.

The netError function is a bit peculiar and doesn't really conform to the rules of Lingo. If everything is fine (no errors occurred), netError doesn't return a binary validation (0 or 1, TRUE or FALSE)—it returns a text string: "OK". If an error occurred, then netError returns an error code: a number indicating the probable cause of the error. If the operation hasn't even started yet or is still in progress, the function simply returns an empty text string: "".

Let's add a test to netMIAW to check for the possibility of an error. We'll keep it simple for the sake of demonstration, but in a commercial product, you would test the error number returned by netError and take an action appropriate to the situation. In real-world projects, you can find yourself spending almost as much time creating Lingo to elegantly handle errors as you do programming the actual interface. Fortunately, if you design your handlers well, you will be able to use the same error-handling routines in project after project without having to write one from scratch every time.

1. *Modify the frame behavior for frame 1 as shown here in bold:*

```
on exitFrame
  global myNetID
  if netDone(myNetID) = FALSE then
    go to the frame
  else
    if netError(myNetID) <> "OK" then
      alert "Network error is" && netError(myNetID)
      -- code here to handle the error
    else
      nothing -- go to the next frame
    end if
  end if
end
```

2. *Save your movie; then rewind and play it.*

The movie should play without a hitch. To test your error code, you can try changing the name of the file you are preloading to the name of a nonexistent file, or you can try dropping your network connection (but be sure to clear the cache, too) and running the movie. In either case, you should see an alert box containing the number of the error code for the problem.

Other net event Lingo

We've set the stage for the next chapter, in which we'll use both NetLingo and Director's built-in network capabilities to create more sophisticated Shockwave movies. But if you'd like to experiment more with net events, try these NetLingo elements:

- getNetText and netTextResult work as a pair. When you know that the file you are going to download is a text file, use the getNetText function to retrieve it. Then, when the operation is successfully completed, use netTextResult to access the contents of the file. For example, to update the contents of a text or field cast member, you might use a command such as this:

  member(9).text = netTextResult(thisNetID)

- netAbort([ID code or URL]) is the command that drops the current network operation immediately, without waiting for it to complete. It can be specified either by the netID or by the exact URL of the location a network operation is attempting to access.

You can try the next two commands in the Message window. They both return information about the specified net event:

- netLastModDate ([ID code]) returns (as a text string) the date the file accessed by the net event was last modified.

- netMIME ([ID code]) returns the MIME type (Multipurpose Internet Mail Extension) of a specified file.

CALLING INFORMATION:
You can get information about the date and type of a network file.

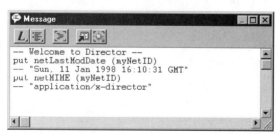

POINTS TO REMEMBER

The rules start mutating in the rarefied atmosphere of network-savvy Lingo and Director 7 features. Keep yourself clear on these concepts:

- Director 7's primary file management capabilities are **network aware**. You can open movies and Casts stored directly in an online environment; no need for Web browsers, file transfer applications, or any other intermediary.

- Cast members can also be created from media **imported** directly from the network. The same goes for MIAW movies.

- A number of veteran **Lingo elements** are now applicable to network navigation, such as the property the searchPaths. This property functions with URLs as well as with local hard-drive directories, though care should be used not to burden searches with slower network operations.

- **NetLingo** is a specialized genre of Lingo created especially for online operations. It requires the presence of the NetLingo Xtra to function fully.

- Events involving network operations can almost never be carried out instantaneously, which is why Director treats them somewhat differently. **Net events** are best viewed more as procedures than as single occurrences. You can start them, check on them from time to time, and even cancel them before they're done.

- Since net events proceed at an unpredictable pace, they don't always conclude in the same order in which they were launched. That's why each is assigned a unique **netID**. The netID of a network operation should be saved and then used in later network Lingo commands such as netDone and netError.

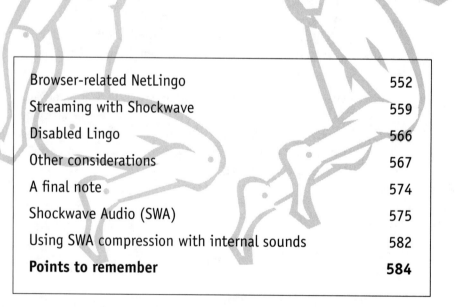

CHAPTER 15

DEEPER INTO SHOCKWAVE

WAY BACK IN CHAPTER 5, YOU GOT ACQUAINTED WITH THE BASICS OF Shockwave, information you needed to know to convert your Director movies to Shockwave movies. In the last chapter, you got the hang of manipulating data in a networked environment, using NetLingo and some of Director 7's powerful capabilities. Between those two chapters, you've picked up quite a bit of Lingo and Director programming techniques. Now it's time to take a closer look at Director 7's tools and techniques for incorporating Shockwave productions into the networked environment. We'll start with a survey of browser-related NetLingo, and then we'll examine Shockwave's asynchronous streaming features. Finally, we'll examine general Shockwave-related issues.

BROWSER-RELATED NETLINGO

There's still a good deal more NetLingo to be added to your scripting arsenal. In this section, we'll look at commands and properties that are especially relevant in the context of Net-aware productions. We'll focus on Shockwave, but much of what is contained in this chapter also applies to other Director movies and to projectors that extend at least a partial presence into the online world. For instance, you could have a CD-ROM production that pulls in data behind the scenes from networked sources and then coordinates media (including Shockwave movies) for display in a browser. NetLingo offers some powerful combinations of capabilities.

> You can have more than one network operation underway at any given point, but keep in mind two principles that, if obeyed, should cut down on problems. First, try to limit the number of ongoing network operations to no more than four at a time. Second, try to avoid directing multiple operations to the same URL at the same time.

Stopping NetLingo

Before we get into new methods for online access, let's consider those times when you don't want your network operations to take place. For example, while you're still in the dry dock of the authoring environment, you may not want your NetLingo executing and generating frequent error messages. Or maybe you're just tired of Director bringing up your network connection software every time you test your movie. Director has a solution in the form of the runMode function and the system property the environment.

The runMode function returns a text string that indicates whether the file is currently playing as a Director movie, a projector file, a Shockwave movie, or a Java applet. The respective values returned are Author (meaning the file's still in Director), Projector (the movie is running as a projector), Plugin (the movie is running in Shockwave form), or Java Applet (the movie is playing as a Java applet).

For our purposes, the environment can return the same values but also has the capability of returning other information about the system. To get the same information that `runMode` supplies, you use `runMode` with the environment. Try this in the Message window:

```
put the environment.runMode
```

TIP

The recently added system property, **the environment**, gives us a clue to where Director might be going in the future. This property combines (so far) the results of the **the platform** and **the colorDepth** properties and the **runMode** function. Because of the syntax **the environment** uses, Macromedia developers can add other properties to it without losing any existing functionality. I expect to see **the platform**, **the colorDepth**, and **runMode** disappear from the documentation in some not-too-distant release of Director, eventually being completely replaced with **the environment**. It's best that you start using it now.

Using either `runMode` or `the environment`, you can test for how the movie is running and then make sure that certain lines of code will execute only when the production has been shocked (or only when some other condition occurs, for that matter). For example, you could use an `if...end if` construct such as the following:

```
if the environment.runMode contains "Author" then
   sprite(1).member = member "placeholder1"
else
   importFileInto(member 1, "http://www.mySite/myFile")
end if
```

Now the `importFileInto` command will occur only when the movie is running outside of the authoring environment. You can use a similar check when you want a certain action to occur only under certain conditions. For example, you can check whether the user's system is running in 32-bit mode, and if it is, you might display some fancy graphics. For 8-bit mode, you could use a different set of graphics that would look better under those conditions.

Navigation tools

Although you can't assume system-level control of the end user's computer, you can use NetLingo to steer around the networked environment from within the currently open browser.

The command goToNetPage is especially useful, although perhaps a little misleadingly named. It'll search for and open not just an HTML page, but any online file displaying a valid MIME type (such as a Shockwave movie, a JPEG graphic, or a Java applet). If executed from within Shockwave, the browser simply goes to the specified location. If issued when no browser is open, Director (or the projector file) will attempt to locate and launch the browser specified in the Network Preferences dialog box. The syntax is straightforward: gotoNetPage "[URL]". However, there are a few interesting twists: If you add a targeted name file, the browser will open the new file in a second window. Thus, the line

gotoNetPage "MarthaKuhl.html", "My Friend"

would open the specified file in a window named My Friend. If there happened to be an open window by that name, the command would simply replace the current contents with the new file.

Similar but subtly different is the command goToNetMovie, which is specific to Shockwave movies. Why bother to use it, when you can get the same result from goToNetPage? Because goToNetMovie also lets you start playback of the movie from any named marker within the Score; just add the name of the marker to the URL of the movie, expressed as a symbol (preceded by a # sign). Here's an example:

goToNetMovie "MarthaKuhl.dcr#Union"

When a goToNetMovie command is issued, the currently playing movie continues to play until the new movie is ready. If you issue a second goToNetMovie command while the first one is still in progress, the second directive will override the first. You can use goToNetMovie while authoring or testing on a local disk or network, but the Shockwave movie to which you are going must be in a folder named dswmedia.

Text-wrangling NetLingo

The set of functions getNetText, postNetText, and netTextResult are the workhorses for getting text from an online source. The getNetText function retrieves the text from the file specified by the URL and loads it into memory (either Director's or the browser's, depending on where the movie is playing). The text string (not the file) can then be retrieved with the netTextResult function. The postNetText function is similar to getNetText, but it sends a post request to the specified URL.

The netTextResult function is a little different from other Net functions in that it works only with the last getNetText or postNetText operation. Because of the amount of memory that can be required for storing the text results, Director discards the results of a getNetText or postNetText operation when a new operation is started. netTextResult returns a valid result only if the last operation is complete (as indicated by the functions netDone and netError).

You can download text with a command line such as this:

```
myID = getNetText(mySite & "myFile.txt")
```

Then you can check the operation and retrieve the text with a command such as this:

```
if(netDone(myID)=TRUE) and (netError(myID)="OK") then
  member("myText").text = netTextResult()
end if
```

You can also specify the netTextResult operation with a Net ID, but doing so is probably not worthwhile because the value is discarded when the next operation begins.

Status Lingo

Here's a fun one: the command netStatus. When you put this command to work in a Shockwave movie, a specified text string will appear in the status area of the browser window—in most browsers, that's the area in the lower-left corner that displays useful information such as the download status or the target HTML of a rolled-over link. During authoring in Director, netStatus messages are displayed in the Message window. You might be tempted to put all kinds of clever little fortune-cookie sayings in there, but the intent of these messages is to give you an easy way of informing the end user about the process in progress.

A STATUS QUOTE:
Most browsers have a status bar in their window, to which you can write using the Lingo term netStatus.

You can use two methods to determine the status of network operations. Using the new getStreamStatus function, you can retrieve information about a network operation in the form of a list (lists are covered in the next chapter). It's best to see this in action, so let's write a couple of quick handlers to demonstrate it.

1. *Open a new movie in Director.*

2. *Create a movie script with the following handler:*

```
on startMovie
  global myID
  clearCache
  myID = preloadNetThing("http://www.demystified.com/pic1.gif")
end
```

This launches a preload operation when the movie starts. We clear the cache so the next handler will have time to see changes as they happen. Otherwise, the operation will be over so fast that we won't get much in the way of results.

3. *Add the following* exitFrame *handler to a frame behavior in the behavior channel of frame 1.*

```
on exitFrame
  global myID
  put getStreamStatus(myID)
  go to the frame
end
```

4. *Play the movie for a few seconds and then stop it.*

5. Open the Message window and scroll through the contents.

CHANGING STATUS:
Use getStreamStatus
to see the changing
status of an operation.

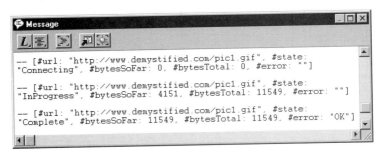

In the Message window, you will see several lines of output from the
getStreamStatus call. Each output line (although it may be wrapped)
contains five sets of values, each headed by a symbol. The values and
their symbols are pretty much self-explanatory. Check *A Lingo Lexicon*
(Appendix C) for the possible values for each element.

The second method to track a network operation's status uses the same
set of information but differs in how you implement it. You can create a
streamStatus handler in a movie script and then inform Director that
you want to use it with the tellStreamStatus function. With
tellStreamStatus set to TRUE (FALSE is the default), Director periodically calls the streamStatus handler and passes the five status elements as
parameters. The streamStatus handler used to be the only method available, but now, with the new getStreamStatus function, you have the ability to determine exactly when you want to receive the status information.

Preference Lingo

In the last chapter, we noted how commands like downLoadNetThing were
disabled in Shockwave—because of the security implications involved,
browsers don't give you the power to write directly to local drives on the
end user's system. Well, there's one small but important exception:
Shockwave can write to and read from text files stored in a directory designated for Shockwave preferences. The term *preferences* is a mild inaccu-
racy, since these files can contain any kind of information you want. If
you're designing an online game, you might use the files to store the previous scores of a returning player. If you're building a Shockwave-based
training system, you might use the files as a means of personalizing information by storing the user's name and recent test results. You can also use

preferences to keep track of how many times someone has visited your site (just update the tally each time) or even where a person has gone within your site.

Shockwave isn't the only technology that's used to perform this kind of limited intrusion. Perhaps you've heard of *cookies*, which are essentially JavaScript versions of the same thing. The difference is that most browsers have some means of notifying the end user that cookie writing is going on (usually with an option to stop it), whereas Shockwave reads and writes transparently.

To create a preferences file, you don't need to resort to elaborate file I/O contortions. Using a preferences file is actually similar to using variables, in that you create the file by simultaneously naming and filling it. For instance, this line establishes a file called visit.txt containing whatever text string happens to be in the local variable userChoices:

```
setPref "visit.txt", userChoices
```

It isn't necessary to include the path name for the file (because there's only one place it'll be stored), but the only accepted extensions for the file name are .txt and .htm. It's a good idea to stick to the eight-dot-three approach to file naming (you're in cross-platform territory, after all).

When you're choosing a name, keep in mind that you may not be the only Shockwave creator writing to the end user's preferences directory; if someone else chooses to write a file with the same name as yours, your original will be overwritten. For that reason, you might want to devise your own unique naming arrangement. I usually add as a prefix the first five numbers of my office phone number; hence, I'd use 33285vst.txt rather than visit.txt.

The syntax you use to read from a preferences file is variable-like as well. You use getPref as the pointer to the target file, and you don't import the file so much as use it to fill a text string container (a variable, cast member, or position within a list). Here's an example:

```
member( "userName").text = getPref ("33285vst.txt")
```

You can use **getPref** and **setPref** not only with Shockwave but also with projectors and while authoring. Unfortunately, these functions each put the preferences file in a different location, although the file is always put in a folder named Prefs. Even Shockwave places the file in a different location, depending on the browser that is running and the system it is running on. Fortunately, **getPref** always knows where to look, so the exact location can be invisible to your program. Also, if the Prefs folder does not exist, it is created automatically. While authoring, look for the Prefs folder in your Director 7 folder (or wherever you installed Director). If you are running a projector, look for the Prefs folder in the same folder as your projector. This last location can be a problem if you are running from a CD-ROM; be careful not to try to write to any read-only media.

STREAMING WITH SHOCKWAVE

Of all the innovations in recent versions of Shockwave, probably none was more welcome than the ability to bypass long download times. Shocked movies can start playing as soon as the components for the first frame have been received, with additional downloading happening in the background while the movie plays. But **streaming Shockwave** isn't a cure-all; you still need to deploy your cast members carefully and make judicious use of streaming-specific scripting and construction techniques.

The first step in working with streaming Shockwave is deciding if it's necessary (or desirable) at all. One of the main factors to consider is the *latency period* built into the opening moments of your production—that is, the period before the end user can reasonably expect to see something happen.

Let's say your Shockwave movie is a video game. If the first screen has several text fields describing the rules of play and the previous high score, there might be a considerable latency period while the end user reads it all and figures out that clicking the New Game button will start the action. That might seem like ample time to stream the rest of the movie.

But what if the end user is a repeat player, and he or she quickly gets into the habit of ignoring the opening screen and clicking New Game immediately? The latency period you were counting on would be gone, and the end user would encounter a game with several pieces missing.

On the other hand, if you're guaranteed a chunk of time between when playback starts and when another scene is needed, you may have a prime candidate for streaming. A good example of this is an interactive story: Even if the end user gets impatient and clicks out of Chapter 1 to Chapter 2, that should still give you plenty of time to stream Chapter 3.

There's a definite hierarchy to streaming, an orderly procession of elements down the bandwidth pipeline. First the movie's information is downloaded. This includes the Score, sprite information (everything you find in the Properties dialog boxes), scripts and behaviors, transitions, and Tool Palette buttons and shapes. All these are loaded before the movie begins playing. Font members, which are new to Director 7, are also loaded at this time to ensure that they will be available for any text that requires them. After the movie's information is downloaded, the movie's bulk data is loaded, including the bitmaps, vector shapes, fields, text, sound, and video. These elements are loaded in the order they appear in the Score, not in the order they're placed in the Cast. (That's one of the benefits of Director's optimization when the Shockwave movie is created.) Elements that are in the Cast but not referenced by the Score are loaded last. This includes elements in all internal Casts.

What this means is that to get the maximum benefit from streaming, you should have a short Score, with the first few frames containing simple elements to occupy the end user until the images arrive. It also means that if you change a member's media with Lingo, that media may not be loading when you want it unless you specifically use a network command such as preloadNetThing to bring the media into memory.

Streaming options

To establish the streaming status of a Shockwave movie, you need to access the Movie Playback Properties dialog box—from the Modify menu, select Movie and then Playback.

THE SOURCE OF THE STREAM:
Establish the streaming behaviors of individual movies in the Movie Playback Properties dialog box.

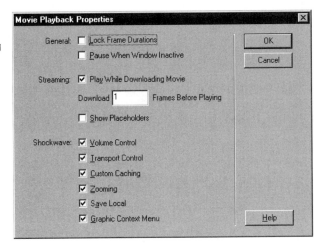

The items in which we are interested are the three selections under the heading Streaming. To enable streaming for your movie, select the Play While Downloading Movie option. If this option is not checked, the movie will not begin playing until the entire movie is downloaded.

The second option specifies the number of frames downloaded before the movie begins playing. That's the number of frames you want completely downloaded (graphic cast members and all) before playback begins. This value affects only movies that you have designated as streaming. If you design your movie for Shockwave, which means you have an introductory segment that plays while other media is downloading, you should set this value so that all of the required media for your introductory segment is loaded before the movie begins playing. If your movie is more compli-cated than that, you will need to experiment to determine the best setting for your movie.

The Show Placeholders option also gets things underway as soon as pos-sible but with a twist: If sprites are missing their source cast members, they'll be displayed as bounding boxes only. The effect may be a little less visually appealing than invisibility, it has the benefit that it enables execu-tion of scripts that may be attached to those sprites. A button sprite, for instance, can be clicked even if its image has yet to arrive.

These playback selections can be set or changed at any time before the Shockwave movie is created. If you are still authoring, these settings will also take effect in your movie when you preview it in a browser. Remember to use Save and Compact on your movie before testing it in a browser if you want the streaming to function correctly.

In the Movie Playback Properties dialog box, under the heading Shockwave, are six options that can be used for setting such things as the display of a volume control for movies playing in Macromedia's upcoming Shockwave Player. By the time you read this, the player may be available. Check the Macromedia Web site for current information.

Streaming in the Score

If you've opted for streaming, your next step is to examine your production with an eye toward possible bandwidth bottlenecks. You'll likely want to keep playback and streaming more or less in sync at some points in the production. Fortunately, Director provides the scripting tools that you can use for this on a frame-by-frame basis.

Streaming Lingo

An important streaming-related function, frameReady(), lets you know whether the entire population of a frame, or range of frames, has been downloaded from a network environment and is ready for immediate local playback. It's a good "look-before-you-leap" tool when you're using streaming files; use it to make sure that at least a key portion of a movie segment is in place before calling it during playback. The frameReady function returns TRUE if the media is ready or FALSE if the media is not yet available.

Here's an example of a script using frameReady. In this case, playback continues to loop until a given Score segment (frames 200 through 225) is available:

```
on exitFrame
    if frameReady (200, 225) then
        go frame 200
    else
        go to the frame
    end if
end
```

When the syntax `frameReady()` is used (no included parameters), the function returns the binary status of the download of the file as a whole (as opposed to the status of a specified frame).

Next consider the `mediaReady` property, which performs the same stream-monitoring function for specific cast members. You can test a specific cast member, or you can test a sprite to see if the cast member used for that sprite is available. Although you can use `mediaReady` to create stalling loops, it's even handier for establishing stand-ins for missing cast members, as in the following:

```
if sprite(1).mediaReady = FALSE then
  sprite(1).member = member("standIn")
end if
```

Streaming-related behaviors

As you saw in Chapter 5, *Introducing Shockwave*, the Library Palette supplies a number of behaviors that make quick work of using Lingo to control streaming. We used a couple of these streaming behaviors in Chapter 5, but we didn't cover all of them. Many of these use the `frameReady` function or `mediaReady` property.

STREAMING BEHAVIORS:
You can use behaviors from the Library Palette to simplify the creation of streaming movies.

Director's four looping behaviors allow you to loop back to a frame (or loop on the current frame) until the specified media has been downloaded. When the media is ready, the playback head proceeds to the next frame. One feature that might not be obvious about the looping behaviors is that when the required media is not already available, the behaviors issue a `preload` command to load the media. All four of these behaviors should be placed in the behavior channel rather than attached to a sprite.

* `Loop until Next Frame Is Available` tests to see if all the media for the next frame is downloaded.

- `Loop until Media in Frame Is Available` allows you to specify a particular frame to see if all the media for that frame is downloaded.

- `Loop until Media in Marker Is Available` is a little different than it sounds. The media being checked for readiness is actually a range of frames, starting with the frame you specify (by the marker label) through the following marker in the Score. If the marker you specify is the last marker in the movie, all media for the rest of the movie (starting at the current frame) is preloaded.

- `Loop until Member Is Available` tests to see if a specific cast member is downloaded before proceeding.

Three jumping behaviors are also available for streaming; each loops on the frame containing the behavior (which will be the current frame) until the specified media has been downloaded. When you install the behavior, you can specify the jumping location: the next frame, a specific frame, or a specific marker. Note that the jump location and the location of the media being checked can be entirely different. Like the looping behaviors, the jumping behaviors issue a `preload` command if the specified media is not yet available. Also, as with looping behaviors, jumping behaviors should be placed in the behavior channel.

- `Jump When Media in Frame Is Available` tests the media of a specific frame for readiness.

- `Jump When Media in Marker Is Available`, like `Loop until Media in Marker Is Available`, actually checks a range of frames. The range starts with the marker you specify and continues through the following marker in the Score. If the marker you specify is the last marker in the movie, all media for the rest of the movie (starting at the current frame) is preloaded.

- `Jump When Member Is Available` tests a specific cast member to make sure it has been downloaded.

The result of using the single placeholder behavior, `Show Placeholder`, is similar to the result of choosing the Show Placeholders option in the Movie Playback Properties dialog box: a placeholder appears at the location of a sprite until the media for that sprite is loaded. There are some differences between the two, however:

- Using the Library Palette behavior, you can specify a vector shape as the placeholder. You have the option of a box (the same as you get using the Movie Playback Properties dialog box), a circle with a slash through it (like the international No symbol), or a custom vector shape. You must supply the custom shape and name it *Show Placeholder Custom.*

- The behavior affects only the sprites with the behavior attached. You can use any of the three available choices for placeholders for any particular sprite.

- If you turn on the Show Placeholders option in the Movie Playback Properties dialog box as well as attach a behavior to a sprite, the attached behavior takes precedence.

- You can have only a single custom vector shape in your movie for use as a placeholder, and it has to be named *Show Placeholder Custom.* You can work around this limitation by swapping the media for the Show Placeholder Custom cast member so that different placeholders are used for different frames. You can also open the script for the Show Placeholder behavior and do some serious tinkering to make it accept a placeholder with a different name.

- You can't use the Show Placeholder behavior on a sprite in the first frame.

Two progress bar behaviors can be used when you want to supply the user with information about the downloading of a movie or linked cast member (and to give the user something to watch while the media downloads). To use either behavior, attach it to a bitmap or to a rectangular shape sprite. The sprite will be displayed with increasing width as the object downloads. You can also use a field or text sprite to show the percent downloaded.

- `Progress Bar for Streaming Movies` depicts the downloading of the current movie.

- `Progress Bar for URL Linked Media` shows the progress for linked media. The linked media can be either a cast member or media that is loaded via Lingo.

Disabled Lingo

In Chapter 14, I mentioned that some Lingo has been made intentionally nonfunctional in Shockwave, mostly for security reasons. Here's a full rundown of the currently *verboten* Lingo.

Lingo disabled for security reasons

The following Lingo elements are disabled for security reasons:

- You can't use the open command to launch an external application.

- On the Windows side, attempts to pass text strings to the Media Control Interface (MCI) with the command mci won't be recognized. See Appendix C for more information on mci.

- The MacOS-specific openResFile and closeResFile commands won't work, because tinkering with resource files on that platform is an easy way to wreak havoc.

- Printing with the printFrom command is disabled. Once a movie is shocked, movie printing becomes the province of the browser.

- Also disabled are any commands that affect system-level operation of the end user's machine, such as colorDepth, shutdown, restart, and even quit.

- You can't open a local file that isn't in the Prefs folder.

- You can't save a movie with the saveMovie command or save a Cast with the save castLib command.

- You can't use the pasteClipboardInto command to paste content from the clipboard.

Lingo unsupported in browsers

The following Lingo elements are not supported in browsers:

- You can't use any Lingo pertaining to the creation of custom menus.

- You can't use any Lingo for managing MIAWs.

- A few file-related terms that, while technically still functional, aren't especially useful because they can't handle URLs as specified locations. These are `searchCurrentFolder`, the `searchPaths`, and `getNthFileNameinFolder`.

OTHER CONSIDERATIONS

Following are a few other issues to keep in mind during the Shockwave authoring process.

Managing the plug-in issue

In most cases, the viewer-side technology for Shockwave is provided via a plug-in file (or the comparable ActiveX control). The plug-in is free, available to anyone using the Web, and easy to download if you don't already have it. It even comes bundled with current Windows and Macintosh operating systems as well as with major browsers. Although it's getting to the point where most people who use the Web have Shockwave, it's still not safe to assume that everyone does, nor that they have the most recent version that your movie requires. To be a gracious host to your online visitors, it helps to do two things: Offer to the Shockwave-less an opportunity to download the plug-in, and provide those that decline an alternative page.

Testing for Shockwave

What happens when a browser *sans* Shockwave encounters a Shockwave file? It depends on the browser, but Shockwave and plug-ins are so integrated into browsers these days that most of them will automatically detect a missing plug-in and will either put up a dialog box to let the user choose to download the required files or will display a placeholder with a caption such as "Click here to get the plugin."

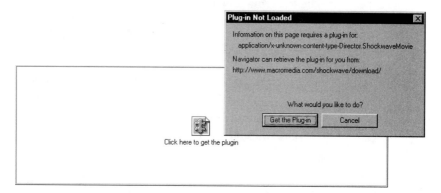

Remember that you can tell Director to create your HTML document for you when you create a Shockwave movie. If you take a look at the contents of that document, you will see lines referencing Macromedia and Shockwave. For example, this line tells Netscape where to find the plug-in if the user does not already have it:

```
pluginspage="http://www.macromedia.com/shockwave/download/"
```

If you choose to provide alternative pages for your Web site that use non-shocked movies, you can try a number of methods.

First of all, you may want to avoid the whole issue of downloading the plug-ins. In that case, you'll probably want to write some JavaScript in your HTML document. Using JavaScript, you can test for the existence of the necessary plug-ins and display source files depending on the result.

Another method is to park a modest Shockwave movie on the page, which loads before anything else. That movie doesn't have to contain anything more than a script similar to this:

```
on enterFrame
    gotoNetPage "IsShocked.html"
end
```

Follow the logic? If Shockwave is installed, the movie will run, and it will open up a new page in the browser containing further Shockwave files. If the end user doesn't have Shockwave, the movie simply won't run, keeping the current page open in the browser. The current page can suggest that the user's viewing pleasure will be enhanced with Shockwave, while still offering the option of viewing a non-shocked version.

Providing the plug-in

If visitors to your site don't have Shockwave compatibility, it behooves you to provide them with a way to get it. The plug-ins are free, and anyone is allowed to download them, but you're expected to direct users to a Macromedia Web site to retrieve them. If you need to bundle Shockwave with your software, you are required to have a Shockwave license and distribution agreement (see the Macromedia Web site for details on licensing). Bundling Shockwave with your software is useful for sites that want Shockwave content to play on the intranet without allowing Internet access.

To direct your users to the Macromedia Shockwave download site, use the URL www.macromedia.com/shockwave/download/. You should also check out the site at www.macromedia.com/support/shockwave/ info/linking/ for information about directing your users to that site. There you will find a number of "Get Shockwave" graphics that you're encouraged to use as the button for your link.

Streaming Shockwave movies do not always outperform nonstreaming movies. Particularly for small movies, turning streaming off may actually improve performance. You'll always need to test your movie under different circumstances to see which works best. Likewise, you may find that in some cases you don't want to use Shockwave at all. A Shockwave movie is in a compressed format, and that means that it will have to be decompressed before playing. Full-format .dir and .dxr files may occupy more file space than their .dcr equivalents, but since there's no need to decompress, they may actually provide a better level of performance. It's an option worth tinkering with, especially when you're confident of relatively high-bandwidth access.

Sizing up the Stage

One big factor in Shockwave efficiency is the size of the Stage. In a free-standing Director movie, you probably want the Stage to be big enough to command attention, but it's a different story inside the confines of a Web browser. Your work is nicely framed within the window of the host application, so why make the Stage any larger than what's necessary to capture the action? If that makes for an unattractive rectangle, you can change the apparent proportions by matching your movie to the browser's background or by "sandwiching"—placing inline graphics above and/or below the Stage to blend into a visual whole.

When contemplating width, keep in mind that many people are still using monitor settings of 640 x 480. If you design your movies for that size, you will need to cut them down even smaller to allow for the real estate taken up by the browser window, and because the end user needs some space to move the window around on the desktop. On the other hand, a quick survey of existing Web sites indicates that most are being designed for larger monitors or higher resolutions. If these sites are viewed with a 640 x 480 setting, the user will need to scroll horizontally as well as vertically to see much of the page.

The size you design to depends pretty much on your target audience. If you are creating a snazzy Web site that you expect to be visited by mostly those with the latest hardware, you can design for the larger size. If you need to consider all users, design for the smaller screen size. Just remember to also leave about 25 to 30 percent of the monitor size for the browser.

Whatever proportions you choose, it's a good idea to make sure that the EMBED and OBJECT tags in HTML specify display dimensions identical to the Stage size, as demonstrated here:

```
<EMBED WIDTH = 600 HEIGHT = 200 SRC = "MYSHOCK.DCR">
```

Notice that the size you specify in the HTML tags doesn't have to match the actual size of the file being displayed. If you cut the dimension sizes in half in the EMBED tag, the movie will be shrunk proportionately but its playback will suffer, because Shockwave will have to recalculate its display formula on the fly. So don't succumb to the temptation to squeeze in a movie by shaving its dimensions; resize the Stage instead.

Using text

Director has improved the handling of text cast members so much that they will generally be your first choice for displaying text. Field text still provides the smallest cast members, but regular text can look so much better that it's well worth the slightly extra download time. This is a major change from previous versions of Director, in which text cast members were converted to bitmaps when you converted a movie to a projector or a Shockwave movie, with a resulting increase in file size and loss of functionality. Now text is stored as strings and displayed in the desired font when the movie plays. In addition, text is anti-aliased as it is displayed, to give a much better look than plain field text. Anti-aliasing is especially important for font sizes larger than 14 points. Finally, you can embed fonts for text to make sure that your user's system displays the text in your chosen font. Given these improvements, it now makes more sense to use Director text for displaying large text than to use the bitmap images that many sites use for text.

For large blocks of small text, where anti-aliasing is generally undesirable, you may still want to use field text. Since field text is displayed using system fonts, you'll want to take care to limit your font choices to those likely to be present on the end user's system. For a serif font, use Times or Times New Roman. For a sans serif font, Helvetica is best. Both of these are standard font families on the Windows and MacOS platforms. Unlike fonts in HTML (which can't be set for specific point sizes), your field text can be set to specific point sizes, so you'll probably achieve more cross-platform consistency within the Shockwave Stage than you will in the rest of the page. Nevertheless, it's a good idea to avoid layouts in which type placement is critical (such as two side-by-side columns). Instead, give the text some air to account for variations in the end user's fonts.

Although you can include fonts with your movies, including an embedded font requires space and time to download. Each embedded font requires from 12K to 25K. That's pretty small, considering what you get, but it still adds up in a Shockwave movie. Remember that fonts download before any other cast members, so including a number of fonts in your Shockwave movie can really delay the start of your movie.

The proper palette

Although you can make a Shockwave movie with 16-bit (and even 32-bit) cast members, you probably don't need to do so—many Web surfers out there are still using 8-bit color monitors, and all Web surfers get impatient waiting for large files to download. I recommend sticking with 8-bit cast members unless you're developing for a specialized audience. On the other hand, don't make the mistake of trying to save a few more kilobytes by sampling 8-bit artwork down to 4-bit or 1-bit. You probably won't be satisfied with the results, and the file won't get any smaller. (Shockwave compression is effectively optimized for 8-bit.) What's more important than the bit depth of the image is the actual number of colors used, which is why the alternatives of dithering and color substitution should be explored.

To dither or not to dither?

As noted in earlier chapters, **dithering** is a means of approximating a color that's missing from a palette, by interpolating specks of light or dark that the eye blends together to create the impression of another color. But dithering has drawbacks: The effect isn't always appropriate (sometimes it makes everything look as speckled as a robin's egg), and it results in larger file sizes than the nondithered equivalents.

So when should you choose to dither? Well, there are two circumstances in which it might seem necessary:

- *When you must use a color that isn't on the palette.* If the backdrop dithers because it's a shade of blue not found in the current palette, why not see if there's another shade of blue that would do just as nicely? If you're creating the artwork as well as importing it, you can avoid this situation entirely by starting with a palette based on the palette used by browsers. In Director, this is the included Web 216 palette. Similar palettes are also available or included with most graphics applications, including Photoshop. When making color choices, don't stray from the Web palette. Unless you must use a shade of chartreuse that simply can't be approximated from the palette, there's no reason to dither.

- *When the artwork requires more shades than there are available.* If your artwork uses numerous subtle gradations of tone (as in shadows or the dappled leaves of a tree in autumn), the limitation isn't which 8-bit palette you use; it's 8-bit palettes themselves. This is especially true when it comes to flesh tones; anything less than a full range of shading turns people into mannequins. In these circumstances, dithering is definitely called for.

Ah, but *where* should the dithering occur? Not all conversion processes are the same. You can have dithering done automatically by Director if you select the Dither option when importing, but you'll probably get better results if you perform dithering from within Fireworks (bundled with Director) or a third-party application such as Photoshop or DeBabelizer.

A pre-shock checklist

Before you shock your movie, check the following:

- *Are there any unused cast members?* Director's Find options makes finding unused cast members easy. From the Edit menu, select Find and then Cast Member. In the Find Cast Member dialog box that appears, select the Usage (Not Used in Score) option. A list of any unused cast members (unused by the Score) will appear. Be careful, though. Before you toss out a cast member, make sure it's unused not only by the Score but by scripts as well.

- *Are there any unneeded Score frames?* If possible, eliminate not only those Score frames that contain surplus sprites but also the empty frames separating scenes (you need to keep your system of markers intact, though).

- *Are there any unneeded channels?* In the Movie Properties dialog box, you can set the number of Score channels. Set this value to include as many channels as you need but no more than you need.

- *Are there any unnecessarily large graphic cast members?* Run through the Cast in the Paint window to make sure nothing's been accidentally set to an incorrect bit depth.

- *Are input text and field cast members set to contain empty strings?* Putting in a stopMovie script that automatically sets cast members to contain empty strings might be a good idea while you are authoring. You don't need to include text in a cast member if you use Lingo to load the member when your movie runs.

- *Are any extraneous Xtras bundled with the movie?* Check the Movie Xtras dialog box.

- *Is the Stage size correctly set?*

- *Is any disallowed Lingo used in scripts?*

- *Are fonts embedded, if needed?*

- *If you're using streaming, does the Movie Playback Properties dialog box have the correct settings?*

- *Have you tested you movie?* Test your movie under as many conditions as possible. Try to make it fail, to see whether the movie handles errors correctly. Play it with both slow and fast modems to see whether performance is acceptable in both cases. Check it on systems set to all available color depths.

A FINAL NOTE

Shockwave, like Director, is a technology in transition. Macromedia is working hard to make it more powerful and reliable, and updates and enhancements won't necessarily be released on the same cycle as new versions of Director. For that reason, I recommend that you get into the habit of periodically scanning the Shockwave Help & Resources section of the Macromedia Web site, located at `www.macromedia.com/support/shockwave`.

It's here that you'll find the latest official documentation on Shockwave, as well as an abundance of pointers on the technicalia of achieving consistent integration with all the various Web browsers out there.

Want to get even deeper into Shockwave? Pick up another Macromedia Press title, *Shocking the Web*, by Cathy Clarke, Lee Swearingen, and David K. Anderson. This is a genuine recommendation, not a publisher-inserted plug. Much of the material on Shockwave out there is fluffy in the extreme, but this book is packed with dozens of real-world examples, documented as case histories and provided in open-code format.

SHOCKWAVE AUDIO (SWA)

Shockwave Audio (SWA) isn't part of Shockwave *per se*; it's a separate technology that can be incorporated not only into Shockwave movies but also into any network-savvy Director production. SWA is essentially a sound-only compression standard, which varies from other standards in that it's optimized for the demands of streaming playback from an online file (although it works just as well from disk). It offers extremely high compression rates: An SWA file can be up to 176 times smaller than the original file. But just as important, SWA files can be played back as slowly as 8K per second, which makes SWA a feasible option for low-bandwidth connections. An additional plus is the host of Lingo commands provided solely for managing SWA files.

Generally, Shockwave files are stored external to the movie. The movie then streams the audio when required. Internal sound, though not streamable, can also be compressed with the same Shockwave compression. This yields a smaller overall movie and decreases the download time. Streaming Shockwave and Shockwave-compressed internal sounds require different methods of implementation. We cover them both in the following sections.

The compression used for Shockwave is MPEG Layer III. It is a perceptual audio-coding compression, meaning it works by removing data that the human ear probably wouldn't hear anyway. Lower frequencies that are masked by higher frequencies, for example, can be safely removed and still retain most of the original sound quality. Other schemes for compressing audio also exist. For example, some schemes are dedicated to speech; they are based on the human vocal tract and attempt to maintain the quality of voice sounds when compressing audio.

Converting to SWA for streaming

Before you can set up an audio file for streaming, you need to convert it to SWA format. The conversion process depends on which system you are working: Windows or Macintosh. For the Macintosh, you need to open your audio file in Sound Edit 16 and export it as an SWA file. For Windows, the Xtra to perform the conversion is included in Director.

In this section, we cover the SWA conversion process as performed within Director under Windows, but Macintosh users will find relevant information here also, so read on.

To convert an audio file under Windows, you must start with a WAV file. Other sound formats, such as AIF files, won't convert. You access the conversion dialog box from the Xtras menu.

Macromedia recommends creating your original audio files with a sampling rate of 22 kHz, 16-bit monaural. There is nothing to be gained by dropping to 8-bit, since the files are converted to 16-bit before compression.

1. From the Xtras menu, select Convert WAV to SWA.

The Convert .WAV Files To .SWA Files dialog box appears, with three general areas displayed. The upper-left area shows the names of the files you plan to convert, after you have selected them using the Add Files button. The lower area lets you choose the files for conversion and the location where the new files will be written. The upper-right area specifies the compression settings; this is where you enter your settings for the conversion.

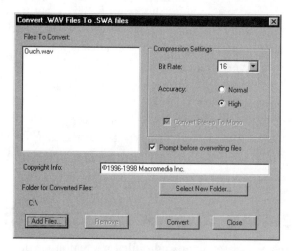

It's important to note that the Bit Rate setting you choose for compressing audio is not related to the sampling rates you use when originally creating an audio file. The Bit Rate setting is used to determine the size and quality of the compressed file. A higher bit rate gives better quality, but with a substantial increase in file size and streaming time. To determine what Bit Rate setting to use, you need to consider both your creation's end use and the probable system of the end user. The bit rate is given in Kbps and can vary from 8 to 160. Following is a list of general guidelines for selecting a bit rate:

- At 64 Kbps and above, there is essentially no loss of quality. At 64 Kbps, you can expect about a 12:1 reduction in file size. For streaming sounds at these bit rates, you will need speeds comparable to a T1 connection.

- 32 to 56 Kbps ranges from FM stereo quality to CD quality. At 32 Kbps, you can expect about a 24:1 reduction in file size. These settings can be used with streaming from CD-ROMs or ISDN lines.

- 16 to 24 Kbps is your likely choice for streaming from the Internet. You can expect compression ratios of about 48:1 and sound quality approximating monaural FM.

- 8 Kbps gives quality similar to what you hear on a phone line. Except for some sound effects for which quality doesn't matter, you should avoid bit rates this low.

The Accuracy setting can be either High or Normal; a High setting gives better quality but takes a little longer to compress. There is no difference in file size. In my experience, there's no reason to settle for the Normal quality—you need to compress a file only once, but it gets played over and over, so stick to the High quality.

Converting stereo to monaural reduces file size in half (assuming that it was stereo to begin with). For Bit Rate settings of 48 or less, sounds are automatically converted to monaural. Unless you have special need for stereo, as in a high-quality game, you will probably be satisfied with monaural.

Now let's see how the Convert .WAV Files To .SWA Files dialog box works. Its interface is a little different from that of most dialog boxes, so it helps to walk through it once.

2. Click the Add Files button in the lower-left of the dialog box.

This opens a standard Open dialog box (labeled Select .WAV Files To Be Converted To .SWA). You can select a file (or Shift-click to select several files) and then click Open to add the file to your list of files to convert.

There are a number of WAV files on the Demystified CD in the Sounds folder, or you can use one of your own.

3.   *Select a file in the Open dialog box and then click Open.*

The file or files should be listed in the left window (Files To Convert) of the Convert .WAV Files To .SWA Files dialog box.

Next we need to specify where the files are to be placed. Below the line Folder for Converted Files is the current location at which the files will be stored. If you want to use a different location, you can change this:

4.   *Click the Select New Folder button.*

The Select an Output Folder for SWA dialog box opens.

5.   *Choose a folder for your output files and then click Select Folder.*

6.   *Set the Compression Settings of your choice and then click the Convert button.*

You should see a status bar indicating how the conversion is proceeding. When the conversion is complete, you can check in the designated destination folder, and you should see a file there with the same name as your original, but with the .swa file extension. The conversion process doesn't allow you to specify a name for the new SWA file.

Working with SWA

Once you have files that have been converted to SWA, the process of linking those files to your movie is fairly simple. Upload the audio files (they should have the suffix .swa) to the appropriate online location, and then incorporate them into your Director production as cast members. This is done by selecting Shockwave Audio from the Media Element submenu of the Insert menu. You'll see a dialog box like this one:

HEAR, MY DEAR:
Shockwave Audio (SWA) files can join the cast as links from their online URLs and play in any of eight sound channels.

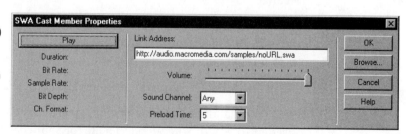

The SWA Cast Member Properties dialog box lists a default SWA file at a Macromedia Web site. For checking and playing with streaming, this is as good a file to use as any. If you wish, you can upload one of your own audio files to a Web site available to you, or you can stream from your local disk.

- You can specify the URL of the SWA file in the Link Address field. The default is a page on Macromedia's Web site that features sample SWA files. If you want to use a local file, click the Browse button to select the location and file on your system.

- Volume is set here as well. SWA volume levels can also be set using the volume cast member property, which is specific to Shockwave Audio cast members.

- The Sound Channel pop-up menu contains a surprise: You get to choose from eight channels, not the standard two that show up in the Score. If you select Any, the sound will play in whatever channel happens to be free at the time. It's easier to use this option than to keep track of what's where in eight channels, but SWA Lingo controls may require you to name a specific channel.

- Preload Time determines how large a chunk of the file should be downloaded before streaming playback begins. Director reads from the preload buffer to play the audio while continuing to write to the buffer as the file downloads. Ideally, the reading should never catch up with the writing, or breaks in the sound playback will occur. You can set the preload time from 1 second to 60 seconds. The higher the Bit Rate setting you chose when you created the SWA file, the slower the file will download and the longer the preload time setting you'll need to use.

> It's best not to use streaming SWA audio and a streaming Shockwave movie at the same time, because both work by attempting to monopolize your system's downloading and processing resources. Instead, wait until a movie's streaming is complete before playing streamed SWA audio. (You can use **frameReady** to test for this.)

Once you've finalized the options and clicked OK, the SWA file is imported into your Cast just like any other cast member. But there's a big difference between these and regular audio cast members. While the latter can be placed only in the Score's two sound channels, SWA cast members must be placed in *one of the main sprite channels*. They don't appear on the Stage, but they belong there nonetheless. The channel you chose for playback in the SWA Cast Member Properties dialog box (if any) has no correlation to the number of the sprite channel in which the cast member resides. You cannot place streaming audio in the sound channels.

Note that we used the Insert menu to import the SWA file rather than using Import from the File menu. You can also use the Import method, but you won't be able to use streaming or SWA Lingo if you do.

SWA and Lingo

You don't need to place an SWA cast member in the Score to play it. In fact, you are probably better off using Lingo to control when the sound preloads and when (and how) it plays. In the very simplest form, all you need are the play member and stop member commands, but a few extra commands will enable you to take full advantage of SWA.

For best results, you'll want to do some preloading of your SWA file before you (or the user) plays it. For this, you can use the preLoadTime property and the preLoadBuffer commands, which work hand in hand.

- preLoadTime is a property of the SWA cast member and is the same property that you set in the SWA Cast Member Properties dialog box. With Lingo, you can check the current value or set it to a new value.

- Once the preLoadTime property is set to your satisfaction, use the preLoadBuffer command to actually perform the preloading.

For example, you might want to preload a sound before the playback head enters the frame where the user can access the sound through a button. In that case, you might create a handler such as this:

```
on exitFrame
  member("mySound").preLoadTime = 4
  preLoadBuffer(member "mySound")
end
```

Next, you need to determine whether the sound has actually been pre-loaded. For that, you have the state cast member property. The state property can tell you quite a bit about the current status of an SWA streaming cast member, including whether the preloading has finished, whether an error occurred, and whether the file is playing or paused. The state property has a value of 2 when preloading is successfully completed, so you can check for that in another handler like this:

```
on exitFrame
  if member("mySound").state = 2 then
    go to frame the frame + 1  -- where the sound is
  else
    if member("mySound").state = 9 then  -- error
      alert "Can't find the sound."
      go to frame "noSound"  -- screen with no sound
    else
      go to the frame  -- not loaded yet
    end if
  end if
end
```

The *Lingo Lexicon* contains a complete list of possible values for the status property. Once the SWA file has been successfully preloaded, you can use the commands play, pause, and stop to control the sound, as in the following three command lines:

```
play member("mySound")
pause member("mySound")
stop member("mySound")
```

Another important SWA property is percentPlayed. With it, you can determine how much of a sound has actually played or, more importantly, whether the sound has finished playing. The value returned is a number representing the percent of the sound that has played. The number ranges from 0, for none played, to 100, indicating the playing is completed. You can test the percentPlayed property in an if...then construct such as this:

```
if percentPlayed <> 100 then
  go to the frame
end if
```

Other SWA Lingo that you will find useful includes the following:

- Use the `duration` property to determine how long a sound will play. You must begin the sound streaming (or at least preload the buffer) before `duration` will return an accurate result.

- Use the `volume` SWA property to set (or check) the volume at which the SWA sound plays. Values range from 0 (no sound at all) to 255.

- You can determine or change the file associated with an SWA cast member with the `URL` property. This property works only when the cast member is not being played.

- If the `state` property reports that an error has occurred, you can use `getError` or `getErrorString` to retrieve more information about the error.

- The `percentStreamed` property tells you the percentage of a sound that has been streamed.

USING SWA COMPRESSION WITH INTERNAL SOUNDS

Here's another way to put at least part of the technology of Shockwave Audio to work. One of the standard Xtras shipped with Director 7 is Shockwave for Audio Settings, which should appear in your Xtras menus. This doesn't churn out SWA files or make use of any of the specialized Lingo; it just uses some of the Shockwave compression algorithms to save the conventional sounds imported as internal cast members within your movie.

While you can't stream internal sounds, using this Xtra gives you compression rates similar to those for SWA files. If you use a lot of internal sounds in your movie, compressing sounds can significantly decrease your file size and the time required to download from the Internet.

CRUNCHTIME:

The Shockwave for Audio Settings Xtra lets you use some of Shockwave's compression techniques to compact the internal audio files in any Director movie.

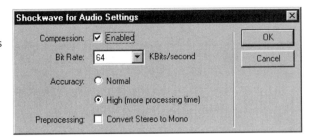

You can specify the compression settings at any time, but compression doesn't take place until you create a projector or Shockwave movie. To enable compression, check the Compression Enabled check box in the Shockwave for Audio Settings dialog box. For projectors, you will also need to make sure that compression is turned on in the Create Projector Options dialog box before you actually create the projector. The Bit Rate, Accuracy, and Preprocessing (Convert Stereo to Mono) settings are similar to the same settings for converting files to SWA.

You get to choose only one compression setting for all of the internal sounds of a movie. You can't decide to compress some sounds and not others, or use some settings for some cast members and different settings for others. If your movie contains internal sounds that are compressed, remember that you will need to include the Xtras for decompressing and playing the sounds. This should be handled automatically by Director when you are authoring—including sounds in your movie—and choosing to compress them should cause Director to automatically include the necessary Xtras.

For more information about Xtras, see Chapter 21, *Extracurricular Lingo: Xtras*.

POINTS TO REMEMBER

- Use the **environment.runMode property construct** to determine whether a movie is running as a Shockwave movie and to prevent commands from executing if it is not.

- To **direct navigation** within the browser, use goToNetPage or goToNetMovie.

- Use getNetText to **retrieve text from the Internet** to the cache. When the text is successfully downloaded, retrieve the contents using netTextResult.

- The netStatus command allows you to place information in the **status area** of a browser.

- The one exception to the rule against downloading to the end user's system is the **preferences file**. You can write to and read from any number of basic text files, which will be stored in Shockwave's Preferences directory. When using preferences files, it's a good idea to come up with your own system for giving them unique names, since many other authors may also be placing preferences files, and a name duplication could overwrite your work.

- One of the recent improvements of Shockwave is the ability to **stream** files rather than just download them in a single lump. Movies can begin playback as soon as the elements for the first frame are in place.

- The streaming behavior of an individual movie is set in the **Modify Playback dialog box**, accessible from the Modify menu. To enable streaming for your movie, select the **Play While Downloading Movie option**.

- If you need to prevent your movie from proceeding until sufficient media has downloaded, you can use the Lingo terms **frameReady** and **mediaReady**, or some of the behaviors included in the Library Palette.

- Audio files can be converted to **Shockwave Audio (SWA)**, which can then be streamed like streaming Shockwave movies.

- A movie's internal sounds cannot be streamed, but they can be **compressed** using SWA compression. This makes the movie smaller and allows it to download faster.

BOOK 3:

SPECIAL TOPICS

CHAPTER 16

LINGO AND LISTS

AS YOUR BOSS AND YOUR BOSS'S BOSS WILL PROBABLY TELL YOU, effective organization is the key to getting things done. This rule really does apply to programming. As your scripting grows more complex, you'll feel an ever more acute need to carry out your data wrangling in an orderly, methodical fashion.

Fortunately, Lingo allows you to keep lists: dynamic, changing, and ultimately flexible lists of elements on the Stage and in memory—and these lists are among the most powerful tools you'll encounter. In this chapter, we'll look at the creation, care, and feeding of both linear and property lists in the scripting environment. Then we'll discuss symbols and some specialized Lingo for getting the most from your lists.

UNDERSTANDING LISTS

Having a thorough understanding of lists is your key to unlocking Lingo's advanced functions. That's not because lists are all that powerful or impressive in themselves; rather, it's because well-written list scripts are a vital ingredient in managing multiple windows, content, data, parent and child objects, and a host of other things you'll find yourself wanting to keep track of. Without lists, ambitions breed complications that inevitably cause performance problems and even outright bugs.

What is a list?

LIST:
A "group variable" that can contain multiple values independent of one another.

Simply put, a **list** is a kind of **variable**, which is like a bucket of data that you can pour out and dip into at any point in your movie. The variables you've encountered thus far can hold only one value at a time: For example, myVariable could contain "Jason" or "butterscotch" or "3.1415," but the only way it could contain all three at once is by melding them into a whole ["Jasonbutterscotch3.1415"]. A list is a means of handling values as a unit without losing track of their individual identities.

Like other variables, a list can be global or local, but it's really more like a spice rack than a bucket. You can place multiple values in their own compartments and change or retrieve them independently of other values. You can also rearrange the value containers into any order you choose. Thus, if a list contains ["Jason", "butterscotch", "3.1415"] and you want to change "butterscotch" to "cilantro," it isn't much trouble to do so.

Has the concept not yet jelled in your mind? Try looking at it this way: A list is like a used car lot: there's always a bunch of cars in the lot, although individual cars come and go. Sometimes the lot may have more cars than at other times, and sometimes the cars are more expensive than at other times. Like a car lot, a list is a strategically assembled framework for discrete units of some thing. A list has its own identity, which can persist no matter what subsets it contains or what relation the values bear to one another.

Who needs lists?

Who needs lists? You do! It's possible to manage multiple items by dropping them into (and yanking them out of) a text string, but that's a limited and cumbersome approach and it doesn't use RAM resources as efficiently as lists do. Here are a few examples of uses you might encounter for a well-scripted list in Lingo:

- Let's say the end user is free to wander at random throughout your production, but you need to keep track of the precise order and number of locations the user visits during the course of the interaction. A list can silently compile such a map, adding the frame number of each new location as it's accessed. You can then use the list to create a Back button that the user can click to retrace her steps.

- If a number of parameters need to be accessed more or less at the same time (such as the name, window type, and rect coordinates of a Movie in a Window), you can group those parameters in a list for ease of scripting.

- Lists can also contain (and be contained by) other lists, which means you can't beat 'em for organizing data that might otherwise be too unruly to manage. For instance, you can write a list containing all of a student's answers to a quiz and then place that list in another list of all students' answers.

Linear and property lists

Before we get any more specific, you'll need to be clued in to an important distinction between Director's two kinds of lists: **linear lists** and **property lists**.

- A linear list (yes, that's semiredundant) might look something like these two examples:

```
myList = [1975, 1942, 1999]
myOtherList = ["Martha", "Kuhl", 5551212, 94609]
```

You can see that a linear list is a number of elements separated by commas. Each element can be a number, variable, string, or anything else that you can put into a variable.

- A property list lets you jam two units of data into each entry, separated by a colon (:), as in

  `myPList = ["Gross":1500, "Houghton":950, "Kuhl":2700]`

  What's the point? To the left of the colon is the **property**—you define the property, but it is used primarily for organizational purposes. To the right of the colon is the **value**—the data to be stored, retrieved, or modified. For instance, you can create a property list in which the names of employees are stored as values and their Christmas bonuses from last year are stored as properties. Then you can sort by property to determine who got paid the most (or least, for that matter).

COOL LINES AND HOT PROPERTIES: A linear list contains one value per entry, whereas a property list uses colons to associate two values in a single entry.

Why make the distinction seem so important? Because a number of Lingo elements apply to only one kind of list and not the other, and if you inadvertently blur and blend the data types, your scripts just won't work. You'll need to decide which type is appropriate for the task at hand and then stick with it.

WORKING WITH LISTS

As with any other variable, you create a list by using it—by giving it a name and at the same time designating its contents. The standard syntax for a linear list is this:

`listName = [entry1, entry2, etc.]`

The square brackets are crucial, since they're what Lingo uses to recognize a list. When you want to dispose of a list (or create an empty list prior to any entries), set the list's values to null using an empty bracket statement, such as *listName* = []. To empty a property list, use a colon as the sole text: *listName* = [:]. You can create lists prior to populating them; in fact, it's a good idea to initialize the ones your movie will be using in a `startMovie` handler.

A sample linear list

We don't need to build a movie to start working with lists. Since they're variables, they reside in RAM, and we can access them just as well using the Message window.

1. ***Open the Message window. Enter this line:***

`roster = ["Bill", "Alice", "Jimmy", "Janet"]`

You've created and populated a list called `roster`, with four entries, all of them text strings. You can confirm this in the Message window.

2. ***Enter the following in the Message window:***

`put roster`

The Message window should return `["Bill"`, `"Alice"`, `"Jimmy"`, `"Janet"]`. If any of the entries read `<Void>` instead, they weren't entered correctly as text strings. In that case, repeat step 1, paying special attention to the placement of the quotation marks.

AVOID THE <VOID>: The keyword `<Void>` is returned when a list hasn't been initialized (as in the first case) or when an entry cannot be interpreted in Lingo (as in the second case, in which the text strings include no quotation marks). Note the slightly different result for the entry Quote, which is a keyword in its own right.

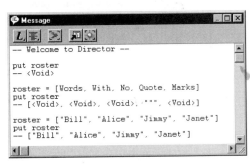

Once a list is established, a number of operations can be performed on it. Some Lingo commands are specific to lists, and sometimes you'll have a choice of using either the specialized Lingo or some syntax more like that of other programming languages.

Accessing a list element

The easiest way to access an element in a list is just to reference the list name and the number of the element's placement in the list. The first element in a list is numbered 1, the second is 2, and so on.

1. *Enter the following line in the Message window:*

```
put roster[2]
```

The Message window should return "Alice".

You can also use the Lingo list command getAt to achieve the same result. The getAt command takes two arguments: the name of the list and the position in that list. Note in the line of code in step 2 that it uses parentheses, not square brackets.

2. *Enter the following line in the Message window:*

```
put getAt(roster, 2)
```

The value returned is the same with either syntax. You can just as easily assign the value of a list element to a variable.

3. *Enter the following lines in the Message window:*

```
temp = getAt(roster, 3)
put temp
```

Sometimes you know (or think you know) the value of a list element, and you want to know the position the element occupies in the list. For this, you can use Lingo's getOne function.

4. *In the Message window, enter this:*

```
put getOne (roster, "Janet")
```

This time the result should be 4, since "Janet" is the fourth item in the list. The getOne function searches for the first item match; had there been another "Janet" later in the list, the function still would have stopped at entry 4. If the list contained no match at all, the result returned would have been zero (0).

There is no alternative syntax for the getOne function.

Changing a list

Another great thing about lists is that once they're established, you can change the values of elements, insert new entries at specific locations, remove elements at specific locations, and even rearrange the elements. First we'll look at how to change a value.

Suppose that Bill quits his job and is replaced by Martin. It's easy to modify the list to reflect the change (the [1] is essential for replacing Bill and not someone else).

roster = ["Bill", "Alice", "Jimmy", "Janet"]

1. **In the Message window, enter this:** *"Martin"*

```
roster[1] = "Martin"
put roster
```

The change has been made. If you prefer to use list Lingo, you can use the setAt command, as in the following example: *changing list value*

```
setAt (roster, 1, "Martin")
```

Either of these syntaxes work just fine while you are authoring, but what if the change should happen while the program is running? In that case, you wouldn't automatically know the location of Bill in the list. The getOne function we looked at in the preceding section comes to the rescue.

```
roster[getOne(roster, "Bill")] = "Martin"
```

That's easy enough, and the first time you use a similar construct in a program, you'll feel like you really have a handle on this Lingo business. (Congratulations in advance!)

Now we have Martin, but Margaret also needs to be added to our list (we just hired her). We don't want to replace anyone—just add Margaret to the list. Most likely we'd just put her at the end of the list, in which case we would use the append command.

2. **In the Message window, enter this:** *Add to the list*

```
append (roster, "Margaret")
put roster
```

The append command puts the new element ("Margaret") at the end of the list, and we don't even need to know the number of the last member to do this. However, if we want to add someone in the middle of the list (at 4 in this case), we can use the <u>addAt</u> command.

3. Enter the following lines:

```
addAt (roster, 4, "Esperanza")
put roster
```

CHANGING THE LIST:
You can make just
about any type
of modification to
a list.

```
┌─ Message ──────────────────────────── _□×
│  L.Ξ  Σ  🗗🔅
│
│ roster[1] = "Martin"
│ put roster
│ -- ["Martin", "Alice", "Jimmy", "Janet"]
│
│ append (roster, "Margaret")
│ put roster
│ -- ["Martin", "Alice", "Jimmy", "Janet", "Margaret"]
│
│ addAt (roster, 4, "Esperanza")
│ put roster
│ -- ["Martin", "Alice", "Jimmy", "Esperanza", "Janet", "Margaret"]
│
└────────────────────────────────────────
```

Now the new name, Esperanza, should show up in the list at the location specified (item 4). If you add an element past the end of the list, Director automatically fills in the intermediate elements and gives them the value zero (0).

Sorting a list

After you add a number of people to your list, suppose you want to be able to walk through the list in alphabetic order. Rather that writing code that will figure out the order (alphabetic or numeric), you can use the Lingo list command `sort`.

1. Enter the following lines in the Message window:

```
sort roster
put roster
```

Now, with that simple command, the list is sorted alphabetically. With sorted lists you get to use the `add` command. The `add` command is kind of a combination of the `append` and `addAt` commands. If the list is unsorted, the addition will occur at the end of the list, just as with the `append` command. But if the list is sorted, the new entry will go in its proper location in alphanumeric order.

2. *Enter the following lines:*

```
add (roster, "Lynn")
put roster
```

A SORT OF LIST:
You can sort a list in
alphanumeric order
and add elements in
their sorted places.

```
🅟 Message                                              _ □ ✕
  ᴸⁱ 🅴  🗷  🖳🗔
addAt (roster, 4, "Esperanza")
put roster
-- ["Martin", "Alice", "Jimmy", "Esperanza", "Janet", "Margaret"]

sort roster
put roster
-- ["Alice", "Esperanza", "Janet", "Jimmy", "Margaret", "Martin"]

add (roster, "Lynn")
put roster
-- ["Alice", "Esperanza", "Janet", "Jimmy", "Lynn", "Margaret", "Martin"]
◄ ▮                                                    ► ▮
```

List manipulation

One of the best reasons for using lists is that Director lets you walk
through them and apply the same set of Lingo instructions to each of the
list elements. The repeat construct make this process almost automatic.
Unfortunately, we can't use a repeat loop in the Message window, so
we'll need to write a script for this example. We can use a new movie, and
we'll define and access the list in a startMovie handler.

1. *Open a new movie, and then open a Movie Script window.*

2. *Enter the following* startMovie *handler:*

```
on startMovie
  roster = ["Bill", "Bob", "Mel"]
  repeat with var in roster
    put var
  end repeat
end startMovie
```

3. *Play the movie; then stop it. (If looping is turned off, it stops by
   itself.)*

In the Message window you will see the three elements of the roster list
displayed. Each element rests on a separate line because each is a result of
a separate put command. The repeat command sets the variable (I called
it var) to each element of the list in turn, passing through all the elements. This is a simple example, but you get the idea. In general, you'd
define the list as a global variable, and then you could perform repeat
actions on the list in other handlers, anywhere in your movie.

A REPEAT PERFORMANCE:
The repeat command allows you to perform the same commands on every element of a list.

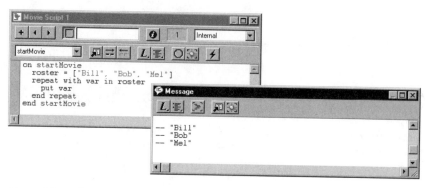

One of the advantages of the repeat loop that we just used is that it automatically knows when the last element of the list is being accessed. If you are accessing elements without a repeat loop, you need to keep track of the number of elements in a list and make sure that you don't try to access a nonexistent element. If you try to access a list element beyond the last element, you will get a script error (while authoring) or an Out of Range error (in a projector). To keep from accessing a nonexistent element, you can use the count function to find the number of elements in a list.

4. *In the Message window, enter these lines:*

```
roster = ["Bill", "Bob", "Mel"]
put count(roster)
put roster[count(roster)]    -- OK
put roster[count(roster)+1]   -- will generate error
```

PAST THE END:
Accessing a list element that doesn't exist will result in an error.

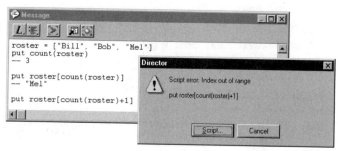

Here are some other list operations with which you can experiment. All of these require only one argument: the name of the list.

• getLast retrieves the very last entry in the list.

• max and min return the maximum and minimum values in a list.

Long lists

Typing lists works fine for the short lists that we're using in these demonstrations, but often you will need to create lists that are a lot longer than these examples. If our bonus list contains everyone in a company, it could easily include hundreds of people, and the list could be changing constantly as new people are hired, moved, and retired.

One solution is to put the list elements into a field cast member. You can format the field contents just as you have been formatting lists in the Message window: Surround the entire list in square brackets and separate list elements with commas. Don't add any Return characters in the list, but let the lines wrap as needed. Once you have the field cast member, you can use the value function to assign it to a variable.

1. *Create a field cast member in cast slot 5 of your movie and add the following line in it:*

```
[1, 2, 3, 4, 5, 6, 7, 8, 9]
```

2. *In the Message window, enter the following lines:*

```
myList = value(field 5)
put myList
```

Better still is to store the list in an external file and then read the file into a field. That way, the file can be updated whenever it's necessary, without your having to modify the movie. You can use the getNetText and netTextResult functions to retrieve the file contents, either from a local file or from the Internet. You can also use the fileIO Xtra, included with Director, or other Xtras to read and write to files. Chapter 21 covers the use of the fileIO Xtra.

Duplicating lists

Copying or duplicating lists involves a small complication that you haven't run into before in your work with variables. To understand this, you need to understand the distinction between accessing by *value* and accessing by *reference*. Everything we have done with variables so far has been by value. We can see this for variables in the Message window.

1. *Enter the following lines in the Message window:*

```
var1 = 10
var2 = var1
```

```
put var2
var2 = 12
put var1
put var2
```

We created a variable, var1, and assigned it a value of 10. Next, we created a second variable, var2, and assigned to it the value of var1. Changing the value of var2 has no effect on the value of var1 because they are separate: Each has its own location for the value in Director's memory.

ACCESS BY *VALUE*.

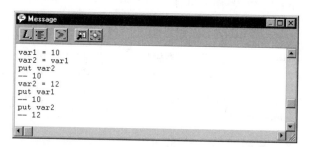

When we try this same set of commands using variables that contain lists, we'll get a different result. That's because each variable refers to the same list—both variables will refer to the exact same location in Director's memory. If you make a change to either list variable, the change will show up in both variables. Again, we can see this in the Message window.

2.   *Enter the following lines in the Message window:*

```
listA = [10, 20, 30, 40]
listB = listA
put listB
listB[2] = 55
put listA
put listB
```

ACCESS BY *REFERENCE*.

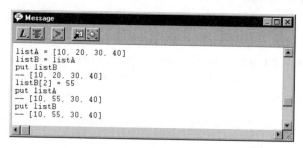

As you can see, the change to listB is reflected in both list variables. Director manages lists by default in this manner to conserve memory, since lists can be one of the larger data elements of a movie.

But that doesn't mean that you necessarily want to work with lists in this way. Suppose you want to copy a list, make changes to it, and have the option of comparing the two lists or even reverting back to the original list? Lingo provides the duplicate function just for this purpose. The duplicate function makes a copy of a list that is totally independent of the original. One more trip to the Message window will show this.

3.   Enter the following lines in the Message window:

```
listC = duplicate(listA)
put listC
listC[2] = 1999
put listC
put listA
```

A DUPLICATE LIST:
Use the duplicate function to create a second, identical list.

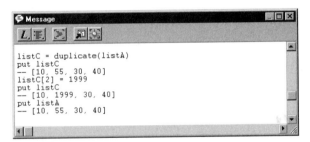

A sample property list

Keeping track of individual units of data is all well and good, but some data has significance only in context. That's what property lists are for: to add a second unit of information. Let's take that hypothetical list of employees and Christmas bonuses and put property lists into practice.

1.   In the Message window, enter this line:

```
bonus = ["Gross":1500, "Houghton":-350, "Kuhl":2700]
```

Now each name (each property) has a numeric value associated with it, on the right side of each colon. This is the value of the property, and in this case it stands for the dollar amount of each bonus. (Houghton took an advance, so his figure is a negative number.)

2. *Enter these two lines:*

```
put getProp (bonus, "Kuhl") into temp
put temp
```

The result should be 2700, which happens to be Kuhl's bonus from last year.

You could also retrieve this same information without the use of getProp.

3. *Enter the line*

```
put bonus["Kuhl"]
```

DELVING INTO DATA:
With the getProp command, you can extract the value associated with a given property in a property list.

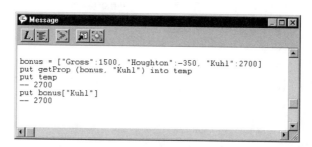

```
bonus = ["Gross":1500, "Houghton":-350, "Kuhl":2700]
put getProp (bonus, "Kuhl") into temp
put temp
-- 2700
put bonus["Kuhl"]
-- 2700
```

Here are some more property list tricks. Let's say we want to find out the smallest bonuses paid last year.

4. *Enter this line:*

```
put min (bonus)
```

The function min retrieves the smallest property value in the list, in this case returning -350. That gives us the number but not the name associated with it. For that we'll need to add another script line.

5. *Enter this line:*

```
put getOne (bonus, -350)
```

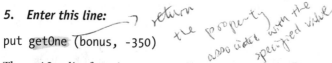

return the property associated with the specified value

The getOne list function returns the property associated with the specified value. If the value is not found in the list, getOne returns zero (0).

For other Lingo pertaining to linear and property lists, see Appendix C, *A Lingo Lexicon*.

Everything you can do with linear lists you can do with property lists: change values, add elements, sort the list, and then some. Sometimes you can use the same Lingo commands for both types; sometimes you use slightly different commands for property lists. For example, getAt works with linear lists only, **getProp** works with property lists only, and getaProp combines the two into a single command that works with both linear and property lists.

Using symbols

SYMBOL:
A text string handled in memory as though it were a single character.

One trick that comes in handy in the realm of lists is the use of **symbols** rather than text strings to identify properties. Symbols are shown by the pound sign (#) that precedes them, as in #Alice or #Jim.

What is a symbol? In the context of lists, it's a grouping of numbers and/or letters that Director treats as a single character. It's as if you were able to add a twenty-seventh letter to the alphabet or a new integer to the series 0 through 9. It's not a variable because it doesn't "contain" anything, but by virtue of its custom nature, a symbol can contain meaning for you. For instance, type this in the Message window:

```
bonus = [#Gross:1500, #Houghton:-350, #Kuhl:2700]
put getOne (bonus, -350)
```

The Message window returns #Houghton, which yields you pretty much the same information as when you performed the same operation with a text string. But here's another experiment for the Message window:

```
set newBonus to [Mike:3,Alex:4,Seth:2]
put newBonus
```

Notice the transformation in the illustration just below. In the case of property lists, text strings that are not safely insulated within quotation marks are automatically converted into symbols. Keep this in mind, or you're likely to end up with scripts invoking "widget", widget, and #widget, which could be either separate entities or inadvertent incarnations of the same thing.

SIMPLIFY WITH SYMBOLS:
Symbols, indicated by the # sign, are processed more efficiently than text strings. In property lists, unquoted text is automatically converted to symbols.

```
🌀 Message                                          _ □ ×
 L 🗐  🗏   🎵 🖳

bonus = [#Gross:1500, #Houghton:-350, #Kuhl:2700]
put getOne (bonus, -350)
-- #Houghton

set newBonus to [Mike:3,Alex:4,Seth:2]
put newBonus
-- [#Mike: 3, #Alex: 4, #Seth: 2]
```

The advantages of employing symbols are twofold: You don't get bogged down in making sure that each entry has the right number of quotation marks in the right places, and Director needs less RAM to manage symbols than it needs for text strings. In the case of large lists with a multitude of entries, that can translate to faster performance.

If you want, you can convert a symbol into a string using the string function.

> Symbols aren't just for lists. They can be contained in (and retrieved from) any type of variable. They're especially useful when you want Lingo to perform a status check as quickly as possible, as in a script for a game that compares a current score to the previous top score each time a point is made.

Lists containing lists

As we mentioned earlier in this chapter, the elements contained in lists can also be lists themselves. Why would you want a list within a list? Because it increases your ability to organize. Imagine, for example, that you want to keep track of all the players in your new Director-built game. For each of them you need to know the name, password, last score, and highest score. You could create a new list for each player that runs your movie, or you could create a single property list whose properties are people and whose values are lists. Here is an example of how you might set up such a list.

In the Message window, enter the following lines:

```
gameList = [:]  -- new, empty list
addProp(gameList, #Mike, [#pwd:"ssorg", #last:1240, ¬
#high:1434])
put gameList
addProp(gameList, #Nan, [#pwd:"brub", #last:2187, #high:2187])
put gameList
put gameList[#Mike][#high]
gameList[#Mike][#high] = 2332
put gameList
```

We began by creating an empty property list, and then we added elements to the list. As you can see, looking at the entire list can quickly become difficult. Getting individual elements (or changing them), though, is almost as easy as getting elements from a one-dimensional list.

LISTS IN LISTS:
The elements in a linear or property list can themselves be lists.

```
gameList = [:]
addProp(gameList, #Mike, [#pwd:"ssorg", #last:1240, #high:1434])
put gameList
-- [#Mike: [#pwd: "ssorg", #last: 1240, #high: 1434]]
addProp(gameList, #Nan, [#pwd:"brub", #last:2187, #high:2187])
put gameList
-- [#Mike: [#pwd: "ssorg", #last: 1240, #high: 1434], #Nan: [#pwd:
"brub", #last: 2187, #high: 2187]]
put gameList[#Mike][#high]
-- 1434
gameList[#Mike][#high] = 2332
put gameList
-- [#Mike: [#pwd: "ssorg", #last: 1240, #high: 2332], #Nan: [#pwd:
"brub", #last: 2187, #high: 2187]]
```

POINTS TO REMEMBER

Here's an overview of the essential concepts introduced in this chapter:

- A **list** is a multipart variable. Values can be deposited in locations in the variable without disturbing values in other locations.

- There are two types of lists. A **linear list** is a simple set of values; a **property list** lets you associate a property with each value, such as fish:"fresh" or States:50.

- Lists can store more than text strings. They can also hold **symbols,** which are groupings of characters (such as #Carol or #Stumpy) that Director handles as a single character.

- When a text string (such as a word) is entered in a property list but not placed in quotation marks, it is automatically **converted to a symbol** by Director. When scripting with lists, keep in mind the distinction among widget (which could be the name of a script or variable), "widget" (a text string), and #widget (a symbol).

- Lists can contain **other lists.**

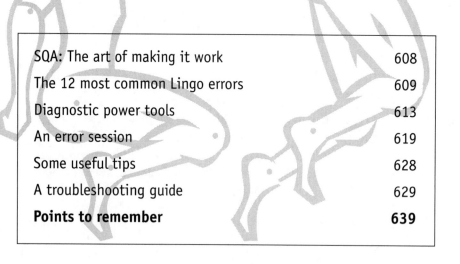

CHAPTER 17

Debugging and Troubleshooting

With complexity comes perplexity. That's a fact of life, and one that holds true when it comes to Director production and Lingo scripting. The more tools at your disposal, the more opportunities you have to futz things up. It's only natural.

This chapter is devoted to the process of unfutzing. We'll start with a look at a number of the most common reasons that scripts go awry. Next we'll look at strategies for debugging Lingo code. Then we'll tackle general Director operations with a troubleshooting guide, which addresses many of the problems that can arise before, during, and after playback.

SQA: The art of making it work

Now that you're getting more ambitious in your Lingo work, it's inevitable that fewer of your scripts will execute correctly the first time around. Fortunately, Director 7 provides a number of tools to help you track down errors in their lairs, and we'll take a look at them in this chapter. We'll also survey some of the most common manifestations of Murphy's Law in Lingo scripting—and then segue into a troubleshooting guide that should help you through some of the thornier (and more persistent) problems you'll encounter when working with Director.

But first, a bit of background on the process of improving the quality of your production. Like it or not, once you distribute your Director work to others, you're in the software business. Your work won't be judged solely on its content and originality, but also on its ability to perform efficiently and consistently, with no unpleasant surprises for the end user. If you want your work to be appreciated, you'll need to build your skills in **software quality assurance**—what's usually referred to as SQA, or sometimes just QA. This chapter gives you an overview of the methodologies often used in this process, and the tools you'll need to make the process work for you.

Testing, troubleshooting, and debugging

First let's make a distinction among three terms that are often used synonymously. **Testing** is the act of finding something wrong (or, if you're lucky, confirming that *nothing* is wrong). **Troubleshooting** is the act of determining exactly how things went wrong—that is, what factors contributed to the unexpected performance. **Debugging** is the act of fixing what's wrong.

An effective tester doesn't need to know much about Director (in fact, some of the most effective testers are often complete neophytes in multimedia). Troubleshooting requires at least an overall knowledge of the way Director (and software in general) works, and attempting to fix those bugs requires real scripting skills. If at all possible, the person or persons responsible for scripting in the first place should attempt to make the fixes. No one else is more familiar with the idiosyncrasies of the scripting or less likely to introduce new bugs while trying to kill off old ones.

The 12 most common Lingo errors

In my experience, if Lingo scripting goes awry, it's usually because one or more of the following errors has occurred. Try eliminating these factors before you start looking for more esoteric explanations:

- A Lingo element is misspelled. Lingo isn't case-sensitive (so capitalization doesn't matter), but if you misspell the variable myVar as miVar, you may have inadvertently created the variable miVar. When working with long Lingo such as the emulateMultiButtonMouse, keep errors (and finger fatigue) to a minimum by using the pull-down Lingo menus in the Script window.

- Nested end and if statements are missing. Keep an eye on the script while it's automatically formatted in the Script window. If two or more consecutive lines are flat against the left margin, that's a sign that Lingo can't parse the script as written. Usually, what's missing are a sufficient number of end and if statements to balance the number of scripts and layers of conditionality. And remember: In most cases of conditionality, you can use the case statement structure to create a somewhat tidier script (see Chapter 11: *Deeper into Lingo*).

WRONG DOG?
Although the mouseUp handler might look okay at a glance, the nesting is incorrect and the walkTheDog handler doesn't indent correctly.

```
on mouseUp
  global theday, sleepIn
  if theday = 1 then
    walkTheDog
  else
    if sleepIn then
      sleepIn
      snore
    end if
end mouseUp

on walkTheDog
member("toDo").text = "Walk the dog."
end
```

- The script works—it just doesn't do what you want it to do. This one has happened to me more often than I'd care to admit. If you're not getting an error message when you run the script, that usually means that the syntax is correct but your expectations aren't. Look at your work with an eye toward tracing its true function. Perhaps you're plucking the wrong entry from a list, or the action you're looking for in frame 20 is happening in frame 200.

- You're trying to manipulate the wrong data type. Using a property designed exclusively for a Shockwave Audio cast member (such as `member(1).volume = 128`) isn't going to work on a still graphic. In many such cases, Lingo recognizes the mismatch and displays an error message similar to this one:

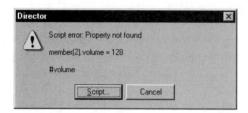

You can't always rely on Director to find your error, however. I tried the command `sprite(1).volume = 128` on a graphic sprite (it should work on a digital video only), and Director did not complain.

- Global and local variables are used incorrectly. If you think you are using a global variable but never declare it as such, you may have created only a local variable with the same name. Similarly, if you don't need a global variable, use only a local variable. It's easy to inadvertently change the value of a global variable when you don't mean to.

- The wrong script type has been selected. You can choose one of three script types: behavior, movie, and parent (set in the script's Properties dialog box). A parent script may be impeccably written—but if its type isn't set to parent, it won't work when you try to initialize child objects from it. Likewise, changing a movie script to a behavior script will usually keep it from executing correctly.

- Outmoded Lingo is used. Each new edition of Director brings with it changes to both Director and Lingo, and version 7 is no exception. For instance, consider the term `the castNum`. It was commonly used in Director 4, declared outmoded (but still tolerated) by version 5, and not recognized at all by Director 6. Now the correct term is `the memberNum`.

One modification that seems to be causing a lot of confusion is the use of `member x of castLib y`. It used to be that `member (x) of castLib y` would work, but that construction now generally causes an error. The preferred syntax is member (x,y), or member x of castLib y (no parentheses).

You'll sometimes see discrepancies between what Director officially supports and what seems to work in practice. The **the castNum** sprite property, for example, was listed as obsolete in the Director 6 *Lingo Dictionary* and is not listed at all in the Director 7 *Lingo Dictionary*. When I try **the castNum** on my version of Director 7, though, it still seems to work just fine. Be warned though; there's no guarantee that it will work in any future version. Get in the habit of changing from old Lingo to new Lingo as soon as possible. On the other hand, if you spend time perusing the online discussion groups, you may occasionally find people discussing Lingo that has never been documented and yet seems to work. Macromedia seems to slip new Lingo into Director versions before telling the general public about it.

- Incorrect syntax is used. If you place an argument before rather than after a function or property, your script is bound to derail. Likewise, a script that points a property to the wrong realm (such as a script that looks for a system-level property such as colorDepth on the sprite level) will probably invoke an error message, in this less-than-clear form:

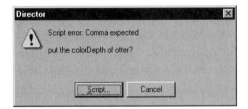

In this case, the problem isn't really that a comma is expected; you can place as many commas as you want in the space indicated by the question mark, and Lingo still won't parse the script. What Director is trying to do is look for a custom function by that name, and the reference to commas is simply a request for more parameters.

If you have doubts about your syntax and the documentation doesn't help, try switching between the old Lingo syntax and the new dot syntax. Even if your command still doesn't work, often you will get a more meaningful (or at least different) error message:

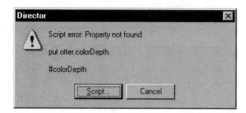

- Instructions result in conflicting control. Make sure that you don't use commands in one handler whose instructions conflict with the instructions in another handler also called. If you use two mouseUp behaviors for a single sprite, for example, both will be called when the sprite is clicked.

- The script controls a similar—but not the appropriate—sprite. Sometimes a script fails to control a sprite not because the Lingo is wrong, but because the sprite isn't derived from the cast member that you think it's derived from. (Did you get all that?) Experimentation and false starts can create multiple cast members that appear identical but have separate identities.

- An element is too large to be controlled. If Director consistently crashes when a particular media element is being manipulated, perhaps Director is choking on the element itself.

- Scripting points to absolute, not relational, values. If you write sprite(3).memberNum = 120, your script will probably work—until you move the cast member from frame 120 to 121. A relational identification is preferable, such as member ("Cuddles the Bear").

The runners-up...

The following stumbling blocks don't pop up so often, but they're still worthy of notice:

- Uninstalled extracurricular Lingo is used. Many Xtras come bundled with Director, and others are available from Macromedia or other third-party sources. Some of these Xtras come with their own custom Lingo syntax; some Xtras have the sole purpose of pumping up your available Lingo vocabulary. If these Xtras aren't correctly installed or properly bundled (with projector or Shockwave files as well as with the Director movies), a script that's correct in theory will suddenly stop working. See Chapter 21: *Extracurricular Lingo: Xtras* for more information on Xtras.

- Platform limitations need to be considered. Placing a MacOS-specific command in a script intended for Windows (or vice versa) will result in Lingo that's syntactically sound but nonfunctional. Likewise, you'll need to be cognizant of the terms that work in a Director movie or a projector, but don't work when the production is in Shockwave form.

- RAM entities have not been disposed of properly. Once created, many items residing in RAM (global variables, lists, child objects, MIAWs, and object instances of Xtras) will persist in memory until you explicitly dispose of them by setting their values to empty. Just because something's no longer in use or in physical evidence doesn't mean it's making no demands on Director's memory.

- The wrong Cast has been used. The advent of multiple Casts makes Director much more versatile, but it also makes it easier to get confused about the location of a movie element. If an item seems to have disappeared or has transmogrified into something else entirely, it may be because you've opened the wrong Cast (or neglected to open the right one).

DIAGNOSTIC POWER TOOLS

You're already familiar with the Message window, which lets you both test and trace Lingo as it executes. But that's just one of the tools Director 7 provides to track scripting in action. In this section, we'll look at four other windows in the light of their diagnostic abilities: the Memory Inspector, the Watcher window, the Debugger, and our stalwart standby, the Script window.

The Memory Inspector

Need to keep a watch on how RAM is being used in your movie? The Memory Inspector is already on the job. This windoid keeps permanently displayed a dynamic map of memory use within Director.

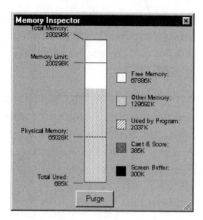

- *Total Memory* or *Memory Limit* tells you how much total memory is available, via virtual memory or software such as RamDoubler.

- *Physical Memory* shows you how much physical RAM is installed in your system.

- *Total Used* is an indication of how much total RAM is being used by your movie (not including the Director application).

- *Free Memory* lets you know how much more memory is available in your system.

- *Other Memory* shows the amount of memory being used by the system and all other open programs.

- *Used by Program* measures the memory used by the Director application; it doesn't include the memory used by the current movie.

- *Cast & Score* lets you know how much memory is reserved by cast members and information in the Score. It also includes linked cast members currently loaded into memory.

- *Screen Buffer* indicates how much memory Director is using as a buffer zone while animating sprites. Bigger buffers usually mean smoother animation, since the motion can be calculated before the sprite reaches the Stage.

- *Partition Size* is visible on the Macintosh Memory Inspector window, but not in Windows. It tracks how much memory has been allotted to Director (a number that can be reset by the user).

- The *Purge* button purges just about everything from its share of RAM, except what's been defined as having an unload value of Never. This purging doesn't affect memory allocated to other applications.

While the Memory Inspector is helpful, it's not as accurate or useful as it might be. You might have better luck using the Memory Lingo, as discussed in Chapter 22. Memory Lingo includes commands for checking memory usage and availability. Whenever you are debugging your projects and suspect that memory might be part of the problem, you can use these commands to populate test fields of the Message window with accurate and updated information.

The Script window

Eight tools are available in the Script window. You've seen some already, but a few are new. Since some of these are helpful in figuring out where you've gone wrong, let's peruse them from left to right.

- *Go to Handler* takes you to a specific handler. Highlight a handler name in the script and then click this button to go to the handler where it resides in the script.

- *Comment* inserts comment marks to deactivate all highlighted lines. Comment marks tell Lingo to ignore those lines of code.

- *Uncomment* removes any comment marks from highlighted lines.

- *Alphabetical Lingo Menu* displays Lingo elements alphabetically. Choose an element to insert it in your script at the cursor.

- *Categorized Lingo* displays Lingo elements grouped by features. You can choose to insert them in your script at the cursor.

- *Toggle Breakpoint* lets you insert or remove breakpoints from your script. Breakpoints are useful in determining where to pause a movie for debugging, and we will cover them shortly. You can also insert a breakpoint by clicking the left border of the Script window at the appropriate line.

- *Watch Expression* adds the highlighted variable or expression to the Watcher window's list of things to keep an eye on.

- *Recompile* recompiles all your scripts right then and there. Basically, this ensures that Director runs your scripts as they are currently written; it returns an error alert if something doesn't parse.

The Watcher window

While your movie is playing, chances are your globals, lists, and other expressions are changing values to reflect different conditions. The Watcher window lets you track these values (or even change them) as your Lingo unfolds, while playing the movie and when using the Debugger.

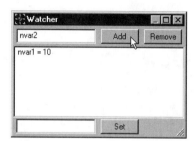

You can add variables or expressions to the list in the window simply by typing them in the upper entry field and clicking Add, or by highlighting them in your scripts (or in the Debugger) and clicking the Watch Expression button. If the value of an item in the list is unavailable, the value <void> will appear after the equal sign that usually precedes a value. Being able to pinpoint just where a value is not what you want it to be can be a valuable asset in the debugging process.

If a value is different from what you want, you can also use the Watcher window to change the value. Select the line containing the variable, enter a new value in the lower entry field, and click Set.

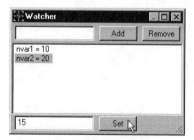

The Debugger window

When Director encounters a problem executing some aspect of a script, an alert box appears on the screen and cryptically attempts to tell you what went wrong. The alert box gives you three choices: Debug, Script, and Cancel. Cancel does nothing, but the movie is stopped. The Script button opens a Script window showing the script, with the cursor at the line where the error occurred. Nothing new in these two actions, but the Debug button opens the Debugger and a whole new realm of problem-solving capabilities for you. Using the Debugger, you can trace the execution of a program as it progresses line-by-line or handler-by-handler. It's a little like the Trace option in the Message window, but in a much handier form. You can also open the Debugger window from the Window menu or cause it to open by setting breakpoints in your scripts.

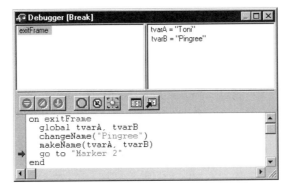

When the Debugger opens after a problem occurs, it shows you the current line of Lingo and indicates the problem area with a green arrow. It also provides some additional information:

- The *Handler History pane*, at the top left, shows the current handler and the handler(s) from which the handler was called (if applicable).

- The *Variable pane*, at the top right, indicates variables and property settings in the current handler as they existed when the error occurred.

- The *Script pane* is the largest pane; it displays the current handler, including the line of Lingo where the problem occurred. If you get to the Debugger because you set a breakpoint, you may also see a red dot at the left of the current line.

What's a **breakpoint**? It's a location in a script where you want Director to stop processing the Lingo—a temporary stopper dropped into a script so you can narrow down the problem by limiting the action. Breakpoints are especially useful when a handler performs many functions at the same time; you can pinpoint precisely the function that's going awry. When Director hits a breakpoint, it halts program execution in a manner that allows the program to be started again, and it opens the Debugger window. At that point, you can actually execute lines of the script a single command at a time—meanwhile watching how things in your program act or change.

> Remember that you can't actually change values or edit scripts in the Debugger window. To add your revisions, you'll have to open the Message window, the Watcher window, or the scripts.

The Debugger offers eight additional tools, some of which you'll recognize from other windows. Here's a rundown from left to right:

- *Step Script* allows you execute the next line of the script. If the command is a call to a handler, this function steps over the handler—the commands in the handler are executed as a unit, and you don't get to see each line executed. This is useful when you're sure that the handler is not responsible for the problem at hand.

- *Step Into* can be used for those occasions when you're not certain that a handler is bug-free. It steps into and runs the questionable handler, giving you line-by-line control of execution.

- *Continue Script* sets the movie running again without any control from the Debugger (unless more breakpoints or errors are encountered).

- *Toggle Breakpoint* inserts or removes a breakpoint from the highlighted line of script. Often a handler will be called repeatedly, such as from within a repeat loop. Once you are certain that the handler works correctly, you don't need to watch it run the next thousand times.

- *Ignore Breakpoint* tells Lingo to pass by breakpoints in your scripts.

- *Watch Expression* adds the highlighted variable or expression to the Watcher window.

- *Watcher Window* opens the Watcher window, so you can add or subtract an expression or a variable from your monitoring list or even change values.

- *Go to Handler* leaves the Debugger and takes you to the Script window of the highlighted handler or line of code.

AN ERROR SESSION

Now that we've had a quick look at some of the tools for debugging, it's time to take a look at how they work in practice. We'll start with the Message window, which is surprisingly helpful (and easy to use) for debugging. We'll then get into breakpoints and the Debugger window.

*1. **Open the movie Debug.dir in the Tutorials folder on the CD.***

This movie doesn't do a whole lot—it just sets some variables and calls some handlers. This is exactly what we need to get acquainted with the debugging process. In fact, if you run the movie as is, you won't see anything happening.

*2. **Take a look at the movie script in cast slot 1 and the frame behavior in frame 10.***

The movie script here has three handlers: startMovie, changeName, and makeName. The startMovie handler sets some global variables and jumps to frame "Next". At frame 10 (labeled *Next*), the frame behavior calls the other two handlers of startMovie. The changeName handler changes the global variable tvarB. The makeName handler creates a list variable from the variables tvarA and tvarB.

*3. **Open the Message window and click the Trace button. Run the movie.***

*4. **Scroll the Message window to find the line** --> go to frame "Next".*

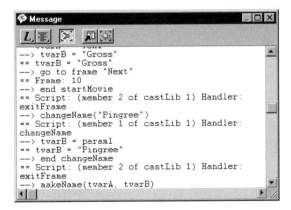

Lines that start with an arrow (a double dash and right angle bracket) are Lingo commands that have been executed. Lines that begin with a double equal sign show what has happened in the movie. For example, `--> tvarB = param1` is a command that was executed. The following line, `== tvarB = "Pingree"`, indicates that `tvarB` was assigned the value `"Pingree"`.

Using the trace

All this information in the Message window can be very useful, although overwhelming. Generally, you'll see hundreds of commands in the window, which makes it difficult to sort out the useful from the extraneous. Fortunately, Director provides some Lingo that can simplify the process. First and foremost is the movie property the trace. This property lets you use Lingo, rather than the Trace button, to decide when tracing information should be displayed. Here's how to use the property:

1. *Make sure the Message window is open. Then press Control-A (Windows) or Command-A (Macintosh) to select all the contents of the window. Press the Delete key to remove the contents.*

2. *Deselect the Trace button in the Message window.*

3. *Open the movie script and add the lines shown here in bold to the* startMovie *handler:*

```
on startMovie
  the trace = TRUE
  clearGlobals
  global nvar1, nvar2, tvarA, tvarB
  nvar1 = 10
  nvar2 = 20
  tvarA = "Toni"
  tvarB = "Gross"
  go to frame "Next"
  the trace = FALSE
end startMovie
```

4. *Run the movie.*

Now only the commands executed between the time the trace is turned on and the time the trace is turned off are displayed in the Message window. This approach is particularly useful when you suspect that a problem is within a certain segment of your code.

5. ***Remove the trace lines from the*** `startMovie` ***handler.***

A couple of other movie properties can also be useful on occasion. The `traceLogFile` property lets you designate a file to receive output sent to the Message window. Viewing the trace information in an external editor, for example, gives you search functionality that you don't have in the Message window. As of this writing, however, the log file isn't actually written to until Director closes, which makes the log file a little less useful. On the other hand, the log file can be used with projectors as well as when authoring. This feature can be extremely helpful when your projector seems to behave differently from the movie while you're authoring.

The `traceLoad` movie property can be set to display information about cast members as they load—either in the Message window or in the trace log file. Normally, no information is displayed (`traceLoad = 0`). Setting `traceLoad` to `1` displays the names of cast members, and setting it to `2` displays a whole lot of extra information. Again, there seems to be a bit of trouble in the present incarnation because the `traceLoad` information appears in the Message window only when you open a new movie (or even worse, as you quit Director). Macromedia knows about these problems, so you can expect them to be rectified in short order.

Using the Message window

The `put` and `alert` commands are surprisingly useful for debugging because they are so quick and easy to use. They both can supply the same sort of information, but you use one or the other according to what you want to happen. The `put` command displays a designated string (which may include values) in the Message window, and the movie keeps running; you can follow along in the Message window as the movie runs. The `alert` command's dialog box can show the same information, but the movie is paused while the alert box is displayed. This gives you a chance to take a look at the current condition of the Stage to ensure that what you see there is what you expected. Are you wondering if a line in an `if...then` construct is ever being reached? Stick a `put` command in there and you'll know immediately.

Both the `showGlobals` and `showLocals` commands display information about variables in the Message window. The `showGlobals` command displays the values of all current global variables. The `showLocals` command provides information about all local variables used in the current handler. Here's how you use them:

1. *Open the movie script and add the lines shown here in bold:*

```
on makeName name1, name2
  put "Now in makeName handler."
  nameList = [name1]
  add nameList, name2
  put "The global variables are:"
  showGlobals
  put "The local variables are:"
  showLocals
end makeName
```

2. *Clear the Message window and then run the movie. Make sure the Trace button is deselected.*

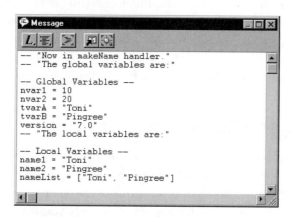

The Message window tells you that you arrived at the makeName handler (you might have been wondering) and gives you a full rundown on the current status of variables. In a more complicated situation, where one handler calls other handlers, you can check the variables at the start and at the end of the handler to see if values have changed as you expected.

Using breakpoints

Finally we get to play with breakpoints and the Debugger window. When you think about it, this is pretty nifty stuff—being able to pause a movie in full play and check (or change) the current status. Then, if you want to, you can run the movie a single line at a time. It's a bit more work, and it takes a bit more practice, but it can be ever so much more rewarding than the Message window's Trace function.

Let's begin by adding breakpoints to our movie:

1. ***Open the movie script and click somewhere in the line*** clearGlobals ***in the*** startMovie ***handler.***

2. ***Click the Toggle Breakpoint button.***

A red circle should appear to the left of the line, indicating that a breakpoint has been set there. You can also set (or unset) a breakpoint by clicking that same area to the left of a line. Note that you aren't allowed to set a breakpoint at every line of a script. Lines beginning with keywords, such as the lines beginning with on and global, don't accept breakpoints.

Breakpoints are handler specific, so setting a breakpoint in the startMovie handler will let us step through that handler but not through other handlers.

Just so we get a good idea of how breakpoints work, we'll also place a breakpoint in the frame behavior in frame 10:

3. ***Open the frame behavior in frame 10. Place a breakpoint at the line*** changeName("Pingree").

4. ***Close the Script window. Rewind and play the movie.***

As soon as Director reaches a command line in a script that contains a breakpoint, it halts execution and opens the Debugger window. As you can see in the following illustration, the Debugger window displays a green arrow superimposed over a red circle to the left of the line with the breakpoint.

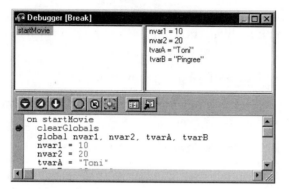

The Handler History pane, at the upper left, shows that we are in the startMovie handler. If the breakpoint was located in a handler called by a handler called by another handler (and so on), the handler hierarchy would be shown in that pane.

The Variable pane, at the upper right, shows the value of variables as they currently exist within the handler. Since we've already run this movie (in authoring mode), the globals are already set to the values they had when the movie last stopped. That's why I placed the clearGlobals command in the script: to reset the variables each time the movie runs. This also tells you that the movie stopped *before* the command with the breakpoint was executed. As you will see, after the clearGlobals command has been executed, the global variables will all have the value <void>.

5. Click the Step Script button (the button on the far left).

The green arrow, indicating the next command that will be executed (the globals line doesn't count), moves down in the script. You can see the effect of the clearGlobals command in the Variable pane—the values are all now <void>.

6. Click the Step Script button four more times.

Each time the button is clicked, another variable's value is set, and that value appears in the Variable pane.

7. Double-click the variable nvar1 in the Script pane, and then click the Watch Expression button.

The Watcher window opens, and the selected variable, with its current value, is displayed. We can change that value from the Watcher window:

8. *Click the* nvar1 *variable in the Watcher window.*

9. *In the Set field, enter* **12**. *Then click the Set button.*

The Watcher window shows the new value for nvar1, but the Debugger window still shows the old value.

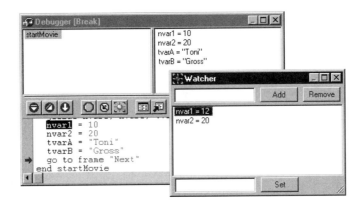

10. *Click the Step Script button in the Debugger window (watch the green arrow while you do this).*

This time, the green arrow doesn't move, but the nvar1 variable is updated to its new value. From now on in this movie, the nvar1 variable will have the value 12 (unless it's changed by you or by some other command).

11. *Click the Step Script button a few more times until the green arrow points to the line* end startMovie.

The last command line that was executed was go to frame "Next". If you look at the Score window, you will see that the playback head is in fact at frame 10. It's important to realize that even though we are still in the startMovie handler, we can be executing commands that affect the movie's playback or make changes elsewhere in the movie.

If we click the Step Script button one more time, we will leave the startMovie handler. At that point, without any more breakpoints, the movie would continue playing out of the control of the Debugger. We placed another breakpoint in the exitFrame handler of the frame behavior in frame 10, so the movie continues to that point and halts again.

12. *Click the Step Script button one more time to end up in the* exitFrame *handler.*

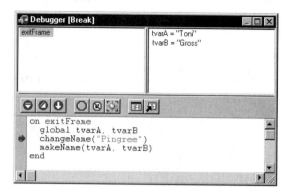

As you can see, the Variable pane shows only the variables used in this handler. Since they are global variables, they already have values, without their being set within this handler. Also note that the Handler History pane shows we are in the exitFrame handler. The green arrow points to the line changeName ("Pingree"). That's a call to another handler, so now it's decision time. Do we click the Step Button and step over the code in that handler? Or do we click the Step Into Script button and run that handler under the control of the Debugger? This time, let's just step over the handler:

13. *Click the Step Script button again.*

The green arrow moves down one line in the exitFrame handler. But look at the Variables pane of the Debugger. The value of tvarB has changed from "Gross" to "Pingree", indicating that the code in the changeName handler was indeed executed.

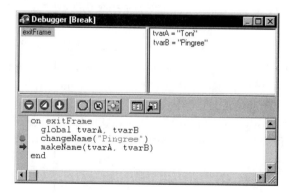

Now we have the choice of whether to step over or step into the makeName handler. Let's step into this one.

14. *Click the Step Into Script button.*

The Debugger now shows the makeName handler. You'll see no breakpoints here, but we are still running under control of the Debugger because we are still in the exitFrame handler, as well—and the exitFrame handler *did* have a breakpoint. The Handler History pane shows that we are in the makeName handler, which is running from within the exitFrame handler.

HANDLER IN A HANDLER:
The Handler History pane shows when you are running a handler nested in other handlers.

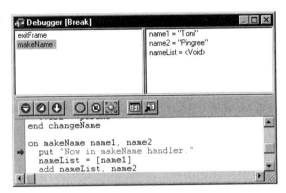

You can use the Handler History pane's information to review just how you got to where you are in the program:

15. *In the Handler History pane, click on* exitFrame.

The Debugger shows the exitFrame handler in the Script pane. The arrow, which is no longer green but is dimmed, shows you where you left that handler.

HANDLING HISTORY:
Clicking a handler name in the Handler History pane shows you that handler.

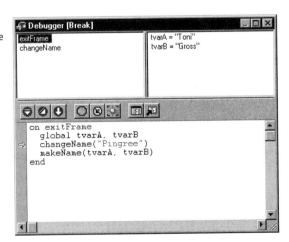

16. *Click* makeName *in the Handler History pane to return to the* makeName *handler.*

Take some time to play with the Debugger so you are familiar with how it works. Set or remove breakpoints in your scripts. Change values in the Watcher window or the Message window to see how various values affect the running movie. Try debugging other Director movies. You should feel so comfortable with the Debugger that you never hesitate to use it when you find or suspect bugs in your programs.

SOME USEFUL TIPS

Before we go on to the troubleshooting guide, you need to consider a few serious hints about writing your code and debugging your programs. If you follow these four guidelines, you will make your programming and debugging experience a whole lot simpler.

- **Include comments.** You really can't add too many comments in your code. When you or someone else needs to inspect your code to track down a bug, these comments can save days of work. The hours you spend trying to decipher what some arcane code is doing (or supposed to be doing), when you just want to fix some small bug, may be some of the most unpleasant hours you'll ever spend programming.

- **Use meaningful variable names.** Whenever possible, give variables names that reflect their functions: lastName is much more meaning-ful than ln or x23. For global variables, it's a good idea to use a lower-case *g* as the first letter—for instance, glastName. That way, you won't inadvertently use a local variable when you think you are using a global variable.

- **Change one thing at a time.** While debugging, don't fall into the trap of making a number of possible fixes all at once. Instead, make the one change that will most likely fix the problem. If that doesn't work, change the code back before trying a new possibility. If you try to make a number of changes at once, you'll probably end up introduc-ing more bugs than you are fixing.

- **Work from a backup.** Always make a copy of your movies before you start making serious changes in an attempt to fix bugs. If you don't like the direction your changes have taken, you can always revert to the original. If you are forced to try to undo all your changes, you will often miss something and end up introducing additional bugs or complications.

A TROUBLESHOOTING GUIDE

Here's an attempt to organize and centralize some problem-solving expertise that might come in handy during your SQA adventures. I've used a symptom/solution structure and arranged the suggestions according to the phase of operation in which the problem is most commonly encountered.

Troubleshooting issues for Shockwave and NetLingo aren't covered here. You'll find those issues in Chapter 14: *Scripting with Net-Savvy Lingo.*

Problems during construction

SYMPTOM: *I can't seem to import external files into the Cast.*

POSSIBILITIES: • Do you have the right file type selected in the Import dialog box? You can search for only one file type at a time; others won't show up until you change the selection in the pop-up menu.

• If you do have the right file type selected in Import but your target files still don't appear, perhaps they don't have a correct internal format. Graphic files seem to work best when saved as PICT or BMP files, and the preferred sound formats are AIFF and WAV.

• Some media types can be recognized by Director only when a specialized Xtra is installed. For instance, the PhotoCaster Xtra adds the capability of importing multiple layers of a Photoshop file as individual cast members. If you used to be able to import a media type but now can't, check your Xtra inventory.

SYMPTOM: *I can't seem to select and move sprite segments.*

POSSIBILITY: • You may have the Director 5 Style Score Display preference set without the Allow Drag and Drop option enabled. I recommend using the Director 7 style for the Score. Check the preferences settings from the File menu by selecting Preferences and then Score.

SYMPTOM: *Graphic cast members are displayed incorrectly on the Stage.*

POSSIBILITIES: • Are the cast members mapped to the appropriate color palette? Check the entries in their Properties dialog boxes and make sure that the palette channel doesn't contain an unwanted palette.

• Are they set to the correct color depth? Again, check their Properties dialog boxes (or check the color depth directly in the Paint window).

• Check the Score-level ink effects of any sprites derived from the cast member. Have any inappropriate effects been applied?

SYMPTOM: *Sprites have disappeared from my Stage.*

POSSIBILITIES: • Check the location of your playback head. Maybe you inadvertently moved to a different frame in the Score.

• Check the channels that the sprites are supposed to occupy. Perhaps the sprites were deleted, or perhaps the button that toggles visibility for each channel has been switched off.

• If the sprites are in their channels, check their locations in the Sprite Properties dialog box. Maybe they've been moved outside the visible area of the Stage.

• Analyze the layering of sprites on the Stage and in the Score. The desired sprites may have been eclipsed by other sprites placed in front of them.

• If the sprites still seem to be in their channels, check the Score-level ink effect. Maybe an obscuring effect has been applied, such as Transparent or Lightest/Darkest.

• The sprites may have been accidentally deleted. Sometimes the Score window is the active window when you think some other window is active, and changes you think you are making in one place are actually being made somewhere else.

SYMPTOM: *Sprites pasted into cells in the Score don't show up in the center of the Stage.*

POSSIBILITY: • The centering of a sprite on the Stage is based on its source cast member's registration point. Check it in the Paint window.

SYMPTOM: *Xtras are not showing up in the Xtras menu.*

POSSIBILITIES: • Are the Xtra files located in your Xtras folder?

• Is your Xtras folder named Xtras?

• Is the folder located in the same folder as your Director application?

• If the Xtras in question are transitions, they won't show up in the Xtras menu but in the Frame Transition dialog box instead.

Problems during playback

SYMPTOM: *During playback, a cast member seems to jump or otherwise act jittery.*

POSSIBILITIES: • Analyze each frame of the animation using the Step Backward and Step Forward buttons of the Control Panel. Maybe one or more sprites have accidentally been moved. Delete them from the Stage and then use In-Between to fill in the resulting gaps in the segment.

• A jump or flash can occur if some sprites in the sequence are assigned a different ink effect than the others. Temporarily switch the Display mode in the Score to Ink, and look for any notation inconsistencies in the segment.

• Is the cast member being controlled by conflicting scripts or child objects?

SYMPTOM: *The cursor seems to blink or appear sporadically.*

POSSIBILITIES: • The cursor disappears when the Score displays a frame that has no interactivity (no click-oriented script attached to any sprite on the Stage). One way to get around this is to attach to a sprite a script that actually does nothing, like this:

```
on mouseDown
nothing
end
```

- You might also try closing the Cast and Score windows. Having them open while you are testing your movie can sometimes cause undesirable cursor rambunctiousness.

SYMPTOM: *The animation of an individual cast member seems too slow.*

POSSIBILITIES:
- Did you use one of the In-Between commands to create the animation? Perhaps you selected too many frames over which to extend the motion. The fewer frames occupied by an animation, the quicker it runs during playback. (However, too few frames result in choppiness.)

- What Score-level ink effects are applied to the sprites? Some are more RAM-intensive than others. You might want to apply some effects only to the beginning and ending sprites in a segment.

SYMPTOM: *Overall animation seems too slow.*

POSSIBILITIES:
- Is sufficient RAM allocated to Director (Macintosh only)?

- Are cast members loaded at the beginning of the movie or on an "as needed" basis? The latter is recommended but can lead to display delays. Try setting other Preload values in the Cast Properties dialog box to see if this makes a difference. Cast Properties is on the Modify menu.

- Do you have too many sprites being animated at once? Animating more than one or two sprites in the same frame really takes a toll on RAM.

- Are you playing digital video or sounds? These both put a strain on resources and can slow down animation that occurs at the same time.

- Is the Message window open and is the Trace option enabled? Tracing script execution usually causes a major slowdown in performance, because you're asking Director to send you a message describing every step as it occurs.

- Check your movie tempo in the Frame Properties: Tempo dialog box displayed from the Modify menu.

SYMPTOM: *It takes forever for my movie to start playing.*

POSSIBILITIES:
- If you have a large Cast and cast members are loaded at or before the first frame of a movie, you're in for a wristwatch or hourglass session. Instead, set the Preload pop-up menu in the Casts Properties dialog box to When Needed.

- Bundling Xtras into a projector can cause delays in the projector playing. Instead, include an Xtras folder with your projector and place needed Xtras there.

SYMPTOM: *I can't hear my movie sounds!*

POSSIBILITIES:
- Do you have your computer's volume turned down at the system level?

- Are your speakers disconnected? If they have their own power supply, is that supply plugged in?

- If you're running Windows, is your sound card functional? Try running another application that uses sound and see if that is mute as well.

- Are one or more of the sound channels disabled in the Score? Check to see if the little dimples at the left of the Score window appear depressed.

- Is there a script affecting the soundEnabled property? You may need to write another script turning it back on.

- Are you using linked sound files? Check the source files themselves. Maybe they've been modified, damaged, or moved.

- If this is the first sound channel that's disappeared, have you puppeted a sound lately? You'll need to return control of that channel to the Score with the command puppetSound 0.

SYMPTOM: *Transitions seem too slow (or too fast).*

POSSIBILITY:
- Experiment with both the time setting and chunk value in the Frame Transition dialog box. If the Smoothness setting is too high, Director cannot always match the specified duration.

SYMPTOM: *A Lingo-controlled sprite action doesn't seem to occur.*

POSSIBILITY:
- Did you include the command updateStage in your script? Without it, the Stage will not be redrawn until the playback head enters a new frame. This command is necessary whenever you want your scripting to manifest results immediately; even puppetSound commands require playback head movement or an updateStage command for prompt execution.

SYMPTOM: *A sprite remains on the Stage long after it has passed from the Score.*

POSSIBILITIES:
- Did you puppet the channel? Remember that any operations you perform on a sprite in the puppeted channel will persist until you return control of that channel to the Score. See *A Lingo Lexicon* (Appendix C) for instructions on how to turn off puppeting. (Note that this consideration applies to sounds in the first sound channel as well.)

- Does the sprite have the Trails feature enabled in the Score window? A sprite with Trails turned on will persist on the Stage even after it has disappeared from the Score.

General performance problems

SYMPTOM: *My movie doesn't look right when it's played back on another system.*

POSSIBILITY:
- Is the playing system's monitor set to the same color depth as the system you used when building your movie? Remember that you can use Lingo to test for the color depth with the property the colorDepth.

SYMPTOM: *Director takes an interminably long time, not just to play my movie, but to respond to my commands—even moving or resizing a window is glacially slow.*

POSSIBILITIES:
- Since the performance limitation applies to the application as a whole (and not just to playback), it's likely that your system's RAM is overburdened. Check your memory use. Are too many other applications open?

- Perhaps Director's portion of the system RAM is too small. On the Macintosh, you can reallocate RAM by opening the Director application's Info window (click the Director icon in the Finder and then choose Get Info from the File menu) and typing a new value in the Preferred Size field of the Memory Requirements area.

- Maybe the sluggishness is caused by Director's attempt to read all cast members into memory at once. Check the Cast Properties window (under the Modify menu) to see when cast members are loaded. If the Preload option is currently set to After Frame One or Before Frame One, try changing the setting to When Needed.

Script-centered problems

SYMPTOM: *My script seems to be ignored by Director. It's not executed at all.*

POSSIBILITIES:
- Did you mistakenly enter the script in the Text or Field window rather than the Script window? They do look similar.

- Did you comment out your script? Remember that Director ignores any lines in the Script window that are preceded by two dashes (--).

- If it's a frame behavior, is it placed in the correct Score cell?

- Does the script contain handlers intended for execution when a low-level event occurs, such as startMovie? If so, the script should be designated a movie script, not a behavior script. You can check (and change) the status in the script's Properties dialog box.

- Is the script located at a point in the messaging hierarchy where the relevant event is not passed?

- If the event message should be passed to this script but isn't, make sure that the scripts preceding it in the hierarchy are using the pass command.

SYMPTOM: *When I try to execute a script, I get a message similar to this one:*

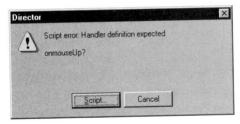

POSSIBILITIES:
- Check your spelling of the handler name. Perhaps it's incorrect.

- If the spelling is correct, perhaps the called handler is inaccessible. Check to see that it's been placed in a movie script rather than a behavior script.

- If the text the message says is incorrect is something you thought was official Lingo, check the online Help search engine to find the Lingo definition. If you can't find it, perhaps it's Lingo that your version of Director no longer supports.

SYMPTOM: *When I try to execute a script, I get this message:*

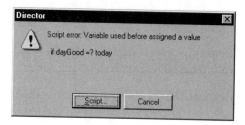

POSSIBILITIES: • If the variable in question is a local variable, it must be initialized
before it can be used. Initialize variables by setting them to a value—
even if that value is null (as in myVariable = 0).

• If the variable is a global one, it must be declared as a global before it
is used. For example:

```
on exitFrame
  global myVariable
    if myVariable = 3 then beep
    else go to the frame
    end if
end
```

Export-related problems

SYMPTOM: *My projector won't run.*

POSSIBILITIES: • Are you trying to run the projector on an inappropriate system? Take
note: Pre-Power PC Macintoshes and pre-Windows 95 or pre-
Pentium II processors are not officially supported by Director 7.

• Perhaps the file itself is bad (incorrectly copied or saved on faulty
media). Try creating another projector from the source movies with
the same settings.

SYMPTOM: *Sounds and/or digital video cast members are missing from my projector.*

POSSIBILITY: • Those cast members were probably linked to external files. Did you
include those files in the same folder as the projector?

SYMPTOM: *My projector application quits unexpectedly when running.*

POSSIBILITY: • Go back to the Score of the movie from which your projector was created. Look at the very end. Is there a control on any level to return the playback head elsewhere or to keep it looping? A Director movie will simply stop when the playback head runs out of frames to process, but a projector will quit.

SYMPTOM: *My projector seems to run more slowly than the original movie.*

POSSIBILITIES: • Are you comparing the performance of both on the same system?

     • On the Macintosh, try resetting the memory allocation for the projector. When Director creates the projector, it allocates the estimated minimum RAM required to run, but you're allowed to second-guess it. From the Finder, click to select the icon for the projector and then choose Get Info from the File menu.

SYMPTOM: *The cursor, evident in the source movie, disappears in the projector file made from the movie.*

POSSIBILITY: • Cursors sometime disappear in projector files when the files are played on monitors set to a greater color depth than the bulk of the movie—for example, a movie made with 8-bit color will play back in 8-bit color on a monitor set to 16-bit color, but the cursor may not appear. The solution is to reset the monitor to the lower screen depth. You might also be able to keep the problem from occurring in the process of creating the projector; select the Reset Monitor's Color Depth to Match Movie's option (Macintosh only) in the Create Projector dialog box.

Cross-platform problems

SYMPTOM: *My files work fine on the Macintosh, but not when I port them to the Windows platform.*

POSSIBILITIES: • Did you use the eight-dot-three naming convention for Windows? Names should be no longer than eight letters, followed by a period and the extension (a three-letter code that identifies the file type).

In the case of Director movies, the extension should be .dir, as in Myfile.dir. Windows 95 allows longer file names, but you'll minimize hassles by sticking with the eight-dot-three protocol. For maximum compatibility, use the same name (extension and all) on the MacOS side as well.

- Is Director looking for the files in the correct location? Maybe it's looking for resources based on the path name, but that path name is no longer valid on the new platform. You can check the path name by entering put the moviePath in the Message window.

SYMPTOM: *The monitor displays strange colors when the movie is played on a new platform.*

POSSIBILITIES:
- Are you using the default system palette? The palettes differ between platforms, so to be displayed correctly on the new platform, the movie may be switching the active palette. This would affect the display of the desktop on the new platform.

- Does the new platform have the required display capabilities? If a movie contains 32-bit color and it's played back on a system capable of only 8-bit color, the display will probably be unacceptable. Higher bit-depth art (such as 16- and 32-bit cast members) could choke the less capable system, causing it to freeze or crash.

SYMPTOM: *My digital video cast members don't appear.*

POSSIBILITY:
- If you're going from MacOS to Windows, do you have QuickTime for Windows installed on the Windows system? It's needed for playback. Windows supports both the QuickTime and AVI standard (and many machines also have MPEG cards), so you'll need to be straight on the type of digital video used. The MacOS does not support the AVI standard, however.

POINTS TO REMEMBER

As always, we'll wrap up with some key concepts to keep in mind:

- The **Message window** should be your first stop when you're trying to understand just what Lingo code is doing. When the **Trace option** is enabled, it provides behind-the-scenes annotation of how scripts are interpreted and executed.

- The **Memory Inspector** tells you how your RAM is being allocated and gives you an idea of how to use that RAM more efficiently.

- The **Watcher window** tells you the values of your globals, lists, and expressions and allows you to change those values.

- The **Script window** has several tools that are useful for debugging, including the Toggle Breakpoint button, the Watch Expression button, and the Recompile button.

- The **Debugger window** assists you in determining where the problem is in your scripting. The Debugger has three sections: the Handler History pane, the Variable pane, and the Script pane.

- When **troubleshooting**, take the time to consider simple causes of problems before you assume more complex ones. Examine your assumptions as well as the problem; sometimes the solution is born when you accurately define what's going wrong.

Universal Import:
Conquering with coolness

IF THERE'S ONE THING MACROMEDIA HAS LEARNED FROM PREVIOUS releases of Director, it's this: New features matter only if multi-media professionals start putting them to use. So how do you motivate veteran programmers to climb back up the learning curve? By commissioning some of the best of them to show off their programming chops—and show off Director's new features at the same time. Here's a look behind the scenes at a Director 7 demo program that's definitely not dull.

PROJECT BACKGROUND

Before a new version of Director is released to the public, it's thrown to the wolves: a volunteer pack of professionals who test, use, and evaluate the proto-product while it's in the beta (pre-release) stage. Members of this "beta list" group don't get paid (unless you count a free T-shirt), but they do get the satisfaction of helping to shape the next generation of Director, and they often get a head start on familiarity with the new features.

So it's no surprise that as the release date approached, Macromedia product manager Kevin Ellis turned to the beta list members at 415 Productions to put their newfound knowledge to the test. Karl Ackermann, a senior programmer at the San Francisco–based production company, was charged with coding a series of movies showcasing the new capabilities of Director 7, for eventual distribution as informational and inspirational examples. (You can find them online at *www.macromedia.com/software/director/productinfo/newfeatures*.)

One of these movies is intended to demonstrate what Macromedia is calling Director 7's Universal Import feature: the ability to import and integrate 40 different multimedia file formats. In fact, not only are an unprecedented number of media types now recognized, but Director 7 is exceptionally sophisticated when it comes to managing them: Animated GIFs (a mainstay of Web graphics) can be imported, linked to (as external cast members) and modified. Apple Computer's QuickTime VR not only integrates seamlessly but all of its 3D-savvy capabilities (panning, tilting) are also supported. And if you want Flash assets to behave like conventional graphic cast members? No problem. While not exactly universal, Director 7's media management skills are indisputably impressive.

THE METHODS

Import features may be *conceptually* impressive, but they're all but impossible to truly demonstrate via a single online movie—how do you show importation when you have no idea what types of files reside on the end user's hard drive? Ackermann and his 415 compatriots opted to show the results of the process rather than the process itself: a "happy landscape" of a multitude of media types, all coexisting nicely. To fulfill this concept, they took the following tacks:

1. *A perpetual pan*. Although true QuickTime VR isn't featured in the movie (that would significantly limit its audience), a similar sense of environmental exploration is evoked by having the end user pan back and forth in a parade of objects that seems much bigger than the Stage itself. Unlike the continuous-loop animation of the Levi's screensaver in Project Profile 2, this one lets the user reverse direction at will.

2. *Scripted sprite animations*. To underscore the connection between raw media types and their manifestations onscreen, 415 opted to populate the landscape with an array of floating desktop icons. Click on each, and it will become an example of a specific media type: The sound file icon becomes an actual sound, and so forth.

3. *Relative motion control*. Those fun sprite animations represent motion within motion: They need to unfold while the sprites themselves are zooming left or right on the stage, all at a rate consistent with the rest. What's more, that rate needs to be modified depending on whether the object is in the foreground (and therefore subjectively moving faster) or on the background (moving more slowly). It's a tall order made easier with the use of behaviors.

Preparing the landscape

The landscape begins with a greensward: a single 1200-pixel-wide cast member representing the earth and horizon line. Since the movie's stage is only 480 pixels wide, this color field provides the outside-the-box effect needed for seamless panning. By moving this image (and all images associated with it) back and forth within the Stage, the illusion of viewer motion is created.

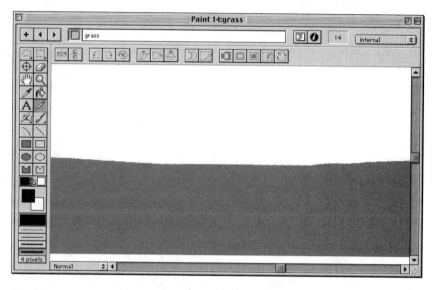

To add more visual interest to the flat plain, six more cast members provide the sprinking of individual grass blades. Other landscaping devices (clumps of trees, boulders, and distant hills) are animated sprites that make their first appearance as icons. It takes a lot of clicking to reveal the full details of the scene.

Planning the panning behavior

To move the scene in either direction, the movie follows the lead of the cursor, moving in a speed directly proportional to its distance from the center. Place the cursor in the middle and panning stops; shoot it over to either edge and it zooms. How is this effect achieved? By a behavior script that performs the following steps:

1. It determines the exact center of the Stage and performs the necessary cursor tracking calculations to determine current position relative to that center.

2. It calculates a "speed factor"—a determination of exactly how fast panning should be, given current cursor position.

3. It tracks (and changes) the horizontal location of each sprite on the Stage. Vertical locations don't matter for the purposes of this script, as all movement is side-to-side only.

4. All sprites are also assigned a *virtual Z* value: the imaginary-yet-perceived distance of the item from the viewer. The hills in the distance, for instance, have a higher *Z* value than the snoozing dog in the foreground. For the sake of simplicity, these are bundled into layer groups, roughly corresponding to foreground, middle ground, distance, and far horizon.

5. The horizontal motion of sprites (the rewriting of the **locH** value) is calculated at speeds proportional to the layer group of each. The higher the virtual Z, the less apparent motion.

6. In order to pull this off, a *master sprite* is also called for: the reference point that controls the left or right motion of the pan. Once it reaches either edge, the motion stops. This is done by creating the property **pMaster** and assigning it (in this case) to the standing dog. Without a master sprite, the panning could continue long past the point of any items still appearing on the Stage.

How are these daunting tasks carried out? With a behavior called PANNING, modified by Ackermann from the original code of Chris Xiques. Here's a closer look at some of its problem-solving methodologies.

The cursor speed list

The relation of cursor location to panning speed is determined by a simple list that gets read into RAM as part of the method **mSetParams** and called with the behavior property **pSpeedFactors**:

```
  set pSpeedFactors=¬
[¬
0:6,¬
40:4,¬
80:3,¬
120:2,¬
160:2,¬
200:1,¬
```

```
240:0,¬
280:0,¬
320:-1,¬
360:-2,¬
400:-2,¬
440:-3,¬
480:-4,¬
2000:-6¬
```

Note how the negative numbers reflect exactly the positive numbers, providing for both left and right movement. These values are set into motion with the object script called **pan**:

```
on pan me
  set ix = findPosNear(pSpeedFactors, the mouseH)
  set curDX=getAt(pSpeedFactors, ix)

  if the left of sprite pMaster <= pMaxLeft AND curDX<0 ¬
then exit
  if the right of sprite pMaster >= pMaxRight AND curDX>0 ¬
then exit

  set the X of mySelf = float(the X of mySelf) + ¬
((curDX*pScrollSpeed)/the Z of mySelf)
  set the locH of sprite mySprite = the X of mySelf
end
```

This use of the **findPosNear** function is what keeps the script from bogging down in a mass of computations. Unlike **findPos** (which performs an exact match), this function searches for the closest match between a given value and a value in a list; if you give it 47 and the list contains only 40, that's the number it will retrieve—or more correctly, it will retrieve the list position of that number.

The PANNING behavior uses a set list for another task: the grouping of layers that pan at the same speed (the **pLayers** property). You can check it out for yourself in the movie's Script window.

Associating icons with animations

Take a look at the movie before running it: You'll notice that all the sprites appear in their post-click visual form; that is, they look the way they'll look after the end user has clicked on them. Now start the movie: You'll see the same sprites transformed into simple icon images. What happened?

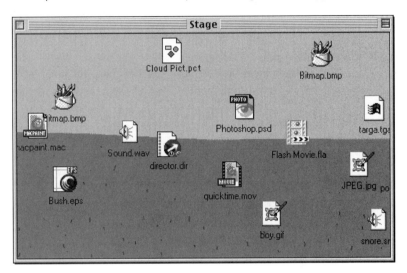

Some basic behavior scripting has happened, that's what. In the custom methods portion of the behavior script, each sprite is associated with both its original cast member (**mShowMediaMember**) and another cast member, that of the corresponding media type icon in cast slots 18 though 39 (**mShowIcon**). The substitution is a sprite-by-sprite event, and which sprites are in which state is tracked by a custom property, dubbed **pState**. Here's the commented code:

```
on mMakeIcon me
   pState = #icon -- Remember that you're in icon mode
   mShowIcon me    -- Display the icon cast member
   mStopSound me   -- If you're playing a sound, stop it
end

on mMakeMediaMember me
   --
   pState = #mediamember -- Remember that you're in media type mode
   mShowMediaMember me    -- Display the media type cast member
   mPlaySound me          -- Play the appropriate sound loop (if any)
end
```

```
on mShowIcon me
  -- Replace the current cast member with the icon member
  set the member of sprite the currentSpriteNum to pIconMember
end
```

```
on mShowMediaMember me
  -- Replace the curent cast member with the media type member
  set the member of sprite the currentSpriteNum to pMediaMember
end
```

Since many of the cast members are inherently animated (GIF89s, Director movies, etc.), their action takes place on the stage as soon as each sprite's **pState** value is updated to **mShowMediaMember**. That's a whole lot of action going on, courtesy of two behavior scripts. A pretty eloquent example of the power of behaviors, don't you think?

Notes for exploration

Because of its reliance on lists and object scripts, the Universal Import movie can withstand substantial tinkering and still remain playable. Here are a few suggestions for further fun with the open source file:

1. Try rearranging the sprites on the Stage before you start the movie: Stick a tree in the sky or the dog on the mountain top. What happens to them relative to each other, both horizontally and vertically?

2. Change the **pMaster** property to the cast number of another sprite. What happens then?

3. Transfer sprites from one depth-of-field layer to another by physically moving them up or down the channel hierarchy in the Score; you'll find they're clustered in convenient groupings. What happens when you move something from the extreme background to the foreground? Or vice versa?

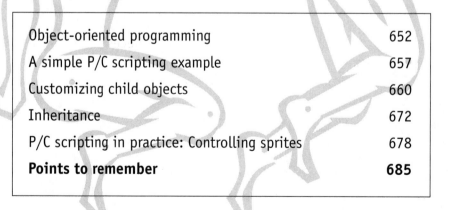

CHAPTER 18

PARENT/CHILD LINGO

5th. that can be seen or touched
material thing

ALTHOUGH MACROMEDIA HAS INTEGRATED <u>OBJECT-ORIENTED PROGRAMMING</u>
throughout Director, most of the OOP has been behind the scenes
and invisible to you. Starting with this chapter, you can use
parent/child Lingo to take control and begin creating objects
yourself. The parent/child approach lets you establish a general
framework for performance in one Lingo script and then create
limitless permutations and variations with ease. There are just a
few new concepts at the core of this approach, but it's well
worth mastering them to gain a new realm of possibilities.

In this chapter, we'll tackle those core concepts and then
apply them to practical contexts. We'll leverage the principles
still further with the introduction of ancestors and inheritance,
and finally we'll use list Lingo to put all the pieces into a
manageable whole.

OBJECT-ORIENTED PROGRAMMING

functions = dated)

The Lingo we've used up to this point is powerful and, placed in an historical perspective, very sophisticated. The use of handlers and functions in Lingo makes it a **structured** language. Essentially, structured languages allow you to include some specific functionality in your code by writing handlers (or buying them) to perform the action. You can then call the handlers from anywhere in your movie. If you need the same functionality in another movie, you can copy those handlers and place them in your new movie. Structured programming has given you the ability to write extremely complex applications productively. And that's what it's all about—being able to create the applications you want in a timely manner.

As programs grew ever more sophisticated and complex, even structured programming wasn't providing the basis for the productivity that was needed. So **object-oriented programming**, or **OOP**, was born. Whereas structured programming allows you to localize a functionality into a handler (other programming languages call them functions, procedures, or subroutines), object-oriented programming allows you to encapsulate both instructions (handlers) and data into an **object**.

This object-oriented programming may at first sound intimidating. But really very few new concepts are involved. As you do in structured programming, in OOP you still use variables, write handlers, and test or set properties. The difference is that you can now combine these in new ways to create objects, and these objects have their own functions and their own properties. That's right; not only can you use Director's properties, but you can also define your own.

OOP in action

Here's another reason not to be intimidated—you've already been using OOP. Way back in Chapter 4, we used a behavior from the Library Palette called Turn Towards Mouse. We applied that behavior to only one sprite, but we could just as easily apply it to more than one. Let's give this a try and then see what we learn from the experience.

1. Open a new movie in Director.

2. *In the Paint window, create two objects. They can be any shape and color you want; just make sure that you'll be able to tell if they rotate (a solid circle, for example, won't do).*

3. *Place the two shapes in channels 1 and 2 of frame 1.*

4. *From the Library Palette, find the Turn Towards Mouse behavior (it's in the Interactive subcategory of Animation). Drag it onto the sprite in channel 1.*

If you don't find the Turn Towards Mouse behavior in your version of the Library Palette, don't dispair. Some Director packages don't include all behaviors, but you can use a version of this one included with the source files for this book. See the "Getting the Behavior" section, following the end of this section, for directions.

5. *In the Parameters dialog box that appears, set the Turn parameters to Towards the Mouse and Always. Then click OK.*

Notice that the Turn Towards Mouse behavior appears in the Cast.

6. *Drag the Turn Towards Mouse behavior from the Library Palette to the sprite in channel 2. Set the Turn parameters to Away from Mouse and While the Mouse Is Down. Set the Otherwise parameter to Remain in the New Position.*

7. *Turn on looping (or add a looping behavior in the behavior channel of frame 1), and then run the movie. Move the mouse around, with the mouse button up and with it down.*

Both sprites rotate as you move the mouse (one rotates only with the mouse button down). Now look at the Cast again. There's only one Turn Towards Mouse behavior, right? What you see is a single script (the behavior) with the ability to provide functionality for two different sprites and to do it in a different manner for each sprite.

Behaviors and the parent/child (P/C) objects are implemented in different ways, but the same principles apply to both. One script, the behavior, represents raw capability. It doesn't create the entity, but it describes how a theoretical entity should behave. That's the **parent** script. From the parent script, with some help from you or Director, **child objects** are created. When you generate these child objects, they reside entirely in Director's RAM, live as long as you want them to, and do whatever you require of them, based on the rules you create in the parent script. You build their personalities by creating them with a special set of rules for responding to input, which you define in the parent script. In the experiment we just programmed, the Turn Towards Mouse behavior is the parent script. When needed, a separate instance of the behavior is created for each sprite. Each instance has its own parameters, which turn out to be the object's **properties**.

The main difference between behavior (parent) objects and child objects is that behaviors are attached to sprites and automatically spring to life (Director does it) when the Score requires them. Child objects, on the other hand, are created when you, the programmer, decide to create them. If you want to associate a child object with a sprite, you need to define that association explicitly.

Getting the behavior

This section is applicable only if you were unable to find the required behavior in the Library Palette.

Director 7 is available in a number of flavors (or packages): upgrades (full or standalone), an educational version, and a studio version. The studio version and the full upgrade version include a number of extra elements, including Fireworks (for image editing), Peak LE (Macintosh) or SoundForge XP (Windows) for sound editing, and a full compliment of behaviors in the Library Palette. The standalone upgrade and educational versions contain only a limited set of Lingo behaviors in the Library Palette, and they don't include the Turn Towards Mouse behavior. To access and use that behavior, and follow along with the exercise, you can perform the following steps:

1. *Save your current movie.*

2. *From the File menu, choose Open to open the movie FollowTheMouse.dir on the Demystified CD-ROM.*

3. *In the Cast, find the Turn Towards Mouse behavior (it should be in Cast slot 4) and select it.*

4. *From the Edit menu, select Copy.*

5. *Reopen the movie you were working on.*

6. *Select an unused cast member slot in the Cast window. From the Edit menu, select Paste.*

The behavior can now be used in your movie. When instructed to place the behavior, instead of dragging it from the Library Palette, you can drag the cast member from the Cast to the specified location.

Nice, but why?

To see how child objects are useful, let's take a look at a couple of real-world examples. First, imagine that you are building a word processor. Any word processor worth its salt will let you edit multiple documents simultaneously. Do you launch a complete new word-processing application for each document? Not if you have objects, you don't.

Consider the properties that are inherent to the word processor, regardless of the document being edited:

- The size of the desktop

- The toolbars displayed and the elements on those toolbars

- The tools available, such as spell-check or a thesaurus

Now consider the properties of each document—properties that are unique to the document and that can be changed without affecting the properties of another document that is also open:

- The contents of the document

- The current font and style

- The cursor location

- The size of the document in the document window

- Any text that may be selected

There are a lot more properties, but you get the idea. The point is that when a new document is opened, the word processor launches a new child process to handle that document. The main application is the word processor. The parent script contains all the handlers needed to deal with any document. And each child object runs by the rules of the parent script but also encapsulates the data and values of properties individual to the particular document. You can create as many child processes as you want, limited only by the resources of the computer on which the program is being run.

Here's another example. Assume you have a program that can be used simultaneously by a number of people. To implement your Back button, your program needs to keep for each user a list that details where that user has been in the program. When the user moves to a new location, the preceding location is placed at the end of the list. If the user clicks the Back button, the last element of the list is used to navigate to that location, and then that element is removed from the list. Because you don't know how many users your program will have to accommodate, you write a parent script with all of the functions for creating and handling a list and then create a child object for each user. Each user gets a separate list that is independent of the other lists in existence, yet each list has access to the functionality necessary to maintain it. Again, your program can have a great number of users and lists, limited only by the operating system resources.

The list discussed above is called a **stack** by programmers. The usual analogy for describing a stack is that it's like a stack of plates. The last plate added to the stack is the first one taken off. Stacks are so commonly used that many programming languages include commands just for dealing with them. These terms are usually **push** and **pop**—you push an element onto the stack and pop an element off.

One more example, and then I promise we'll get into some actual creation. This time, imagine you are creating a shoot-em-up game. As the game progresses and the skill level increases, you place more and more spaceships on the screen. You can place all the functionality of the spaceships into a parent script while still allowing each ship to behave differently. Each ship has its own point value, shield strength, current position, and so on. The ship objects all can behave differently, as determined by the unique values of their individual properties, but each ship has the same set of parent properties, and the handlers defined by the parent script use those values to determine the ship's actions. Again, you can have a multitude of spaceships, limited only by the system's resources.

Why bother with P/C scripting? Because a parent can have many children, and a parent script can sketch out general principles while each child's properties provide the specifics. Parenthood isn't cloning; there's room for variations and adaptation, and that means you can create virtually limitless permutations from a single source. With this next Lingo leap on the learning curve, you'll be learning the gene therapy of the Director universe.

> Lingo isn't the only language that lets you do this kind of programming. If you're proficient in Java or C++, you may already be familiar with many of the concepts in this chapter, albeit under different names: *class* instead of parent, *instance* instead of child object, *instance variable* (or *member variable*) instead of property variable, *method* instead of handler, and *super class* (or *base class*) rather than ancestor script. Conversely, if you decide in the future to tackle those languages, you're getting a head start here; strip away the syntax differences, and you're dealing with essentially the same principles.

A SIMPLE P/C SCRIPTING EXAMPLE

P/C really is a simple concept. And to prove it, let's do some parent/child scripting. We're going to omit some common elements in this first example, but we'll add them later.

1. Create a new Director movie.

Since we're not actually going to be playing the movie, the Stage size or color doesn't matter.

2. Open a Script window and enter these two handlers:

```
on getAround
  put "I get around using feet."
end getAround
```

```
on getCovering
  put "I'm covered with fur."
end getCovering
```

3. Name this script Animal.

Keep an eye on your keystrokes. With P/C scripts, you're making up the rules as well as implementing them, and that means Director doesn't always have the standard recourse of dialog boxes to warn you that it doesn't understand what's supposed to be happening. You'll be doing a lot of typing in this chapter (both in the Script window and in the Message window), so try to be accurate and consistent, paying special attention to quotation marks and spacing.

4. In the Properties dialog box for the script, use the pull-down menu to change the script type to Parent. ← *movie script window*

CHOOSING YOUR PARENTS: When writing parent scripts, don't forget to designate them as such by selecting the Parent type in the Properties dialog box.

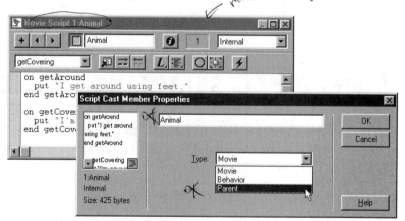

Congratulations! You've just created a parent script that consists of two handlers. Now it's time to use that parent script to create child objects. To create a child object, you use the new function. You assign the value returned by new to a variable (or a list). This variable provides access to the child object when you need it. The primary syntax for creating child objects is as follows:

variable = new (script *"Parent Script"*)

5. Open the Message window and enter the following:

```
dog = new (script "Animal")
cat = new (script "Animal")
```

Now two child objects are born, both from the same parent script, both with the same capabilities, and both (unfortunately) with the same properties (none). You've created these objects in the dry dock of the Message window, but these new commands could just as easily be placed in any Lingo location. Now let's see if we can get the child objects to do something.

6. In the Message window, enter the following:

```
getAround dog
getCovering dog
```

The object performs as instructed:

IT'S A DOG'S LIFE:
Calling a handler with the object variable as a parameter tells Director to execute that handler.

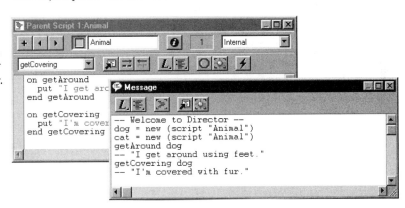

It's important that you understand that the handler executed is *not* the handler in the script named Animal. It contains exactly the same code, but it's actually an *instance* of that script. You can, in fact, add handlers to the parent script while the program is running. Even though the parent script has changed, existing child objects will not be affected since they reside completely in RAM.

7. In the Message window, enter:

```
getAround cat
```

Since cat has the same parent, and since we made no allowances for object variations, the result from the cat object is the same as for the dog object:

```
-- "I get around using feet."
```

CUSTOMIZING CHILD OBJECTS

Our exercise has produced a bona fide parent script and two child objects, but we're still some distance from illuminating all the practical possibilities. We could create dozens of objects from our parent, but they'd all still have the same personality. How can we make each one truly unique?

Adding custom properties

The answer is to declare **custom properties** and allow each child object to have its own value for these properties. If we can identify the points of individuality in the parent script, we can supply the necessary customizing information with each child object.

To illustrate this, let's imagine that we are building a variation on the animal-vegetable-mineral game. Users can enter an item (animal, vegetable, or mineral) and some information about it. Other users can try to guess what the item is. As each item is specified, we want to create an object that stores the information and provides us with a means of retrieving that information in a useful format. We don't intend to create the whole game, just the parent scripts necessary to implement the child objects.

First we need to determine the properties that identify each parent. For example, with Animal, we already have its covering and its means of locomotion. To that we can add maybe a name and a color. As each child object is created, the values for these properties will be passed in as arguments of the new function. We need to create a parent script that has the ability to accept them.

So far, we have worked with global variables and local variables. Global variables are available to any handler and can persist as long as the application is running. Local variables are available only for the handler in which they are defined and persist only as long as that handler is running. What we need is a variable that belongs to a child object but is accessible from outside the object as long as that object exists: a **property variable**. To declare a property variable, you use the `property` keyword and declare the variables at the start of a parent script.

1. *Add the following line to the* Animal *parent script. Be sure to insert it at the top of the script,* outside of any handler.

```
property theName, theColor, covering, movement
```
← *custom properties*

What's going on in this declaration? It's establishing a template for individuality. The Lingo declares four custom properties (theName, theColor, covering, and movement), which means that when a child object is birthed from this script, the script will keep track of values attached to those properties. The actual nature of the properties is determined by what happens to those values (in the custom handlers elsewhere in the script), so think of custom properties as sort of "personalized variables" for child objects.

Now that we have the property variables declared, we need to assign to them some values. This is generally done in an on new handler in the parent script. Although we didn't include one in our previous parent script example, every parent script should have an on new handler. The on new handler is called whenever a new child object is being created and is the logical spot for object initialization. The declaration contains an argument for each of the property values being passed in, plus a special argument that is always the first argument. This argument, which by custom is called me, is used to refer to the current object. You don't supply a value for me; Director does that for you when the child object is created.

2. *Add the following* on new *handler after the property declaration:*

```
on new me, myName, myColor, myCovering, myMovement
  --assign values to properties
  me.theName = myName
  me.theColor = myColor
  me.covering = myCovering
  me.movement = myMovement
  return me  -- return the identifier for this object
end
```
concludes the creation of the object

The instructions placed in the on new handler are carried out exactly once, when the child object is created. Any other handlers can be executed at any time. The statement return me concludes the creation of the object. This return command ensures that the object variable we set when we create the child object contains a reference to the new object. The me is a shorthand way of designating the object of invocation. Remember me is the name we all share, no matter what our official names happen to be.

The concept of **me** is actually quite useful. It's a keyword that allows you to refer to a child object without actually naming it—which is handy when you plan on applying the script to any number of instances. It's like referring to an unborn child as Junior; you can designate the nursery as "Junior's Room" and even build up Junior's wardrobe, long before the kid arrives. And if you have a large family, all of your children may have taken turns being Junior.

In truth, **me** isn't official Lingo, even though it's in the Lingo Dictionary. It's just the name of the local variable that's commonly used to store the identity. You could just as easily use **it** (or **Junior**), but **me** is recognized by most Lingo programmers as a special keyword.

What might strike you as a bit confusing in the handler is the part about me.theName = myName and so forth. That's simply a way of letting us set the custom properties at the moment of birth. By adding variables (arguments) on the new line and then matching those variables to properties, we're telling Lingo to treat arguments that follow new in the birth script as property values. Strictly speaking, the me. part of the assignment statement is not required, and you will see that some other people's code does not contain it. There are times, however, as we'll see when we get into parents of parents, when me. is required. Because it emphasizes that the variables are really properties, we will continue to use this syntax.

Now let's add some handlers to our parent script so the child objects can perform some function. We already have two handlers for Animal, but we need to change those also.

3. ***In the Animal script, delete the*** getAround ***and*** getCovering ***handlers and then add the following four handlers:***

```
on getAround me
  put "I move around with" && me.movement & "."
end

on getCovering me
  put "I'm covered with" && me.covering & "."
end
```

```
on getName me
  put "I am a" && me.theName & "."
end

on getColor me
  put "The color of this" && me.theName &&
  "is" && me.theColor & "."
end
```

concatenate with a space in front

ignore it and continue typing

All these handlers use the put command to display information in the Message window, but that's just for demonstration purposes. They could just as easily perform other tasks such as managing lists or controlling sprites. In that respect, they aren't any different from the custom handlers we create outside of parent scripts.

That's it for now for the Animal parent script. Now let's return to the Message window to create some child objects and see whether we can run them through their paces. Remember that our arguments for new, in order, are name, color, covering, and movement.

4. In the Message window, enter the following lines:

```
ch1 = new(script "Animal", "dog", ¬
"brown", "fur", "paws")
ch2 = new(script "Animal", "Cardinal", ¬
"red", "feathers", "wings")
```

Remember that even though we show lines entered in the Message window as using the continuation symbol, you can't really do that—and you don't need to. Unlike in the Script Editor window, in the Message window you can just let long lines wrap. When you press Enter (Windows) or Return (Macintosh), Director will correctly interpret the wrapped line.

Now we have two child objects: ch1 and ch2. If we were creating these child objects in a real program, we would probably be maintaining a list of the objects. That way we could add or remove references to the objects as needed without losing track of them. For our demonstration, we can probably keep track without a list. Let's see if we really do have two objects with distinct properties but the same functionality.

5. In the Message window, enter the following lines:

```
ch1.getName()
ch2.getName()
ch1.getColor()
ch2.getColor()
```

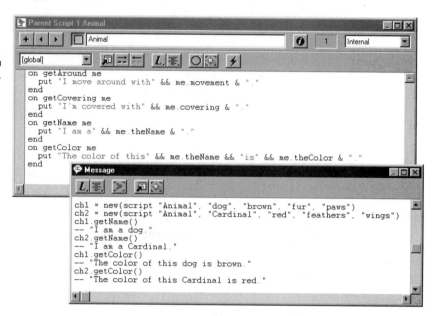

Everything is working just as it should be. You can play with your child objects by calling their other handlers. The results should continue to show the individuality of the two objects.

Here again, I want to point out variations you may see if you look at P/C code that others have written. I like the syntax used in step 5 because it emphasizes the object and property nature of what is going on. You might, however, see the same statements written in these equivalent forms:

```
ch1.getName()
getName ch1
getName(ch1)
```

The following statement will not work because it lacks parentheses, and Director will try to find a property variable rather than a handler:

```
ch1.getName
```

Another parent

That takes care of the Animal parent script (for now). That same parent script doesn't exactly fit our concept of vegetables. After all, most carrots don't get around much. So we can use a second parent script to create vegetable objects. This time we will use three properties: name, color, and edible part.

1. **Select an empty slot in the Cast and open the Script window.**

2. **Enter the following declarations and handlers:**

```
property theName, theColor, part

on new me, myName, myColor, myPart
  -- assign values to properties
  me.theName = myName
  me.theColor = myColor
  me.part = myPart
  return me  -- return the identifier for this object
end

on getName me
  put "I am a" && me.theName & "."
end

on getColor me
  put "A" && me.theName && "is colored" && ¬
me.theColor & "."
  end

on getPart me
  put "You eat the" && me.part && ¬
  "of this vegetable."
end
```

3. **Close the Script window Then name the script Vegetable.**

4. **Open the Cast Member Properties dialog box for the script and change the script type to Parent.**

5. *Create a Vegetable object by entering the following line in the Message window:*

```
ch3 = new(script "Vegetable", "carrot", "orange", "root")
```

There's nothing new in terms of syntax here, but we have created a new parent type or class. The child object ch3 is of class Vegetable. It has a lot of similarities to Animal objects, including an identical getName handler, but it also has differences. You can access the Vegetable object just as you did the Animal objects.

6. *Enter the following lines in the Message window:*

```
ch3.getName()
ch3.getPart()
```

VEGETABLE HAS CLASS: Although similarities exist, our Vegetable object has a different parent than our Animal objects.

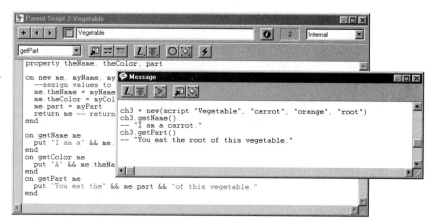

You may have been asking yourself, "When I made those function calls, how did Director know to run the handlers in the correct child object?" We've now made a call to getName for three different objects that include two different parents. How does Director keep things straight? The answer is that our object variable, such as ch3, specifies the correct child object. And the value of the object variable is automatically set from the value passed to the new handler (and returned by it) when the new object is created. We can illustrate this further by trying to make a call to getName without an object identifier:

7. *In the Message window, enter the following line:*

```
getName
```

As you can see, Director doesn't like it and responds with an error message.

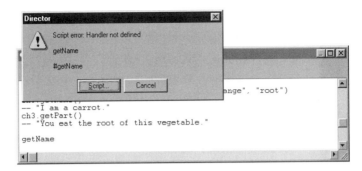

Why does Director complain that the getName handler is not defined rather than complaining about the lack of an object identifier? Because you can have yet another getName handler in your movie—one in a movie script instead of a parent script.

8. *Open a movie script and place in it the following handler:*

```
on getName
  put "I'm not an object."
end
```

9. *Now enter the* getName *call in the Message window.*

The call to getName works fine because Director keeps track for us of just which handler should be getting called. Your other calls, such as to ch3.getName(), will still find the appropriate handler.

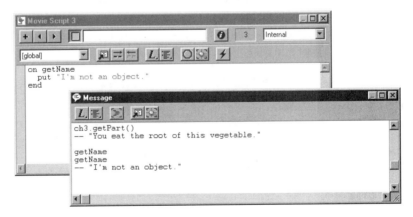

Just because we have so far been accessing an object's handlers only from outside the object doesn't mean that such needs always to be the case. A handler in the object can call another handler in the object or a handler in a movie script.

10. *Change the* on new *handler in the Vegetable parent script by adding the lines shown here in bold:*

```
on new me, myName, myColor, myPart
  -- assign values to properties
  me.theName = myName
  me.theColor = myColor
  me.part = myPart
  -- call the other handlers
  me.getName()
  me.getColor()
  me.getPart()
  return me  -- return the identifier for this object
end
```

11. *Reinitialize the* ch3 *object variable by reentering the following line in the Message window (or you can find where you did it before, place the cursor at the end, and press Enter in Windows or Return on the Macintosh):*

```
ch3 = new(script "Vegetable", "carrot", "orange", "root")
```

We need to perform this reinitialization because, as mentioned earlier, child objects live entirely in RAM. Once the child object has been created, making changes to the parent script has no effect on the child object. Reinitializing the ch3 object variable creates a new child object, even though the object variable was used before. As the new child object is created, the new handler is executed, including the three handler calls we just added.

CALLING ALL HANDLERS: One handler in an object can call other handlers. The called handlers can be internal to the object or in a movie script, but Director searches through the object's internal handlers first.

Accessing properties

Obviously, we can use an object's properties from within the object, since each of the put commands we wrote into the handlers does just that. But we can also get at them, both for testing and setting, from outside of the object. The syntax is the same as for other properties we have used. Here's the dot-syntax version:

```
objectVariable.property = someValue
```

And here are the older styles:

```
the property of objectVariable = someValue
set the property of objectVariable = someValue
set the property of objectVariable to someValue
```

We're dealing with properties here, not handlers, so the use of parentheses would be incorrect and would produce an error message from Director.

The following example demonstrates that we can set and retrieve the theName property's value. We also can use the getName function to verify that the object knows that its property has changed.

1. **In the Message window, enter the following lines:**

```
ch3.theName = "weed"      → sets the property of the object
put ch3.theName           → equivalent of ch3.theName
getName ch3
```

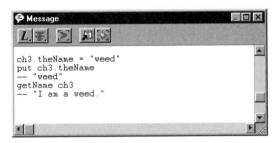

```
ch3.theName = "weed"
put ch3.theName
-- "weed"
getName ch3
-- "I am a weed."
```

2. **Here's how it's done in the older style. In the Message window, enter the following lines:**

```
the theColor of ch3 = "green"
put the theColor of ch3
set the part of ch3 to "nothing"
getPart ch3
```

Don't do it!

Accessing an object's properties directly is a no-no, except for debugging purposes.

Big caveat! I seriously debated whether or not to even mention in this chapter the ability to access a child's properties from outside the child. I decided in favor of doing so partially because it is useful for demonstrating that values are being set, but mostly because you may find it useful when you are debugging your programs. In real life, you should not write programs that access a child object's properties directly.

One of the main rules of object-oriented program design is *information hiding*. The principle of information hiding is that if you want to access an object's properties, you must ask the object to retrieve the information for you or to make the changes for you. In other words, you should include a handler in the object that will perform the necessary tasks. The commands that make the request should know nothing about the internal workings of the object; otherwise, much of the reliability and extendability of objects are lost. In OOP, this situation is called having a *public interface* and *private handlers*. All exchanges with a child object should take place through the public interface. The internal workings of the object, the private handlers, should not be accessed directly. That allows your program to modify the private elements as needed, without breaking things in the program.

Here is an example. In your stock portfolio manager program, suppose you have a StockValue property (which is private) and a public interface handler named getNetStockValue:

```
on getNetStockValue me
  return me.StockValue
end
```

The value returned by getNetStockValue is used by the accounting side of the software to figure taxes. Suddenly, the IRS decides to use a new formula for determining a stock's value. (The old way was too easy to understand.) You, the programmer, go in and make some modifications to the private handler:

```
on getNetStockValue me
  return calcValue(me.StockValue)
end
```

Any parts of your program that use the stock's value will continue working exactly the same as before, except they will receive the corrected value. They don't even need to know that modifications have been made. If your program had been accessing the StockValue property directly, it would be getting the wrong information or it would need to perform the revised calculations everywhere StockValue was used.

Disposing of child objects

Once created, a child object will hang around in Director's RAM until all references to it are removed, which means that you have the duty of consigning your creations to oblivion. In our previous examples, we included only one reference to each child object—to ch3, for example. You can remove the ch3 object by changing the value of ch3, but the best way to remove it is to set the variable to VOID:

```
ch3 = VOID
```

Because we use only the single reference, that single line would remove the ch3 child object. If you include more than the one reference in your code, you need to make sure that you cover them all. For example, if you're keeping track of your objects in a list you will need to delete the list element that references the object. Here's an example:

```
box = new(script "Container")
mybox = box
box = VOID
mybox.getSize()  --works fine
box.getSize() -- produces an error
-- because box doesn't reference an object
mybox = VOID  --now the object is gone
mybox.getSize()  --Error, no object
```

In the overall scheme of things, objects take up little space in a movie's RAM—considering it takes a lot of text (code) to equal even a small graphic. Still, accumulating too many idle objects will have a negative impact on your playback performance. What's worse, some objects can make a royal mess of your code if allowed to linger too long. Since objects stay in memory as long as Director's running, they can be set to work on any movie that happens to open after they're initialized. This is a strength—you can spread objects across several movies—but it's also a liability. If you create an object that moves around the sprite in channel 7 of one movie, unless it disappears when the movie disappears, it's likely to start moving around the sprite in channel 7 in subsequent movies.

INHERITANCE

Using child objects is an excellent way of handling numerous related items. But where OOP really starts paying dividends is when you introduce **inheritance** into the project. In some respects, we already have inheritance: You can say that each child object inherits the properties and handlers of the parent script. But the chain of inheritance can go back still further, to preceding generations.

In Director, inheritance is implemented using ancestor scripts. When a parent script has an ancestor, the properties and handlers of that ancestor are available to the parent and its child objects, plus the ancestor can have an ancestor, and so on. Elements of each ancestor are available to every element below them in the hierarchy (all of their descendants).

Even better, more than one parent script can have the same ancestor script. That means we can group related parents under a common ancestor and place all of the elements common to both in that ancestor. If we need to include another related parent in our program, we can add it easily without having to duplicate all of the functionality that is provided by the ancestors.

Using ancestor scripts

Adding an ancestor to a parent script is a two-part process. First we write the ancestor script and designate it as a parent script. Then we place the ancestor property in a parent script (the descendant, not the ancestor) and assign it to the ancestor script. Let's see how this works:

1. *Open your existing parent script Vegetable. Find and select the two handlers* getName *and* getColor*, and then cut them (Control-X Windows; Command-X Macintosh).*

2. *Use the New Script button (the + button) to create a new script. Paste the two handlers into the new script.*

This script is going to be our ancestor script, and these two handlers will be the handlers it contains.

3. *At the beginning of the script, before (and outside) the handlers, add this property declaration:*

```
property theName, theColor
```

Not only are we placing some of our handlers in the ancestor script, we're also moving some properties there.

4. *Use the Cast Member Properties button to change the script type from Movie to Parent. Then name the script **AllTypes.***

Your ancestor script should look like the one shown here.

ANCESTORS ARE PARENTS:
Ancestor scripts are parent scripts and contain property variables and handlers.

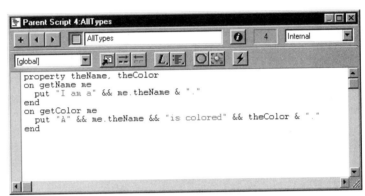

```
property theName, theColor
on getName me
  put "I am a" && me.theName & "."
end
on getColor me
  put "A" && me.theName && "is colored" && theColor & "."
end
```

Although we don't use one here, your ancestor script could also contain a new handler. If you use a new handler, just make sure to also include the line return me.

5. *Return to the Vegetable parent script and change the property declaration to read as follows:*

```
property part, ancestor
```

We have removed the theName and the theColor properties because we now have them in the ancestor script instead. We also added the property ancestor. Now we need to modify the new handler to include a statement that assigns the ancestor script to the ancestor property. The statement uses the new function, and the syntax is the same for assigning ancestors as for creating child objects.

6. *Add the statement setting the ancestor **property to the** new **handler in the Vegetable script, as shown here in bold. It should be the first line in the handler.***

```
on new me, myName, myColor, myPart
  me.ancestor = new(script "AllTypes")
  -- assign values to properties
  me.theName = myName
  me.theColor = myColor
  me.part = myPart
  -- call the other handlers
  me.getName()
  me.getColor()
  me.getPart()
  return me  -- return the identifier for this object
end
```

Although the ancestor assignment need not be the first line of a new handler, there are some conditions that require it to be first in this particular case. Since we moved the theName property to the AllTypes script, our new handler knows nothing about that property until the ancestor is assigned. Trying to access the theName property before the ancestor is set will result in a script error.

> Remember how we said that using the **me.** to prefix a reference to a property is not always optional? Here's an example. When a property is declared in an ancestor script, the **me.** prefix is required. Otherwise, Director will think you are declaring (or accessing) a variable and won't bother to look in the ancestor script for a property.

7. Reinitialize the ch3 **child object or enter the following line in the Message window:**

```
ch3 = new(script "Vegetable", "carrot", "orange", "root")
```

The handler calls in the new handler are executed just as expected. You can also call the handlers and access all of the child object's properties from the Message window.

8. In the Message window, enter the following lines:

```
ch3.getColor()
put ch3.theColor
```

```
Message                                          _ □ ×

ch3 = new(script "Vegetable", "carrot", "orange", "root")
-- "I am a carrot."
-- "A carrot is colored orange."
-- "You eat the root of this vegetable."

ch3.getColor()
-- "A carrot is colored orange."
put ch3.theColor
-- "orange"
```

To get full benefit from our ancestor, we need to modify the Animal parent script so that it, too, takes advantage of the ancestor.

9. **In the Animal script, remove the** getName **handler (but leave the others).**

10. **Modify the property declaration to read as follows:**

```
property covering, movement, ancestor
```

11. **Add the ancestor assignment at the top of the** new **handler:**

```
me.ancestor = new(script "AllTypes")
```

12. **Reinitialize or reenter the** ch1 **child object declaration:**

```
ch1 = new(script "Animal", "dog", ¬
"brown", "fur", "paws")
```

As you probably noticed, we left the getColor handler in the Animal parent script. So which one gets executed? Think about it logically: For inheritance to work properly, what we want is more generalized functions in ancestors and more specific functions in descendants. If a child differs in some way from the ancestor, we need to be able to modify the child without affecting any other descendants of the ancestor. And that is exactly the ability that we have. When we make a call to getColor, Director looks first in the child's handlers as defined in its parent script. Failing to find the handler (as was the case with Vegetable), Director will look through the handlers as defined by the ancestor scripts. You can test this.

13. **In the Message window, enter the follow lines:**

```
ch1.getColor()
put ch1.theColor
```

**ANCESTOR DEFERS
TO CHILD:**
A handler defined in
a child's parent script
takes precedence over
a handler with the
same name defined in
an ancestor's script.

```
ch3.getColor()
-- "A carrot is colored orange."
put ch3.theColor
-- "orange"

ch1.getColor()
-- "The color of this dog is brown."
put ch1.theColor
-- "brown"
```

When to use inheritance

Now that we have introduced inheritance to our child objects, it's time to step back and take another overall look at the use of objects. Two of a programmer's biggest problems with OOP are trying to use OOP when it's not really applicable and not using it when it is available. Remember that the purpose of OOP is threefold: to reduce complexity, increase reusability, and increase productivity. Adding objects and ancestors just because you can, will often be counterproductive. Similarly, using child objects without using inheritance often means that you are using only a small portion of the OOP capabilities.

Let's look at why our example of the animal-vegetable-mineral game works. Although we include only a couple of handlers in the AllTypes ancestor script, we could have included a lot more. We could track the user who posed the question, the user who is trying to guess the answer, the number of guesses, and the size of the object. All these are properties that the Animal and Vegetable objects have in common, and we could place those properties and functions in a central location. We could easily have duplicated those functions in the Animal and Vegetable objects without too great a productivity loss, but then when we add Mineral, we would have to duplicate them all again—and then again when we add the Spiritual objects (is that cheating?). Even when a child object needs a different functionality (the getColor function of the Animal parent, for instance), we can make that modification without losing the encapsulation of the AllTypes ancestor.

Here's another example—and a bad one by design. This time we are dealing with cities. In our design, we have houses, which are our child objects. Houses have an ancestor script for buildings, which have an ancestor script for city blocks, which have an ancestor script for districts, which have an ancestor script for cities. At first glance, it seems as though this would be an ideal case for OOP. After all, a natural progression and hierarchy is apparent. But this plan wouldn't work, and trying to make it work would probably waste a lot of your time.

So how do you know when a scenario such as this one is inappropriate? You apply the "type of" versus "contains" test. Here's how it works: You have ElementA and ElementB. If ElementA is a type of ElementB, then ElementB is a natural as an ancestor. If ElementB contains ElementA, you should think about using lists instead of inheritance. Let's apply this to our cities example:

- Are houses a type of building? They sure are, and that makes buildings a natural as an ancestor of houses. Other subclasses of buildings would be offices, self-storage units, garden sheds, and termite mounds. Set up a parent script for houses, another for offices, and so on. They can all share a common ancestor of the class building.

- Are buildings a *type* of city block? Not at all. Blocks *contain* buildings. There are other elements to city blocks (sidewalks, fire hydrants, trees), but how much do they really have in common? So trying to implement inheritance up to the city block level won't work. This isn't to say that you can't implement city blocks as a parent script, because you can and quite likely would. Each child object of the city block parent would be a specific city block. And each child object can contain a list (probably a property list—pun intended) that specifies the buildings on that block. The child object can also contain a list of fire hydrants. Remember that lists can contain elements of any type, so we can place objects in a list. A house or an office object can be placed in the list with all of its properties and functionality intact. (Some people call objects that contain lists of objects **container objects**.) The important point is that although objects are being used, there is no attempt to apply inheritance where it isn't appropriate.

- Are city blocks a type of district? Again, the obvious answer is no. So again, even though we would likely implement districts through a parent script, there would be no attempt to use districts as an ancestor of city blocks or of buildings.

That takes care of the problem of trying to use inheritance where it's inappropriate. The other big problem for progammers is failing to use inheritance where it *should* be used. If your program design specifies a parent script for lawyers and another for doctors, you should seriously be thinking about a "people" or "professional" ancestor script. Whenever you have parent scripts, try to find some commonality that will let you encapsulate their functionality. Often such commonality is not obvious at first. To make it easier, don't focus just on your items but also on what handlers they require. It may turn out that many seemingly unrelated parents all use lists and so can use the same set of handlers for adding to, deleting from, sorting, and printing lists.

P/C SCRIPTING IN PRACTICE: CONTROLLING SPRITES

Our exercises in parents, children, and ancestors have thus far been confined to the Message window. This underscores the fact that the objects created by these methods are creatures of RAM, but the next step is to use them to control physical aspects of a production. This is one of the areas for which the real power of P/C scripting starts to shine through.

1. **Open the movie BigFunPC.dir in the Tutorials folder of the CD.**

OBJECTS FOR SPRITES:
These Swifty images can be brought to life by first creating child objects that control movements and then linking those objects to the sprites on the Stage.

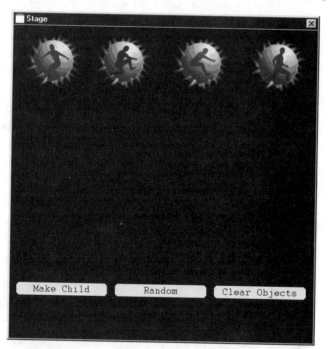

2. *Run the movie. Click the Make Child button four times.*

With each click of the Make Child button, another object is created and set to controlling one of the sprites. As the object is created, it is given initial values to control the direction, location, and speed properties of the object. It is also assigned a channel number. The channel number determines the channel of the sprite that the object will control. The Random button sets new values for the speed and location properties. The Clear Objects button deletes all of the current objects. With no objects, the sprites are no longer controlled and no longer move.

3. *Stop the movie and display the Cast window.*

All of the programming for this movie has been done for you. We have three parent scripts, or if you want, two parents (Fall and Scoot) and an ancestor (allSprites). We use two parent scripts because some sprites will move down (Fall), and some sprites will move left to right (Scoot), and our movement handlers differ for the two different directions. These three scripts contain the property declarations and the handlers needed to set properties and control the sprites. The cast script for the Make Child button contains the code for creating the objects (so we no longer need to use the Message window).

Let's take a look at the scripts and see what's familiar and what's new.

First look at the allSprites script (Cast slot 1). This script will be used as the ancestor:

```
property Channel, Speed, Place

on setSpeed me, mySpeed
  me.Speed = mySpeed
end

on setPlace me, myPlace
  me.Place = myPlace
  me.doPlace()  -- set the location
end

on setChannel me, myChannel
  me.Channel = myChannel
end
```

```
on enlist me
  global spriteList
  add the actorlist, me
  add spriteList, me
end
```

Here we are following our design rules and encapsulating as much as possible in a common ancestor. The only property that must be declared in the parent scripts is the `ancestor` property. Notice also that we have included handlers for setting the properties. These form our public interface, and all access to an object's properties should occur through these handlers.

We never have occasion to retrieve the property values, so we don't have any handlers for that. The handlers for setting the speed and channel are totally straightforward.

The `setPlace` handler is a little different in that it contains a call to the `doPlace` handler. The `doPlace` handler sets the sprite's initial location, and falling and scooting sprites each have their own `doPlace` handler. For that reason, we placed a `doPlace` handler in each parent script.

The last handler in allSprites is the `enlist` handler, in which we maintain our list of objects that have been created. As you progress in your use of P/C scripting, you'll find that much of the necessary sophistication lies not in the object scripting, but in the writing of lists to manage the objects once they have been created. The `spriteList` list is a normal list, and we store it as a global variable. The `actorList` list is a special list built into Director as a movie property. It is designed to store only child objects, so don't use it for storing other elements. What makes it really special is that any object in `actorList` receives a `stepFrame` message each time the playback head enters a frame. If you place a `stepFrame` handler in the child object's parent script (which we do) or ancestor script, that handler will be called each time the `stepFrame` message is received. That makes the `actorList` and `stepFrame` handler excellent candidates for controlling animation.

We use two lists because a program could have other child objects controlling other types of sprites (although we don't do that here). We could track our falling and scooting sprites with the `spriteList` list, and use the `actorList` list to control all animating sprites.

Now take a look at the Fall parent script in Cast slot 2:

```
property ancestor
on new me
  me.ancestor = new(script "allSprites")
  me.enlist() -- manage lists
  return me
end

on stepFrame me
  if sprite(me.Channel).locV > (480+40) then
    sprite(me.Channel).locV = (1-40)
  else
    sprite(me.Channel).locV = ¬
    (sprite(me.Channel).locV) + me.Speed
  end if
end

on doPlace me
  sprite(me.Channel).locH = me.Place
end
```

The new handler designates the ancestor script for the child and calls the enlist handler (in that ancestor) to update the spriteList and actorList lists. In the stepFrame handler, all of the movement takes place for the animation. Basically, the handler says that if the spite is going off the bottom of the Stage, put it at the top. Otherwise, move it down by an amount determined by the Speed property. We call this property Speed because the bigger the jump, the faster the sprites seem to move.

We play a few tricks with the numbers. The 480 is the Stage's height, and the 40 is about half the height of the sprite, so (480+40) means the trailing edge of the sprite is (at least) almost gone. Making this script work for any size Stage or sprite is an exercise for you to do. You really should write the script with variables for the Stage and sprite dimensions, and you should make it obvious to anyone what is going on (by commenting your code). Using hard-coded numbers like this is very poor programming practice.

The Scoot parent script is exactly like the Fall script if you switch locH for locV (and vice versa) everywhere in the script. That difference is why we used two separate parent scripts.

Now let's take a look at the script for cast member 9, the Make Child button:

```
on mouseUp
  global spriteList
  myCount = count(spriteList)
  if myCount < 4 then  -- only 4 sprites
    ran = random(2)  -- 1 falling, 2 sideways
    if ran = 1 then
      obj = new(script "Fall")
    else
      obj = new(script "Scoot")
    end if
    -- set the properties
    obj.setChannel(myCount+1)
    obj.setSpeed(random(25))
    obj.setPlace(random(480))
  end if
end
```

We start by determining how many child objects we already have using the count function. We know only four sprites are available, so once we have all four assigned to a child object, we stop creating new objects.

Next we use a random call to determine if the sprite should go down or sideways. Depending on the random value, we create an object with the proper parent. Notice that we assign the child object to a local variable. When this mouseUp handler finishes, that local variable no longer exists. Our child object still exists, since we have references to it in our lists, but we aren't leaving around unneeded references that we might have to track down when we want to get rid of the objects.

Finally we set the properties. The sprites are located in channels 1 through 4, which corresponds to the objects' locations in the list. Since myCount contains the number of the last item in the list, we add 1 to myCount for the current sprite. (Again, you should represent the sprite channels with variables. If you move the sprites around in the Score, this script would break.) The speed and location are set to random values.

The other scripts in the movie are pretty standard, but the Random button script is worth taking a look at because it uses a repeat loop that's different from any we have used so far:

```
on mouseUp
  global spriteList
  repeat with obj in spriteList
    obj.setSpeed(random(25))
    obj.setPlace(random(480))
  end repeat
end
```

Here the loop is executed once for each object in a list. The syntax is as follows:

```
repeat with [variable] in [some list]
```

On each pass through the repeat loop, the variable is set to the value of the corresponding list element. In our case, that element is a child object. Using that object reference, we can set new values for the object's properties. Again, notice that we use only the public interface to access the properties.

TIME TO ENLIST:
When you create multiple child objects, you can use lists to keep track of them. The actorList list lets you specify which objects get the stepFrame message, as these objects have done.

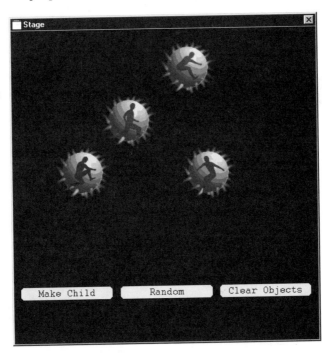

Other P/C scripting possibilities

Now that you're up and running, try these variations by making modifications to the BigFunPC movie:

- Move the starting location of the sprites off the Stage. After you do this, the sprites will appear to be created when you click the Make Child button instead of just being moved around the Stage.

- Set the Channel property of all sprites to channel 1. Now you'll have more than one child object controlling the same sprite. What do you think will be the result?

- Add a Delete Child button that removes a child object and moves that sprite off the Stage. Remember to remove the reference to the child object from both lists.

- Add more sprites. Either use the existing cast members or use cast members of your choice. Modify the Make Child button script so that these new sprites can also be used.

- Use a Direction property that determines the sprite's direction. Then use the Direction property to combine the two parent scripts into one parent script. If you really want to get fancy, instead of just two values (down or sideways), allow the sprites to move in any direction. You can do this by allowing the Direction property to be set to vary over 360 degrees and then move each sprite horizontally and vertically according to that value.

- Add a Rotation property that makes the sprites rotate while they move.

POINTS TO REMEMBER

Here's an overview of the essential concepts introduced in this chapter:

- To create a child object, first write a **parent script**. Use the new command to create the child object from the parent script.

- **Property variables** are declared with the property keyword.

- The **me variable** is generally used to specify a particular child object.

- Child objects not only have parents; they can also have **ancestors**. Ancestors are specified by setting a child object's ancestor property. Child objects can use properties defined in their parent script and in the parent's ancestors. This is called **inheritance**.

- Child objects don't have physical manifestations; they exist entirely in RAM. When all references to the child object are erased, the child object is removed from memory.

- The **actorList** list is a built-in list for Director. Objects in actorList receive a stepMovie message every time a frame is reached.

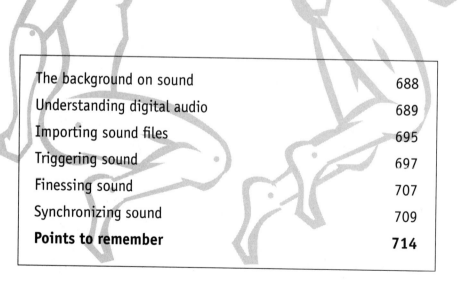

CHAPTER 19

LINGO AND AUDIO ELEMENTS

DIGITIZED SOUNDS AREN'T EASY TO INTEGRATE INTO THE MULTIMEDIA MIX. That's primarily because they're born elsewhere, in other applications. Once they arrive in Director, they can have dozens of different internal configurations, each of which affects their compatibility and impact on overall performance.

In this chapter, we'll begin by looking at the essentials of working with audio: the dominant file formats, the primary quality parameters, and the different ways in which Lingo can be used to trigger and finesse sound files. You'll learn how to overcome the two-channel sound barrier and how to use Lingo to synchronize audio playback with other media elements.

THE BACKGROUND ON SOUND

Dealing with sound is one of the quirkier aspects of working with Director today. In addition to the fact that the application limits you to only two sound channels in the Score, a number of other issues tend to frustrate budding multimedia producers:

- How do I synchronize the sound to the action?

- Why does sound play differently on different machines?

- Which file formats should I use?

- Why do some files sound better than others?

- Why do my sound files end abruptly or not play at all?

These are some of the questions we'll tackle in this chapter. The focus here is on Director's built-in audio capabilities (and the Lingo to manage them). And to beef up your sound-wrangling skills, you should also tackle the next chapter (*Lingo and Digital Video*), since one way to get more control over sounds is to save them as audio-only digital video movies. In addition, check out the discussion of sound compression and playback with Director 7's streaming Shockwave Audio in Chapter 15: *Deeper into Shockwave*.

Working with audio in Director 7 takes some patience and fortitude, but if it's any consolation, it used to be an even greater hassle. Sounds are now treated as cast members, but in previous versions they had to be installed as resources in the file and accessed via a pull-down menu. That's because of Director's roots as a video game prototyping tool; in the early days, the sounds it managed were simple bloops, beeps, and explosions (in fact, you used to have a choice of explosions built right into the menu). The ability to play longer sounds was soon added, but in the old lo-fi days of computing, even a short music clip didn't make too much of a demand on processing. Today, however, CD-quality sound is commonplace on personal computers, which means that every software designer producing for general distribution has to become a bit of an audio engineer as well.

UNDERSTANDING DIGITAL AUDIO

A number of new parameters are involved in Director-based audio, each of which can have a significant impact on the quality or performance of your presentation—so take your fingers off the keyboard and take some time to get clear on the following concepts.

File formats

For the budding multimedia developer, the best way to make sure a sound will work with Director is to save it as an **Audio Interchange File Format (AIFF)** file before inserting it into a Cast. If a sound isn't in AIFF, a sound editing program such as Macromedia's SoundEdit 16 can probably convert it. Director can also work with WAV-formatted sounds (either compressed or uncompressed), Shockwave audio, AU, MP3, and Macintosh sounds, but I suggest that you stick with AIFF files until you get a firm grip on the art of using sounds. After you are up and running with AIFF sounds, you can add other types (and QuickTime sounds, too). That way, if something starts breaking, you will have a better idea of where the problem may lie.

Besides the sound type, four other factors can affect the performance and quality of a sound file:

- The **sampling rate** of the sound

- The **bit depth** at which the sound was recorded

- The choice of **stereophonic** or **monophonic** encoding

- The **compression rate** of the sound file

Sound sampling rates

The **sampling rate** is similar to the resolution of a graphics file—the higher the rate, the more accurately the sound is documented. Just as higher resolution images look less blurry than low-res versions, a sound with a higher sampling rate sounds more true to life. To convert an audio signal to digital, the value of the audio signal must be checked, or sampled, a large number of times per second. The sampling rate (measured in kilohertz, or kHz) is the frequency with which samples are taken. A sound sampled at 22.050 kHz, for example, saves the audio value 22,050 times per second.

Just as all pictures don't need to have crystal clarity, not all sounds need to be sampled at the highest rate possible. You can incorporate CD-quality sound into your production—but if it's running on a laptop with tiny internal speakers, the extra quality just translates into a waste of disk space and RAM—it won't be heard.

Most full-featured sound editing programs give you at least these rates to choose from:

- *5.5125 kHz*, roughly the sound quality of your standard telephone call

- *11.025 kHz*, approximately the level of broadcast television audio (without Surround Sound)

- *22.050 kHz*, essentially the quality you could expect from an FM radio station with good reception

- *44.100 kHz*, the standard for compact disc recording

- *48.000 kHz*, the standard for digital audio tape (DAT) recording

Some older Macintosh models used slightly variant sample rates for medium- and high-quality sound: 11.127 and 22.225 kHz, respectively. Most MacOS sound-management software compensates for this discrepancy, but PC sound cards may balk at playing such files. If you're authoring for cross-platform playback, stick to 11.025 and 22.050 kHz.

So what sampling rate is right for your sounds? For working with Director sounds, you should stick to those sampled at 11.025, 22.050, and 44.1 kHz. And while most newer computers will support 44.1 kHz stereo sound, unless you have special requirements you probably won't need that. For best results, stick to 22.05 kHz for your sounds. If your sounds are recorded at 44.1 kHz you can convert them to 22.05 kHz using a program such as SoundEdit 16. This is known as **downsampling**, a process that converts an audio file to a smaller file size with the same quality you'd experience if you originally sampled the audio at the lower rate.

It's also possible to convert from a lower to a higher rate, but since no information is added, the only difference will be an unnecessarily larger file. And file size is important; a half-second uncompressed 11.025 kHz sound that takes up 11K of disk space will occupy 44K at the 44.1 kHz setting.

Because of the way Windows handles sound, attempting to play simultaneous sounds recorded at different sampling rates can result in a time lag (latency) before sounds begin. You may find that attempting to save file space by recording some sounds at a lower sampling rate than others will result in unacceptable performance problems. So even though some sound effects, such as a button click, really don't need the quality you get with 22.05 kHz, trying to save such a small amount of space will probably create more problems than it will solve. Best to stick to 22.050 kHz sound for all your sounds.

Sound bit depth

To return to the graphics metaphor, if the sampling rate is roughly analogous to the resolution of an image, the sound's **bit depth** is similar to color bit depth. Bit depth is a measure of how much data space is used to store a given portion of the item: The more space, the less is lost in the translation.

Today's multimedia sound commonly offers two bit-depth modes: 8-bit and 16-bit. At 8-bits, a sound sample has 256 possible values; at 16-bits, the values have 65,536 possible steps—so you get a lot more information in 16-bit sounds. While the file size for 16-bit sounds is twice as big as that for 8-bit sounds, the tradeoff is generally well worth it in terms of quality.

As with sampling rates, you should stick with a single bit rate for all your sounds. Even though some sounds, such as a button click, don't require 16-bit quality, you'll find that using a single bit rate provides the best results for the least amount of trouble. As a further incentive, any sounds that use Shockwave compression (either by compressing your movie's internal sounds or by using external Shockwave sounds) will automatically be converted to 16-bit sound depth. Any size gain you thought you were achieving by using 8-bit will be lost, and you will have lost sound quality in the process. So stick with 16-bit sound depth for all of your sounds.

Although all recent Macintosh computers can handle stereo 16-bit sound straight from the factory (just plug in the speakers), audio capabilities under Windows can vary wildly from machine to machine. There's a booming market in sound cards for the PC, some of which provide 44.1kHz, 16-bit, stereo, CD-quality sound, and some of which sound only slightly better than those walkie-talkies you had as a kid. (If there's no sound card installed at all, Microsoft's Speaker Driver for Windows, which is even more rudimentary, will attempt playback.) Many multimedia producers package their products with a list of recommended sound cards. You'll see a lot of references to Sound Blaster or Sound Blaster–compatible, which means 16-bit, 44.1kHz, stereo sound.

Stereo or mono?

Another factor determining sound file size is whether you use **stereophonic** or **monophonic encoding**. In general, opting for mono over stereo cuts the file size in half.

When should you use stereo, and when should you use mono? Macromedia recommends using mono unless you have special circumstances that require stereo. (By the way, Macromedia also *strongly* recommends sticking with 22.05 kHz, 16-bit mono sound.) If the original sound has been recorded in stereo, you can easily convert the sound to mono using a program such as SoundEdit 16 without any loss in quality.

Some people think that even on the cheap, tinny speakers found on most computers, stereo sounds warmer and commands more attention; others believe the extra file size is wasted. It's really a matter of what's pleasing to your ears, so you might want to experiment. Generally, however, you should consider using stereo in the following cases:

- You are using high-quality sound, such as a symphony recording, and the sound itself is the main focus, rather than being used as background sound.

- You are using the stereo channels as effects. For example, when you want to give the impression of movement, you can have a sound start on one channel and then fade out on that channel as the sound fades in to the other channel.

Register Today!

Return this
Microsoft Windows 95 Resource Kit
registration card for:

✔ a Microsoft Press® catalog

✔ exclusive offers on specially priced books

U.S. and Canada addresses only. Fill in information below and mail postage-free. Please mail only the bottom half of this page.

1-55615-678-2A   *Microsoft Windows 95 Resource Kit*   *Owner Registration Card*

_____

NAME

_____

INSTITUTION OR COMPANY NAME

_____

ADDRESS

_____

_____

CITY   STATE   ZIP

Microsoft®*Press*

Quality Computer Books

For a free catalog of
Microsoft Press® products, call
1-800-MSPRESS

BUSINESS REPLY MAIL
FIRST-CLASS MAIL   PERMIT NO. 53   BOTHELL, WA

POSTAGE WILL BE PAID BY ADDRESSEE

MICROSOFT PRESS REGISTRATION
MICROSOFT WINDOWS 95 RESOURCE KIT
PO BOX 3019
BOTHELL   WA   98041-9946

You can save monophonic sound at a high-level sampling rate and bit depth, but should you? If the source sound is mono, upping the other quality parameters will produce as accurate a reproduction as possible—and when you're working with mono, that might translate into optimum playback.

Calculating audio file size

These five factors determine the size of a sound file: the sound's inherent length, the sampling rate used, the bit-depth resolution, the choice of stereo or mono encoding, and the compression factor. With that many variables, you might think it would be difficult to determine the actual size of a sound file, but in fact it's quite easy to predict. Just apply this formula:

Length in seconds × **Sample rate** × **(Bit depth) / (8 bits per byte)**

This formula produces the length of a mono file. To calculate the size of a stereo clip, just double the result. So if a 15-second sound bite were sampled at 22.05 kHz in 16-bit mode, the equation would be

$15 \times 22050 \times \left(\frac{16}{8}\right) = 661500$ bytes

If the sound in question is stereo, you'd double that to 1,323,000, or 1,323,000 bytes. Divide *that* by 1024 to get the slightly more comprehensible kilobyte count, which rounds off to 1292K or 1.3MB. Your mileage may vary, but this formula should prove a reliable estimate of the end result. If your files are significantly larger or smaller, that may be an indication that you haven't achieved your desired quality level.

Using audio compression

Since sound files can get very big very quickly, you can choose from among several **compression** methods for squeezing them down. But just as with graphics compression methods, there's always a trade-off when you use them. A compressed file may be smaller, but this reduction might be achieved at the expense of either sound quality or access speed.

If your sound editing application supports compression standards, you might want to experiment to see which standard works best for you—but as always, experiment on a copy of the file, not the original. MACE compression is no longer supported in Director, but other types, such as IMA-compressed AIFF files, are supported. Shockwave audio compression may be your best bet since Director is now designed around Shockwave to a large extent.

With different compression standards and different compression ratios, sound quality can vary wildly. With Shockwave, for example, you can use compression ratios of up to 12:1 without any appreciable decrease in sound quality. Compression ratios of 24:1, and even above, can produce sound quality that is still significantly better than what can be achieved by reducing the sampling rate and sound bit depth. This results from the use of perceptual coding techniques that work with what a person hears rather than just randomly losing data.

If your audio files are in a compressed format that Director doesn't support, consider opening and converting them within SoundEdit 16. Or check to see whether an Xtra has been written to support a required file type.

If your project is capable of using Shockwave Audio, you have a number of powerful compression options available; the capability to play streaming, high-quality sound compressed to modem-friendly sizes is one of Shockwave's strengths. For more information, see Chapter 15: *Deeper into Shockwave*.

You should be aware, however, when using Shockwave Audio for compression on sounds in the Cast, that the compression doesn't actually take place until the projector is created, the movie is saved as a Shockwave movie, or the movie is updated with the Update Movies command from the Xtras menu. Since compression can substantially alter the quality of a sound, you should make sure that you test your movie under the correct conditions.

IMPORTING SOUND FILES

Sound files enter the Cast database through the same portals as any other cast member: the Import dialog box and the Insert menu. Shockwave compressed external files will generally be linked to your movie via the Insert menu. For other sounds, use the Import dialog box. If Sound is selected in the Files of Type pull-down menu of the Import dialog box, files of that type (that is, AIFF, WAV, and SWA files) will show up in the central window.

SOUND FOUND:
From the Import dialog box, you can choose sounds and place them in Casts as either integral or linked elements.

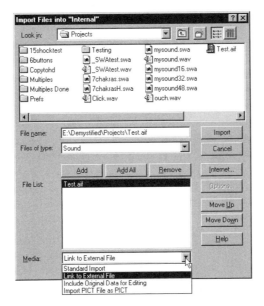

On a Macintosh, if you want to audition the sounds before importing them, select the Show Preview check box. The Import dialog box will expand to include a Preview control bar; if the file is in a compatible format, you can hear it by clicking here.

Note the Media pop-up menu at the bottom of the dialog box. If you select Link to External File rather than Standard Import, the sound will be imported as a linked internal cast member (the other options aren't relevant to sounds). Choosing this option has its advantages: A linked cast member can actually belong to several movies at once, since it's the link that's imported. That keeps the file size of your movie down as well, although you could achieve essentially the same effect by importing the file into an external Castlib and sharing that Cast among movies.

Using linked sound files also has its downside: You have to make sure that your files stay in the same relative location as the corresponding movie, or Director will have trouble finding them. Also, the looping feature is disabled with linked sounds.

If you change the location of a linked file and need to reconnect the sound cast member with its source file, click the File Name button in the Cast Member Properties dialog box. You'll see an open dialog box that allows you to navigate to the file's new location. You can also use this feature to swap in an entirely new file.

THE SOUND SOURCE:
Click the File Name button (the path name in the center of the box) to update the link to an external sound file.

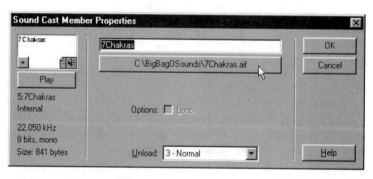

If you want to edit an audio cast member directly while it's still imported into a Cast, don't forget that you can use the Editors Preferences dialog box (from the File menu) to set an external editor for just about any media type. You may want to designate one preference for AIFF sounds and designate the preferences separately for other sounds (if you're using any).

If you're using streaming Shockwave audio (SWA), you have an additional choice. You can either import an SWA file as you import other cast members, or you can insert the SWA file as covered in Chapter 15: *Deeper into Shockwave*. To insert an SWA file, choose Media Element from the Insert menu and then choose Shockwave Audio. If you choose to import SWA files into your Cast rather then inserting them, the sounds will play just like other sounds, but you lose the ability to manage the sounds using Shockwave Lingo—including such controls as preloading and streaming. Shockwave sounds that are imported are converted from their Shockwave compressed format to Director's internal format.

Streaming versus internal audio

In addition to keeping movie size to a minimum, for what other reasons would you choose to insert rather than import a sound file? The key factor to consider is **streaming,** or loading files sequentially into memory.

External streaming SWA files are streamed when played in Director. That means the application grabs the beginning part and starts playing the sound and then continues to process the data during playback—files are processed in a continuous stream rather than in one big chunk. Imported sounds, in contrast, demand blocks of RAM large enough to hold them in their entirety.

The rule of thumb is this: Keep your longest or largest files external; let them stream during playback. Import sound effects and other short or low-resolution sounds—or anything requiring quick triggering on multiple occasions—as internal sounds.

TRIGGERING SOUND

The simplest way to incorporate sound into your productions is to do what we did in Chapter 4: Add a sound sprite to one of the two sound channels, and then place an instruction in the tempo channel to wait until the sound has finished playing. But since everything else stops in its tracks until the performance is over, this method is really useful only for brief feedback sounds and quick effects.

A few other approaches to sound let you blend it more smoothly into the multimedia whole. We'll take a look at them now.

Multicell sound segments

If you spread sprites of the same sound cast member across a series of contiguous cells, the sound will play until the playback head passes out of the last cell (unless a tempo channel command dictates otherwise). This implies two things:

- If you want a sound to play in its entirety during playback, you need to know how many frames it will occupy at your current playback tempo.

- If you want a sound to retrigger (play from the top), you can't place it next to another sprite from the same sound in the same channel. The workaround is to alternate placement in the two channels, as shown in the illustration:

STRAIGHT AND STAGGERING:
To retrigger a sound without a time gap, you must place it in a new sound channel.

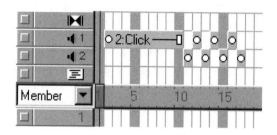

In the Score in the illustration, the first sound will play only once, for a duration of nine frames. The second sound will play seven times, since the gap between filled cells causes Director to treat each instance as a new start. (We're assuming that for this example, the Tempo channel is set to allow each sound to play completely. We'll get to that shortly in the section "Synchronizing Sound.")

Estimating duration

Because Director is frame-based rather than time-based, a 6-second sound might occupy 6 frames or 60, depending on the tempo settings of your movie. If you want to get an accurate reading of the number of frames your sound requires, try this four-step process:

Use the In-Between command to fill the channels with sound sprites in a segment.

1. Place the sound in the first frame of an otherwise blank movie. Make sure this movie has the same tempo setting as the one in which the sound will eventually reside.

2. Extend the sound across numerous frames. If your sound is longer than a few seconds, make the segment hundreds of frames long.

3. Rewind and play the movie.

4. As the sound stops, click the Stop button on the control panel. Then check the frame counter in the panel's lower-left corner. Depending on your reaction time, the value should be within a few frames of the sound's stopping point.

When placing the sound in your movie, you might want to add a few extra frames to the end of the segment. It's often less jarring for viewers to experience a brief pause than an abrupt end.

Using looping

When a sound needs to be stretched out longer than its inherent duration (or when it needs to play indefinitely), don't forget about looping. Any internal sound can be made into a loop by selecting the Loop check box in the sound's Properties dialog box. If you want a sound to loop at some points and play only once at others, you can set the loop property using Lingo. Setting the loop property to TRUE will cause the sound to loop, while setting the property to FALSE will prevent the sound from looping.

If you're jumping from one movie to another, the sound playing in the last frame will continue to play until the new movie begins. If the sound in that channel is looped, the loop will continue—which makes for a nice effect, smoothing the transition. You can even use the **sound fadeOut** command to further smooth the transition.

The puppetSound command

We've already dabbled a bit with puppeting sounds; they're good to use as aural feedback (like the button click sound) and as transitions (a puppeted sound can play while a new movie or window is being loaded).

The term *puppet* comes from older versions of Lingo, when puppeting was required to enable Lingo to control any Score element. Basically, a channel is made a puppet, and that means Lingo pulls the strings and can override instructions in the Score. Director 7 is much more sophisticated, and autopuppeting is now included, so using the puppetSprite command is usually no longer necessary. But the puppetSound command is still used to play sound cast members using Lingo and also to return control of a sound channel to the Score. The syntax is as follows:

```
-- play a sound
puppetSound [whichChannel], ["whichSound"]
puppetSound [whichChannel], [castnumber]
-- stop sound and return control to Score
puppetSound [whichChannel], 0
```

We can check this out with a quick movie.

1. *Open a new movie in Director and name it* **Sounds.dir.**

2. *Import some sounds. Use Standard Import so the sounds are internal, and make sure that Click.wav (on the Demystified CD) is one of the sounds.*

On the Director Demystified CD, you'll find a Sounds folder containing a number of sounds you can use. The Click.wav file is a quick button-click sound. Go ahead and import several sounds so you can experiment with them to find one that won't drive you crazy if you hear it over and over. The Cellopia sound is nonirritating.

3. *Use Paint to create a cast member and then name it* **Button.** *Place Button on the Stage.*

4. *Open a cast script for the Button cast member and enter the following handler:*

```
on mouseUp
  puppetSound 2, "Click"
  updateStage  -- not really necessary
end
```

5. *Place a* go to the frame *behavior in frame 1 of the behavior channel to loop the movie there.*

6. *Use the Properties dialog box to turn on looping for your alternate sound.*

7. *Drag your alternate sound to sound channel 1 of the Score.*

8. *Run the movie, and click the button.*

You should hear a click sound whenever you click the button. Don't worry if you notice a time lag between the button click and the click sound; we'll fix that later. Because we used two different channels for the sounds, we get to hear both at the same time. We use the updateStage command, even though it isn't necessary in our movie, to remind us that there are times when it *is* necessary. For example, if your program spends a lot of time in a script, it may be a while before the playback head moves—updateStage triggers the sound just as going to a new frame does.

9. *Stop the movie and change the Button script to play a different sound—one that is fairly long, such as Mechanic.*

10. Run the movie again, and click the button.

This time you get to hear both sounds playing for some time. If you think this is handy, you should know that you can play up to eight sounds at the same time.

Although only two physical sound channels are available, you can use Lingo to access up to six additional channels.

11. Add another button to your movie (name it Stop) with the following mouseUp *handler:*

```
on mouseUp
  puppetSound 2, 0  -- turn off the button sound
end
```

12. Run the movie, and click the Button button and the Stop button. You should be able to start and stop the sound you are puppeting in channel 2.

When working with puppeted sounds, the most common error you should watch out for is failure to return control with puppetSound 0. If you do not give control back to the Score, sounds in the Score will not play correctly. Even if you turn right around and puppet a sound in the same channel, nothing is lost by getting into the habit of unpuppeting a channel.

The soundBusy command

Another common error to watch for is puppeting a sound in a channel that is already being used. In our example program, for example, a background sound appears in channel 1. If we play the Click sound in channel 1 (we used channel 2), it will override the background sound. When the Click is finished, the background sound will not automatically start again, even though it still resides in the Score. You can test this using the Message window.

1. Run the movie.

2. In the Message window, enter the following:

```
puppetSound 1, "Click"
puppetSound 1, 0  -- return control to the Score
```

As you can hear, the background sound does not pick up where it left off. As mentioned earlier, when one sound finishes playing in a particular Score channel, Director considers that channel's sound already played.

Sound will not begin again until a blank cell is encountered in that channel. Even then, the sound would begin again from the start—there is no way for Director to begin playing the sound again where it left off (although you can make it do this by using a sound-only digital video). If you are using many sounds in your movie, often playing sounds at the same time and including sounds in the Score, you will need to develop a scheme for tracking which channel you want to use.

If you want to determine which channels are in use, you can use the soundBusy function, which returns a pronouncement on whether or not a sound in a certain channel is currently playing: it returns TRUE if it is, and FALSE if it isn't. A simple repeat loop can be used to search through the possible channels to find one not in use. This handler starts at the highest numbered channel to lessen the chance of interfering with a sound in a sound channel.

```
on getChannel
  global maxChannel  -- set at start up
  repeat with channel = maxChannel down to 0
    if soundBusy(channel) then
      nothing
    else
      exit repeat
    end if
  end repeat
  if channel = 0 then
    return 0  -- no channel available
  else
    return channel  -- contains the number we want
  end if
end
```

The soundBusy function is also useful in scripts when you want something to wait until a sound has finished playing or to happen only when a sound is active.

The sound playFile command

Lingo offers a third layer of sound control. Use the command sound playFile to play a sound directly from its external file—no need to import it into the Cast or even to puppet it. All you need to do is specify the channel and the name of the file (include the full path name if it's located outside of your movie's folder), as in this example:

```
-- Macintosh
sound playFile 2, "My HD:My Movie:Intro Music"
-- Windows
sound playFile 2, "C:\My Movie\Intro Music"
-- Both, but sound in same folder as movie
sound playFile 2, "Intro Music"
```

You can also use the @ operator if you want to specify a relative path name.

When a sound is played in this manner, it'll continue until the sound has finished, until the playback head encounters a resident sound in the designated channel, or until you issue the command puppetSound [*channel number*], 0.

In theory, **sound playFile** can be used to launch several external sound files at once. In practice, though, you can't get a good sound if more than one file is being read at a time. Since the sounds are streamed from disk rather than from memory, having to read the disk at two locations is more than Director can handle without some degradation. The same holds true if you try to play a sound file while a digital video is playing or while cast members are being loaded.

The soundDevice command

How many sound channels can you invoke? Director 7 allows up to eight simultaneous sounds to play on both Macintosh and Windows computers. The number you can actually use depends on available memory, but most systems should allow all eight. Playing simultaneous sounds is a pretty amazing feat when you think about it. While the Macintosh has long been designed to handle more than one sound, Windows never was (and still isn't)—and really isn't designed to do much with sounds at all. That's why Windows machines require a sound card to get sound from anything but the internal speaker. Unfortunately, the variety of sound cards and standards for Windows means playing sound can get complicated (or interesting, depending upon your point of view).

To get simultaneous sounds, Director (and other applications) uses a device driver to mix the requested sounds before sending them to the sound output device (the sound card or whatever). That way, the output device sees only the single sound, which is what it's designed for. But this is an evolving process, and it's probably changing as you are reading this. Here's where we stand as this book goes to press.

THE SOUNDDEVICE AND SOUNDDEVICELIST: Director now lets you check and set the device for mixing simultaneous sounds.

The `soundDeviceList` built-in list was introduced in Director 7 to display the possible devices that can be used for playing sound. Remember: We're talking mixing devices (device drivers), not sound cards or other output hardware. You should take a look at this list in the Message window.

1. In the Message window, enter

```
put the soundDeviceList
```

On the Macintosh, you will see only one choice: **MacSoundManager**. Be happy—that's all you need. On Windows systems, you could see up to three items on the list:

SOUND DEVICES ON PARADE: Depending on the Director version and system setup, Windows users may have as many as three sound devices to choose from.

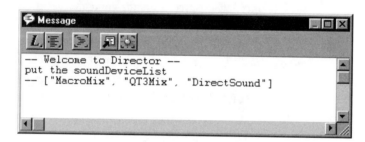

These sound devices are used for Windows machines only.

- The `soundDeviceList` list for all Windows machines should show **MacroMix**. MacroMix will work on any Windows machine but will produce less-than-spectacular results. In particular, users may experience a long latency period (lag time) before sounds start to play—as much as half a second, depending on the user's system. That may not matter for some sounds, but for a mouse-click sound, a half second will make the sound seem displaced from the action.

- The **QT3Mix** device should also show up in the list. It has two advantages over MacroMix: It has a much shorter latency period, and it allows QuickTime audio to mix with other sounds. QT3Mix also requires that QuickTime 3 be installed on the system playing the movie.

- The **DirectSound** device may or may not show up in the list. If it doesn't, it's probably because you have an early version of Director 7 that didn't contain the DirectSound Xtra. If that's the case, you should definitely get the free 7.0.2 update from the Macromedia Web site. DirectSound is really the device of choice; it has low latency and mixes with QuickTime 3 sounds. It requires that DirectX version 5 or later be installed on the user's machine.

The RSX device is no longer used. RSX functioned by writing to DirectSound, which is now written to directly.

With as many as three devices available, you need a way to test and set the device. That's where Director 7's new soundDevice property comes in. Try displaying the current value in the Message window.

2. In the Message window, enter

```
put the soundDevice
```

Macintosh users should always see MacSoundManager. Windows users will see either MacroMix or DirectSound. If the DirectSound Xtra is included in your version of Director and DirectX (version 5+) is installed on your system, the default should be DirectSound. Otherwise, the soundDevice defaults to MacroMix. The default order is based on levels of priority, and DirectSound has a higher priority level than MacroMix, which has a higher level than QT3Mix.

One more thing and then we'll try to figure out which device to use.

3. In the Message window, enter

```
the soundDevice = "quick brown fox"
put the soundDevice
```

Interesting, isn't it? As you can see, when an invalid sound device is specified, the entry doesn't "stick." If your default soundDevice property came up MacroMix, try setting the soundDevice to DirectSound. That entry isn't accepted either (if it had been, it would have been the default). So we have learned that there is no harm trying a different sound device—if it works, so be it; otherwise, the property automatically switches back to the default device.

So how do you know which device to use? Well, here's what the programmers at Macromedia say:

- If your priority is to mix QuickTime 3 and Director sounds, use QT3Mix. DirectSound can handle this, but it won't work in a few cases (such as when the user has gone into the QT3 control panel and has set the output to Wave instead of DirectSound). QT3Mix will always mix Director sound with QuickTime 3 sound.

- Otherwise, attempt to set the soundDevice to DirectSound.

- Test the soundDevice. If DirectSound doesn't stick, the property will default back to MacroMix.

- If the soundDevice comes back with MacroMix (which has a higher priority than QT3Mix), attempt to set it to QT3Mix.

- If QT3Mix doesn't stick, you're stuck with MacroMix.

- For Windows NT, there is no DirectX version 5, so DirectSound will not work.

> If you were experiencing a delay with the Click sound as you executed the steps earlier in this section, try changing **the soundDevice** and then redo the steps. If you were using MacroMix and can switch to QT3Mix (I'm assuming you didn't have DirectSound or there would be no latency), you should see a marked improvement.

The soundKeepDevice property

SOUNDKEEPDEVICE:
The soundKeepDevice property is for Windows only.

The soundKeepDevice system property, when its value is set to TRUE, prevents Director from releasing the sound device, so it doesn't need to be reloaded for the next sound. This results in a huge performance improvement for DirectSound and, presumably, QT3Mix. The default value is TRUE for Director 7.0, but it's FALSE in version 7.0.2 to allow Flash sounds to be mixed with other sounds.

An unfortunate side effect of this property, however, is that you can't use sounds that do not play using DirectSound (including Flash sounds and the system beep, for example). Also, users may find that other applications running concurrently with your movie cannot play sound while Director keeps the sound device.

All of this is still being worked out and is changing. In fact, some early versions of Director may not have a functioning soundKeepDevice property that the programmer can change. In this case, check with Macromedia about a maintenance release for your version of Director that includes soundKeepDevice.

Just to be on the safe side, you might want to set the soundKeepDevice to FALSE whenever you don't expect to be using sound intensively.

FINESSING SOUND

Lingo, too, can control the dynamics of sound. Here are a few tricks to add to your scripting toolkit.

Adjusting volume

You can dictate the sound volume during playback in two ways: Use the property the soundLevel to make a global adjustment to all sounds, or use the volume system property to set a level for a specific sound channel. We've already noted the property the soundEnabled, which can turn all sounds on and off.

The soundLevel property

Using the soundLevel property is the scripting equivalent of reaching into the host computer's Sounds control panel and resetting the overall volume. You can choose from among eight possible settings, 0 (muted) through 7 (maximum volume). The syntax is as follows:

```
the soundLevel = [0 through 7]
```

This modification persists even after the user quits your movie, so you might want to write housekeeping scripts that determine the present volume levels upon startup and then reset the volume to those levels when the movie stops (which is a good idea, since it's not nice to implement changes that remain after your production has shut down). You can retrieve the current settings at any time using the command put the soundLevel.

```
currentLevel = the soundLevel
```

On systems with externally adjustable external speakers, the soundLevel combines with the volume set on the speakers. Adjusting the soundLevel may produce unacceptable results for the user who is also listening to a CD or has a radio card. For that reason, you should probably leave the soundLevel alone and make your sound volume adjustments through the volume property.

The volume system property

Using the volume system property, you can set the volume for channels on an individual basis. This means you can set the volume for the two Score sound channels for sounds in the Score as well as set the volume for any channel you access using puppetSound or sound playFile.

The range of volume is far more refined here than with the soundLevel property, ranging from 0 (mute) through a maximum of 255. To set the property, specify both the channel and the volume, as in the following example (note that you can't use the dot syntax with this property):

```
the volume of sound 2 = 125
```

This property can also be tested, like this:

```
currentVol = the volume of sound 4
```

If you're developing for cross-platform delivery, don't count on sound levels being consistent throughout. In general, Windows tends to distort sounds at the higher volume levels, making them sound even louder than they are. Whatever means you choose to set the sound level, be sure to test your movie thoroughly on a number of differently configured systems.

Sound fades

Nothing smoothes out the abruptness of a sound better than fading it in and out of an optimum volume. Thanks to the commands sound fadeIn and sound fadeOut, it's easy to achieve that fading effect. Both of these commands work on all available channels, control each channel separately, and allow the period of the fade to be set.

To fade in a sound over a period of time, specify both the channel and the time period (expressed in ticks), like this:

sound fadeIn 3, 120

This would ramp up the sound in channel 3, arriving at its inherent volume after 2 seconds (120 ticks). This duration could also be expressed as (2 * 60).

The sound fadeOut command follows the same syntax. For both commands, if no duration is given, the fade effect is spread across a default period, which is the current tempo setting divided by 60 and then multiplied by 15. You'll probably want to place sound fadeIn and sound fadeOut in separate scripts.

SYNCHRONIZING SOUND

One of the more impressive features of Director is its capability to read **cue points** in sound files (AIFF and WAV files), QuickTime digital video, and Shockwave Audio. What's the big deal? Cue points are a means of annotating the file and thereby subdividing the linear whole. In this respect, they're pretty much analogous to the marker system in Director's Score window. By providing tempo settings and Lingo that let you test for and track these points, you can create a new degree of synchronization with other media.

Director is unable to create cue points internally; you need to use an appropriate external editor for that. On Windows systems, the Sound Forge 4.0 (or later) and Cool Edit 96 (or later) applications can both place cue points in a sound file. Cue points are called *markers* or *regions* in those applications. On the Macintosh, use SoundEdit 16 or Peak LE.

Probably the easiest method of synchronizing animation with sound or video is to use the tempo channel. Let's give that a try first.

1. *Import the file 7Chakras.aif into your movie. This AIFF file already contains some cue points.*

2. *Drag the 7Chakras cast member into sound channel 2 in the Score.*

3. *Double-click the tempo channel for the frame that contains 7Chakras.*

4. *In the Frame Properties: Tempo dialog box, click Wait for Cue Point.*

5. *From the Channel pull-down menu, select 7Chakras.*

6. *Use the Cue Points pull-down menu to view the available cue points.*

WHAT'S MY CUE?
The Tempo dialog box shows all of the available cue points for a sound or digital video.

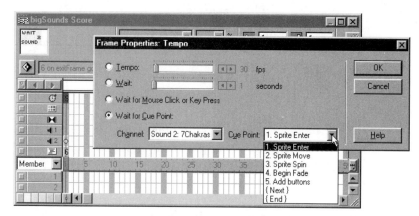

A number of cue points were placed in the 7Chakras.aif file, but a couple of others are available by default to all sound and digital video cast members: Next and End. You can use End even if the cast member contains no cue points, because the end of the sound is treated as a cue point. End keeps the playback head in a frame until a sound finishes. Use Next when you want to wait on a cue point, but you don't care which cue point it is—just the next one that's encountered. Next also considers the end of play to be a cue point, allowing the playback head to continue its journey.

By using the tempo settings, you can tell Director to hold on a frame until your desired cue point is reached, after which the playback head will move on. This lets you start animation or take other actions based on the location in the sound. Notice in the Cue Point list that each of the cue points is associated with a number. These numbers correspond to the cue's position in the list and can be used with Lingo to synchronize animation or other processes.

You can also determine the cue points in a cast member using Lingo. For this, you have two related properties: cuePointNames and cuePointTimes.

7. *In the Message window, enter the following statements:*

```
put member("7chakras").cuePointNames
put member("7chakras").cuePointTimes
```

Both properties return a list relating to the cue points of the specified cast member. The names are listed in the order they appear in the sound (or QuickTime digital video). The times are given as milliseconds from the start of the sound to the location of the cue point. The times and names are in corresponding order in the lists; and for both names and times, their locations in the lists correspond to the cue point numbers shown in the Tempo dialog box. The cue point numbers are used by Lingo elements to identify the cue points.

JUST THE FACTS:
Lingo can retrieve the names and times of cue points in a cast member.

```
-- Welcome to Director --

put member("7chakras").cuePointNames
-- ["Sprite Enter", "Sprite Move", "Sprite Spin", "Begin
Fade", "Add buttons"]

put member("7chakras").cuePointTimes
-- [4202, 8103, 14419, 27608, 39543]
```

Three other scripting elements useful with cues are the system message and event handler on cuePassed, the property mostRecentCuePoint, and the function isPastCuePoint. Each gives you the ability to handle cue points in different situations using Lingo.

on cuePassed

The cuePassed message is sent each time a cue point is passed. The cue point can be located in a sound in the sound channels, in a sound played with sound playFile or puppetSound, or in an SWA or a digital video in a sprite channel. You can write an on cuePassed handler to perform actions whenever a cue point is encountered.

1. *Add the following handler to the frame behavior of your movie:*

```
on cuePassed me, channelID, cueNumber, cName
  put "The channel number is" && channelID
  put "The Name is" && cName
end
```

2. *Run the movie with the Message window open and visible.*

After a few seconds, you should start seeing reports in the Message window about which cue points have been encountered. Notice that the channel is reported as Sound2, which differentiates the channel from the sprite channels.

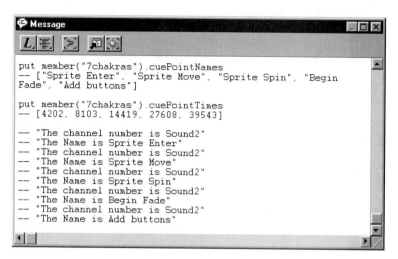

3. **Enter the following line in the Message window (while the movie is running):**

puppetSound 4, "7Chakras"

Now you should see reports on cue points in channel Sound4 as well as for Sound2.

mostRecentCuePoint

If you want to check for yourself to determine which cue point has been passed, you can use the mostRecentCuePoint property. This gives you more control over scripting when you may or may not take actions on a cue point, depending on other factors. For example, you may be using a sound file to give hints to a user answering a question. Using mostRecentCuePoint, you can determine which was the last hint given before the user answered.

For a sound playing, the syntax is as follows:

sound([soundChannel]).mostRecentCuePoint

1. **Comment out the** on cuePassed **handler in your movie.**

2. **Restart you movie and enter (repeatedly) the following line in the Message window:**

put sound(2).mostRecentCuePoint

If you are quick enough, the return value should be 0 because no cue point has been passed. Each subsequent time you enter the statement, you'll get a value showing the number of the cue point that was last encountered. If you need to know the name of the cue point, you use the number returned to find its position in the list of cue point names returned by cuePointNames:

```
x = sound(2).mostRecentCuePoint
put getAt(the cuePointNames of member "7Chakras", x)
```

isPastCuePoint

The isPastCuePoint function can be used in two ways, depending on the arguments you give it. Here's the syntax:

```
isPastCuePoint([soundOrSprite], [cueID])
```

If *cueID* is an integer, the value returned is TRUE if the cue point with that number has been passed. But if *cueID* is the name of a cue point, the function returns the number of times that the cue point specified has been passed. If more than one cue point in a sound has the same name, all cue points with that name are counted.

Counting the cue points can be useful, for example, if you want to loop a sound for a certain amount of time. The sound should have looping turned on, so it loops; and then you can turn the sound off after it has played the required number of times:

```
if (isPastCuePoint(sound 2, "elevator")) = 5 then
    puppetSound 2, 0
end
```

This will override the looping capabilities of the file playing in sound channel 2 as soon as the cue point named "elevator" has been passed for the fifth time.

By setting a number of cue points to the same name in a sound, you can determine how far into the sound you are, in chunks rather than in specific time.

POINTS TO REMEMBER

Once again, a recapitulation of the salient points:

- Sound quality can be determined by the **sampling rate**, the **bit depth** of the file (8-bit or 16-bit are the most prevalent), whether the file is **stereophonic** or **monophonic**, and the file's **compression rate**.

- Sounds in the sound channel are retriggered when a **gap** is encountered.

- Sound files can be either internal (within a Director Cast) or linked to an external source. External files are **streamed**, or read in from disk while they're playing back. An internal file is loaded into RAM as a whole.

- Use **puppetSound** to play a cast member sound. Use **sound playFile** to play a sound in an external file.

- Unless you want to wait until the playback head moves, you'll need to use updateStage in your sound-related scripts to achieve immediate results.

- You can use Lingo to set the **volume** of a sound and to **fade** sound in and out.

- Both the Score (using the tempo) and Lingo let you interpret the **cue points** encoded into sounds and digital videos. You can use these points to write synchronization scripts for audio and other media during playback.

SIMPLE INVADERS I

CREATED BY ELAN DEKEL

DESIGN BY

BEN BARNETT & ALEX ORRELLE

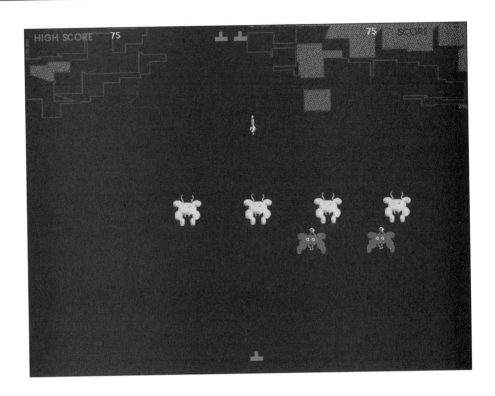

Simple Invaders:
Engineering alien encounters

LIKE OTHER ART FORMS, VIDEO GAMES HAVE THEIR CLASSIC GENRES—
and the "alien invasion" is one of those. If you've ever set foot
in a video arcade, you've seen the onslaught of extraterrestrials
descending to the surface of Earth, deterred only by the nimble
manipulation of some heavy artillery. Saving the planet: it's
a dirty job, but someone (preferably with an ample supply of
quarters) has got to do it.

This project invokes the classic format to demonstrate Director's strength as a programming tool, using a handful of animation techniques, lists, and parent-child objects to achieve the playability that used to require thousands of lines of complex code. *Simple Invaders* is an eloquent example of the potential of script-based authoring—and its single-frame structure makes it ideal for online playback via Shockwave.

PROJECT BACKGROUND

Director is the engine behind thousands of CD-ROM–based and online games, but rarely is it used for games of the "shoot-em-up" variety, such as *Tomb Raider* or *Duke Nukem*. How come? Because the pace of action is ever increasing, as is the number of graphic elements. As a result, low-level languages such as C are usually used to free up processor resources for image management.

But that doesn't mean that Director has no place in the game development process. Because of its ease of use and deft integration of graphic and scripting environments, it's an ideal choice for creating game prototypes. Someone with an idea, some design chops, and a grasp of Lingo can churn out an impressive proof-of-concept demo in a surprisingly short time. The speed of interaction may not be as fast as in a commercially released product, but most of the bells and whistles will be in place.

Simple Invaders doesn't qualify as a proof-of-concept demo, if only because it was created by Israel-based programmer Elan Dekel primarily as an exercise. Since the gameplay itself isn't original, it puts the focus on how things were achieved, rather than on what is happening on the screen. The challenge was to incorporate all the features commonly seen in video games (updated scores, character animation, visual and audio special effects) entirely from within the Director platform, and within a modest file size as well; when converted to a Shockwave movie, the final production weighs in at a modest 221K. With *Simple Invaders*, Dekel demonstrates the advantage of versatility and ease-of-use over sheer, raw speed.

THE DESIGN

From a graphic design standpoint, only four elements needed to be created: the backdrop, the aliens, the animated missiles, and a single-frame opening screen (a fifth element, the missile launcher, was kept a simple block icon). For these, Dekel turned to friends Ben Barnett and Alex Orelle.

At first only one alien was designed, the somewhat more sinister green one, dubbed Dodo. But when it was clear that the project called for more visual variety, a second, unnamed alien was quickly whipped up: Barnett and Orelle opened up a copy of the three images representing Dodo in Adobe Photoshop and then changed most of the green to red. A new set of eyes were layered over (creating a slightly more comical effect), and the result was, like the original, imported as 8-bit dithered artwork. To further differentiate the two aliens, the artwork for each was imported into cast slots in a slightly different order. As the animation scripts cycled through their images, this had the effect of making each seem to move in a distinctive pattern, although the difference is more in sequence than in style.

THE TENTACLED TWO:
A second alien was created by modifying a copy of the first, and the sequence of images was varied to produce a nonsynchronous motion.

When it came to designing the backdrop, the artwork was confined to a small rectangle in the upper quadrant of the Stage, blended into the background color of the movie. This wasn't done to save file size, but for performance reasons: the sprites of the aliens never overlap a background sprite, which means that Director never needs to devote number-crunching resources to calculating a layered display or ink effect.

To get a sense of how sprite overlapping can slow things down, try this experiment: In channel 1 of the frame named start, move the backdrop so that it's directly behind the active area of the alien sprites. Then apply a processor-intensive ink effect (such as Lightest) to both backdrop and aliens.

THE SCRIPTING TERRAIN

To begin the programming process, Dekel identified the need for scripts that perform the following distinct tasks:

- *Automatic animation.* The aliens need to wag their tentacles, and they need to move downward in a coordinated rank and file. Likewise, the missiles need to move upward when launched, blazing all the while.

- *User-based action.* The missile launcher needs to be moveable along a horizontal coordinate, and some means of firing needs to be provided.

- *Event interpretation.* When has a missile scored a direct hit? When has an alien successfully landed? Scripts are needed to determine these key events and to dictate what action should be taken as a result.

- *Scorekeeping.* Rather than place a set value on hitting an alien, Dekel decided to put a premium on proximity: The closer to the ground the alien gets, the more points awarded when it's hit. Scripts have to keep running tallies of aliens hit, of launchers used, and of the top score of preceding games.

These tasks called for a judicious use of global variables to pass values and of lists in which to store those values. And since the appearance and performance of aliens and missiles depends on choices made by the end user, they were best created with parent-child scripts. You'll find these in cast slots 2 and 3.

The scripting schematic

Once the required pieces were identified, the next step was to determine how they would interrelate. What script would call subsequent scripts, and what values would they need to pass? The best way to make the necessary connections was to focus on the three main modes of the movie: when it's newly launched, when gameplay is underway, and when a game is over. Each of these may involve a multitude of events (in the Lingo sense), but they are the three distinct parts of the user experience.

SCRIPTING INITIAL TASKS

As usual, most of the necessary parameters and functions are established in a handler for the **on startMovie** event. In it, Dekel set the initial values for the key global variables, emptied the text fields pertaining to score display, and issued a **preLoadCast** command to speed up loading of the Cast. As he mentions in his commented-out statements, his concern with preloading is not the graphics cast (which is minimal), but the sound effects; if they aren't preloaded, there could be a delay the first time they're used.

```
set MaxHighScores = 15
-- the number of high scores to save in the high-score list
set MissileSpeed = 15
-- vertical speed of the missile
set sInc = 5
-- the speed of the battle station
set MaxAliens = 8
-- the number of aliens (the more, the slower it will run)
set MaxMissiles = 2
-- (1 to 5 missiles) the more missiles, the easier the game
set bstationSprite = 48
-- the battle station sprite
set highscore = 0
set the text of field "highscore" = "0"
set the text of field "score" = "0"
set the text of field "highscorelist" = " "
preLoadCast
-- load all the cast members so we don't wait for SFX
```

A number of factors affecting gameplay (number of aliens, speed of missiles) were meticulously established as settable values, and yet the end user has no means of setting them. Try adjusting these values in the Script window and then see if you can figure out a way to add value-setting capabilities to the interface. Better yet, use these globals to create escalating values for each consecutive game, making each one more difficult to play and win. At present, only one factor (the speed of the aliens) increases cumulatively.

THE GAME BEGINS...

To get the gameplay underway, Dekel employs two handlers, **newGame** and **InitWave**. The first calls the second, but only after establishing beginning values and navigating to the frame named start, which is where the gameplay takes place.

The handler **InitWave** is one of three that manage the waves of alien invaders (the others are **NewWave** and **SameWave**). It starts the action by invoking no less than 18 global variables and then attends to a number of tasks. First it sets still more parameters, mostly for globals:

```
set the text of field "score" = string(score)
set AlienY = 100
set Alast = MaxAliens
set Afirst = 1
set initpoints = initpoints + 10
set points = initpoints
puppetsprite bstationsprite,true
```

Note that only one sprite is puppeted at this point—the one belonging to the battle station, or missile launcher. Note the first line, which places the text of the score field into a text string of the same name. That's another time-saver, since the score will need to be updated quickly, and it's faster to modify a text string in memory than to continuously write to a slot in the Cast.

YOU GOTTA GIVE 'EM CREDIT: The startup screen for *Simple Invaders* is actually the largest graphic cast member in the production.

The next task is to initialize two lists, one for each type of child object that will be created during play:

```
set alienList = []
set missileList = []
```

It's not enough to name the list, however—the individual slots within each need to be created. This is done by populating them: with empty values (that is, zeros) in the case of the missile list, and with child objects in case of the alien list.

```
repeat with i = 1 to MaxMissiles
    addat(missileList,i,0)
end repeat
set numaliens = MaxAliens
repeat with i = 1 to MaxAliens
    addat(alienList,i,birth(script "Alien",i+1))
    updatestage
end repeat
```

Why the slightly different approach for missiles and aliens? Because the former don't need to appear on the screen all at once; they represent the latent reserve of an arsenal. The aliens, on the other hand, are about to show up in force. But in both cases the lists are filled sequentially, using the **addAt** syntax in conjunction with a **repeat** loop set to a range of values (with the end range established by a global variable).

As you can tell from the lack of dot syntax, *Simple Invaders* was written prior to version 7 of Director. In addition, Dekel used an approach to parent-child scripting that's technically out of date but still worth knowing about: Objects are created with the syntax **birth(script "Alien")** rather than the more current **new(parent "Alien")**, and the script itself is saved as a movie script rather than as a parent script. The approach may be outmoded, but it isn't obsolete; the movie runs fine under version 7 without modification, a testament to Macromedia's commitment to maximum backward compatibility.

Finally, the handler performs some more strategic puppeting:

```
repeat with i = 40 to 45
    puppetsprite i,false
end repeat
```

What's in these four channels that needs to get unpuppeted? Check it out for yourself. You'll find four sprites derived from the initial missile cast member, placed in the Score but conveniently parked outside the visible area (698 pixels from the left edge of a 640-pixel Stage). This is another of Dekel's clever approaches to maximizing performance, because the sprites are loaded into memory along with the rest of the frame, even when they're not appearing. Other scripts make them visible by changing their coordinates, but their appearance is swifter than if they'd been manifested by resetting a sprite's **memberNum** property. The sprites for the aliens are also tucked away in this fashion but in the opposite direction. (Check out the Property dialog box of any of the sprites in channels 2 to 20.)

LOUNGING IN LIMBO:
As you'll note in the
Score, the alien sprites
are on the Stage at all
times—they just start
out placed in locations
past the visible area.

The last bits of business in **InitWave** perform a similar trick but in reverse. The sprites in channels 30 and 31 contain two of the three missile launcher icons that reside in the upper portion of the Stage, indicating the number of launchers left to the end user. Since the game ends when no launchers remain, there's always at least one in place. These lines make either one or both disappear (depending on the **numShips** variable) by scooting their horizontal coordinates to the nether regions of the Stage (a full 360 pixels from the right edge).

```
puppetsprite 30,true
puppetsprite 31,true
if numShips < 2 then set the loch of sprite 31 = 1000
if numShips < 1 then set the loch of sprite 30 = 1000
```

The parent scripts

Let's take a look at the two parent scripts Dekel wrote to control the "unpredictable" aliens and the missiles. Neither really call for behavioral variations: Missiles always shoot in the same direction, and aliens just keep marching until they're blasted away. But the parent-child approach is ideal because both need to be virtually unlimited in number. That's why the parent scripts don't pass a lot of unique parameters to each child object—just enough to give each a unique location. The rest of the action is contained in a set of general rules, universally applied to children.

Here's the way aliens are born, again with code commentary by Dekel:

```
property x,sp
-- each instance has an X-coordinate and a sprite number
on birth me,mysp
    global AlienY, MaxAliens
    set sp = mysp      -- mysp contains the sprite number
                        -- of the alien
    puppetsprite sp,true
    set the stretch of sprite sp = false
    set alien = sp - 1  -- the aliens sprites start at sprite 2
    -- figure out the starting position of the alien on
    -- the screen
    if alien <= (MaxAliens/2) then
        -- we have 2 rows of aliens
        set x = alien * 100
        set the locv of sprite sp = AlienY
        -- AlienY contains the Y coord of the aliens
    else
        set x = (alien - (MaxAliens/2)) * 100
        set the locv of sprite sp = AlienY + 50
        -- aliens on the second row are lower down
    end if
    set the loch of sprite sp = x
    return me
end
```

The aliens are placed on the stage in two even rows, each containing exactly half of the contingent (as set in **MaxAliens**), and neither overlapping the other. Giving birth to the missiles is a simpler matter, since they're not arrayed in visible space. Instead, each shows up at the same point: just above the missile launcher.

```
property x,y,sp    -- we need to keep each missile's
                    -- X and Y coords and its sprite number
on birth me,mysp
    global bstationSprite
    set sp = mysp + 39
    puppetsprite sp,true
    set disposeme = 0
    -- start the missile just above the battle station
    set x = the loch of sprite bstationSprite
```

```
        set y = the locv of sprite bstationSprite - 20
        set the loch of sprite sp = x
        set the locv of sprite sp = y
        return me
    end
```

Note how each missile child object is initialized with a value called **disposeme**, which is set to 0 during the birth process. This value becomes an important hook for triggering postlaunch behavior.

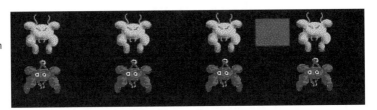

SLIME ON THE LINE: Through careful list management, each alien child object controls a sprite in a unique location on the Stage.

The motion scripts

Once the screen has been populated, it's time for action. Since the gameplay takes place in a single frame, all this happens courtesy of animation scripts. For example, the invaders' deliberate descent is dictated by the animate handler within the alien parent script. The first part of this controls movement across and down the screen.

```
on animate me
    global alienList, Alast, Afirst, AlienY, inc, ¬
MaxAliens, points, numShips
    set x = x + inc  -- move the alien sideways
    -- if an alien hits the edge of the screen, reverse the
    -- direction of all the aliens and drop them down
    if x>=620 then
        set inc = -inc
        set AlienY = AlienY + 30
        set points = points + 5
    else if x<20 then
        set inc = -inc
        set AlienY = AlienY + 30
        set x = x + inc + inc
        set points = points + 5
    end if
end
```

The next portion of the handler tends to the character animation, the motion created by cycling through a range of cast members. This is the kind of Lingo that could easily be adapted to a behavior script had Dekel needed to deploy it for a broader range of characters.

```
set alien = sp - 1
if alien <= (MaxAliens/2) then
    -- loop through the alien casts
    set tmp = the castnum of sprite sp
    set tmp = tmp+1
    if tmp > 19 then set tmp = 16
    set the castnum of sprite sp = tmp
    set the locv of sprite sp = AlienY
else
    if tmp > 25 then set tmp = 22
    set the castnum of sprite sp = tmp
    set the locv of sprite sp = AlienY + 50
end if
set the loch of sprite sp = x
```

If you examine the missile parent script, you'll see a similar handler called **Manimate**. But that's just the half of it; another script needs to turn the instructions into motion by repeatedly issuing calls to **animate** and **Manimate**. You'll find that in the frame script applied to the start frame:

```
-- animate the aliens
set tmp1 = count(alienList)
repeat with i = 1 to tmp1
    set tmp = (getat(alienList,i))
    if not (tmp=0) then animate tmp
end repeat
-- animate the missiles
set tmp1 = count(missileList)
repeat with i = 1 to tmp1
    set tmp = (getat(missileList,i))
    if not (tmp=0) then Manimate tmp
end repeat
go to the frame
```

This script accesses the lists created for both missiles and aliens, passing the **animate** (or **Manimate**) trigger individually to each object within the list. Because these lists already exist, there's no need to resort to the **actorList** variable (which we used in Chapter 18). Instead, this handler is called every time the playback head loops back into the frame.

User control

When the game's afoot, the end user can really do only two things: shoot missiles (an inexhaustible supply is assumed) and move the missile launcher back and forth. Rather than rely on mouse movements, Dekel chose to provide this control directly through the keyboard. This approach has the advantage of using the **keyDown** and **keyUp** events to test for simple, unambiguous conditions.

```
on keyDown
    global keyDir
    if the key = " " then
        FireMissile
    else if the key = "," or the key = "<" then
        set keyDir = 1
        MoveMe "left"
    else if the key = "." or the key = ">" then
        set keyDir = 2
        MoveMe "right"
    else if the key = "q" or the key = "Q" then
        checkHighScore
        go to frame "game over"
    end if
end
on keyUp
    global keyDir
    set keyDir = 0
end
```

The global variable **keyDir** is then passed to the frame script in start, which uses it to update the launcher display. The **startMove** script contains handlers that define **FireMissile** and **MoveMe**.

Playing the game and keeping score

Okay, so the aliens are moving, the launcher is lurching left and right, and the missiles are flying. That makes for a nice visual effect, but a game requires additional behavior. That's why the missile parent script includes lines that detect when a hit has been scored and performs subsequent actions. First, it checks to see if a missile sprite intersects an alien sprite:

```
repeat with i = 1 to MaxAliens
-- loop through the alien sprites
    if sprite sp intersects (i+1) then     -- gotcha!
    set score = score + points              -- increment score
    set the text of field "score" = string(score)
    if score > highscore then       -- do we have a high-score?
        set highscore = score
        set the text of field "highscore" = string(highscore)
    end if
    set numaliens = numaliens - 1
    puppetsound "gotcha"
    updatestage
    set disposeme = 1
    set the loch of sprite (i+1) = 1000
```

The intersection has been detected, the score updated, and a sound played. Since the missile has done its duty, the object is disposed of by setting its **disposeme** value to 1. The physical alien (the sprite that had been controlled by that object) is whisked off the Stage to the limbo location of 1,000 pixels from the left edge.

Next, the stakes are upped slightly. The next lines react to the hit by slightly increasing the speed of the remaining aliens—which is why the aliens get more aggressive as their numbers get fewer. In fact, on machines with fast processor speeds, they can become almost a blur.

```
if inc > 0 then set inc = inc + 1
else set inc = inc - 1
```

Now it's time for the vanquished alien to disappear—not the sprite (which is back in limbo), but the child object itself. This is done by replacing it with a zero placeholder in the list **alienList**:

```
-- remove alien from alien list
deleteat(alienList,i)
addat(alienList,i,0)
-- if all the aliens have been hit, then start a new game
if numaliens = 0 then NewWave
```

But what of the missile itself? Since missiles can disappear in two ways
(by hitting an alien or sailing above the Stage), Dekel devised scripting
that handles both permutations:

```
if y < 0 or disposeme then
    set the loch of sprite sp = 1000
    puppetsprite sp,false
    set tmp = sp-39
    deleteat(missileList,tmp)
    addat(missileList,tmp,0)
```

This means that if the missile's Y coordinate (vertical) is zero—or if its
disposeme value is true—it too will be whisked to limbo and cleared from
the child objects in **missileList** with a zero substitution.

GAME OVER!

When does the game end? There are three rounds (one for each missile
launcher), and each round ends when at least one of the aliens finally hits
the ground. The **animate** handler in the alien parent script tests for that
condition with these lines:

```
if the locv of sprite sp > 430 then
    -- clean out the alien list
    repeat with i = 1 to MaxAliens
        set the loch of sprite sp = 1000
        deleteat(alienList,i)
        addat(alienList,i,0)
    end repeat
    puppetsound "endgame"
    updatestage
    set numShips = numShips - 1
```

The variable **numShips** is a leftover from the early stages of the project, when the missile launcher was conceived of as a spaceship. To distinguish between end of round and end of game, these lines were added:

```
if numShips >= 0 then
    SameWave
else
    CheckHighScore
    go to frame "game over"
end if
```

IN RETROSPECT

Ultimately, *Simple Invaders* lives up to its name: It's a no-frills application, unlikely to command much attention from video-gamers used to the 3D exploits of Lara Croft and her like. Yet what's in the movie doesn't represent a dead end, but a sound starting point for extending your own scripting skills. There are a number of possibilities for enhancements, and you're heartily encouraged to try them. Consider these, for instance:

- What, no *explosions*? When an alien is shot (or makes a successful landing), no animation marks the event—just a sound effect. One useful enhancement would be to add appropriate visual effects, and perhaps make them vary in size and intensity: a quick palette switch to briefly turn the Stage into a crimson landscape, for instance.

- How about a *multiple-player* version? The single-frame game itself wouldn't need modification, just the scripts that track and display the scores. Another variation, a Shockwave version that tracks the all-time high scores of multiple users, could be created simply by continually updating an external HTML text file.

- How about adding *customizable creatures*? Thanks to Director 7's multiple cast management features, it would be easy to substitute in any number of designs for the aliens. How about letting the end users choose—or better yet, providing them with an option to design their own aliens? And the customization need not be limited to appearance; behaviors can be written to encapsulate any number of different personality types.

- And how about providing *true network-based interplay*? Since Director 7 allows cast and script resources to be distributed anywhere on the Internet (or any networked environment), one person could be designing monsters to fling at any number of players. How about some real-time text chat happening at the same time? Or how about reporting all high scores to a central Web location? You could play a duel in Vancouver today and then learn that your next competitor awaits you in Vladivostock.

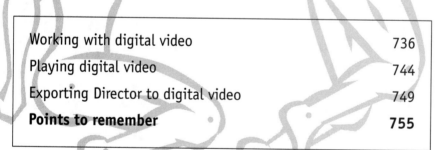

CHAPTER 20

LINGO AND DIGITAL VIDEO

MOVIES WITHIN MOVIES—THAT'S ONE OF THE STRENGTHS OF DIRECTOR. Director can place full-motion video right in the middle of your productions.

In this chapter, we'll zero in on the capabilities and liabilities of digital video in the authoring environment. We'll navigate through the multiple layers of format and performance options, and we'll look at the issues involved in incorporating video. We'll come full circle by discussing how to reverse the process and turn a Director movie into a digital video.

WORKING WITH DIGITAL VIDEO

In the preceding chapter, you studied the role of digital audio in your Director productions. Now that we're moving on to digital video, keep in mind that the two have a lot in common: Both try to place a time-based medium in the midst of a frame-based medium, and both can be created by a large number of applications at various compression and quality settings. But when it comes to digital video, you're confronted with many more aspects to control than you are with digital audio. This may seem overwhelming at first, but actually it's liberating; in fact, some programmers choose to place their sounds in nonvideo form (sounds without images) because of the greater control they can wield over playback.

In the next few pages, we'll be looking at the methodology of working with digital video, primarily with the two most common digital video types: **QuickTime** and **AVI**. AVI (which stands for audio video interleave) is sometimes also known as Video for Windows, or VFW. Other digital video file types include QTVR (QuickTime Virtual Reality) and QD3D (QuickDraw 3D). On the Macintosh, you can import MPEG files if you have installed the QuickTime MPEG extension. On Windows computers, an Xtra such as the MPEG Xtra or DirectMedia Xtra is required to play MPEGs.

In this chapter, we'll refer to all video types as digital video and focus on QuickTime. Where there is a functional difference, we'll refer to a specific file type.

When you're considering incorporating digital video into a production, remember that if you use QuickTime, the end users viewing your production will have to have QuickTime 3 (for Windows or MacOS) installed on their systems. Also, AVI files must be converted to QuickTime if they are to be played on a Macintosh.

Director 7 supports QuickTime 3 (QT3) and will support QuickTime 4 when it's released, but Director no longer supports QuickTime 2.x. Older QuickTime files (those produced with versions prior to QT3) will need to be updated before you can incorporate them into your Director 7 productions.

Digital video improvements

Director continues to make improvements in its ability to handle video.

Actually, some of what we discuss here was introduced in Director 6.5, but it's all nevertheless pretty new. Director continues to make improvements in its handling of digital video, as do the developers of QuickTime and other Xtras. Here's a rundown on some of the new capabilities you will find:

- Support for new file formats such as QTVR v2.0, AVI, Flash movies, and animated GIF files

- Ability to set the rotation and scale of a digital video sprite while Director is running (using Lingo)

- Use of 1-bit cast members as masks to create irregular shapes for displaying a digital video

- Support of loop points to loop only a portion of a digital video

- New Lingo to control a digital video's properties and determine how it plays

Importing digital video movies

You import a digital video movie as a cast member in the usual fashion (via the Import dialog box or through the Insert menu), but you need to keep in mind a few things:

- Because they're usually hefty in size, digital video movies are always imported as linked rather than embedded cast members. For that reason, you should place the external file in a more-or-less permanent location before importing, to save yourself the trouble of having to update links later.

CODEC:
A compression and decompression standard used to store digital video.

- Digital video files can be saved using a variety of compression/decompression schemes known as **codecs**. Much of a video's quality and performance characteristics will be determined by how it was saved, so you should be familiar with the various codec options offered by the application in which the file was created.

- Only the most basic editing (single-frame cutting and pasting) can be performed on a digital video movie once it's imported into the Cast, so any movie you create should be as complete and final as possible before it becomes part of a Director production. Of course, if you edit a digital video movie after importation, it'll still play (so long as it hasn't been moved or renamed).

> Because QuickTime and AVI movies can be used in the same production, you might get confused about which digital video is in which format. You can always clear things up by using the Lingo property **the digitalVideoType of member**, which will return a symbol indicating the type: either **#quicktime** or **#videoforwindows.**

To make the discussion in this chapter easier to follow, let's start by importing a couple of digital video files. If you search around your system files, you can probably find some video files that either came with your operating system or with some software you purchased. You'll also find some on the Demystified CD.

1. *Create a new Director movie and name it* **Digital.dir.**

2. *From the File menu, select Import. The Import Files dialog box opens.*

3. *In the Files of Type field (the Show field on the Macintosh), choose QuickTime.*

4. *In the upper portion of the Import Files dialog box, navigate to the DigitalVideo folder on the Demystified CD.*

Notice that when QuickTime files are specified, both QuickTime files and AVI files are displayed. The logic behind this is that either type of digital video file can be imported as a QuickTime cast member.

5. *Select SpaceQT.mov, click Add, and then click Import.*

The file is imported immediately, without any additional questions or prompts (although it may take a few moments). If you look at the Cast, you'll see that the picon for the new cast member has a QuickTime subicon, and that the subicon has an extra image on its left, indicating that the cast member is linked to an external file.

6. *Import SpaceAVI.avi in the same manner.*

This time when you click Import, you are prompted (*Windows only*) to choose between importing the file as a QuickTime cast member or an AVI cast member. Choose QuickTime.

7. Windows only: *Import SpaceAVI.avi again. This time choose to import the file as an AVI cast member.*

> When you import an AVI file on the Macintosh, it's automatically converted to a QuickTime cast member. When you import an AVI file under Windows, you have the choice of importing the file as a QuickTime or an AVI cast member.

Now you have a couple of files to play with in your movie. On a Macintosh, they are both QuickTime files. Under Windows, you have an identical digital video source file as both a QuickTime and an AVI cast member; this will give you the opportunity to experiment with both formats to see if you can find some performance or quality differences.

8. *Double-click a digital video cast member.*

If you chose a QuickTime cast member, the QuickTime window appears and includes a control bar that you can use to view the video. If you double-click an AVI cast member, the AVI Video window appears without a control bar for playing the video. You can play the AVI video by double-clicking the image in the AVI Video window.

Digital video options

Before you place any digital video sprites in the Score, you should survey the source cast member's Properties dialog box. You'll find that it includes many more options than you've encountered in other Properties dialog boxes.

- For QuickTime cast members (Macintosh and Windows), select the cast member in the Cast window and then click the Cast Member Properties button. In the Xtra Cast Member Properties dialog box that appears, click the Options button. The QuickTime Xtra Properties dialog box appears.

- For AVI cast members, select the cast member and then click the Cast Member Properties button. The Digital Video Cast Member Properties dialog box appears.

The parameters in the dialog boxes for QuickTime and AVI cast members are identical:

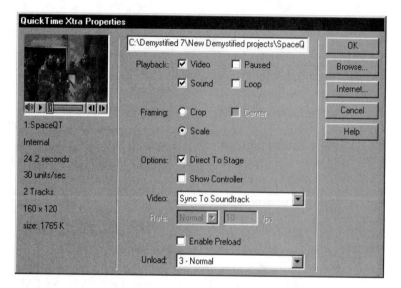

HOT PROPERTIES: The QuickTime Xtra Properties dialog box has a number of playback options (many of which can also be set and changed via Lingo).

For QuickTime cast members, the image of the digital video in the upper-left corner of the Properties dialog box includes a control bar so you can play the video in a small-sized version. This feature isn't available for AVI cast members. Under the image is additional information about the digital video: the number of seconds it will play at normal speed, the units per second, the number of tracks (QuickTime can have more than one audio or video track), the size in pixels, and the file size.

The Browse and Internet buttons along the right edge of the dialog box allow you to change the link to a different digital video file or to relink the cast member if the file has been moved.

The center area contains the options that you can set for the digital video.

- Under Playback, the *Video* option ensures that the visual portion of the digital video will be shown on the Stage. As mentioned in the previous chapter, sometimes you will use QuickTime for audio-only cast members. When you don't have (or don't want) video, disabling Video will improve performance.

- The *Sound* option must be checked for the video's soundtrack to play during playback. If you have a silent video, deselect Sound to increase performance.

- *Paused* means "paused at start." When enabled, Paused keeps the video from beginning to play as soon as it appears on the Stage. You can start the video later using Lingo.

- *Loop* causes continuous repeat playback of the video. If you want the video to play only once, do not check this option.

- When the *Crop* option (under Framing) is selected, resizing the video's sprite on the Stage won't change the proportions of the video itself. Instead, the sprite's bounding box becomes a sort of window to the video, displaying only the part that shows through.

A CROP IN THE FIELD:
When the Crop option is checked, resizing the sprite displays only a portion of the video (left). When Scale is selected, the image is resized to fit the new dimensions (right). The center image shows the original video sprite.

- *Scale*, when checked, performs the opposite action of Crop. The digital video will be placed on the Stage with proportions that match the shape of the sprite. Unless you maintain the original proportions, the video content will be distorted.

- The *Center* option becomes available when Crop is selected. When this option is checked, cropped videos are centered in the resized sprite.

- Selecting *Direct to Stage* (under Options) is probably the best way to ensure optimum performance of your video, but there are some considerations that might keep you from enabling this option every time. It gives the video playback priority, playing it on the very top level regardless of its sprite's position in the Score's channel hierarchy. This means any other elements superimposed on the video won't be shown. Another side-effect is that Score ink effects will have no effect on the video.

- *Show Controller* becomes available when Direct to Stage is checked. This option displays the controller bar, the area of playback buttons standard to digital video. When this option is off, only the digital video itself is displayed. If you choose to show the controller, the video will always be paused at the start, the same as if you had selected the Paused option. You can still play the movie using Lingo.

KEEPING CONTROL: You can give the end user playback control by including the QuickTime controller bar in the sprites derived from your digital video.

- *Enable Preload* (the check box near the bottom of the dialog box) can make a big difference in playback performance. When this option is selected, Director loads the entire video into RAM (as opposed to playing it from its linked file). If there's not enough RAM for the entire video, Director will preload as much as it can.

- The *Unload* list box provides the standard options for removing a cast member from memory when the memory is needed for other cast members.

The Video pull-down menu provides these two options:

- The *Sync to Soundtrack* option addresses the difference between digital video playback and Director's frame-by-frame operation. When computer processing resources (available RAM, CPU speed, and so on) aren't sufficient to play every frame in the digital movie at the given rate in the allotted time span, the digital video will make up the difference by strategically dropping video frames. The result is a movie that retains its timing, but at the risk of becoming jerky or abrupt. On the plus side, the sound is always played and stays synchronized with the video.

- *Play Every Frame* provides an alternative approach to inadequate resources. When this option is chosen, the video will deal with the problem of slow video display by simply slowing down playback, so that all frames will be displayed. Because this approach would essentially trash any coherent sound track, the sound is disabled.

If you choose to go the route of playing every frame, you need to give your digital video a strategy to replace the one you've overridden. That's why the Rate pull-down menu becomes active and provides three choices:

- *Normal* sets playback to the internal frame rate of the video (not the tempo of the Director movie).

- *Maximum* doesn't force the video to the top level of playback the way Direct to Stage does, but it does throw as many resources as possible toward speedy playback.

- *Fixed* lets you set playback to a uniform number of frames per second, which you specify in the *fps* field.

Many of the attributes you can set in this Properties dialog box can also be controlled via Lingo. In fact, there's probably more Lingo for setting video parameters than for any other type of media. Check *A Lingo Lexicon* for definitions of properties such as **center of member**, **the controller of member**, and **directToStage**.

For the very best digital video performance, you'll want to use Direct to Stage and play the video without any scaling. If you do scale the video sprite to a different size, use the video sprite's Properties dialog box to set the size to half-scale increments (such as 50% or 25%) or integer multiple increments (such as 200%). Odd sizes for scaling (such as 64%) can seriously affect the video's playback performance.

Checking the Enable Preloading option in the Properties dialog box, or preloading the Cast member using Lingo, may make this unnecessary. Also, because the video is being streamed from disk, the beginning of a video is sometimes jumpy. For best results, include a half-second or so of blank video at the start of your video source and fade it (also done in the source) into the actual content.

PLAYING DIGITAL VIDEO

Unlike sounds, which have their own sound channels (plus the virtual sound channels), digital video sprites reside in the numbered sprite channels of the Score. You can add a digital video sprite to the Score in the same manner that you add any other type of cast member to the Score: Drag the cast member to the Score channel or drag it to the Stage. When the playback head reaches a frame with a digital video, the video will begin playing (assuming Paused wasn't selected as one of the digital video's properties). The video will continue playing as long as the playback head is within a frame that contains the sprite. As with sounds, you can extend the sprite in the Score to cover as many frames as are needed to display the entire video, or you can take greater control by using the tempo channel, cue points, and Lingo.

Let's try playing one of our digital videos:

1. *Select the SpaceQT.mov file in the Cast and bring up its QuickTime Xtra Properties dialog box.*

2. *In the Playback options area, make sure that Video and Sound are checked and that Paused and Loop are not. Also make sure that Direct to Stage and Sync to Soundtrack are selected and that Show Controller is not checked. Close the Properties dialog box by clicking OK.*

3. *Drag the SpaceQT.mov cast member from the Cast to channel 1, frame 1 of the Score.*

4. *Open the Tempo dialog box for frame 1. Choose Wait for Cue Point and select End as the cue point to wait for.*

5. *Play the movie.*

The movie should stay on frame 1 while the digital video plays. The digital video should play in its entirety, and when it is finished, the Director movie should stop (unless Looping is turned on in Director's control panel). That's it; you just played a QuickTime movie!

When a digital video plays, the tempo for the video is independent of the frame rate (tempo) of the Director movie. Setting a different tempo in the tempo channel has no effect on the playback of a digital video.

Using Lingo to play a digital video

Playing a digital video by just using the Score is okay, but you gain a lot more control once you introduce Lingo into the equation. With Lingo, you can control when the video starts and stops, play it from one specified movie time to another, pause it, play it in reverse or at different speeds, and play designated tracks of the video.

The movieRate property

Starting, stopping, and pausing are the most common actions you'll be performing using Lingo. Those three are all controlled with the movieRate digital video sprite property. If we change our Director movie a bit, we can test the movieRate property in the Message window.

1. *In your Digital.dir movie, remove both the tempo channel sprite and the digital video sprite in channel 1.*

2. *Modify the properties of SpaceQT.mov by checking the Paused check box. Now the digital video will not automatically start when the playback head reaches the frame that contains the digital video sprite.*

3. *Drag the SpaceQT.mov cast member to frame 1, channel 1 of the Score.*

4. *Add a frame behavior to the Score to loop on frame 1.*

5. *Start the movie.*

As you can see, the SpaceQT digital video is not playing, even though the Director movie is running.

6. *With the movie still running, enter the following line in the Message window:*

```
put sprite(1).movieRate
```

As you can see, the value returned is 0. The value is a floating-point number, which allows you, for example, to set the speed at which the movie plays to half speed (0.5). Setting the movieRate property to 1 will play the video at its normal speed; –1 will play the video at normal speed but in reverse.

7. *Enter the following line in the Message window:*

```
sprite(1).movieRate = 1
```

The video should begin playing. To pause the video, set movieRate to 0:

```
sprite(1).movieRate = 0
```

Now start the video again by resetting movieRate to 1. When the video starts playing again, it should begin playing at the same location where it was paused. This is different from the playback of sounds, for example, where you are forced to restart the playback from the beginning (except for streaming SWA sounds).

The movieTime property

Not only can you pause and restart a digital video, you can jump to any location in the video using the movieTime sprite property. The movieTime value is given in ticks: $\frac{1}{60}$ of a second. The value of movieTime at the beginning of a digital video is 0. The value at the end is determined by the length of the video, which you can access from the video's Properties dialog box. The movie's length is given in seconds, so multiply by 60 for a value in ticks. You can also access the length of a digital video through Lingo by using the duration property, which reports the video's length in ticks.

You can experiment with the movieTime property in the Message window to check the current location in a video or to jump to a new location.

1. **Start your Director movie and enter the following line in the Message window:**

```
put sprite(1).movieTime
```

If your digital video is rewound and not running, 0 should be returned as the value.

2. **Start the video. Then enter** put sprite(1).movieTime **repeatedly. You should get a different value each time until the end of the video.**

3. **Set** movieTime **to a location somewhere in the middle of the video. Then start the video again:**

```
sprite(1).movieTime = 600
sprite(1).movieRate = 1
```

As you can see, the movie begins right where you set it using movieTime. Using the movieTime property, you can start wherever you want to in a video and then repeatedly test to see that your desired ending location has been reached.

Cue points

Digital video works with cue points almost exactly as sound does. You can set cue points in a QuickTime file using SoundEdit 16 for use on Windows or Macintosh systems (although SoundEdit runs only on the Macintosh). AVI files don't support cue points. After you have placed cue points in your digital video cast member, you can use the tempo settings to wait for a cue point or you can use the same cue point Lingo that you used with sounds:

- on cuePassed

- cuePointNames

- cuePointTimes

- mostRecentCuePoint

- isPastCuePoint

Cue point Lingo is discussed in detail in Chapter 19: *Lingo and Audio Elements*.

Masks for digital video

Instead of using the entire sprite bounding box to display the video, as we've done so far, you can create a mask for the cast member and the video will appear only in the area of the mask (or more correctly, only in the area *not* in the mask). A mask is defined by creating a 1-bit, black-and-white cast member and assigning it to the digital video cast member, using the mask property. Note that this is a cast member property, not a system or sprite property. Once set, and as long as you don't unset it, the mask of a cast member applies to any sprite in your movie that was created from that cast member.

1. *Open the Paint window and create a black filled shape of your choice. It can have an irregular outline if you want.*

2. *Close the Paint window. Name the new cast member QTMask.*

3. *Select the QTMask cast member in the Cast; then, from the Modify menu, select Transform Bitmap.*

4. *In the Transform bitmap dialog box, select 1-bit for the Color Depth setting and choose Remap Colors. Close the dialog box.*

You don't place the mask on the Stage; you assign it to the cast member. Director decides where it appears on the stage by aligning the cast member's registration point with the upper left of the video's sprite. Since our mask cast member uses the default registration point (the center), only about a quarter of the mask will actually fall within the bounds of the video sprite's rectangle. We want to change that.

5. *Open QTMask in the Paint window again and change the registration point to somewhat above and to the left of the sprite. Close the Paint window.*

6. *Save your movie. Sometimes Director gets confused if you don't.*

7. *Start your Director movie and enter the following in the Message window:*

```
member("SpaceQT").mask = member("QTMask")
sprite(1).movieRate = 1
```

The video plays, but only the area defined by the black pixels of the mask is visible. You can set the visible area to "not the mask" by using the invertMask property:

8. *In the Message window, enter*

```
member("SpaceQT").invertMask = TRUE  -- false is the default
```

Now the video plays in the entire area of the sprite's bounding box except for the area defined by the mask. Remember that you can set the registration point of a cast member using Lingo (use regPoint), so you can set up scenes where the mask actually moves around with the movie playing in it—something like looking through a peephole or a spyglass.

Other digital video Lingo

A number of other Lingo elements are useful for controlling digital video. You can play with them at your leisure; here are their uses:

- quickTimeVersion will tell you the version of QuickTime installed on the user's system. This lets you determine whether the required version is installed before the user attempts to play a digital video.

- currentTime tells you how far into a digital video you are. The time is recorded in milliseconds, the same as that returned by cuePointTimes when you are manually timing cue points.

- duration returns the total time, in ticks, for a digital video cast member.

- volume sets the sound volume of a digital video sprite.

- `rotation` and `scale` set the rotation and scale of a QuickTime sprite. Although these can be changed while a digital video is playing, you'll probably find that repeated rotations, for example, provide a less-than-desirable effect.

A number of properties relate to a digital video's tracks. You can find information about a digital video's tracks and even control tracks individually. Here are some of the more useful track properties:

- Use `trackCount` to determine the number of tracks in a digital video. Use `trackType` to determine whether a track is video, sound, text, or music.

- To determine the starting and stopping times of a track in a digital video, use `trackStartTime` and `trackStopTime`.

- Use `setTrackEnabled` to turn a track on or off. Use `trackEnabled` to determine whether a track is set to play.

EXPORTING DIRECTOR TO DIGITAL VIDEO

The flow of digital video to Director movies also works in reverse: It's a simple matter to turn all or part of your production into a digital video movie—which can, in turn, be imported back into another Director movie.

Exporting to digital video is recommended only for straightforward, linear animations. Any interactivity, such as button scripts and frame scripts, will be lost in the translation.

Why would you want to turn a Director movie into a digital video movie? It's useful for importing into other applications, or even for exporting to videotape (many digital video–based media management applications have facilities for video offload). Exporting to digital video is also useful when you want to use digital video's frame-dropping approach to synchronization rather than Director's plod-through-all-frames style.

When it comes to encapsulating animations for use on the Stage, a digital video version is often more efficient than the equivalent film loop. That's because the loop brings with it all of its component cast members (each of which needs to be loaded into RAM), whereas the digital video is a single cast member (which should load in a single gulp). You should experiment to find which strategy works best for your projects.

To convert from Director to digital video, you start by selecting Export from the File menu to access this dialog box:

WRITING THE RANGE:
In the Export dialog box, you can specify which portion of your Director production should be translated into the QuickTime format.

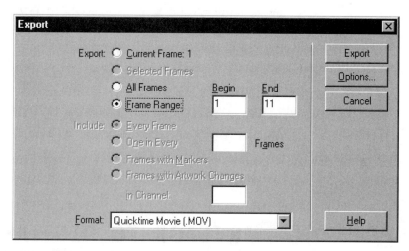

The options available in the Export dialog box are determined by the destination file type you choose—the selection in the Format list. You can export the movie as a QuickTime digital video, an AVI digital video (Windows only), or a sequence of bitmapped graphics (BMP files under Windows; PICT, PICS, or Scrapbook on the Macintosh). We focus here on exporting to QuickTime, but many of the parameters apply to all export formats. For QuickTime, use the Format pop-up menu to choose QuickTime Movie.

The next step is to choose the range of frames you want to convert and the method of selecting frames within that range. For the Include option, you can specify every frame, all frames with markers, and frames at designated intervals (the One in Every option). You can even capture only those frames in which a change is registered in a specific visual channel.

When you have determined which frames you want to capture, click the Options button. This brings up the QuickTime Options dialog box and a whole new set of parameters specific to QuickTime.

GOING TO THE MOVIES:
The QuickTime Options
dialog box provides
you with a number
of settings that will
determine the size
and quality of your
digital video export.

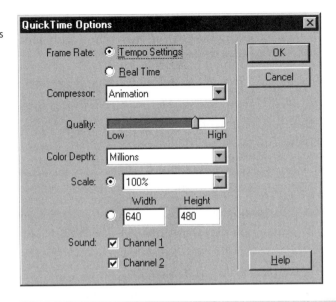

The AVI (Windows) version of this export process is completely stripped down. When the Options dialog box appears, your only setting option is the export rate in frames per second. Also, when you export to AVI, no sound is exported.

Some of these choices are easy to make: The color depth of the QuickTime movie should probably be the same as the source movie's color depth. And if you have sounds in both sound channels, you'll want to enable those check boxes. But other options bear a bit of explanation.

- Under Frame Rate, *Tempo Settings* takes its cue from the information in the tempo channel, translating that speed into the fps of the resulting digital video file. This is the option to choose when you want to lock in speeds, even when the actual playback in Director is slower.

- *Real Time* records the digital video movie exactly as the Director movie unfolds on your system—if the tempo setting is 60 fps but the actual playback lags at 5 fps, the latter is what you'll get. You need to actually play the movie before exporting it, since Director keeps track of the duration of each frame the last time it was played and uses that information for the export.

- The *Quality* slider bar determines the degree of fidelity to the original. The farther to the right, the higher the quality (and the larger the resulting file size).

- The *Scale* options let you define a video size different from the Stage; 100% is the existing Stage size and is the default.

When creating a movie for export to a digital video, remember the following:

- Only sounds from the sound channels of the Score go into the video; sounds played through Lingo are not exported.

- Sounds must be imported with the Standard Import option; cast member sounds that are linked to the external file will not be exported.

- Sounds that have their loop property set will not loop in the video. To create the impression of looped sound, you will need to place the sound in multiple frames, alternating between sound channels 1 and 2 (remember that sound channels must have a break for the same sound to play again).

- Animation created by moving sprites using Lingo will not be exported. Animation must be created by placing sprites in the Score and using tweening to animate them.

- Setting a sprite's rotation and skew in the Score works fine, but you cannot use Lingo to get the same effect.

Compressor options

In the QuickTime Options dialog box, the Compressor pop-up menu offers a number of codec choices, depending on the video hardware and software you have installed on your system. The one that's best for you depends on the final disposition of your digital video movie.

- *Animation* is optimized for segments featuring simple sprite motions and a minimum of transition and sound play instructions. It's also a good choice if your segment has mostly computer-generated artwork (as opposed to photographs or other artwork originally in analog form). This option compresses the file on average at a rate of 4:1 (the compressed version is approximately one-fourth the size of what it would be without compression).

- *Cinepak* is a standard codec for high-quality digital video. This option is recommended if you have a lot of 16-, 24-, and 32-bit images, or if you plan on transferring the resulting movie to videotape. The average compression ratio is about 10:1.

- *Component Video* (Macintosh only) is a codec created primarily for capturing raw video footage. About the best reason for using it here would be if you plan to combine the resulting file with other footage saved in the same format. This compression ratio is about 2:1.

- *Graphics* is optimized for 8-bit color. Consider it an alternative to the Animation codec; it provides better compression (about 11:1), but files take longer to decompress.

- *None* ensures maximum quality by performing no compression at all. Of course, this is the bulkiest solution, but it's a good option when you plan to apply another codec standard in a digital video editing application.

- *Photo-JPEG* is a standard compression format for digitized images from an analog medium, such as scanned photographs. This compression ratio ranges from about 10:1 to 20:1.

- *Video* is Apple's original codec for QuickTime video. At 5:1, it doesn't compress as well as Cinepak, but it's recommended if you plan eventually to port the resulting QuickTime movie across platforms. This codec is optimized for 16-bit and 24-bit color images.

- *Intel Indeo Video* produces lossless compression and high quality—especially if you happen to have a video card with a special Intel chip installed. This codec is designed to work with specialized hardware. It'll work without it, but at greatly reduced speeds.

Again, experimentation is the rule. You might want to make several versions of your video and then compare their size, quality, and performance. Take the estimates of compression ratios given here as rules of thumb only—the actual result you'll get depends on the contents of the digital video movie that's being created.

Export

After you set all the options, you can export the file.

Click the Export button in the Export dialog box. A Save File dialog box opens prompting you to name the file and the file's location on your system. When you click Save, Director warns you about disabling screen savers, which can interfere with the export process. (For a simple movie, the process is quick enough that screen savers should not be a problem, however.)

Once the export is complete, you are back in Director with your original movie. You can open your new QuickTime video using whatever QuickTime viewers you have installed on your system, or you can import the new video into a Director movie and play it in Director. Give it a try!

Don't forget that the ability to synchronize Lingo with internal cue points can be applied to QuickTime video as well as digital audio files. See the section on synchronizing sound in Chapter 19 for a rundown on the methods and terminology.

POINTS TO REMEMBER

Here's a recapitulation of the important stuff:

- The quality of a digital video movie is determined by its internal compression/decompression standard, or **codec**.

- The **Properties dialog boxes** of digital video cast members have a lot of parameters for you to set. If your video isn't performing as expected, check Properties first for solutions.

- Additionally, **Lingo properties** abound for the purposes of controlling digital video cast members; many of them are scriptable equivalents of the options in the Properties dialog box. Check the *Lingo Lexicon* or *Lingo Dictionary* for a full listing and definitions.

- You can **export** a Director movie as a digital video movie, but you'll lose any interactivity. The quality of the final product is once again determined by the choice of codec.

- The **cue point recognition** feature of Director works for QuickTime movies as well as audio files. This gives you more options when it comes to synchronizing playback.

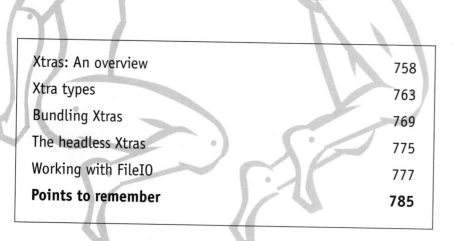

CHAPTER 21

EXTRACURRICULAR LINGO: XTRAS

ALTHOUGH YOU MAY NOT HAVE BEEN AWARE OF IT, YOU'VE BEEN USING Xtras since you started using Director. Xtras are software module add-ons that you can apply to the basic Director program. Xtras are among the most powerful means of enhancing the capabilities of Director, but with this power comes complexity. Because each of these software modules is written to perform a different task, each tends to play by its own set of rules.

In this chapter, we'll tackle the issues involved in putting Xtras to work: how to add them to your movies, how to decode their methods of operation, and how to write scripts that adapt those methods for your purposes.

XTRAS: AN OVERVIEW

Because of its support of object-oriented programming, Director has a certain modularity. When a new, specialized capability is needed, a new unit of software can be written to provide it, without having to re-create the entire core Director program. This is one of Director's strengths—its power can be continually enhanced, not just by the software engineers at Macromedia but by anyone with a bright idea and some programming smarts. These external software extensions are called **Xtras**, and they are similar to the plug-ins used by Photoshop, browsers, and other applications.

Xtras come in a number of flavors. Some are Lingo-specific and are accessed through Lingo commands. Others provide their own user interface, which lets you use them without having to master the subtleties of scripting. What's more, such interfaces fit seamlessly into the Director interface: Just pull down the Xtras menu and you'll find many of them ready to access. Other Xtras provide functionality that occurs automatically, such as when you place a QuickTime video in the Cast.

Some Xtras are even more integrated. Transition-related Xtras don't even use an interface of their own; they simply add more choices to the Transition menu. As time goes by, expect even more Xtras to intertwine with Director. One of your tasks will be to keep track of when you're working in the application itself vs. when you're tapping into an Xtra.

Xtras tend to come in two broad categories: the plug-and-play kind (those with their own interface or those too straightforward to need one) and the kind I call the "headless" Xtras. These headless Xtras have no interface and a complicated method of deployment. Although I can't show you how to cope with all of them, I'll try to give you some general principles for getting a grip on most Xtras.

Since many Xtras are third-party software, they may be subject to limitations on their use. Those provided by Macromedia with your copy of Director are intended for unimpeded use, but other developers may expect to be paid licensing fees for the employment of their software in a commercial project. Review the rights messages in the documentation, and read the readMe file when you can find one. Having to pay licensing fees or royalties may be a major consideration in deciding whether or not to use an Xtra. Many Xtras written for Director 6 will not function in Director 7. If you are obtaining Xtras, make sure that the manufacturer has certified them for use in Director 7. Also, some of the available Xtras are freeware or shareware, which may mean that they haven't been as thoroughly tested as some retail products (on the other hand, considering the state of some retail software...). In any case, allow sufficient time in your project development for the necessary learning curve and for thorough testing.

Xtras: The new standard

Earlier versions of Director contained a second set of extensions called **XObjects**. In Director 6.*x*, Xtras replaced XObjects, and in Director 7, XObjects are considered obsolete. Here are some of the reasons why Xtras have become the standard:

- *Custom user interfaces.* Xtras function like full-fledged subapplications: They can have their own control panels, dialog boxes, and help files.

- *Cross-application extensibility.* Because Xtras support the Macromedia Open Architecture (MOA) standard, an Xtra can also work in other Macromedia products. For instance, transition Xtras can be used in Authorware, and some graphical special-effect Xtras also work in XRes and FreeHand. This increases the potential market for third-party developers.

- *Ease of cross-platform development.* Since the MOA standard applies to Macromedia products for the Macintosh and Windows operating systems, creating versions of Xtras for both platforms is easy.

In essence, Macromedia hopes a mini-industry will arise to create and market Xtras—which, when you think about it, is a smart way of expanding the versatility of Macromedia's products without spending gazillions on research and development. Although it's not a huge industry segment, it's a niche some savvy software firms are happily occupying.

> If you're a programmer and you want to learn how to write your own Xtras, check out *XDK for Director 7 (Xtras Developer's Toolkit for Director 7)*, which is available at the Macromedia Web site. It includes examples, source code, and debugging tools for the Windows and Macintosh platforms.

Installing Xtras

Installation of Xtras can mean two separate things: installing them on your system so you can use Xtras while you're authoring, and installation (or bundling) with your final product so the Xtras are available when your product is played.

For the most part, installation on your system requires only that the Xtra be placed in the Xtras folder of the Director application. If you look on your system, you'll find a number of Xtras already in the Xtras folder. Some were created by Macromedia for use with Director, others were supplied by third parties to accompany Director, and still others were supplied as demo versions that supply some functionality (but not as much as when you purchase the complete version).

XTRAS FOR DIRECTOR:
To install Xtras for use while authoring, place them, or the folder that contains them, in Director's Xtra folder.

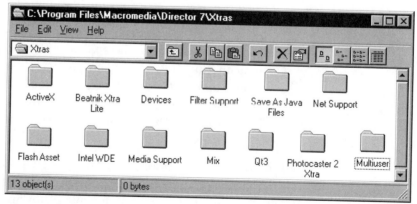

Putting an Xtra to work is simple: Just drag a copy to the Xtras folder and then fire up Director 7. The Xtra will show up where it's supposed to. When you don't want to use the Xtra anymore, just remove it from the Xtras folder. When Director launches, it considers an Xtra installed if it's located in the folder named Xtras that's on the same level (that is, in the same folder) as the application itself. Xtras buried up to five layers deep in nested folders within this folder will still be recognized. You might want to take advantage of this feature to help you keep your Xtras organized.

Prior to Director 6, Xtras could also be placed in another location, a common folder intended to be shared by other Macromedia applications. Now, however, Director does not search this shared folder upon startup. On MacOS machines, the unsupported location was the Xtras folder tucked within the Macromedia folder in the System folder. Under Windows 95 and NT, the folder was Xtras in Macromedia in Common Files in the Files folder. Under Windows 3.1, it was Xtras within MACROMED. If you're in the habit of placing Xtras in any of these locations, you're likely to run into problems in Director 7.

Dealing with Xtras for your final product takes more consideration than installing Xtras for authoring. Any Xtra required by a movie must be installed on the user's system. That means the user must already have it, you must supply it, or you must provide the user a means to get it. Deciding what Xtras are needed and how to provide them is the subject of the section "Bundling Xtras" later in this chapter.

The Xtras you have

In addition to looking at the Xtras folder to see what Xtras you have available, you can use the Movie Xtras dialog box from within Director. Open a new movie, and then, from the Modify menu, select Movie and then Xtras. You will see the Xtras that Director considers the default set needed for your movie, but they aren't all the Xtras; they're just the most commonly used Xtras. If you perform some authoring action that uses another Xtra that isn't in the list, Director adds it to the list (although you will need to add scripting Xtras manually). For example, if you have a third-party Xtra that supplies custom transitions, the Xtra won't show up in the list until you use one of the custom transitions.

XTRAS FOR YOUR MOVIE:
The Movie Xtras dialog
box contains the list of
Xtras needed for your
current movie.

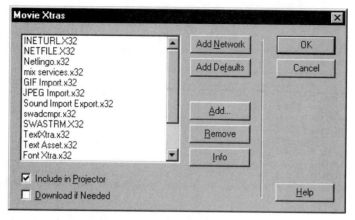

Selecting an Xtra in the Movie Xtras dialog box may or may not give you
an active Info button. When the button is available, you can click it to get
additional information about that specific Xtra. This information is from
the Web, so you'll need to be connected to the Internet for access. Other
information about Xtras may be included in readMe files included with
the Xtras or in help files supplied through the Xtra's interface.

To see the rest of the Xtras installed on your system, click the Add button
in the Movie Xtras dialog box. The Add Xtras dialog box appears, listing
other available Xtras.

EXTRA XTRAS:
The Add Xtras dialog
box shows all of the
available Xtras not
already included in the
Movie Xtras dialog box.

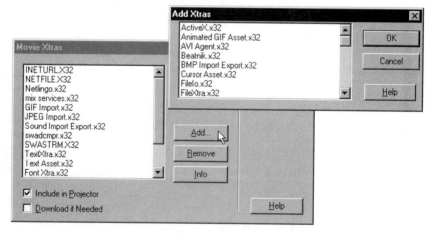

Each Xtra occupies its own chunk of RAM, so if you install a lot of Xtras,
you may want to increase the RAM your computer has allocated to
Director (Macintosh only). Some Xtras are more RAM intensive than

others; for example, a Lingo Xtra may occupy only a few bytes of memory, while a database Xtra may require almost as much RAM as Director itself.

> The Xtras folder has an additional feature that you might find handy: It can be used for more than just Xtras and plug-ins. If you place a Director movie or external Cast file in the folder, it appears under the Xtras menu when Director is launched. Selecting a Director movie from the Xtras menu will open the movie as a Movie in a Window (MIAW). Casts placed in the Xtras folder are especially handy. You can create external Casts that contain handlers or images (such as buttons) that you commonly use in your projects and then place the Cast in the Xtras folder. When you select the Cast from the Xtras menu, the Cast will open in Director, allowing you to copy elements you want to use into the Casts of your movie.

The Director 7 CD contains folders named Xtra Partners and Goodies. These folders contain demo versions of Xtras and utilities that give you an idea of what is available in the way of third-party Xtras. The Web is also a useful place for finding out what Xtras are available; you'll find a variety of freeware, shareware, and retail Xtras. Often they can be downloaded directly, or you can play with a downloadable demo version. Here are some sites to check out for lists of Xtras:

- http://www.macromedia.com/support/director/
- http://www.director-online.com/

Appendix F also lists a number of sites for obtaining useful Xtras.

XTRA TYPES

Xtras come in numerous flavors—and identifying the particular flavor, or type, of Xtra can often cause some confusion. The confusion arises because Xtras can be categorized according to how they are used (plug-and-play versus "headless" Xtras), how they are implemented (on a programming level), or their intended purpose. We can look at Xtras from all three points of view, but what should be most important to you is that an Xtra fulfills some purpose—not that it fits into some type.

Plug-and-play versus headless Xtras

I make the somewhat arbitrary distinction between plug-and-play and headless Xtras because, although some Xtras are almost transparent in their use and may be supplied with their own interface, others require implementation through a Lingo-like interface. An example of a plug-and-play Xtra is one that adds new transitions to Director. You place the Xtra in your Xtras folder, and the next time you start Director, the transition will appear in the Transition dialog box. Examples of headless Xtras are FileIO and MUI Xtras. Both of these require you to create a child object, which then provides access to the functions you need. The distinction between plug-and-play versus headless Xtras is mine, not Macromedia's, but it can be a helpful demarcation as you're using them.

Xtras by programming type

Xtras use capabilities that are built into Director, and it's often useful to make a distinction based on which technology they use.

External Cast Xtras

If you create an external Cast from within Director and then place the Cast file in the Xtras folder, the Cast will show up in the Xtras menu when you run Director. In this way, you can create database Casts that contain useful images and handlers that you may want to use in various projects. Open a Cast using the Xtras menu, and drag any element you need into the Casts of the movie you are working on.

MIAW Xtras

Anyone who is conversant with Lingo can create an **MIAW Xtra**. You create a Director movie and then place it in the Xtras folder. The movie shows up in the Xtras menu. If you open the movie, it shows up as an MIAW, with Lingo providing the ability for the Xtra to affect Director functions.

MOA Xtras

MOA stands for **Macromedia Open Architecture**. Director has built into it an **application programming interface** (API) that allows programmers to write Xtras in the C/C++ programming language that interact with

Director through calls to the API. These Xtras can modify Director features or add entirely new features. Because they are written in C, they can implement functions in Director that are difficult to accomplish using Lingo. A database, for example, can be created within Director, but such a database will likely be slow and inefficient. Using C, however, the database can be implemented as an Xtra that will perform many times faster.

MIX Xtras

MIX stands for **Macromedia Information Exchange**. MIX Xtras are used to import and export file types not built into Director. Macromedia, for example, develops MIX Xtras to support new graphics formats, new sound formats, and other media formats as they are developed. The Xtras are implemented through Director's standard Import and Export menu items, although the Xtra may provide an interface of its own. MIX Xtras are typically used to import files while authoring, but they also must be included with your movies that use linked graphics or sound.

Xtras by purpose

Director uses five types of Xtras, categorized by their purposes: cast member Xtras, import Xtras, transition Xtras, scripting Xtras, and tool Xtras.

Cast member Xtras

Cast member Xtras, also called **sprite Xtras**, enable Director to control media types that it can't otherwise manipulate. A sprite Xtra provides the application with the data it needs to incorporate new kinds of cast members, so if a new video or sound technology emerges, Director should be able to add it to the multimedia mix. Some sprite Xtras work through the standard Import dialog box (available via the File menu). Other sprite Xtras appear on the Insert menu; these usually offer their own Import-style dialog box. Still other sprite Xtras require Lingo to control the sprite.

One example of a sprite Xtra is PhotoCaster, from Media Lab, Inc., which is included with Director 7. It imports graphic images from Photoshop files, which might not seem like a big deal since Director 7 reads that format automatically. But PhotoCaster can take a multiple-layer Photoshop file and import each layer as a separate cast member, each with the accurate registration points necessary to re-create the composite image on the Stage. What's more, all items in the layers are neatly anti-aliased onto a blank background, eliminating the fuzzy halo effect that often accompanies imported external artwork. For designers who frequently work with Photoshop, this Xtra can save many tedious hours of image tweaking. The PhotoCaster dialog box is accessed from the Insert menu under Media Lab Media.

THE LAIR OF THE LAYERS:
The PhotoCaster Xtra imports individual layers of Photoshop images as nicely fringe-free cast members.

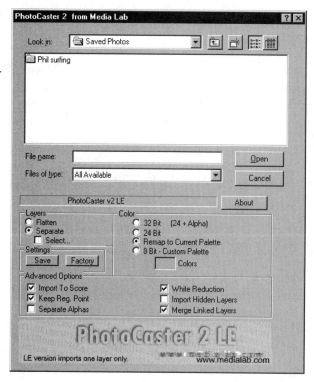

You'll often find an authoring version as well as a distribution version of a sprite Xtra in your Xtras folder. If that's the case, only the distribution version should be supplied with your movie. The Shockwave 7 download contains all of the standard sprite Xtras necessary for the most common file types, so most Shockwave movies don't require any sprite Xtras to be included.

Import Xtras

Import Xtras give Director the capability of importing media into a movie. When your movie cast members have links to external files, the file is imported every time the movie runs, and the necessary import Xtra must be available. That means you must include the Xtra with your movie.

Transition Xtras

http://www. metroradio-com.hk

Director comes with an extensive suite of transition effects, but you can expand that with **transition Xtras**. These show up as additional entries in the Frame Properties: Transition dialog box, just like other transitions, and you can access and finesse them just as you can the built-in transitions. That's why I don't consider most transition Xtras to be headless: They don't have an interface of their own, but that doesn't matter because they borrow an existing one.

One example of a transition Xtra is the DM XTreme Transitions collection, from Dedalomedia Interactive (see DMTools.com on the Web). Once installed, the available transitions show up in the Transitions dialog box along with the other transitions. I especially appreciate the Ripple Fade and Rollup transitions.

ROLL OUT THE TRANSITIONS:
Third-party transition Xtras can give you some easy-to-use but very impressive transitions.

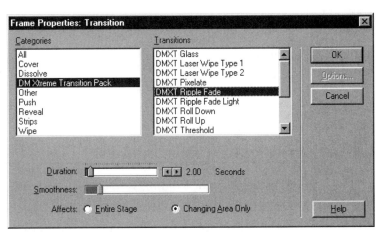

Scripting Xtras

Some Xtras are designed to extend the Lingo vocabulary by engineering new functions and providing Lingo-like syntax to carry them out. The scripting terminology isn't always official Lingo, but it can be interwoven with the genuine article through scripting as long as the Xtra is present. These are known as **scripting Xtras**, or **Lingo Xtras**.

A good illustration of a third-party Lingo Xtra is the Buddy API Xtra by Magic Modules (see www.mods.com.au/budapi). This Xtra provides more than 100 Windows API and Macintosh toolbox functions, including (but not limited to) tools for the following purposes:

- Finding, opening, copying, deleting, and printing files

- Controlling applications external to Director

- Getting operating system version information

- Getting processor information

Much of the control you've wished for over elements external to Director becomes available with the Buddy API Xtra. Once you have access to the functions provided in the Buddy API Xtra, you'll find a thousand uses for them.

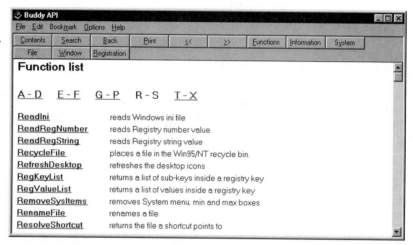

Two other important scripting Xtras are included with Director:

- The NetLingo Xtra provides much of the program's network access capabilities. If all of a sudden your production's Web-related functions don't work, it may be because this unit's missing.

- The FileIO Xtra provides the ability to read and write files from Director. We delve extensively into the FileIO extra later in this chapter.

Unlike other Xtra types, scripting Xtras can be opened and closed with Director still in session, via scripts incorporating the Lingo commands openXlib and closeXlib. See their entries in *A Lingo Lexicon* (Appendix C) for details. Scripting Xtras placed in the Xtras folder are opened automatically, but you can use openXlib to open Xtras in other locations.

NetLingo, FileIO, and Buddy API are examples of global scripting Xtras; install them, and the specialized Lingo they provide works just like any other bit of Lingo. Using them is like creating a bunch of global handlers that are instantly recognized and understood.

Tool Xtras

Other Xtras function as enhancements to Director itself, presenting an interface window that works well with the application's look and feel; because they're built for authoring, they're called **tool Xtras**. Tool Xtras help you while you are authoring, but they have no role while the movie is playing. For that reason, you don't need to distribute tool Xtras with your movies. Examples of tool Xtras include a spell checker that checks the spelling in your text fields, debugging tools that function along with the Debugger window and Message window, and a dialog box creation tool that uses a graphical user interface for design and then provides the Lingo for implementing the dialog box in your movie.

Classification of Xtra types isn't an exact science, and you won't learn any hard and fast rules. You'll hear scripting Xtras called Lingo Xtras, sprite Xtras called cast Xtras, and so forth. But it doesn't matter what you call them, so long as you understand how to use them.

Because Xtras make their contributions relatively seamlessly, you can easily forget that Xtras are there. But by taking advantage of their power, you're required to make a commitment: If the Xtra used isn't somehow provided for every version of your movie, playback will come screeching to a halt. This goes for projectors as well—you'll need to include the necessary Xtras when you distribute them.

BUNDLING XTRAS

With the exception of tool Xtras, which by definition are for authoring only, chances are you'll need to make sure the Xtras your movie uses are available with your production. Just how you do this depends on how your final production is delivered.

For Shockwave and "slim" projectors (projectors that use the Shockwave system player), most of the common Xtras required by a movie are included in the Shockwave player or installed when Shockwave 7 is installed. This includes the Xtras for importing BMP, PICT, JPEG, and GIF images; handling text; playing sound; and managing Shockwave Audio. End users will need the Shockwave player to play your movie at all, but once they have it, no other Xtras may be needed.

If your movie requires Xtras that are not included in the Shockwave installation, users will need to install them on their system before your movie will play. For Shockwave movies, this is accomplished by checking an Xtra's Download If Needed check box in the Movie Xtras dialog box. This will cause the Shockwave movie to prompt the user to allow the download of the necessary files—if the user agrees, the download occurs automatically. Only the information required to download the required file (the file's Internet location) is included in the Shockwave movie, so the movie size (and download time) is not adversely affected. For projectors that use the Shockwave player, Xtras can be provided in two ways, as described later for stand-alone projectors.

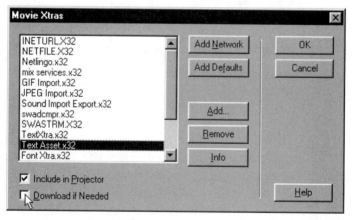

Information needed for downloading Xtras is contained in a file named Xtrainfo.txt (which is in the same folder as your Director application). This file may contain several types of information about each Xtra, although not all Xtras require all types of information. The Xtrainfo file contains the name of the file containing an Xtra, which is often different than the Xtra's name as shown in the Movie Xtras dialog box and generally differs between Windows and the Macintosh. Also included in the file is the URL of the site on the Internet from which the Xtra can be downloaded and the URL where you can get more information about the Xtra (for the Info button in the Movie Xtras dialog box). Any Xtra supplied with Director will have an entry in the Xtrainfo file, as should any Xtras that are properly installed at a later date. Remember, the information about which Xtras are required for your particular movie is stored within the movie (and can be accessed through the Movie Xtras dialog box). The information in the Xtrainfo.txt file contains information about all Xtras installed, not just those used by your current movie.

When you check the Download if Needed option for Xtras, Director will attempt to contact the download site listed in the Xtrainfo.txt file and download the Xtra. This insures that the given URL is correct, that the Xtra can be downloaded, and that you have the latest version of the Xtra. What you see as the download occurs is approximately what the end user will see, except the end user will be prompted to permit the download and will have the opportunity to prevent it. Xtras that will be downloaded in this manner must be packaged (by their manufacturer) with a digital signature that guarantees the file to be safe using the Verisign security system. The file download uses the Verisign secure download process to guarantee security. To be available to Shockwave, the Xtra must also designated Shockwave Safe by the original developer (again, designated by a digital signature in the file). Shockwave Safe means the Xtra will not attempt to perform any actions not permitted by net movies, as discussed in earlier chapters on Shockwave.

If you distribute Shockwave movies in a medium other than the Web, the movie won't automatically connect to the Internet and attempt to download the required Xtras. If the user is not connected, your movie will hang as it attempts to make the required connection. To avoid this, you may be better off providing any necessary Xtras as part of your installation process.

Since they don't have access to the Shockwave player, stand-alone projectors require that all necessary Xtras be provided. You can provide Xtras for projectors (both stand-alone and slim) in one of two ways: by placing them in a folder named Xtras (in the same folder as your movie) or by including them (bundling them) with the projector. Which method is best is open to debate—some prefer bundling (Macromedia seems to suggest this), whereas some developers recommend using the Xtras folder.

Including Xtras with a projector increases the size of the projector file and increases the time required to load the file. Also, you will need to re-create the projector if you decide that another Xtra is required. Including an Xtras folder with the projector means that you can add additional Xtras to the Xtras folder without re-creating the projector, but it also means that you have to make sure that the Xtras folder ends up in the same location as your projector.

> Although it will sometimes work, you shouldn't attempt to both provide an Xtras folder and bundle Xtras in a projector. Stick to one method or the other. Trying to do both will generally cause your movie to fail to run or will create an error if it does run.

To bundle an Xtra with a projector, check the Include in Projector check box for the Xtra in the Movie Xtras dialog box. All Xtras listed in the Move Xtras dialog box that have the Include in Projector option checked will automatically be included when you create the projector. This is true for both stand-alone projectors and slim projectors, although stand-alone projectors will require Xtras that a slim projector doesn't need.

A LASTING LINK:
When you link to Xtras via the Movie Xtras dialog box, those Xtras will automatically be bundled with your production when you convert it to a projector.

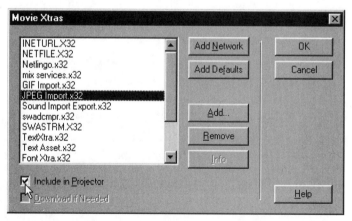

You may need to experiment to determine which Xtras are needed for your project. If you include all of the Xtras in Director's Xtras list as shown in the Movie Xtras dialog box, you can expect your movie to run. If you use an Xtra that's not in Director's default list, Director will automatically add it to the Movie Xtras list. An exception to this rule is when you use an unlisted Lingo Xtra; in this case, you will have to add the Xtra to the list manually. To add an Xtra to the list, click the Add button in the Movie Xtras dialog box, select the Xtra you need in the Add Xtras dialog box, and then click OK. To remove an Xtra from the list, select the Xtra and then click the Remove button. During your experimentation, you can click the Add Defaults button to add all the default Xtras back in, including any of the default Xtras that you may have removed.

Whether you choose to include Xtras in your projector or to include them separately in an Xtras folder, use the list in the Movie Xtras dialog box as your guide. The decision process is probably going to be a lot more difficult for your small projects, like those testing what you learn in this chapter, than it will be for large projects. In a large project, you will probably be using most of Director's built-in capabilities and will therefore require most of the default Xtras. The difference between including all of the Xtras and including only the minimum needed for a small project is probably about 600K and is important only if you are downloading the file or trying to fit it onto a diskette. Here are some guidelines:

- The network Xtras (INetURL, NetFile, and NetLingo) are required if you are accessing the Internet. NetFile is also required for accessing local Shockwave Audio files.

- GIF Import and JPEG Import are required only if you have linked cast members of that type.

- Font Xtra and Font Asset are required only if you include fonts in your movie.

- The Sound Import Export Xtra is required for accessing external sounds, including Shockwave Audio.

- The files swadcmpr and SWASTRM (SWA Decompression and SWA Streaming on the Macintosh) are required for external SWA sounds and for movies that use Shockwave-compressed sounds.

- No Xtras are needed for internal sounds (that is, sounds that are not linked) unless Shockwave compression is used.

When you use the Movie Xtras dialog box to examine linkages, you may find that Director has included some Xtras that you don't think you need. Take care when removing them; they may be necessary to the operation of the movie, and removing them may make your production bomb bait. However, if it's a third-party Xtra that you don't remember using, it may have been added inadvertently. Some Xtras automatically add cast members to the Cast even when they've been idly selected. Director will add a link on such an occasion, but you can delete both it and any cast members that may have been created.

Xtras "stick" to your movies.

If you are creating a project with multiple movies, you don't need to include Xtras in every movie. Xtras initialized in one movie stay around as long as the projector is running. Include the Xtras you will need in the first movie, and they will be available to all subsequent movies to which you link.

If your project requires an Xtra that is not available to it, you will see an alert box reporting the missing Xtra during testing.

Xtra errors:
When you test your movie, Director will report any missing Xtras.

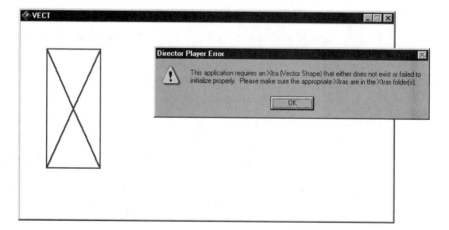

If an Xtra is missing, Director will typically still try to play the movie. Exactly what happens depends on the type of Xtra that is missing:

- For sprite Xtras, director will display a red X shape in place of the sprite that could not be accessed.

- For transition Xtras, the requested transition will be replaced with a jump-cut.

- Sounds requiring a missing Xtra won't play.

- For missing scripting Xtras, attempting to access a handler requiring the Xtra will result in a "Handler not found" error message.

Xtras can be a complicated subject, requiring complete books for a full examination. For additional information on Xtras, here are two worthy books to check out:

- *Xtravaganza!: The Essential Sourcebook for Macromedia Xtras* by Chuck Henderson (Peachpit Press)

- *The Director Xtras Book* by Rich Shupe (Ventana Communications Group, Inc.)

THE HEADLESS XTRAS

Now we come to the more difficult class of Xtra: the headless variety. For the most part, these follow the same rules of installation and bundling as other Xtras—they're just a little harder to put to work because they lack a user interface. Here are some examples:

- *NetLingo* provides a great deal of the online networking capabilities of Director 7. We've discussed these capabilities in Chapters 5, 14, and 15. The NetLingo commands are also included in this book's *A Lingo Lexicon* appendix and in Director's *Lingo Dictionary*.

- *FileIO* lets you both read from and write to standard text files placed anywhere on the local system. (To get networked text, you'll need to use NetLingo commands, which are described in Chapter 14:

Scripting with Net-Savvy Lingo.) Since fileIO is very practical but rather inscrutably documented by Macromedia, we'll focus on this Xtra in a moment.

- *MUI* lets you create custom dialog boxes containing check boxes, radio buttons, scrolling text fields, and other elements. This Xtra is even more poorly documented than FileIO, so if you need to use custom dialog boxes, you might consider procuring a third-party Xtra or utility that provides the same functionality implemented through a graphical user interface.

If a headless Xtra has no user interface—no presence in the Xtras menu or elsewhere in Director outside of the Movie Xtras dialog box—how can you tell when the Xtra is installed? Simple: Enter the command showXlib in the Message window to get a printout of all open XLibraries and their contents (the Xtras).

showXlib

A description similar to this should be returned:

```
-- XLibraries:
--    Xtra: Beatnik
--    Xtra: FileXtra
--    Xtra: UiHelper
--    Xtra: JavaConvert
--    Xtra: QuicktimeSupport
--    Xtra: NetLingo
--    Xtra: Multiuser
--    Xtra: XmlParser
--    Xtra: Mui
--    Xtra: fileio
--    Xtra: ActiveX
```

XLIBRARY:
A type of file that contains one or more Xtras or DLLs.

Using this command will return the exact name of each Xtra, which may not be precisely the same file name used for the Xtra as seen in the Movie Xtras dialog box. For instance, the Xtra library may be named fileio, but it may show up in the Movie Xtras dialog box as FileIO.x32 (for Windows) or FileIO PPC Xtra (for the Macintosh). If you poke around in your Xtras folder, you should find an Xtra corresponding to each of the items in the returned list.

Xtras as objects: A key concept

The other question that headless Xtras bring to mind is this: If there's no user interface, how do you get these Xtras to work?

In some cases (such as NetLingo), there's no manipulation at all for you to do; these Xtras simply add needed functionality. Even those that do have user-settable aspects don't have to follow a set methodology; there are no rules that must be obeyed by Xtra authors. But in most cases, the conceptual framework for putting an Xtra to work is this: *Treat the Xtra as a parent script.* Remember the discussion of parent/child scripting in Chapter 18? Many of the principles of P/C scripting apply here.

To use a typical headless Xtra, you

1. Create a child object derived from an Xtra.

2. Pass commands to and from that child object.

3. Dispose of the object when you're done with it.

You can't open multiple copies of the same Xtra, but you can create multiple child objects derived from one Xtra, all running simultaneously. Xtras, however, aren't like typical parent scripts in that you don't set a number of parameters during the birth process; you just give the object a name. One object born of an Xtra has the same innate characteristics as the next—but you don't have to use all those characteristics every time. Once you have created the child object, you can modify the object using the Xtra's built-in functions, as we'll see in the following example for FileIO.

WORKING WITH FILEIO

Enough of the theory. Let's put the parent/child methodology to work by tackling FileIO, Director's main tool for reading and writing files. We'll start by initializing a new child object we'll call scribe. But before we do that, let's open a new movie in Director and save it. Doing this will set the moviePath system property, and that will make it easier to talk about the file we will be creating (because we'll be using the moviePath to define the newly created file's location on your system). It doesn't matter what you call the movie, but you'll be putting the new text file in the same folder as the movie.

1. *Open Director and save the movie.*

2. *In the Message window, enter this line:*

```
put the moviePath
```

On my system, the path returned is C:\Projects\. You will see a different path, depending on the system you are working on and the location where you saved your movie.

Now we're ready to create the child object for accessing a file.

3. *In the Message window, enter the following:*

```
scribe = new (xtra "FileIO")
```

Nothing observable should happen, but behind the scenes, the object has been created. Before we can start putting this object through its paces, we need to know how to communicate with it. What terms and syntax does it recognize?

If we have a well-documented readMe file at hand, these questions may be easily answered. But if not (and we don't), the trick is to look at the instructions encoded within the Xtra.

4. *In the Message window, enter the following:*

```
put interface(xtra "FileIO")
```

This should produce a torrent of information. You might want to cut and paste it into a text file, or even print it, so you can read it in a more manageable form. I've taken the liberty of italicizing portions for the sake of clarity:

```
-- "xtra fileio
new object me
    -- create a new child instance
-- FILEIO --
fileName object me
    -- return fileName string of the open file
status object me
    -- return the error code of the last method called
error object me, int error
    -- return the error string of the error
setFilterMask object me, string mask
    -- set the filter mask for dialogs
```

openFile object me, string fileName, int mode
    -- opens named file. valid modes: 0=r/w 1=r 2=w
closeFile object me -- close the file
displayOpen object me
    -- displays an open dialog and returns the selected fileName
    -- to lingo
displaySave object me, string title, string defaultFileName
    -- displays save dialog and returns selected fileName to
    -- lingo
createFile object me, string fileName
    -- creates a new file called fileName
setPosition object me, int position
    -- set the file position
getPosition object me
    -- get the file position
getLength object me
    -- get the length of the open file
writeChar object me, string theChar
    -- write a single character (by ASCII code) to the file
writeString object me, string theString
    -- write a null-terminated string to the file
readChar object me
    -- read the next character of the file and return it as an
    -- ASCII code value
readLine object me
    -- read the next line of the file (including the next
    -- RETURN) and return as a string
readFile object me
    -- read from current position to EOF and return as a string
readWord object me
    -- read the next word of the file and return it as a string
readToken object me, string skip, string break
    -- read the next token and return it as a string
getFinderInfo object me
    -- get the finder info for the open file (Mac Only)
setFinderInfo object me, string attributes
    -- set the finder info for the open file (Mac Only)
delete object me
    -- deletes the open file

```
+ version xtraRef
    -- display fileIO version and build information in the
    -- message window
* getOSDirectory
    -- returns the full path to the Mac System Folder or
    -- Windows Directory
```

So we have a plethora of data—but what does it all mean? Well, all the
object me entries are indicators of the parent/child structure, so mentally
substitute the name of the object there. That leaves us with a list of commands and at least a hint of the appropriate syntax (in this particular
case, the crucial use of parentheses isn't mentioned). A quick look at one
of the lines will help us decipher what we are seeing:

```
openFile object me, string fileName, int mode
    -- opens named file; valid modes: 0=r/w 1=r 2=w
```

The name of the function is openFile. It takes three arguments: The first
is me, the reference to the object; the second is a string; and the third is an
integer (int). The two dashes are like a comment symbol and tell us that
what follows is a description of the function. In this case, we are told that
the function opens a file, and we are given the allowable values for the
third argument (we'll deal with those in a minute). From the information
we see about openFile, we could write a command line such as this:

```
openFile(scribe, "myFile", 0)
```

Or, in dot syntax:

```
scribe.openFile("myFile", 0)
```

Although the parentheses aren't shown in the output of the interface
function, they are required when using the dot syntax (and strongly recommended in both cases).

Creating an external file

Let's tinker some more by adding a few commands to our scribe object.

5. *In the Message window, enter this line:*

```
scribe.createFile (the moviePath & "Prose.txt")
```

See the importance of the parentheses? We're passing the command
createFile to scribe and specifying the name of the file to be created.
I added the suffix .txt to mark the file as a text file, but this isn't strictly

necessary; you can place any valid file name in the title text string. Mind you; createFile or any of the other special terms that come bundled with FileIO aren't really Lingo—they're just keywords that will be recognized in this context.

Did it work? Let's find out:

6. Switch to the desktop-level view of your system (the Windows desktop or the Macintosh Finder). Open the folder in which you saved the Director movie.

Somewhere in the directory, the file Prose.txt should appear. If you didn't save your movie (and set the moviePath), the file will likely have ended up at the top level of your hard drive. If you can't find it, try searching your drive with your system's Find command.

If you examine the file's properties or attributes, you'll see that the file is empty. That's because we've only created it. We'll have to pour some text into it before it starts taking up space.

Opening the file

Before we can write to the file, we need to open it. To do that, we use openFile, which we looked at earlier:

```
openFile object me, string fileName, int mode
    -- opens named file. valid modes: 0=r/w 1=r 2=w
```

When we looked at openFile earlier, we glossed over the values for the mode: r stands for read, w stands for write, and r/w stands for read or write. Thus, if we set the mode to 0, the file can be both read and written to. If we set it to 1, the file can only be read, and if we set it to 2, the file can only be written to. These distinctions are tailored after other languages (such as C), where this sort of file-access specification is common.

Let's open the file so that we can both read and write to it:

7. In the Message window, enter this line:

```
scribe,openFile(the moviePath & "Prose.txt", 0)
```

Again, nothing happens that we can readily see, but the file is opened. Although we have the ability to read and write to the file, we still have yet to do either. If we wanted to open a file that already exists, we would have used the openFile command, but not the createFile command. The createFile command is used for creating a new file where one did not previously exist.

If all this work without visible results is starting to unnerve you, try entering `put scribe.fileName()` in the Message window. It should return the name of the file as a text string. You can use this `put` entry at any point in the text-wrangling process.

Writing to the file

Let's try putting some text into our text file.

8. In the Message window, enter this line:

```
scribe.writeString ("Director 7 Demystified!")
```

You'll note that we don't need to name the file in the command line, just the object that has the file currently open. That's because FileIO objects can't open more than one file at a time, so any further specification would be extraneous. In this case, you've typed in the text string directly, but that's only one approach. You could also enter the entire contents of a string or of a field or text cast member, with a line like this:
```
scribe.writeString(member("Short Story Field").text)
```

Did it work? It's time to confirm. There's no Save File command in the interface documentation, so it's likely that the best way to save our changes to the file is by closing it.

9. In the Message window, enter this line:

```
scribe.closeFile()
```

Again, you don't enter any arguments because only one file can be affected.

10. From the desktop, use a word processing application to open the file Prose.txt.

If your word processor is capable of reading a simple text file (most are), you ought to see your own prose captured in the file. If this hasn't worked, see the section "I/O errors" a little later in this chapter.

Reading from the file

That takes care of the O part of FileIO. How about the I? That's a pretty straightforward process as well: Just open the file and read it into Director as a text string. You can park the text string in a number of locations: in a variable, in a position in a list, or in a text or field cast member. Make sure you quit your word processor before proceeding, because we won't be able to open the file if it's in use by another application.

— cast member

11. Create a field cast member and name it myText.

12. In the Message window, enter the following:

```
scribe.openFile (the moviePath & "Prose.txt", 0)
member("myText").text = scribe.readFile()
put member("myText").text
```

0 = r | w
1 = r
2 = w

Your deathless prose now springs into a new role as a cast member! Note that you've imported the actual text into the cast member, not forged a link to the external file. If you want your movie to reflect changes made to the text file, you'll need to go through the process of assigning the file's contents to the cast member again.

Disposing of the object

The scribe object has been pretty handy; we were able to assign six tasks to it, all of which it handled equally well. But like other objects, instances of Xtras stick around and take up memory unless you specifically get rid of them, which is what you should do now.

13. In the Message window, enter this line:

```
scribe = 0
```

I/O errors

Because so much about accessing external files is not directly under your control, errors are a lot more common when you use FileIO than when you use standard Lingo. A file you want to create may already exist; the file you want to write to may be read-only—an almost endless list of things can go wrong. Although so far in this book we haven't been doing it (to keep things simple), it's a good idea for you to check after each FileIO command to see whether an error occurred—and if an error did occur, you should have a handler on hand to take care of the problem. If the user specifies a file and the file can't be opened, for example, you should be ready to prompt the user to name a different file.

The FileIO Xtra includes the status command that you can use to make sure that things are working correctly. The status command returns a code referring to the last command executed. If status returns 0, you know that no error occurred. Otherwise, something went wrong. You should include a handler in your code that you call whenever something doesn't work (use a case statement that uses the returned error code to determine what to do). For your own information, or to display an error message to the user, you can use FileIO's error command, which returns a string describing the error. Here's how that might look in the Message window:

```
scribe.openFile("DoesNotExist", 0)
put status(scribe)
-- -37
put scribe.error(-37)
-- "Bad file name"
```

More FileIO commands

Those are the highlights of FileIO in a nutshell. As you can see from the interface documentation, several other intriguing capabilities exist. You might want to experiment with them, using the same syntax as described here and taking care to dispose of the objects when you're done. Here are some useful hints:

- You can read (or write) a file one piece at a time. For example, you can read only a single character from the file, using readChar.

- Consider the concept of the current position in an open file. When you first open the file, the current position is 0, the start of the file (actually, before the start). If you issue a readChar command, it returns the character following the current position (in this case, the first character). The current position is then moved to the next position, and another call to readChar will read the next character (not the same one again). In this manner, you could step through a file, reading it one character at a time.

- The getPosition command tells you the current position in the file. The setPosition command allows you to move to a specific location.

- Often you will want to append text to the end of a file. The getLength command tells you the number of characters in the file—a number you can then use with setPosition:

  ```
  scribe.setPosition(scribe.getLength())
  ```

  Writing to the file will now place the new contents at the end of the file.

- If you want the movie's user to determine where to place the file, the FileIO Xtra can simplify that process. The displayOpen command will cause a standard Open dialog box to pop up. When the user clicks the Open button, the file name (including the path) is returned. The file isn't actually opened at this point; you need to handle that with the `openFile` command. The `displaySave` command performs the same function except that it pops up a Save dialog box instead of an Open dialog box.

POINTS TO REMEMBER

Here are some of the key points of this chapter:

- Xtras come in five main flavors: **cast member Xtras**, **import Xtras**, **transition Xtras**, **scripting Xtras**, and **tool Xtras**.

- To install an Xtra, you need to include a copy of it in Director's **Xtras folder**, which should be in the same folder as the Director application.

- You may need to **bundle** Xtras with any projectors derived from your movie. You can do this by bundling the Xtras into the projector (in the Modify Xtras dialog box, select Include in Projector) or by including an Xtras folder with the projector.

- The **Shockwave player** provides all of the common Xtras. For most projects, it's likely that you won't need to include any Xtras with your Shockwave movie or slim projector (a projector that uses the Shockwave player to play).

- Some Xtras come with their own **user interface**. Others are **headless**, offering functionality but requiring a good amount of Lingo manipulation to set them into action.

- Treat FileIO and similar Xtras like **parent scripts**. You need to create a child object of each Xtra and then set that object to work.

- Don't forget to **dispose**! Like all child objects, Xtra-derived objects will persist in RAM unless you get rid of them after their usefulness has passed.

- **Instructions** on how to use a headless Xtra are usually encoded in the Xtra itself. You can read these instructions in the Message window by using the `interface` function. Some Xtras come with help files or a readMe file.

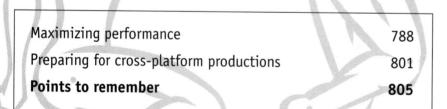

CHAPTER 22

PROFESSIONAL TOPICS AND TECHNIQUES

BY NOW, YOU'RE PROBABLY MORE THAN READY TO LEAVE THE REALM OF theory and tutorials for real-world experience. That's why we'll devote this chapter to the topics and challenges that often arise when a project becomes a product—a piece of software in its own right, ready to get down to business in any number of contexts, on any number of desktops.

We'll start by looking at the general issue of performance: how to maximize your multimedia elements for optimum playback. Then we'll wrap up with a rundown of the factors you'll consider when developing for both Windows and the MacOS platforms.

MAXIMIZING PERFORMANCE

Even after all the elements of a Director production are in place, a lot of fine-tuning usually remains to be done—especially if the final product is intended to run on a broad range of machines. Too often multimedia programmers have been frustrated by a movie that worked fine while it was being built but started slowing down and getting out of sync as soon as it was loaded onto someone else's computer. Another source of angst is the movie that performs wonderfully until one last, modest feature is added; like the straw that breaks the camel's back, that addition inexplicably slows playback to a crawl.

These problems can't be avoided entirely, but they can be kept to a minimum if you rigorously analyze and regularly review and update the measures taken to maximize performance in your production. This section offers some general principles to keep in mind.

Memory management

In Chapter 1 we touched briefly on the Unload priority feature, which lets you perform a sort of RAM triage on cast members by designating which ones should stay permanently in memory and which ones should be removed as soon as possible. We haven't used this feature in our tutorials, since none of them have made heavy RAM demands, but you should get familiar with this tool as your productions get larger in scale and scope. When Director decides that memory is running short, it removes some elements from memory so that others can be loaded. The least recently used cast members are the first ones to be unloaded. This is generally a good system, but it doesn't always match the needs of your production.

Cast members already in memory appear on the screen almost immediately, while loading or reloading a cast member can cause a short delay. So even if your production never seems to be running low on memory, you may want to make sure that certain cast members stay in memory. Also, remember that although some commonly used cast members don't seem to be experiencing loading delays, the reloading of those members will also slow down the loading of new cast members in a frame. Think of segments of your movie as a whole. If you know a large graphic will require some extra time to load, you can facilitate that by making sure that other members are still in memory and don't need to be reloaded. If you know that all the cast members used in a section of your movie won't be used again, drop those members from memory so more memory will be free for new cast members.

Each cast member has a purge priority property. You can set a cast member's purge priority in its Properties dialog box while you are authoring, but you can also use Lingo to change the priority on the fly. That lets you give a cast member a low purge priority in segments of your movie where you frequently use it and then change the priority for sections where it's rarely or never used.

Set the Unload priority for each cast member in its Properties dialog box, accessible via the pop-up menu at the bottom of the dialog box.

A SELECTIVE MEMORY: Set the Unload priority of individual cast members.

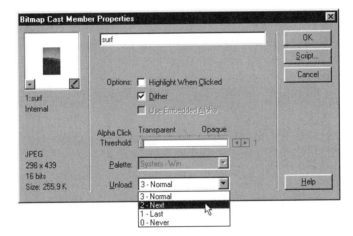

The higher the purge priority you give a cast member, the more likely it is to be removed from memory. These are your choices:

- *3 - Normal* leaves the purge decision to Director's discretion. This is the default option and means that Director can remove the cast member whenever it needs the memory.

- *2 - Next* means that the cast member will be purged after cast members with Normal priority are purged.

- *1 - Last* means that Director will purge a cast member only when it becomes absolutely necessary to free up the RAM space it occupies.

- *0 - Never* dictates that once loaded, the cast member will remain in memory for as long as the movie or projector is open.

> Don't use the Never purge priority unless you find it absolutely necessary. Even then, use Lingo to set the priority and change it to a higher priority as soon as possible. Situations can occur in which preventing Director from freeing up RAM will result in a crash—a worse scenario than a frame that is displayed slowly. Instead, set the purge priority of cast members that you want to stay loaded to 1 - Last. They'll stay in memory until Director desperately needs the RAM.

Setting the loading point

Another memory management tool is found in each Cast's Cast Properties dialog box (choose Cast Properties from the Modify menu). That's where you can specify exactly when cast members in that Cast should be loaded into RAM: whenever they turn up in the Score, after the first frame of the movie (that is, when it starts playing), or before playback begins.

CAST LOADING :
Set the loading point in a Cast's Cast Properties dialog box.

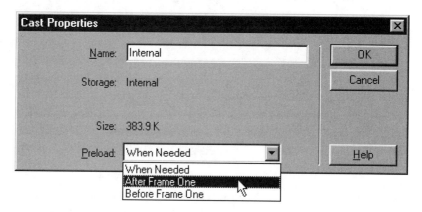

Choosing When Needed is appropriate in most instances, since Director loads the cast members in the order they appear in the Score and thus ensures that elements needed for the beginning of a movie are quickly available. The downside of When Needed is that Cast loading is an ongoing process that can introduce a series of delays, especially if the user can jump around in the movie. The After Frame One setting loads the cast members for the first frame as quickly as possible and then proceeds to load other cast members (in the order they are used in the Score) up to the limit of available RAM. This gets you the first frame, but it can result in a delay in going to other frames. On the plus side, because a large number of cast members are loaded, animation can be improved. The Before Frame One setting is similar to After Frame One but doesn't bother to display the first frame before loading. This approach is useful if you want to jump right into an animation and need all necessary members loaded. Before Frame One is good for situations in which you're jumping from one movie to another movie, the second movie using the Cast into which you're loading. You can place a custom cursor or a message of the "Please Wait" variety in the last frame of the old movie, which will be displayed until Director is ready to launch the new movie.

Memory Lingo

Several Lingo elements are useful for loading and unloading cast members, checking the status of loading, and even determining how your movie is handling loading and memory. We've used some of these in previous chapters; others are mentioned here for the first time. You should be familiar with the following elements.

Save your Director files (including all Casts) before you start messing around with memory. Better yet, use Save and Compact. One obvious reason to do this is to save the heartbreak of losing data if you crash your system. Also, some functions don't perform correctly if cast members have never been saved. For example, setting **the traceLoad = 2** (as shown in the following paragraphs) will crash Director 7.0 if cast members haven't been saved, although that problem should be fixed in the Director 7.0.2 update. Problems have also been reported with the **loaded** and **preload** commands in the 7.0 release.

The purgePriority cast member property overrides the priority set in a cast member's Properties dialog box. The values are the same as those given in the dialog box, but you use only the priority number, not the name. The following example sets the purge priority for a cast member named StartButton to Normal, which is level 3:

```
member("StartButton").purgePriority = 3
```

The traceLoad movie property is useful for delving into just when members get loaded into (or unloaded from) memory. The information is placed in the Message window unless a log file is specified using the traceLogFile system property. The default value is 0, which displays no information. Setting traceLoad to 1 displays a cast member's name when it is loaded or unloaded:

```
member 1 of castLib 1 ("StartButton") was loaded into memory.
member 6 of castLib 1 ("SpaceQT") was purged from memory.
```

Setting traceLoad to 2 displays a lot more information. Not only do you get the cast member's name and the frame number in which the member was loaded (or purged), you get information about when, which file, and the amount of seeking the hard drive had to do to find the information. Use traceLoad = 2 when you want to really fine-tune your production: You can arrange how your files are placed on a CD for the best performance.

TRACING YOUR LOAD:
The traceLoad
property gives you a
wealth of information
about when cast
members are loaded
and purged.

```
-- Welcome to Director --
the traceLoad = 2

Time = 6436234 msec (5234 msec later).
Movie "Trace" is on frame 1 (freeBytes = 69309412, 21308 bytes consumed).
member 1 of castLib 1 ("Oval") was loaded into memory.
Member is in movie "E:\Demystified\Projects\Trace.dir"
File seek info: No file access occurred.

Time = 6436410 msec (176 msec later).
Movie "Trace" is on frame 2 (freeBytes = 69283416, 25996 bytes consumed).
member 2 of castLib 1 was loaded into memory.
Member is in movie "E:\Demystified\Projects\Trace.dir"
File seek info: Seeked 204 to find member at file pos 13348.  Read in 648 bytes.
```

Several Lingo elements are available for preloading cast members. The preLoad command loads cast members used in a specified range of frames:

- preLoad (without any arguments) loads all cast members referenced in the Score from the current frame to the end of the movie.

- preLoad *[frameX]* (one argument) loads all cast members referenced in the Score from the current frame to the frame specified by the argument.

- preLoad *[frameX]*, *[frameY]* (two arguments) loads all cast members referenced in the Score from the frame specified by the first argument to the frame specified by the second argument.

The preLoadMember command works in a similar fashion but references specific cast members or a range of cast members:

- preLoadMember (without any arguments) loads all cast members in the movie.

- preLoadMember *[memberX]* (one argument) loads the specified cast member. You can also specify a particular Cast, as in preLoadMember "John Kuhl" of castLib "Family".

- preLoadMember *[memberX], [memberY]* (two arguments) loads a range of cast members beginning with the cast member specified in the first argument through the member specified in the second argument.

The preLoadMember command requires that the arguments used be valid. Referencing an empty cast slot or using an invalid name will result in a script error (although empty slots are permitted within a range of cast members).

Note that for both **preLoad** and **preLoadMember**, the full preloading requested may not be completely successful. It all depends on how much memory is available. Director loads cast members only until it runs out of memory; then it stops. To determine the amount of preloading that actually occurred, use the **result** function, as in:

```
preLoad 21, 142
put the result
-- 129
```

You can determine whether media have been successfully loaded in a number of ways—which one you choose depends on the situation. The frameReady function and mediaReady property are generally used when media is being downloaded from the Internet. To test to see if a particular cast member is in memory, use the loaded property:

```
put member("BigPic").loaded
-- 1
```

The loaded property returns TRUE (1) if the cast member is loaded into memory or FALSE (0) if it is not.

Instead of allowing Director to designate when (and which) cast members should be removed from RAM, you can specify when certain media should be purged. The unLoad command is used to purge cast members when you are referencing them by frame number:

- unLoad (without any arguments) purges all cast members referenced in the Score from all frames of the movie.

- unLoad *[frameX]* (one argument) purges all cast members used in the specified frame.

- unLoad *[frameX]*, *[frameY]* (two arguments) purges all cast members used in the range of frames spanned by the two arguments.

The unLoadMember command allows you to purge cast members by referencing them by either cast slot number or name:

- unLoadMember (without any arguments) purges all cast members in the movie.

- unLoadMember *[memberX]* (one argument) purges the specified cast member.

- unLoadMember *[memberX]*, *[memberY]* (two arguments) purges a range of cast members beginning with the cast member specified in the first argument and continuing through the member specified in the second argument.

Although traceLoad may erroneously report the unloading of script cast members, certain types of cast members are never unloaded: scripts, fonts, shapes, and transitions.

Several functions can help you determine how much memory is available to Director at any given time as well as how much memory is required for a segment of frames. Unfortunately, these functions are less useful than they might at first appear for a number of reasons.

First of all, you need to consider the total amount of memory available versus the amount of any *contiguous* memory. As Director loads and unloads cast members, it doesn't gather up unused areas of memory. This means that although a lot of memory may be available, it may be spread around as small chunks rather than contained in a large continuous piece. A new cast member is always loaded into a single, contiguous area, which may require the purging of cast members to create an area sufficiently large. (Occasionally this can even lead to situations in which Director needs to unload some members to fit in new ones and then unload the new ones to fit in the old ones again—a process called *churning*.)

The freeBytes function returns the amount of total bytes of free memory, contiguous or not. The freeBlock function returns the number of bytes in the largest area of contiguous free memory. If your movie seems to be loading cast members slowly, a check of memory with freeBlock may show that free memory has become fragmented into many small chunks. Your only real recourse is to issue an unLoad command to free up all memory, even though many cast members might need to be immediately loaded back in. As the cast members are reloaded, Director will attempt to arrange them adjacently, hopefully leaving an adequate area of contiguous free memory.

The ramNeeded function provides the number of bytes of memory needed for the cast members used in a specific range of frames. Its results are subject to two shortcomings: They don't take into account any elements that may be loaded via Lingo, and they don't deduct out of the total any elements that are already loaded into memory. If you can calculate adjustments for these two variables, you can use ramNeeded to make projections about how your movie will perform.

Graphics management

To keep your graphic cast members from occupying needlessly large amounts of RAM, watch out for these problems:

- *Excess color depth.* Graphics are often saved at a greater bit depth than is necessary. Remember that when you're importing or creating in the Paint window, Director gives new cast members a color depth that matches your current monitor settings, not the inherent color depth of the graphic. That's how 8-bit artwork can end up as 24-bit, and so on. So check your collection of Casts: Can that black-and-white design be converted to 1-bit, and can that simple color box be shifted to 8-bit?

> If a graphic cast member needs to be only one color, keep in mind that you can make it as small as possible by saving it as a 1-bit (that is, a black-and-white) cast member and then using the foreground color chip in the Tool Palette to colorize the sprites derived from it (you can also use the Lingo property **the forecolor of sprite**). But because 1-bit color produces a decidedly blocky image, it's best used for artwork that doesn't require subtle shading or anti-aliased edges.

- *Extraneous areas.* If any of your artwork has more space surrounding it in the Paint window than will be visible on the Stage, you can save RAM by trimming off the unseen areas. Likewise, make sure your animations don't needlessly duplicate areas; copy and modify only the moving parts.

- *Unused cast members.* Does your cast collection include some stray cast members, perhaps remnants from a prototype or some earlier draft? To cut down on file size, seek them out and clear their slots.

- *Reuse cast members.* If a portion of a large piece of artwork changes, don't import several versions of the artwork. Instead, make "patches" that can be strategically and seamlessly placed over the image.

If you have nonscripted sprites that remain on the Stage for a sequence of frames without moving, you can place them in only the first frame of the sequence and apply the Trails Score ink. That way, the sprites will still be displayed, but Director won't have to update them in each frame.

Sound management

With so many different ways to play sounds in a Director movie, it can be hard for you to tell which might be the best approach at any particular time, a problem magnified in Windows, where you can't be sure if your user even has a sound card installed. But since sound is seldom omitted entirely and is often one of the most RAM-intensive aspects of a multimedia production, it is wise to pay attention to these principles:

- *Keep it short.* If the sound lends itself to natural pauses (such as breaks in narration), use those pauses as points to divide a large file into multiple smaller files.

- *Don't oversample.* Storing sounds at an unnecessarily high sampling rate is just a waste of storage space and RAM. Spoken-word files may be perfectly acceptable at 11 kHz, and most computers aren't equipped to play back DAT-quality sound anyway.

- *Use the same sampling rate.* The sound devices used to combine sound are much more efficient if all sounds use the same sampling rate.

- When speedy playback is an issue, *use embedded instead of linked sounds*. They may enlarge the file size of your productions, but they also load more quickly. Extremely large files, however, are usually best kept in an external file and either used as a linked cast member or triggered with the sound playFile command.

- *Be careful about compression*. Compressed sounds do not travel well between platforms. Test and retest your cross-platform files.

Having a sound play while a movie is loading is a common way to ease transitions between movies. Be wary, however, of asking Director to play external sound files or large internal ones when calling other movies. Puppeting a short, looped sound is a better use of resources when CD-ROM drives (and their slower access times) are involved.

Digital video management

Much of the inherent quality of a QuickTime or an AVI movie cast member depends on the application in which it was created. The image quality, internal special effects, and compression ratios all affect the overall performance of digital video, and much, if not all, of the creation is out of the programmer's control. However, you can take some steps to ensure optimum performance in the context of a Director production:

- Enable the Direct to Stage option in the digital video movie's Cast Member Properties box.

- Substitute digital video for Director animations when appropriate. In some circumstances, a digital video movie performs better than a Director animation of the same actions. Since the movie is a single cast member and the animation might involve dozens of individual cast members, playback of the digital video is often less RAM intensive than tracking the choreography of sprites.

- Make sure that a copy of QuickTime is bundled with your production or that you provide the user with the means to download it.

Script management

Although scripts don't take up much storage space, Director can expend a lot of RAM resources keeping track of them and the results of their executions. Here are some rules of thumb for streamlined script deployment:

- *Don't write too many on idle event handlers.* They can quickly bog down your Director programs.

- *Don't use repeat loops to kill time while you're waiting for something to happen,* such as while downloading a file. The repeat loop can tie up the processor and make the system appear to be unresponsive. Instead, loop on a frame and make a test on each exit of the frame.

- *Avoid using updateStage* unless it's clearly needed to make your script work. Why force Director to update the Stage when nothing has changed?

- *Don't access a function more times than is necessary.* It takes time for Director to find and retrieve information implicit in a function. Instead, call the function once and store the results in a variable; then access that variable. Don't reprise the process unless you have reason to believe the value has changed.

- *Empty global variables* when they're no longer needed by setting them to VOID.

- *Empty lists when they are no longer needed.* Large lists can take up a good deal of RAM. When a list is no longer needed, set the list to VOID.

- *Dispose of RAM-resident entities* (Xtras, MIAWs, child objects) when you're through with them. Don't just suppress their display. Make sure you remove all references to child objects or they will remain in memory.

Don't forget to comment your code! Commented lines don't take up any more execution time, and there's no better way to annotate your efforts. It's worthwhile to laboriously document scripts (although it may seem a chore, especially at the end of a project, when you're tediously familiar with them), because weeks or months from now you may need to retrace your steps in a hurry. At that point, you'll thank yourself for having made the extra effort.

Save and Compact

You can't fully evaluate the performance of your Director-based production unless you've saved it recently with Save and Compact (as opposed to using the Save command). Save simply records everything in the Director file as it currently is, whereas Save and Compact optimizes the file for playback in its current configuration. It does this by analyzing where cast members appear in the Score and then reordering the position of their data within the movie file to better reflect the order of deployment during playback. In other words, the data documenting the cast member that appears in frame 1 may be stored closer to the beginning of the file than that of another cast member that doesn't show up until frame 17. Note that the order of elements in the Cast database isn't affected—just their organization on the bits-and-bytes level.

Since the Save and Compact command is already working on the bits-and-bytes level, it also takes the opportunity to fit the data together in the most efficient configuration, which is why a file will often shrink slightly after being saved with Save and Compact.

By the way, you don't have to wait for the end of your project to use Save and Compact. It's no different from Save except as noted, although it does take a few moments longer to carry out.

Linkage management

When you get ready to distribute a production, you're preparing to wrest it away from the environment in which it was developed—that is, your computer and your configuration of Director. Since Director 7 can be extended in so many directions, you need to take care that all capabilities survive the move to the outside world. This usually means taking care to preserve linkages. Here are a few issues for your checklist:

- Are you using multiple Casts? All external cast files are going to have to travel with the movies that use them and be located in the same relative location in the file structure. You can use the Cast dialog box (from the Modify menu, select Movie and then Casts) to change the linkages if necessary.

- What about Xtras? Make sure to include an Xtras folder with your project that contains all of the necessary Xtras. If you bundle Xtras into your projectors, make sure that all necessary Xtras are marked Include in Projector (from the Modify menu, select Movie and then Xtras). Never use both an Xtras folder and Xtras bundled together into a projector.

- Path name problems are fairly easy to resolve with Director 7; just use the property the searchPaths to make sure the application searches in the right place for the appropriate files. This is why it's important to test your production on a system separate from the one used to create it; unless your movie is removed from the original context, it's hard to tell if it is obeying new linkages to the final versions of support files (the ones that will travel with it) or simply using the original path names. Don't include URLs in the searchPaths as doing so can greatly slow down Director's search for files. For the same reason, don't include too many locations in the searchPaths.

One of the most common mistakes people make when preparing for distribution in Windows is assuming that the drive letter remains a constant: A: for the floppy drive, D: for the CD-ROM drive, and so on. The fact is that drive letters can be changed, and if someone does so, that person can inadvertently prevent your production from maintaining its links. It's best to use a Lingo script to find the appropriate drive letters and adjust the **searchPath** property accordingly.

Don't forget to check you production for viruses. Your customers will never forget or forgive you if you send them a virus that corrupts their hard drive or causes other problems. While you're at it, be sure to run an application such as Norton Disk Doctor on your files to be sure that they have retained their integrity.

PREPARING FOR CROSS-PLATFORM PRODUCTIONS

In theory, the differences between Macintosh-based and Windows-based Director movies are minimal. In reality, there are complications (as usual). Although the folks at Macromedia did an admirable job of smoothing the transition between platforms, there's no hiding the fact that the Macintosh can do some things a Windows-capable PC can't, and vice versa; incompatibilities and problems in translations inevitably occur. It's a relatively easy matter to become aware of these differences and compensate for them, and it's definitely easier to compensate than to rebuild your production from scratch on each platform, which is the porting option with some other multimedia software.

The primary platform differences

Some things just aren't the same for both the realms of Windows and Macintosh. Here are some of the primary inconsistencies you'll encounter in the porting process:

- *Colors* display differently. Even if you've taken care to use compatible palettes, some colors may show up darker or lighter than you want.

- *Sounds* are more complicated to include under Windows, so try to be sure that the necessary devices are installed on a Windows machine. Volume settings can also differ considerably between the two platforms, and since sound capabilities aren't standardized on PCs, there's no guarantee that the end user's computer will be capable of anything more than simple system sounds. Stick to AIFF, WAVE, and SWA for external sounds.

- *Transitions* may occur at different speeds, and some may differ widely between the two systems (pixel dissolves are noticeably different, as are fades). Preview all transitions on each platform to make sure you're still achieving the desired effect.

- Some RAM-intensive *Score-level ink effects* will slow down playback even more under Windows. This is especially evident with the inks Add, Add Pin, Blend, Darkest, Lightest, Subtract, and Subtract Pin.

- *Stretched sprites* (those resized to dimensions different from their source cast member's) have a negative impact even on Macintosh playback; on Windows, they can greatly slow things down.

- *Custom menus* don't transfer smoothly, since menus have different features in Windows and on the Macintosh. Test for the platform and create menus specific to the type of system your movie is running on.

- *Text*, in all its glorious forms, is especially painful. *Fields* are tricky, since their display depends on external font files installed on the host machine. Small text anti-aliases badly on the Windows side and becomes noticeably "soft" and difficult to read, so avoid anti-aliasing text of sizes smaller than 14 points.

Sound issues

Internal sounds should play on both Windows and Macintosh systems. For external sounds, stick to AIFF, WAVE, and SWA sounds if you want them to play on both platforms. All sounds should be recorded using only the PC-compatible sampling rates (11.025, 22.05, or 44.1KHz) rather than any of the Macintosh-specific sampling rates.

When playing simultaneous sounds under Windows, performance will depend on the device driver used. The MacroMix device, for example, may result in an unacceptably long lag time (latency) between when you want a sound to start playing and when it actually starts. If you use sound fades, you may find differences between the two platforms, so test them thoroughly.

Volume is another consideration. On the PC, sounds can be distorted greatly at the high end of the scale, so it's best to set the volume to the medium range and let the end users pump it up if they want. QuickTime movies and SWA sounds have their own internal volume levels, and in Windows that volume is calculated relative to the settings of the sound driver—which means that such sounds may play more loudly or softly than they do on the Macintosh, where sound levels are relatively consistent. You'll likely need to do a few trial transfers and tweak accordingly.

QuickTime issues

Director 7 supports only QuickTime 3 (or higher), so QuickTime 2.x digital video will need to be converted to QT3. QT3 supports MPEG on the Macintosh, but not under Windows. (You'll need a third-party Xtra for that.) When you import AVI files, you have the option of converting them to QuickTime, but in any case, AVI files need to be converted to QuickTime to play on the Macintosh. For best results, and to simplify your porting process, stick to one format (either QuickTime or AVI). Using a combination of formats will increase the testing you will need to perform on each platform.

Custom menu limitations

Lingo scripts using the menu keyword should work as expected, with these exceptions:

- Type style displays (Bold, Italic, Underline, Outline, and Shadow) are not transferable.

- Macintosh Command-key and Windows Control-key equivalents (that is, shortcuts) should automatically be converted to their counterparts on each platform. You shouldn't need to write different scripts to support each platform.

- The @ character used to create the Apple symbol and menu applies only on the Macintosh. There is no equivalent character for Windows, so this character should be avoided on cross-platform menus.

Mapping fonts with Fontmap.txt

Director 7 now allows you to embed fonts as cast members in your productions. The fonts are compressed, so they don't take up too much space and are good for custom fonts. Still, they take up space and can slow the downloading and playback of movies since fonts are loaded into memory before actual playback begins. An alternative (actually, you can use a combination of both) is to include a mapping file with your production.

If you've looked in the home directory of your copy of Director, you may have noticed a file named Fontmap.txt. This isn't a Director movie—it's just a plain text file. It's intended to be read on both the Macintosh and

Windows platforms, and it's where Director looks to learn how to resolve font differences between the platforms.

When a movie is launched, Director reads from this file to create an internal font map—a list of font equivalents. If you open it with a word processor, you'll see the current defaults:

```
Mac:Chicago  => Win:System
Mac:Courier  => Win:"Courier New"
Mac:Geneva => Win:"MS Sans Serif"
Mac:Helvetica  => Win:Arial
Mac:Monaco => Win:Terminal
Mac:"New York"  => Win:"MS Serif" Map None
Mac:Symbol  => Win:Symbol
Mac:Times  => Win:"Times New Roman" 14=>12 18=>14 24=>18 30=>24

Win:Arial  => Mac:Helvetica
Win:"Courier"  => Mac:Courier
Win:"Courier New"  => Mac:Courier
Win:"MS Serif"  => Mac:"New York" Map None
Win:"MS Sans Serif"  => Mac:Geneva
Win:Symbol  => Mac:Symbol
Win:System  => Mac:Chicago
Win:Terminal  => Mac:Monaco
Win:"Times New Roman"  => Mac:"Times" 12=>14 14=>18 18=>24
24=>30
```

If you'd like, you can add to or modify this list using this syntax:

```
Mac:Font  => Win:Font
Win:Font  => Mac:Font
```

You can also specify which font sizes should be substituted, as in the line shown above that maps Windows' Times New Roman font to the Macintosh's Times font. If you don't want to remap the font's special characters (the dingbats and bullets and such), add the command MAP NONE to the mapping line.

Individual characters can also be mapped for substitution, but you'll need to cite them by their individual ASCII codes. The Fontmap.txt file deals with a few of these:

```
Mac: => Win: 128=>196 129=>197 130=>199 131=>201 132=>209
Win: => Mac: 128=>222 129=>223 130=>226 131=>196 132=>227
```

Although Fontmap.txt is the default source for the font mapping table, you can designate another file in the Movie Properties dialog box. Just make sure that it's a text file and that its contents follows the syntax shown above.

Points to remember

Here's a closing recap:

- Maximize the performance of your Director-based production by using memory management techniques. Set the correct **Unload** value for individual cast members, and set the appropriate **loading point** for Casts as a whole. Also, make sure that graphic cast members aren't saved at excessive color depth and that all unneeded cast members are deleted from your movies.

- Use the **Save and Compact** command rather than Save for a possible performance increase and reduction in file size.

- Cut the disk from a **virus-free, file-optimized hard drive** (or partition thereof).

- If you distribute **protected versions** of your Director movies, they can be used—but not opened or modified—by others. Take care to keep unprotected versions of your files, though, in case you want to make changes.

- Before distributing your production, take pains to make sure that all **linkages**—to external casts, multiple movie files, and Xtras vital to the production—are maintained on the distributable version. Don't forget that the property the searchPaths can be used to maintain these linkages.

- Pay special attention to, and test extensively, all **sound and QuickTime digital video** to make sure that they play adequately on both **Windows and Macintosh platforms**.

REFERENCE

APPENDIX A

DIRECTOR RESOURCES ON THE INTERNET

THE DIRECTOR DEMYSTIFIED WEB SITE

`http://www.demystified.com`

After three English editions and various versions in other languages, we realized that the *Director Demystified* books needed their own presence on the Web. Demystified.com is a modest but growing site, dedicated to keeping our readership up-to-date. It's where you'll find:

- **Tutorial movies.** All the tutorial movies on the CD-ROM have downloadable counterparts here.
- **Target files.** If you want to get really net-savvy with Director 7, you'll need to practice connecting online media in your productions. As you may have noticed while reading Chapters 14 and 15, we've placed those resources online at our site.
- **Sample movies.** Here you'll find open-code versions of Director productions for your perusal. If you're proud of a movie you've done, send it to us and we may share it here.
- **Updates and corrections.** If some portion of our text is invalid (either because we made a mistake or Macromedia changed the rules), we'll post new information and pointers for workarounds.
- **Ordering information.** Want Demystified in Italian? How about Chinese? We'll also tell you how to order additional English copies of Demystified direct from the publisher.
- **Useful links.** Look here for links to demos from other developers, developers of Xtras, and other development tools.

OTHER DIRECTOR-ORIENTED WEB SITES

Thousands of Web sites use Director movies (in Shockwave incarnations), but only a few are devoted to providing in-depth resources for the Director producer and Lingo programmer. Here are my favorites—with the proviso that in the hypershifting world of the Web, things tend to change, move, and disappear. If any of these URLs are invalid, try a Web search using the name as a keyword.

The Director Web

http://www.mcli.dist.maricopa.edu/director/

Alan Levine's meticulously maintained site has been growing on the Web for years, and its depth of content makes it absolutely invaluable for budding Directorphiles. It offers searchable archives of sample movies, Xtras, and XObjects, and even a topic database of subjects discussed on the Direct-L mailing list. For sheer volume of illustrations, inspirations, and answers, it's almost as useful as Macromedia's site. You'll also find a number of links here to other useful sites.

Director Technotes

http://www.macromedia.com/support/director/ts/nav

All of Macromedia's sprawling site (http://www.macromedia.com) is worth browsing on a regular basis, but the Technotes section should be one of your first destinations if you have a burning issue that needs immediate resolution. It presents the compiled experience of the tech support staff in an easy-to-search format, arranged by topic in Q&A form.

Another good Macromedia site is

http://www.macromedia.com/support/director/dev_index.fhtml

which ties you to a number of learning categories and other Director-related material.

Director Online

http://director-online.com

Director Online has links, articles, product reviews, and answers to readers' questions from the Multimedia Handyman—a pretty snazzy and nice site. Check it out for articles by "Doug" and reviews of Xtras.

Dr. Diego's FAQ

http://www.xtramedia.com/lingoTips.shtml

The folks at XtraMedia have compiled this forum for the pseudonymous Dr. Diego, "the daring digital sleuth who tracks down answers to the hard questions." This site is home to dozens of well-written tips and techniques on Lingo and XObjects.

UpdateStage

http://www.updatestage.com/

Gretchen MacDowell's excellent site is simple yet substantial, essentially a compilation of insights she's achieved while working as a professional Lingo programmer. It's updated regularly, and past issues are archived and accessible by topic. This is also a good site for lists of quirks and bugs, as well as their workarounds.

Lingo Users Journal

http://www.penworks.com/LUJ/index.html

Lingo Users Journal was a print-based publication, and is now in the process of converting to all online. Things at this site are in flux, but it's a good place for sample back issues in downloadable form, as well as online versions of Lingo used in the publication's articles. Keep an eye on this site and support the Penworks people and their contribution to Lingo programming.

Lingo help: DaLingoKid

http://www.jervo.com/pages/dalingokid.html

This is an intriguing site that offers personal help from a "super hero alter ego" named DaLingoKid (who perhaps bears a resemblance to programmer/college student Jervis Thompson). If you have a specific Lingo scripting problem, you can ask him to help you solve it. Time permitting, he'll create and post a small Director movie solving the problem (or illustrating the principle) and post it on his site; you can peruse the archive of existing movies as well. No attitude or obfuscatory prose here—just a friendly expert who's happy to share his expertise with others.

THE DIRECT-L LISTSERV

Direct-L is an electronic mailing list that is, in the words of its FAQ, "the main Internet-based forum for information-gathering, technical advice, ranting, raving, and whining about Director." With more than 2,000 subscribers from around the world, it's a sort of e-mail–based seminar/convention/shoptalk session for some of the most talented users of Director out there.

Because it's a mailing list, not a newsgroup, you can't just cruise by and check it out; you need to go through a subscription procedure (see the next section). Everyone on the list has to receive everything anyone else mails to the list, so read the FAQ (it's on the Director Web site) and try to be considerate. Don't attach samples of your movies to your postings, and if you have a question, search to see if it has already been answered in the archives or the FAQ.

Joining Direct-L

To subscribe, send an e-mail message consisting solely of these two lines to the address listserv@uafsysb.uark.edu:

SUBSCRIBE DIRECT-L *[your name and e-mail address]*
SET DIRECT-L DIGEST

The message should have no subject and no signature file, if possible.

Important: This address is not the same address as the list itself. The list's address is direct-l@uafsysb.uark.edu.

Including the line SET DIRECT-L DIGEST means you'll get the day's traffic on the list in a single compiled and indexed piece of e-mail. If you leave off this line, you'll receive each list posting as a separate e-mail, which can mean 50 or more pieces of mail a day—use your e-mail filter to sort them.

Unsubscribing

To remove yourself from the list, send e-mail containing the message SIGNOFF DIRECT-L to the address listserv@uafsysb.uark.edu.

THE LINGO-L LISTSERV

The Lingo-L list is similar to the Direct-L list but is dedicated solely to the Lingo programming aspects of Director. Subscribing to Lingo-L is similar to subscribing to Direct-L in terms of receiving many messages or daily digests. To subscribe to Lingo-L and to find out about other aspects of the list, you can find information at the *Lingo User's Journal* site: http://www.penworks.com/LUJ/lingo-l.cgi.

OTHER INTERESTING SITES

http://www.Shockrave.com

Dedicated to Shockwave, this site has cartoons of various kinds, from charmingly simple to quite complex, all created with Director.

http://www.Chinwag.com/html/mailing_lists_1.html

Another mailing list, this one calls itself "an open discussion list for developers using Macromedia's Shockwave and Director tools." There is also a companion site for Flash users:

http://www.Chinwag.com/html/mailing_lists_0.html

APPENDIX B

THE LINGO GRAVEYARD

LINGO AT REST...

Every new version of Director brings changes, especially to the Lingo vocabulary. Outmoded Lingo gets retired, and new Lingo is put forth to replace the old. Here's a list of "dead" Lingo, accompanied (where applicable) by version 7 replacements. Note that some of these commands still work under Director 7—Macromedia doesn't just throw things away without providing some backward compatibility. Still, there's generally a reason that commands are retired, the best one being that something else is provided that works better. Remember: Even if some Lingo element still works now, it may not work in the next upgrade. If you expect your productions to be around for a while, stick to the Lingo that currently is 100 percent supported.

One of the biggest changes in recent Lingo history is the redefinition of the term *cast*. Back in the days when only one cast could be open at a time, this term referred to cast members within the Cast window. Now that multiple casts can be active, *cast* is used to refer to the casts *themselves*, while cast members are denoted with *member*. Hence, the castNum of sprite becomes the memberNum of sprite, and so forth. Terms like the castLib and the castLibNum continue to use *cast*, as they pertain to programming on the cast level.

behavesLikeToggle
This used to determine whether a button behaved like a pushbutton or toggle button. It has no current equivalent.

birth
This used to describe child objects born from parent scripts. It was changed to new in version 5 of Director, when it was still recognized, but not preferred, by Macromedia. It's not recognized at all by Director 7.

castmembers
See the number of members cast property.

castNum of sprite

See the member of sprite and memberNum of sprite properties instead.

castType

See the type of member cast member property.

center of cast

See the center of member cast member property.

closeDA

Unrecognized now, this MacOS-specific command closed any desk accessories open on the host system. Since the desk accessory file format has long been abandoned by the MacOS in favor of control panels and Apple menu items, it's no big loss.

colorQD

This function once determined whether the host Macintosh had color display capability (QuickDraw). Functional in version 5, it is now obsolete.

continue

Worked in conjunction with the pause command, also obsolete, to resume playback. Use go to the frame + 1 instead.

dontPassEvent

This interrupted the standard flow of event messages in the message hierarchy. Its replacement is the clearer stopEvent command—which is actually a little more powerful since it can also work on the sprite script (or score script) level.

duplicate cast

See the duplicate member command instead.

duration of cast

See the duration of member SWA property.

enabled of member/sprite

Disappeared with the Button Editor.

erase cast

See the erase member command instead.

factory

This was an early form of object-oriented programming that hasn't been much used since version 3. Lists and parent-child objects effectively replaced factories, and now the term is officially dead.

fileName of cast

See fileName of member instead.

fullColorPermit

An obsolete property concerned with RAM buffers.

getLatestNetID

No longer necessary since net Lingo commands return the NetID (which you should save).

initialToggleState

Was used when buttons made with the now obsolete Button Editor could be toggle buttons.

labelString of member

Determined the label of a button cast member.

machineType

See the platform system property and the environment system property.

mouseCast

Another casualty of the great cast meaning shift, this has now been officially replaced by mouseMember.

movie

See the movieName movie property.

openDA

This command used to open a desk accessory file, and like its sister closeDA, it is now defunct.

openResFile

See the recordFont command.

pathName

See the moviePath movie property.

pause

Macromedia is nudging out this old standby in favor of go to the frame, which does the same thing.

pauseState

Determines if a movie is paused using the pause command, now also obsolete.

quickTimePresent

See the quickTimeVersion function.

setButtonImageFromCastMember

Another button function that has disappeared.

setCallBack

Worked with XCMDs, which preceeded even the now defunct Xobjects.

sound close

Stops the sound playing in a sound channel. Use puppetSound [whichChannel], 0 instead.

spriteBox

This used to change the coordinates of the bounding box of an individual sprite. Use rect of sprite instead.

stretch of sprite

Was used to allow changes in a sprites dimensions, now defunct.

textAlign

Used to set the allignment of text in a Text or field cast member. Use the alignment property instead.

textFont

Used to specify the font of text in a field cast member. Use the font property instead.

textHeight

Used to specify the height of lines in a field cast member. Use the lineHeight property instead.

textSize

Used to specify the size of the font in a field cast member. Use the fontSize property instead.

textStyle

Used to specify the style (bold, etc.) of text in field cast member. Use the fontStyle property instead.

when...then statements

Discontinued in version 5, the when...then statements were replaced with the more efficient if...then and case and otherwise constructs.

XFactoryList

See the showXLib command.

APPENDIX C

A LINGO LEXICON

The following is a compilation of elements in the Lingo language, as supported by version 7 of Macromedia Director for the Windows (versions NT, 95, and 98) and Macintosh operating system (MacOS) platforms. Although the online help guide and Macromedia's *Lingo Dictionary* are excellent references, these pages are intended to provide another perspective on the complexities (and occasional perplexities) of Lingo.

Here are a few things to note:

- All entries are *categorized by type* rather than alphabetically (although entries are arranged alphabetically within each category). In the case of multiword terms, organization is by the *dominant word*; for example, the `pattern of member` will be found under "P" in the Properties category, not under "T" or "M."

- The type categories are *thumb tabbed* for easy reference.

- *Additional information* is provided whenever possible. For instance, the codes for all built-in patterns are given in the entry for the property the `pattern of member`.

- Some *unofficial Lingo* is also listed. These terms aren't officially supported by Macromedia, but they are still useful in some contexts. Tread cautiously when using them, of course.

All entries are also listed alphabetically in the index for this book.

Although this lexicon does *not* include Lingo that is entirely obsolete, it does include technically obsolete elements that Director can still interpret (usually with pointers to the terms that have replaced the obsolete ones). For a list of discontinued Lingo, see Appendix B: *The Lingo Graveyard*.

Lexicon format

Each definition follows this format:

Elements: `Lingo [nonLingo]`

All words in `this typeface` are part of the defined Lingo element and need to be entered exactly as shown. Everything in the italicized type and square brackets *[like this]* is also part of the syntax but varies with the particular use of the statement and needs to be replaced (including the italicized brackets) with content specific to the statement. When working with Lingo, pay special attention to correct spelling and spacing and the use of commas, parentheses ( ), and non-italicized brackets [ ].

Purpose: This section gives a general description of the use of the Lingo element, plus any additional information that might be pertinent.

In context: This section gives an example of how the element might be used, as well as additional information needed to provide a context for the example construct.

Notes: This section includes any additional information, such as when to use or when not to use an element.

See also: Often one Lingo element is closely related to other Lingo elements. When you should consider other Lingo elements at the same time, this section will direct you to the relevant locations.

Other Lexicon nuances

In the script examples (in the "In Context" sections), lines beginning with a double hyphen are not intended for user entry. Typically, they are the responses given by Director in the Message window; occasionally, they are comments that further describe what is happening: for example,

```
put abs (-30 + -60)
-- 90
```

Two points that may confuse the neophyte are the use of the me keyword and the listing of parameters. In almost all cases, me is not an integral part of the Lingo term; it's a keyword that allows certain elements to refer to themselves without describing themselves explicitly (for example, the memberNum of sprite me, rather than the memberNum of sprite 47). See the definition of me, as well as the discussion of the concept in Chapter 18, for further clarification.

When parameters are given following a Lingo term, as in

on streamStatus *[URL, state, bytesSoFar, bytesTotal, error]*

the parameter names aren't official names that need to be spelled correctly; they're just brief descriptors of the information provided in that particular order. You could write a script that reads

on streamStatus mickey, minnie, elmo

and it would work just fine, so long as you remember that the mickey variable contains the URL data, minnie contains a status message on download progress, and elmo tells you how many bytes have been downloaded so far. Feel free to apply your own labels to parameters, but use them consistently.

Director 7 introduced **dot syntax**, or **dot property notation**. This format provides improved readability and more closely resembles the syntax used by other object-oriented languages, such as C++. We try to give examples of an element's syntax in both the dot syntax and the older syntax. If you are new to Lingo, you should try to stick to the newer syntax. If you have been using Lingo in previous versions of Director, the old syntax will still work just fine. Use whichever syntax feels comfortable to you.

EVENT HANDLERS

Event handlers are the keywords that denote a script intended for execution during a particular event. Each begins with the word on. If you encounter a script line beginning with on that doesn't appear in this section (for example, on thisHappens), chances are the line refers to a custom handler (thisHappens).

on activateWindow

Elements: on activateWindow
          [statement line(s)]
        end

Purpose: This event handler is triggered when a movie currently running as a Movie in a Window (MIAW) becomes active (when it is moved to the foreground by the end user, since MIAWs can be open yet run in the background).

In context: This script produces a system beep when the movie is opened in a MIAW and the user clicks its window to make it active in the foreground:

```
on activateWindow
    beep
end
```

Notes: This handler should be placed in a movie script of the movie that becomes the MIAW (rather than the movie that opens the MIAW). When the movie plays on its own (that is, when it is not called as an MIAW), this handler is ignored.

See also: The on deactivateWindow, on closeWindow, on moveWindow, and on openWindow handlers; the activeWindow property; and the open command.

on alertHook

Elements: on alertHook *[me, error, message]*
          [statement line(s)]
          return *[0 or 1]*
        end

Purpose: This handler is called when an error occurs while a Director movie is running and allows the movie to announce that something has gone wrong or take other actions. It automatically receives three arguments: *me,* the instance argument; *error,* a text string that should help to identify the cause of the error; and *message,* a text string that is suitable for display in an alert box. The return value determines whether an alert box will automatically appear when the error occurs (1 means no, 0 means yes). With alerts turned off, you can still use the alert command to display your own message in an alert box. The alertHook hander should be placed in a parent or behavior script. For the handler to be called, you must set the alertHook system property to the parent script, as in the following:

```
the alertHook = new(script "myAlert")
```

In context: This script makes sure the automatic alert display is turned off and then displays an alert box containing a custom message:

```
on alertHook me, error, message
   alert "The problem is:" && message
   return 1
end
```

Notes: Since this handler must be placed in a parent script to work, the keyword me is integral to this handler.

on beginSprite

Elements: on beginSprite *[me]*
           [statement line(s)]
      end

Purpose: This handler was one of Director 6's most useful new features, and it continues to be most useful in Director 7, as it lets you easily attach scripts to individual sprites and sprite segments. It recognizes when the playback head encounters a new sprite (that is, one that wasn't present in the last frame played). When used in frame scripts, it takes no argument; it will simply execute if one or more new sprites is encountered. To attach the action to a specific sprite, incorporate on beginSprite into a behavior script. In such cases, you must include the keyword me.

In context: This behavior script triggers three beeps when the playback head encounters the sprite it's attached to:

```
on beginSprite me
   beep 3
end
```

Notes: Keep in mind that the beginSprite event is declared not only at the sprite's physical beginning in the Score, but at any time the playback head newly occupies a frame that contains the sprite. If the sprite consists of a sprite segment stretched out over several frames in the Score, on beginSprite will be triggered even if the playback head bypasses the initial portions and jumps into the midst of the segment.

on closeWindow

Elements: on closeWindow
           [statement line(s)]
      end

Purpose: This event handler is triggered when the user closes a movie currently running as a Movie in a Window (MIAW) by clicking the close box.

In context: This script will produce a dialog box when the user closes a MIAW:

```
on closeWindow
        alert "Goodbye! It was fun!"
end
```

Notes: This handler should be placed in a movie script of the movie that becomes the MIAW (rather than the movie that opens the MIAW). When the movie plays on its own (that is, when it is not called as an MIAW), this handler is ignored.

See also: The on `activateWindow`, on `deactivateWindow`, and on `openWindow` handlers.

on cuePassed

Elements: on cuePassed *[me,] [channelID, cuePointNumber, cuePointName]*
              [statement line(s)]
          end

Purpose: This handler is triggered when a sound or sprite passes an internal cue point during playback (to learn about embedded cue points, see Chapter 19). You can pull information from the parameters or use the parameters to test for certain conditions.

The *me* parameter should be used when the handler is included in a behavior script (frame or sprite). The parameter *channelID* refers to the number of the channel in which the playback is taking place. The parameters *cuePointNumber* and *cuePointName* indicate the internal identification of the cue point itself.

In context: This frame behavior uses the handler to capture the name of a cue point (from a file playing in sound channel 2) and perform an action when a particular point is reached:

```
on cuePassed me 2, number, name
   if name = "crescendo" then
      go to the frame + 1
   else nothing
   end if
end
```

Notes: For sprite behaviors, only the sprite containing the cue point receives the cuePassed message. When using Shockwave Audio sounds, it's better to refer to them by sprite channel number instead of by sound channel number, because although they play in a sound channel, they appear as sprites in the Score. Be clear whether you're referring to audio channels or to sprite channels.

See also: The isPastCuePoint function and cuePointNames and cuePointTimes properties.

on deactivateWindow

Elements: on deactivateWindow
              [statement line(s)]
          end

Purpose: This event handler is triggered when a movie currently running as a Movie in a Window (MIAW) is deactivated (that is, when it remains open yet the end user moves it to the background).

In context: This script plays a system beep sound when a MIAW is moved to the background by a click on another window:

```
on deactivateWindow
   beep
end
```

Notes: This handler should be placed in a movie script of the movie that becomes the MIAW (rather than the movie that opens the MIAW). When the movie plays on its own (that is, when it is not called as an MIAW), this handler is ignored.

See also: The on `deactivateWindow`, on `closeWindow`, and on `openWindow` handlers.

on endSprite

Elements: on endSprite *[me]*
                            [statement line(s)]
                    end

Purpose: This counterpart to the on `beginSprite` event handler is triggered when the playback head enters a new frame and finds that one or more of the sprites in the previous frame are no longer present. If used in frame scripts, it takes no argument. To attach the action to a specific sprite, incorporate it into a behavior script. In such cases, you must include the keyword me.

In context: This behavior script triggers a housekeeping script called updateScoreList when playback of the sprite it's attached to ends:

```
on endSprite me
    updateScoreList
end
```

Notes: The endSprite event is initiated not only at the physical ending of the sprite in the Score, but whenever the playback head moves to a frame without the sprite. If the sprite consists of a sprite segment stretched out over several frames in the Score, on `endSprite` will be triggered even if the playback head bypasses the final portions by jumping out of the midst of the segment. It is executed after the exitFrame event.

on enterFrame

Elements: on enterFrame *[me]*
                            [statement line(s)]
                    end

Purpose: All statement lines contained in this handler will be executed when the playback head enters a frame. When used as a frame script (that is, when it is placed in the behavior channel cell of a frame), it will be evoked only during playback of that frame. When used in a movie script, it will be applied globally to all frames, unless an individual frame has an on `enterFrame` handler of its own, in which case the frame script will be executed instead. When used in a behavior script, it will be passed the object reference me. Sprite behaviors always receive the enterFrame message, even if there is a frame or movie script containing the handler.

In context: This script could be used in a frame that loops back on itself to move the sprite in channel 2 to the left across the Stage:

```
on enterFrame
    sprite(2).locH = sprite(2).locH - 1
end
```

Notes: There's no need to use the `updateStage` command, as the Stage is automatically updated whenever a new frame of the Score is entered.

on EvalScript

Elements: on EvalScript *[script parameters, if any]*
                          [statement line(s)]
                  end

Purpose: This event handler is in a class of its own. It's designed for Shockwave movies, and it responds to the event in which a Web browser sends an "evaluate script" message in response to a JavaScript, Visual Basic script, or script written in some other scripting language using the `EvalScript` syntax. Since `EvalScript` messages can pass parameters containing text strings that can be interpreted as Lingo, this handler is a means of programming interaction between a browser and the Shockwave movie.

In context: This script captures the text string passed by a browser script's `EvalScript` calling statement (the parameter `theWord`) and then executes that string as a Lingo command. This effectively passes control of the Shockwave movie to the browser script, at least for the purpose of issuing simple commands like `quit` or `pause`.

```
on EvalScript theWord
    theOrder = word 1 of theWord
    do theOrder
end
```

Notes: Remember that unlike Lingo, JavaScript is case sensitive, so pay close attention to capitalization (especially the "E" in `EvalScript`).

on exitFrame

Elements: on exitFrame
                          [statement line(s)]
                  end

Purpose: All statement lines contained in this handler will be executed when the playback head exits the frame to which it is attached. When used as a frame script (that is, when placed in the script channel cell of a frame), it will be evoked only during playback of that frame. When used in a movie script, it will be applied globally to all frames, unless an individual frame has an `on exitFrame` handler of its own, in which case the frame script will be executed instead. Individual sprites may also have an `on exitFrame` handler in a behavior script. Both sprite and frame behaviors will receive the `exitFrame` message. Behavior scripts will receive the object reference `me`.

In context: This script stops the sound file playing in sound channel 2 and then moves the playback head to the frame marked with the Adios marker:

```
on exitFrame
    puppetSound 2, 0
    go to frame "Adios"
end
```

HANDLERS

Notes: on exitFrame is a good location for housekeeping scripts such as those that eliminate elements no longer needed (such as scripts that turn off puppet status).

on getBehaviorDescription

Elements: on getBehaviorDescription
              [statement(s)]
              end

Purpose: This handler notes a modest event: the act of inspecting a behavior in the Behavior Inspector. That's when Director searches for information about the behavior to place in the Inspector's Description field. Used in conjunction with the return keyword, this handler can be used to provide explanatory text when creating your own behaviors.

In context: This script attaches a useful descriptive label to a behavior:

```
on getBehaviorDescription
    return "Makes a sprite turn blue"
end
```

See also: The on getPropertyDescriptionList, on getBehaviorTooltip, and on runPropertyDialog handlers.

on getBehaviorTooltip

Elements: on getBehaviorTooltip
              [statement lines(s)]
              end

Purpose: This handler is placed in a behavior to define the tooltip that will show up when the mouse stops over the behavior's icon in the library palette. The text of the tooltip is the string returned by the handler. If no getBehaviorTooltip handler is used in a behavior, the text of the tooltip is the name of the behavior's cast member.

In context: This statement causes the tooltip to display Popcorn Bowl:

```
on getBehaviorTooltip
    return "Popcorn Bowl"
end
```

See also: The on getPropertyDescriptionList, on getBehaviorDescription, and on runPropertyDialog handlers.

on getPropertyDescriptionList

Elements: on getPropertyDescriptionList
              [statement(s)]
              end

Purpose: When creating custom reusable behaviors, the getPropertyDescriptionList handler defines which properties will show up in the Properties dialog box when a user drags the behavior onto a sprite or double-clicks the behavior in the Behavior Inspector. When building reusable behaviors, this is the prime vehicle for allowing their custom properties to be set. The elements in the Parameters dialog box are defined as elements of a property list. The list is then returned by `getPropertyDescriptionList`. See Director 7's online Help for instructions on creating a behavior's property list.

In context: If you place the following handler in a behavior script and then drag the behavior onto a sprite, you should see the Properties dialog box appear. The property list created in the handler causes a single property to show up in the Properties dialog box with the label "Your Age," an initial value of 3, and a type of integer. To see this work, test the handler without any other handlers in your behavior.

```
on getPropertyDescriptionList
    set pList = [:]
    addProp pList, #myProperty, ¬
        [#default:3, #format:#integer, #comment:"Your Age"]
    return pList
end
```

Notes: If the behavior contains a `runPropertyDialog` handler, then the Properties dialog box will not be displayed.

See also: The on `getBehaviorTooltip`, on `getBehaviorDescription`, and on `runPropertyDialog` handlers.

on `hyperlinkClicked`

Elements: on `hyperlinkClicked` *[me,] [data, range]*
                      [statement lines(s)]
                 end

Purpose: Hyperlinks are created in text fields using the Text Inspector. At that time, information is entered in the Hyperlink Data field. When the hyperlink text is clicked, the `hyperlinkClicked` message is sent, and the `hyperlinkClicked` handler takes appropriate action based on the input parameters: *me*, used only if the handler is in a behavior script, is the object identifier; *data* is the string specified in the Text Inspector; and *range* delineates the hypertext string that was clicked. The hypertext string is extracted using the syntax `thisMember.char[range[1]..range[2]]`.

In context: This handler, in a behavior script, uses the *data* parameter as a marker identifier to specify the location to jump to. It also displays an alert box showing the hypertext string that was clicked.

```
property spriteNum
on hyperlinkClicked me, where, span
    go to frame where
    thisMember = sprite(spriteNum).member
    hyperString = thisMember.char[span[1]..span[2]]
    Alert "The hypertext is:"&& hyperString
end
```

HANDLERS

on idle

Elements: on idle
              [statement line(s)]
          end

Purpose: Director executes the statements contained in this handler when no other handler is being called. In other words, the idle event occurs whenever no other event is occurring, unless a different duration has been set. It's possible to set the duration of idle with the property the idleHandlerPeriod, but by default, the idle message is sent as often as possible.

In context: This handler places a variable (to be defined elsewhere) in a text field intended to be updated as often as possible:

```
on idle
   global timeRemaining
   member ("Time Display").text = timeRemaining
   updateStage
end
```

Notes: The updateStage command must be specifically invoked; otherwise, the Stage won't be redrawn until the Score enters a new frame.

Considering that idle occurs more often than any other event, scripts with this handler will be executed almost continuously. Therefore, this handler is not a good place for processor-intensive Lingo (such as puppetTransition). Whenever possible, take advantage of handlers like on mouseWithin.

See also: The idleHandlerPeriod property.

on keyDown

Elements: on keyDown
              [statement line(s)]
          end

Purpose: Statements in this handler execute when a keyboard button is pressed (as opposed to the mouse button). The on keyDown handler can be located in a number of locations, and the message is sent to them in the following order: primary event handler, editable field script, field cast member script, frame script, and movie script. Once an on keyDown handler is found, no other locations receive the message unless the pass command is used.

In context: This script checks to see which key has been pressed (using the key function) in a situation where the correct answer is 2:

```
on keyDown
   if the key = "2" then
      member("response").text = "Good answer!"
   else
      member("response").text =  "Sorry! Try again."
   end if
end
```

Notes: The keyDown message is sent whenever any character key is pressed—a letter key, a function key, or a key on the numeric keypad. Some keys, such as the Control or Command key, Shift key, and Alt or Option key, when pressed by themselves, do not cause the message to be sent.

See also: The key, keyCode, keyPressed, commandDown, and optionDown functions and the keyDownScript property.

on keyUp

Elements: on keyUp
         [statement line(s)]
      end

Purpose: Statements in this handler execute when any keyboard button (as opposed to the mouse button) is pressed and then released. The on keyUp handler can be located in a number of locations, and the message is sent to them in the following order: primary event handler, editable field script, field cast member script, frame script, and movie script. Once an on keyUp handler is found, no other locations receive the message unless the pass command is used.

In context: This script checks to see which key has been pressed in a situation where the correct answer is 2:

```
on keyUp
   if the key = "2" then alert "Good answer!"
     else alert "Sorry! Try again."
   end if
end
```

Notes: The keyUp message is sent whenever any character key is released—a letter key, a function key, or a key on the numeric keypad. Some keys, such as the Control or Command key, Shift key, and Alt or Option key, when pressed by themselves, do not cause the message to be sent.

See also: The key, keyCode, keyPressed, commandDown, and optionDown functions and the keyDownScript property.

on mouseDown

Elements: on mouseDown
         [statement line(s)]
      end

Purpose: Statements in this handler execute when the mouse button (as opposed to any keyboard button) is pressed. The mouseDown handler can be located in a number of locations, and the message is sent to them in the following order: primary event handler, sprite behavior script, cast member script, frame script, and movie script. Once a mouseDown handler is found, no other locations receive the message unless the pass command is used.

In context: This script animates a button cast member when clicked, by switching the cast member with an adjacent cast member (a pushed-down version), and makes a button-click sound:

```
on mouseDown
    currSprite = the clickOn
    thisOne = sprite(currSprite).memberNum
    sprite(currSprite).memberNum = thisOne +1
    puppetSound "Switch"
end mouseDown
```

Notes: Place a mouseDown handler in a movie script if you want mouse clicks to have the same effect throughout the movie. You can override the movie script's actions by placing a mouseDown handler in a location that Director checks first, such as a sprite behavior.

See also: The on mouseUp and on mouseEnter handlers and the clickOn and mouseDownScript properties.

on mouseEnter

Elements: on mouseEnter
            [statement line(s)]
      end

Purpose: This handler is triggered when the end user's mouse cursor enters the area of a sprite. The event message is sent once, at the time of the actual event. You can use it in score scripts or attach it to behavior scripts (in which case, use the syntax on mouseEnter me to make it self-referential).

In context: This behavior script is a quick and easy way to create a rollover—a change in the appearance of a button even before it's clicked:

```
property spriteNum
on mouseEnter me
    sprite(spriteNum).member = "clickMe"
end
on mouseLeave me
    sprite(spriteNum).member = "notOver"
end
```

Notes: Keep in mind that unless the sprite uses the Matte ink, the event occurs when the mouse rolls over the sprite's bounding box, which may or may not have the same visible dimensions as the sprite's physical appearance on the Stage.

See also: The on mouseLeave and on mouseWithin handlers.

on mouseLeave

Elements: on mouseLeave
            [statement line(s)]
      end

Purpose: This handler is the logical counterpart to on mouseEnter, and like it in every way except that it operates when the end user's mouse leaves the given sprite's area.

In context: See on mouseEnter.

See also: The on mouseEnter and on mouseWithin handlers.

on mouseUp

Elements: on mouseUp
           [statement line(s)]
        end

Purpose: Statements in this handler execute when the mouse button (as opposed to any keyboard button) is released.

In context: When a button cast member ceases to be clicked, this script animates it by switching it with an adjacent cast member (a pushed-up version) and makes a button-click sound:

```
on mouseUp
  currSprite = the clickOn
  thisOne = sprite(currSprite).memberNum
  sprite(currSprite).memberNum = thisOne -1
  puppetSound "Switch"
end mouseUp
```

Notes: A clicked sprite does not receive the mouseUp event if the user moves the mouse off of the sprite before releasing the button. See the on mouseUpOutside handler.

See also: The on mouseDown and on mouseEnter handlers and the clickOn, mouseUp, and mouseUpScript properties.

on mouseUpOutside

Elements: on mouseUpOutside
           [statement line(s)]
        end

Purpose: This handler anticipates a two-step function from the end user. It executes when the user presses the mouse button while over a sprite and then releases the button after moving the cursor off of the sprite.

In context: This behavior script associates a certain sound with this action:

```
on mouseUpOutside
  puppetSound "Amen!"
end
```

on mouseWithin

Elements: on mouseWithin
           [statement line(s)]
        end

Purpose: This event handler provides a useful alternative to scripting with the on idle event when continuous action is required. The event is declared (and this handler is executed) repeatedly, so long as the end user's mouse remains within the confines of the given sprite's bounding box. The mouse button does not need to be down. Unless the Matte ink is applied to the sprite, the entire bounding box of the sprite is used.

In context: This sprite behavior script will move the sprite around with the mouse without the mouse button's being down:

```
property spriteNum
on mouseWithin
    sprite(spriteNum).locH = the mouseH
    sprite(spriteNum).locV = the mouseV
end
```

See also: The on mouseEnter and on mouseLeave handlers.

on moveWindow

Elements: on moveWindow
         [statement line(s)]
     end

Purpose: Use this handler to execute statements when the user moves a Director MIAW window. Place the handler in a script in the MIAW movie. This handler has no effect when the Stage is moved.

In context:

```
on moveWindow
    puppetSound "whoosh"
end
```

on openWindow

Elements: on openWindow
         [statement line(s)]
     end

Purpose: This handler is similar to on moveWindow but is tied to the action of opening the MIAW window. Since that, in effect, begins the user session for the movie in the window, this is a good handler to use for housekeeping purposes, much like the on startMovie handler.

In context: This handler shows the date and time that the window is opened:

```
on openWindow
    member("Time").text = the time
    member("Date").text = the long date
end
```

on prepareFrame

Elements: on prepareFrame
             [statement line(s)]
         end

Purpose: The prepareFrame event occurs each time the playback head enters a frame. It's triggered when Director is preparing a new frame, but before the frame's contents are drawn on the Stage (and before the enterFrame event occurs). Because the frame's contents are not yet displayed, this handler is a good location for scripts that populate or manage the contents of that frame. Since it can take the me argument, you can write behavior scripts with it as well.

In context: This script sets the location of a sprite before it appears on the Stage:

```
on prepareFrame
   sprite(5).locH = 100
   sprite(5).locV = 230
end
```

See also: The on enterFrame handler.

on prepareMovie

Elements: on prepareMovie
             [statement line(s)]
         end

Purpose: This handler recognizes that there's a period in which Director is getting ready to run a movie. It executes at the point when Director has finished preloading any cast members requiring preloading—but before it has composed the first frame of the movie or created behavior instances for sprites in that frame.

In context: This script initializes a few global variables and updates one (gLevel) passed from the preceding movie:

```
on prepareMovie
   global gScore, gTime, gLevel
   set gScore = 0
   set gTime = 0
   set gLevel to (gLevel + 1)
end
```

Notes: This handler executes a fraction of a second or so sooner than on startMovie. Why should you bother with the distinction? It pretty much depends on what's in the first frame of the movie being opened. If you're using global variables to store data that's passed on to behavior scripts in that frame (or using any authoring-level Lingo), use on prepareMovie instead.

HANDLERS

on resizeWindow

Elements: on resizeWindow
　　　　　　　[statement line(s)]
　　　　　　end

Purpose: This event handler is triggered when the user resizes a movie currently running as a Movie in a Window (MIAW)—that is, when the user drags the resize corner of the window to change its proportions. Obviously, it works only on MIAWs opened in resizable windows.

In context: This script will play a sound when the user resizes a MIAW's window:

```
on resizeWindow
    puppetSound 2, "Creak"
end
```

Notes: This handler should be placed in a movie script of the movie that becomes the MIAW (rather than the movie that opens the MIAW). When the movie plays on its own (that is, when it is not called as an MIAW), this handler is ignored. It functions only when applied to MIAWs whose window type is resizable rather than fixed.

See also: The on deactivateWindow, on closeWindow, and on openWindow handlers and the windowType of window property.

on rightMouseDown

Elements: on rightMouseDown
　　　　　　　[statement line(s)]
　　　　　　end

Purpose: Use this handler to specify what will occur when, in Windows, the end user presses the right button on a multibutton mouse. On the MacOS, which uses a single-button mouse, this event is interpreted as the pressing of the mouse button while the Control key is down. The MacOS event is recognized, however, only if the emulateMultiButtonMouse property (there's a mouthful) is set to TRUE.

In context: This script uses the mouse button (or button-key combination) to toggle the system sound on and off:

```
on rightMouseDown
    set the soundEnabled to not (the soundEnabled)
end
```

See also: The emulateMultiButtonMouse property.

on rightMouseUp

Elements: on rightMouseUp
                [*statement line(s)*]
            end

Purpose: The functional counterpart of on rightMouseDown, this handler applies to the release of the right mouse button (Windows) or the release of the mouse button while the Control key is pressed (MacOS).

In context:

```
on rightMouseUp
   the soundLevel = 130
end
```

Notes: On the MacOS side, you'll need to make sure the property the emulateMultiButtonMouse is set to 1, or TRUE, for this event to be recognized.

on runPropertyDialog

Elements: on runPropertyDialog me, *[ListName]*

Purpose: Used for creating custom reusable behaviors, this handler works hand in hand with the getPropertyDescriptionList handler. The getPropertyDescriptionList handler specifies the properties displayed in the Properties dialog box; the runPropertyDialog handler can set the values of those properties for a particular behavior instance. If the runPropertyDialog handler is not defined in the behavior, Director displays the Properties dialog box whenever the behavior is attached to a sprite. In other words, if you want the Properties dialog box to appear whenever you attach the behavior to a sprite, do not use a runPropertyDialog handler.

In context: This handler sets a value for the propName property without having the Properties dialog box displayed:

```
on runPropertyDialog myList
   setaProp myList, #propName, 1
   return myList
end
```

on savedLocal

Elements: on savedLocal
                statement(*s*)
            end

Purpose: This property is provided to allow for enhancements in future versions of Shockwave.

See also: The allowSaveLocal property.

on startMovie

Elements: on startMovie
        [statement line(s)]
     end

Purpose: Statements in this handler execute when the movie they belong to is ready to begin playing. Specifically, the startMovie handler is run after a prepareMovie handler and before any enterFrame handler.

In context: This script makes sure that data fields are blank by placing nothing (EMPTY) in their cast members; then it sets the volume to a medium level:

```
on startMovie
   member ("EnterTemp").text = EMPTY
   member ("TempDone").text = EMPTY
   the soundLevel = 5
end
```

Notes: An on startMovie script will be executed whenever playback of the movie begins, whether the user is viewing it from the beginning or jumping in at any point from another movie. Keep in mind that any on prepareMovie handler scripts will be executed slightly sooner.

The on startMovie handler must be in a movie script—not a behavior—in order to function. Make sure the title in the Script window says Movie Script. If it doesn't, change the handler from a behavior script to a movie script via the Type menu in the script's Cast Member Properties dialog box.

on stepFrame

Elements: on stepFrame
        [statement(s)]
     end

Purpose: The statements in this handler are executed whenever the playback head enters a frame or the updateStage command is executed. However, two criteria must be met for the handler to run: The handler must be in the script of an object instance, and the instance must be included in the actorList. Only objects in the actorList receive this stepFrame message. The stepFrame handler is useful for controlling actions that you want executed frequently on a specific set of objects, such as the animation of a sprite controlled by an object. When you no longer want an object to receive the stepFrame message, remove its reference from the actorList.

In context: This parent script can be used to create a child object that is automatically placed in the actorList. The sprite in the channel designated when the object is created will be moved to the left on the Stage every time the playback head enters a new frame (or reenters the same frame).

```
property channel
on new me, chan
   me.channel = chan
   add the actorList me
   return me
end

on stepFrame
   sprite(channel).locH = ¬
   sprite(channel).locH - 1
end
```

Notes: The stepFrame message is sent before the prepareFrame message.

See also: The actorList property.

on stopMovie

Elements: on stopMovie
                    [statement line(s)]
                end

Purpose: Statements in this handler execute when the movie they belong to halts playback. This can be either when the movie plays through to the end or when the movie branches to another movie.

An on stopMovie script is a good location for housekeeping commands such as those to set global variables, save data, close resource files, and dispose of Xtra objects, behavior objects, or anything else that might persist in memory. If you're designing a project with multiple movies, remember that many elements (such as windows and Movies in a Window) persist unless they are explicitly disposed of.

In context: This script makes sure that the sound capabilities of the computer are not turned off before proceeding:

```
on stopMovie
   set the soundEnabled to TRUE
end
```

Notes: Movies playing as Movies in a Window (MIAWs) do not have their stopMovie handlers executed when their window is closed or deleted (using the close window or forget window command).

The on stopMovie handler must be in a movie script—not a behavior—in order to function. Make sure the title bar of the Script window says Movie Script. If it doesn't, change the handler to a movie script via the Type menu in the script's Cast Member Properties dialog box.

HANDLERS

on streamStatus

Elements: on streamStatus *[URL, state, bytesSoFar, bytesTotal, error]*
[statement line(s)]
end

Purpose: This handler can be used to determine or report on the progress of a downloading stream from the Internet. The parameters are as follows: *URL* states the universal resource locator address of the object. The *state* parameter relays the state of the object downloading—it can return the string value "Connecting", "Started", "Error", "InProgress", or "Complete". The *bytesSoFar* parameter denotes the number of bytes retrieved so far. The *bytesTotal* parameter relays the total number of bytes overall. The *error* parameter determines whether an error has occurred, returning 0 or FALSE if there is no error, 1 or TRUE if there is an error, and an empty string (" ") if the download is still in progress. The event is declared when the relevant information is conveyed to the movie containing the script—that is, a streamStatus event occurs when the server passes notification that the streaming has started (in which case, the *state* parameter changes to "InProgress".

In context:

```
on streamStatus url, state, bytes
    member("status").text =  "The file"&& url &&¬
      "is currently" && state
end
```

Note: This event will be recognized only if the property the tellStreamStatus is set to TRUE and the handler is placed in a movie script.

on timeOut

Elements: on timeOut
[statement line(s)]
end

Purpose: Use this handler to place commands that will be executed when the keyboard or mouse is idle for a specified period of time. This handler must be placed in a movie script.

In context:

```
on timeOut
    alert "Hey! Anybody home?"
end
```

Notes: Remember that the timing of the timeOut event depends on the value set in the property the timeOutLength. You can also automatically execute a script whenever a timeout is declared by designating that script with the property the timeOutScript. Since that script is considered a primary event handler, instructions placed in an on timeOut handler script would be executed afterward.

See also: The timeOutLength and timeOutScript properties.

on zoomWindow

Elements: on zoomWindow
          [statement line(s)]
      end

Purpose: This event handler is triggered when the user resizes a movie currently running as a Movie in a Window (MIAW) by clicking the Windows Minimize/Maximize check box or Macintosh Zoom button.

In context: This script plays a sound when the MIAW is resized via Minimize/Maximize or Zoom:

```
on zoomWindow
    puppetSound 2,"Whoosh"
end
```

Notes: This handler should be placed in a movie script of the movie that becomes the MIAW (rather than the movie that opens the MIAW). When the movie plays on its own (that is, when it is not called as a MIAW), this handler is ignored. It functions only when applied to MIAWs whose window type is resizable rather than fixed.

HANDLERS

COMMANDS

Commands are the direct orders of Lingo, the terms that point to specific actions. Some are freestanding and self-explanatory (like updateStage), while others are used in conjunction with other Lingo elements to perform a variety of tasks.

abort

Elements: abort

Purpose: When this command is used, Lingo immediately exits the handler containing it, without processing any of the script lines that follow it. If a handler containing abort has been called by another handler, Lingo will quit executing both the called and the calling handlers. If you want execution to continue on the level of the calling handler, use the exit keyword instead.

In context: This handler checks to makes sure that the current monitor has a color depth of 16-bit or greater. If it doesn't, the handler is aborted.

```
on loadBigPicture
    if the colorDepth <16 then
        abort
    end if
    sprite(17).member = "Van Gogh"
end
```

Notes: Using abort will not cause the application to quit or the system to shut down.

See also: The exit keyword.

add

Elements: add [listName, value]

Purpose: This command modifies the population of a linear list to include the specified value. If the list is unsorted, the new entry will be attached to the end of the list. For sorted lists, the value is placed in the proper sorted order.

In context: These two command lines first establish a list (pets) and then add another value to that list:

```
pets = [3, #dog, #night]
add pets, 7
```

The resulting list is [3, #dog, #night, 7]. Had this list been sorted using the sort command, the list would be [3, 7, #dog, #night], symbols coming last in alphanumeric order.

Notes: This command is intended for linear lists. For property lists, use addProp.

See also: The append and sort commands.

addAt

Elements: addAt *[listName, positionNumber, value]*

This command modifies the population of a linear list to include the specified value. The second argument in the command line specifies the position of the new entry in the list.

In context: These two command lines first establish a list (pets) and then add another value to that list at the first position:

```
pets = [3, #dog, #night]
addAt pets, 1, 7
```

The resulting list is [7, 3, #dog, #night].

Notes: This command works only with linear lists and will return an error if used with a property list. For property lists, use addProp. Adding an element to a sorted list will cause the list to be considered unsorted.

See also: The deleteAt command.

addProp

Elements: addProp *[listName, propertyName, value]*

Purpose: This command is used to insert new entries into a property list. If the list is unsorted, the new entry is added to the end of the list; if it is sorted, the entry is added in alphanumeric order.

In context: These two command lines first establish a property list (ballStats) and then add another value to that list:

```
ballStats = [#runs:2, #hits:8, #errors:7]
addProp ballStats, #shoeSize, 9
```

This resulting list is [#runs: 2, #hits: 8, #errors: 7, #shoeSize: 9].

See also: The deleteProp command.

addVertex

Elements: addVertex*[member(mRef), pointIndex, pointLocaton,]¬*
               [controlLocH, controlLocV]

Purpose: This vector shape command is used to add a new vertex to an existing vector shape cast member. The *pointIndex* parameter specifies the location of the new vertex in the list of the member's vertices. The *pointLocation* parameter specifies the location of the new vertex relative to the origin of the vector shape. The optional control parameters specify the location of the control handles for the new vertex and affect the curvature of the lines between the vertices.

In context: The following line adds a vertex point in the vector shape Seth between the first and second existing vertex points, centered horizontally and 25 pixels above the center of the vector shape:

```
addVertex(member("Seth"), 2, point(0, -25))
```

Notes: The origin of a vector shape is different than the registration point and can be defined using the originH and originV properties.

See also: The moveVertex and deleteVertex commands and the vertexList property.

alert

Elements: alert *[text of message]*

Purpose: When executed, this command produces a system beep and displays a standard dialog box. The message can contain a maximum of 255 text characters.

In context:

```
alert "This is an example of an alert box."
```

Notes: When an alert box is on the Stage, no other actions (including making other applications active) can be undertaken until OK is clicked or Enter or Return is pressed.

append

Elements: append *[listName, value]*

Purpose: This command attaches a new entry to the end of the linear list, regardless of whether the list has been sorted.

In context: These three command lines establish a list (pets), sort the list, and then append another value to that list:

```
pets = [#dog, 3, #night]
sort pets
append pets, 7
```

The resulting list is [3, #dog, #night, 7]. Had the add command been used instead, the list would be [3, 7, #dog, #night].

Notes: This command is intended for linear lists. For property lists, use addProp.

See also: The add command.

beep

Elements: beep *[numberOfBeeps]*

Purpose: This command triggers a system sound on the host computer.

On Windows machines, the sound used for the beep is the one designated in the system's Sound Properties dialog box. On MacOS systems, the beep is the sound specified in the user's Sound control panel; playback volume is also specified by the user. If the system volume is muted (set to 0), the beep will be shown by a flash of the menu bar.

In context: This line triggers four beeps:

```
if the key = "4" then beep 4
```

Notes: You may encounter inconsistent results when using this command on the Windows platform—the *numberOfBeeps* parameter is generally ignored. To ensure multiple beeps under Windows, you will need to use multiple beep commands and a pause long enough for the sound to play between each command.

See also: The beepOn property.

before

See: The put...before command.

call

Elements: call #*[handler name]*, *[script]*[*,params...*]

Purpose: This is what I call a "pointing" command: It reaches outside the context of the handler that contains it to trigger another handler—in this case, one within an object script.

In context: If an object named lovechild has been created with hippie as an ancestor, and the hippie script includes a hairlength handler, this would return that handler's value:

call #hairlength, lovechild

Notes: This command can call handlers in behavior scripts, parent scripts, and ancestors. The *script* parameter can be a single script instance or a list of script instances. In the latter case, the message is sent to each script instance in the list.

callAncestor

Elements: callAncestor #*[handler name]*, *[script]*[*,params...*]

Purpose: Like call, this is another "pointing" command. This command lets you assign a handler to be executed not by a child object, but by the object's ancestor script. Of course, the ancestor needs to have been written to recognize the handler; otherwise, an error alert will appear, but only if the command is sent to a single ancestor. (If you use callAncestor to point the execution command to multiple ancestor scripts, no error alert will occur if the handler isn't defined.)

In context: If an object named lovechild has been created with hippie as an ancestor, and the hippie script includes a hairlength handler, this would return that handler's value:

call #hairlength, lovechild

Notes: The *script* parameter can be a single script instance or a list of script instances. In the latter case, the message is sent to each script instance in the list.

cancelIdleLoad

Elements: cancelIdleLoad *[idleLoadTag value]*

Purpose: This command keeps cast members with the specified load tag from being loaded during Director's idle moments—that is, while nothing else is happening.

In context: This statement will keep all cast members with the load tag of 50 from loading during an idle period:

cancelIdleLoad 50

See also: The idleLoadTag property.

COMMANDS

clearCache

Elements: clearCache

Purpose: This command clears Director's Network cache, the memory reserve file used for networking operations. It works only on Director movies and projector files, since Shockwave movies rely on the network cache settings of the browsers in which they operate.

In context: This script clears the cache when the end user hasn't been active for a while (the period defined in the timeOut handler):

```
on timeOut
   clearCache
end
```

Notes: If a file is still in use, it won't be cleared from the cache when this command is executed.

clearError

Elements: clearError (member *[whichFlashMember]*)

Purpose: This Flash command resets the error state of a streaming Flash cast member to 0. When an error occurs (as indicated by a -1 value for the member's state property), you can use the getError function to determine what type of error occurred. After checking the error (and, hopefully, correcting it), you can then use the clearError command to reset the cast member's error state, causing Director to attempt to open the Flash member if it is needed again.

In context: This handler uses getError to determine whether a network error occurred while loading a Flash movie named Katelyn. If an error occurred, a Movie in a Window is played to prompt the user to connect to the Internet, and the main movie branches back to the Family segment, where the attempt to load the Flash movie can be retried. Director will not attempt to load the Flash movie until the error state is cleared.

```
on isFlashLoading
   if getError(member "Katelyn") = #network then
      clearError(member "Katelyn")
      open window "getNetwork"
      go to frame "Family"
   else
      go to frame "niece"
   end if
end
```

See also: The state property and the getError function.

clearFrame

Elements: clearFrame

Purpose: This Score-recording command clears the contents of the currently active frame in the Score. The frame itself is not deleted (as in deleteFrame)—only the contents of its channels.

In context: This handler tests to see if the amount of available RAM is greater than 1 megabyte. If it isn't, the current frame is cleared.

```
on clearIfNoRAM
   beginRecording
      if the freeBytes<1024*1024then
         clearFrame
         updateFrame
      end if
   endRecording
end clearIfNoRAM
```

Notes: This command applies only to Score-generation sessions, as denoted by the use of the commands beginRecording and endRecording.

clearGlobals

Elements: clearGlobals

Purpose: This command empties the contents of all global variables (with the exception of the version variable), setting them all to VOID.

In context: This handler performs some housekeeping chores before moving on to a new movie:

```
on stopMovie
   disposeRearWindow
   clearGlobals
   set the soundEnabled to TRUE
end
```

Notes: Using clearGlobals is a good housekeeping measure when several movies are coordinated in a single user session. Clearing the global variables at the end of a movie lets the following movie create its own set of global variables.

close window

Elements: close window *[name or windowList #]*

Purpose: This command disposes of an open window's display on the host computer while retaining it in memory. The window can be referred to by name or by its number in the windowList property.

In context:

```
on stopPlaying
   close window "Session Status"
end
```

or:

```
on stopPlaying
   close window 7
end
```

See also: The open window and forget window commands and the windowList function.

closeXlib

Elements: closeXlib *[file name]*

Purpose: This command closes an open XLibrary file (the files in which Xtras reside). If no particular file is specified, all open XLibrary files will be closed.

In context: This command line closes a specific XLibrary file in a folder named Support in the same folder as the movie. Note the use of the @ operator to specify the complete path name, which is necessary when the XLibrary is not in the same folder as the current movie.

```
closeXlib "@:Support:ColorXtra"
```

This command line closes all open XLibraries:

```
closeXlib
```

Notes: In the example, the path name is in the Macintosh format, using colons(:) as separators. Windows path names use backslashes (\) rather than colons (:), but Director will make the necessary conversion for either system whenever the @ operator is used.

See also: The openXlib and showXlib commands.

copyToClipBoard

Elements: copyToClipBoard member (*[whichMember]*)

Purpose: This command transfers a copy of a cast member to the host system's clipboard. The cast member can be referred to by name or cast number.

In context: These lines both perform the same function:

```
copyToClipBoard member("First One")
copyToClipBoard member (1)
```

Notes: Only cast members (not sprites or text strings) can be copied to the clipboard using this command.

See also: The pasteClipBoardInto command.

crop

Elements: crop member(*[whichMember]*), *[cropRect]*

Purpose: This command is used with bitmap cast members to crop their size to a given rectangle. The cast member may be specified by name or number.

In context: These commands crop an existing bitmap cast member to the size of a sprite and then assign the cast member to that same sprite:

```
w = sprite(12).width
h = sprite(12).height
crop member("Loving Couple"), rect(20, 33, w+20, h+33)
sprite(12).member = "Loving Couple"
```

These commands capture a section of the Stage, with the section defined by an existing sprite:

```
member("Stage").picture = the picture of the stage
crop member("Stage"), the rect of sprite("section")
sprite("section").member = "Stage"
```

Notes: A bitmap will remain in the same relative position after cropping because the registration point doesn't move.

cursor

Elements: cursor *[cursor code]*

                 cursor [*[cast member]*]

                 cursor [*[cast member, mask cast member]*]

Purpose: You can use this command to specify a standard system cursor or to designate a cast member as a custom cursor. In addition, you can name a second cast member to be the mask of that cursor.

Here are the codes for cursor designation:

0	No custom cursor (returns cursor choice to the computer)
-1	Arrow cursor
1	Insertion (I-beam) cursor
2	Crosshair cursor
3	Thick cross (crossbar) cursor
4	Wristwatch cursor (Macintosh only)
4	Hourglass cursor (Windows only)
200	Blank cursor (no cursor is displayed)

In context: This script sets the cursor to a crosshair:

```
on enterFrame
   cursor 2
end
```

This line sets the cursor to the cast member in cast slot 17. Note the square brackets.

```
cursor [17]
```

This line sets the cursor to the cast member in cast slot 17 and names the adjacent cast member as the mask:

```
cursor [17, 18]
```

Notes: A nonsystem cursor must be created as a cast member (or series of cast members, if a mask is used). For complex cursor shapes, a mask is generally required to prevent white areas from being transparent.

COMMANDS

To function as a custom cursor or mask, a cast member must meet the following criteria:

- It must be 1-bit (single-color) graphic.
- It must be confined to a square area of 16 by 16 pixels or less. If the cast member is larger, only the upper-left portion will be shown.

See also: The `cursor` sprite property and the `rollOver` function.

delay

Elements: `delay` *[duration]*

Purpose: This command stops a movie's playback head from moving for a defined period of time. The delay period is expressed in terms of ticks (¹⁄₆₀ of a second). When a delay period is active, the only user action recognized by Director is quitting the movie (Control-Alt-period for Windows, Command-period for Macintosh). Since this command relates to playback, it is best used in an `on enterFrame` or `on exitFrame` script.

In context: This command delays the movie for 10 seconds:

`delay 600`

Another way to state this is:

`delay (10*60)`

Notes: Unlike `go to the frame`, the delay state ignores all mouse clicks. Scripts will still run while the delay is in effect.

To instigate a pause in playback while allowing user interaction, use the `timer` or `ticks` property and loop on a frame until the desired amount of time has passed.

See also: The `startTimer` command and the `timer` and `ticks` properties.

delete

Elements: `delete` *[text chunk]*

Purpose: This command removes an element of text (a character, word, item, line, or paragraph) from a specified text string or text cast member.

In context: This script tests to see if the user has erroneously put the title "Mr." into text cast member First Name. If so, the "Mr." is stripped, but the rest of the name remains.

```
if member("First Name").word[1] = "Mr." then
    delete member("First Name").word[1]
end if
```

See also: The `char...of`, `item...of`, `line...of`, and `paragraph` keywords.

deleteAll

Elements: `deleteAll` *[list name]*

Purpose: This command deletes all values from a linear or property list while keeping the list type definition. Lists remain either linear or property, depending on their previous use.

In context:

`deleteAll petList`

deleteAt

Elements: deleteAt *[name of list]*, *[position number]*

Purpose: This command removes a specified item from a specified list. This command will result in an error if the specified list element does not exist. Use the count function to determine whether an element exists.

In context: If the list petList consists of ["dog", "cat", "Studebaker", "fish"], then this command will remove the third item:

```
if count(petList)>= 3 then
   deleteAt petList, 3
end if
```

See also: The count function.

deleteFrame

Elements: deleteFrame

Purpose: This Score-modifying command deletes the currently active frame from the score.

In context: This handler tests to see if the amount of available RAM is greater than 1 megabyte. If it isn't, the current frame is deleted.

```
on clearIfNoRAM
   beginRecording
      if the freeBytes<1024*1024*1024 then
         deleteFrame
      end if
   endRecording
end clearIfNoRAM
```

Notes: This command applies only to Score-generation sessions, as denoted by the use of the commands beginRecording and endRecording.

deleteOne

Elements: deleteOne *[listName, listValue]*

Purpose: This command removes the first occurrence of a specified entry in a linear or property list. All subsequent occurrences of that entry (if any) are not disturbed.

In context: If the list petList consists of ["dog", "sheep", "sheep", "fish", "sheep"], then this command will remove the first instance of "sheep":

```
deleteOne petList, "sheep"
```

If a property list Mike consists of [#name:"Gross", #hair:"Yes"], then the following command will remove Mike's hair.

```
deleteOne Mike, "Yes"
put Mike
-- [#name:"Gross"]
```

Notes: For property lists, the associated property is also removed, but don't attempt to use the property name instead of the property value in the command.

deleteProp

Elements: deleteProp *[name of list]*, *[property or number]*

Purpose: The command deletes an element from a linear or property list. For property lists, specify the property name. For linear lists, specify the number of the element in the list.

In context: These two command lines establish a property list (ballStats) and then delete a value from that list:

```
set ballStats = [#runs:2, #hits:8, #errors:7, #shoeSize, 9]
deleteProp ballStats, #errors
```

The list now contains [#runs: 2, #hits: 8, #shoeSize: 9].

Notes: In the case of multiple items bearing the same property identifier, only the first item will be deleted. The deleteProp command, when used with a linear list, is synonymous with deleteAt.

See also: The addProp command.

deleteVertex

Elements: deleteVertex (member *[memberRef]*, *[vertIndex]*)

Purpose: This command removes an existing vertex from a vector shape cast member. The vertex is specified by its index number in the member's vertexList property.

In context: This line will remove the second vertex point in the vector shape Seth:

```
deleteVertex member("Seth"), 2
```

See also: The addVertex and moveVertex commands and the originMode and vertexList properties.

do

Elements: do *[expression]*

Purpose: This command takes a text string and treats it as a Lingo command. If you have Lingo commands stored in a list, text field, or external file, you can extract and execute them.

In context: The first script line establishes a list (myList); the second retrieves the second entry in that list and executes it as a Lingo command:

```
cmdList = ["quit", "beep", "count myList"]
do getAt(cmdList, 2)
```

The result is a single system beep.

Notes: The string to be executed can consist of multiple lines. Each line will be treated as a Lingo command and will be executed.

downloadNetThing

Elements: downloadNetThing *[URL, localfile]*

Purpose: This command is used to control the download of a file from a networked environment for later use (without the pesky download time delay). You supply the appropriate URL address of the file to be downloaded; it can be an HTML page, Director movie, graphic image, or anything that resides on an FTP or HTTP server. The *localfile* parameter indicates the path name and file name for the file on the local disk—the location where you want the file to be parked (if the file doesn't yet exist, it will be created).

In context: This script line (yes, it's one line) fetches a file called Swiftytext from the given URL address and stores it on the host computer in a file of the same name:

```
downloadNetThing "http://www.demystified.com/movies/Swiftytext", ¬
the moviePath&"Swiftytext"
```

Notes: It would be wise to use netDone to see if the download is complete. Also, note that downloadNetThing is disabled in Shockwave movies for security purposes (no sneaky background file transfers without the end user's cooperation).

duplicateFrame

Elements: duplicateFrame

Purpose: This Score-modifying command duplicates the currently active frame from the Score and then makes the new version (placed after the frame being copied) the active frame.

In context: This handler inserts 99 new copies of the first frame in a Director movie:

```
on makeABunch
   go to frame 1
   beginRecording
      repeat with x = 1 to 99
         duplicateFrame
      end repeat
   endRecording
end makeABunch
```

Notes: This command applies only to Score-generation sessions, as denoted by the use of the commands beginRecording and endRecording. It is synonymous with the insertFrame command.

duplicate member

Elements: duplicate member *[source] [, destination]*

Purpose: This command creates a duplicate of an existing cast member (specified by name or cast number). If no destination is given, the new cast member will be placed in the first available cast slot.

In context: The first command line duplicates cast member Spelling in the first free slot. The second places a duplicate of cast member 2 in cast slot 10.

```
duplicate member("Spelling")
duplicate member 2, 10
```

Notes: Duplicated cast members are given the same name as their source cast members. The duplicate command is recommended only for use during authoring.

enableHotSpot

Elements: enableHotSpot sprite([*whichQTVR*]), [*hotSpotID*], [*TOrF*]

Purpose: This QTVR command determines whether a specified hot spot for a specified QTVR sprite is enabled (TRUE) or disabled (FALSE).

In context:

```
enableHotSpot sprite("Office"), 2, TRUE
```

Notes: Use the ptToHotSpotID function to determine the ID of a hotspot at a specific point.

See also: The ptToHotSpotID QTVR function.

erase member

Elements: erase member *[member name or number]*

Purpose: This command clears a cast member (specified by name or cast number), emptying its contents and deleting its name (if any).

In context: The first command line erases the first occurrence of cast member Spelling in the Cast. The second erases the cast member in cast slot 10.

```
erase member "Spelling"
erase member 10
```

Notes: When more than one cast member has the same name, erase member will delete only the first one bearing that name. This command is recommended only for use during authoring.

externalEvent

Elements: externalEvent ("*textstring*")

Purpose: Another "pointing" command, externalEvent can be used to communicate with the end user's browser application from a Shockwave movie. Many scripting languages (such as JavaScript, ActiveX, VBScript, and LiveConnect) are usually delivered to the browser in the form of text strings embedded in an HTML file, but externalEvent will let you pass those same text strings from within the context of Lingo. Since the rules of interaction vary widely for each scripting language, there is no one set way of using this term. For instance, ActiveX processes it as an event, whereas LiveConnect parses it as a call to a function. However, one proven way to work with it is to use in it conjunction with an interpretive code added to an HTML script. For in-depth documentation on the use of externalEvent with particular languages and browser configurations, see the Director Technotes Web site.

In context: This script passes a text string containing a custom JavaScript handler name and two parameters (note how they're contained within single quotation marks):

```
on javaBlue
    externalEvent ("TurnBlue ('button1', 'button2')")
end
```

Notes: Support of scripting languages varies from browser to browser, so you may have problems if you try to pass a text string that the host browser can't interpret. What's more, there's no easy way to determine whether or not the browser has done anything with the data you've passed; the best you can do is include instructions to pass data back to the Shockwave movie and use the on evalScript handler to recognize that communication.

See also: The on evalScript handler and the mci command (Windows only).

finishIdleLoad

Elements: finishIdleLoad *[load tag]*

Purpose: If the loading into RAM of cast members with a specified load tag value has been interrupted (as when an MIAW has been deactivated), this command will resume the loading process where it left off.

In context:

finishIdleLoad 40

See also: The idleLoadTag and idleLoadMode properties.

forget window

Elements: forget window *[name or windowList #]*

Purpose: This command disposes of a window from display and application RAM. For the window to be deleted, it must not be referred to by multiple variables. The window can be referred to by name or by its number in the windowList property.

In context:

```
on stopMovie
    forget window "Session Status"
end
```

Or:

```
on stopMovie
    forget window 7
end
```

See also: The close window and open window commands and the windowList function.

COMMANDS

getPref

Elements: getPref(*fileName*)

Purpose: The companion command to setPref, the getPref command retrieves the contents of the named file. For security reasons, Shockwave movies are allowed to write to a user's system only using setPref, and the file can then be retrieved with getPref (although Director movies and projectors can also use both getPref and setPref). The file is a standard text file, and only the file extensions .txt and .htm are used. No path name is required (or allowed), as the location is determined by the application.

In context: This handler retrieves the contents of preferences file r32user.txt:

```
on checkUser
   userInfo = getPref("r32user.txt")
end
```

See also: The setPref function.

go

Elements: go {to} {frame} *whichFrame*
          go {to} movie *whichMovie*
          go {to} {frame} *whichFrame* of movie *whichMovie*

Purpose: This command moves the playback head to the indicated location: a specified frame in the current movie or another movie. The frame can be specified by number or marker name (when present).

In context:

```
go to frame 156
go frame "Main Loop"
go frame "Main Loop" of movie "Info"
```

Notes: The keyword to is not required, but it is often used for clarity.

go loop

Elements: go loop

Purpose: This command causes the playback head to loop back to the last frame possessing a marker. If the current frame contains a marker, the playback head loops back to the current frame. If there is no marker in the current frame or to the left of the frame, the movie loops to the first marker to the right of the current frame. If there is no marker in the movie, the playback head loops back to the beginning of the movie.

In context:

```
go loop
```

See also: The go next and go previous commands.

go next

Elements: `go next`

Purpose: This command causes the playback head to move to the next frame possessing a marker. If there are no markers to the right of the current frame, the playback head moves to the first marker to the left, if there is one (including the current frame), or to frame 1, if there are no markers in the movie.

In context:

`go next`

See also: The `go loop` and `go previous` commands.

go previous

Elements: `go previous`

Purpose: This command causes the playback head to move to the previous frame possessing a marker. If the current frame has a marker and there are no markers to the left of the current frame, the movie loops on the current frame. If the current frame does not have a marker and there are no markers to the left, the playback head moves to the first marker to the right. If there are no markers in the movie, the playback head loops to frame 1.

In context: This button script moves the playback head to the previous marker:

```
on mouseUp
   go previous
end
```

goToFrame

Elements: `goToFrame (sprite` *[whichFlashSprite, frame]*`)`

Purpose: This command plays a Flash movie sprite beginning at the frame identified by the *frame* parameter. The frame may be specified by either an integer indicating the frame number or a string indicating a frame label. The goToFrame command is equivalent to setting a Flash movie sprite's `frame` property.

In context: This command branches to frame 10 within a Flash movie in channel 6:

`goToFrame(sprite 6, 10)`

gotoNetMovie

Elements: `gotoNetMovie` *[URL address]*

Purpose: This command loads a Shockwave movie residing on an HTTP or FTP server and then plays it. This command can also be specified so that playback begins at a designated point in the movie.

In context: This script line opens a movie at the specified universal resource locator (URL) address:

`gotoNetMovie "http://demystified.com/examples/swifty1.dcr"`

COMMANDS

This line opens the same movie, but at the point of the internal marker entitled Jumping. Note the use of the pound (#) symbol to preface the label name.

```
gotoNetMovie "http://demystified.com/examples/swifty1.dcr#Jumping"
```

Notes: If you issue another gotoNetMovie command while the first one is still in progress, the second directive will override the first. When you are testing your movie using local media, the file must be placed in a folder named dswmedia.

GotoNetPage

Elements: gotoNetPage *[URL] [, targetName]*

Purpose: Like its sister command gotoNetMovie, this directive searches and opens an online file (a Shockwave movie, HTML page, or anything else displaying a valid MIME type). You can use the optional HTML parameter *targetName* to designate where you want the page to be loaded: to a new window or to a frame within the browser.

In context: This script line loads the HTML document scooty.html into a new browser window named Boot:

```
gotoNetPage "http://www.demystified.com/scooty.html", "Boot"
```

Notes: If this command is issued when a browser isn't open, Director (or the projector file) will attempt to locate and launch a browser. If you want to specify a particular browser, you might want to launch it first using the open command.

halt

Elements: halt

Purpose: When this command is used, Lingo immediately exits the handler containing it, without processing any of the script lines that follow it. Playback of the movie will then stop.

In context: This handler checks to makes sure that the current monitor has a color depth of 16-bit or greater. If it doesn't, the handler is exited and playback stopped.

```
on loadBigPicture
    if the colorDepth <16 then
        halt
    end if
    sprite(7).member = "Van Gogh"
end
```

Notes: Using halt will stop movie playback, but it will not cause the Director application to quit during authoring or the host system to shut down. If a handler containing halt is called by another handler, Lingo will quit executing both the called and the calling handler. If you want execution to continue on the level of the calling handler, use the exit keyword instead.

hilite

Elements: hilite *[text chunk]*

Purpose: This command selects a given portion of a text container by displaying it on the Stage with the system's highlight color (specified in the Windows Display Properties dialog box or the Macintosh Color control panel).

In context:

```
hilite line 7 of member "Poem Text"
```

Notes: Don't confuse this command with the hilite of member property.

hold

Elements: hold sprite *[whichFlashSprite]*

Purpose: This Flash command stops a Flash movie sprite that is playing in the current frame but allows any audio to continue to play.

In context: This behavior script stops the Flash movie sprites playing in channels 1 through 5 without preventing any audio in those channels from playing:

```
on mouseUp
   repeat with i = 1 to 5
      hold sprite i
   end repeat
end
```

See also: The movieRate property.

importFileInto

Elements: importFileInto member(*[memberRef]*), *[file]*

Purpose: This command retrieves a file into the Cast database at a given slot; the cast member will then have the same name as the source file.

In context: This command places a PICT file named Bella Rosa into cast slot 3:

```
importFileInto member 3, "Bella Rosa"
```

Notes: This command will work on all file types that can be imported using the Import dialog box. If the cast member slot to which the file is being imported is already occupied, its contents will be overwritten.

insertFrame

Elements: insertFrame

Purpose: This Score-modifying command duplicates the currently active Score frame and places the new frame after the current frame. The new version then becomes the active frame.

In context: The following handler inserts 99 new copies of the first frame in a Director movie.

```
on makeABunch
  go to frame 1
  beginRecording
    repeat with x = 1 to 99
      insertFrame
    end repeat
  endRecording
end makeABunch
```

Notes: This command applies only to Score-generation sessions, as denoted by the use of the commands beginRecording and endRecording. It is synonymous with the duplicateFrame command.

installMenu

Elements: installMenu *[cast member]*

Purpose: This command adds a custom menu to the host system's menu bar while the movie is running. The name and contents of that menu must be entered in a field cast member; specification of the cast member can be by name or slot number.

In context:

installMenu 9

installMenu "About this CD-ROM"

See also: The menu: keyword.

mci

Elements: mci *["string"]*

Purpose: Use this command to communicate with the media control interface developed by Microsoft for use in Windows-based multimedia. MCI is basically a means of controlling external devices; it can issue commands to start, stop, and play a number of hardware products, such as tape decks, video discs, and even VCRs. The MacOS ignores mci commands.

In context: This sample script line instructs a video disc player (identified by the device type videodisc) to play a specified track on the disc currently in the device:

mci "play videodisc track 29"

Notes: Microsoft recommends against using the 16-bit MCI interface. Third-party Xtras can be found to provide the same functionality.

move member

Elements: move member *[source]*, *[destination]*

Purpose: This command relocates a current cast member (specified by name or cast number). If no destination is given, the new cast member will be placed in the first available Cast slot.

COMMANDS

In context: The first command line moves cast member Spelling to the first free slot. The second places cast member 2 in cast slot 10.

```
move member "Spelling"
move member 2, 10
```

Notes: This command is recommended for use while authoring but not while a movie is running.

moveToBack

Elements: moveToBack window *[windowName]*

Purpose: Relocates a given open window (such as an MIAW) to the rearmost layer of windows, thereby rendering it inactive.

In context:

```
moveToBack window "Command Center"
```

Notes: The window must be specified by its name, not by the name of the movie playing in the window.

See also: The windowList property.

moveToFront

Elements: moveToFront window *[windowName]*

Purpose: Relocates a given open window (such as an MIAW) to the foremost layer of windows, thereby rendering it active.

In context: This command uses the windowList property to reference a window:

```
windowName = getAt(the windowList, 2)
moveToFront window windowName
```

Notes: The window must be specified by its name, not by the name of the movie playing in the window.

See also: The windowList property.

netAbort

Elements: netAbort *[URL or netID]*

Purpose: Hold everything! That's what this command conveys in the networked environment. It issues an immediate halt to a network operation—streaming file downloads, text retrieval, and so on. You can use either the URL address of the targeted document or the unique net ID issued by Lingo to the particular operation.

In context: This script line stops any NetLingo action that's been directed to the given URL address:

```
netAbort "http://www.demystified.com/index.html"
```

The next script assumes that a list is kept of the net IDs of all currently running network operations. All operations are then halted.

```
on holdEverything
  global netIDList
  num = count(netIDList)
  if num <> 0 then
    repeat with i = 1 to num
      netAbort i
    end repeat
  end if
end
```

Notes: Using the net ID is the quickest way to stop activity, although the URL method will work as well. Since you can't hard-code in specific net ID data (it's assigned on the fly by Director), it's a good idea to write a global variable that captures and contains the value as each network operation is started.

netStatus

Elements: netStatus "*[message string]*"

Purpose: When this command is put to work in a movie running in a browser, a specified text string will appear in the status area of the browser window; in most browsers, that's the area in the lower-left corner that displays useful information such as the download status or the target HTML of a rolled-over link.

In context:

netStatus "Now downloading the file."

Notes: During authoring in Director, netStatus messages are displayed in the Message window. This command does not work in the projector format.

nothing

Elements: nothing

Purpose: As its name implies, this command directs Lingo to do nothing—in the context of the handler it occupies. This command often is used to balance nested if statements.

In context: This handler checks to see if the mouse is currently over the sprite in channel 1. If it is, the handler then checks to see if the current system volume level is set to less than 6. If the volume is indeed below this threshold, the handler resets the level before playing a sound file (Warning!). A third if statement checks to make sure that the sound isn't currently playing before it's played again—otherwise, the beginning of the sound would be retriggered with every idle event. A fourth statement stops the sound from playing as soon as the mouse is no longer over the sprite.

```
on idle
  if rollOver(1) then
    if the soundLevel < 6 then
      set the SoundLevel to 6
    else nothing
```

```
        if soundBusy (1) then nothing
        else puppetSound "Warning!"
    else sound close 1
end
```

nudge

Elements: nudge(sprite *whichQTVRSprite*, #*direction*)

Purpose: This QTVR command is used for navigating a QTVR sprite. The QTVR sprite is nudged in the direction specified by #*direction*. Possible values for #*direction* are #down, #left, #right, #up, #upLeft, #upRight, #downLeft, and #downRight.

In context: The following command nudges the QTVR sprite Showcase downward and to the left:

```
nudge (sprite "Showcase", #downLeft)
```

open

Elements: open *[document]* with *[application]*

open *[application]*

Purpose: This command opens an application (other than Director) or opens a document with a specified application.

In context: This script line opens a file named Text (in the same folder as the movie) with the application Notepad. Note that the entire path name of the application is given.

```
open "Text" with "C:\Windows\Notepad"
```

This line opens only the application MacThing in the same folder as the movie:

```
open "MacThing"
```

Notes: Unless an application's location is contained in the system's search path, the application either must be in the movie's folder, or the full path name must be specified. Third-party Xtras provide a much better interface for running external applications.

open window

Elements: open window *[name]*

Purpose: This command opens a Director movie or existing window object in the form of a window (a Movie in a Window, or MIAW) that plays in front of the currently running movie.

In context: This button script opens a window named Countdown. If no window or movie named Countdown is found, Director displays an Open dialog box.

```
on mouseUp
    open window "Countdown"
end
```

Notes: Director 7 has had some trouble with MIAWs. When authoring, an open Message window may prevent a window from opening in the foreground.

See also: The `close window` and `forget window` commands and the `windowList` function.

openXlib

Elements: `openXlib` *[fileName]*

Purpose: This command opens an XLibrary file, making the contained Xtras available to Director.

In context: This command line opens the XLibrary file ColorXtra. Note that a complete path name is given (this is necessary when the XLibrary is not in the same folder as the current movie).

`openXlib "My CD-ROM:Support:ColorXtra"`

See also: The `closeXlib` and `showXlib` commands and the `interface` function.

pass

Elements: `pass`

Purpose: This command modifies the standard flow of event messages in the message hierarchy, allowing an event message to be passed to additional scripting levels when otherwise the event would stop at the present level. The `pass` command prevents other commands following it in a handler from executing, so it should either be the last command or placed in a conditional structure where no other commands are expected to execute once the `pass` command is reached.

In context: This movie script instructs Director to ignore all keystrokes except the exclamation point (!). Whenever the exclamation point is typed by the user, it's displayed normally; other keys do nothing.

```
on startMovie
   set the keyDownScript to "exclamationOnly"
end
on exclamationOnly
   if the key = "!" then pass
   else stopEvent
end
```

Notes: Since only primary event handlers are normally passed on once a handler is encountered, the `pass` command is especially useful for making sure that two or more scripts on different levels are executed. For instance, a button may have a cast script that dictates its animation when clicked, and a behavior script containing navigation instructions. In that case, the behavior script would need to contain a `pass` command.

See also: The `stopEvent` command.

pasteClipBoardInto

Elements: pasteClipBoardInto member *[cast member]*

Purpose: This command places the current contents of the host system's clipboard file into a specified cast slot. The slot can be specified by name or slot number.

In context:

```
pasteClipBoardInto member "Text Display"
pasteClipBoardInto member 47
```

Notes: A specific slot must be named. If the slot specified is already occupied, its contents will be overwritten. If those contents are of a data type other than that which is on the clipboard, the slot's data type will change to match the type of the item being pasted.

For Shockwave movies and for movies with the safePlayer property set to TRUE, the user is provided with a warning dialog box and allowed to cancel the operation. The pasteClipBoardInto command is not supported for movies playing over the Internet.

pause member

Elements: pause member *[cast member name]*

Purpose: When triggered, this command pauses playback of a Shockwave Audio cast member. Play can then be resumed by issuing a play member command.

In context:

```
pause member "background sound"
```

Notes: When paused, the Shockwave Audio file will return the status code 4 when tested by the property the state of member.

See also: The stop member and play member commands and the state of member property.

pause sprite

Elements: pause (sprite *[whichGIFSprite]*)

Purpose: This command causes an animated GIF sprite to pause in its playback and remain in the current frame.

See also: The resume and rewind commands.

play

Elements: play *[frame name or number]*
play frame *[name or number]*
play movie *[name]*
play frame *[number]* of movie *[name]*
play sprite *[FlashSprite]*

Purpose: This command moves the playback head to a specific frame in the current movie or another movie. The frame can be specified by number or marker name (when present). The play command differs from the go command in that Director stores information about the location where the play command was issued so the calling movie can pick up again when the played movie finishes. While not strictly required, every play command should have a matching play done command in the played movie to avoid using up Director's memory by the storage of unnecessary return information. For Flash sprites, place the sprite from the beginning, or from the current location if the sprite has been stopped using the stop command.

In context: This handler plays a segment of the current movie and then two movies in succession. Note that the handler is suspended until the movie or segment being played finishes. This is different than the approach used in the go command, which would play only the first frame of the first segment and first movie.

```
on mouseUp
  play frame 156
  play "Main Loop"
  play frame "Main Loop" of movie "Info"
end mouseUp
```

Notes: The word frame is not required, but it often is used for purposes of clarity.

See also: The play done and downloadNetThing commands.

play done

Elements: play done

Purpose: This command is the counterpart to the play command. When Director encounters this command, it ends playback of a sequence or movie and returns to the point at which the play command was executed.

In context:

```
on mouseUp
  play done
end
```

Notes: Use play done for movies or sequences that may be entered from a number of different locations, such as a Help file. Make sure to issue play done commands for each play command to minimize RAM waste.

postNetText

Elements: postNetText(*[url, propertyList]* *[,serverOSString]* *[,serverCharSetString]*)
postNetText(*[url, postText]* *[,serverOSString]* *[,serverCharSetString]*)

Purpose: This command is similar to the getNetText command but is generally used when working with forms. The postNetText command sends a POST request to the specified URL. The server's return information is retrieved using the netTextResult function, as with getNetText. The elements in the property list are equivalent to HTML form field names (the property name) and field values (the property value).

The *serverOSString* and *serverCharSetString* parameters are optional and have to do with conversion of text depending on the operating system of the server. For most applications, these parameters are not required.

In context: This statement omits the two optional parameters:

```
netID = postNetText("www.demystified.com\users.cgi",¬
newUserList)
```

See also: The getNetText, netTextResult, netDone, and netError functions.

preLoad

Elements: preLoad
preLoad *[ending frame number]*
preLoad marker "*[marker]*"
preLoad *[from frame]*, *[to frame]*
preLoad *[movie]*

Purpose: This command attempts to load into memory all cast members appearing in the specified frames before proceeding. If no frames are specified, all cast members in the movie will be preloaded. Preloading stops when the specified cast members are loaded or when memory is full. Use the result function to obtain the result returned by preLoad, which is the frame number of the last frame that was loaded.

In context: The first command line preloads cast members appearing in frames 1 through 119. The second preloads cast members up to the frame marked Main Intro, and the third line preloads only cast members in frames 25 through 50.

```
preLoad 119
preLoad marker "Main Intro"
preLoad 25, 50
```

Notes: This command is useful for optimizing playback performance. Cast members referenced through Lingo but which do not appear in the Score are not affected by this command.

See also: The preLoadMember and unLoad commands and the result function.

preLoadBuffer

Elements: preLoadBuffer member *[SWACastmember]*

Purpose: This command is used to preload a Shockwave Audio file before the file is played. Only the first part of the file is preloaded, as determined by the cast member's preLoadTime property. After issuing this command, you should check the cast member's state property to determine whether the preload is complete and was successful.

In context: These statements specify that three seconds of the SWA file Whale Snort should be preloaded before playback begins; then preloading into memory begins:

```
member("Whale Snort").preLoadTime = 3
preLoadBuffer (member "Whale Snort")
```

Notes: Many of an SWA cast member's properties are unavailable to your program until the cast member has successfully been preloaded.

See also: The preLoadTime and state properties.

COMMANDS

preLoadMember

Elements: preLoadMember
             preLoadMember *[name or number]*
             preLoad *[from member]*, *[to member]*

Purpose: This command attempts to load into memory all specified cast members before proceeding. If no range of cast slots is specified, all cast members in the movie will be preloaded. Preloading stops when the specified cast members are loaded or when memory is full. Use the result function to obtain the result returned by preLoad, which is the number of the last cast member that was loaded.

In context: The first command line preloads the cast member in cast slot 1. The second line preloads the cast member named Company Logo, and the third line preloads cast members 14 through 40.

```
preLoadMember 1
preLoadMember "Company Logo"
preLoad 14, 40
```

See also: The preLoad and unLoad commands and the result function.

preLoadMovie

Elements: preLoadMovie *[Name]*

Purpose: This command loads into memory the whole of a specified movie (RAM permitting), which can speed the execution time of a subsequent go to or play movie command.

In context:

```
preLoadMovie "Company Overview"
```

Notes: For movies being downloaded from the Internet, use downLoadNetThing or preLoadNetThing.

preloadNetThing

Elements: preLoadNetThing *[URL]*

Purpose: Like downLoadNetThing, this command lets you download a file from a networked environment—but in this case, the file is loaded not to the end user's hard drive, but to Director's or the browser's cache.

In context: This script line fetches a Shockwave movie called Swifty1.dcr from the URL address shown and preloads it into the browser cache:

```
loadID = preLoadNetThing "http://www.demystified.com/movies/Swifty1.dcr"
```

Notes: Use netDone to see if the download is complete. Note that downLoadNetThing is disabled in Shockwave movies for security purposes (no sneaky background file transfers without the end user's cooperation).

COMMANDS

printFrom

Elements: printFrom *[frame][, frame] [, percentage]*

Purpose: Use this command to print a frame or range of frames in a movie. If no reduction percentage is given, the frame or frames will be printed at 100 percent. Allowable reductions are 100, 50, and 25 percent.

In context: The first line prints a single frame (267). The second line prints all frames from 150 through 267 at a 50 percent reduction:

```
printFrom 267
printFrom 150, 267, 50
```

proxyServer

Elements: proxyserver *[server type,* "ipaddress"*, portnumber]*
               proxyserver ( )

Purpose: Here's a command for those well versed in Web server configuration and terminology. This command, when triggered, will set the values for an FTP or HTTP proxy server. The *server type* parameter should be either #ftp or #http (note the designations as symbols). The *ipaddress* parameter must be a string and designates the Internet port address; use the actual numerical address (for example, ì288.54. 253.00î) rather than any named domain associated with that address. The *portnumber* parameter can be replaced with the number of a specified port. If you use proxyserver(), the command will call the settings of an FTP or HTTP proxy server, if available.

What's the purpose of this command? It's primarily a means of passing configuration parameters to Web server software, which means it can be used (in conjunction with the appropriate access codes) to change the accessibility of files being served. For instance, if you were operating on the Internet behind a firewall of limited access, you could use the proxyServer command to retrieve data from beyond the firewall.

In context:

```
proxyServer #http "288.54. 253.00"
```

puppetPalette

Elements: puppetPalette *[paletteMem][, speed][, range]*

Purpose: Use this command to override the currently active palette. Director will use the puppeted palette until you return control to the Score with the command puppetPalette 0. If you want to fade into the new palette, add a number corresponding to the speed of the fade, from 1 (slowest) to 60 (fastest). You can also add a second statement specifying the range of frames over which the change should occur.

In context: The first command line performs a simple palette switch. The second line puppets the palette at a median speed, over a range of 11 frames (350 through 360).

```
puppetPalette "Crazy Quilt"
puppetPalette "Crazy Quilt", 30, 350-360
```

Notes: It isn't possible to set color cycling or full-screen fade effects on puppeted palettes. Movies playing in a browser always use the browser's palette.

COMMANDS

puppetSound

Elements: puppetSound *[channel, memberRef]*
            puppetSound *[channel]*, 0

Purpose: This command overrides the current contents of a sound channel and plays the sound indicated instead. To stop a sound or return control of the channel to the Score, use the command puppetSound channelNum, 0. If no channel number is given, the channel is assumed to be channel 1.

In context: This command plays the Button Click sound in channel 3:

puppetSound 3, "Button Click"

Notes: A sound begins playing only when the playback head moves or the updateStage command is executed. To provide a timely sound, such as a button click sound, you may need to use the updateStage command.

puppetSprite

Elements: puppetSprite *[channel number, TRUEorFALSE]*

Purpose: This command turns on or off the puppet status of the designated visual channel. Director 6 introduced the concept of autopuppeting, which removed much of the need for puppeting a visual channel. Puppeting is still required when you want Lingo to control a sprite after the sprite is no longer in the Score. Without puppeting, Lingo changes to a sprite last only so long as the sprite is in the Score; then the sprite (and the changes) disappear. With puppeting, both the sprite and the changes remain in effect until the channel is unpuppeted.

In context: This behavior script makes the channel containing the clicked sprite a puppet:

property spriteNum
on mouseDown
   puppetSprite spriteNum, TRUE
end mouseDown

Notes: Remember that it's the channel that's puppeted, not the sprite in the channel. And don't forget to turn off the puppet status of the channel when you're through manipulating it with Lingo.

puppetTempo

Elements: puppetTempo *[speed]*

Purpose: Use this command to override the currently active tempo and substitute a new one.

In context: This script line sets the tempo to 20 frames per second:

puppetTempo 20

Notes: Unlike most other puppeting Lingo, puppetTempo does not need to be explicitly turned off in order to return control to the Score. Instead, the tempo will persist until another tempo command is encountered, either in the channel or via Lingo.

puppetTransition

Elements: puppetTransition *[ID code] [, duration] [, size][, area]*

Purpose: Use this command to trigger transitions via Lingo control. The *ID code* parameter specifies the transition as shown below. The other parameters are optional. The *duration* parameter (expressed in quarter seconds) specifies the time the transition takes to complete. The *size* parameter indicates the number of pixels in a chunk (from 1 to 128), although this value will be ignored by transitions that don't use chunks. To apply the transition to the entire Stage rather than just the changing area, set the *area* parameter to FALSE.

Here are the codes for built-in transitions:

01	Wipe right	28	Random columns
02	Wipe left	29	Cover down
03	Wipe down	30	Cover down, left
04	Wipe up	31	Cover down, right
05	Center out, horizontal	32	Cover left
06	Edges in, horizontal	33	Cover right
07	Center out, vertical	34	Cover up
08	Edges in, vertical	35	Cover up, left
09	Center out, square	36	Cover up, right
10	Edges in, square	37	Venetian blinds
11	Push left	38	Checkerboard
12	Push right	39	Strips on bottom, build left
13	Push down	40	Strips on bottom, build right
14	Push up	41	Strips on left, build down
15	Reveal up	42	Strips on left, build up
16	Reveal up, right	43	Strips on right, build down
17	Reveal right	44	Strips on right, build up
18	Reveal down, right	45	Strips on top, build left
19	Reveal down	46	Strips on top, build right
20	Reveal down, left	47	Zoom open
21	Reveal left	48	Zoom close
22	Reveal up, left	49	Vertical blinds
23	Dissolve, pixels fast (not for monitors set to 32-bit color)	50	Dissolve, bits fast (not for monitors set to 32-bit color)
24	Dissolve, boxy rectangles	51	Dissolve, pixels (not for monitors set to 32-bit color)
25	Dissolve, boxy squares		
26	Dissolve, patterns	52	Dissolve, bits (not for monitors set to 32-bit color)
27	Random rows		

In context: This statement performs a Reveal right transition lasting 2 seconds, with a chunk size of 16, applied to the entire Stage:

puppetTransition 17, 2, 16, FALSE

To puppet a nonstandard transition (one supplied by a transition Xtra) or any other transition that appears as a cast member, designate the transition with the keyword member and the cast number, as in the line shown on the next page.

COMMANDS

```
puppetTransition member 342
```

Notes: The transition channel does not need to be made a puppet before puppetTransition is used.

put

Elements: put *[expression or function]*

Purpose: Use this command for testing expressions or retrieving property or function values in the Message window.

In context: The first put line displays the current contents of the function the long date. The second one returns the binary status of the soundEnabled property. The third one calculates the expression 6 times 9:

```
put the long date
-- "Monday, December 6, 1999"
put the soundEnabled
-- 1
put 6*9
-- 54
```

put...after

Elements: put *[expression]* after *[textString or chunkExpression]*

Purpose: This command adds the designated expression (converted to a string) to the end of a designated text container or after a chunk expression in a text container. If there are calculations or other operations to be performed on the expression, they will be executed before the expression is added to the text string.

In context: This line adds another entry to the string in the variable myVar, currently containing "rock, paper, scissors":

```
put ", rainhat" after myVar
```

The variable myVar now contains "rock, paper, scissors, rainhat". Note that the inserted expression includes both a comma and a space; otherwise, the variable would return "rock, paper, scissorsrainhat".

The following command uses a chunk expression to determine the location to place the text after:

```
put " hammer" after char 4 of myVar
```

This results in the string "rock hammer, paper, scissors, rainhat".

put...before

Elements: put *[expression]* before *[textString or chunkExpression]*

Purpose: This command adds the designated expression (converted to a string) to the beginning of a designated text container or before a chunk expression in a text container. If there are calculations or other operations to be performed on the expression, they will be executed before the expression is added to the text string.

In context: This line adds another entry to the string in the variable myVar, currently containing "rock, paper, scissors":

```
put "rainhat, " before myVar
```

This returns "rainhat, rock, paper, scissors". Note that the inserted expression includes both a comma and a space; otherwise, the variable would return "rainhatrock, paper, scissors".

See also: The put...after command.

put...into

Elements: put *[expression]* into *[textContainer]*

             put *[expression]* into *[variable]*

Purpose: You can use this command to place an expression in an existing text container (such as a text field, list, or variable). It can also be used to create or fill a variable, though this usage is considered obsolete.

In context: This command line places a text string in the text cast member Menu:

```
put "Tofu Twinkies" into field "Menu"
```

This line evaluates an expression before placing the result (expressed as a string) in the field cast member myField:

```
put "moe"&&"moe"&(3*9) into myField
```

```
The content of the field is now "moe moe27".
```

Notes: This command overwrites any other contents in the target container.

qtRegisterAccessKey

Elements: qtRegisterAccessKey(*[categoryString, keyString]*)

Purpose: Use this command for encrypted QuickTime media. This command allows the key for the encrypted media to be registered, making all QuickTime media encrypted with that key accessible to the movie. The key is application specific; it is not a systemwide key. After the application unregisters the key or shuts down, the media will no longer be accessible.

Notes: For security reasons, there is no way to display a listing of all registered keys.

See also: The qtUnRegisterAccessKey command.

qtUnRegisterAccessKey

Elements: qtUnRegisterAccessKey(*[categoryString, keyString]*)

Purpose: Use this command for encrypted QuickTime media. This command allows the unregistration of a key for encrypted media, making the encrypted media no longer accessible.

See also: The qtRegisterAccessKey command.

COMMANDS

quit

Elements: quit

Purpose: This command causes Director to close both the current movie and the application and return to the desktop.

In context: This script performs a few housekeeping tasks before quitting:

```
on mouseUp
    forget window "Control Panel"
    set the soundLevel to 7
    quit
end
```

See also: The restart and shutDown commands.

recordFont

Elements: recordFont(*memberVar, font* ,[*style*],[*sizes*] ,*characters*)

Purpose: This command embeds a TrueType or Type 1 font as the specified cast member and makes the font accessible to the movie. Once embedded, these fonts can be used just as if they were installed on the system that is playing the movie. The recordFont command is the Lingo equivalent of embedding a font using the Director interface (from the Insert menu, select Media Element and then Font). The parameters are as follows:

memberVar: The reference to a cast member, which should be obtained using the new function.

font: The name of the original font (installed on the authoring system) to be recorded.

style: A list of symbols indicating the styles of the font to be included; possible values are #plain, #bold, and #italic. If this argument is the empty list ([ ]), #plain is used.

sizes: A list of integers giving the sizes of the bitmaps to be recorded. If this parameter is empty, no bitmaps will be generated. Bitmap fonts typically look better than non-bitmap fonts at smaller point sizes (below 14 points), but they take up more memory than non-bitmap fonts.

characters: A string of all the characters to be included. If this parameter is an empty string, all characters in the font will be included. If only certain characters are included, then other characters used will appear as empty boxes.

In context: These statements embed only the elements of the font Crazy that are needed to display the string "Welcome Home!".

```
newFont = new(#font)
recordFont(newFont, "Crazy", [], [], "Welcome Home!"
```

Notes: The *style* and *sizes* parameters are lists. They must be included (even if empty) as argument placeholders and must use the square bracket syntax of lists.

Macromedia states: "Since recordFont resynthesizes the font data rather than using it directly, there are no legal restrictions on Shock Font distribution."

See also: The new function.

restart

Elements: restart

Purpose: This command closes the file and all currently open applications and (Macintosh only) shuts down and then restarts the host computer.

In context:

```
on desperationHandler
  restart
end
```

Notes: For Windows, this command is identical to the quit command.

See also: The quit and shutDown commands.

resume sprite

Elements: resume(sprite *GIFSpriteNumber*)

Purpose: This command causes an animated GIF sprite to resume playing after being paused. Playback continues, beginning at the frame after the current frame.

In context:

```
resume (sprite 3)
```

See also: The pause sprite and rewind commands.

rewind sprite

Elements: rewind sprite *[whichSprite]*

Purpose: This command rewinds a Flash or Animated GIF movie sprite, returning to frame 1. The command can be used even when the sprite is playing.

In context: This handler implements a Rewind button for an animated GIF sprite playing in channel 7:

```
on mouseUp
  rewind sprite 7
end
```

See also: The frame property.

save castLib

Elements: save castLib *[name of cast]*
save castLib *[name of cast, pathname: newName]*

Purpose: This command saves changes made to a specified Cast database. If only the name of the Cast is given, the changes will be saved to that Cast's file. If another file name (and optional path name) is given, the changed version will be written to that file. If no such file currently exists, it will be created.

In context: This statement saves changes to a Cast named MainCon:

```
save castLib "MainCon"
```

COMMANDS

This statement saves the changes to a new file in the open movie's folder, leaving the source cast file in an unmodified state:

```
save castLib "MainCon", "NewFile"
```

saveMovie

Elements: saveMovie

saveMovie *[name of movie, pathname:newName]*

Purpose: When used alone, this command saves any changes made to the currently open movie. When used with another name, a copy of the movie is saved under that name. Use a path name to create the new copy in a location outside of the current folder.

In context:

```
saveMovie "My Drive:User Versions:MyMovie"
```

scrollByLine

Elements: scrollByLine member *[cast member, amount]*

Purpose: When this command is used with a field or text cast member, you can specify the number of lines scrolled up or down by setting a number for the parameter *amount*. When the amount is positive, the field scrolls down; when the amount is negative, the field scrolls up.

In context: This script line scrolls the text down seven lines:

```
scrollByLine member "User List", 7
```

Notes: Lines are defined by their appearance in the cast member, not by the existence of a Return character.

scrollByPage

Elements: scrollByPage member *[cast member, amount]*

Purpose: Like its sister command scrollByLine, this command lets you scroll up or down in a field or text cast member according to an amount set and plugged into the *amount* parameter, but by page instead of by line. When *amount* is positive, the field scrolls down, and when it is negative, the field scrolls up.

In context: This script line scrolls the text to display the previous page:

```
scrollByPage member "User List", -1
```

Notes: A page is equal to the amount of text that appears in a text or field sprite.

sendAllSprites

Elements: sendAllSprites ([#message, args...])

Purpose: This command allows you to send a custom message to all of the sprites on the Stage. All behaviors of all sprites receive the message unless the stopEvent command is issued. If more than one behavior contains a handler for the message, the consequences are unpredictable. This command is a bit of overkill, and you are probably better off sending a message to only the sprites you want to receive the message using sendSprite.

In context: This timeOut handler sends the message updateLocation to all sprites. The message includes the parameters 4 and -2.

```
on timeOut
    sendAllSprites (#updateLocation, 4, -2)
end
```

See also: The sendSprite command.

sendSprite

Elements: sendSprite(*[whichSprite, #message, args...]*)

Purpose: This command enables you to send a custom message to all of the scripts attached to the specified sprite. If no handler is found for the message, or if the pass command is used, the message will continue on up the standard message hierarchy.

In context: This handler sends the message showTime to the sprite Timer along with two arguments, "late" and 0:

```
on timeOut
    sendSprite ("Timer", #showTme, "late", 0)
end
```

See also: The sendAllSprites command.

set...=

Elements: set *[property]* = *[expression]*
                set *[variable]* = *[expression]*

Purpose: This command is equivalent to the set...to command. The set keyword is not required for use with the = operator (it is mandatory when used with the to keyword).

In context: The following three lines are equivalent:

```
myVar = "Hello there!"
set myVar = "Hello there!"
set myVar to "Hello there!"
```

set...to

Elements: set *[property]* to *[expression]*
                set *[variable]* to *[expression]*

Purpose: When used with a settable property (as opposed to a property that can be tested but not set), the property will be changed to the condition specified in the expression. In conjunction with a variable, the contents of the variable are changed to the value of the expression. The variable is created if it does not already exist.

COMMANDS

In context: This button script creates an animation effect by switching the cast member of the button with a cast member in the next adjacent cast slot:

```
on mouseUp
    put the clickOn into currSprite
    set sprite(currSprite).member to ¬
    sprite(currSprite).member + 1
    updateStage
end
```

setaProp (for child objects)

Elements: setaProp *childObject, property, value*
　　　　　childObject.property = *value*

Purpose: Use this command to associate a value with a property in a child object (or the object's ancestor property). If the property currently exists in the child object, its value will be replaced by the new value; if it doesn't exist, both the property and its value will be added to the object. To use the dot syntax version, the property must already exist.

In context: These commands first add a new property to a child object (with the value 10) and then change the value of that new property:

```
setaProp childRef, #newProp, 10
childRef.newProp = 99
```

setaProp (for property lists)

Elements: setaProp *list, property, value*
　　　　　list [*#property*] = *value*
　　　　　list.property = *value*

Purpose: Use this command to associate a value with a property in a property list. If the property currently exists, its value will be replaced by the new value; if it doesn't exist, both it and the property will be added to the list (must exist with dot syntax).

In context: This first command line establishes a property list (ballStats), the second and third lines then each add a new property to the list, and the fourth line changes the value of a property:

```
ballStats = [#runs:2, #hits:8,#errors:7]
setaProp ballStats, #shoeSize, 9
ballStats [#hatSize] = 7.25
ballStats.runs = 3
```

This script returns [#runs: 3, #hits: 8, #errors: 7, #shoeSize: 9, #hatSize: 7.2500].

setAt

Elements: setAt *[list], [position number], [value]*

Purpose: This command replaces an item in a specified list location. It is applicable to both linear and property lists.

In context: This command line replaces the third entry of a linear list composed of symbols:

```
put myList
-- [#Bonnie, #Susie, #Mommy, #Sis]
setAt myList 3, #CowboyJoe
put myList
-- [#Bonnie, #Susie, #CowboyJoe, #Sis]
```

Notes: When setAt is specified to replace a value in a location that doesn't exist (for example, at position 101 in a 100-item list), the action taken depends on the list type. For a linear list, the list will be expanded with blank entries to achieve sufficient size. For a property list, an error message will be displayed.

setPref

Elements: setPref *[fileName, fileText]*

Purpose: This command allows a Director application (particularly Shockwave) to write a file to the user's system. For security reasons, Shockwave movies running in a browser are severely restricted in their ability to write information on the user's local media. The exception is allowed by the use of the setPref command.

The first argument gives the name of the file. No path name is required or allowed, because only certain locations are allowed. For Shockwave movies, the file is placed in a folder named Prefs (which is created, if needed), which resides in the browser's Plug-In Support folder. For Director or projector movies, the file resides in a Prefs folder in the same folder as the application. The file created is a standard text file, and the only file extensions allowed are .txt and .htm.

The companion to the setPref command is the getPref command, which retrieves the text of the named file. The getPref command will look in the same location that setPref uses for the file.

In context: This handler saves the contents of the field cast member currentUser in a file named r32text:

```
on exitFrame
    setPref "r32text", member("currentUser").text
end
```

Notes: Files created by setPref are not private and may be overwritten by other applications, so use a unique name for the file.

See also: The getPref function.

setProp

Elements: setProp *[list]*, *[property]*, *[value]*
             list*[property]* = *value*

Purpose: Use this command to associate a value with a property in a property list. If the property currently exists, its value will be replaced by the new value; if it doesn't exist, an error will result. The setaProp command is preferable to this command because it will add a property if the property does not already exist.

In context: These two command lines establish a property list (ballStats) and then change one of the properties:

```
set ballStats = [#runs:2, #hits:8, #errors:7]
setProp ballStats, #hits, 9
```

This script returns [#runs: 2, #hits: 9, #errors: 7].

See also: The setaProp command.

setTrackEnabled

Elements: setTrackEnabled (sprite *[sprite]*, *[track]*, *[true or false]*)

Purpose: This command determines whether a particular track of digital video is able to play, according to its setting: TRUE (1) or FALSE (0). Disabled sound tracks will be muted and video tracks will not be updated on the Stage.

In context: This statement turns off track 2 of sprite 3:

```
setTrackEnabled(sprite(3), 2, FALSE)
```

See also: The trackEnabled property.

showGlobals

Elements: showGlobals

Purpose: This debugging command can be used to check the current value of global variables . It returns (in the Message window) a display of all current global variables, including Director-set variables (such as version).

In context:

```
showGlobals
-- Global Variables --
user = "Mike Gross"
ballStats = [#runs: 3, #hits: 8, #errors: 7]
version = "7.0"
```

Notes: You can use showGlobals in the Message window since all global variables are accessible there, even after the movie stops running. Variables created in the Message window are global variables.

See also: The clearGlobals and showLocals commands and the global keyword.

showLocals

Elements: showLocals

Purpose: This debugging command is used to check the current values of local variables. It returns a display (in the Message window) of all current local variables. Use showLocals in the handler whose local variables you want to check.

In context:

```
showLocals
-- Local Variables --
myVar = 9
myNextVar = 1
yetAnotherVar = 47
```

Notes: In contrast to showGlobals, using the showLocals command in the Message window is of limited value because the handler containing the local variables must still be running.

See also: The showGlobals command.

showProps

Elements: showProps member *whichFlashOrVectorMember*
          showProps sprite *whichFlashOrVectorSprite*

Purpose: This command is useful when authoring to debug movies containing vector shapes and Flash movies; it displays in the Message window a list of all the properties of the vector or Flash cast member or sprite. When it is applied to a sprite, only sprite properties are displayed. When it is applied to a cast member, all cast member properties are displayed.

In context: This is a partial listing of the properties of a vector shape cast member (the total output was 33 lines long):

```
showProps member("myVector")
directToStage:      0
centerRegPoint:     1
regPoint:           point(58, 40)
defaultRect:        rect(0, 0, 116, 80)
imageEnabled:       1
antialias:          1
scale:              100.0000
originMode:         #center
```

Notes: This command does not work for projectors or Shockwave movies.

showResFile

Elements: showResFile

Purpose: This is a debugging command, usable only in the Message window. It returns a display of all open resource files. It is for Macintosh only and generally is considered obsolete.

In context:

```
showResFile
-- Resource files: current=4608 sound=0 app=4608
---- doc=-1 shared=-1
-- Res: Times Type: fnt Id:9471 Home: 1788
```

showXlib

Elements: showXlib

showXlib *[name of Xlib file]*

Purpose: When used in the Message window, this command displays a list of the Xtras contained in an Xlib file, or all open XLibraries if no file is specified.

In context: This is the output under Windows; the output on a Macintosh will be slightly different:

```
showXlib
-- XLibraries:
--   Xtra: FileXtra
--   Xtra: UiHelper
--   Xtra: JavaConvert
--   Xtra: QuicktimeSupport
--   Xtra: NetLingo
--   Xtra: Multiuser
--   Xtra: XmlParser
--   Xtra: Mui
--   Xtra: fileio
--   Xtra: ActiveX
```

shutDown

Elements: shutDown

Purpose: On the Macintosh, this command closes the file and all open applications and then shuts down the host computer. On Windows systems, it shuts down the current application (either Director or a projector application).

In context:

```
on sessionOver
    shutDown
end
```

See also: The quit and restart commands.

sort

Elements: sort *[name of list]*

Purpose: Use this command to place the contents of a list in alphanumerical order. If the list is a property list, the sorting will be in alphabetical order of the properties. For a linear list, the values are sorted.

In context:

```
Zoo = ["zebra", "emu", "narwhal"]
sort Zoo
put Zoo
-- ["emu", "narwhal", "zebra"]
```

Notes: Once the sort command has been applied to a list, you can maintain the list's order while adding new entries by using the add or addProp command.

sound fadeIn

Elements: sound fadeIn *[channel]*
               sound fadeIn *[channel]*,*[duration]*

Purpose: This command fades in the sound in the specified channel over a specified period of time. The time (duration) is given as ticks—$1/60$ of a second. If no duration is specified, the default is approximately 15 times the tempo ticks, up to a maximum of about 4 seconds (240 ticks). Thus, the slower the tempo, the faster the fade in.

In context: This handler fades in a sound in channel 3 over a period of 2 seconds:

```
on mouseUp
    sound fadeIn 3, 2*60
    puppetSound 3, "Horn Fanfare"
end
```

Notes: If the sound fadeIn command is in a frame behavior and the sound is in a Score sound channel, put the command in a frame before the sound starts. When puppeting sounds, place the sound fadeIn command before the puppetSound command in a handler. Otherwise, the sound will start loud, drop to zero, and then fade in.

The sound fadeIn command may be problematic (especially under Windows) if the fade is interrupted before it finishes. Interrupting the fade may result in the channel's sound volume being stuck at the current level or zero. Use the volume property to test and reset the volume.

See also: The sound fadeOut command and the volume property

sound fadeOut

Elements: sound fadeOut *[channel]*
               sound fadeOut *[channel]*,*[duration]*

Purpose: This command fades out the sound in the specified channel over a designated period of time. The time (duration) is given as ticks—$1/60$ of a second. If no duration is specified, the default is approximately 15 times the tempo ticks, up to a maximum of about 4 seconds (240 ticks). Thus, the slower the tempo, the faster the fade out.

In context: This command fades out a sound in channel 3 over a period of 2 seconds:

```
sound fadeOut 3, 2*60
```

Notes: The sound fadeOut command may be problematic (especially under Windows) if the fade is interrupted before it finishes. Interrupting the fade may result in the channel's sound volume being stuck at the current level. Use the volume property to test and reset the volume.

See also: The sound fadeIn command and the volume property

COMMANDS

sound playFile

Elements: sound playFile *[channel number, file]*

Purpose: Use this command to play external sound files (files not installed in the Cast). Since the files are not preloaded into RAM before playing, this command keeps memory requirements to a minimum when playing large sound files. For sounds stored on the Internet, it's a good idea to download the file first using downLoadNetThing or preLoadNetThing.

In context:

sound playFile 1, "D:\My Kiosk\My Music\Intro.aif"

Notes: When the sound file isn't in the same folder as the movie, don't forget to use the file's complete path name.

Because the application is accessing the disk to play the sound, avoid playing more than one sound (using sound playFile) or playing a digital video or loading cast members at the same time. The extra disk accessing can cause the sound or video to break up.

sound stop

Elements: sound stop *[channel number]*

Purpose: Obsolete but still working, this command stops the sound file currently playing in the designated channel. Use puppetSound instead.

In context:

sound stop 2

See also: The puppetSound command.

startTimer

Elements: startTimer

Purpose: This command begins an accounting of a duration by setting the property the timer to 0. The lastClick, lastKey, lastRoll, and lastEvent timers are also reset to zero.

In context: These handlers check to see how long a key was pressed:

```
on keyDown
    startTimer
end keyDown
on keyUp
    put "The key was down for"&& the timer &&"ticks."
end
```

Notes: There is only one timer property. If you need to use multiple timers, you can use the ticks property to track multiple events.

See also: The timer and ticks properties.

stop

Elements: stop sprite *whichFlashSprite*

Purpose: This command stops the designated Flash movie from playing.

In context: This command stops the Flash movie sprite playing in channel 7:

stop sprite 7

See also: The hold and play commands.

stopEvent

Elements: stopEvent

Purpose: This command prevents other handlers in the message hierarchy from receiving an event. The only locations where this is needed are in primary event handlers (which otherwise always pass events) and sprite behaviors (where events are otherwise passed to other behaviors for the same sprite). The command affects only the event that triggered the handler in which it was placed; subsequent events are not affected.

In context: This handler checks to see if a sound is playing in channel 2 and prevents the mouseEnter event from being passed to the sprite's other behaviors if it is:

```
on mouseEnter
    if soundBusy(2) then
        stopEvent
    end if
end
```

Notes: This command replaces the dontPassEvent command, which is now obsolete.

See also: The pass command.

stop member

Elements: stop member (*[cast member]*)

Purpose: When this command is triggered, playback of a Shockwave Audio streaming cast member will halt, without the possibility of resuming play at the same point.

In context:

stop member "narration track 1"

Notes: Use this command to change the Shockwave Audio properties streamName, preLoadTime, and URL of member, since a cast member of this type must be stopped for those properties to be modified.

See also: The pause member and play member commands.

stream

Elements: stream(member *[FlashSprite, Bytes]*)

Purpose: Use this command when you want to manually stream a portion of a specified Flash movie cast member into memory. If you do not specify the number of bytes to stream, using the *Bytes* parameter, Director tries to stream the number of bytes set by the

COMMANDS

cast member's `bufferSize` property. You can use the `stream` command for a cast member regardless of the cast member's `streamMode` property.

In context: This command line attempts to stream 24,000 bytes of the Flash movie fDog. The actual number of bytes that were successfully streamed is saved in the variable `bytesStreamed`.

```
bytesStreamed = stream(member("fDog"), 24000)
```

Notes: The `stream` command returns the number of bytes actually loaded into memory.

substituteFont

Elements: substituteFont(*[textMember, oldFont, newFont]*)

Purpose: This command can be used to substitute fonts in a text cast member if the current font is not available. All text chunks that use *oldFont* will have their font changed to *newFont*.

In context: This handler checks for any missing fonts that are used in the text cast member BigText and replaces all missing fonts with the font Courier:

```
on prepareFrame
    mList = member("BigText").missingFonts
    repeat with i in mList
        substituteFont(member("BigText"), i, "Courier")
    end repeat
end
```

See also: The `missingFonts` property.

tell

Elements: tell *[windowObject]* to *[statement]*

tell *[windowObject]*
     [statement(s)]
end tell

Purpose: This command is used to pass Lingo statements from one window object to another. For example, it can be used in an MIAW to pass Lingo statements back to the Stage (the root movie) or to another MIAW.

In context: This button script for an MIAW tells the root movie (the `stage`) to run the handler checkAnswer, a handler in the root movie. The checkAnswer handler's result is then retrieved using the `result` property, the result then being used to set the `stageColor` property. Only the checkAnswer statement is passed to the root movie. The other statements are executed by the MIAW.

```
on mouseUp
    tell the stage to checkAnswer
    isOK = the result
    if isOK then the stageColor = 0
end
```

This button script for an MIAW tells another MIAW to change the graphic for a sprite and change the color of the stage. Because these statements are included in a tell...end tell construct, both statements are executed by the receiving MIAW.

```
on mouseUp
   tell "runSwifty"
      sprite(1).member = "girlSwifty"
      the stageColor = 0
   end tell
end mouseUp
```

Notes: In previous versions of Director, you were limited to sending messages from the root movie to an MIAW or vice versa. To communicate between MIAWs, you needed to use the root movie as an intermediary. With Director 7, you can now send messages directly from one MIAW to another.

See also: The windowList property

unLoad

Elements: unLoad *[frame number or range of frames]*

Purpose: This command purges from current RAM all cast members applied to the Stage in the given frame or range of frames. If no frames are specified, it will purge the contents of all frames in the movie.

In context: This command line clears all cast members currently loaded into RAM that appear in frames 1 through 250:

unLoad 1, 250

Notes: Frames can be specified by frame numbers or by marker names (when applicable).

See also: The preLoad, preLoadMember, and unLoadMember commands and the purgePriority property.

unLoadMember

Elements: unLoadMember *[name or number, or range thereof]*

Purpose: This command purges from current RAM all specified cast members. If no cast members are specified, the entire Cast contents in the currently active movie will be cleared from memory. The Casts or cast members will not themselves be affected—just their status of being loaded into RAM.

In context: This statement clears a single cast member. Note that a Cast can be specified.

unLoadMember member "Dog" of castLib "Pets"

This statement clears all cast members from cast slots 1 through 100:

unLoadMember 1, 100

Notes: Cast members that have been modified without having been saved cannot be unloaded from memory.

See also: The unLoad, preLoad, and preLoadMember commands and the purgePriority property.

COMMANDS

unloadMovie

Elements: unLoadMovie *[movie]*

Purpose: This command removes a movie from Director's (or a projector's) RAM, which is helpful if you are short on memory. You can use a URL as a reference for the file if it's in Shockwave form. If there is no movie in RAM, the value –1 is returned.

In context:

```
if ramNeeded (1, lastFrame) > the freeBytes then
    unloadMovie "http://www.demystified.com/movies/Swifty2.dcr"
end if
```

updateFrame

Elements: updateFrame

Purpose: In a Score-generation script, this command is used to enter changes in a given frame and move on to the next.

In context: In the first 99 frames of a Score, this handler changes the color of the sprite in the first channel to a random color:

```
on moChanges
    beginRecording
        repeat with x = 1 to 99
            go to frame x
            set the forecolor of sprite 1 to random(256)
            updateFrame
        end repeat
    endRecording
end moChanges
```

Notes: This command applies only to Score-generation sessions, as denoted by the use of the commands beginRecording and endRecording.

updateStage

Elements: updateStage

Purpose: This command triggers a redraw of the Stage of the currently active movie. If this command is not used, the Stage will not be redrawn until the playback head enters a new frame. This command is commonly used in scripts that delay movement of the playback head for long enough to create a noticeable lag between an action and the reaction (such as a button click and the button's sound). Consider it Lingo shorthand for "do this now."

In context:

```
on mouseDown
    puppetSound 2, "Hamster Squeal"
    updateStage
    myBigHandler
end
```

Notes: The updateStage command causes the prepareFrame and stepFrame messages to be sent.

zoomBox

Elements: zoomBox *[channel], [channel] [,duration]*

Purpose: This command produces an unusual result: A rectangular dotted outline zooms from the sprite in the first designated channel to the sprite in the second, in an effect similar to the "zoom open" animation of the standard Macintosh window or Windows Minimize/Maximize check box. The duration of the effect is expressed in ticks; each duration is the interval between subsequent expanded and moving versions of the zoom lines.

In context: This script applies the zooming effect, moving it from the sprite in visual channel 1 to that in channel 2, with a duration of 5 ticks between updates of the effect:

```
on enterFrame
   zoomBox 1, 2, 5
end
```

Notes: Note that the duration of the overall effect cannot be given—just the duration of the period between updates. If no duration is given, the default should be one tick, but this setting may be problematic.

COMMANDS

FUNCTIONS

abbr, abbrev, abbreviated

See: The date and the time functions.

abs

Elements: abs (*[numeric expression]*)

Purpose: This mathematical function returns the absolute value of the given numeric expression. This function is useful for converting negative numbers into positive numbers or for producing a positive result from an expression involving negative numbers.

In context:

```
put abs (-2.2)
-- 2.2
put abs (20 + -60)
-- 40
```

atan

Elements: atan (*[numeric expression]*)

Purpose: This mathematical function returns the arctangent of the expression in the parenthetical statement. The result is given in radians and is between –PI/2 and +PI/2 (see the sin function for a discussion of radians and how to convert degrees to radians).

In context:

```
put atan (3)
-- 1.2490
```

See also: The sin and cos functions and the PI constant.

cacheDocVerify

Elements: cacheDocVerify (*[value]*)

Purpose: This function determines how information is replenished in a networked environment. There are two possible values: #always and #once (default). #once means get the information one time and thereafter use the information in Director's cache. #always means always check the online information to see if there is a newer version.

In context: This statement line returns the current status of cache refreshing:

```
put cacheDocVerify()
-- #once
```

Notes: This function applies only to Director and projector movies. It isn't available for Shockwave movies, since they use network browser settings.

cacheSize

Elements:　cacheSize (*[size or nothing]*)

Purpose: This function sets Director's networking cache to a specified size (expressed in kilobytes). When you use the cacheSize () syntax, the current cache size is returned. This is a changeable function, which is not quite the same thing as being a settable property. When you change the function, the appropriate syntax is cacheSize (newSize), not set the cacheSize to newSize.

In context:

```
put cacheSize ()
-- 2000
cacheSize (4000)
put cacheSize ()
-- 4000
```

Notes: This function works only for movies in projector or Director form. Shockwave movies won't be affected by any changes to the networking cache because they operate from another cache, the one belonging to the end user's Web browser application.

charPosToLoc

Elements:　charPosToLoc (member *[name or number]*, *[number]*)

Purpose: In field cast members, this function determines the coordinates occupied by a given character in the field and returns the value as a point. It cannot be applied to text cast members. The character is identified by a number indicating its order in the string of text.

In context: This statement determines the coordinates of the fourth character in the text currently occupying the field:

```
put charPosToLoc (member "Answer field", 4)
-- point(21, 14)
```

Notes: The point is given in pixels and specifies the distance from the upper-left corner of the field cast member. In other words, the point returned refers to the location in the cast member, not the location on the Stage. Thus, all characters have a location, even if they are not visible in the cast member's representation as a sprite on the Stage, and moving the sprite on the Stage does not affect the charPosToLoc return value.

chars

Elements:　chars (*[string]*, *[first]*, *[last]*)

Purpose: This function retrieves a character or series of characters from within a specified text string.

In context: If the variable myVar contains "sword, fish, trombone", then this line retrieves the fifth through eighth characters (note that spaces are treated as characters):

```
put chars(myVar, 5, 8)
-- "d, f"
```

Notes: If chars is directed to retrieve characters that don't exist (for example, the tenth character of an eight-character string), an empty string is returned for that portion. In the following example, although characters 4 through 10 are requested, only characters 4 and 5 are returned:

```
myVar = "12345"
put chars(myVar, 4, 10)
-- "45"
```

charToNum

Elements: charToNum (*[string]*)

Purpose: This function returns the ASCII character code equivalent of the first character of a given text string expression.

In context: These statements produce the same result: the ASCII code for the capital letter "A":

```
put charToNum ("Alex")
-- 65
put charToNum ("A")
-- 65
```

Here's a handler that uses charToNum (and numToChar) to convert a string argument to all uppercase. This is accomplished by subtracting 32 (the distance between "A" and "a" in ASCII code) from a lowercase letter's ASCII code. Only letters are affected.

```
on toUpper theString
   repeat with i = 1 to length(theString)
      num = charToNum(char i of theString)
      if num >= 97 and num <= 122 then   -- only lowercase letters
         num = num - 32
      end if
      ch = numToChar(num)
      put ch into char i of theString
   end repeat
   return theString
end
```

See also: The numToChar function.

color

Elements: color(*#rgb*, *[redValue, greenValue, blueValue]*)
color(*#paletteIndex*, *[paletteIndexNumber]*)
rgb(*[rgbHexString]*)
rgb(*[redValue, greenValue, blueValue]*)
paletteIndex(*[paletteIndexNumber]*)

Purpose: This element is both a function and data type. Director 7 has introduced the concept of color objects to enable more accurate specification of colors. Colors can now be specified as absolute RGB color values (as well as indexes into a palette). This enables better color coordination across palettes, systems, and monitor color depth. Color objects are useful for setting the background color of sprites, the color of the Stage, and (to a limited extent) the foreground color of a sprite.

In context: These commands create new color objects:

```
newObj1 = color(#rgb, 120, 10, 35)
newObj2 = paletteIndex(20)
put newObj1
-- rgb( 120, 10, 35 )
```

These commands set the color of the Stage. This is equivalent to setting the Stage color in the Movie Properties dialog box.

```
(the stage).bgcolor = newObj1
(the stage).bgColor = color(#rgb, 0,0,0)
```

Individual color components can be set:

```
newObj1.red = 88
put newObj1
-- rgb( 88, 10, 35 )
```

Color objects also allow mathematical operations:

```
put newObj1
-- rgb( 88, 10, 35 )
put newObj1 + 20
-- rgb( 108, 30, 55 )
newObj1.green = newObj1.green - 10
put newObj1
-- rgb( 88, 0, 35 )
```

Color objects can be converted from one color type to the other:

```
newObj1.colorType = #paletteIndex
put newObj1
-- paletteIndex( 142 )
```

See also: The bgColor property.

the commandDown

Elements:　the commandDown

Purpose: This function reports whether the Control key (Windows) or Command key (Macintosh) is currently pressed. It is a binary function (1 indicates TRUE, and 0 indicates FALSE).

In context: The following button script carries out one action if the button is simply clicked (the custom handler buttonClick), and another action (a jump to marker Special Place) if the mouse click occurs when the Control key (or Command key) is down.

FUNCTIONS

```
on mouseUp
  if the commandDown then
    go "Special Place"
  else
    buttonClick
  end if
end
```

constrainH

Elements: constrainH (*[channel number], [coordinate number]*)

Purpose: Use this function to determine whether a given point is currently within the horizontal boundaries of the sprite in a specified channel. If the point (expressed as a pixel coordinate) is between the left and right edges of the sprite, its value will not be changed. If, however, it is to the left of the leftmost edge, the value returned will be that of the edge rather than the point. If the point is to the right of the rightmost edge, that edge's horizontal coordinate will be given instead.

In context: These three statements in the Message window reflect the same sprite in the same location: the left edge is at 90 pixels and the right edge is at 180 pixels. The coordinate passed to constrainH is clipped if it is outside the sprite.

```
put constrainH (1, 55)
-- 90
put constrainH (1, 120)
-- 120
put constrainH (1, 205)
-- 180
```

This statement moves a sprite in channel 2 to the position of the mouse, but constrained within the boundaries of sprite 1:

```
sprite(2).locH = constrainH(1, the mouseH)
```

Notes: Because it limits values to a certain range, this function is useful for scripting that constrains sprites to the boundaries of another sprite. The sprite used with the constrainH function is the constraining sprite.

See also: The constrainV function and the constraint, left, and right properties

constrainV

Elements: constrainV (*[channel number], [coordinate number]*)

Purpose: Use this function to determine whether a given point is currently within the vertical boundaries of the sprite in a specified channel. If the point (expressed as a pixel coordinate) is between the top and bottom edges of the sprite, its value will not be changed. If, however, it is above the topmost edge, the value returned will be that of the edge rather than the point. If the point is below the bottom edge, that edge's horizontal coordinate will be given instead.

In context: These three statements in the Message window reflect the same sprite in the same location: the top edge is at 100 pixels and the bottom edge is at 220 pixels. The coordinate passed to constrainV is clipped if it is outside the sprite.

```
put constrainV (2, 80)
-- 100
put constrainV (2, 110)
-- 110
put constrainV (2, 240)
-- 220
```

Notes: Because it limits values to a certain range, this function is useful for scripting that constrains moveable sprites.

See also: The constrainH function and the constraint, left, and right properties

the controlDown

Elements: the controlDown

Purpose: This function reports on whether a Control key (sometimes displayed as Ctrl) is currently pressed. It is a binary function (1 indicates TRUE, and 0 indicates FALSE).

In context: This button script carries out one action if the button is simply clicked (the custom handler buttonClick), and another action (a jump to marker Special Place) if the mouse click occurs when the Control key is down:

```
on mouseUp
    if the controlDown then
        go "Special Place"
    else
        buttonClick
    end if
end
```

cos

Elements: cos ([angle])

Purpose: This mathematical function returns the cosine of the specified angle enclosed in parentheses. The angle is given in radians (see the sin function for a discussion of radians and how to convert degrees to radians).

In context:

```
put cos (3)
-- -0.9900
```

See also: The atan and sin functions and the PI constant.

FUNCTIONS

count

Elements: count ([name of list])
        count(theObject)
        object.count
        textExpression.count

Purpose: This function determines the quantity of the contents of a number of Director objects: the number of elements in linear and property lists, the number of chunks of a text expression, and the number of properties in a child object's parent script (ancestor scripts don't count).

In context:

```
countdown = [10,9,8,7,6,5,4,3,2,1]
put count (countdown)
-- 10
member(2).text = "Welcome home!"
put member(2).text.chars.count
-- 13
put (the globals).count
-- 12
```

See also: The number functions.

date (formats)

Elements: date([string])
        date([integer])
        date([year, month,day])

Purpose: This function and data type provides a standardized date format that facilitates date manipulation and platform independence and accommodates different international display formats. Dates in this format can be compared and manipulated mathematically, and date elements (such as the month) can be extracted easily. Years are given as four digits; months and days are given as two digits (although the comma-separated version will accept single-digit months and days).

In context: These three commands create equivalent dates:

```
dDate = date("19990521")
dDate = date(19990521)
dDate = date(1999, 05, 21)
```

This statement extracts the month:

```
put dDate.month
-- 5
```

Mathematical operations are performed in terms of days. These statements determine the number of days between the current date and the first day of the year 2000:

```
thisDate = date(19990503)
put date(2000,01,01) - thisdate
-- 243
```

See also: The date (system clock) function and systemDate property.

the date (system clock)

Elements: the date
the abbr date
the abbrev date
the abbreviated date
the short date
the long date

Purpose: This function returns the current date, as set in the host computer's system clock. Note that the date and the short date are functionally equivalent; abbr and abbrev are shorthand for *abbreviated*. The systemDate property returns the current date as a date data type.

In context:

```
put the date
-- "5/3/99"
put the long date
-- "Monday, May 03, 1999"
put the abbr date
-- "Mon, May 03, 1999"
```

the doubleClick

Elements: the doubleClick

Purpose: This function reports whether the two most recent mouse clicks qualified as a double-click. It is a binary function (1 indicates TRUE, and 0 indicates FALSE).

In context: This button script carries out an action only if the mouse click that triggers the mouseUp event is the last part of a double-click:

```
on mouseUp
   if the doubleClick then
      alert "Hooray!"
   end if
end
```

See also: The clickOn property.

duplicate

Elements: duplicate (*[name of list]*)

Purpose: This command-like function, limited to lists, returns a copy of the specified list without modifying the original. Think of it as a Save As function for list management.

In context: This statement places the current contents of the list GuestList into the variable toRSVP:

```
toRSVP = duplicate (GuestList)
```

Notes: If you don't use the duplicate function, assigning a list to a second variable creates a pointer to the original list—any changes made through the second variable apply to the original list.

endFrame

Elements: sprite([*whichSprite*]).endFrame

Purpose: This function returns the frame number of the end frame of the sprite's span; it is useful in determining the span of a particular sprite in the Score. The playback head must currently be on a frame that contains the sprite.

In context: This statement in the Message window reports the ending frame of the sprite in channel 3:

```
put sprite(3).endFrame
```

Notes: You cannot set the frame number value.

See also: The startFrame function.

exp

Elements: exp ([*number*])

Purpose: This mathematical function returns the value e (the natural logarithm base) raised to the power given as the parameter (which may be an integer or floating-point number). This function is the counterpart to the log function.

In context:

```
put exp (3)
-- 20.0855
put log(exp(3))
-- 3.0000
```

externalParamCount

Elements: externalParamCount ()

Purpose: This function returns the number of parameters being passed to a Shockwave movie (running in a browser) from an EMBED or OBJECT tag in HTML source code.

In context:

```
if externalParamCount () > 0 then
   set myVar to externalParamValue ()
   put myVar
end if
```

See also: The externalParamName and externalParamValue functions.

externalParamName

Elements: externalParamName (*parameter*)

Purpose: When this function is used, the name of a particular parameter in a list of external parameters from an HTML EMBED or OBJECT tag is returned. If *parameter* is an integer, the command will return the parameter name corresponding to that location in the list. If *parameter* is a string, the command will return the same string if a matching parameter name is found in the list. If no matching parameters are found, VOID is returned.

In context:

```
if externalParamName (1) = "Refresh" then
    myVar = externalParamValue ("Refresh")
    put myVar
end if
```

Notes: This function works only with Shockwave movies running from within a browser.

See also: The externalParamCount and externalParamValue functions.

externalParamValue

Elements: externalParamValue (*parameter*)

Purpose: Brother to externalParamName, this function returns a value from the external parameter list in an HTML EMBED or OBJECT tag. If *parameter* is an integer, the command returns the value at that location in the list. If *parameter* is a string, the command returns the value associated with the first instance of the string in the list (or VOID if the name is not found).

The methodology is the same as for externalparamName.

See also: The externalParamName and externalParamCount functions.

findEmpty

Elements: findEmpty (member *[cast name or number]*)

Purpose: This function locates the nearest vacant cast slot after the specified cast member. If the given slot is itself vacant, its number will be returned.

In context:

```
put findEmpty (member "Horn Fanfare")
-- 6
put findEmpty (member 11)
-- 12
```

findLabel

Elements: findLabel (sprite *[FlashSpriteRef, label]*)

Purpose: This Flash movie function determines the frame number associated with the given *label* parameter. If the label is not found in the Flash movie (or is in a portion of the movie not streamed in yet), the value returned is 0.

In context:

```
put findLabel(sprite "myFlash", "main")
```

findPos

Elements: findPos (*[list name], [property]*)

Purpose: This property list function locates the position occupied by a given property in the specified list.

In context: The following script finds the list location of the property #Sis in the list myList. It returns 3, since that property is third in the list.

```
myList = [#Bonnie: 300, #Susie: 150, #Sis:2]
put findPos (myList, #Sis)
-- 3
```

Notes: If the property exists in more than one location in the list, this function will locate only the first instance. If no property matches, this function returns VOID.

findPosNear

Elements: findPosNear (*[list name], [property]*)

Purpose: This function is for use with sorted property lists only. It returns the position occupied by the specified property in the specified list if the property exists, or the position of the closest alphabetical match if the property does not exist.

In context: This script searches for the property #s, which doesn't exist in the list myList. Instead, the function returns 2, since the second entry is the closest approximation.

```
sort myList
put myList
-- [#a: 4, #c: 1]
put findPosNear(myList, #b)
-- 2
```

Notes: If the property exists in more than one location, this function will locate only the first instance.

flashToStage

Elements: flashToStage (sprite *[whichSprite, point]*)

Purpose: This function is used to determine which Director Stage coordinate is underneath a Flash movie coordinate. Note that a Flash movie's coordinates are determined by the original size when the movie was created and can be affected by stretching, scaling, or rotation of the Flash sprite. For Flash movies, as with the Stage, the point (0,0) is the upper-left corner.

In context: This command determines the Director coordinates on the Stage for a Flash sprite's upper-left corner:

```
put flashToStage(sprite 4, point(0,0)
```

See Also: The stageToFlash function.

float

Elements: float (*[expression]*)

Purpose: This mathematical function evaluates an expression and returns the resulting number is as a floating-point number (that is, it includes a decimal point).

In context:

```
x = 22
put float (3*x)
-- 66.0000
```

See also: The floatPrecision property.

floatP

Elements: floatP (*[number]*)

Purpose: This function determines whether the number enclosed in parentheses is a floating-point number (that is, a number that includes a decimal point). It is a binary function, returning 1 (TRUE) if the given number is a floating-point number, or 0 (FALSE) if it is not.

In context:

```
put floatP (3.1514)
-- 1
```

the frame

Elements: the frame

Purpose: This function determines the frame currently displayed on the Stage.

In context: This script jumps the playback head to a location 19 frames before the current frame:

```
on exitFrame
   go to the frame -19
end
```

frameReady

Elements: frameReady ()
              frameReady (*frame number*)
              frameReady (*first frame, last frame*)

Purpose: This streaming-related function lets you know whether a frame or range of frames has been downloaded from a network environment and is ready for immediate access on the local drive. It's a good "look before you leap" tool when you use streaming files—use it to make sure at least a key portion of an element is in place before calling it during playback.

This function can be tested but not set. When the syntax frameReady () is used, it returns the binary download status of the file as a whole (as opposed to a specified frame): 1 means the download is complete, and 0 means it is either incomplete or has not begun.

In context: This script, which might reside in a Shockwave movie, limits playback to a loop until the next crucial Score segment (frames 200 through 225) is available:

```
on exitFrame
    if frameReady (200, 225) then
        go frame 200
    else go to the frame
end
```

Notes: Important! The frameReady function can be used only when the Streaming property of the file being downloaded is set—in the Playback properties dialog box (under the Modify menu), either Use Media as Available or Show Placeholders must be checked.

See also: The mediaReady property.

framesToHMS

Elements: framesToHMS (*[frames]*, *[tempo]*, *[drop frame T/F]*, *[fractional seconds T/F]*)

Purpose: This function evaluates the specified range of frames and returns an estimation of the hours, minutes, and seconds required to play it back under the current parameters. It requires four arguments:

- The number of frames.

- The playback tempo.

- A TRUE or FALSE statement turning drop-frame compensation on or off. Drop-frame compensation is a method for correcting frame-rate discrepancies between standard video playback (30 fps) and some modes of color video encoding (which are slightly less than 30 fps). This value is relevant only if the given tempo is 30 fps, but it must be given nonetheless.

- A TRUE or FALSE statement turning fractional-second calculation on or off. When this argument is set to TRUE, remaining frames adding up to less than a second will be given in timings of hundredths of a second. When it is set to FALSE, a count of the remaining frames is given.

In context: These statements calculate the running time of the same movie at two different frame rates (24 and 30 fps), with both drop frames and fractional seconds turned off:

```
put framesToHMS (9014, 24, FALSE, FALSE)
-- " 00:06:15.14 "
```

```
put framesToHMS (9014, 30, FALSE, FALSE)
-- " 00:05:00.14 "
```

Notes: Durations calculated with this function can be relevant for both Director movies and digital video files.

FUNCTIONS

the freeBlock

Elements: the freeBlock

Purpose: This function retrieves the size of the largest block of system RAM available in a contiguous segment, expressed in kilobytes. This function is useful for determining whether the host computer has sufficient RAM for a memory-intensive movie.

In context:

```
put the freeBlock
-- 2703108
```

Notes: To retrieve all available RAM (not just contiguous blocks of RAM), use the freeBytes.

the freeBytes

Elements: the freeBytes

Purpose: This function retrieves the current amount of available free RAM, expressed in kilobytes. It is useful for determining whether the host computer has sufficient RAM available for a memory-intensive movie.

In context:

```
put the freeBytes
-- 2891364
```

Notes: Unlike the freeBlocks, this function retrieves all available free RAM, not just contiguous blocks of unused RAM.

getaProp

Elements: getaProp (*[list name]*, *[position/property]*)

Purpose: In the case of a linear list, this function returns the value in the given list position (the equivalent of the getAt function). In the case of a property list, it returns the value that is assigned to the first occurrence of the property in the list. This function returns VOID if the item is not in the list.

In context: Here's an example with a linear list:

```
set popQuiz = ["T", "F", "Yes", "T", "T"]
put getaProp (popQuiz, 3)
-- "Yes"
```

Here's an example with a property list:

```
set popQuiz = [#T:1, #F:2, #F:3, #T:4]
put getaProp (popQuiz, #F)
-- 2
```

Notes: When the given value is not in the list, this function returns VOID. Except for this, it is identical to the getProp function when used with a property list.

getAt

Elements: getAt *([list name], [position])*

Purpose: This function retrieves a particular value from a list (linear or property) by specifying the position the value occupies in that list.

In context:

```
set popQuiz = ["T", "F", "F", "T", "T"]
put getAt (popQuiz, 2)
-- "F"
```

Notes: This function causes an error if the *position* argument is greater than the number of elements in the list.

getError

Elements: getError *(cast member)*

Purpose: This Shockwave Audio and Flash movie function returns an error code to help you determine the source of a malfunction (if one has occurred). These are the (somewhat cryptic) code values for SWA members:

0   OK (no error)
1   Memory (insufficient RAM or memory malfunction)
2   Network (connection or data transfer problem)
3   Playback device (system sound capabilities failure)
99   Other

These are the return values for Flash movie members:

FALSE	No error occurred.
#memory	There was insufficient memory to load the member.
#fileNotFound	The file could not be found.
#network	A network error prevented the file from loading.
#fileFormat	The file is of the wrong type, or an error occurred during reading.
#other	Some other error occurred.

In context:

```
put getError (member "Elena") into myVar
if myVar > 0 then go to the frame "error"
```

Notes: Director sets a cast member's state property to -1 when an error occurs. Use the state property to determine whether an error occurred; then use getError to determine the nature of the error.

getErrorString

Elements: getErrorString *(cast member)*

Purpose: Like getError, this Shockwave Audio function returns an error code, but this function returns a text string describing the status, rather than a numerical code.

In context:

```
put getErrorString (member "Elena") into myVar
put myVar
-- "OK"
```

getHotSpotRect

Elements: getHotSpotRect(sprite *[whichQTVRSprite], [hotSpotID]*)

Purpose: Use this QTVR function to determine the approximate bounding rectangle for the hot spot specified by hotSpotId. The value returned is of type rect. This function returns rect(0, 0, 0, 0) if the specified hot spot doesn't exist or is not visible on the Stage. It returns the bounding rectangle for the visible portion of a hot spot if the entire hot spot is not visible.

In context:

```
put getHotSpotRect(sprite "office", 4)
-- rect(10, 40, 50, 65)
```

getLast

Elements: getLast (*[list name]*)

Purpose: This list function retrieves the final value from a specified linear or property list.

In context:

```
set popQuiz = ["T", "F", "F", "T", "T"]
put getLast (popQuiz)
-- "T"
```

getNetErrorString

Elements: getNetErrorString(*[xtraObject, code]*)

Purpose: This function returns a string describing an error code encountered in a network operation. If the error code given is invalid, this function returns a string indicating an error of unknown type. All codes are negative integers except for 0 (indicating no error).

The following are possible error codes:

-2147216223	Unknown error.
-2147216222	Invalid movie ID.
-2147216221	Invalid user ID.
-2147216220	Invalid password.
-2147216219	Incoming data has been lost.
-2147216218	Invalid server name.
-2147216217	Server or movie is full; no connections available.
-2147216216	Bad parameter.
-2147216215	No socket manager present.
-2147216214	No current connection.

FUNCTIONS

FUNCTIONS

-2147216213	No waiting message.
-2147216212	Bad connection ID.
-2147216211	Wrong number of parameters.
-2147216210	Unknown internal error.
-2147216209	Connection was refused.
-2147216208	Message buffer is full.
-2147216207	Invalid message format.
-2147216206	Invalid message length.
-2147216205	Message is missing.
-2147216204	Server initialization failed.
-2147216203	Server send failed.
-2147216202	Server close failed.
-2147216201	Connection is a duplicate.
-2147216200	Invalid number of message recipients.
-2147216199	Invalid message recipient.
-2147216198	Invalid message.
-2147216197	Server internal error.
-2147216196	Error joining group.
-2147216195	Error leaving group.
-2147216194	Invalid group name.
-2147216193	Invalid server command.
-2147216192	Error changing user level.
-2147216191	Error in database.
-2147216190	Invalid server initialization file.
-2147216189	Error writing to database.
-2147216188	Error reading from database.
-2147216187	User ID not found in database.
-2147216186	Error adding new user.
-2147216185	Database is locked.
-2147216184	Data record is not unique.
-2147216183	No current record.
-2147216182	Record does not exist.
-2147216181	Moved past beginning or end of database.
-2147216180	Data not found.
-2147216179	No current tag selected.
-2147216178	No current database.
-2147216177	Can't find configuration file.
-2147216176	Current database record is not locked.

getNetText

Elements: getNextText ("*URL*")

Purpose: This function begins retrieval of a text file on an HTTP or FTP server. You can use netDone to determine when the process is complete and netTextResult to retrieve the data. The function returns a unique ID number that should be saved for use with other net functions.

In context: This command line fetches the text at the given URL:

```
netId = getNetText ("http://www.learn2.com/myText")
```

To see the text, however, you need a script like this:

```
on place
   if netDone(netId) then
      member("result").text = netTextResult(netId)
   end if
end
```

See also: The netDone and netTextResult functions.

getNthFileNameInFolder

Elements: getNthFileNameInFolder(*[path], [number]*)

Purpose: You can use this long-named function to retrieve the name of a particular file or folder in a particular location. You must specify the path to the folder containing that file and then specify the numerical position of the file. An empty string is returned if the file's *number* is greater than the number of files and folders in the specified folder.

In context: The following section of code will create an alphabetically sorted list containing the names of all files and folders in the folder containing the current movie:

```
fileList = []  -- initialize list
x = 0 -- initialize counter
repeat while TRUE
   x = x + 1
   fname = getNthFileNameInFolder(the moviePath, x)
   if fname = EMPTY then exit repeat
   append(fileList, fname)
end repeat
sort fileList
```

getOne

Elements: getOne (*[list name], [value]*)

Purpose: In the case of a linear list, this function returns the position number of the first entry whose value matches the value given. In the case of a property list, it returns the first property that is assigned that value.

In context: Here's an example for a linear list:

```
popQuiz = ["T", "F", "Yes", "T", "T"]
put getOne (popQuiz, "Yes")
-- 3
```

Here's an example for a property list:

```
popQuiz = [#T:1, #F:2, #F:3, #T:4, #T:5]
put getOne (popQuiz, 2)
-- #F
```

Notes: If the value is not found in the list, 0 is returned.

getPos

Elements: getPos (*[list name]*, *[value]*)

Purpose: For linear lists, this function is identically to the getOne function. In the case of a property list, it returns the numerical position of the first property that is assigned that value.

In context:

```
popQuiz = [#T:1, #F:2, F:3, #T:4, #T:5]
put getPos (popQuiz, 2)
-- 2
```

Notes: If the given value is not in the list, this function returns 0.

getProp

Elements: getProp(*list, property*)
             list.property

Purpose: This function is limited to property lists. It returns the value of the first entry that is assigned the given property.

In context:

```
set popQuiz = [#T:1, #F:2, #F:3, #T:4]
put getProp (popQuiz, #F)
-- 2
```

Notes: If the given value is not in the list, this function returns an error message. Except in this regard, it is identical to the getaProp function when used with property lists.

getPropAt

Elements: getPropAt (*[list name]*, *[position number]*)

Purpose: This function is limited to property lists. It returns the property attached to the entry at a given location in the list.

In context:

```
popQuiz = [#T:1, #F:2, #F:3, #T:4]
put getPropAt (popQuiz,3)
-- #F
```

getStreamStatus

Elements: getStreamStatus(*[netID]*)
             getStreamStatus(*[URLString]*)

Purpose: This function returns a property list containing information about a current network streaming operation. This property list is in the same format as is used by the streamStatus handler. The properties of the list are as follows:

#URL   The URL location used to start the network operation.

#state   The current status. The value can be a string consisting of Connecting, Started, InProgress, Complete, Error, or NoInformation.

#bytesSoFar   Current number of bytes retrieved.

#bytesTotal   Total number of bytes in the stream, if known.

#error   Empty string ("") if the download is still in progress, OK if it completed successfully, or an error code if the download ended with an error.

In context: These statements start a network operation using getNetText and then check on the operation using getStreamStatus:

```
netID = getNetText¬
("http://www.demystified.com/text1.txt")
put getStreamStatus(netID)
-- [#url: "http://www.demystified.com/text1.txt",
#state: "Connecting", #bytesSoFar: 0,
#bytesTotal: 0, #error: ""]
```

See also: The on streamStatus handler and the tellStreamStatus function.

hitTest

Elements: hitTest(sprite *[flashSprite]*, *[point]*)

Purpose: This function is used to determine what part of a Flash movie is over a point on the Director Stage. The Stage location is given as a point. The return value is one of the following:

#background   The point corresponds to the background of the Flash movie sprite.

#normal   The point lies within a filled object.

#button   The point lies within the active area of a button.

In context: This script checks what part of the Flash sprite the mouse is currently over:

```
put hitTest(sprite 3, the mouseLoc)
-- #background
```

FUNCTIONS

HMStoFrames

Elements: HMStoFrames *([duration], [tempo], [drop frame T/F], [fractional seconds T/F])*

Purpose: This function evaluates the specified duration of time (expressed in hours, minutes, and seconds) and calculates the number of frames necessary to match that duration with playback using the given parameters. It requires four arguments:

- The time specified as an HMS format string.
- The playback tempo.
- A TRUE or FALSE statement turning drop-frame compensation on or off. Drop-frame compensation is a method for correcting frame rate discrepancies between standard video playback (30 fps) and some modes of color video encoding (which are slightly less than 30 fps). This value is relevant only if the given tempo is 30 fps, but it must be given nonetheless.
- A TRUE or FALSE statement turning fractional-second calculation on or off. When this argument is set to TRUE, remaining frames adding up to less than a second will be given in timings of hundredths of a second. When it is set to FALSE, a count of the remaining frames is given.

In context: These statements calculate the frame count of movies with the same running time but two different frame rates (24 and 30 fps), with both drop frames and fractional seconds turned off:

```
put HMStoFrames ("01:05:20", 24, FALSE, FALSE)
-- 94080
put HMStoFrames ("01:05:20", 30, FALSE, FALSE)
-- 117600
```

Notes: Durations calculated with this function can be relevant for both Director movies and digital video files. This function is the counterpart to the framesToHMS function.

idleLoadDone

Elements: idleLoadDone *([load tag number])*

Purpose: This function reports on the progress of loading all cast members with a given load tag (a grouping value for joint loading into RAM). If all cast members with the load tag have been loaded, it returns 1 (or TRUE). If the loading is not yet complete (or not undertaken at all), it returns 0 (or FALSE).

In context: This statement sends the playback head to a specific frame while cast members with a load tag of 40 are loaded:

```
if idleLoadDone (40) = 0 then go to "Wait"
```

ilk

Elements: ilk *([entity name], [type symbol])*
            ilk *([type symbol])*

Purpose: You can use this function to determine the type of a given entity: a list (linear or property), a point, or a set of rect coordinates. If the entity type matches that of the given symbol, the function returns 1 (or TRUE). If it doesn't, it returns 0 (or FALSE). Six types of symbols return meaningful values: #color, #date, #linearlist, #proplist, #point, and #rect. Caution: The symbol #list can be used, but it always returns 1 (TRUE).

In context: These first two statements determine that the entity popQuiz is indeed a property list, but not a linear list. The last statement determines that the variable myDate contains an element of type #date:

```
put ilk (popQuiz, #proplist)
-- 1
put ilk (popQuiz, #linearlist)
-- 0
put myDate.ilk(#date)
-- 1
```

inflate

Elements: inflate (*[rect], [added width], [added height]*)

Purpose: This function changes the dimensions of a rect coordinate grouping to reflect a new width or depth value. The increase in size is actually twice the number given as a parameter since the width, for example, is increased both to the left and to the right.

In context: This statement adds 200 pixels (100*2) to the horizontal dimension of the given rect newRect:

```
oldRect = rect(100, 100, 150, 250)
newRect = inflate(oldRect, 100, 0)
put z
-- rect(0, 100, 250, 250)
```

Notes: Despite its name, inflate can also be used to shrink a rect (just use negative rather than positive numbers).

inside

Elements: inside (*[point], [rectangle]*)

Purpose: This function returns a judgment on whether a given point is within the area described by a given rectangle. If it is, the response is 1, or TRUE; if not, the response is 0, or FALSE.

In context: This Message window statement determines whether the last mouse click (the clickLoc) was within the area of a sprite (it wasn't):

```
put inside(the clickLoc, the rect of sprite 1)
-- 0
```

integer

Elements: integer (*[numeric expression]*)

Purpose: This rounding function takes a decimal value and returns the nearest whole number.

FUNCTIONS

In context:

```
put integer (3.1415*2)
-- 6
```

integerP

Elements: integerP (*[expression]*)

Purpose: This function determines whether a given expression is a whole number (as opposed to a decimal value, text string, or property). It is a binary function, returning 1 if TRUE or 0 if FALSE.

In context:

```
put integerP (3.1415)
-- 0
put integerP (3)
-- 1
```

interface

Elements: interface(*xtra [XtraName]*)

Purpose: This function provides access to the description and available methods for an Xtra. The information is extracted from the Xtra.

In context: This statement uses the Message window to determine the methods to be used with the fileIO Xtra. Only the first few lines of output are shown.

```
put interface(xtra "fileIO")
-- "xtra fileio -- CH 18apr97
new object me -- create a new child instance
-- FILEIO --
fileName object me -- return fileName string
of the open file
status object me -- return the error code of
the last method called
```

Notes: This replaces the mMessageList function, which is now obsolete.

intersect

Elements: intersect(*[rectangle], [rectangle]*)

Purpose: When one rectangular area overlaps another, this function returns the rect coordinates of a third rectangle, the one defined by the intersecting area.

In context:

```
put sprite(1).rect
-- rect(13, 96, 163, 208)
put sprite(2).rect
-- rect(32, 160, 182, 272)
put intersect(sprite(1).rect, sprite(2).rect)
-- rect(32, 160, 163, 208)
```

isPastCuePoint

Elements: isPastCuePoint *([sprite or sound], [cuePointID])*

Purpose: You can use this function to keep track of how many times a particular cue point has been passed during the playback of a looping sprite. (To learn about embedded cue points, see Chapter 19.) The parameter *cuePointID* is either the name of a cue point in quotation marks or the point's number (counting from the beginning of the track). The parameter *sprite or sound* refers to the number of the sprite channel or the sound channel.

What the function returns depends on whether you're dealing with a named or numbered cue point. If the ID is a name, the function returns a count of the number of times the point has been passed during playback (or more correctly, the number of times a point with that name has been passed; if a name is duplicated, both cue points are counted). If it's a number, the response is binary: 0, or FALSE, means the point hasn't been passed; 1, or TRUE, means it has (there's no count of the number of times).

In context: These script lines adjust the volume of a looping sound file each time the cue point Drumroll is passed in sound channel 2 and then move the playback head when the cue point has been passed five times. Note the use of the parentheses in the second usage.

```
if isPastCuePoint (sound 2, "Drumroll") then
   set the volume of sound 2 to ((the volume of sound) - 5)
end if

if (isPastCuePoint (sound 2, "Drumroll"))= 5 then
   go to frame 300
end if
```

Notes: This function is compatible with SoundEdit, QuickTime, and Xtra files that support cue points. Try not to confuse cue points (which are embedded in the tracks of linear playback files) with the marker points within Director's Score window. And don't forget that SWA and QuickTime sprites appear as sprites, so it's best to refer to them by sprite channel number.

See also: The on cuePassed handler and the cuePointNames, cuePointTimes, and mostRecentCuePoint properties.

the key

Elements: the key

Purpose: This function returns the identity of the last key pressed by the user while the movie was running.

In context: This button script emits a system beep when the button is clicked, but only when the last keystroke was an "X":

```
on mouseUp
   if the key = "X" then beep
   end if
end
```

the keyCode

Elements: the keyCode

Purpose: Like the key, this function identifies the last key pressed by the user while the movie was running—but the key is expressed by the numerical key code used by the computer's operating system (this code may not be identical to the ASCII character code).

In context: This statement determines that the right arrow key was pressed:

```
put the keyCode
-- 124
```

Notes: This function is useful for certain keys (such as the arrow keys and function keys) that are not recognized by the key function.

keyPressed

Elements: keyPressed(*[keyCode or string]*)

Purpose: This function determines whether a particular key is being pressed. If the specified key is pressed, then the function returns 1 (TRUE); otherwise, it returns 0 (FALSE). The keyPressed function can be called from within repeat loops (whereas the key function cannot).

In context:

```
on mouseWithin
   if keyPressed("z") = 1 then
      showStats
   end if
end
```

See also: The keyPressed property

label

Elements: label(*[marker expression]*)

Purpose: This function returns the number of a frame to which a given marker is attached, or 0 if there is no such label.

In context:

```
put label ("Introduction")
-- 23
```

the last

Elements: the last *[chunk]* in *[expression]*

Purpose: This function isolates the final chunk in a text expression. A chunk is a discrete unit of text—a line, word, character, or delimited item. The expression can be contained in a text cast member, variable, or script line.

In context:

```
put the last word of "User Name"
-- "Name"
```

the lastClick

Elements: the lastClick

Purpose: This function returns the amount of time passed since the last time the mouse was clicked, expressed in ticks ($\frac{1}{60}$ of a second).

In context:

```
put the lastClick
-- 434
```

the lastEvent

Elements: the lastEvent

Purpose: This function returns the amount of time passed since the last time a user event occurred (a mouse click, mouse movement, or keystroke). This duration is expressed in ticks ($\frac{1}{60}$ of a second).

In context:

```
put the lastEvent
-- 324
```

Notes: User events should not be confused with event messages sent through the Lingo hierarchy.

the lastKey

Elements: the lastKey

Purpose: This function returns the amount of time passed since the last time a keyboard key was pressed, expressed in ticks ($\frac{1}{60}$ of a second).

In context:

```
put the lastKey
-- 3
```

See also: The key and keyCode functions.

the lastRoll

Elements: the lastRoll

Purpose: This function returns the amount of time passed since the last time the mouse was moved, expressed in ticks ($\frac{1}{60}$ of a second).

In context:

```
put the lastRoll
-- 1797
```

FUNCTIONS

length

Elements: length ([*text or numerical string*])

Purpose: This function returns a count of all the characters (including spaces and special characters) in a given string.

In context:

```
put length ("Director Demystified")
-- 20
put length ("123456789")
-- 9
```

See also: The count function.

lineHeight

Elements: lineHeight (member [*name or number*], [*line number*])

Purpose: This function determines the height, in pixels, of a specified line of text in a field cast member. It cannot be applied to text cast members.

In Context: This statement determines that the height of the type in the third line of text in the field Answer field is 11 pixels:

```
put lineHeight (member "Answer field", 3)
-- 11
```

See also: The lineHeight property.

linePosToLocV

Elements: linePosToLocV (member [*name or number*], [*line number*])

Purpose: This function measures the distance (in pixels) from the topmost edge of a field cast member to a specified line of text within the cast member. It cannot be applied to text cast members.

In context: This statement determines that the third line of text in the field Answer field is 22 pixels from the top of the field's cast member:

```
put linePosToLocV (member "Answer field", 3)
-- 22
```

list

Elements: list ([*value 1*], [*value 2*], [*etc.*])

Purpose: This function declares a linear list that contains the values enclosed in the parentheses. This function creates the same list as accomplished using square brackets ([ ]).

In context: This script creates a list variable named myList:

```
myList = list ("Bread", "Cheese", "Eggs")
```

listP

Elements: listP (*[item]*)

Purpose: This somewhat confusing function determines whether the given item qualifies as a list, a rect, or a point. It is a binary function, returning 1 if TRUE or 0 if FALSE.

In context:

```
myList = ["mouse","cat","cheese"]
put listP (myList)
-- 1
myPoint = point(10,20)
put listP(myPoint)
-- 1
```

locToCharPos

Elements: locToCharPos (member *[name or number]*, point (*[coordinates]*))

Purpose: In field text cast members, this function determines which individual character is closest to (or occupying) a given location in that cast member. It cannot be applied to text cast members. The character is identified by a number indicating its order in the string of text. The point is relative to the cast member's upper left, which is point (0,0).

In context: This statement determines that the character occupying (or closest to) a given point (10 pixels across and 150 pixels down from the field cast member's upper-left corner) is the fortieth character in the text currently occupying the field:

```
put locToCharPos (member "Answer field", point (10, 150))
-- 40
```

locVToLinePos

Elements: locVToLinePos (member *[name or number]*, *[distance in pixels]*)

Purpose: In field text cast members, this function determines which line of text is closest to (or occupying) a given distance (in pixels) from the topmost edge of that cast member. This function cannot be applied to text cast members.

In context: This statement determines that the third line of text in the field Answer field is the line occupying (or closest to) the vertical point 22 pixels from the top of the field's bounding box:

```
put locVToLinePos (member "Answer field", 22)
-- 3
```

log

Elements: log (*[decimal number]*)

Purpose: This function returns the natural logarithm of the given number.

In context:

```
put log (103.1)
-- 4.6357
```

See also: The exp function.

the long date

See: The date function.

map

Elements: map ([rect1], [rect2], [rect3])

Purpose: This function extrapolates a new rect coordinate grouping with width or depth values that bear the same relationship to [rect1] that [rect2] bears to [rect3].

In context:

```
put the rect of the stage into rect1
set rect2 to offset (rect1,100, 100)
set rect3 to offset (rect2,100, 100)

put map (rect3, rect2, rect1)
-- rect(196, 172, 836, 652)
```

mapMemberToStage

Elements: mapMemberToStage (sprite [sprite], [pointOnStage])

Purpose: This function uses the specified sprite and point to return an equivalent point within the dimensions of the Stage. This function is the counterpart of the mapStageToMember function. Both functions take into account any transformations made to the sprite, so you can use these functions to determine whether a particular area of a cast member has been clicked. For example, a click one-fourth of the sprite's width from the left will translate to coordinates one-fourth of the cast member's width from the left, even if the dimensions of the sprite have been changed.

In context:

```
put mapMemberToStage(sprite 1, point(91,71))
-- point(141, 178)
```

Notes: If the specified point is outside of the dimensions of the cast member, then VOID is returned.

See also: The map and mapStageToMember functions.

mapStageToMember

Elements: mapStageToMember(sprite [sprite], [pointOnStage])

Purpose: This function converts the *pointOnStage* parameter from Stage coordinates to the coronets of the sprite's cast member. Because this function takes into account any transformations made to the sprite, you can use this function to determine whether a particular area of a cast member has been clicked. For example, a click one-fourth of the sprite's width from the left will translate to coordinates one-fourth of the cast member's width from the left, even if the dimensions of the sprite have been changed.

In context: This script translates the point clicked to the relative location on the sprite's cast member:

```
put the clickLoc
-- point(191, 178)
put mapStageToMember(sprite 1, the clickLoc)
-- point(141, 71)
```

Notes: If the specified point on the Stage is not within the sprite, this function returns VOID.

See also: The map and mapMemberToStage functions.

marker

Elements: marker ([*numerical value*])
            marker ([*string*])

Purpose: This function returns the frame number of a marker in the Score. If a marker name is used for the parameter, then the return value is the number of the frame that contains the marker. If a number is used for the parameter, then a value is returned based on the locations of markers relative to the curate frame: Marker (+1) refers to the next frame with a marker, and marker (-1) designates the last preceding frame that has a marker associated with it. If the current frame has a marker, marker (0) can be used to refer to the frame itself; otherwise, marker (0) is the equivalent of marker (-1).

In context:

```
go to marker (-5)
```

max

Elements: max ([*list*])

Purpose: When used in conjunction with a list, this function retrieves the item with the highest value. If the list is numerical, max returns the highest number; if it is a text list, this function returns what would be the last entry if the list were sorted by alphabetical order.

In context:

```
set myList = list ("dog", "cat", "cheese")
put max (myList)
-- "dog"
set myList = list (5, 22, 0.97)
put max (myList)
-- 22
```

See also: The min function.

FUNCTIONS

maxInteger

Elements: the maxInteger

Purpose: This function documents the maximum whole integer that can be managed by the host system—the largest number it can count up to, in terms of tallying or tracking (larger numbers can be expressed as floating-point numbers).

In context:

```
put the maxInteger
-- 2147483647
```

min

Elements: min (*[list]*)

Purpose: When used in conjunction with a list, this function retrieves the item with the lowest value. If the list is numerical, min returns the lowest number; if it is a text list, this function returns what would be the first entry if the list were sorted by alphabetical order.

In context:

```
set myList = list ("dog", "cat", "cheese")
put min (myList)
-- "cat"
set myList = list (5, 22, 0.97)
put min (myList)
-- 0.97
```

See also: The max function.

the mouseXX

See: Lingo elements previously considered functions are now considered system properties. See the mouseChar, mouseDown, mouseH, mouseItem, mouseLine, mouseLoc, mouseMember, mouseUp, mouseV, and mouseWord properties.

moveVertex

Elements: moveVertex (*member [member]*, *[vertexIndex]*, *[horiz]*, *[vertical]*)

Purpose: This function moves the vertex of a vector shape cast member to another location. It specifies the horizontal and vertical coordinates for the move relative to the current position of the vertex point.

In context: This statement shifts the first vertex point in the vector shape Seth 15 pixels to the right and 20 pixels up from its current position:

```
moveVertex(member "Seth", 1, 15, -20)
```

Notes: Changing the location of a vertex through this function affects the member's shape in the same way as does dragging the vertex in the Vector Shape editor.

See also: The addVertex and deleteVertex commands, the moveVertexHandle function, and the originMode and vertexList properties.

moveVertexHandle

Elements: moveVertexHandle *(member [member, vertexIndex, handleIndex, horiz, vertical])*

Purpose: This function moves the vertex handle of a vector shape cast member to another location. As with moveVertex, the horizontal and vertical coordinates for the move are relative to the current position of the vertex handle, which in turn is relative to the vertex point it controls.

In context: This statement shifts the second control handle of the first vertex point in the vector shape Seth 12 pixels to the right and 10 pixels down:

MoveVertexHandle(member "Seth", 1, 2, 12, 10)

Notes: Changing the location of a control handle affects the shape in the same way as dragging the handle in the Vector Shape editor.

See also: The addVertex and deleteVertex commands, the moveVertex function, and the originMode and vertexList properties.

netDone

Elements: netDone ()

netDone *[netID]*

Purpose: As the name indicates, this function lets you know when a net-based action (such as getNetText, preloadNetThing, gotoNetMovie, or gotoNetPage) is completed. To check on the status of the last network operation undertaken, you can use netDone() (though this approach is not recommended). To retrieve information on an particular network operation, you'll need to invoke the operation's unique net ID returned by the network command when the operation started. The value returned is 1 (or TRUE) if the operation is completed (or if the browser terminates the operation for any reason). A value of FALSE (or 0) is returned if the network operation is underway.

In context: This script keeps the playback head in a looping pattern until the netDone status indicates that the network operation is complete:

```
on exitFrame
   if netDone (myNetID) = FALSE then
   go to the frame
   else go frame "Huzzah!"
   end if
end
```

See also: The netError, getNetText, preloadNetThing, and netTextResult functions and the gotoNetMovie command.

netError

Elements: netError ()

netError *[netID]*

Purpose: Another means of testing the status of a network operation, this function documents whether an error has occurred. Using netError () lets you test the last network operation (though this approach is not recommended). As with netDone, you should use the unique network ID returned by the command starting the network operation as the parameter. If everything went successfully, the string "OK" is returned; otherwise, an error number is returned. If no network operation has begun, the empty string is returned.

In context:

```
put netError (myNetID)
-- "OK"
```

netLastModDate

Elements: netLastModDate ()

Purpose: This function retrieves the "date last modified" information bundled with an HTTP-encoded file, expressed as a text string. This information is not always available and, in that case, the empty string is returned. This function can be used only if netDone and netError report that the last network operation has successfully completed.

In context:

```
set myVar = netLastModDate ()
put myVar
-- "Fri, Jul 10, 1998 12:22:23 PM GMT"
```

Notes: This function can be tested but not set. Also, you can't use net IDs to retrieve an earlier operation's modification date; Director flushes this information from memory as soon as another operation begins.

netMIME

Elements: netMIME ()

Purpose: This function retrieves the MIME type (image/jpeg, application/x-director, and so on) of the most recently downloaded HTTP- or FTP-encoded item.

In context:

```
on myMIMECheck
   set myMIME = netMIME()
   if myMIME = "image/gif" then
      go to frame "display pretty picture"
   end if
end
```

Notes: This function can be used only if netDone and netError report that the last network operation has completed successfully. This function can be tested but not set.

netTextResult

Elements: netTextResult ()
            netTextResult ([netID])

Purpose: This function returns the text string retrieved by a network operation. It can be called only if the last operation is complete (as indicated by such functions as netDone and netError). You can also specify the operation with its net ID, but the specification will be moot because the value is discarded when the next operation begins.

In context:

```
on exitFrame
    if netDone (myNetID) = TRUE then
        put netTextResult into field "manifesto"
    end if
end
```

new

Elements: new

Purpose: This term can serve as both a function and an event handler, depending on its use. It can be used to refer to the process of creating a child object or to a new cast member.

When a child object is created, new can be used to point to its parent script and to ascribe particulars to any custom properties contained in that script. When the parent script includes an on new handler, its contents will be executed when each child object is initialized (that is, born). For more details, see Chapter 18.

In context: The first script creates a child object Eric, with its parent script being Hypochondriac. The second script is a portion of that parent script, which establishes three properties while initializing the object.

```
set Eric = new(script "Hypochondriac","Aquarius", "Green", "Crewcut")
```

```
property sign, color, haircut
on new me, mySign, myColor, myHaircut
    set sign = mySign
    set color = myColor
    set haircut = myHaircut
    return me
end new
```

the number of chars in

Elements: the number of chars in *[text chunk]*

Purpose: This function counts all characters in the given text element.

In context: This script returns a count of characters in the quoted text string:

```
put the number of chars in "Director Demystified"
-- 20
```

This script counts a cast member's characters:

```
put the number of chars in member("main").text
-- 411
```

Notes: This function counts each keystroke item in the selected elements, including spaces, as a character.

the number of items in

Elements: the number of items in *[text chunk]*

Purpose: This function counts all items in the given text element. Be default, an item is defined as a unit delimited by a comma (this can be changed using the `itemDelimiter` property). If the text chunk doesn't contain any commas, it is counted as a single item.

In context: This script returns a count of items in the quoted text string:

```
put the number of items in "Director Demystified"
-- 1
```

This script counts a cast member's items:

```
put the number of items in member("main").text
-- 3
```

the number of lines in

Elements: the number of lines in *[text chunk]*

Purpose: This function counts all lines in the given text element. A line is defined as any text delimited by a Return keystroke.

In context: This script returns a count of lines in the quoted text string:

```
put the number of lines in "Director Demystified"
-- 1
```

This script counts a cast member's lines:

```
put the number of lines in member("main").text
-- 25
```

the number of words in

Elements: the number of words in *[text chunk]*

Purpose: This function counts all words in the given text element. A word is defined as any text delimited by spaces.

In context: This script returns a count of words in the quoted text string:

```
put the number of words in "Director Demystified"
-- 2
```

This script counts a cast member's words:

```
put the number of words in member("main").text
-- 48
```

numToChar

Elements: numToChar (*[numerical expression]*)

Purpose: This function returns the ASCII code equivalent—that is, the character—of the given number. This function can be applied to one character at a time.

In context:

```
put numToChar (162)
-- "¢"
```

See also: The charToNum function.

objectP

Elements: objectP (*[expression]*)

Purpose: You can use this function to determine whether a name is currently assigned to an object in memory (a child object, Xtra, or window).

In context: This script tests whether a child object called ColorObj is currently in memory; if it is not, the script creates that object:

```
if not (objectP (ColorObj)) then
    ColorObj = new(script "Color Choice")
end if
```

offset (strings)

Elements: offset (*[text string], [text string]*)

Purpose: This function compares the first text string against the second and returns the count of the character where the first string begins within the second. If the second text string does not contain the first at any point, the function returns 0.

In context: This statement finds the first string 12 characters into the second string:

```
put offset ("myst", "Director Demystified")
-- 12
```

Notes: In both strings, spaces are counted as characters. On the Macintosh, this function is not sensitive to case or to diacritical marks.

offset (rect)

Elements: offset (*[rect], [new width], [new height]*)

Purpose: This function extrapolates a new rect coordinate grouping, with width and depth values relative to another rect. The new rect is offset toward the top right of the Stage.

In context: This statement creates a rect offset by 100 pixels (both vertically and horizontally) from the coordinates of the Stage:

```
mainRect = (the stage).rect
newRect = offset (mainRect,100, 100)
put mainRect
-- rect(160, 120, 672, 504)

put newRect
-- rect(260, 220, 772, 604)
```

Notes: To offset in the opposite direction (toward the bottom left), use negative numbers as the offset values.

the optionDown

Elements: the optionDown

Purpose: This function determines whether the Alt key (Windows) or Option key (Macintosh) is currently being pressed. It can be used in scripting that interprets Alt-key or Option-key combinations. It is a binary function (1 indicates TRUE, and 0 indicates FALSE).

In context: This button script carries out one action if simply clicked (the custom handler buttonClick) and another (a jump to marker Special Place) if the mouse click occurs when the Alt or Option key is down:

```
on mouseUp
   if the optionDown then go "Special Place"
   else buttonClick
end
```

Notes: On Windows projectors, the optionDown function returns TRUE only if a second key is also pressed (in addition to Alt). If you need to check for the Alt key or Option key by itself, use controlDown or shiftDown instead.

param

Elements: param (*parameter position*)

Purpose: When one or more parameters have been associated with a handler, this function can be used to refer to a parameter not by name, but by the order in which the parameters were established. This function is useful for creating handlers that can accept an indeterminate number of parameters.

In context: This script returns the third parameter associated with it. Note that the handler itself declares no parameters.

```
on soldier
   put param(3)
end
```

FUNCTIONS

Even though no parameters are declared in the handler, the third parameter passed in will be displayed:

```
soldier (john, sarge, 5551212)
-- 5551212
soldier ("hut", "hut", "hike")
-- "hike"
soldier (454, 895, 20202)
-- 20202
```

the paramCount

Elements: the paramCount

Purpose: Use this function to count the total number of parameters being sent to the current handler.

In context: This handler script does nothing but return the parameter count. Note that the handler itself does not declare parameters.

```
on marching
    put the paramCount
end
```

Now here's what happens when the handler is called with four parameters:

```
marching (1, 2, 3, 4)
-- 4
```

pictureP

Elements: pictureP (*[variable]*)

Purpose: This function can be used to determine whether a cast member is a picture (a bitmap, text, or PICT). If the function returns 1, or TRUE, the cast member is a picture. If it returns 0, or FALSE, the cast member is of another data type. This function can't be invoked for a cast member directly, but only for a variable containing the picture of member property of that cast member.

In context:

```
set testMe = member ("Sniffle").picture
put pictureP (testMe)
-- 1
```

Notes: As with other Lingo ending in the letter "P," the suffix is short for predicate, indicating the self-referential nature of the function (which can also be referred to as a property).

point

Elements: point (*[horizontal coordinate]*, *[vertical coordinate]*)

Purpose: This function and data type serves as a two-position subvariable containing the horizontal and vertical coordinates of a given point on the Stage.

FUNCTIONS

In context:

```
put point (640, 480) into theEdge
put theEdge
-- point(640, 480)
```

pointInHyperlink

Elements: pointInHyperlink (sprite *[whichSprite]*, *[point]*)

Purpose: This text sprite function returns TRUE or FALSE to indicate whether the specified point is within a hyperlink in the text sprite.

In context: This command uses the Message window to test whether the mouse is over a hyperlink.

```
put pointInHyperlink(sprite 4, the mouseLoc)
-- 1
```

Notes: This function is especially useful for changing the cursor when the cursor is over a hyperlink.

See also: The cursor command and the mouseLoc function.

pointToChar

Elements: pointToChar (sprite *[whichSprite]*, *[point]*)

Purpose: This function returns the number of the character in a text sprite that corresponds to a point on the Stage. If the point is not contained in the sprite, this function returns –1.

In context:

```
put pointToChar(sprite 3, the mouseLoc)
-- 43
```

Notes: This function is especially useful for determining the character currently beneath the cursor.

See also: The mouseLoc, pointToWord, pointToItem, pointToLine, and pointToParagraph functions.

pointToItem

Elements: pointToItem (sprite *[sprite]*, *[point]*)

Purpose: This function returns the number of the item in a text sprite that corresponds to a point on the Stage. If the point is not contained in the sprite, this function returns –1.

By default, items are separated by commas, but this setting can be changed using the itemDelimiter property.

In context:

```
put pointToItem(sprite 3, the mouseLoc)
-- 2
```

Notes: This function is especially useful for determining the item currently beneath the cursor.

See also: The itemDelimiter property and the mouseLoc, pointToChar, pointToWord, pointToLine, and pointToParagraph functions.

pointToLine

Elements: pointToLine(*sprite [whichSprite]*, *[point]*)

Purpose: This function returns the number of the line in a text sprite that corresponds to a point on the Stage. If the point is not contained in the sprite, this function returns –1.

Lines are always separated by returns in the text cast member.

In context:

```
put pointToLine(sprite 3, the mouseLoc)
-- 3
```

Notes: This function is especially useful for determining the line currently beneath the cursor.

See also: The mouseLoc, pointToChar, pointToWord, pointToItem, and pointToParagraph functions.

pointToParagraph

Elements: pointToParagraph (*sprite [whichSprite]*, *[point]*)

Purpose: This function returns the number of the paragraph in a text sprite that corresponds to a point on the Stage. If the point is not contained in the sprite, this function returns –1.

Paragraphs are separated by Return characters.

In context:

```
put pointToPargraph(sprite 3, the mouseLoc)
-- 2
```

Notes: This function is especially useful for determining the paragraph currently beneath the cursor.

See also: The mouseLoc, pointToChar, pointToWord, pointToItem, and pointToLine functions.

pointToWord

Elements: pointToWord (*sprite [whichSprite]*, *[point]*)

Purpose: This function returns the number of the word in a text sprite that corresponds to a point on the Stage. If the point is not contained in the sprite, this function returns –1.

Words are separated by spaces.

In context:

```
put pointToWord (sprite 3, the mouseLoc)
-- 38
```

FUNCTIONS

Notes: This function is especially useful for determining the word currently beneath the cursor.

*See also:*The itemDelimiter property and the mouseLoc, pointToChar, pointToItem, pointToLine, and pointToParagraph functions.

power

Elements:　power ([number], [exponent])

Purpose: This mathematical function raises the value specified by *number* to the power *exponent*.

In context: This statement raises 2 to the eighth power:

```
put power (2, 8)
-- 256.0000
```

ptToHotSpotID

Elements:　ptToHotSpotID (sprite [QTVRSprite], [point])

Purpose: This function returns the ID number of the hot spot of a QTVR movie sprite at the given point. If no point corresponds to the specified point, the return value is 0.

quickTimeVersion

Elements:　quickTimeVersion()

Purpose: This function returns the version number of the latest version of QuickTime installed on the system. If the latest version is prior to QuickTime 3.0, then the value 2.12 is always returned. The return value is a floating-point number. The parentheses are required even though there are no parameters—failure to use the parentheses will return information about the QuickTime Xtras, not the version number.

In context: This statement assigns the QuickTime version to a variable:

```
QTver = quickTimeVersion()
```

Notes: This function replaces the QuickTimePresent function.

ramNeeded

Elements:　ramNeeded ([frame number], [frame number])

Purpose: You can use this function to determine how much RAM will be needed for playback of a given range of frames. The value is expressed in bytes (divide by 1024 to convert to kilobytes).

In context: This statement determines the RAM needed for playback of frames 1 through 5 of the active Director document:

```
put ramNeeded (1, 5)
-- 349604
```

Notes: This function may understate the required RAM because of elements that are used through Lingo that are not in the Score.

random

Elements: random (*[number]*)

Purpose: This function generates a random number, with the number specified used as the upper limit of numbers to choose from. The lowest possible number is 1.

In context: This statement retrieves a random number in the range 1 through 255:

```
put random (255)
-- 76
```

This statement retrieves a random number in the range 5 through 20:

```
put random (16) + 4
-- 18
```

rect

Elements: rect (*[left]*, *[top]*, *[right]*, *[bottom]*)
rect (*[corner point]*, *[corner point]*)

Purpose: This function and data type is a coordinate grouping, describing a rectangular area. It is used for such purposes as establishing the size of sprite bounding boxes and the windows of Movies in a Window (MIAWs). The function can take two arguments (one for each of opposite corner points) or four arguments (one for each side).

In context:

```
sprite("Martha").rect = rect(118, 264, 166, 324)
```

See also: The rect sprite, member, and window properties.

the result

Elements: the result

Purpose: This function retrieves the return value from the last handler executed. This function is used mostly for obtaining values from handlers in movies playing in a window (MIAWs) or as a debugging tool.

In context: Here's a simple movie-level handler that generates a random number within the range of color choices:

```
on pickAColor
   return random (255)
end
```

Note the use of the keyword return.

Now here are statements in the Message window that execute the handler and retrieve the result:

```
pickAColor
put the result
-- 116
```

FUNCTIONS

A better method is to assign the return value to a variable:

```
myVar = pickAColor
put myVar
-- 116
```

rollOver

Elements: the rollOver

        rollOver (*[sprite]*)

Purpose: This function can be used to determine whether the mouse cursor is over a sprite. The property can be used in either of two forms:

When preceeded by the, do not use parentheses. This form will return the number of the channel of a sprite the mouse is over, or 0 if the mouse is not over a sprite.

When used with a parameter in parentheses (but not with the keyword the), the parameter specifies a sprite's channel. If the mouse is over the specified sprite, the function returns TRUE. Otherwise the function returns FALSE.

In context: This handler checks to see whether the mouse is over the sprite in channel 2. If it is, the movie branches to the frame labeled Bingo.

```
on exitFrame
   if rollOver (2) then
      go to frame "Bingo"
   else
      go to the frame
   end if
end
```

You can use a handler such as the folowing to take a specific action depending upon which sprite the mouse is over:

```
on exitFrame
   thisSprite = the rollOver
   case thisSprite of
      0: go to the frame
      1: go to frame "Frosty"
      2: go to frame "Summer"
      otherwise
         go to the frame
   end case
end
```

See also: The mouseEnter, mouseLeave, and mouseWithin handlers; and the mouseMember property.

the selection

Elements: the selection

Purpose: This function can be used to test the contents of a portion of text currently selected (highlighted) in a field sprite. It returns the highlighted area as a text string.

In context:

```
if the selection = "Your name here" then
    set the text of field "Input" to "Type!"
end if
```

See also: The selection text cast member property.

the short date

See: The date function.

sin

Elements: sin (*[expression]*)

Purpose: This mathematical function determines the sine of the angle specified in *expression*. The angle parameter must be expressed in radians.

In context:

```
put sin (430*2.1)
-- -0.9785
```

Notes: Director's trigonometric functions use radians rather than degrees for angles when used as input or when they are returned as output. The following two handlers will perform the conversion from degrees to radians and vice versa:

```
on degreeToRadian degree
    return (degree * PI/180)
end degreeToRad

on radianToDegree radian
    return (radian * 180/PI)
end
```

See also: The cos and tan functions and the PI constant.

soundBusy

Elements: soundBusy (*[number]*)

Purpose: This function can be used to test whether a sound is currently playing in the channel expressed by *number*. If it is, it returns 1 (or TRUE); if no sound is playing, it returns 0 (or FALSE).

In context:

```
if soundBusy (2) = TRUE, then sound stop 2
```

Notes: This function is valid only after the playback head has moved or an updateStage command has been executed.

FUNCTIONS

sqrt

Elements: sqrt (*[number]*)

Purpose: This mathematical function returns the square root of the number enclosed in parentheses.

In context:

```
put sqrt (3.1415)
-- 1.7724
```

the stageBottom

Elements: the stageBottom

Purpose: This function returns the bottom edge of the Stage in the active movie, expressed in pixels from the top edge of the active area of the end user's monitor.

In context: This statement determines the true depth of the Stage by subtracting the property the stageBottom from the property the stageTop:

```
put the stageBottom - the stageTop
-- 384
```

the stageLeft

Elements: the stageLeft

Purpose: This function returns the left edge of the Stage in the active movie, expressed in pixels from the left edge of the active area of the end user's monitor.

In context: This statement determines the true width of the Stage by subtracting the property the stageLeft from the property the stageRight:

```
put the stageRight - the stageLeft
-- 512
```

the stageRight

Elements: the stageRight

Purpose: This function returns the right edge of the Stage in the active movie, expressed in pixels from the left edge of the active area of the end user's monitor.

In context: This statement determines the true width of the Stage by subtracting the property the stageLeft from the property the stageRight:

```
put the stageRight - the stageLeft
-- 512
```

stageToFlash

Elements: stageToFlash (*sprite [whichSprite]*, *[point]*)

Purpose: This function is used to determine which Flash movie coordinate is over a Director movie Stage coordinate. Note that a Flash movie's coordinates are determined by the original size when the movie was created and can be affected by stretching, scaling, or rotating the Flash sprite. For Flash movies, as with the Stage, the point (0,0) is the upper-left corner.

In context: This command determines the Flash movie coordinates corresponding to a point on the Stage:

```
put stageToFlash(sprite 4, point(100,230))
```

See also: The flashToStage function.

the stageTop

Elements: the stageTop

Purpose: This function returns the top edge of the Stage in the active movie, expressed in pixels from the top edge of the active area of the end user's monitor.

In context: This statement determines the true depth of the Stage by subtracting the property the stageBottom from the property the stageTop:

```
put the stageBottom - the stageTop
-- 384
```

startFrame

Elements: sprite(*[whichSprite]*).startFrame

Purpose: This function returns the frame number of the beginning frame of the sprite's span and is useful in determining the span of a particular sprite in the Score. The playback head must currently be on a frame that contains the sprite.

In context: This statement returns the starting frame of the sprite in channel 3 in the Message window:

```
put sprite(3).startFrame
```

Notes: You cannot set this value.

See also: The endFrame function.

string

Elements: string (*[expression]*)

Purpose: This function converts the given expression to a text string, complete with quotation marks. It's useful for placing the results of calculations or list operations into display fields. The expression can be a number, numeric expression, list, symbol, or another non-string expression.

In context:

```
put string (#oxmallet)
-- "oxmallet"
put string (17*24)
-- "408"
```

See also: The stringP and value functions.

stringP

Elements: stringP (*[expression]*)

Purpose: You can use this function to test whether a given expression is officially a text string. It is a binary function, returning 0 (or FALSE) if the expression is not a text string and 1 (or TRUE) if it is.

In context:

```
put stringP (#oxmallet)
-- 0

put stringP ("oxmallet")
-- 1
```

swing

Elements: swing (sprite *[whichSprite]*, *[pan]*, *[tilt]*, *[fieldOfView]*, *[speed]*)

Purpose: This function provides a smooth transition to a new viewing location in a QTVR movie containing a VR Pano. The *pan*, *tilt*, and *fieldOfView* parameters are given in degrees. The *speed* parameter is a number from 1 to 10 that specifies the speed at which the swing occurs (with 1 being the slowest). The actual speed at which the swing occurs will be determined by the user's system and the current movie conditions.

Notes: To determine whether the swing has completed, use the pan property to see if the current pan matches the requested pan.

See also: The pan property.

symbol

Elements: symbol (*[text string]*)

Purpose: A handy conversion utility, this function changes a given text string into a symbol, complete with the special # character.

In context:

```
put symbol("oxmallet")
-- #oxmallet
```

This script achieves the same result:

```
set myVar = "oxmallet"
put symbol (myVar)
-- #oxmallet
```

symbolP

Elements: symbolP (*[expression]*)

Purpose: To discover whether an expression is a symbol, use this function, which will return a binary value: 1 (or TRUE) if the expression is a symbol, or 0 (or FALSE) if it isn't.

In context:

```
put symbolP (MyVar)
-- 0
put symbolP (#MySymbol)
-- 1
```

tan

Elements: tan (*[angle]*)

Purpose: This mathematical function calculates the tangent of a given angle. The supplied angle must be in radians.

In context:

```
put tan (6.2833)
-- 0.0001
put tan (57.295)
-- 0.9248
```

Notes: See the sin function for a description of the use of radians as well as a handler for converting degrees to radians and vice versa.

tellStreamStatus

Elements: tellStreamStatus

Purpose: This function enables or disables the continuous reporting of all network operations to scripts using the handler on streamStatus.

In context: This script line turns off the status reports:

```
tellStreamStatus = 0
```

See also: The on streamStatus handler.

the ticks

Elements: the ticks

Purpose: This function documents the time period since the host computer was started, expressed in ticks (¹⁄₆₀ of a second).

In context:

```
put the ticks
-- 1205643
set timeNow = the ticks /60/60
put timeNow
-- 335
```

Notes: This function is useful for maintaining a set of timers.

the time

Elements: the time
the abbr time
the abbrev time
the abbreviated time
the short time
the long time

Purpose: This function returns the time, as set in the internal clock of the host computer. As with the date function, there are variations that return the time in different formats.

In context:

```
put the time
-- "4:14 AM"
put the short time
-- "4:14 AM"
put the abbreviated time
-- "4:14 AM"
put the long time
-- "4:14:38 AM"
```

Notes: In the United States, the short time and the abbreviated time are identical.

union

Elements: union (*[rect]*, *[rect]*)

Purpose: This function measures the two given rect coordinate groups and then returns a calculation of a third rect: one of the minimum size required to enclose the two.

In context:

```
set rect1 to rect (100,400,313, 313)
set rect2 to rect (200,500,400, 400)
put union (rect1, rect2)
-- rect(100, 400, 400, 400)
```

value

Elements: value (*[text string]*)

Purpose: Use this function to convert the contents of text strings to numerical values. If a string doesn't parse as a numeric value, Void is returned instead.

In context:

```
put value ("5")
-- 5
put value ("five")
-- <Void>
put value ("2" & "*2")
-- 4
```

voidP

Elements: voidP (*[variable]*)

Purpose: You can use this function to see whether a variable has been initialized by having a value assigned to it—even if that value is empty. If the variable has not been initialized (given an initial value), the function returns 1 (or TRUE); if it has, the function returns 0 (or FALSE).

In context: In the first script line, an uninitialized variable is tested (it doesn't yet exist). Then the variable (myVar) is initialized, but with an empty value. Even though the variable contains nothing, the fact that it formally exists changes the status of voidP.

```
put voidP (myVar)
-- 1
set myVar to ""
put voidP (myVar)
-- 0
```

Notes: This function is useful when creating variables, since it can be used to ensure that no variable of the same name already exists.

windowPresent

Elements: windowPresent (*[MIAW name]*)

Purpose: This function determines whether a given MIAW window is open. If it is, the function returns 1 (or TRUE); if is isn't, the function returns 0 (or FALSE).

In context: This statement displays a warning message if a specified movie isn't currently running as an MIAW:

```
if windowPresent ("Running") = 0 then alert ¬
    "Sorry, that movie isn't open right now."
```

Notes: The name cited for this function must be the name of the MIAW (as shown in the windowList property), which can differ from the name of the movie playing in that window.

xtra

Elements: xtra "*[name]*"

Purpose: This is a function, although it may seem like a keyword. It returns a child instance of the parent script of an Xtra. Use it in conjunction with the new function to initialize new instances of an Xtra.

In context:

```
fileGet = new (xtra "FileIO")
```

See also: The new function.

FUNCTIONS

PROPERTIES

actionsEnabled

Elements: the actionsEnabled of sprite *[FlashSprite]*
sprite(*[FlashSprite]*).actionsEnabled
the actionsEnabled of member *[FlashMember]*
member(*[FlashMember]*).actionsEnabled

Purpose: This property determines whether the actions in a Flash movie are enabled. The property is TRUE (enabled) by default. This property applies to Flash movie cast members and sprites.

In context: This statement sets the actionsEnabled property of the Flash movie smallFlash to FALSE:

```
sprite("smallFlash").actionsEnabled = FALSE
```

Notes: This property can be both tested and set.

See also: The buttonsEnabled and clickMode properties.

the activeCastLib

Elements: the activeCastLib

Purpose: This property represents the number of the cast library of the foremost cast window during authoring.

In context:

```
put the activeCastLib
-- "4"
```

Notes: This property can be tested but not set.

the activeWindow

Elements: the activeWindow

Purpose: This property indicates the window that currently has a script running and is useful to enable a window to reference itself. Note that this is different from the window that has the active title bar and that is the foremost window (see the frontWindow property).

In context: This handler sets the Stage color of the active window to blue and the other windows to gray:

```
on activateWindow
    repeat with win in (the windowList)
        if win = the activeWindow then
            the stageColor = 108
```

```
        else
           tell win
              the stageColor = 248
           end tell
        end if
   end repeat
end
```

Notes: This property can be tested but not set.

See also: The frontWindow property.

the actorList

Elements: the actorList

Purpose: This property is a list of all child objects that will receive a stepFrame message each time the playback head enters a new frame. You must explicitly add (or remove) your child objects to (or from) the list. You can use regular list Lingo to add or remove items in this list, or you can clear all objects by setting the actorList to [ ], which denotes an empty list.

In context: This command creates a child object and at the same time adds it to the actorList. Note that the actorList is the only reference to the child object (there is no variable, for instance), and that if the object is removed from the list, it will cease to exist.

```
   add the actorList, new (script "spaceship")
```

Notes: It's a good idea to clear the actorList upon closing each movie, because Director doesn't purge it automatically.

See also: The stepFrame handler.

alertHook

See: The on alertHook handler.

alignment of member

Elements: the alignment of member *[memberRef]*
              member(*[memberRef]*).alignment

Purpose: This property, limited to field and text cast members, determines which alignment (or justification) is used to display characters within a particular cast member. It is equivalent to selecting the Alignment buttons in the Text or Field dialog box. The value for fields can be left, center, or right. For text, the value can be #left, #right, #center, or #full.

In context:

```
member ("fResults").alignment = "center"
member("tLesson").alignment = #full
```

Notes: The cast member must include at least one character (even if only a space) for this property to be active. This property can be both tested and set.

allowCustomCaching

Elements: the allowCustomCaching

Purpose: This property is not currently implemented. It is provided for intended future enhancements and will contain information about a private cache.

allowGraphicMenu

Elements: the allowGraphicMenu

Purpose: This property determines whether graphic controls in the context menu can be used when the movie is played in a Shockwave environment. The default setting is TRUE; setting this property to FALSE results in only a text menu display.

In context:

set the allowGraphicMenu to FALSE

Notes: This property can be both tested and set and defaults to TRUE.

See also: The allowSaveLocal, allowTransportControl, allowVolumeControl, and allowZooming properties.

allowSaveLocal

Elements: the allowSaveLocal

Purpose: This property is not currently implemented. It is provided for intended future enhancements and will determine whether the Save menu control will be available when the movie is playing in a Shockwave environment.

Notes: This property can be both tested and set and defaults to TRUE.

See also: The allowGraphicMenu, allowTransportControl, allowVolumeControl, and allowZooming properties.

allowTransportControl

Elements: the allowTransportControl

Purpose: This property is not currently implemented. It is provided for intended future enhancements of Director.

allowVolumeControl

Elements: the allowVolumeControl

Purpose: This property is not currently implemented. It is provided for intended future enhancements of Director and will determine whether the menu's Volume control will be functional when a movie is playing in a Shockwave environment.

allowZooming

Elements: the allowZooming

Purpose: This property is not yet implemented. It is provided for intended future enhancements of Director.

alphaThreshold

Elements: member([*memberRef*]).alphaThreshold
          the alphaThreshold of member [*memberRef*]

Purpose: This property determines how a bitmap's alpha channel affects mouse-click detection. For values from 1 through 255, the mouse click is detected if the pixel in the alpha map at the clicked location has a value that is equal to or greater than the value of the alphaThreshold property. A value of 0 makes all mouse clicks detectable.

In context: This statement specifies that clicks on a sprite derived from the bigPic cast member will be detected on areas where pixels in the alpha channel have a value of 144 or greater:

member("bigPic").alphaThreshold = 144

Notes: This property can be both tested and set.

See also: The useAlpha property.

ancestor

Elements: ancestor = new (script "[*name*]")

Purpose: This property lets you designate a script in addition to the parent script of a child object or behavior from which parameters and handlers can be inherited (for an introduction to ancestor scripting, see Chapter 18).

In context: This parent script declares ancestor as a property and then sets that property to the script "Kamehameha". The script also sets the value of the aWhere property in the ancestor using the special property me.

```
property sign, color, haircut, ancestor
on new me, myColor, myHaircut
    set color = myColor
    set haircut = myHaircut
    set ancestor = new (script "Kamehameha")
    me.aWhere = "Hawaii"
    return me
end new
```

See also: Chapter 18: *Parent/Child Lingo.*

antiAlias

Elements: member([*memberRef*]).antiAlias
          sprite([*spriteRef*]).antiAlias

Purpose: This property determines whether a sprite is rendered to the Stage using anti-aliasing. The default setting is TRUE, which provides anti-aliasing. Although anti-aliasing can result in better display quality, it can also put a drain on system resources and slow the animation. For text, anti-aliasing also depends on the text point size and the value of the antiAliasThreshold property.

PROPERTIES

In context:

```
member("bigText").antiAlias = TRUE
```

Notes: This property applies to text, vector shapes, and Flash movies. The `antiAlias` property can be both tested and set.

See also: The `antiAliasThreshold`, `quality of sprite`, and `quality of member` properties.

antiAliasThreshold

Elements: member(*[textMemberRef]*).antiAliasThreshold

Purpose: Anti-aliasing is more important for text at larger point sizes and may make smaller text less readable. This property lets you set a point-size threshold for anti-aliasing; all text of equal or greater point size will be anti-aliased. For this property to have an effect, the `antiAlias` property of the text cast member must be TRUE.

In context: These statements enable anti-aliasing and set the threshold to 18 points:

```
member("bigText").antiAlias = TRUE
member("bigText").antiAliasThreshold = 18
```

Notes: This property defaults to 14 points.

See also: The `antiAlias` property.

the applicationPath

Elements: the applicationPath

Purpose: You can use this property to get a string that relays the location of the folder containing the active Director application (not the movie running).

In context:

```
put the applicationPath
--"C:\Macromedia\Director\Director 7\"
```

Notes: This property can be tested but not set.

autoMask

Elements: member(*[cursor]*).autoMask

Purpose: This property has the same effect as the automask check box in the Cursor Properties Editor while authoring. If `autoMask` is TRUE, then all white pixels in the animated color cursor are transparent and allow the elements beneath the cursor to show through. If `autoMask` is FALSE, the white pixels are opaque.

In context:

```
member("myCursor").autoMask = TRUE
```

Notes: This property can be both tested and set.

autoTab of member

Elements: the autoTab of member *[memberRef]*
        member(*[memberRef]*).autoTab

Purpose: This property is the Lingo equivalent of setting the Tab to Next Editable Item check box in a field or text cast member's Properties dialog box. A setting of TRUE (or 1) means that pressing the Tab key will move the cursor to the next editable sprite on the Stage; a setting of FALSE (or 0) means the cursor will not advance.

In context:

member("Answer Field").autoTab = TRUE

backColor of member

Elements: the backColor of member *[memberRef]*
        member(*[memberRef]*).backColor
        the backColor of sprite *[spriteRef]*
        sprite(*[spriteRef]*).backColor

Purpose: This property establishes the background color of field and button cast members and 1-bit sprites. The value is expressed as the number the color occupies in the active color palette. Using this property with other cast types will produce no results.

In context:

put the backColor of member 1
-- 15
set the backColor of member "Push Me" to 255

Notes: Changing the backColor property of sprites with a bit depth of greater than 1-bit is not recommended as the results are not predictable. Use the new bgColor property instead.

See also: The bgColor, color, and backgroundColor properties.

backgroundColor

Elements: member(*[vectorRef]*).backgroundColor
        the backgroundColor of member *[vectorRef]*

Purpose: This property determines the background color of a vector cast member (and sprites derived from it). The color must be given as a color data type.

In context: This statement sets the vector's background color to pure red and then to the color in the current palette at position 35:

member(7).backgroundColor = rgb(255, 0, 0)
member(7).backgroundColor = paletteIndex(35)

Notes: This property can be both tested and set.

See also: The bgColor property and the color function.

the beepOn

Elements: the beepOn

Purpose: When this property is set to TRUE, a system beep will sound whenever the mouse is clicked outside of the area of active sprites on the Stage. *Active* refers to sprites with scripts attached to them (at either the Cast or Score level).

In context:

```
set the beepOn = TRUE
```

Notes: This property can be both tested and set. Its default value is FALSE. It's best placed in frame or movie scripts.

bgColor

Elements: sprite(*[spriteRef]*).bgColor
the bgColor of sprite *[spriteRef]*
the bgColor of the stage
(the stage).bgColor

Purpose: For sprites, this property determines the background color of the sprite. It is equivalent to setting the background color using the tool palette. The color specified is a color data type. This is an improvement on the backColor property because it can be applied to sprites of any color depth and is independent of the color depth of the monitor.

For the Stage, this property is equivalent to setting the Stage color in the Movie Properties dialog box.

In context: This statement sets the background color of a bitmap sprite to pure blue:

```
sprite("myPic").bgColor = rgb(0, 0, 255)
```

Notes: This property can be both tested and set for all sprite types.

See also: The color function and the backColor, backgroundColor, and stageColor properties.

bitRate of member

Elements: member(*[memberRef]*).bitRate
the bitRate of member *[memberRef]*

Purpose: This cast member property returns the bit rate of a particular Shockwave Audio cast member, expressed in kilobytes per second (Kbps). The bit rate is an aspect of the file's compression, set in the file's Compression Settings dialog box. It is not the same bit depth as the original sampling rate of the sound itself.

In context:

```
put the bitRate of member "Doowop"
-- 8
```

Notes: This property will return a value of 0 until file streaming starts, or the file is preloaded using the preLoadBuffer command. This property can be tested but not set.

See also: The bitsPerSample property.

PROPERTIES

bitsPerSample

Elements: member(*[memberRef]*).bitsPerSample
the bitsPerSample of member *[memberRef]*

Purpose: This cast member property returns the original bit depth of a particular Shockwave Audio cast member.

In context:

put member("Big Kahuna").bitsPerSample

Notes: This property can be tested only after the sound begins streaming or the file is pre-loaded using the preLoadBuffer command. It cannot be set.

See also: The bitRate property.

blend of sprite

Elements: sprite(*[spriteRef]*).blend
the blend of sprite *[spriteRef]*

Purpose: You can use this property to establish the blend value of a given sprite. Specifying the value, from 0 to 100, is equivalent to selecting the Blend value in the Sprite Properties dialog box.

In context:

set the blend of sprite 7 to 88

Notes: This property can be both tested and set.

See also: The blendLevel property.

blendLevel

Elements: sprite(*[spriteRef]*).blendLevel
the blendLevel of sprite *[spriteRef]*

Purpose: You can use this property to establish the blend value of a given sprite. This is similar to using the blend property or setting the Blend value in the Sprite Properties dialog box, except the scale of the values ranges from 0 to 255.

In context:

sprite(7).blendLevel = 150

Notes: This property can be tested and set.

See also: The blend of sprite property.

border

Elements: member(*[fieldRef]*).border
the border of member *[fieldRef]*

Purpose: This field cast property can be used to set the thickness of the border of a field cast member in pixels.

In context: The first statement gives the field "Results" a border 12 pixels thick, and the second gives it no border at all:

```
member("Results").border = 12
member ("Results").border = 0
```

Notes: This property can be both tested and set.

See also: The boxDropShadow property.

bottom

Elements: sprite(*[spriteRef]*).bottom
            the bottom of sprite *[spriteRef]*

Purpose: This property determines the bottom of the bounding box of the given sprite, expressed in vertical coordinates from the top of the Stage.

In context:

```
put the bottom of sprite 5
-- 251
```

Notes: This property can be both tested and set.

See also: The top, height, left, right, locH, and locV properties.

bottomSpacing

Elements: *[chunkExpression]*.bottomSpacing

Purpose: This property sets the spacing applied to the bottom of paragraphs in a chunk portion of a text cast member. Note that the actual spacing between two paragraphs is the total of the bottom spacing of the first paragraph, the top spacing of the second paragraph, plus the default spacing. The default value is 0. Setting the value to an integer greater than 0 increases the spacing. A value less than 0 decreases the spacing.

In context: This statement closes the gap between paragraphs for the first six paragraphs of the cast member:

```
member(6).paragraph[1..5].bottomSpacing = -3
```

Notes: The default value (0) results in default spacing between paragraphs.

See also: The topSpacing property.

boxDropShadow

Elements: member(*[memberRef]*).boxDropShadow
            the boxDropShadow of member *[memberRef]*

Purpose: This property, limited to field cast members, can be used to set the size of a drop shadow effect when applied to the border of a bounding box of a field. The property can be set to 0 (no drop shadow), or a shadow thickness in pixels can be specified.

In context: This statement sets the shadow of a field's box to a width of 5 pixels:

```
member("Time Field").boxDropShadow = 5
```

Notes: This property should not be confused with the `dropShadow` member property, which applies the effect not to the bounding box but to the characters themselves.

See also: The `border` property.

boxType

Elements: `member([memberRef]).boxType`
         `the boxType of member [memberRef]`

Purpose: This property, limited to text and field cast members, returns a symbol (indicated by the # character) that designates the type of box used to display a field. It is the Lingo equivalent of setting the Framing options in the cast member's Properties dialog box.

Here are the codes for the box types:

```
#adjust
#scroll
#fixed
#limit
```

In context:

```
put the boxType of member "Answer field"
-- #adjust
```

Notes: This property can be both tested and set.

broadcastProps

Elements: `member([memberRef]).broadcastProps`
         `the broadcastProps of member [memberRef]`

Purpose: This property determines whether changes made to a Flash movie or vector shape cast member are applied to any existing sprites created from the cast member. The default value is TRUE, meaning any change to the cast member is also made to the sprites and to any new sprites that are created. When this property is set to FALSE, only new sprites are affected by new changes.

In context:

```
member("mugFlash").broadcastProps = FALSE
```

Notes: This property can be both tested and set. It seems to affect only some vector and Flash movie properties.

browserName

Elements: `browserName [pathname]`
         `browserName()`
         `browserName(#enabled, [TrueOrFalse])`

Purpose: This property returns or establishes the path name of the preferred browser in use by Director—that is, the browser selected in the Network Preferences dialog box. When you use the browserName () method, you will receive the name of the currently selected browser. When you use the browserName (#enabled, trueorfalse) method, you can specify whether the browser is automatically launched when the goToNetPage command is executed.

In context:

```
put browserName ()
-- "Abishag:Netscape Navigator™ Folder:Netscape Navigator™ 3.01"
```

Notes: Keep in mind that this property is one of the few that can't begin with the. It can be both tested and set.

bufferSize

Elements: member(*[flashRef]*).bufferSize
              the bufferSize of member *[flashRef]*

Purpose: This property determines the size of the buffer used for a linked Flash movie whose preLoad property is set to FALSE. It essentially determines how many bytes are streamed into memory at a time. The value must be an integer. The default is 32768 bytes (32K).

In context: These commands set the preLoad property of a Flash cast member to FALSE, thereby allowing the movie to be streamed. The buffer size for the streaming is then set to 64K.

```
member("forestFlash").preload = FALSE
member("forestFlash").bufferSize = 65536
```

Notes: This property can be both tested and set.

See also: The bytesStreamed, preLoadRAM, and streamMode properties and the stream command.

buttonsEnabled

Elements: sprite(*[flashRef]*).buttonsEnabled
              the buttonsEnabled of sprite *[flashRef]*
              member(*[flashRef]*).buttonsEnabled
              the buttonsEnabled of member *[flashRef]*

Purpose: This property determines whether the buttons in a Flash movie are active. By default, the buttons are active (TRUE). The actionsEnabled property must also be set to TRUE for buttons to be active.

In context: This script determines whether frame 40 of a Flash movie is ready for playing, and, if so, enables the buttons:

```
if frameReady(sprite("oceanFlash"), 40) then
   sprite("oceanFlash").buttonsEnabled = TRUE
end if
```

Notes: This property can be both tested and set.

See also: The actionsEnabled property.

the buttonStyle

Elements: the buttonstyle

Purpose: This property affects the overall behavior of buttons (created with the tool palette) during playback of a movie—in particular, what happens when the end user clicks one button and then moves to others without releasing the mouse button.

When this property is set to FALSE (or 0), user feedback is list style: The first and all subsequent buttons will be highlighted as the user rolls the cursor over them with the mouse button held down. If the mouse moves over another button while the mouse button is down and the mouse button is then released, the new button will receive the mouseUp message. This is the default setting.

When this property is set to TRUE (or 1), user feedback will be dialog style: Only the initial button clicked will be highlighted, and releasing the mouse button over another button will not cause that button's mouseUp script to be executed.

In context:

the buttonStyle = True

Notes: This property can be both tested and set; it is not attributable to individual button cast members, but to general behaviors on the Stage.

buttonType of member

Elements: member(*[memberRef]*).buttonType
            the buttonType of member *[memberRef]*

Purpose: This property, limited to button cast members, returns a symbol (indicated by the # character) that designates the display type of a button. It is the Lingo equivalent of setting the Type options in the cast member's Properties dialog box. It applies only to buttons created with the Tool Palette.

Here are the codes for the button types:

#pushButton
#checkBox
#radioButton

In context:

put the buttonType of member "Push me!"
-- #pushButton

Notes: This property can be both tested and set.

bytesStreamed

Elements: member(*[flashRef]*).bytesStreamed
            the bytesStreamed of member *[flashRef]*

Purpose: This property determines the number of bytes of a Flash movie cast member that have been streamed into memory.

PROPERTIES

In context:

```
put member("bigFlash").bytesStreamed
```

Notes: This property can be tested only, not set, and is functional only while the Director movie is playing.

See also: The `bufferSize` and `percentStreamed` properties and the `stream` command.

castLibNum of member

Elements: `member([memberRef]).castLibNum`
    `the castLibNum of member [memberRef]`

Purpose: This cast member property specifies the number of the Cast that contains a particular cast member.

In context:

```
put the castLibNum of member "Kermit"
--"4"
```

Notes: This property can be tested but not set.

See also: The `name (of castLib)`, `number (of castLib)`, and `number (of castLibs)` properties.

castLibNum of sprite

Elements: `sprite([spriteRef]).castLibNum`
    `the castLibNum of sprite [spriteRef]`

Purpose: Use this property to determine which castLib is associated with a particular sprite in the currently active frame. Unlike the `castLibNum` member property, this property can be changed for sprites.

In context: This statement changes the castLib for a sprite. The sprite will now be derived from the cast member with the same `memberNum` property in the new castLib.

```
sprite(6).castLibNum = 3
```

Notes: This property can be both tested and set.

See also: The `name (of castLib)`, `number (of castLib)`, and `number (of castLibs)` properties.

castMemberList

Elements: `member([cursorRef]).castmemberList`
    `the castmemberList of member [cursorRef]`

Purpose: This cursor cast member property enables you to determine (or set) the cast members used in an animated color cursor. Cast members in the list must be valid 8-bit bitmaps; other elements will be ignored. Each element in the cursor list will correspond to a frame in the animated cursor, appearing in the same order as the list.

In context: These commands show the contents of a cursor list (for a cursor in cast member 4) and then change the list by adding another bitmap:

```
put member(4).castMemberList
-- [(member 2 of castLib 1), (member 3 of castLib 1)]
member(4).castMemberList = [member 2,member 3,member 7]
```

Notes: This property can be both tested and set.

See also: The cursorSize property.

center

Elements: member([*memberRef*]).center
              the center of member [*memberRef*]

Purpose: This property is limited to digital video cast members and Director movies imported as cast members into other movies. It is often used in conjunction with the crop member property.

When the crop member property is TRUE, any resizing of derived sprites on the Stage will crop the video window (only the area defined in the sprite bounding box will show through). If at the same time the center property is set to TRUE, the area shown in the cropped window will be centered on the actual size of the video. If the center property is FALSE, the upper left of the video will appear in the spite, and the lower and rightmost areas will be cut to fit.

In context:

```
member ("QuickTime1").center = TRUE
```

Notes: This property can be both tested and set. The default setting is 0, or FALSE.

See also: The crop property.

centerRegPoint

Elements: member([*memberRef*]).centerRegPoint
              the centerRegPoint of member [*memberRef*]

Purpose: This property determines whether the center of a vector shape, Flash movie, or bitmap cast member is used as the registration point (TRUE, the default), or whether the cast member's current point value is used (FALSE). When you change the registration point of the cast member using the regPoint property, the centerRegPoint property is automatically set to FALSE.

In context:

```
member("globeVector").centerRegPoint = TRUE
```

Notes: This property can be both tested and set.

See also: The regPoint property.

the centerStage

Elements: the centerStage

Purpose: This movie property affects the movie opened subsequent to the current movie. It establishes whether the Stage of that movie is centered on the host computer's monitor.

When the `centerStage` is set to FALSE, the subsequent Stage will be positioned according to the current Stage Location coordinates in its Movie Properties dialog box.

In context:

```
on mouseUp
    set the centerStage to FALSE
    play movie "Help File"
end
```

Notes: This property can be both tested and set, with the default being TRUE (centered). It can test the currently open movie, but when it is set, the change will apply only to the following movie. Settings used during projector creation may override this property.

changeArea of member

Elements: member(*[TransitionRef]*).changeArea
              the changeArea of member *[TransitionRef]*

Purpose: This property is the Lingo equivalent of setting the Change Area option in the Transition dialog box. It applies to transition cast members only. When this property is set to TRUE (or 1), the transition is applied only to the area changing on the Stage. When this property is set to FALSE (or 0), the transition is applied to the Stage as a whole.

In context:

```
put the changeArea of member "Scratchy"
-- 1
```

Notes: This property can be both tested and set, with the default being whatever was set in the Transition dialog box.

channelCount

Elements: member(*[SoundRef]*).channelCount
              the channelCount of member *[SoundRef]*

Purpose: This property can be used to establish whether sound cast members have a single sound channel (monophonic) or two channels (stereophonic).

In context: This statement determines that the Dog snore sound file was imported into the active cast as a single-channel sound:

```
put member("Dog snore").channelCount
-- 1
```

Notes: This property can be tested but not set.

charSpacing

Elements: *[chunkExpression]*.charSpacing

Purpose: This property modifies the default spacing between characters in the chunk portion of a text cast member. The default value is 0 (no modification). A value greater than 0 increases the spacing between characters; a value less than 0 decreases the spacing.

In context: This statement increases the spacing between characters in the first paragraph of cast member 6:

```
member(6).paragraph[1].charSpacing = 2
```

Notes: This property can be both tested and set.

See also: The bottomSpacing and topSpacing properties.

the checkBoxAccess

Elements: the checkBoxAccess

Purpose: You can use this movie property to limit the degree of user feedback when a standard radio button or check box (the kind created with Director's tool palette) is clicked by the end user. This property has three states:

0   User can turn the items on and off.

1   User can turn the items on, but not off.

2   User cannot change the items; control is by scripts only.

In context: This script freezes a user selection after it is made:

```
on mouseUp
    put the text of member 3 into userText
    open window "countdown"
    set the checkBoxAccess to 1
end
```

Notes: This property can be both tested and set, with the default being 0 (user on/off control). This is a moviewide property and cannot be set for individual radio buttons or check boxes.

the checkBoxType

Elements: the checkBoxType

Purpose: This movie property applies only to the standard check box button (the kind created with Director's tool palette), providing some options in the behavior of those check boxes. This property has three states:

0   Fills the check box with an "X."

1   Fills the check box with an unfilled black square.

2   Fills the check box with a solid black square.

In context: This script changes the display type of a check box just as it's being clicked:

```
on mouseDown
    set the checkBoxType to 2
end
```

Notes: This property can be both tested and set, with the default being 0 (filled with an "X"). This is a moviewide property and cannot be set for individual check boxes.

PROPERTIES

the checkMark

Elements: the checkMark of menuItem *[item]* of menu *[name or number]*

Purpose: When you've installed custom menus in a movie, you can use this property to toggle on and off those little selection check marks that can appear next to menu items. You might want to use this property to indicate that a command has already been selected or that an option is already enabled.

In context: This custom handler (called in the menu script) turns off the sound and then adds a check mark to the Sound Off menu item on the Sound menu:

```
on turnOff
    set the soundEnabled to FALSE
    set the checkMark of menuItem "Sound Off" of menu "Sound" to TRUE
end
```

Notes: This property can be both tested and set, with the default being FALSE (no check mark displayed). It must be placed in a script directly called by the menu item itself; using it in a button or frame script will have no effect on the menu display.

See also: The installMenu command and the menu keyword.

the chunkSize of member

Elements: member(*[TransitionRef]*).chunkSize
the chunkSize of member *[TransitionRef]*

Purpose: This transition property is the Lingo equivalent of setting the Smoothness option in the Transition dialog box. It applies to transition cast members only. It can be set on a sliding scale from 1 (maximum smoothness of transition) to 128 (minimum smoothness). You can set a value greater than 128, but it will produce the same results as the maximum setting.

In context:

```
set the chunkSize of member "Scratchy" to 128
```

Notes: This property can be both tested and set, with the default value being whatever is set in the Transition dialog box.

the clickLoc

Elements: the clickLoc

Purpose: This property contains the coordinates of the Stage location of the cursor when the mouse was last clicked. The location is expressed as a point, in pixels, from the left and top edges of the Stage.

In context:

```
put the clickLoc
-- point(289, 260)
```

clickMode

Elements: sprite(*[flashRef]*).clickMode
the clickMode of sprite *[flashRef]*
member(*[flashRef]*).clickMode
the clickMode of member *[flashRef]*

Purpose: This property (which can be applied to Flash sprites and cast members) determines when a Flash movie sprite receives a mouse-click event or mouse-over event (mouseEnter, mouseLeave, or mouseWithin). This property has three possible values:

#boundingBox: A mouse-click or mouse-over event is determined by the sprite's bounding box.

#opaque: The default value. A mouse-click or mouse-over event is determined by the opaque areas of a sprite if the sprite has its ink effect set to Background Transparent. Otherwise, the setting is identical to #boundingBox.

#object: A mouse-click or mouse-over event is determined by the sprite's filled areas (not counting any background area). This setting is independent of the sprite's ink setting.

In context: This command sets the sprite's ink effect to Background Transparent and clickMode to #opaque. The sprite will now be able to detect mouse clicks over any opaque portion of the sprite, and rollover events will be determined by the border of the opaque areas.

```
sprite("surfFlash").ink = 36
sprite("surfFlash").clickMode = #opaque
```

Notes: This property can be both tested and set.

the clickOn

Elements: the clickOn

Purpose: This movie property returns the channel number of the last active sprite clicked. An active sprite is one that has a sprite or cast member script attached to it. A click on the Stage returns 0.

In context: This statement centers the sprite last clicked at the location of the mouse:

```
sprite(the clickOn).loc = the mouseLoc
```

Notes: Remember that only a scripted sprite will return an accurate clickOn value. If the last sprite clicked has no script attached, the clickOn will return 0. To cause sprites with no scripts to be detected, attach an empty script to the sprite.

closed

Elements: member(*[vectorRef]*).closed

Purpose: This property determines whether the specified vector shape cast member is closed or open. It is useful for building a vector shape with a vertex-by-vertex process and then closing the member. Remember that only closed shapes can be filled. A value of TRUE indicates that the shape is closed; FALSE indicates that the end points are open.

In context: These statements close a vector shape and then fill it with green:

```
member("circleVect").closed = TRUE
member("circleVect").filled = TRUE
member("circleVect").fillColor = rgb(0, 125, 0)
```

See also: The addVertex, deleteVertex, and moveVertex commands and the filled, fillColor, and fillMode properties.

color

Elements: sprite(*[spriteRef]*).color
the color of sprite *[spriteRef]*

Purpose: This property specifies the foreground color of the sprite. It is similar to the foreColor property but differs in that the color is specified as a color data type and is independent of the monitor color depth setting and the sprite's color depth.

In context: This statement sets the foreground color of a sprite to red:

```
sprite(3).color = rgb(255, 0, 0)
```

Notes: This property can be both tested and set.

See also: The color, bgColor, and foreColor properties.

the colorDepth

Elements: the colorDepth

Purpose: This property determines the current color depth setting of the monitor on the host computer. When more than one monitor is attached, the colorDepth refers to the monitor that displays the Stage. However, when this property is set, the color depth changes on all attached monitors. At present, there are six possible states:

1	1-bit color: black and white
2	2-bit color: 4 colors
4	4-bit color: 16 colors
8	8-bit color: 256 colors
16	16-bit color: 32,768 colors
32	32-bit color: 16,777,216 colors

In context:

```
put the colorDepth
-- 8
```

Notes: This property can be tested on both Windows and Macintosh platforms but set only on the Macintosh. The standard default value is the current setting for the host computer's main monitor.

constraint

Elements: sprite(*[whichSprite]*).constraint
            the constraint of sprite *[whichSprite]*

Purpose: This property determines whether a moveable sprite is currently constrained (cannot be moved outside the boundaries of another sprite). To release the constraint on a sprite, set the boundary sprite to 0, or none.

In context: This script limits the movement of the sprite in channel 8 to the dimensions of the sprite (which could be an invisible shape) in channel 14:

```
on enterFrame
    set the constraint of sprite 8 to 14
end
```

Notes: This property can be both tested and set, with the default being FALSE, or 0. If you're constraining a graphic sprite, you'll find that the outside edge corresponds to the sprite's registration; for a shape sprite, the edge is the top-left corner. Settings for a sprite's locH and locV properties will not be applied if they are outside the limits set by the constraining sprite.

See also: The constrainH and constrainV functions and the locH and locV properties.

the controller of member

Elements: the controller of member *[QTmemberRef]*

Purpose: Limited to digital video cast members with the Direct to Stage option enabled, this property determines whether the Stage display of the video includes a controller area (Play, Pause, and Rewind buttons, and so on). It is the script equivalent of selecting Show Controller in the cast member's Info window.

In context: This script line ensures that the playback controls of a digital video cast member are shown on the Stage:

```
member("QuickTime1").controller = 1
```

Notes: Remember that this property won't work unless the digital video cast member has the Direct to Stage option enabled. It can be both tested and set, with the default being 0 (no controller). This property works with QuickTime and QuickTime for Windows, but not with Video for Windows.

See also: The directToStage property.

copyrightInfo

Elements: member(*[SWAmemberRef]*).copyrightInfo
            copyrightInfo of member *[SWAmemberRef]*

Purpose: This property determines the copyright text of a Shockwave Audio (SWA) cast member. The information is available only after the SWA sound begins playing or after the file has been preloaded using the preLoadBuffer command.

In context: This statement displays the SWA file's copyright information in a text field:

```
member("info").text = member("swaJazz").copyrightInfo
```

Notes: This property can be tested but not set.

the cpuHogTicks

Elements: the cpuHogTicks

Purpose: This property has nothing to do with parasites and pork. This property defines the period (expressed in ticks, or 1⁄60 of a second) that Director can reserve, or "hog," processor time before turning it over to the system—which presumably needs it to perform background tasks or to attend to other open applications. The default is 20 ticks. Setting a higher value may improve performance within your Director production but may slow things down elsewhere.

In context:

```
set the cpuHogTicks = 200
```

Notes: Macintosh only. For some applications that require rapid keyboard input (some games, for example), this property may actually slow performance since Director typically checks for multiple keyboard input less frequently than the operating system does.

crop

Elements: member([dvMemberRef]).crop
                 the crop of member [dvMemberRef]

Purpose: This property is limited to digital video cast members and Director movies imported as cast members into other movies. It is equivalent to selecting Framing (Crop/Scale) in the cast member's Properties dialog box.

When the crop of member is TRUE, any resizing of derived sprites on the Stage will crop the video window (only the area defined in the sprite bounding box will show through). If the property is FALSE, resizing the bounding box will deform or scale the video window the fit the new dimensions.

In context:

```
member("QuickTime1").crop = TRUE
```

Notes: This property can be both tested and set.

See also: The center property.

cuePointNames

Elements: member([memberRef]).cuePointNames
                 the cuePointNames of member [memberRef]

Purpose: This property produces a list of names given to internal cue points in cast members. If a cue points exists but is unnamed, an empty string ("") will be returned for that list element.

In context:

```
put the cuePointNames of member "soundtrack"
-- ["hat", "hamster in blender", "cheese"]
```

Notes: Director can interpret the internal cue points of AIFF, WAV, and SWA sounds, and QuickTime movies. SWA files must be already streaming or preloaded using the preLoadBuffer command. Note that this property will not register the internal marker points of Director movies that have been converted to QuickTime movies. For more information about working with internal cue points, see Chapters 19 and 20.

This property can be tested but not set.

See also: The cuePointTimes and mostRecentCuePoint properties and the isPastCuePoint function.

cuePointTimes

Elements: member(*[memberRef]*).cuePointTimes
           the cuePointTimes of member *[memberRef]*

Purpose: This property returns a list of cue points in a particular cast member, in milliseconds, from the starting point of the cast member's source file.

In context:

```
put the cuePointtimes of member "Synch"
-- [0, 4466, 7300, 13000, 17000, 21833]
```

Notes: Director can interpret the internal cue points of AIFF, WAV, and SWA sounds, and QuickTime movies. SWA files must be already streaming or preloaded using the preLoadBuffer command. Note that this property will not register the internal marker points of Director movies that have been converted to QuickTime movies. For more information about working with internal cue points, see Chapters 19 and 20.

This property can be tested but not set.

See also: The cuePointNames and mostRecentCuePoint properties and the isPastCuePoint function.

the currentSpriteNum

Elements: the currentSpriteNum

Purpose: This property provides the channel number of a sprite associated with the most recent event message (such as a mouseDown or mouseWithin event message). It provides a useful shortcut for referring to an onscreen element. The property's value is valid only when the property is used in sprite behaviors and cast member scripts.

In context: This script uses the currentSpriteNum property to make any sprite transparent as soon as it's clicked. It works equally well no matter which sprite it's attached to.

```
on mouseDown
    set the ink of sprite (the currentSpriteNum) to 1
end
```

Notes: This property, while still functional, has been superseded by the spriteNum property. The spriteNum property enables a more objected-oriented approach to writing behaviors.

This property can be tested but not set.

See also: The spriteNum property.

currentTime

Elements: sprite(*[spriteRef]*).currentTime
the currentTime of sprite *[spriteRef]*
the currentTime of sound *[soundRef]*

Purpose: This property returns the total playing time for a particular sound sprite or QuickTime sprite, expressed in milliseconds.

In context:

```
put the currentTime of sprite 2
-- 176
```

Notes: Remember that Shockwave Audio sounds appear in sprite channels even though they play as sounds, so it's best to refer to them by their sprite numbers.

This property can be tested but not set.

cursor

Elements: sprite(*[spriteRef]*).cursor
the cursor of sprite *[spriteRef]*

Purpose: This property determines which cursor appears when the mouse pointer rolls over a given sprite. You can use a standard cursor resource or designate a cast member as a cursor. In addition, you can name a second cast member as the mask of that cursor. To specify a cursor resource, use this format:

sprite(*spriteRef*).cursor = *cursorCode*

Here are the cursor codes:

0	No custom cursor (returns cursor choice to the computer)
-1	Arrow cursor
1	Insertion (I-beam) cursor
2	Crosshair cursor
3	Thick cross (crossbar) cursor
4	Wristwatch cursor (Macintosh only)
4	Hourglass cursor (Windows only)
200	Blank cursor (no cursor is displayed)

To specify a cast member as a cursor (and optional cursor mask), use the following format. Note that square brackets are required to specify the cast members for the cursor.

sprite(*spriteRef*).cursor = [*memberRef, maskMemberRef*]

In context: This line sets the cursor of the sprite in channel 8 to a crossbar:

```
sprite(8).cursor = 3
```

This command returns control of the cursor to the operating system:

```
sprite(8).cursor = 0
```

This command sets the cursor to the cast member in cast slot 17 and names the adjacent cast member as the mask. Note the square brackets.

```
sprite(8). cursor = [17, 18]
```

Notes: This property can be both tested and set, with the default being 0 (no special cursor). To return cursor determination to the host computer, reset the cursor property to 0. You'll note that unless the sprite's ink is set to Matte, the cursor change is performed when the cursor is over the sprite's bounding box rather than over the area of the sprite itself.

See also: The cursor command; also see Chapter 11 for important information on creating custom cursors.

cursorSize

Elements: member([memberRef]).cursorSize
the cursorSize of member [memberRef]

Purpose: This cursor cast member property determines the size of an animated color cursor cast member. Only two values are permitted: 16, for a 16-by-16 pixel cursor; and 32, for a 32-by-32 pixel cursor. Not all Windows video cards can display cursors of both sizes.

In context: This command sets the cursor size for the cursor in cast member 8 to 16 by 16 pixels:

```
member(8).cursorSize = 16
```

Notes: If the bitmaps used to create an animated color cursor are smaller than the designated size, the bitmaps are displayed at full size. If the bitmaps are larger than the designated size, the bitmaps are scaled to the cursorSize setting.

This property can be both tested and set. The default is 16 on the Macintosh and 32 under Windows.

See also: The cursor command.

day

Elements: (*the systemDate*).day
[*dateVariable*].day

Purpose: This property retrieves the number of the day of the month from the systemDate property or other element using the date data type.

In context: This command determines the current day of the month:

```
put the systemDate
-- date(1999, 5, 16)
put (the systemDate).day
-- 16
```

Notes: This property can be both tested and set for variables containing a date data type. It cannot set the systemDate property. It works only with the systemDate property, not the date function.

See also: The month, year, and systemDate properties, and the date function.

defaultRect

Elements: member([*memberRef*]).defaultRect
            the defaultRect of member [*memberRef*]

Purpose: This cast member property determines the default size of sprites created from Flash movie or vector shape cast members. The size will also be reflected in all current sprites created from the members, unless they have had their bounding boxes modified on the Stage. Values are specified as a rect type.

The value for this property is affected by the cast member's defaultRectMode property. Setting a new defaultRect value automatically sets defaultRectMode to #fixed. Setting defaultRectMode to #flash automatically resets the defaultRect value to the size of the cast member as it was originally created.

In context: These commands first check the member's current defaultRect value in the Message window and then set a new value:

```
put member(6).defaultRect
-- rect(0, 0, 80, 62)
member(6).defaultRect = rect(0, 0, 40, 32)
```

Notes: This property can be both tested and set. The default setting is the size of the cast member as it was originally created.

See also: The defaultRectMode and flashRect properties.

defaultRectMode

Elements: member([*memberRef*]).defaultRectMode
            the defaultRectMode of member [*memberRef*]

Purpose: This cast member property determines whether a sprite created from a Flash movie or vector shape cast member is created using the cast member's original size (as it was created) or the size determined by the defaultRect property. The size will also be reflected in all current sprites created from the members unless they have had their bounding boxes modified on the Stage.

Possible values for the property are as follows:

#flash: Sets the defaultRect property to the size at which the cast member was originally created.

#fixed: Allows a value specified by the defaultRect property to be used as the size for sprites.

The default value for defaultRectMode is #flash. Changing the defaultRect property will automatically set the defaultRectMode value to #fixed. Setting defaultRectMode to #flash will automatically reset the defaultRect property to the size of the cast member as it was originally created.

In context: These commands check the defaultRectMode property of a cast member, change the defaultRect value for the cast member, and then check defaultRectMode again:

```
put member(4).defaultRectMode
-- #flash
member(4).defaultRect = rect(0, 0, 40, 80)
put member(4).defaultRectMode
-- #fixed
```

Notes: This property can be both tested and set. It is automatically set to #fixed when defaultRect is set.

See also: The flashRect and defaultRect properties.

depth

Elements:　member([*memberRef*]).depth
　　　　　　　the depth of member [*memberRef*]

Purpose: This property retrieves the current color depth of a given graphic cast member. There are six possible states:

1	1-bit color: black and white
2	2-bit color: 4 colors
4	4-bit color: 16 colors
8	8-bit color: 256 colors
16	16-bit color: 32,768 colors
32	32-bit color: 16,777,216 colors

In context:

```
put the depth of member "Rainbow image"
-- 32
```

Notes: This property can be tested but not set. To change the color depth of a specific cast member, use the Transform Bitmap command on the Modify menu.

the deskTopRectList

Elements:　the deskTopRectList

Purpose: This system property returns a list describing the dimensions of all monitors currently available to the end user (stated as rect coordinates, in pixels).

In context: In this case, there are two available monitors, of equal size:

```
put the deskTopRectList
-- [rect(0, 0, 832, 624), rect(832, 0, 1664, 624)]
```

Notes: This property can be tested but not set.

the digitalVideoTimeScale

Elements: the digitalVideoTimeScale

Purpose: This systemwide property establishes the basic unit of time used for measuring duration during playback of digital video cast members. The default is 60 units per second, equivalent to the standard system tick. Although this setting will produce accurate playback for most digital video, this property enables you to make adjustments for video recorded in a nonstandard fashion. It is recommended that the digitalVideoTimeScale property be a multiple of a member's timeScale property to precisely track the time when the digital video is playing.

In context: These commands check the movie's time scale and a digital video's timeScale property:

```
put the digitalVideoTimeScale
-- 60
put member(3).timeScale
-- 600
```

Notes: This property can be both tested and set, but it must be applied to a movie as a whole (not to individual digital video cast members).

See also: The timeScale property.

digitalVideoType

Elements: member([*memberRef*]).digitalVideoType
            the digitalVideoType of member [*memberRef*]

Purpose: This property returns a symbol indicating the format type of a given digital video cast member. The possible values are #quickTime and #videoForWindows.

In context:

```
put the digitalVideoType of member "TestQT"
-- #quickTime
```

Notes: This property can be tested but not set.

directToStage

Elements: member([*memberRef*]).directToStage
            the directToStage of member [*memberRef*]
            sprite([*spriteRef*]).directToStage
            the directToStage of sprite [*spriteRef*]

Purpose: This cast member and sprite property is limited to elements that can be played direct to stage: digital video, Flash movies, vector shapes, and animated GIF files. It is equivalent to selecting Direct to Stage in the cast member's Properties dialog box. For Flash movies or vector shapes, set the property for the sprite. For Animated GIF files and digital video, set the property for the member.

When the `directToStage` property is TRUE, the sprite will play in the foreground of the Stage, regardless of its position in the score channel layering. Score inks will have no effect on digital video sprites in this state.

If the property is FALSE, the digital video sprite will be treated like any other sprite.

In context:

```
member("QuickTime1").directToStage = TRUE
```

Notes: This property can be both tested and set. In general, setting the Direct to Stage condition (either manually or with Lingo) will improve the playback and performance of the digital video.

dither

Elements: `member([memberRef]).dither`
            `the dither of member [memberRef]`

Purpose: This bitmap cast member property determines whether a bitmap is dithered when it is displayed on the Stage. It has an effect only if the monitor depth is 8 bits or less. If the property is set to TRUE, then dithering occurs for any color in the image that is not in the current palette. If the property is set to FALSE, no dithering occurs, and Director displays colors in the image using the closest color available in the current palette.

In context:

```
member("myPicture").dither = TRUE
```

Notes: The effects of dithering can vary greatly between bitmap images. You need to test each particular image to see whether dithering is appropriate. Since dithering can affect movie performance, you should set this property to TRUE only when necessary.

See also: The `depth` property.

drawRect

Elements: `window [windowName].drawRect`
            `the drawRect of window [windowName]`

Purpose: This property establishes the size and shape of a movie's window—not the intrinsic Stage size, but the size of the window that movie occupies when opened by an `open window` command. The value is a rect data type, and the rectangular coordinates are listed in this order: left corner, top border, right corner, bottom border.

The original rectangle can be determined from the `sourceRect` property of the window.

In context:

```
put the drawRect of window "countdown"
-- rect(0, 0, 96, 100)
```

Notes: This property can be both tested and set. If you use this property to scale an MIAW, you should be aware that field and text members are not scaled along with other elements. Also, scaling an MIAW may affect its performance.

See also: The `rect` function and the `sourceRect` property.

dropShadow

Elements: member(*[memberRef]*).dropShadow
            the dropShadow of member *[memberRef]*

Purpose: This property, limited to field cast members, can be used to set the depth of a drop shadow for the characters of the text of a field. The property can be set to 0 (no drop shadow), or a shadow thickness in pixels can be specified.

In context: This statement sets the shadow of a field 5 pixels from the text itself (to the lower right):

member("Answer field").dropShadow = 5

Notes: This property should not be confused with the boxDropShadow property, which applies the effect not to the characters themselves, but to the field's bounding box as a whole.

duration

Elements: member(*[memberRef]*).duration
            the duration of member *[memberRef]*

Purpose: This property is limited to transitions, digital video, and Shockwave Audio (SWA) cast members. The value returned depends on the type of the cast member.

For transitions, the duration is the same as the setting for Duration in the Transition dialog box. The value is expressed in milliseconds.

For digital video, the duration is the length, in ticks, of the video.

For streaming SWA, the value is the duration of the sound. This value is 0 unless streaming has begun or the sound has been preloaded using the preLoadBuffer command.

In context:

put member (22).duration
-- 150

Notes: This property can be tested for the three cast member types, but it can be set only for transitions.

editable

Elements: member(*[memberRef]*).editable
            the editable of member *[memberRef]*
            sprite(*[spriteRef]*).editable
            the editable of sprite *[spriteRef]*

Purpose: This property, limited to field and text cast members and field sprites, determines whether the cast member can be edited by the end user when it appears on the Stage. For cast members, it is equivalent to manually selecting Editable Text in the cast member's Properties dialog box. This property can be set for a cast member, in which case it applies to all sprites derived from that cast member. When applied to a field sprite, only that sprite is made editable.

In context: This statement overrides a Properties dialog setting and makes a text field editable by the end user:

```
member("Name field").editable = TRUE
```

Notes: This property can be both tested and set, but setting the property for a text sprite has no effect.

the emulateMultiButtonMouse

Elements: the emulateMultiButtonMouse

Purpose: This movie-level property can be used to resolve the inconsistencies inherent in creating movies for the Macintosh (where a mouse is assumed to have a single button) and Windows (where a multiple-button mouse is the rule). When the property is set to TRUE (or 1), a click on the rightmost button of a Windows mouse will be interpreted as the equivalent of a combination Control-mouse click under the MacOS. When set to FALSE (or 0), such a click will be interpreted as a simple mouse click (no different from a click on the left mouse button).

In context: This statement enables the emulateMultiButtonMouse property:

```
the emulateMultiButtonMouse = TRUE
```

Notes: This property can be both tested and set, with the default being 0 (or FALSE).

the enabled of menuItem

Elements: the enabled of menuItem *[item]* of menu *[menuRef]*

Purpose: When you've installed custom menus in a movie, you can use this property to toggle on and off the disabling of menu items. When disabled (FALSE), a menu item will be dimmed and unselectable.

In context: This custom handler (called in the menu script) turns off the sound and then enables the Sound On menu item in the Controls menu:

```
on turnOff
    set the soundEnabled to FALSE
    set the enabled of menuItem "Sound On" of menu "Controls" to TRUE
end
```

Notes: This property can be both tested and set, with the default being TRUE.

See also: The installMenu command, the menu keyword, and the name and number menu properties.

endColor

Elements: member(*[memberRef]*).endColor
             the endColor of member *[VmemberRef]*

Purpose: This property sets the end color for a vector shape's gradient fill. The color is specified as an RGB value. The endColor property has an effect only on closed vector shapes with the fillMode property set to #gradient. The starting color is set with the fillColor property.

In context: These statements set a gradient for a closed vector shape:

```
on setGradient theVector
  if theVector.closed = TRUE then
    theVector.fillMode = #gradient
    theVector.fillColor = rgb(0,0,255)
    theVector.endColor = rgb(0,255,0)
  end if
end
```

Notes: This property can be both tested and set.

See also: The color function and the fillColor, fillMode, fillCycles, and fillDirection properties.

environment

Elements: the environment

 the environment.*[propertyName]*

Purpose: This system property combines a number of other system properties and provides for future developments in Director by allowing other properties to be included. When used without an argument, this property returns a list of all the properties shown below. When used with a *propertyName* argument, only information about that specific property is returned. The list is already growing—the Macromedia documentation lists three properties, but the latest version (7.0.2) lists seven properties:

#ShockMachine: A binary value, with TRUE indicating that the ShockMachine player is installed on the system.

#platform: A string containing the same information as the platform system property, identifying the user's system. The value can be either Macintosh, PowerPC, or Windows,32.

#runMode: A string identifying the mode under which the movie is running. Possible values are Author, Projector, Plugin, and Java Applet.

#colorDepth: An integer specifying the color depth of the monitor that the Stage appears on (1, 2, 4, 8, 16, or 32).

#internetConnected: Values will be determined in the future.

#uiLanguage: A string specifying the language the system uses, such as English.

#productBuildVersion: A string containing information about Director's version number.

In context: These commands show operation under Director 7.0 and then under 7.0.2:

```
put the environment
-- [#shockMachine: 0, #platform: "Windows,32", ¬
  #runMode: "Author", #colorDepth: 16]
put the environment
-- [#shockMachine: 0, #platform: "Windows,32", ¬
  #runMode: "Author", #colorDepth: 16, ¬
  #internetConnected: #unknown, #uiLanguage: "English", ¬
  #productBuildVersion: "51"]
```

See also: The colorDepth, platform, and runMode properties.

eventPassMode

Elements: sprite(*[FspriteRef]*).eventPassMode
the eventPassMode of sprite *[FspriteRef]*
member(*[FmemberRef]*).eventPassMode
the eventPassMode of member *[FmemberRef]*

Purpose: This Flash property determines under what circumstances mouse events are passed to the Flash movie's behaviors. Possible values are as follows:

#passAlways: Always pass mouse events (the default).

#passButton: Pass mouse events only when a button in the Flash movie is clicked.

#passNotButton: Pass mouse events only when a nonbutton object is clicked.

#passNever: Never pass mouse events.

In context: This statement sets the Flash movie's property to receive mouse clicks only on the movie's buttons:

member("birdFlash").eventPassMode = #passButon

Notes: This property can be both tested and set.

See also: The buttonsEnabled property.

the exitLock

Elements: the exitLock

Purpose: This property applies not to movies, but to projector files created from movies. When set to TRUE, it prevents the end user from quitting to the Finder or desktop by pressing the standard key combinations (Control-period, Control-Q, Control-W, or Esc in Windows; or Command-period, Command-Q, or Command-W on the Macintosh). If this property is set to FALSE, the default, the user will be able to quit the projector.

In context:

```
on startMovie
   set the exitLock to TRUE
end startMovie
```

Notes: This property can be both tested and set and has a default setting of FALSE. Since it keeps savvy users from shutting down the program, it's useful for kiosks and other productions that are supposed to run without interruption. However, be sure to script in *some* means of quitting—unless you're willing to restart the computer every time you want to quit.

fieldOfView

Elements: sprite(*[QTVRspriteRef]*).fieldOfView
fieldOfView of sprite *[QTVRspriteRef]*

Purpose: This QTVR sprite property determines the sprite's current field of view. The value is given in degrees.

Notes: This property can be both tested and set.

See also: The pan property and the swing function.

fileName (of castLib)

Elements: castLib *[castRef]*.fileName
            the fileName of castLib *[castRef]*

Purpose: This property specifies the full file name and path name of a Cast database. In the case of internal Casts, the text string returned will be the name and path name of the currently open movie.

In context:

```
put the fileName of castLib "New Controls"
-- "Phils:Director 7:New Controls"
```

Notes: This property can be both tested and set. This property accepts URLs as file names as well as local files. To avoid delays while a file downloads from the Internet, you should use the downLoadNetThing or preLoadNetThing command to retrieve the file before it is needed.

fileName (of member)

Elements: member(*[memberRef]*).fileName
            the fileName of member *[memberRef]*

Purpose: When a cast member is linked to an external file (as opposed to being wholly contained by Director), this property establishes the name (and path name, when applicable) of that file.

In context:

```
on mouseUp
   set the fileName of member "movie" to "The Home ¬
Front:Applications:Director 4.0:Introduction"
end
```

Notes: This property can be both tested and set. Once set, the source file will remain the designated file until the application quits or the property is reset.

This property accepts URLs as file names as well as local files. To avoid delays while a file downloads from the Internet, you should use the downLoadNetThing or preLoadNetThing command to retrieve the file before it is needed.

fileName (of window)

Elements: window *[windowRef]*.fileName
            the fileName of window *[windowRef]*

Purpose: When used in a multiwindow movie, this property determines which movie is displayed in a given window. This is useful when you want the window to bear a different name than the movie, or when you want subsequent movies to play using the same set of window coordinates.

In context: This button script establishes a window named Control, sets its coordinates, designates the movie Countdown to play in the window, and then opens that window:

```
on mouseUp
    set the rect of window "Control" to rect(292, 200, 388, 300)
    set the fileName of window "Control" to "Countdown"
    open window "Control"
end
```

Notes: This property can be both tested and set. This property accepts URLs as file names as well as local files. To avoid delays while a file downloads from the Internet, you should use the downLoadNetThing or preLoadNetThing command to retrieve the file before it is needed.

fillColor

Elements: member(*[memberRef]*).fillColor

Purpose: This vector shape cast member property determines the color used to fill a closed vector shape. The value is specified as an RGB value. The property is applied to the vector shape only if the cast member's fillMode property is set to #solid (in which case, the fill color is defined) or #gradient (in which case, the gradient's start color is defined). If this property is used to define a gradient, the endColor property is used to specify the gradient's ending color.

In context: These statements set a gradient for a closed vector shape:

```
on setGradient theVector
    if theVector.closed = TRUE then
        theVector.fillMode = #gradient
        theVector.fillColor = rgb(0,0,255)
        theVector.endColor = rgb(0,255,0)
    end if
end
```

Notes: This property can be both tested and set.

See also: The color function and the closed, endColor, fillMode, fillCycles, gradientType, and fillDirection properties.

fillCycles

Elements: member(*[memberRef]*).fillCycles

Purpose: This vector shape cast member property determines the number of cycles that the colors in a vector shape's gradient pass through. The value is specified as an integer from 1 (the default) through 7. The property is applied to the vector shape only if the shape is closed and the cast member's fillMode property is set to #gradient.

In context:

member("vShape").fillCycles = 3

Notes: This property can be both tested and set.

See also: The color function and the closed, endColor, fillMode, fillColor, gradientType, and fillDirection properties.

PROPERTIES

fillDirection

Elements: member(*[memberRef]*).fillDirection

Purpose: This vector shape cast member property determines the degree to which the gradient in a filled vector shape is angled. The value is specified as an integer or a floating-point number and returned as a floating-point number. The property is applied to the vector shape only if the shape is closed and the cast member's fillMode property is set to #gradient.

In context: This statement sets the angle of the gradient to 45 degrees.

```
member("vShape").fillDirection = 45
```

Notes: This property can be both tested and set.

See also: The color function and the closed, endColor, fillMode, fillCycles, gradientType, and fillColor properties.

filled

Elements: member(*[memberRef]*).filled
              the filled of member *[memberRef]*

Purpose: This property, limited to shape cast members, indicates whether the specified cast member is presently filled with a pattern or color. When set to TRUE (or 1), the shape is filled. When set to FALSE (or 0), the shape is not filled. The nature of the fill is determined by the member's pattern property.

In context:

```
set the filled of member "Box" = 1
```

fillMode

Elements: member(*[memberRef]*).fillMode

Purpose: This vector shape cast member property determines whether a closed vector shape is filled or not, and if filled, whether the fill is solid or a gradient. The value is specified as a symbol, and allowed values are as follows:

#none: The interior of the shape is transparent.

#solid: The interior of the shape has a single fill color.

#gradient: The interior of the shape uses a gradient between two colors.

In context: These statements set a gradient for a closed vector shape:

```
on setGradient theVector
  if theVector.closed = TRUE then
    theVector.fillMode = #gradient
    theVector.fillColor = rgb(0,0,255)
    theVector.endColor = rgb(0,255,0)
  end if
end
```

Notes: This property can be both tested and set. This property is not applied to open vector shapes, which cannot be filled.

See also: The color function and the closed, endColor, fillColor, fillCycles, gradientType, and fillDirection properties.

fillOffset

Elements: member(*[memberRef]*).fillOffset

Purpose: This vector shape cast member property determines how the center of a gradient is offset within the vector shape. The offset is in pixels, and the value is specified as a point. The property is applied to the vector shape only if the shape is closed and the cast member's fillMode property is set to #gradient.

In context: This statement shifts the offset of a gradient 10 pixels down and 20 pixels to the right:

```
member("vCoffee").fillOffset = point(20,10)
```

Notes: This property can be both tested and set.

See also: The color function and the closed, endColor, fillMode, fillCycles, fillScale, gradientType, and fillColor properties.

fillScale

Elements: member(*[memberRef]*).fillScale

Purpose: This vector shape cast member property determines the scale or spread of a gradient applied to a vector shape. The spread determines how much the colors blend in the gradient. The value is specified as an integer or a floating-point number. The default is 100. A value of 0 creates a fill with a sharp break between the start and end colors (no mixing or blending). The property is applied to the vector shape only if the shape is closed and the cast member's fillMode property is set to #gradient.

In context: This handler starts a vector shape as two solid colors and then gradually blends the colors:

```
on scaleit theVector
   repeat with x = 1 to 100
     theVector.fillScale = x
     updateStage
   end repeat
end
```

Notes: This property can be both tested and set.

See also: The color function and the closed, endColor, fillMode, fillCycles, fillOffset, gradientType, and fillColor properties.

firstIndent

Elements: *[chunkExpression]*.firstIndent

Purpose: This property sets the indentation applied to the first word of paragraphs in a chunk portion of a text cast member. The default value is 0 (no indent). Setting the value to an integer greater that 0 increases the indentation. A value less than 0 decreases the indentation, resulting in a hanging indent.

In context: This statement indents the first five paragraphs of the cast member:

```
member(6).paragraph[1..5].firstIndent = 5
```

Notes: This property can be both set and tested. For a hanging indent, you must set the leftIndent property before setting the firstIndent property.

See also: The leftIndent and rightIndent properties.

fixedLineSpace

Elements: *[chunkExpression]*.fixedLineSpace

Purpose: This property sets the height of lines in a chunk portion of a text cast member. The default value is 0 (normal line height). Setting the value to an integer greater than 0 increases the line height by the specified number of pixels. A value less than 0 decreases the spacing between lines.

In context: This statement increases the line spacing in the first five paragraphs of the cast member:

```
member(6).paragraph[1..5].fixedLineSpacing = 3
```

Notes: This property can be both tested and set.

See also: The bottomSpacing and topSpacing properties.

fixedRate

Elements: sprite(*[spriteRef]*).fixedRate
the fixedRate of sprite *[spriteRef]*
member(*[memberRef]*).fixedRate
the fixedRate of member *[memberRef]*

Purpose: This property determines the frame rate at which a Flash movie or Animated GIF file will be displayed. The value specified is an integer, and the default is 15. The playback rate is applied only if the element's playBackMode property is set to #fixed.

In context: This statement increases the frame rate by 5:

```
sprite(15).fixedRate = sprite(15).fixedRate + 5
```

Notes: This property can be both tested and set. Applying the property to a cast member affects all sprites derived from the cast member. Setting the property for a sprite affects only the one sprite.

See also: The playBackMode property.

the fixStageSize

Elements: the fixStageSize

Purpose: You can use this property to override the intrinsic Stage sizes saved with individual movies. When this property is set to TRUE, all subsequent movies will open with Stage dimensions matching the current movie, despite their "actual" dimensions.

In context:

```
the fixStageSize = TRUE
```

Notes: This property can be both tested and set, with the default being 0, or FALSE. It cannot be used to modify the size of a movie currently playing and has no effect on Movies in a Window (MIAWs).

flashRect

Elements: member([*memberRef*]).flashRect
             the flashRect of member [*memberRef*]

Purpose: This property returns the size of a Flash movie or vector shape as it was originally created. The value is given as a rect data type. This property is useful for determining the original size after the size has been changed using the defaultRect property. Setting a Flash movie or vector shape cast member's defaultRectMode property to #flash will reset the default size of the element to the value determined by flashRect.

In context: This script tests whether the currently specified size of a vector shape (as specified by the defaultRect property) is the original size. If it is not, the default size is restored to the original value. Note that using the defaultRectMode setting to modify the size setting leaves the defaultRect property intact (but not currently used).

```
if member(4).rect <> member(4).flashRect then
   member(4).defaultRectMode = #flash
end if
```

Notes: This property can be tested but not set. Linked Flash cast members must have their header loaded into memory for the property's value to be valid.

See also: The defaultRect and defaultRectMode properties.

flipH

Elements: sprite([*spriteRef*]).flipH
             the flipH of sprite [*spriteRef*]

Purpose: This sprite property determines whether a sprite's image is flipped horizontally (around its vertical axis) from the cast member's original orientation. The cast member's registration point is used as the point around which the flip occurs. A value of TRUE means the image is flipped.

In context: This command flips the sprite's image if it is not already flipped:

```
sprite("vDog").flipH = TRUE
```

Notes: This property can be both tested and set. The rotation and skew of the sprite are not affected by a flip.

See also: The flipV, rotation, and skew properties.

flipV

Elements: sprite(*[spriteRef]*).flipV
the flipV of sprite *[spriteRef]*

Purpose: This sprite property determines whether a sprite's image is flipped vertically (around its horizontal axis) from the cast member's original orientation. The cast member's registration point is used as the point around which the flip occurs. A value of TRUE means the image is flipped.

In context: This command flips the sprite's image if it is not already flipped:

sprite("vDog").flipV = TRUE

Notes: This property can be both tested and set. The rotation and skew of the sprite are not affected by a flip.

See also: The flipH, rotation, and skew properties.

the floatPrecision

Elements: the floatPrecision

Purpose: This property establishes the number of decimal places used in floating-point numbers. It does not affect the results of calculations—just the amount of detail displayed.

In context: These statements show the different results of the same calculation (of a tangent of an angle) with this property set to two different values:

```
put the floatPrecision
-- 4
put tan (302*19.7)
-- -0.9823
set the floatPrecision to 8
put tan (302*19.7)
-- -0.98233246
```

Notes: The maximum value of the floatPrecision is 14. This property can be both tested and set, with the default being 4.

font

Elements: member(*[memberRef]*).font
the font of member *[memberRef]*

Purpose: This property, limited to field cast members, can be used to determine or set the typeface used in a field. If multiple typefaces are present in the field, this property will change them all to the specified font. The font should be named in quotation marks and spelled in the same way it appears in your system's Font menu.

In context:

```
set the font of member "Answer field" to "Times New Roman"
```

Notes: This property can be applied to a field cast member only if that field contains at least one character (even just a space character).

fontSize

Elements: `member([memberRef]).fontSize`
           `the fontSize of member [memberRef]`

Purpose: This property, limited to field cast members, can be used to set the size of the type used to display the given cast member on the Stage. The value given is that of the first type size used in the first line of the field. When used to set a field's font size, it resizes all text in the field to that value.

In context:

```
put the fontsize of member "Answer field"
-- 14
```

Notes: This property can be both tested and set, but the field must contain some text (even just a single space character) to be effective.

fontStyle (text members)

Elements: `[chunkExpression].fontStyle`

Purpose: This property sets the style of the font used to display all or a portion of the text in a text cast member on the Stage. The available style parameters are `#plain`, `#bold`, `#italics`, `#underline`, `#shadow`, `#outline`, and `#extend` (you'll need to place them in a list). The additional parameter `#condense` is also available on MacOS systems.

To reset styling to plain formatting, use `#plain`.

In context: The first command sets the display of words five through eight of the cast member's text to both underlined and italic. The second command sets the entire text of the cast member to plain.

```
member(9).word[5..8].fontStyle = [#underline,#italic]
member("Answer Text").fontStyle = [#plain]
```

Notes: This property can be both tested and set. It will have no effect if the text cast member is empty, but it will work if there's even a single space character in the field.

This is a new property for text cast members. Although you can use the old syntax (non–dot syntax) for some chunk expressions, it doesn't work for all chunk expressions. You should stick to the dot syntax when setting this property. Note that the styles must be included as symbols in a list, which is different than when you set `fontStyle` for field cast members (which use a string).

fontStyle (field members)

Elements: `the fontStyle of member [memberRef]`

Purpose: This property sets the style of the font used to display all or a portion of the text in a field cast member on the Stage. The available style parameters are `plain`, `bold`, `italics`, underline, shadow, outline, and extend (you'll need to place them inside quotation marks). The additional parameter condense is also available on MacOS systems.

To reset styling to plain formatting, use plain.

In context: This script sets the display of the cast member's text to both underline and italic:

```
set the fontStyle of member "Surf's Up" to "underline, italic"
```

Notes: This property can be both tested and set.

Although you can use the new dot syntax for some chunk expressions, it doesn't work uniformly. You should stick to the old syntax when setting this property for chunk expressions of fields. Note that the styles must be included a comma-separated text string, which is different than when you set fontStyle for text cast members (which uses a list).

foreColor of member

Elements: member([*memberRef*]).foreColor
the foreColor of member [*memberRef*]
sprite [*memberRef*].foreColor
the foreColor of sprite [*memberRef*]

Purpose: This property establishes the foreground color of text, field, and button cast members and sprites and 1-bit bitmap sprites. The value is expressed as the number the color occupies in the active color palette.

In context:

```
put the foreColor of member 1
-- 15
member ("Push Me").foreColor = 255
```

Notes: This property can be both tested and set. Bitmaps with a color depth greater than 1-bit yield unpredictable results; see the color property instead.

frame

Elements: sprite([*flashRef*]).*frame*
the frame of sprite [*flashRef*]

Purpose: This property sets or retrieves the frame number of a Flash movie being played.

In context: This handler checks to see if the Flash movie has reached the last frame. If it has, the first frame is displayed again.

```
on checkFlash
   if sprite(7).frame >= member("sky").frameCount then
      sprite(7).frame = 1
   end if
end checkFlash
```

Notes: This property can be both tested and set.

See also: The frameCount and state properties.

frameCount

Elements: member(*[flashRef]*).frameCount
          the frameCount of member *[flashRef]*

Purpose: This Flash cast member property retrieves the number of frames in a Flash cast member.

In context: See the frame property.

Notes: This property can be tested but not set.

See also: The frame and state properties.

the frameLabel

Elements: the frameLabel

Purpose: This property determines (as a text string) the name of the marker label for the current frame. If there is no marker label, the value is 0.

In context:

```
put the frameLabel
-- "Clyde"
```

Notes: This property can be both tested and set (it can be set during Score-modification scripting only).

the framePalette

Elements: the framePalette

Purpose: This property determines the color palette assigned to the current frame by returning a numeric identifier. If the palette occupies its own cast slot, that cast number will be given. If the palette is integrated into Director (such as System-Win or Vivid), this property returns a negative number corresponding to one of the following codes:

-1	System palette (System-Mac)
-102	System palette (System-Win)
-101	System palette (System-Win Director 4)
-2	Rainbow
-3	Grayscale
-4	Pastels
-5	Vivid
-6	NTSC
-7	Metallic
-8	Web 216

In context: This statement in the Message window shows that the currently active frame is associated with the custom palette in cast slot 21:

```
put the framePalette
-- 21
```

See also: The puppetPalette command.

PROPERTIES

frameRate

Elements: `member([memberRef]).frameRate`
`the frameRate of member [memberRef]`

Purpose: This property, specific to digital video and Flash movie cast members, can be used to establish the playback speed of the digital video or to check the rate of a Flash movie. For digital video, it is equivalent to selecting the Play Every Frame option in the cast member's Properties dialog box and setting the rate. These options can be communicated with the following codes:

1 to 255   A number in this range sets the rate in frames per second.

0 or -1   Plays at the normal setting.

-2   Plays as quickly as the host computer allows.

For Flash movies, the value of the property is the frame rate at which the movie was originally created.

In context:

```
set the frameRate of member "QuickTime4" to -2
```

Notes: This property can be both tested and set for digital videos, but for Flash movies it can only be tested.

See also: The `fixedRate`, `movieRate`, `movieTime`, and `playBackMode` properties.

the frameScript

Elements: `the frameScript`

Purpose: This property determines the number of the cast member used as the frame behavior attached to the current frame. If there is no behavior, the value is 0. However, this property seems to apply only to scripts placed in the primary internal Cast. Scripts placed elsewhere are identified with a number that, although consistent, does not directly correspond to the cast slot number.

In context: This command retrieves the cast member number of the frame behavior for the current frame:

```
put the frameScript
-- 22
```

Here's how this property identifies a script in cast slot 5 of a secondary internal Cast:

```
put the frameScript
-- 131078
```

Notes: This property can be both tested and set (it can be set during score-modification scripting only).

the frameSound1

Elements: `the frameSound1`

Purpose: This property determines the sound currently residing in the first sound channel of the current frame (identified by cast member number). If the channel is empty, the value is 0.

In context: This script establishes that the sound currently playing in channel 1 occupies slot 15 in the currently open Cast:

```
put the frameSound1
-- 15
```

Notes: This property can be both tested and set (it can be set during score-modification scripting only).

See also: The puppetSound command.

the frameSound2

Elements: the frameSound2

Purpose: This property determines the sound currently residing in the second sound channel of the current frame (identified by cast member number). If the channel is empty, the value is 0.

In context: This script establishes that the sound currently playing in channel 1 occupies slot 14 in the currently open Cast:

```
put the frameSound2
-- 14
```

Notes: This property can be both tested and set (it can be tested during score-modification scripting only).

See also: The puppetSound command.

the frameTempo

Elements: the frameTempo

Purpose: This property determines (as a number representing frames per second) the tempo setting for the current frame. If the tempo channel contains a delay statement (rather than a speed), that statement will not be reported—you'll get the prevailing speed instead.

In context:

```
put the frameTempo
-- 15
```

Notes: This property can be both tested and set (it can be set during score-modification scripting only).

See also: The puppetTempo command.

the frameTransition

Elements: the frameTransition

Purpose: If a transition has been assigned to the frame currently active in the Score, it will have its own cast slot assigned to it in the internal Cast. This property will return that transition's slot number. If there is no transition, it will return 0.

PROPERTIES

In context: This script reports that the transition in the current frame resides in cast slot 3:

```
put the frameTransition
-- 3
```

Notes: This property can be tested at any time, but it can be set during a score-generation Lingo session only.

See also: The puppetTransition command.

the frontWindow

Elements: the frontWindow

Purpose: Use this property to determine which window is in the foreground and has the focus at the current time.

In context:

```
if the frontWindow = "Boss Coming" then tell window ¬
   "Alien Game" to go frame "hide"
```

Notes: This property can be tested but not set. You may receive a VOID message when you're authoring within Director, which means the foreground window is a Tool Palette or another editing windoid.

See also: The activeWindow property, the on activateWindow and on deactivateWindow handlers, and the moveToFront command.

globals

Elements: the globals

Purpose: This system property contains a special property list of all non-void global variables. Each element in the list has the variable name as the property and the variable's value as the property value. The information contained in the list is the same as displayed by the showGlobals command, but the information can be accessed as a list. Although global variables cannot be modified by means of the list, the following list commands can be used to retrieve information: count, getAt, getPropAt, getProp, and getAProp.

In context: These commands use the Message window to collect information about the current global variables:

```
put the globals -- no useful info
-- (the globals)
put (the globals).count
-- 5
put getPropAt(the globals, 5)
-- #version
put getAProp(the globals, #version)
-- "7.0.2"
```

Notes: The globals list can be tested but not set. The list always contains at least the property #version, Director's version number. Using the command put the globals in the Message window does not display the list; use showGlobals instead.

See also: The showGlobals and clearGlobals commands.

gradientType

Elements: member(*[memberRef]*).gradientType

Purpose: This vector shape cast member property determines the gradient type of a vector shape's gradient. The value is specified as a symbol: #linear or #radial. The property is applied to the vector shape only if the shape is closed and the cast member's fillMode property is set to #gradient.

In context:

member("vShape").gradientType = #radial

Notes: This property can be both tested and set.

See also: The color function and the closed, endColor, fillMode, fillColor, fillCycle, and fillDirection properties.

height (of member)

Elements: member(*[memberRef]*).height
            the height of member *[memberRef]*

Purpose: This property returns the height of a specified bitmap or shape cast member, expressed in pixels.

In context:

put the height of member "Scary clown"
-- 623

Notes: This property can be tested but not set.

height (of sprite)

Elements: sprite(*[spriteRef]*).height
            the height of sprite *[spriteRef]*

Purpose: This sprite property determines the height of a specified sprite in the current frame, expressed in pixels. It can be applied to bitmap, animated GIF, Flash movie, vector shape, and shape sprites.

In context:

sprite(7).height = 100

Notes: This property can be tested for all cast types but cannot be used to set button and field text cast members.

As a result of some of the changes in Director, the width and height properties are not always accurate. Using the height and width properties in conjunction with the rect property should give an accurate indication of a sprite's size when it's drawn on the stage:

sprite (*[spriteRef]*).rect.width
sprite (*[spriteRef]*).rect.height

See also: The width, rect, and stretch properties.

PROPERTIES

hilite

Elements: member([*memberRef*]).hilite
                the hilite of member [*memberRef*]

Purpose: This property is limited to standard check boxes and radio buttons (those created with the Tools window). When such a button is selected, the property is set to 1, or TRUE. When the button is deselected (clicked off), the property is 0, or FALSE. This property is useful for testing for user feedback and for turning buttons on and off with Lingo.

In context: This frame script carries out an action when a certain button has been activated, including removing the highlighting from another button:

```
on idle
  if member("No Clowns").hilite = TRUE then
    member("More Clowns").hilite = FALSE
    go to frame "Clowns gone"
  end if
end
```

Notes: This property can be both tested and set.

hotSpot

Elements: member([*CursorMemberRef*]).hotspot
                the hotspot of member [*CursorMemberRef*]

Purpose: This property determines the hot area of an animated color cursor. The hot area, or hotspot, is the 1 pixel in the cursor that is used to determine such things as where a mouse click took place, the coordinates of the cursor's current location, and when a rollover is taking place. For a standard arrow cursor, it makes sense to have the hotspot at the tip of the arrow. For other cursors, other locations may make more sense. The value is specified as a point, with point(0,0) being the upper-left corner.

In context: This script checks the size of a cursor and then sets the hotspot at the cursor's approximate center:

```
if member("STrek").cursorSize = 16 then
  member("STrek").hotSpot = point(8,8)
else
  member("STrek").hotSpot = point(16,16)
end if
```

Notes: This property can be both tested and set. The default value is point(0,0).

See also: The cursor and cursorSize properties and the cursor command.

hotSpotEnterCallback

Elements: sprite([*spriteRef*]).hotSpotEnterCallback
                hotSpotEnterCallback of sprite [*spriteRef*]

Purpose: When a cursor enters a QTVR sprite's visible hotspot, a message is generated, allowing actions to be taken. The hotSpotEnterCallback property determines the name of the message (and the name of the handler that is called). The QTVR sprite receives the message first. If a handler is not found in the sprite's behaviors, the message is passed down the event chain. The message has two arguments: the me parameter and the ID of the hotspot that the cursor entered. To prevent a message from being sent, set this property to 0 (which is also the default).

In context:

```
sprite(7).hotSpotEnterCallback = "HotSpot Sound"
```

Notes: This property can be both tested and set.

See also: The hotSpotExitCallback, nodeEnterCallback, nodeExitCallback, and triggerCallback properties.

hotSpotExitCallback

Elements: hotSpotExitCallback of sprite *whichQTVRSprite*

Purpose: When a cursor exits a QTVR sprite's visible hotspot, a message is generated, allowing actions to be taken. The hotSpotExitCallback property determines the name of the message (and the name of the handler that is called). The QTVR sprite receives the message first. If a handler is not found in the sprite's behaviors, the message is passed down the event chain. The message has two arguments: the me parameter and the ID of the hotspot that the cursor is leaving. To prevent a message from being sent, set this property to 0 (which is also the default).

In context: This command prevents a message from being sent when the cursor leaves a QTVR hotspot:

```
sprite(7).hotSpotEnterCallback = 0
```

Notes: This property can be both tested and set.

See also: The hotSpotEnterCallback, nodeEnterCallback, nodeExitCallback, and triggerCallback properties.

HTML

Elements: member([*memberRef*]).HTML

Purpose: The HTML property of a text cast member is the version of the cast member text formatted with basic HTML tags.

In context: These two put commands show the difference between the ASCII version of text contents and the HTML version:

```
put member(3).text
-- "This is the time to go to the store.
When is my break?
Hello world!"
put member(3).HTML
-- "<html>
<head>
<title>Untitled</title>
</head>
```

```
<body bgcolor="#FFFFFF">
This is the time to go to the store.<br>
When is my break?<p>
Hello world!</body>
</html>
"
```

Notes: This property can be both tested and set.

See also: The importFileInto command and the RTF property.

hyperlink

Elements: [*chunkExpression*].hyperlink

Purpose: When you create a hyperlink in a text cast member, you designate a string (called the hyperlink string) that is the argument sent to a hyperLinkClicked handler. This property determines the contents of that hyperlink string.

To determine the current hyperlink string for an existing hyperlink, the first character of *chunkExpression* must be within the link range in the cast member. If it isn't, then the value is an empty string ("").

When you set this property, the designated *chunkExpression* becomes a new hyperlink. The value you set is the hyperlink string for the new hyperlink. You cannot have overlapping hyperlinks. If the new hyperlink is even partially within the range of an old hyperlink, then the old hyperlink will be removed.

Setting a hyperlink to an empty string ("") will remove it.

In context: This command determines the hyperlink string for a hyperlink that contains character 56 in the text cast member:

```
put member(24).char[56].hyperlink
-- "link2"
```

This command creates a new hyperlink from words 20 through 25 and defines the hyperlink string as "link4":

```
member(24).word[20..25].hyperlink = "link4"
```

Notes: This property can be both tested and set.

See also: The hyperlinks, hyperlinkRange, and hyperlinkState properties.

hyperlinkRange

Elements: [*chunkExpression*].hyperlinkRange

Purpose: Use this text cast member property to determine the range of characters that make up a hyperlink. The first character in *chunkExpression* determines which hyperlink is specified. The property's value is a linear list with two elements. The first element in the list is the character number of the first character in the hyperlink; the second element is the last character in the hyperlink.

In context: This command retrieves the range of a hyperlink that contains the 89th character in the text:

```
put member(14).char[89].hyperlinkRange
-- [82, 104]
```

Notes: This property can be tested but not set. If *chunkExpression*'s first character is not in a hyperlink, the value returned is [0, 0].

See also: The hyperlink, hyperlinks, and hyperlinkState properties.

hyperlinks

Elements: [chunkExpression].hyperlinks

Purpose: Use this text cast member property to determine the range of characters for each hyperlink in the portion of the text cast member defined by *chunkExpression*. The property's value is a linear list, where each list element is a hyperlink range. Each range is a list containing two elements. The first element in the list element is the character number of the first character in the hyperlink; the second element is the last character in the hyperlink.

In context: This command shows all of the hyperlink ranges in an entire text cast member:

```
put member("geology").hyperlinks
-- [[1, 12], [43, 50], [105, 197]]
```

Notes: This property can be tested but not set.

See also: The hyperlink, hyperRange, and hyperlinkState properties.

hyperlinkState

Elements: [chunkExpression].hyperlinkState

Purpose: This text cast member property determines the current state of a hyperlink. The hyperlink in this case is the hyperlink that contains the first character of *chunkExpression*.

Recognized values for the state are #normal, #active, and #visited (although other values are allowed). When the state is #normal, the hyperlink text is displayed in blue and underlined (the default hyperlink state). When the state is #active or #visited, the hyperlink text is displayed in red and underlined, indicating that the hyperlink has been accessed. This property is not automatically set when a hyperlink is clicked; you need to set it in the hyperlinkClicked handler.

In context: This behavior plays a movie when a hyperlink is clicked. The state is set to #active while the movie plays and is set to #visited when the movie returns.

```
property spriteNum
on hyperLinkClicked me, link, range
   num = sprite(spriteNum).memberNum
   member(num).char[range[1]].hyperlinkState = #active
   play movie link
   member(num).char[range[1]].hyperlinkState = #visited
end
```

Notes: This property can be both tested and set.

See also: The hyperlink, hyperlinks, and hyperlinkRange properties.

PROPERTIES

the idleHandlerPeriod

Elements: the idleHandlerPeriod

Purpose: This property determines how much time passes before Director declares an idle event and sends a message to the appropriate handlers. When this property is set to 0, the idle event happens as frequently as possible (the main limitation is the processor speed of the machine running the application). When it is set to integer *x*, then *x* ticks must pass before an idle event occurs. For example, setting the property to 2 means that 2 ticks must pass between idle events (or the idle events may occur up to 30 times per second).

The idle events occur between the enterFrame and exitFrame events. If there is sufficient time between these events for the time specified by the idleHandlerPeriod to elapse, one or more idle events occur (assuming that other actions, such as script execution, do not prevent the movie from being idle).

Time is measured in ticks ($\frac{1}{60}$ of a second).

In context: To ensure that the system waits at least $\frac{1}{10}$ of a second between idle event declarations, use this statement:

```
set the idleHandlerPeriod = 6
```

See also: The on idle handler, the idleLoadDone function, and the idleLoadMode, idleLoadPeriod, idleLoadTag, and idleReadChunkSize properties.

the idleLoadMode

Elements: the idleLoadMode

Purpose: This property determines when the preLoad and preLoadMember commands attempt to load cast members during idle periods. These are the possible values:

0   No idle loading at all.
1   Only between frames, if processor time is available.
2   Only when an idle event has been declared.
3   As often as possible (when doing so would not affect playback performance).

In context: This statement turns off all preloading:

```
set the idleLoadMode = 0
```

See also: The on idle handler, the idleLoadDone function, and the idleHandlerPeriod, idleLoadPeriod, idleLoadTag, and idleReadChunkSize properties.

the idleLoadPeriod

Elements: the idleLoadPeriod

Purpose: This property affects the time (in ticks) that the application waits before servicing the idle load queue. If this property is set to 0 (the default), Director services the load queue as frequently as possible.

In context:

```
set the idleLoadPeriod to 60
```

See also: The on idle handler, the idleLoadDone function, and the idleLoadMode, idleHandlerPeriod, idleLoadTag, and idleReadChunkSize properties.

the idleLoadTag

Elements: the idleLoadTag

Purpose: This property is assigned to cast members that are queued for loading during idle time. You can group cast members for preloading by assigning them a tag number. This tag can be any number; Director won't prioritize idle load groups, but you can use the idleLoadDone function to find out whether all members sharing a given tag have been loaded.

In context:

```
set the idleLoadTag to 42
put the idleLoadTag
-- 42
```

See also: The on idle handler, the idleLoadDone function, and the idleLoadMode, idleLoadPeriod, idleHandlerPeriod, and idleReadChunkSize properties.

the idleReadChunkSize

Elements: the idleReadChunkSize

Purpose: This property determines the maximum number of total bytes of cast members that Director can load during each idle queue service period.

In context:

```
set the idleReadChunkSize to 3072
```

Notes: This property can be both tested and set. The default value is 32K.

See also: The on idle handler, the idleLoadDone function, and the idleLoadMode, idleLoadPeriod, idleLoadTag, and idleReadChunkSize properties.

imageEnabled

Elements: sprite(*[spriteRef]*).imageEnabled
the imageEnabled of sprite *[spriteRef]*
member(*[memberRef]*).imageEnabled
the imageEnabled of member *[memberRef]*

Purpose: This property determines whether a Flash movie or vector shape's sprite images are visible. By default (TRUE), the image is visible. Setting the value of the property to FALSE will prevent the image from appearing. Setting the property for a sprite affects only the sprite's image. Setting the property for a cast member affects all sprites and resets each sprite's imageEnabled sprite property.

In context: These commands make a Flash sprite visible if it has completely streamed into memory (assuming it was made invisible previously):

```
if member(FlashVar).percentStreamed = 100 then
   member(FlashVar).imageEnabled = TRUE
   go to frame "showFlash"
else
   go to the frame
end if
```

Notes: This property can be both tested and set.

ink

Elements: sprite(*[spriteRef]*).ink
the ink of sprite *[spriteRef]*

Purpose: You can use this property to find and change the score-level ink effect applied to a given sprite in the current frame. That ink is expressed in the following codes:

0	Copy
1	Transparent
2	Reverse
3	Ghost
4	Not Copy
5	Not Transparent
6	Not Reverse
7	Not Ghost
8	Matte
9	Mask
32	Blend
33	Add Pin
34	Add
35	Subtract Pin
36	Background Transparent
37	Lightest
38	Subtract
39	Darkest
40	Lighten
41	Darken

In context: This script makes a light-colored sprite disappear on the Stage by changing its ink effect to Transparent:

```
on mouseUp
   puppetSprite 7, TRUE
   sprite(7).ink = 1
   updateStage
end mouseUp
```

Notes: This property can be both tested and set.

interval

Elements: member(*[CursorRef]*).interval
the interval of member *[CursorRef]*

Purpose: This cursor cast member property determines the interval between each frame of an animated color cursor. It has the same effect as setting the Interval field in the Cursor Properties Editor dialog box while authoring. The interval is given in milliseconds (ms); the default is 100 ms. A value of -1 prevents cursor animation and displays the first frame of the cursor.

In context: These handlers in a sprite behavior speed up the cursor animation for cursor Spin while the cursor is over the sprite:

```
on mouseEnter
   member("Spin").interval = 50
end
on mouseLeave
   member("Spin").interval = 150
end
```

Notes: This property can be both tested and set.

See also: The cursor command and the cursor, cursorSize, and hotSpot properties.

invertMask

Elements: member(*[QTmemberRef]*).invertMask
               the invertMask of member *[QTmemberRef]*

Purpose: When a mask is used with a QuickTime video, by default the video appears through the black pixels of the mask only. By setting the invertMask property to TRUE, you can instead display the video through the white pixels.

In context: This command sets a QuickTime video to appear through the white pixels of a mask:
```
member("QTsurfing").invertMask = TRUE
```

Notes: This property can be both tested and set.

See also: The mask property.

isVRMovie

Elements: member(*[memberRef]*).isVRMovie
               isVRMovie of member *[memberRef]*
               sprite(*[spriteRef]*).isVRMovie
               isVRMovie of sprite *[spriteRef]*

Purpose: This property can be used to determine whether a sprite or cast member is a QTVR movie (TRUE) or not (FALSE).

Notes: This property can be tested but not set.

the itemDelimiter

Elements: the itemDelimiter

Purpose: An item delimiter is a special character used to separate items in a chunk expression. The comma is the most common delimiter (and the default), but this property can be used to change it to another character. You can use items to manipulate a chunk expression in the same manner you might manipulate a simple database.

In context: These commands change the item delimiter to the colon, enabling easy parsing of a path name on a Macintosh system (on Windows, use the backslash). Each element in the path is separated by a colon, making each element an item. When using the itemDelimiter

PROPERTIES

property in this fashion, it's a good idea to save the value and then reset the property when you are done.

```
saveIt = the itemDelimiter
set the itemDelimiter = ":"
myPath = the moviePath
put myPath
-- "The Home Front:Applications:Director"
put item 2 of myPath
-- "Applications"
the itemDelimiter = saveIt
```

Notes: This property can be both tested and set. Since most of the time you will use the comma as a delimiter, remember to set this property back to ", " after using it in special circumstances (as in the preceding script).

kerning

Elements: member([memberRef]).kerning

Purpose: This property determines whether text in a text cast member is automatically kerned when the contents of the cast member are changed. The default is TRUE, providing automatic kerning. Setting kerning to FALSE prevents kerning. Kerning also depends on the value of the kerningThreshold property, which specifies the font size at which kerning takes place.

In context:

```
member("Title Text").kerning = TRUE
```

Notes: This property can be both tested and set.

See also: The kerningThreshold property.

kerningThreshold

Elements: member([memberRef]).kerningThreshold

Purpose: This property determines the font size at which kerning can occur in a text cast member. The default is 14, meaning any text of font size 14 or greater can be kerned. For kerning to actually take place, the kerning property must be set to TRUE. You can set kerningThreshold to a different point size (an integer) to enable or restrict kerning.

Notes: This property can be both tested and set.

See also: The kerning property.

keyboardFocusSprite

Elements: set the keyboardFocusSprite = [textSpriteNum]

Purpose: This property determines which editable text or field sprite has the focus for keyboard input. This is similar to using the Tab key to move the focus to an editable sprite, except that the insertion point is not modified and text is not automatically selected. The value is the number of the sprite. A value of 0 means no sprite has the focus, although the user can still change the focus and edit the sprites. A value of -1 returns keyboard focus control to the Score.

In context: This command gives the keyboard focus to sprite 5:

```
set the keyboardFocusSprite = 5
```

See also: The autoTab and editable properties.

the keyDownScript

Elements: the keyDownScript

Purpose: This property designates which Lingo script is to be executed as a primary event handler when the keyDown event occurs. If that script consists of a single line, it can be attached to this property. If the script is more complex, it should be placed in a custom handler, and this property should be used to call that handler.

In context: This script provides a shortcut to access a Help file: If the user presses the question mark (?) key while holding down the Command key, playback will branch to a section marked "Help".

```
on startMovie
    set the keyDownScript to "zutAlors"
end startMovie

on zutAlors
    if (the key = "?") and (the commandDown = TRUE) then play "Help"
end
```

Notes: This property can be both tested and set. To disable a primary event handler, set this property to "", or EMPTY. Remember that primary event handlers such as the one specified by the keyDownScript property will normally pass the message down the event hierarchy after execution. If you want to interrupt the passing-on of the event, use the stopEvent command in the script.

See also: The keyUpScript property and the on keyDown handler.

the keyPressed

Elements: the keyPressed

Purpose: This property identifies which key was last pressed by the end user. If it is called when no key has been pressed, an empty string is returned. What's the difference between the property the keyPressed and the function the key? The property will be updated when keys are pressed while playback is in a repeat loop, whereas the function will not be updated.

In context:

```
on mouseWithin
    if the keyPressed = "x" then
    beep 3
    end if
end
```

Notes: This property can be tested but not set. Note that the character must be cited as a single-character text string (use quotation marks).

the keyUpScript

Elements: the keyUpScript

Purpose: This property designates which Lingo script is to be executed as a primary event handler when the keyUp event occurs. If that script consists of a single line, it can be attached to this property. If the script is more complex, it should be placed in a custom handler, and this property should be used to call that handler.

In context: This script keeps track of the number of keys that have been pressed during the user session by placing a count of keyUp events in a global variable called gKeys:

```
on startMovie
    global gKeys
    gKeys = 0
    set the keyUpScript to "keyCount"
end startMovie

on keyCount
    global gKeys
    gKeys = gKeys + 1
end
```

Notes: This property can be both tested and set. To disable a primary event handler, set this property to "", or EMPTY. Remember that primary event handlers such as the handler designated by the keyUpScript property will normally pass the message down the event hierarchy after execution. If you want to interrupt the passing-on of the event, use the stopEvent command in the script.

See also: The keyDownScript property and the on keyUp handler.

the labelList

Elements: the labelList

Purpose: This property returns a listing of all markers used in the currently open movie. The value is a string, not a list, and each marker is placed on a line of its own. The marker elements are in the same order in which they reside in the Score.

In context:

```
put the labelList
-- "Attractor
Introduction
User Entry
"
```

See also: The label and marker functions and the frameLabel property.

lastChannel

Elements: the lastChannel

Purpose: This movie property retrieves the number of channels in a movie. This value is the number set in the Movie Properties dialog box, not the number of channels actually in use.

In context: This statement displays the number of channels of the current movie in the Message window:

```
put the lastChannel
-- 120
```

Notes: This property can be tested but not set.

the lastFrame

Elements: the lastFrame

Purpose: This property retrieves the number of the last occupied frame in the current movie. You can use it to obtain a quick frame count in the Message window, or to write navigational scripts that jump to the end of the movie even when the movie is under construction, with a fluctuating number of frames.

In context:

```
put the lastFrame
```

left

Elements: sprite(*[spriteRef]*).left
the left of sprite *[spriteRef]*

Purpose: This property gives the onscreen location of the left edge of the given sprite's bounding box, measured in pixels from the left edge of the Stage.

In context: This Message window call determines that the left edge of the sprite in channel 4 is 89 pixels away from the edge:

```
put the left of sprite 4
-- 89
```

Notes: This property can be both tested and set.

leftIndent

Elements: *[chunkExpression]*.leftIndent

Purpose: This property sets the left indentation applied to the text in a chunk portion of a text cast member. The default value is 0 (no indent). Setting the value to an integer greater that 0 increases the indentation by that number of pixels. Negative values are treated as 0.

In context: This statement sets the left indent for the first five paragraphs of the cast member to 10 pixels:

```
member(6).paragraph[1..5].leftIndent = 10
```

PROPERTIES

Notes: This property can be both tested and set. For a hanging indent, you must set the leftIndent property to specify an indent and then set the firstIndent property to a negative number.

See also: The firstIndent and rightIndent properties.

lineCount

Elements: member([*memberRef*]).lineCount
              the lineCount of member [*memberRef*]

Purpose: This property applies to field cast members only. This property returns the number of lines of text currently contained by that cast member—not measured by number of carriage returns but by the cast member's width settings in the Field window.

In context:

```
put the lineCount of member "Gettysburg Address"
-- 87
```

Notes: This property can be tested but not set.

lineDirection

Elements: member([*memberRef*]).lineDirection

Purpose: This property applies only to shapes created with the Tool Palette. It determines the direction of the shape's slope. Two values are possible: If the shape slopes up to the right, the value is 1; if the shape slopes down to the right, the value is 0. Shapes with no slope, such as rectangles or ovals, have a value of 0.

In context:

```
put member("longLine").lineDirection
-- 0
```

Notes: This property can be both tested and set.

lineHeight

Elements: member([*memberRef*]).lineHeight
              the lineHeight of member [*memberRef*]

Purpose: Use this property to determine the height of a line of a field cast member—not the height of the text itself, but the height of the spacing between lines. In desktop publishing programs (and among typographers), this measurement is known as *leading*.

In context: These commands determine the line height and a specific line of a field:

```
put the lineHeight of member "Declaration"
put the lineHeight of line 12 of member("Declaration")
```

Notes: This property can be both tested and set—but if you use it to set line heights, you may find that they revert to original settings once the movie closes. For a modification that will persist throughout the movie, use the lineHeight of member in a movie-level on prepareMovie handler instead.

See also: The alignment, font, fontSize, and fontStyle properties, and the lineHeight function.

lineSize

Elements: sprite(*[spriteRef]*).lineSize
the lineSize of sprite *[spriteRef]*
member(*[memberRef]*).lineSize
the lineSize of member *[memberRef]*

Purpose: This property is specific to geometric shape and line sprites created with the Tool Palette. It establishes the thickness of the border of the sprite, expressed in pixels. If there is no border, the property returns 0.

In context: This button script indicates that a shape has been clicked by giving it a border 5 pixels thick:

```
on mouseUp
    sprite (the clickOn).lineSize = 5
end
```

Notes: This property can be both tested and set.

linked

Elements: member(*[memberRef]*).linked
the linked of member *[memberRef]*

Purpose: This property determines whether a Flash movie or Animated GIF file is stored in the Director Cast or as a linked file. If the element is stored as a linked file, the cast member's pathName property must be set to point to the location of the movie. A value of TRUE indicates that the element is stored as a linked file; FALSE indicates that the element is stored internally.

Notes: This property can be both tested and set.

See also: The fileName and pathName cast properties.

loaded

Elements: member(*[memberRef]*).loaded
the loaded of member *[memberRef]*

Purpose: This property determines whether a given cast member is currently loaded into RAM (that is, is immediately available for display on the Stage). This is expressed as 1 (TRUE) or 0 (FALSE).

In context: This statement indicates that Container is not loaded in memory.

```
put the loaded of member "Container"
-- 0
```

Notes: This property can be tested but not set.

See also: The preLoad and unLoad commands, the freebytes and ramNeeded functions, and the size property.

loc

Elements: sprite(*[spriteRef]*).loc
                the loc of sprite *[spriteRef]*

Purpose: This property returns or establishes (as a single-point coordinate) the location of the given sprite's registration point.

In context: This line moves the sprite 10 pixels down and right from its current position:

```
sprite(7).loc = sprite(7).loc + 10
put sprite(7).loc
-- point(38, 176)
```

Notes: This property can be both tested and set.

See also: The bottom, top, height, width, rect, locV, and locH properties.

locH

Elements: sprite(*[spriteRef]*).locH
                the locH of sprite *[spriteRef]*

Purpose: This property establishes the horizontal location of the given sprite, expressed in terms of the distance (in pixels) from the sprite's registration point to the left of the Stage.

In context:

```
put the locH of sprite 2
-- 234
```

Notes: This property can be both tested and set.

locV

Elements: sprite(*[spriteRef]*).locV
                the locV of sprite *[spriteRef]*

Purpose: This property establishes the vertical location of the given sprite, expressed in terms of the distance (in pixels) from the sprite's registration point to the top of the Stage.

In context:

```
put the locV of sprite 2
-- 182
```

Notes: This property can be both tested and set.

the locZ of sprite

Elements: sprite(*[spriteRef]*).locZ

Purpose: This sprite property can be used to move a sprite forward in the Stage's layering of sprites without having to resort to modifying the channels used. Each sprite is considered to have a dynamic Z-order, which determines when one sprite overlays another—sprites with a lower Z-order number are obscured by sprites in the same location with a higher Z-order number. By default, the Z-order is the same number as a sprite's channel number.

You can set a sprite's `locZ` property to give it a higher (or lower) Z-order number and allow it to be overlayed on top of sprites in higher-numbered channels. The `locZ` property can have values ranging from negative 2 billion to 2 billion. If two sprites have the same `locZ` value, the channel number determines which sprite is on top.

In context: These handlers in a sprite's behavior switch the sprite that is displayed with one normally hidden behind it. The `locZ` values used are arbitrary, but they are large and small enough to ensure that the original sprite is moved back in the `locZ` order when the cursor moves over it and that it is in front again when the mouse leaves the sprite.

```
on mouseEnter
    sprite(12).locZ = -100
end
on mouseLeave
    sprite(12).locZ = 100
end
```

Notes: This property can be both tested and set.

How sprites are layered can determine how mouse clicks are interpreted. Using `locZ` to move a sprite behind a second sprite may prevent the first sprite from receiving mouse clicks and other mouse events.

See also: The `locH` and `locV` properties.

loop

Elements: `sprite([FLashSpriteRef]).loop`
             `the loop of sprite [FlashSpriteRef]`
             `member ([memberRef]).loop`
             `the loop of member [memberRef]`

Purpose: When this property is TRUE, a Flash movie, sound, or digital video will play over again (loop) when the end is reached. When this property is FALSE, the element will play to the end and then stop. Setting this property to TRUE is equivalent to selecting the Loop option in the cast member's Properties dialog box.

For sprites, this property can be applied to Flash movies only.

In context: This handler is executed when a GoOn button is clicked. The script ensures that the Flash movie finishes playing before moving on to the next frame. The `loop` property is turned off to ensure that the Flash movie doesn't restart when the end is reached.

```
on GoOnClicked
    member("loopFlash").loop = FALSE
    repeat while member("loopFlash").percentStreamed < 100
        updateStage
    end repeat
    go to the frame + 1
end goOnClicked
```

Notes: This property can be both tested and set.

loopBounds

Elements:
```
sprite([QTspriteRef]).loopBounds
the loopBounds of sprite [QTspriteRef]
```

Purpose: This QuickTime sprite property allows looping to be set for only a portion of a QuickTime movie. The property's value is a list: The first element in the list is the start point, and the second element is the end point. Both points are integers specifying a time, in ticks (1/60 of a second), in the video. Both time points must be within the range of the video, and the start point must be before (less than) the end point. Otherwise, the loopBounds property is ignored. Also, the loopBounds property is ignored if the movie's loop property is set to FALSE.

In context: This command sets a QuickTime sprite's looping start time to 4 seconds and the looping end time to 9 seconds:

```
sprite(9).loopbounds = [60*4, 50*9]
```

Notes: This property can be both tested and set; the default setting is [0,0].

If you set loopBounds while a QuickTime movie is playing and the movie is currently past the end point being set, the movie will continue to the end and then loop back to the movie's beginning. Otherwise, the loop points will take effect immediately.

See also: The loop property.

margin

Elements:
```
member([memberRef]).margin
the margin of member [memberRef]
```

Purpose: This property, which is limited to field cast members, determines the margin space surrounding the text in the cast member's bounding box. The default is 0.

In context: These commands give a field a bounding box and then set a 4-pixel clear area between the field text and the bounding box:

```
member("Answer field").border = 2
member("Answer field").dropShadow = 2
member("Answer field").margin = 4
```

Notes: This property can be both tested and set.

mask

Elements:
```
member([QTmemberRef]).mask = [memberRef]
the mask of member [QTmemberRef] = [memberRef]
```

Purpose: This property allows you to designate a cast member as a mask for a QuickTime video cast member. The QuickTime element's directToStage property must be set to TRUE for the mask to be applied. The mask cast member must be a 1-bit bitmap (black and white). By default, the video appears through the mask's black pixels, but this can be changed using the invertMask property. Always set the QuickTime cast member's mask property before any sprite is displayed. Altering the mask property while the video is playing can have unpredictable results.

In context: This frame behavior specifies a mask for a QuickTime cast member and designates the white areas of the mask as the areas through which the video will appear. Note that this script is executed in a prepareFrame handler, so the QuickTime sprite is not yet displayed.

```
on prepareFrame
    member(5).mask = member("Stained Glass")
    member(5).invertMask = TRUE
end
```

Notes: This property can be both tested and set. To remove a mask, set the mask property to 0.

Director aligns the mask's registration point with the QuickTime cast member's registration point (which is always the top-left corner). For this reason, you will generally also want to set the registration point of a mask cast member to its upper-left corner. If you resize a QuickTime sprite, the mask is not affected, so you may need to supply a different mask for a resized QuickTime sprite.

See also: The invertMask property.

media

Elements: member([*memberRef*]).media
              the media of member *[memberRef]*

Purpose: This property is difficult to interpret but handy to use. It returns a unique code that identifies a particular cast member in the application's RAM; it has nothing to do with the media *type* of the cast member itself. Since it represents not an absolute value but a temporary location in memory, this code can change when you modify the cast member or move it from one slot to another.

Rather than attempting to decode the code, use it as a means of copying cast members via Lingo. By treating it as a settable property rather than a function, you can make copying (and overwriting) easy.

In context: The first two put statements show the actual results of this function; note that although the cast members were in fact identical, they return separate codes. The last statement copies the contents of cast slot 14 in the currently active cast to slot 15. In such instances, the two cast members will return identical media codes until one or the other is modified.

```
put the media of member 12
-- (media 2fe809e)
put the media of member 15
-- (media 2fe80f8)
member(14).media = member(15).media
```

Notes: This property is fairly RAM intensive, since it requires a new slice of memory each time it's invoked. For that reason, you might want to use it only while authoring (keep it out of projector files and Shockwave movies). Use multiple sprite derivations from a single cast member or set the member sprite property whenever possible.

See also: The ilk function and the type property.

PROPERTIES

mediaReady

Elements: member(*[memberRef]*).mediaReady
the mediaReady of member *[memberRef]*
sprite(*[spriteRef]*).mediaReady
the mediaReady of sprite *[spriteRef]*

Purpose: Is it ready for prime time? That's what this property—useful only for streaming movies or cast files—determines. If a file is currently being streamed from a network environment, this property will report whether a specified cast member has been downloaded and is ready for deployment. If it is, the property will return 1, or TRUE; if not, it will return 0, or FALSE.

In context: This script line plays a frame only if a key cast member has been successfully downloaded from a streamed-media movie. If it hasn't, the playback head will loop to the current frame.

```
on exitFrame
    if member("star").mediaReady = 1 then
        go to frame "Starring Role"
    else
        go to the frame
    end if
end
```

Notes: This property can be tested but not set. You can set movies to be streamed by checking the Play While Downloading Movie box or Show Placeholders box in the Movie Playback Properties dialog box under the Modify menu.

member

Elements: sprite(*[spriteRef]*).member
the member of sprite *[spriteRef]*

Purpose: This property identifies the cast member from which a specified sprite has been derived. It will return the cast slot number and the number of the source cast, but not the name (if the cast member has a name). The member property is similar to the memberNum property, although memberNum does not specify the castLib.

You can specify a new member for a sprite using the member or castLib keyword.

In context: These commands check the member used for a sprite and then set the sprite's member:

```
put the member of sprite 4
-- (member 4 of castLib 1)
sprite(4).member = member("hello")
sprite(4).member = member("hello") of castLib("Sounds")
sprite(4).member = member("hello", "Sounds")
```

Notes: This property can be both tested and set.

Possibly the most common problem encountered by Macromedia's technical support people relates to the setting of a sprite's member and castLib. The preferred syntax is as follows:

```
sprite(x).member = member(whichMem, whichCastLib)
```

The following syntax is also allowed:

```
sprite(x).member = member(whichMem) of castLib(whichCastLib)
sprite(x).member = member whichMem of castLib whichCastLib
```

The following syntax is *not* allowed (note the missing parenthesis for castLib):

```
sprite(x).member = member(whichMem) of castLib whichCastLib
```

memberNum

Elements: sprite(*[spriteRef]*).memberNum
      the memberNum of sprite *[spriteRef]*

Purpose: Use this property to retrieve or change the source cast member of a designated sprite. If you also need to change the castLib, use the member property.

In context: This script animates a button cast member when the button is clicked, by switching it with an adjacent cast member (a pushed-down version) and making a button-click sound:

```
on mouseDown
    currSprite = the ClickOn
    thisOne = sprite(currSprite).memberNum
    sprite(currSprite).memberNum = thisOne + 1
    puppetSound 2, "Switch"
    updateStage
end mouseDown
```

Notes: This property can be both tested and set.

the memorySize

Elements: the memorySize

Purpose: This property retrieves the amount of RAM allocated to Director (or to a projector file) when it was launched. On the Macintosh, this RAM allocation can be set by modifying the Get Info box of the application in the Macintosh Finder. Under Windows, this property gives the total memory available for the system. The value is expressed in bytes; to convert to kilobytes, divide by 1024.

In context:

```
put the memorySize
-- 66519040
```

PROPERTIES

milliSeconds

Elements: the milliSeconds

Purpose: This system property returns the amount of time that has passed since the computer was started. The value is given in milliseconds (¹/₁₀₀₀ of a second). This value is retrieved from the host computer and not tracked by Director, so the accuracy of the value depends on the host machine and its operating system. This property is similar to the older `ticks` property, which returns the time in ticks (¹/₆₀ of a second). Both properties are useful for writing your own timer functions.

In context: These statements check the time and, a few moments later, check it again:

```
put the milliseconds
-- 15893296
put (the milliseconds)/1000
-- 15915
```

Notes: This property can be tested but not set.

See also: The `ticks` and `timer` properties and the `time` function.

missingFonts

Elements: member([*memberRef*]).missingFonts

Purpose: This property provides a list of the names of all fonts that are used in a text cast member but which are missing from the system. Using this information, you can switch fonts when your program is running by using the `substituteFont` command.

Notes: This property can be tested but not set.

See also: The `substituteFont` command.

modal

Elements: window([*windowRef*]).modal
              the modal of window [*windowRef*]

Purpose: This property determines whether the movie in the specified window can respond to elements external to the window (such as handlers residing in another movie currently playing). When the `modal of window` is set to 1 (or TRUE), the movie in the window is "sealed" and will ignore external elements. When this property is set to 0 (or FALSE), the movie will respond to such elements. Generally, you make a window modal when you want to force users to interact with a window and to prevent users from accessing other elements until they do. Always provide a means for the user to take any necessary action and then close the window.

In context:

```
window ("Settings").modal = TRUE
```

Notes: This property can be both tested and set, with the default being 0, or FALSE.

In authoring, as at other times, if you make a window modal, you won't be able to interact with it unless you have provided a means within the window to do so. Remember that you can always close a modal window by using Control-Alt-period (Windows) or Command-period (Macintosh).

modified

Elements: member(*[memberRef]*).modified
the modified of member *[memberRef]*

Purpose: This property can be used to determine whether the given cast member has been modified since it was loaded in the current movie. If it has, this property returns 1 (or TRUE); if it hasn't, it returns 0 (or FALSE).

In context: This statement demonstrates that a cast member has indeed been modified:

```
put the modified of member 117
-- 1
```

Notes: This property is useful for text fields and other elements that may be modified by the end user. You can write scripts that retrieve and retain those modifications if this property is TRUE. This property can be tested but not set.

month

Elements: (*the systemDate*).month
[dateVariable].month

Purpose: This property retrieves the number of the month from the systemDate property or other element using the date data type.

In context: This command returns the current month:

```
put the systemDate
-- date( 1999, 5, 16 )
put (the systemDate).month
-- 5
```

Notes: This property can be both tested and set for variables containing a date data type. It cannot set the systemDate property. It works only with the systemDate property, not the date function.

See also: The day, year, and systemDate properties.

mostRecentCuePoint

Elements: sprite(*[spriteRef]*).mostRecentCuePoint
the mostRecentCuePoint of sprite *[spriteRef]*
sound *whichSound*.mostRecentCuePoint
the mostRecentCuePoint of sound *whichSound*

Purpose: This property documents the most recent internal cue point passed in a sprite derived from a cast member containing internal cues (for example, sound files and QuickTime movies). The value is an integer.

In context:

```
put sprite(7).mostRecentCuePoint
-- 3
```

Notes: This property can be tested but not set. If no cue points are encountered, the value is 0.

motionQuality

Elements: sprite([*QTVRspriteRef*]).motionQuality
               motionQuality of sprite [*QTVRspriteRef*]

Purpose: This sprite property determines the codec quality used when a QTVR sprite is clicked and dragged by the user. The value is a symbol, and the allowable values are #minQuality, #maxQuality, and #normalQuality.

In context: This statement sets the motion quality to the maximum:

```
sprite(5).motionQuality = #maxQuality
```

Notes: This property can be both tested and set.

mouseChar

Elements: the mouseChar

Purpose: When the mouse is rolled over a field sprite, this property returns the number of the character over which the cursor is positioned. Numbering begins at the first character of the text in the field cast member. If the mouse is not currently over a field sprite (or over the border of the field), this property returns –1.

In context: This field sprite behavior highlights the character the mouse is over:

```
property spriteNum
on mouseWithin
    num = sprite(spriteNum).memberNum
    hilite member(num).char[the mouseChar]
end
```

Notes: This property can be tested but not set.

See also: The mouseItem, mouseWord, and mouseLine properties.

mouseDown

Elements: the mouseDown

Purpose: This system property determines whether the mouse button is currently being pressed. It is a binary function, returning 1 (or TRUE) if the mouse button is down, and 0 (or FALSE) if it is not.

In context: This script lets the user skip to another location by holding down the mouse button:

```
on enterFrame
    if the mouseDown = TRUE then go to "Trestles"
end
```

Notes: This property can be tested but not set.

mouseDownScript

Elements: the mouseDownScript

Purpose: This property designates a primary event handler script to be executed when the mouseDown event occurs. If that script consists of a single line, it can be attached to this property. If the script is more complex, it should be placed in a custom handler, and this property should be used to call that handler.

In context: This script keeps track of the number of times the mouse has been clicked during the user session by placing a count of mouseDown events in a global variable called gMouse:

```
on startMovie
   global gMouse
   gMouse = 0
   set the mouseDownScript to "clickCount"
end startMovie
```

```
on clickCount
   global gMouse
   gMouse = (gMouse +1)
end
```

Notes: This property can be both tested and set. To disable a primary event handler, set this property to "", or EMPTY. Remember that primary event handlers such as the handler designated by the mouseDownScript property will normally pass the message down the event hierarchy after execution. If you want to interrupt the passing-on of the event, use the stopEvent command in the script.

the mouseH

Elements: the mouseH

Purpose: This system property and function returns the current horizontal location of the cursor, expressed in terms of pixels from the left edge of the Stage. The mouseH property is useful for checking whether the mouse is over a specific area of the Stage or a sprite.

In context: The first command shows the mouse's horizontal location in the Message window. The second command moves a sprite to the horizontal location of the cursor.

```
put the mouseH
-- 178
sprite(3).locH = the mouseH
```

See also: The mouseV and mouseLoc properties.

the mouseItem

Elements: the mouseItem

Purpose: When the mouse is rolled over a field sprite, this system property returns the number of the item over which the cursor is positioned. If the mouse is not currently over a field sprite or is over a nontext portion of the field, such as the border, this property returns -1. By default, a field item is any chunk separated by commas (though this can be changed using the itemDelimiter property). For example, if the field sprite contains "eenie, meenie, minie, moe", then placing the mouse over minie will return the integer 3.

In context: This script turns the first item in a text field into the equivalent of a button:

```
on mouseUp
    userChoice = the mouseItem
    if userChoice = 1 then go "Wax Up"
end
```

Notes: This property can be tested but not set.

See also: The itemDelimiter, mouseChar, mouseWord, and mouseLine properties.

mouseLevel

Elements: sprite(*[QTspriteRef]*).mouseLevel
the mouseLevel of sprite *[QTspriteRef]*

Purpose: This QuickTime sprite property determines how Director passes mouse clicks on a QuickTime sprite. This property can be applied to all QuickTime elements, including QTVR, which may have different requirements than standard QuickTime digital video. Allowable values are as follows:

#controller: Only mouse clicks on the controller are passed to QuickTime. Mouse clicks on other areas of the sprite are passed to other Lingo handlers. This is the standard behavior for QuickTime sprites other than QTVR.

#all: All mouse clicks on the sprite are passed to QuickTime. No clicks pass to other Lingo handlers.

#none: No mouse clicks on the sprite are passed to QuickTime. Director responds to all mouse clicks.

#shared: All mouse clicks on the sprite are passed to QuickTime and then to other Lingo handlers. This is the default value for QTVR.

Notes: This property can be both tested and set.

See also: The hotSpotId and triggerCallback properties.

the mouseLine

Elements: the mouseLine

Purpose: When the mouse is rolled over a field sprite, this system property returns the number of the line over which the cursor is positioned. If the mouse is not currently over a field sprite or is over a nontext portion of the field, such as the border, it returns -1. A line consists of any range of text followed by a return delimiter.

In context:

```
put the mouseLine
-- 8
lineVar = the mouseLine
```

Notes: This property can be tested but not set.

See also: The mouseChar, mouseWord, and mouseItem properties.

[handwritten note: "loop itenVar = the mouseLine will detect the mouseline of the current field you click."]

PROPERTIES

the mouseLoc

Elements: the mouseLoc

Purpose: This property contains the current position of the mouse as a Director point, with the horizontal component listed first and then the vertical component. The point values are the number of pixels from the Stage's upper-left corner.

In context: This statement centers a sprite's registration point on the current location of the mouse:

```
sprite(4).loc = the mouseLoc
```

Notes: This property can be tested but not set.

See also: The mouseH and mouseV properties.

the mouseMember

Elements: the mouseMember

Purpose: When the mouse is over a sprite, this system property returns the cast number of the sprite's source cast member. If the mouse is not currently over a sprite, it returns Void. Unless the sprite ink is set to Matte, the entire bounding box of the sprite is used. The mouseMember property can also be used to assign the cast member of the sprite currently underneath the cursor to a variable.

In context:

```
put the mouseMember
-- (member 4 of castLib 1)
spriteVar = the mouseMember
```

Notes: This property can be tested but not set.

See also: The member, memberNum, mouseChar, mouseWord, mouseLine, and mouseItem properties and the rollOver function.

mouseOverButton

Elements: sprite (*[spriteRef]*).mouseOverButton
        the mouseOverButton of sprite *[spriteRef]*

Purpose: This Flash sprite property is set to TRUE if the mouse cursor is over a button in a Flash movie sprite. If it isn't, the value is set to FALSE.

In context: This Flash sprite behavior sets the animated color cursor Spin to spinning rapidly when the mouse is over a Flash button:

```
property spriteNum
on mouseWithin
    if sprite(spriteNum).mouseOverButton = TRUE then
      member("Spin").interval = 50
    else member("Spin").interval = 100
end
```

Notes: This property can be tested but not set.

PROPERTIES

the mouseUp

Elements: the mouseUp

Purpose: This system property determines whether the mouse button is currently being pressed. The opposite of the mouseDown, it returns 1 (or TRUE) if the mouse button is up, and 0 (or FALSE) if it is down.

In context: This script lets the user skip to another location by holding down the mouse button:

```
on enterFrame
    if the mouseUp = FALSE then go to "Secret Spot"
end
```

Notes: This property can be tested but not set.

See also: The on mouseUp handler and the mouseUpScript property.

the mouseUpScript

Elements: the mouseUpScript

Purpose: This property designates the primary event handler for the mouseUp event. If that script consists of a single line, it can be attached to this property. If the script is more complex, it should be placed in a custom handler, and this property should be used to call that handler.

In context: This script provides a shortcut to access a Help file: If the user presses the question mark (?) key while clicking the mouse, playback will branch to a section marked "Help".

```
on startMovie
    the mouseUpScript = "zutAlors"
end startMovie

on zutAlors
    if the commandDown = TRUE then go to "Help"
end
```

Notes: This property can be both tested and set. To disable a primary event handler, set this property to "", or EMPTY. Remember that primary event handlers such as the handler designated by themouseUpScript property will normally pass the message down the event hierarchy after execution. If you want to interrupt the passing-on of the event, use the stopEvent command in the script.

the mouseV

Elements: the mouseV

Purpose: This system property and function returns the current vertical location of the cursor, expressed in terms of pixels from the top edge of the Stage. The mouseV property is useful for moving a sprite to the vertical position of the cursor or checking whether the mouse is over specific areas of the Stage or a sprite.

In context:

```
put the mouseV
-- 480
sprite(14).locV = the mouseV
```

See also: The mouseH and mouseLoc properties.

the mouseWord

Elements: the mouseWord

Purpose: When the mouse is rolled over a field sprite, this system property returns the number of the word over which the cursor is positioned. If the mouse is not currently over a field sprite or is over a nontext area of a field sprite, such as the border, this property returns -1. For example, if the text sprite contains "eenie, meenie, minie, moe," then placing the mouse over the word "moe" will return the integer 4.

In context: This field sprite behavior highlights the word in a field that the mouse is over:

```
property spriteNum
on mouseWithin
   num = sprite(spriteNum).memberNum
   hilite member(num).word[the mouseWord]
end
```

Notes: This property can be tested but not set.

See also: The mouseItem, mouseChar, and mouseLine properties.

moveableSprite

Elements: sprite([*whichSprite*]).moveableSprite
             the moveableSprite of sprite [*whichSprite*]

Purpose: This property establishes whether the end user can move a given sprite on the Stage. It is equivalent to choosing the Moveable option in the Score or Sprite Inspector—with the added benefit that you can turn the option on and off under Lingo control. Setting the property to TRUE makes the sprite moveable, and setting it to FALSE prevents the user from moving the sprite.

In context: This sprite behavior makes the sprite moveable if the Control key is down when the mouse moves over the sprite:

```
property spriteNum
on mouseEnter
   if the controlDown = TRUE then
      sprite(spriteNum).moveableSprite = TRUE
   end if
end mouseEner
```

Notes: This property can be both tested and set.

PROPERTIES

the movieAboutInfo

Elements: the movieAboutInfo

Purpose: This property retrieves the information set in the About field of the Movie Properties dialog box. Macromedia says that this property is for future enhancements to Shockwave, but you can use it now as you see fit.

In context: This statement retrieves the movieAboutInfo information in the Message window:

```
put the movieAboutInfo
-- "I wondered what this was for."
```

Notes: This property can be tested but not set.

See also: The movieCopyrightInfo property.

the movieCopyrightInfo

Elements: the movieCopyrightInfo

Purpose: This property retrieves the information set in the Copyright field of the Movie Properties dialog box. Macromedia says that this property is for future enhancements to Shockwave, but you can use it now as you see fit.

In context: This statement retrieves the movieCopyrightInfo information in the Message window:

```
put the movieCopyrightInfo
-- "Copyright Peachpit, Panmedia, and MEL Co."
```

Notes: This property can be tested but not set.

See also: The movieAboutInfo property.

the movieFileFreeSize

Elements: the movieFileFreeSize

Purpose: This property determines the amount of space in a Director movie that is currently used (but not necessary) as a result of changes to cast members and castLibs. This space is basically an artifact resulting from the way Director stores the movie. Using the Save and Compact (or Save As) options on Director's File menu will eliminate this basically wasted space. The amount is expressed in bytes.

In context:

```
put the movieFileFreeSize
-- 9438
```

Notes: When the Save and Compact command is used on a Director movie, all this free space is eliminated; on such a movie, this function returns 0.

See also: The movieFileSize function.

the movieFileSize

Elements: the movieFileSize

Purpose: This property determines the amount of file space a Director movie currently occupies on the storage medium (hard disk and so on). It is expressed in bytes.

In context:

```
put the movieFileSize
-- 20144
```

Notes: This property's value does not reflect changes made while authoring after the last time the movie was saved.

See also: The movieFileFreeSize function.

the movieName

Elements: the movieName

Purpose: This property returns the name of the open movie (the root movie, as opposed to movies playing in windows).

In context:

```
put the movieName
-- "Odyssey Part 2"
```

Notes: This property does not include any path information.

See also: The moviePath property.

the moviePath

Elements: the moviePath

Purpose: This property returns the path name of the folder containing the active root movie (the movie playing on the Stage, rather than movies in windows).

In context: These statements display possible moviePath values in the Message window for a Macintosh system and a Windows system:

```
put the moviePath -- Macintosh
-- "DD CD-ROM:DD Tutorial Movies:"
put the moviePath -- Windows
-- "E:\Demystified\Projects\"
```

Notes: The @ operator provides a comparable path name that is system independent.

See also: The movieName property and the @ operator.

movieRate

Elements: sprite(*[spriteRef]*).movieRate
            the movieRate of sprite *[spriteRef]*

Purpose: This property is limited to digital video cast members. It determines the style of playback when the cast member is displayed on the Stage. There are three basic states for this property:

0   Stops playback of the digital video entirely.

1   Plays at the normal forward rate.

-1   Plays the file in reverse.

Other values are also allowed, with reservation. For example, a value of -.5 plays the file in reverse at half speed, and a value of 2 plays the file at double speed. Playing at nonstandard speeds may exceed the ability of the system to display every frame, causing frames to be skipped or dropped.

In context: This statement causes the movie to play at normal speed, but in reverse:

set the movieRate of member "QuickTime1" = -1

Notes: This property can be both tested and set.

movieTime

Elements: sprite(*[spriteRef]*).movieTime
            the movieTime of sprite *[spriteRef]*

Purpose: This property is limited to digital video sprites. It specifies the current time of the digital video. It can be used to determine the amount of time a digital video sprite has been playing thus far or to set a new time location in the video. The value is expressed in ticks (1/60 of a second).

In context:

put the movieTime of sprite 5
-- 3030

Notes: This property can be both tested and set.

See also: The duration property.

movieXtraList

Elements: the movieXtraList

Purpose: This property retrieves a list of all Xtras included in the Movie Xtras dialog box: either the default set or the set as modified by you. The list is a linear list, but each element in the list is a property list. Here is a simple example of a list element:

[#name: "Sound Import Export.x32"]

In this case, the only property is the #name property.

If an Xtra has been marked as Download If Needed in the Movie Xtras dialog box, the syntax is a bit more complicated:

```
[#name: "TextXtra.x32", #packageUrl:
"http://download.macromedia.com/pub/shockwave/
xtras/TextAsset/TextAsset, #packageFiles:
[[#fileName: "Text Asset.x32", #version: "7.0r198"]
[#fileName: "TextXtra.x32", #version: "7.0r198"]]]
```

This specification has the additional properties #packageUrl, which specifies the location to go to to retrieve the file, and #packageFiles, itself a property list giving the file name and version.

In context: Run this statement for yourself in the Message window to see information about your Xtras:

```
put movieXtraList
```

Notes: This property can be tested but not set.

See also: The xtraList property.

the multiSound

Elements: the multiSound

Purpose: Use this property to determine whether the host computer is capable of playing multichannel sound. For Windows, this requires a multichannel sound card. For the Macintosh, it should be standard. This property returns TRUE if the system can play multichannel sound; otherwise, it returns FALSE.

In context:

```
put the multiSound
-- 1
```

Notes: This property can be tested but not set.

name (of castLib)

Elements: castLib(*[castLibRef]*).name
          the name of castLib *[castLibRef]*

Purpose: This property determines (as a text string) the name of the Cast database with the given castLib number. Each new Cast (whether internal or external) is given a castLib number, usually in the order in which the Cast is created.

In context:

```
put castLib(2).name
-- "Extra cast"
```

Notes: This property can be both tested and set. For the default internal cast, the value returned is Internal unless it has been changed.

See also: The number (of castLib) and number (of castLibs) properties.

PROPERTIES

name (of member)

Elements: member(*[memberRef]*).name
                the name of member *[memberRef]*

Purpose: This property can be used to retrieve, establish, or change the name given to a cast member in the Cast database. If the cast member has no name, this property returns 0. By default, this is the name you give a cast member in the Cast window or Cast Member Properties dialog box.

In context: These commands check, change, and then recheck a cast member's name:

```
put member(19).name
-- "CurrentScore"
member("CurrentScore").name = "Old Score"
put the name of member 19
-- "Old Score"
```

Notes: This property can be both tested and set.

See also: The number member property.

the name (of menu)

Elements: the name of menu *[number]*

Purpose: The numerical order of menus depends on their positions in the cast member for the current menu (as installed by installMenu). This property can be used to retrieve the menu names by referring to that numerical order. These names are the names of menus that appears in the menu bar. An error results if no menu has been installed.

In context:

```
put the name of menu 1
-- "Sound"
```

Notes: This property can be tested but not set. Menus are not supported in Shockwave.

See also: The installMenu command and the name (of menuItem) and number of menus properties.

the name (of menuItem)

Elements: the name of menuItem *[item name or number]* ¬
                of menu *[menu name or number]*

Purpose: This property retrieves or modifies the name of a specific item on a specific menu.

In context: This script changes the name of a menu item when the volume is turned all the way down. An error results if no menu has been installed.

```
on mouseUp
    if the soundLevel = 0 then
    set the name of menuItem "Volume" of menu "Sound" to "Muting On"
    end if
end mouseUp
```

Notes: This property can be both tested and set. Menus are not supported in Shockwave.

See also: The installMenu command and the name (of menu) and number of menus properties.

name (of window)

Elements: window(*[windowrRef]*).name
the name of window *[windowRef]*

Purpose: This property returns the name of the MIAW you name. This property may seem silly at first glance: If you have to list the name of the window in order to return the name of the window, what's the point? Actually, there are two points: The property is settable as well as testable, and it allows you to access windows through the windowList. For example, you can use a repeat loop to apply commands to each MIAW by looping on the elements in the windowList.

In context: This line changes a window name:

set the name of window "Scott" to "Mr. Hartley"

Notes: It's very important to keep in mind that this property changes only the *name* of the window, not the movie playing in the window or the text that appears in the window's title bar. To test or set the title, use the title property.

See also: The title and windowList properties.

name (of Xtra)

Elements: xtra (*[XtraRef]*).name
the name of xtra *[XtraRef]*

Purpose: This property returns the name of the specified scripting Xtra.

In context: This startMovie handler outputs a list of all Lingo Xtras available to the movie. A similar handler could be used to check for the existence of a particular Xtra.

```
on startMovie
   repeat with i = 1 to the number of xtras
      put xtra(i).name
   end repeat
end
```

Notes: This property can be tested but not set.

See also: The number (of Xtras) and xtraList properties.

the netPresent

Elements: the netPresent

Purpose: Since a Director production can be bundled without network-related Xtras, this property determines whether the key Xtras for network-access functions are in place. It's useful for making sure the capability is there before a network operation is launched. This property returns 1 (or TRUE) if the Xtras are in place and recognized; it returns 0 (or FALSE)

PROPERTIES

if they are not. The netPresent property does not determine whether a connection to the Internet currently exists.

In context:

```
if netPresent = 1 then
    getNetText "http://www.demystified.com/sample.txt"
else go frame "Sorry!"
end
```

Notes: This property can be tested but not set. The syntax netPresent() is also used, but this will generate an error if the Net Support Xtras are not available.

netThrottleTicks

Elements: the netThrottleTicks

Purpose: This Macintosh-only property allows you to adjust the compromise between the amount of time spent servicing network operations and the amount of time spent servicing animation and playback. The default value is 15. A higher value favors playback over network operations. A lower value favors network operations over playback. This property is ignored for all but projectors and authoring on the Macintosh.

In context: This statement increases the amount of time spent on network operations at the price of possibly slowing down animation (Macintosh only):

```
the netThrottleTicks = 7
```

node

Elements: sprite(*[QTVRspriteRef]*).node
              node of sprite *[QTVRspriteRef]*

Purpose: This sprite property determines the current node that a QTVR sprite displays.

Notes: This property can be both tested and set.

See also: The nodeEnterCallback, nodeType, and nodeExitCallback properties.

nodeEnterCallback

Elements: sprite(*[QTVRspriteRef]*).nodeEnterCallback
              nodeEnterCallback of sprite *[QTVRspriteRef]*

Purpose: This sprite property determines the name of a handler that will be called when a QTVR movie sprite switches to a new active node. The message is sent with two arguments: the me parameter and the node ID of the new node. When no callback handler should be executed, set this property to 0.

Notes: This property can be both tested and set.

See also: The node, nodeType, and nodeExitCallback properties.

nodeExitCallback

Elements: sprite(*[QTVRspriteRef]*).nodeExitCallback
nodeExitCallback of sprite *[QTVRspriteRef]*

Purpose: This sprite property determines the name of a handler that will be called as a QTVR movie sprite leaves a node and before it enters a new active node. The message is sent with three arguments: the me parameter, the node ID of the node being exited, and the node ID of the new node. When no callback handler should be executed, set this property to 0.

The callback handler should return a value, which is interpreted by Director. The possible return values are #continue (go to the new node) and #cancel (do not go to the new node).

Notes: This property can be both tested and set.

See also: The node, nodeExitCallback, and nodeType properties.

nodeType

Elements: sprite(*[QTVRspriteRef]*).nodeType
nodeType of sprite *[QTVRspriteRef]*

Purpose: This sprite property retrieves the type of the node currently being displayed by the QTVR sprite. The three possible values are #object, #panorama, and #unknown. If the sprite isn't a QTVR sprite, the value should be #unknown, but this property seems to return #panorama for QuickTime movies and 0 for AVI sprites. Other sprite types generate a script error.

In context:

```
put sprite(33).nodeType
-- #panorama
```

Notes: This property can be tested but not set.

See also: The node, nodeEnterCallback, and nodeExitCallback properties.

number (of CastLib)

Elements: castLib(*[castLibRef]*).number
the number of castLib *[castLibRef]*

Purpose: Use this property to determine the number of a Cast. Even when named, a Cast has its own unique cast number, usually determined by the order in which it was created or linked to the movie.

In context:

```
put the number of castLib "Baja"
-- 2
```

Notes: This property can be tested but not set.

See also: The name (of castLib) and number (of castLibs) properties.

the number of castLibs

Elements: the number of castLibs

Purpose: This system property determines the number of Cast databases (both internal and external) currently linked to the present movie. Each new Cast (whether internal or external) is given a castLib number, usually in the order in which it is created.

In context: This repeat loop allows actions on each castLib:

```
repeat with i = 1 to the number of castLibs
    cname = castLib(i).name
    -- some actions
end repeat
```

Notes: This property can be tested but not set.

See also: The name (of castLib) and number (of castLib) properties.

the number (chunkType)

Elements: the number of chars
the number of items
the number of lines
the number of words

See: Under the number of chars, the number of items, etc., functions.

number (of member)

Elements: member([*memberRef*]).number
the number of member [*memberRef*]

Purpose: This property can be used to retrieve the position of a cast member in its Cast database. If the specified cast member does not exist, the dot-syntax version of this property will generate a script error. If the existence of the member is in doubt, use the older-style syntax, which will return –1.

In context:

```
put the number of member "Score"
-- 19
```

Notes: This property can be tested but not set. If more than one cast member has the same name, only the number of the first cast member with that name will be returned.

See also: The member, memberNum and number (of members) properties.

the number of members

Elements: the number of members
the number of members of castLib [*castLibRef*]

Purpose: This property returns the number of the last cast slot occupied by a cast member. If no castLib is specified, this property defaults to the castLib Internal.

In context:

```
put the number of members of castLib "Baja"
-- 22
```

Notes: This property can be tested but not set. Because there can be vacant cast slots before the last cast member, this is not necessarily an accurate count of all cast members.

See also: The member, memberNum, and number (of member) properties.

the number of menuItems

Elements: the number of menuItems of menu *[menu name or number]*

Purpose: This property returns a count of menu items in a specified menu. The menu can be referred to by its name or by its numerical position in the installMenu script. A script error will be generated if no menus are installed.

In context:

```
put the number of menuItems of menu "Sound"
-- 2
```

Notes: This property can be tested but not set. Menus are not supported in Shockwave.

See also: The installMenu command and the number of menus property.

the number of menus

Elements: the number of menus

Purpose: This property returns a count of the number of menus currently installed in the movie. A value of 0 indicates no menus are installed. Use this property to determine whether a menu is installed before using other menu properties.

In context:

```
put the number of menus
-- 4
```

Notes: This property can be tested but not set. Menus are not supported in Shockwave.

See also: The installMenu command and the number of menuItems property.

the number of Xtras

Elements: the number of Xtras

Purpose: This property counts the Lingo Xtras (the ones providing additional scripting capabilities) that the movie has open and available. Remember: Not all Xtras are Lingo Xtras, and not all items appearing on the Xtras menu are Xtras of any kind.

In context:

```
put the number of Xtras
-- 7
```

Notes: This property can be tested but not set.

See also: The name (of Xtra) property.

numChannels

Elements: member(*[SWAmemberRef]*).numChannels
the numChannels of member *[SWAmemberRef]*

Purpose: This Shockwave audio (SWA) cast member property can be used to determine whether the member is stereo (the value is 2, indicating 2 channels) or monaural (the value is 1). This property's value is valid only after the sound begins playing or is preloaded using the preLoadBuffer command.

In context:

```
put member("SWA Rigolletto").numChannels
-- 2
```

Notes: This property can be tested but not set.

obeyScoreRotation

Elements: member(*[FlashMemberRef]*).obeyScoreRotation

Purpose: Director 7 allows Flash movies to be rotated using the Score rotation setting. Flash movies in earlier versions of Director used a Flash rotation property. The obeyScoreRotation property allows you to choose between using the newer Score rotations setting (TRUE) or the older rotation property (FALSE). In either case, whichever source of rotation information is chosen, the other is ignored.

In context: This statement specifies that the rotation of sprites created from the Fhands Flash cast member will rotate according to the information in the Score:

```
member("Fhands").obeyScoreRotation = TRUE
```

Notes: This property can be both tested and set.

The default value is TRUE for all movies created with Director 7.0 or later. Flash assets in movies created in earlier versions of Director will have this property set to FALSE for backward compatibility.

See also: The rotation property.

the organizationName

Elements: the organizationName

Purpose: This property contains the name of the company entered during your installation of Director. For some reason, this property is valid only while authoring and will generate a script error in a projector. Supposedly, it can be used to customize authoring tools.

In context: This script shows the name of the company that was entered, along with the user's name, at the start of the Director 7 installation process:

```
put the organizationName
-- "MEL Co."
```

Notes: This property can be tested but not set. This property generates an error outside of the authoring environment.

See also: The serialNumber and userName properties.

originH

Elements: `sprite([`*spriteRef*`]).originH`
              `the originH of sprite` *[spriteRef]*
              `member([`*memberRef*`]).originH`
              `the originH of member` *[memberRef]*

Purpose: This property determines the horizontal coordinate of the origin point for a Flash movie or vector shape cast member or sprite. The origin point is the point around which scaling and rotation take place. Use this property when you want to set the horizontal and vertical properties independently, or when you want to use floating-point values. To set the horizontal and vertical location as a point, use the `originPoint` property.

This property is valid only if the `originMode` property is set to `#point`. Do not reset the origin point (or set the `originMode` property to `#point`) if you have the `scaleMode` property set to `#autoSize` (Director 7's default value).

In context: This script changes the origin point of a Flash movie if `scaleMode` is not set to `#autoSize`. Otherwise, `originMode` is set to `#centered` (as required).

```
if sprite(4).scaleMode <> #autoSize then
    sprite(4).originMode = #point
    sprite(4).originH = 20
    sprite(4).originV = 40
else
    sprite(4).originMode = #center
end if
```

Notes: This property can be both tested and set. The default value is 0.

See also: The `originV`, `originMode`, `originPoint`, and `scaleMode` properties.

originMode

Elements: `sprite([`*spriteRef*`]).originMode`
              `the originMode of sprite` *[spriteRef]*
              `member([`*memberRef*`]).originMode`
              `the originMode of member` *[memberRef]*

Purpose: This property determines the origin point (or how the point is set) for a Flash movie or vector shape cast member or sprite. The origin point is the point around which scaling and rotation take place. The value is a symbol; the allowable values are as follows:

`#center`: The origin point is at the center (the default).

`#topleft`: The origin point is at the top left.

`#point`: The origin point is determined by the value specified by the `originPoint` property or the `originH` and `originV` properties.

In context: This sprite behavior sets the `originMode` property to `#point` so that the origin point can be changed using the `originPoint` property:

```
property spriteNum
on beginSprite
  sprite(spriteNum).originMode = #point
  sprite(spriteNum).originPoint = point(20, 40)
end
```

Notes: This property can be both tested and set. This property must be set to #center (the default value) if the scaleMode property is set to #autoSize (the default value for Director 7) or the sprite will not be displayed correctly.

See also: The originH, originV, originPoint, and scaleMode properties.

originPoint

Elements: sprite([spriteRef]).originPoint
             the originPoint of sprite *[spriteRef]*
             member([memberRef]).originPoint
             the originPoint of member *[memberRef]*

Purpose: This property determines the coordinates of the origin point for a Flash movie or vector shape cast member or sprite. The origin point is the point around which scaling and rotation take place. Use this property when you want to set the horizontal and vertical properties as a point. To set the horizontal and vertical coordinates individually, use the originH and originV properties.

This property is valid only if the originMode property is set to #point. Do not reset the origin point (or set the originMode property to #point) if you have the scaleMode property set to #autoSize (Director 7's default value).

In context: This sprite behavior sets the originMode property to #point so that the origin point can be changed using the originPoint property:

```
property spriteNum
on beginSprite
  sprite(spriteNum).originMode = #point
  sprite(spriteNum).originPoint = point(20, 40)
end
```

Notes: This property can be both tested and set. Its default value is point(0,0).

See also: The originH, originV, and scaleMode properties.

originV

Elements: sprite([spriteRef]).originV
             the originV of sprite *[spriteRef]*
             member([memberRef]).originV
             the originV of member *[memberRef]*

Purpose: This property determines the vertical coordinate of the origin point for a Flash movie or vector shape cast member or sprite. The origin point is the point around which scaling and rotation take place. Use this property when you want to set the horizontal and vertical properties independently, or when you want to use floating-point values. To set the horizontal and vertical location as a point, use the originPoint property.

This property is valid only if the originMode property is set to #point. Do not reset the origin point (or set the originMode property to #point) if you have the scaleMode property set to #autoSize (Director 7's default value).

In context: This script changes the origin point of a Flash movie if scaleMode is not set to #autoSize. Otherwise, originMode is set to #centered (as required).

```
if sprite(4).scaleMode <> #autoSize then
    sprite(4).originMode = #point
    sprite(4).originH = 20
    sprite(4).originV = 40
else
    sprite(4).originMode = #center
end if
```

Notes: This property can be both tested and set. The default value is 0.

See also: The originH, originMode, originPoint, and scaleMode properties.

pageHeight

Elements:　member([*memberRef*]).pageHeight
　　　　　　the pageHeight of member [*memberRef*]

Purpose: Use this property to obtain the height of the visible contents of a field cast member, measured in pixels. This value is the height of the text shown on the Stage, not the height if the entire cast member were visible.

In context:

```
put the pageHeight of member "HearYe!"
-- 140
```

Notes: This property can be tested but not set. Its name is a bit of a misnomer, since the property measures not the actual height of text in the cast member, but the height of its display in sprites on the screen. Thus, a field cast member could actually be 224 pixels high, but if resized on the Stage to 140 pixels, the pageHeight of member would return 140. You might think that would make this a sprite rather than a member property, but no: Field text can't be resized on a sprite-by-sprite basis. Changing the dimensions of one sprite derived from the cast member changes all the others.

palette

Elements:　member([*memberRef*]).palette
　　　　　　the palette of member [*memberRef*]

Purpose: You can use this property to establish which color palette is used to display a given bitmap cast member. If a custom palette is used, it returns the number of the cast slot that palette occupies. If a built-in palette is used, it returns a negative number corresponding to one of the following codes:

-1　　System palette (System-Mac)

-102　System palette (System-Win)

-101　System palette (System-Win Director 4)

-2　　Rainbow

-3	Grayscale
-4	Pastels
-5	Vivid
-6	NTSC
-7	Metallic
-8	Web 216

In context: These statements in the Message window show that cast member 12 is associated with the custom palette in cast slot 21, and that cast member 13 uses the Web 216 palette:

```
put member(12).palette
-- 21
put member(13).palette
-- -8
```

Notes: This property can be both tested and set.

See also: The framePalette, paletteRef, and paletteMapping properties and the puppetPalette command.

the paletteMapping

Elements: the paletteMapping

Purpose: This property determines just how closely Director attempts to approximate the colors of cast members mapped to a different palette than that of the movie. If this property is set to 1 (or TRUE), whenever a sprite derived from the cast member appears on the Stage, Director will temporarily remap the colors to those closest to those in the movie palette. If this property is set to the default value of 0 (or FALSE), Director will make no attempt to remap the colors—which means that unless a custom palette is applied to the frame, the image may not be displayed correctly. Setting this property to TRUE allows you to display bitmaps using different palettes at the same time, although the effect may not be acceptable for all bitmaps.

In context:

```
set the paletteMapping to TRUE
```

Notes: This property can be both tested and set. Since color remapping on the fly is a pretty processor-intensive procedure, it may be better to permanently remap the cast members using the Transform Bitmap command on the Modify menu.

See also: The palette, framePalette, and paletteRef properties and the puppetPalette command.

paletteRef

Elements: member([*memberRef*]).paletteRef
              the paletteRef of member

Purpose: Use this property to find the palette assigned to a bitmap cast member. Symbols will be returned for system palettes (the ones built into Director), and cast member palettes will be referred to by cast number.

In context:

```
put member(2).paletteRef
-- #systemMac
```

Notes: This property can be both tested and set.

See also: The palette, framePalette, and paletteMapping properties and the puppetPalette command.

pan

Elements: sprite(*[spriteRef]*).pan
                 pan of sprite *[spriteRef]*

Purpose: This property determines the pan of a QTVR sprite. The value is specified in degrees. For a smooth transition to a new pan, use the swing function.

In context: This statement switches the QTVR sprite to view the opposite side:

```
sprite(3).pan = sprite(3).pan + 180
```

Notes: This property can be both tested and set.

See also: The swing function and the fieldOfView property.

pathName

Elements: member(*[FlashRef]*).pathName
                 the pathName of member *[FlashRef]*

Purpose: This property determines the location of the external file for a linked Flash movie cast member. For unlinked cast members, the value of this property is the empty string. If you set the pathName for a currently unlinked Flash cast member, the cast member becomes linked.

In context: This sprite behavior uses a global variable beenThere to track whether a Flash movie has already played. If it has, a different Flash movie is substituted using a path name stored in the global variable Flash2.

```
property spriteNum
on beginSprite
   global beenThere, Flash2
   if beenThere = TRUE then
      x = sprite(spriteNum).member
      member(x).pathName = Flash2
   else
      beenThere = TRUE
   end if
end beginSprite
```

Notes: This property can be both tested and set. You can also use the fileName property to achieve the same result.

See also: The fileName (of member) and linked properties.

PROPERTIES

the pathName (movie property)

See: The moviePath property and the @ operator. The pathName is obsolete and should no longer be used.

pattern

Elements: member(*[memberRef]*).pattern
the pattern of member *[memberRef]*

Purpose: This property determines the pattern associated with a shape cast member. Possible values are the numbers of the pattern chips, counting from the top left as they appear in the patterns palette in the Tools window. The member's filled property must be set to TRUE for this property to have any effect.

In context:

```
put the pattern of member 7
-- 2
set the pattern of member 7 to 4
```

Notes: This property can be both tested and set.

pausedAtStart

Elements: member(*[memberRef]*).pausedAtStart
the pausedAtStart of member *[memberRef]*
sprite(*[spriteRef]*).pausedAtStart
the pausedAtStart of sprite *[spriteRef]*

Purpose: This property is limited to digital video and Flash movie cast members and sprites. When it is set to 1 (or TRUE), sprites will be paused when they first appear on the Stage. When it is set to 0 (or FALSE), sprites will commence playing as soon as they appear. This is equivalent to selecting the Paused at Start check box in the cast member's Info dialog box.

In context: This statement enables the QuickTime movie QT1 to play as soon as its sprite appears on the Stage:

```
member("QT1"). pausedAtStart = TRUE
```

Notes: This property can be both tested and set.

See also: The play command.

percentPlayed

Elements: member(*[memberRef]*).percentPlayed
the percentPlayed of member *[memberRef]*

Purpose: This property returns the percentage of a Shockwave Audio cast member that has played (not streamed) at the time the property is tested. It's valid only after playback of the cast member has begun or the file has been loaded via the preloadBuffer command. The value is given as a number between 0 and 100.

In context: This command reports that only 10 percent of the named file has been played:

```
put the percentPlayed of member "yackyack"
--10
```

Notes: This property can tested but not set.

See also: The percentStreamed property and the preLoadBuffer command.

percentStreamed

Elements: member([*memberRef*]).percentStreamed
the percentStreamed of member [*memberRef*]

Purpose: Similar to the percentPlayed of member, this property detects the percentage of a Shockwave Audio file or Flash movie that has been streamed (not played) into memory.

In context:

```
put the percentStreamed of member "yackyack"
--10
```

Notes: This property can be tested only after the Shockwave Audio file is playing or has been loaded through the preloadBuffer command. It cannot be set.

See also: The percentPlayed property and the preLoadBuffer command.

picture

Elements: the picture of the stage
window ([*windowRef*]).picture
the picture of window [*windowRef*]

Purpose: This property retrieves the bitmap contents of the Stage or of a Movie in a Window (MIAW). Basically, it's a means of capturing a snapshot of the movie that you can then display by assigning the picture to a cast member.

In context: These statements create a new bitmap cast member and then assign the Stage screen capture to the new bitmap:

```
cPic = new(#bitmap)
member(cPic).picture = the picture of the stage
```

Notes: This property can be tested but not set.

See also: The media and picture of member properties.

picture (of member)

Elements: the picture of member [*memberRef*]
member([*memberRef*]).picture

Purpose: Use this property to determine the image (a bitmap, text, or PICT) associated with a given slot in a Cast database. You'll find this property useful as a means of moving images around, as you can assign it to a variable and then pass that variable to other handlers. It's also handy for prescribing the physical appearance of child objects from within parent scripts.

In context: This script places the image of a cast member in a global variable:

`gPassImage = the picture of member("TieGuy")`

Notes: This property can be both tested and set.

the platform

Elements: the platform

Purpose: Use this property to determine the platform on which your movie is being run by the end user. Here are the values that can be returned:

`Macintosh,PowerPC`   PPC Macintosh

`Windows,32`   Windows 95, 98, and NT

Earlier versions of director also returned these (no longer supported) values:

`Macintosh,68k`

`Windows,16`   Refers to all versions prior to Windows 95

In context:

```
put the platform
-- "Macintosh,PowerPC"
```

Notes: This property can be tested but (obviously) not set. Because these property values may be amended in the future, it is recommended that you use a `contains` statement to check these values.

See also: The `runMode` function.

playBackMode

Elements: sprite(*[spriteRef]*).playBackMode
               the playBackMode of sprite *[spriteRef]*
               member(*[memberRef]*).playBackMode
               the playBackMode of member *[memberRef]*

Purpose: This property determines how the frame rate of a Flash movie sprite or Animated GIF cast member is implemented. The value is a symbol; allowed values are as follows:

`#normal`: The movie attempts to play the element at the original tempo. This is the default.

`#lockStep`: The element is played frame for frame with the Director movie.

`#fixed`: The element is played at the frame rate specified by the `fixedRate` property.

In context: These commands sets the frame rate for a Flash movie sprite to 10 frames per second:

```
sprite(4).playBackMode = #fixed
sprite(4).fixedRate = 10
```

Notes: This property can be both tested and set.

See also: The `fixedRate` property.

playing

Elements: sprite(*[FlashRef]*).playing
                    the playing of sprite *[FlashRef]*

Purpose: This property determines whether the Flash movie is currently playing (TRUE) or has stopped (FALSE).

In context: These statements test whether the Flash movie has stopped playing and, if it has, set the movie back to its first frame:

```
if sprite(5).playing = FALSE then
   sprite(5).frame = 1
end if
```

Notes: This property can be tested but not set.

See also: The frame and frameCount properties and the stop and play commands.

posterFrame

Elements: member(*[FmemberRef]*).posterFrame
                    the posterFrame of member *[FmemberRef]*

Purpose: You can use this property to determine which frame of a Flash movie cast member is used as the image for the movie's thumbnail image. The value is the number of the frame to be used. The default value is 1.

In context: This statement uses the last frame of a Flash movie for the thumbnail image:

```
member("Ftree").posterFrame = member("Ftree").frameCount
```

Notes: This property can be both tested and set.

See also: The frame and frameCount properties.

preLoad

Elements: member(*[memberRef]*).preLoad
                    the preLoad of member *[memberRef]*

Purpose: This property is for digital video and Flash cast members only (see the preload commands for preloading cast members). For digital video, when this property is set to TRUE, the cast member will be preloaded into RAM before sprites derived from it appear on the Stage. This is equivalent to selecting the Enable Preload check box in the cast member's Info dialog box.

For Flash movies, a value of TRUE means that the movie must be completely loaded into RAM before the first frame is displayed. A value of FALSE allows the movie to be streamed according to its bufferSize and streamMode properties. This property has no effect on Flash cast members that are not linked to external files.

In context:

```
member("QT1").preLoad = TRUE
```

Notes: This property can be both tested and set.

PROPERTIES

See also: The preLoad and preLoadMember commands for preloading cast members and the bufferSize and streamMode properties.

the preLoadEventAbort

Elements: the preloadEventAbort

Purpose: When set to 1 (or TRUE), this property stops the preloading of cast members if a user event (a mouse click or key press) occurs. If this property is set to 0 (or FALSE), such user events will not interrupt preloading. When preloading large amounts of data, it's a good idea to set this property to TRUE to enable user interaction.

In context:

the preLoadEventAbort = TRUE

Notes: This property can be both tested and set. The default is FALSE.

See also: The preLoad and preLoadMember commands.

the preloadMode of castLib

Elements: the preLoadMode of castLib *[cast]*

Purpose: This cast property determines the specified Cast's current memory management mode (not to be confused with the Purge Priority). It is the Lingo equivalent of setting Load Cast in the Cast Properties dialog box.

There are three possible values:

0	When needed (the default)
1	Before frame 1
2	After frame 1

In context:

set the preLoadMode of castLib "Faces" = 2

Notes: This property can be both tested and set.

the preLoadRAM

Elements: the preLoad RAM

Purpose: This property can be used to specify a limit on the amount of RAM that can be used for the preloading of digital video cast members. It has no effect on the preloading of other types of cast members. When set to 0 (the default), all available RAM can be applied to digital video cast members loading into memory; when set to a specific value, that value becomes the maximum RAM used for digital video management.

In context: This statement limits the amount of RAM used for digital video preloading to 700K:

the preLoadRAM = 700

Notes: This property can be both tested and set. It's useful when you want to ensure that a digital video cast member doesn't inhibit movie performance by monopolizing RAM.

preLoadTime

Elements: `member([memberRef]).preLoadTime`
             `the preLoadTime of member [memberRef]`

Purpose: This property determines the amount of downloading time before streaming playback of a Shockwave Audio member begins, measured in seconds. In other words, if you set this property to 10 seconds, then 10 seconds' worth of audio will be downloaded before the sound starts playing. This is the same as setting the Preload Time field in the SWA Cast Member Properties dialog box. Use this property to ensure that playback does not outrun the continuing loading of a streaming sound.

In context: This command ensures that 11 seconds of sound is already in memory before the sound will start playing.

`set the preLoadTime of member "Ta-Dah!" = 11`

Notes: This property can be set only when streaming of the Shockwave Audio member is stopped. The default duration is 5 seconds.

See also: The `preloadBuffer` command.

productVersion

Elements: `the productVersion`

Purpose: This system property retrieves the version of Director used to create a project.

In context: The following script will return the product version in the Message window:

```
put the productVersion
-- "7.0.2"
```

See also: The `version` keyword.

puppet

Elements: `sprite([spriteRef]).puppet`
             `the puppet of sprite [spriteRef]`

Purpose: This property can be used to establish whether an individual sprite channel is currently puppeted and under the control of Lingo rather than being controlled by the score. In the context of a command, it is the equivalent of `puppetSprite`; it can also be used in the Message window to trace the puppet status.

When the sprite is puppeted, this property returns 1, or TRUE. When it is not puppeted, it returns 0, or FALSE.

In context:

```
put the puppet of sprite 2
-- 0
```

Notes: This property can be both tested and set.

See also: The `puppetSprite` command.

purgePriority

Elements: member(*[memberRef]*).purgePriority
the purgePriority of member *[memberRef]*

Purpose: This property determines the purge priority of the designated cast member. It is equivalent to setting the Unload value in the cast member's Properties dialog box.

There are four possible values:

0   Never (not recommended)

1   Last

2   Next

3   Normal (at the discretion of Director)

In context: This statement determines that cast member Quit will be unloaded from memory only if Directory is severely short of memory.

```
set the purgePriority of member "Quit" to 1
```

Notes: This property can be both tested and set. The value 2, typically referred to as *next*, means next highest priority, not next to be unloaded.

See also: The unLoad and unLoadMember commands.

quad

Elements: sprite(*[spriteRef]*).quad

Purpose: This property determines the four corners of a sprite on the Stage. The value of the property is a linear list of four elements, with each element a Director point. The four elements define, in order, the upper-left, upper-right, lower-right, and lower-left corners (start at the top left and move clockwise). Each point element can be a floating-point number. You can modify the individual points to create perspective, skewing, rotations, and other distortions.

After you have set the quad value of a sprite, the rotation and skew properties can no longer be used (although you can achieve the same effect using the quad value). To return the sprite to its values as determined in the Score (or to use the rotation and skew properties), you can set the sprite's puppetSprite property to FALSE. This works even if the puppetSprite property is already set to FALSE.

In context: This statement displays the sprite's quad value in the Message window:

```
put sprite(1).quad
-- [point(80.0000, 101.0000),
point(206.0000, 101.0000),
point(206.0000, 207.0000),
point(80.0000, 207.0000)]
```

These statements switch the upper-left and upper-right points, essentially tying the sprite in a bow. Note that the list that is changed (qList) is reassigned to the quad property—this is a copy of the list, not a pointer to the quad list.

```
qList = sprite(1).quad
qListT = sprite(1).quad
```

```
qList[1] = qListT[2]
qList[2] = qListT[1]
sprite(1).quad = qList
```

Notes: This property can be both tested and set. The quad property is a bit buggy, especially in early version of Director 7. Using the (undocumented) useFastQuads property has been reported to reduce the prevalence of bugs.

See also: The rect, rotation, skew, and useFastQuads properties.

quality

Elements: sprite(*[spriteRef]*).quality
            the quality of sprite *[spriteRef]*
            member(*[memberRef]*).quality
            the quality of member *[memberRef]*

Purpose: You can use this property to determine whether anti-aliasing is applied to a Flash movie sprite when it is displayed. Anti-aliasing can make the sprite look better, but it may slow down the rendering for some sprites on some slower systems. The value is a symbol; the allowable values are as follows:

#high: The movie always plays with anti-aliasing. This is the default.

#low: The movie always plays without anti-aliasing.

#autoHigh: The sprite starts playing using anti-aliasing. If Director can't keep up with the movie's frame rate, anti-aliasing is turned off. This value gives priority to playback speed rather than visual quality.

#autoLow: The sprite starts playing without using anti-aliasing. If Director determines that anti-aliasing can be applied and that it can still keep up with the movie's frame rate, then anti-aliasing will be applied. This value maintains the frame rate while rendering using anti-alias quality whenever possible.

In context: This command attempts to display the sprite with the best quality, but ensures that the frame rate is maintained:

```
member("simpleFlash").quality = #autoHigh
```

Notes: This property can be both tested and set.

See also: The fixedRate, frameRate, and playBackMode properties.

the randomSeed

Elements: the randomSeed

Purpose: Since a computer is incapable of picking a random number by guessing, a random value is arrived at by starting with a number and then applying that number to a variety of calculations to produce a variable result. That initial number is the seed, and changing it can produce different results if the random function is invoked repeatedly. Using the same seed will produce the same sequence of numbers, which is useful for debugging purposes. For normal playing, allow Director to handle the seed for the movie.

PROPERTIES

In context: The first two sets of random numbers below are identical because the same randomSeed value was used.

```
the randomSeed = 1
put random (5)
-- 3
put random (5)
-- 4
the randomSeed = 1
put random (5) -- same sequence
-- 3
put random (5)
-- 4
the randomSeed = 200
put random (5) -- new sequence
-- 2
put random (5)
-- 3
```

Notes: This property can be both tested and set. For an even higher level of randomness, try tying the randomSeed to a changing value such as the frame or the tick.

rect (member)

Elements: the rect of member *[memberRef]*
member(*[memberRef]*).rect

Purpose: This property returns the rect coordinates (left, top, right, and bottom) of a graphic cast member (bitmaps, shapes, digital video, text, and so on). The rect value is defined in terms of the distance from the upper-left corner of the cast member, so the left and top coordinates are always 0.

In context:

```
put member("gadzooks").rect
-- rect(0, 0, 161, 205)
```

Notes: This property can be tested but set only for field and text cast members. If you set this property for field and text cast members, the new right coordinate will be accepted and the bottom coordinate adjusted so the text is still contained in the cast member.

See also: The rect function and the quad and rect (sprite) properties.

rect (sprite)

Elements: the rect of sprite *[spriteRef]*
sprite(*[spriteRef]*).rect

Purpose: This property returns the rect coordinates (left, top, right, and bottom) of a graphic sprite's bounding box. Unlike the rect property as applied to cast members, the value indicates the coordinates from the upper-left corner of the Stage (0,0).

In context:

```
put sprite (1).rect
-- rect(118, 264, 166, 324)
```

Notes: This property can be both tested and set.

rect (window)

Elements: the rect of window *[windowRef]*
window (*[windowRef]*).rect

Purpose: This property defines the rect coordinates that determine the dimensions of a MIAW. The coordinates are given as (left, top, right, and bottom).

In context: These commands display a window's rect value in the Message window, give the window a new size, and set the window back to the original size as determined by the original source:

```
put window("Credits.dcr").rect
-- rect(256, 230, 752, 538)
set window("Credits.dcr").rect = rect(0, 0, 100, 193)
window("Credits.dcr").rect = window("Credits.dcr").sourceRect
```

Notes: This property can be both tested and set. In fact, you can use it to set the dimensions of a window even before you open a movie in that window. If you make the rect value smaller than that of the original movie, the movie is cropped, not scaled. To scale or pan MIAWs, use the drawRect property.

See also: The drawRect, sourceRect, and windowList properties.

ref

Elements: *chunkExpression*.ref

Purpose: This property gives you an easy shorthand method for referring to a chunk expression in a text cast member. The syntax for a chunk expression can sometimes be long and cumbersome, but you can use the ref property to enter the chunk expression specification once and then save it for multiple uses (without the chance of typing mistakes).

In context: This statement uses the ref property to assign a reference to a text chunk expression to the variable currRef:

```
currRef = member("bigText").paragraph[6].line[1].word[12..25].ref
```

The variable can now be used to access the text chunk:

```
put currref.char[12]
-- "a"
put currref.font
-- "Times New Roman"
```

You can access the entire text contents using the `text` keyword. The first of the following statements will reference the text chunk; the second will only provide (not very useful) information about the property itself.

```
put currRef.text
-- "the text is here"
put currRef  -- not very useful
-- <Prop Ref 2 1121104>
```

regPoint

Elements: `member([memberRef]).regPoint`
`the regPoint of member [memberRef]`

Purpose: This property determines the location of a graphic cast member's registration point, expressed in terms of coordinates from the left and top edges of the cast member's bounding rectangle. The registration point is used to establish the center of sprites derived from cast members.

In context: This script line moves the registration point of cast member Raised Hand. Note that the coordinates are preceded by the word `point`.

```
member(1).regPoint = point(30, 100)
```

Notes: This property can be both tested and set.

right

Elements: `sprite([spriteRef]).right`
`the right of sprite [spriteRef]`

Purpose: This property returns the location of the right edge of the bounding box of the specified sprite, expressed in terms of its distance in pixels from the left edge of the Stage.

In context:

```
put sprite(2).right
-- 568
```

Notes: This property can be tested and set.

rightIndent

Elements: `[chunkExpression].rightIndent`

Purpose: This property sets the right indentation applied to the text in a chunk portion of a text cast member. The default value is 0 (no indent). Setting the value to an integer greater than 0 increases the indentation by that number of pixels. Negative values are treated as 0.

In context: This statement sets the right indent for the first five paragraphs of the cast member to 10 pixels:

```
member(6).paragraph[1..5].rightIndent = 10
```

Notes: This property can be both tested and set.

See also: The `firstIndent` and `leftIndent` properties.

the `rightMouseDown`

Elements: the `rightMouseDown`

Purpose: This system-level property can be used to resolve the inconsistencies inherent in creating for the MacOS (where the mouse is assumed to have a single button) and Windows (where the multiple-button mouse is the rule). This property is set to TRUE whenever the right mouse button (Windows) is down, or whenever the mouse button and Control key (Macintosh, but see *Notes*) are being pressed. Otherwise, the value is FALSE.

In context: The first statement enables the `rightMouseDown` property to function on the Macintosh:

```
the emulateMultiButtonMouse = TRUE
if the rightMouseDown then puppetSound 4,"dingbat"
```

Notes: This property can be tested but not set. For the Macintosh, the `emulateMultiButtonMouse` property must be set to TRUE for the `rightMouseDown` property to recognize the mouse button and Control key combination.

See also: The `emulateMultiButtonMouse` property.

the `rightMouseUp`

Elements: the `rightMouseUp`

Purpose: See the entry for the `rightMouseDown`. This property functions identically, except that it's tied to the moment the mouse button is released.

the `rollOver`

Elements: the `rollOver`

Purpose: See the `rollOver` function.

the `romanLingo`

Elements: the `romanLingo`

Purpose: This property reflects whether the Macintosh operating system is currently employing a single-byte character set (used with English and most European languages) or a double-byte character set (used with Japanese and other ideogrammatic languages).

In context:

```
the romanLingo = TRUE
```

Notes: This property can be both tested and set. The default is set when Director starts, using information from the operating system. Generally, you need to set this property only if you are working on a non-roman system but are using only single-byte characters. In that case, you can gain a performance boost by setting the `romanLingo` property to TRUE.

PROPERTIES

rotation

Elements: member(*[memberRef]*).rotation
the rotation of member *[memberRef]*
sprite(*[spriteRef]*).rotation
the rotation of sprite *[spriteRef]*

Purpose: This property determines the rotation of a QuickTime movie, Animated GIF, or Flash movie cast member or sprite, or a bitmap or vector shape sprite. The value is a floating-point number and specifies the degree of rotation.

A QuickTime movie rotates around the center of the movie's bounding rectangle. Neither the bounding rectangle nor the sprite's controller are rotated. If the sprite's crop property is set to FALSE, the image is scaled to fit in the bounding rectangle (which may result in distortion). If the sprite's crop property is set to TRUE, part of the movie may lie outside of the area of the bounding rectangle. The visible area of the sprite is then seen through the bounding rectangle as through a window.

A Flash movie rotates around its origin point (specified by the originMode property). The bounding rectangle is not rotated, but acts as a window through which the visible area of the movie is seen.

An Animated GIF, bitmap, or vector shape rotate around the registration point of the element. The bounding rectangle is not fixed in size, but adjusts to contain the full rotated image.

In context: This behavior holds the playback head on the same frame until the sprite has rotated five full times:

```
on exitFrame
    if sprite(3).rotation > 5*360 then
        go to frame "rotationDone"
    else
    sprite(3).rotation = sprite(3).rotation + 10
    go to the frame
end
```

Notes: This property can be both tested and set. The default value is 0.

See also: The flipH, flipV, skew, and originMode properties.

RTF

Elements: member(*[memberRef]*).RTF

Purpose: The RTF property of a text cast member is the version of the cast member text formatted with basic RTF formatting tags.

In context: These two put commands show the difference between the ASCII version of text contents and the RTF version:

```
put member(8).text
-- "This is the time to go to the store.
When is my break?
Hello world!"
```

```
put member(8).rtf
-- "{\rtf1\ansi\deff0 {\fonttbl{\f0\fswiss Arial;}
{\f1\froman Times New Roman;}}
{\colortbl\red0\green0\blue0;}
{\stylesheet{\s0\fs24 Normal Text;}
}\pard \f0\fs24{\pard \plain\fs24\fi200
This is the time to go to the store.\par
When is my break?\par
\par
Hello world!\par}}"
```

Notes: This property can be both tested and set.

See also: The HTML property and the importFileInto command.

the runMode

Elements: the runMode

Purpose: This property returns the run mode of the movie—that is, it indicates whether the file is currently saved as a Director movie, projector file, Shockwave movie, or Java applet. The value is a string; possible values are "Author" (the movie is running in Director), "Projector" (the movie is running as a projector), "Plugin" (the movie is running in Shockwave format), and "Java Applet" (the movie is playing as a Java applet).

In context: This script effectively disables the downLoadNetThing command if the movie it's running in is in the Shockwave format:

```
on getthefile
   if the runMode contains "Plugin" then
      alert "Sorry, I can't do that!"
   else downLoadNetThing ("update.txt", "ReadMe.txt")
end
```

Notes: This property can be tested but not set.

safePlayer

Elements: the safePlayer

Purpose: This property determines whether the safety features (designed for Shockwave security) are turned on (TRUE) or not (FALSE). For Shockwave movies, this property is always TRUE.

Warning! Before you try this property on one of your movies, it is important to realize that you cannot undo the property if you set the value to TRUE. Make sure you have a backup copy of your Director file. Consider yourself warned!

For various security reasons, certain actions are disallowed for movies being played over the Internet. For example, files cannot be written to (or read from) the user's system. The following is a rundown of the safety features:

The safePlayer property cannot be reset. *You can't change it back to FALSE, even in the authoring environment.*

You cannot use the open command to start an application.

You cannot read or write files (except you can use the getPrefs and setPrefs commands) or determine the names of files.

You cannot affect the user's system using the colorDepth, quit, restart, or shutdown commands.

You cannot save a movie or cast file using Lingo.

You cannot use the printFrom command to print.

You cannot send strings to Windows MCI by using mci.

Only Xtras registered as safe can be used.

Using the pasteClipboardInto command generates a warning dialog box and permits the user to cancel the operation.

Accessing a URL that does not have the same domain as the movie (such as with getNetText) generates a security dialog box.

Notes: In the authoring environment and in projectors, this property can be both tested and set. The default value is FALSE in these environments.

sampleRate

Elements: member([*memberRef*]).sampleRate
             the sampleRate of member [*memberRef*]

Purpose: This property, limited to sound cast members, retrieves the sample rate (a measure of sound quality) of a specified cast member, in samples per second. For Shockwave Audio (SWA) compressed sounds, the value is the sample rate of the original uncompressed sound.

In context: This statement determines that the sound cast member Mantra was sampled at 22.05 KHz:

```
put the sampleRate of member "Mantra"
-- 22050
```

Notes: This property can be tested but not set.

sampleSize

Elements: member([*memberRef*]).sampleSize
             the sampleSize of member [*memberRef*]

Purpose: This property, limited to sound cast members, retrieves the sample size (a measure of sound quality) of a specified cast member as a number reflecting the bits in the sample (for example, 8-bit or 16-bit).

In context: This statement determines that the sound cast member Mantra is an 8-bit sound:

```
put the sampleSize of member "Mantra"
-- 16
```

Notes: This property can be tested but not set.

scale

Elements: member(*[memberRef]*).scale
the scale of member *[memberRef]*
sprite(*[spriteRef]*).scale
the scale of sprite *[spriteRef]*

Purpose: You can use this property to check or change the scale of a QuickTime, vector shape, or Flash movie sprite. It's useful for zooming the sprite in or out to create interesting visual effects.

For Flash movies and vector shapes, the value is a floating-point number determining the scale as a percentage. The default value is 100 (100 percent). The sprite itself is not scaled—only the view of the element within the bounding rectangle. The scaling is performed around the element's origin as determined by the originMode property setting (the viewScale property always scales the image around the center of the bounding rectangle). The nature of the scaling may be affected by the element's scaleMode property as well. If the scaleMode property is set to #autoSize, the scale property must be set to 100 (the default), or the sprite will not be displayed properly.

For QuickTime movies, the image is scaled within the sprite's bounding box. The bounding box and the controller (if used) are not scaled. The scale property applies only when the crop property of the QuickTime cast member is set to TRUE. The value is given as a linear list containing two floating-point numbers: [horizontalScale, verticalScale]. The default value is 100 percent: [100, 100].

In context: This sprite behavior uses a vector shape to create the effect of an exploding button. When the button is clicked, the cast member is swapped for a vector shape with the scale set to 0. The repeat loop then brings the size of the vector shape up to 100 percent.

```
property spriteNum
on mouseUp
   member("myVector").scale = 0
   sprite(spriteNum).member = "myVector"
   repeat with i = 0 to 50
      member("myVector").scale = member("myVector").scale + 2
      updatestage
   end repeat
end
```

Notes: This property can be both tested and set.

See also: The scaleMode, originMode, and viewScale properties.

scaleMode

Elements: sprite(*[spriteRef]*).scaleMode
the scaleMode of sprite *[spriteRef]*
member(*[memberRef]*).scaleMode
the scaleMode of member *[memberRef]*

Purpose: This property determines how a Flash movie or vector shape is scaled, rotated, skewed, or flipped. The property's value is a symbol; the allowable settings are #autoSize (the default for Director 7), #showAll (the default prior to Director 7), #noBorder, #exactFit, and #noScale. These values provide combinations of functionality that determine when you will want to use a particular value.

The phrase "maintains aspect ratio" implies that the image is not stretched to fit a sprite that is resized, although the image may be shrunk or enlarged.

#autoSize: This is the default for Director 7 (#showall was the default previously). When the sprite is rotated, skewed, or flipped the bounding rectangle is adjusted to fit the sprite (instead of being cropped). This is the only setting that does not crop the image for those operations. This setting requires that the scale, viewScale, originPoint, and viewPoint properties are at their default values. This setting does not maintain the aspect ratio.

#showAll: This was the default prior to Director 7. When the sprite is rotated, skewed, or flipped, the image is cropped to fit the sprite (instead of the sprite's rectangle being reset). This setting maintains the aspect ratio. If a sprite rectangle of other than the default size is used, the image is shrunk or enlarged (while maintaining the aspect ratio) to fit within the sprite. Any areas of the sprite not filled by the image are filled by the sprite's background color.

#exactFit: This setting does not maintain the aspect ratio. The image is stretched to fit the size of the sprite on the Stage.

#noScale: This setting maintains the aspect ratio. The original size of the element is maintained, by cropping, when a nondefault sprite size is used. This setting may have been introduced to provide a more consistent version of #noBorder.

#noBorder: This setting maintains the aspect ratio. It is the same as #noScale, except that if the sprite is resized after a rotation or skew operation, the image is resized, rather than cropped, to maintain the aspect ratio.

In context: These commands determine a sprite's size and then place a Flash movie in the sprite after first ensuring that the image will be stretched to exactly fit the sprite's bounding rectangle:

```
sprite(2).rect = rect(33, 199, 133, 316)
member("Fshoes").scaleMode = #exactFit
sprite(13).member = member("Fshoes")
```

Notes: This property can be both tested and set.

See also: The scale, originMode, and viewScale properties.

the score

Elements: the score

Purpose: The purpose of this interesting property may be hard to glean from the Macromedia documentation. Director movies can be saved as film loop cast members within other movies; this property lets you switch the score of the main movie with the score of the encapsulated one. This property is worth experimenting with.

In context:

```
put the score
-- (media 1c0a316)
set the score = the media of member "other"
```

Notes: This property can be both tested and set. Note that it returns not a name but a reference to an address in memory—which is why, when changing it, you need to invoke the media of member to refer to that unique address.

scoreColor

Elements: sprite(*[spriteRef]*).scoreColor
              the scoreColor of sprite *[spriteRef]*

Purpose: This property determines the color used to display a Score cell. It returns a number from 0 (the leftmost color in the six-color Score palette) to 5 (the rightmost color). Setting the scoreColor property for a sprite can provide a means of identifying related sprites.

In context:

```
put the scoreColor of sprite 1
-- 4
```

Notes: This property can be both tested and set. The default value is 0.

the scoreSelection

Elements: the scoreSelection [*[first channel]*, *[last channel]*, *[first frame]*, *[last frame]*]

Purpose: Use this property to designate which channels in the Score are selected. You can name the channels by channel number, but unnumbered channels have these unique value designations:

Frame script channel	0
Sound channel 1	-1
Sound channel 2	-2
Transition channel	-3
Palette	-4
Tempo channel	-5

This property takes arguments in the form of a list: The first number should be that of the first sprite of the range of channels, and the second should be the last channel. The range of frames is similarly described by the third and fourth numbers.

PROPERTIES

In context: Here's how you'd select channels 5 through 15 in frames 250 through 350:

theScoreSelection = [[5, 15, 250, 350]]

This statement selects the same cells as the preceding script, but it also selects frames 100 through 150 of channel 1:

theScoreSelection = [[5, 15, 250, 350], [1, 1, 100, 150]]

Notes: This property can be both tested and set. Note the use of double brackets to indicate a list within a list. You can select discontinuous areas in the Score by placing multiple list subsets within the outer brackets (but separate them with commas).

the script (of menuItem)

Elements: the script of menuItem *[itemRef]* of menu *[menuRef]*

Purpose: When you've installed custom menus in a movie, you can use this property to link the execution of a handler to an individual item in the menu.

In context: This script line (called in the menu script) executes the turnOff handler when the Sound Off menu item is selected:

set the script of menuItem "Sound" of menu "Controls" to "turnOff"

Notes: This property can be both tested and set.

See also: The installMenu command and the menu keyword.

scriptInstanceList

Elements: sprite(*[spriteRef]*).scriptInstanceList
              the scriptInstanceList of sprite *[spriteRef]*

Purpose: This property generates a list of script references attached to a sprite, which can be handy when attaching, finding, or deciding which behaviors should go with which sprites. This property is valid only while the movie is running; otherwise, the list is empty.

In context: This script will display the value of the scriptInstanceList property in a field named Diagnose when the sprite is clicked:

```
property spriteNum
on mouseDown
    member("Diagnose").text = the scriptInstanceList of sprite (spriteNum)
end
```

Notes: This property can be both tested and set.

the scriptNum

Elements: the scriptNum of sprite *[number]*

Purpose: This property identifies the Score script attached to a given sprite, expressed in terms of the number given to that script in the Cast. When no script is attached to the sprite, the property returns 0.

In context:

```
put the scriptNum of sprite 1
-- 13
```

Notes: This property can be both tested and set (during Score recording).

scriptsEnabled

Elements: member(*[memberRef]*).scriptsEnabled
the scriptsEnabled of member *[memberRef]*

Purpose: This property, limited to linked Director movies imported as cast members into other movies, determines whether the scripting in the linked movie is enabled when the movie is played back within the context of the current movie; it is the Lingo equivalent of setting the Enable Scripts option in a linked movie's Properties dialog box. When this property is set to TRUE (or 1), the linked movie's scripts are enabled. When it is set to FALSE (or 0), the linked movie plays back as an animation (sequence of sprites) only.

In context: This statement prevents the scripts in the linked Director movie 5HELP from executing when the movie plays:

member("5HELP").scriptsEnabled = FALSE

Notes: This property can be both tested and set.

scriptText

Elements: member(*[memberRef]*).scriptText
the scriptText of member *[memberRef]*

Purpose: This property retrieves or modifies the script attached to a cast member. If there is no attached script, it returns a set of empty quotation marks. If the cast member is itself a script, that script is quoted as a whole. This property is useful for changing the contents of a script while the movie is playing.

In context: This statement uses the text of field commands to replace the script in member TestBehavior:

member("TestBehavior").scriptText = member("Commands").text
member("TestBehavior").scriptType = #score

Notes: This property can be both tested and set. The text of scripts is removed when a movie is converted to a projector or compressed for Shockwave, so the scriptText property will return an empty string in those situations. The value, however, can still be set, and the new script text will be compiled so that is can be run.

scriptType

Elements: member(*[memberRef]*).scriptType
the scriptType of member *[memberRef]*

Purpose: This property, limited to Lingo script cast members, returns a symbol (indicated by the # character) designating the type of script. It is the Lingo equivalent of setting the Type options in the cast member's Properties dialog box.

Here are the codes for the script types:

#movie
#parent
#score

PROPERTIES

In context:

```
put the scriptType of member "Obey!"
-- #score
```

Notes: This property can be both tested and set.

scrollTop

Elements: member([*memberRef*]).scrollTop
               the scrollTop of member [*memberRef*]

Purpose: This property helps control the visible contents in the sprite of a field cast member. It defines the distance (in pixels) from the top of the text (in the cast member) to the top of the text in the sprite. Setting this property to 0 displays the text at the beginning of the cast member. By changing the value of this property, you can display different sections of text in the sprite. This property is useful for creating custom scroll bars and for automatically scrolling text (such as the credits at the end of a movie).

If the boxType value for the field is set to #scroll (or the field's Framing value is set to Scrolling in the Properties dialog box), the scroll bar is automatically adjusted as the visible text is scrolled in the field.

In context: This handler scrolls the contents of the field cast member Credits. Starting the scrollTop setting with a negative number means the field starts out blank, and the lines then appear to slide up from the bottom. The totalPixels and fieldPixels values, which have been set elsewhere, are used to determine the height of the total text and the height of the field, respectively.

```
on doCredits
global totalPixels, fieldPixels
   member("Credits").scrollTop = - fieldPixels
   repeat with i = 1 to totalPixels + fieldPixels
      member("Credits").scrollTop = ¬
      member("Credits").scrollTop + 1
   end repeat
end doCredits
```

Notes: This property can be both tested and set.

See also: The boxType and lineCount properties and the count and lineHeight functions.

the searchCurrentFolder

Elements: the searchCurrentFolder

Purpose: This property determines whether the current folder (the last folder opened) is searched when Director attempts to locate a file. It is a binary function, with the default being 1, or TRUE.

In context:

```
put the searchCurrentFolder
-- 1
```

Notes: This property can be both tested and set.

See also: The searchPaths property and the @ operator.

searchPath

See: This property is no longer used; use searchPaths instead.

searchPaths

Elements: the searchPaths

Purpose: This system property establishes a list of alternative paths for Director to search when looking for an external file to open. These locations are in the form a of list; when Director cannot find a file in the current folder, it will look for the file in the listed paths. Using the searchPaths property, you can designate a set of folders that will be searched for your movie's linked elements, with the following caveats: Designating full path names for linked elements is faster; setting too many folders in the list can slow down performance; Windows and Macintosh use different path specifications; using URLs in the property can *really* slow down performance (so don't do it).

In context: This script finds the type of system the movie is running on and sets the searchPaths property accordingly:

```
if (the platform) contains "Windows" then
    the searchPaths = ["C:\myMovie\sounds",¬
    "C:\myMovie\video"]
else
    the searchPaths = ["hard drive:myMovie:sounds",¬
    "hard drive:myMovie:video"]
end
```

Notes: This property can be both tested and set.

See also: The searchCurrentFolder property and the @ operator.

selectedText

Elements: member(*[memberRef]*).selectedText
            the selectedText of member *[memberRef]*

Purpose: This property returns an object that can be used to refer to the selected chunk of text in a text cast member. You can then use the object to refer to the chunk's properties, including the text contents.

In context: This sprite behavior uses the selected variable to store a reference to the selected text. It then checks to see if the selected text contains the word *turnip* and takes appropriate action depending on the results.

```
property spriteNum
on mouseUp
    mem = sprite(spriteNum).memberNum
    selected = member(mem).selectedText
    if selected.text contains "turnip" then
        member("Response").text = "Correct"
```

```
    else
      member("Response").text = "Try again"
    end if
end
```

Notes: This property can be tested but not set. To set the selected text for a text cast member, use the `selection` property.

See also: The `selection` (text cast member) property.

selection (cast property)

Elements: `castLib ([castRef]).selection`
               `the selection of castLib [castRef]`

Purpose: This cast property determines which cast members in the specified cast are selected. The value is a list, with each element being another list containing the start and end slots of the selected members.

In context: This statement selects cast members 5 through 10 in castLib 1:

`castLib(1).selection = [[1, 10]]`

This statement selects cast members 5 through 10, and 15 through 20, in castLib 1:

`castLib(1).selection = [[5, 10], [15,20]]`

Notes: This property can be both tested and set.

See also: The `castLibNum`, `name` (of castLib), `number` (of castLib), and `number` (of castLibs) properties.

selection (text cast member property)

Elements: `member([memberRef]).selection`

Purpose: This property determines the selected text in a text cast member. The value is a linear list with two elements: the number of the starting character and the number of the ending character.

In context: This sprite behavior sets the focus on a text sprite and selects characters 2 through 4:

```
property spriteNum
on beginSprite
  mem = sprite(spriteNum).member
  the keyboardFocusSprite = spriteNum
  member(mem).selection = [2,4]
end
```

Notes: This property can be both tested and set.

See also: The `selectedText` property. For fields, see the `selStart` and `selEnd` properties and the `selection` function.

the selEnd

Elements: the selEnd

Purpose: This property is used with the currently editable field to establish the portion of text that is selected (shown in reverse). It is usually used in conjunction with the selStart property.

In context: This statement selects 10 characters of an editable field:

```
set the selEnd to the selStart + 10
```

Notes: This property can be both tested and set, with the default being 0. For reliable results, the selStart property should be set before the selEnd property.

See also: The hilite command, the selection function, and the editable and selStart properties. For text cast members, see the selection property.

the selStart

Elements: the selStart

Purpose: This property is used with editable text fields to establish the portion of text that is selected (shown in reverse). It is usually used in conjunction with the selEnd property.

In context: This statement selects 10 characters of an editable text field:

```
set the selEnd to the selStart + 10
```

Notes: This property can be both tested and set, with the default being 0. For reliable results, the selStart property should be set before the selEnd property.

See also: The hilite command, the selection function, and the editable and selEnd properties. For text cast members, see the selection property.

serialNumber

Elements: the serialNumber

Purpose: This property contains the serial number entered during your installation of Director. Supposedly, it can be used to customize authoring tools.

In context:

```
put the serialNumber
```

Notes: This property can be tested but not set. This property generates an error outside of the authoring environment.

See also: The organizationName and userName properties.

shapeType

Elements: member([*memberRef*]).shapeType
            the shapeType of member [*memberRef*]

Purpose: This property, limited to shape cast members (filled or unfilled), returns a symbol (indicated by the # character) designating its shape type. It is the Lingo equivalent of setting the Shape options in the cast member's Properties dialog box.

Here are the symbolic codes for shape types:

```
#rect
#roundRect
#oval
#line
```

In context:

```
put the shapeType of member "box"
-- #roundRect
```

```
set the shapeType of member "box" to #roundRect
```

Notes: This property can be both tested and set.

the shiftDown

Elements: the shiftDown

Purpose: This system property determines whether the Shift key is currently pressed. It can be used in scripts that interpret Shift-key combinations. It is a binary function (1 indicates TRUE; 0 indicates FALSE).

In context: This button script performs one action if the button is simply clicked (the custom handler buttonClick), and another action (playback branches to the Special Place marker) if the mouse click occurs when the Shift key is down:

```
on mouseUp
    if the shiftDown then
        go to "Special Place"
    else
        buttonClick
    end if
end
```

size

Elements: member([*memberRef*]).size
the size of member [*memberRef*]

Purpose: This property returns the amount of file storage space occupied by a given cast member, expressed in terms of bytes (to convert to kilobytes, divide by 1024). This is the number you will see in the cast member's Properties dialog box. For external (linked) files, the number represents overhead (header information and so on), not the actual file size.

In context:

```
put the size of member "Sitting Swifty"
-- 3066
```

Notes: This property can be tested but not set.

See also: the ramNeeded and freeBytes functions and the memorySize property.

skew

Elements: sprite(*[spriteRef]*).skew

Purpose: This property determines the angle at which a sprite is skewed (the angle at which the vertical edges are tilted). The value is a floating-point number representing the angle in degrees, with angles between 0 and 90 degrees skewed to the right, angles between 90 and 180 degrees skewed to the right and down (flipped), and so on. Negative angles are also allowed, with angles between 0 and -90 degrees skewed to the left, and so on. This is similar to setting the Skew value for a sprite in the Score.

In context: This frame behavior starts a sprite as a horizontal line (skew = 90) and then makes the sprite appear to rise up to the left. The registration point of the sprite is assumed to be its lower-left corner.

```
on enterFrame
   sprite(3).skew = 90
   repeat with i = 1 to 90
      sprite(3).skew = (sprite(3).skew) - 1
      updateStage
   end repeat
end
```

Notes: This property can be both tested and set. The sprite is skewed around its registration point, where applicable.

See also: The flipH, flipV, and rotation properties.

sound

Elements: sprite(*[spriteRef]*).sound
              the sound of sprite *[spriteRef]*
              member(*[memberRef]*).sound
              the sound of member *[memberRef]*

Purpose: This property is limited to digital video, Director movies imported as linked cast members in the active movie, and Flash movies. It determines whether playback of a sprite includes sound (TRUE) or not (FALSE). It is equivalent to selecting or deselecting the Sound check box in the cast member's Properties dialog box.

In context:

```
member("QTMovie1").sound = TRUE
```

Notes: This property can be both tested and set, with the default being TRUE, or 1 (sound on).

See also: The soundEnabled, soundLevel, and volume properties.

soundChannel

Elements: member([*memberRef*]).soundChannel
            the soundChannel of member *[memberRef]*

Purpose: This property is for Shockwave Audio (SWA) cast members only and determines the sound channel in which the SWA sound will play. The value is an integer specifying the channel (typically 1 through 8). A value of 0 tells Director to use the highest-numbered sound channel not in use.

In context: This statement specifies that the SWA sound Verdi will play in sound channel 6:

member("Verdi").soundchannel = 6

Notes: This property can be both tested and set.

soundDevice

Elements: the soundDevice

Purpose: This property can be used to change the sound mixing device on Windows systems, or to check the current sound device on Windows or Macintosh systems (the Macintosh has only one sound device). Use the soundDeviceList property to check the devices available on the system. If you attempt to change the soundDevice property setting to a nonfunctioning sound device, the change will be ignored.

In context: This statement attempts to set the sound device on a Windows system to DirectSound:

the soundDevice = "DirectSound"

Notes: This property can be both tested and set. See Chapter 19 for a discussion of how to determine which sound device to use.

See also: The soundDeviceList and soundKeepDevice properties.

soundDeviceList

Elements: the soundDeviceList

Purpose: This property retrieves a linear list of the available sound devices for the current system. For the Macintosh, this list always contains only the MacSoundManager device. For Windows, the list contents may vary but will always contain the MacroMix device (others will be included depending on the system configuration).

In context: This statement displays a typical sound device list for a Windows system:

put the soundDeviceList
-- ["MacroMix", "QT3Mix", "DirectSound"]

Notes: This property can be tested but not set. See Chapter 19 for a discussion of how to determine which sound device to use.

See also: The soundDevice and soundKeepDevice properties.

PROPERTIES

the soundEnabled

Elements: the soundEnabled

Purpose: When this property is set to FALSE, the system's sound capabilities are turned off. When it is set to TRUE, sound is heard at the level set in the host machine's Sound control panel or set using the soundLevel property.

In context:

the soundEnabled = FALSE

Notes: This property can be both tested and set, with the default being 1, or TRUE.

See also: The soundLevel and volume properties.

soundKeepDevice

Elements: the soundKeepDevice

Purpose: Setting this system property to TRUE allows Director to maintain control of the sound device after a sound finishes. When it is set to FALSE, the sound driver may be unloaded and require reloading the next time a sound plays. The default is TRUE for Director 7.0, which generally improves performance but may interfere with the sound functionality of other applications running concurrently with the Director movie. For version 7.0.2, the default is FALSE, to allow for Flash movie sounds to mix with other sounds.

In context: This statement sets the soundKeepDevice property to FALSE:

the soundKeepDevice = FALSE

Notes: This property can be both tested and set.

See also: The soundDevice and soundDeviceList properties.

the soundLevel

Elements: the soundLevel

Purpose: This property sets or returns the current volume level, as set in the host computer's system level sound control. It is expressed as a number from 0 (mute) to 7 (maximum volume).

In context: This script saves the current sound level and then sets the volume to a median setting:

oldSoundLevel = the soundLevel
the soundLevel = 4

Notes: This property can be both tested and set.

It's not always a good idea to reset a system's volume level since other applications may also be playing sounds. You are better off setting the volume of individual movie elements. If you do change the system volume level, you should test it (and save it) first and then reset the original level when the movie exits.

See also: The soundEnabled and volume properties.

sourceRect

Elements: window (*[memberRef]*).sourceRect
the sourceRect of window *[memberRef]*

Purpose: When a movie is running in a window and has been resized, this property can retrieve the coordinates of that movie's original Stage (as opposed to the size of the window in which it's currently playing). The coordinates are left edge, top edge, right edge, and bottom edge, expressed in terms of the distance in pixels from the edges of the host computer's monitor.

In context: These commands first check sourceRect for a movie in the Message window and then set the movie's Stage size and location to the movie's original settings:

```
put the sourceRect of window "Running"
-- rect(160, 141, 672, 483)
window("Running").rect = window("Running").sourceRect
```

Notes: This property can be tested but not set. You can set a window's size and location using the rect (of window) property while the movie is running or by using the Movie Properties dialog box while authoring.

See also: The rect function and the left, bottom, top, right, height, width, and rect (of window) properties.

the spriteNum

Elements: the spriteNum of sprite *[channel number]*
the spriteNum of me

Purpose: This property returns the number of the sprite in the given sprite channel. Use this property in behaviors by declaring it as a property. This property can be used to write scripts that pass the accurate sprite number, no matter how many times they're moved around in the Score. This makes it ideal for parent-child scripting and for writing behaviors.

If the behavior contains an on new handler, the new handler should explicitly set the value of spriteNum from information passed in as an argument. Otherwise, allow Director to automatically set the value.

In context: These behaviors perform the exact same function of changing the cast member used for a sprite. The second handler shows how the spriteNum property can be assigned to a variable to simplify scripting.

```
property spriteNum
on mouseEnter
    sprite(spriteNum).memberNum = sprite(spriteNum).memberNum + 1
end

property spriteNum
on mouseEnter me
    thisSprite = sprite(me.spriteNum)
    thisSprite.memberNum = thisSprite.memberNum + 1
end
```

See also: The me keyword.

the stage

Elements: the stage

Purpose: This property refers to the root movie—the movie that opens windows in which other movies appear. It can be used with Stage properties and with the `tell` command to pass Lingo from a window movie to the root movie.

In context: This script passes a text string from a window movie to the root movie:

```
on mouseDown
    tell the stage to put "I'm Running!" into field "Report"
end
```

This statement shows how you can use the `stage` property to access other properties:

```
(the stage).title = "Shark Bait"
```

Notes: This property can be tested but not set.

the stageColor

Elements: the stageColor

Purpose: This property establishes the current color of the movie's Stage. It is equivalent to setting a Stage color from the color chip in the Movie Properties dialog box. The color is expressed as a number (relating to that color's position on the current palette).

In context: This statement changes the Stage color to a mauve (number 31 on the Macintosh 8-bit System color palette):

```
the stageColor = 31
```

Notes: This property can be both tested and set. To find the number of a color, click it in the Color Palettes window; the number will be displayed in the lower-left corner. The color of the Stage can also be set using the syntax `(the stage).bgColor = ` *colorDataType*

See also: The `bgColor` property.

startTime

Elements: sprite(*[QTspriteRef]*).startTime
             the startTime of sprite *[QTspriteRef]*

Purpose: This is a digital video property. You can use it to determine where playback begins in a digital video. By default, this property is set to 0, and playback begins at the start of the movie. The value is given in ticks ($\frac{1}{60}$ of a second) from the start of the video.

In context: This statement, which would be placed in a `prepareFrame` handler, skips the first 5 seconds of the digital video movie in channel 7:

```
set the startTime of sprite 7 = (5 * 60)
```

Notes: This property can be both tested and set. Some people report that they have better luck using the `movieTime` property.

See also: The `duration`, `movieTime`, and `stopTime` properties.

state

Elements: member([*memberRef*]).state
state of member [*memberRef*]

Purpose: This property documents the current status of a Shockwave Audio (SWA) or Flash movie cast member by returning a descriptive code. For SWA, the codes are as follows:

0	Stopped
1	Preloading
2	Preloading has completed successfully
3	Playing
4	Paused
5	Playback is completed (done)
9	Generic error (no clear explanation)
10	Insufficient memory

For Flash movies, the codes are valid only while Director is running. Possible values are as follows:

0	Not in memory
1	Loading header
2	Header loaded successfully
3	Media is currently loading
4	Media is loaded
-1	An error occurred

In context: This script mutes the second sound channel if the Shockwave audio file is playing:

```
on enterFrame
    if the state of member "Zing!" = 3 then
        set the volume of sound 2 to 0
    end if
    if the state of member "Zing!" = 5 then
        set the volume of sound 2 to 150
    end if
end
```

Notes: This property can be tested but not set.

See also: The clearError command and the getError and getErrorString functions.

static

Elements: sprite([*spriteRef*]).static
the static of sprite [*spriteRef*]
member([*memberRef*]).static
the static of member [*memberRef*]

Purpose: This Flash movie property determines when a Flash sprite is redrawn. If the movie image is static (that is, not animated), you can increase performance by not requiring the sprite to be redrawn at each frame. The default value is FALSE, indicating that the Flash movie is not static and the sprite should be redrawn. A value of TRUE indicates that the sprite should be redrawn only when it is moved or resized on the Stage.

In context: This statement sets the static property to TRUE:

```
sprite("carFlash").static = TRUE
```

Notes: This property can be both tested and set, but set the static property to TRUE only when the Flash movie sprite does not intersect other moving Director sprites. If the Flash movie intersects moving Director sprites, the Flash sprite may not be redrawn correctly.

staticQuality

Elements: sprite(*[QTVRRef]*).staticQuality
staticQuality of sprite *[QTVRRef]*

Purpose: This property determines the codec quality used for a static panorama image. Allowed values are #minQuality, #maxQuality, and #normalQuality.

In context:

```
sprite("QTVRcoralReef").staticQuality = #maxQuality
```

Notes: This property can be both tested and set.

the stillDown

Elements: the stillDown

Purpose: This system property indicates whether the end user is pressing the mouse button. It returns 1 (or TRUE) so long as the button is down and 0 (or FALSE) when the button is up.

In context: This handler prevents the playback head from moving while the mouse button is down:

```
on mouseDown
  puppetSound 2, "Quick move"
  sprite(15).member = member("Arrows right")
  updateStage
  repeat while the stillDown = TRUE
    nothing
  end repeat
end
```

Notes: This property can be tested but not set.

See also: The mouseDown property.

stopTime

Elements: sprite([*spriteRef*]).stopTime
               the stopTime of sprite [*spriteRef*]

Purpose: This digital video property determines how much of a video will be played by setting the ending point within the video. The duration is expressed in ticks ($\frac{1}{60}$ of a second) from the start of the video. Can be used with the startTime property, which sets the starting point.

In context: This statement, which would be placed in a prepareFrame handler, sets the end point of video display at 30 seconds after the first frame of the video:

sprite (7).stoptime = (30 * 60)

Notes: This property can be both tested and set.

See also: The duration, movieTime, and startTime properties.

streamMode

Elements: member([*memberRef*]).streamMode
               the streamMode of member [*memberRef*]

Purpose: This Flash movie cast member property determines how a linked Flash movie cast member is streamed into memory. The value is a symbol; the allowable values are as follows:

#frame: Part of the Flash movie is streamed each time the playback head advances. This is the default value.

#idle: Part of the Flash movie is streamed each time an idle event occurs, but at least once for each time the playback head moves.

#manual: Streaming is under the control of the stream command.

In context: This statement increases the Flash movie streaming by setting the streamMode property to #idle:

member("handsFlash").streamMode = #idle

Notes: This property can be both tested and set.

See also: The stream command and the state and streamSize properties.

streamName

Elements: member([*memberRef*]).streamName
               the streamName of member [*memberRef*]

Purpose: This property specifies a file name or URL for a Shockwave Audio streaming cast member.

In context: This statement makes a file on the Internet the URL of the SWA cast member VoiceOver:

member("VoiceOver").streamName = "http://myteach.com/training1.swa "

Notes: This property can be both tested and set. This property is similar to the URL property

See also: The URL property.

streamSize

Elements: member([*memberRef*]).streamSize
             the streamSize of member [*memberRef*]

Purpose: This Flash movie property retrieves the total number of bytes of the specified cast member that will need to be streamed to play the entire movie.

In context: This statement determines the size of the fishFlash movie:

```
put member("fishFlash").streamSize
-- 2283
```

Notes: This property can be tested but not set.

See also: The bufferSize, bytesStreamed, and percentStreamed properties.

strokeColor

Elements: member([*memberRef*]).strokeColor
             the strokeColor of member [*memberRef*]

Purpose: This property determines the stroke color of a vector shape. The value is an RGB color data type.

In context: This statemet sets a new stroke color for the vector shape Bridge:

```
member("Bridge").strokeColor = rgb(255, 255, 0)
```

Notes: This property can be both tested and set. This is the same as setting the stroke color of the shape in the Vector Shape Editor.

See also: The color function and the backgroundColor, endColor, fillColor, and strokeWidth properties.

strokeWidth

Elements: member([*memberRef*]).strokeWidth

Purpose: This property determines the stroke width for a vector shape's framing stroke. The value is specified in pixels and is floating-point number between 1 and 1399.

In context: This statement sets the stroke width to 15 pixels:

```
member("pear").strokeWidth = 15
```

Notes: This property can be both tested and set.

See also: The color function and the backgroundColor, endColor, fillColor, and strokeColor properties.

the switchColorDepth

Elements: the switchColorDepth

Purpose: This property can be used to determine whether, when a Director movie is loaded, the monitor of the host MacOS machine is reset to the movie's color depth.

PROPERTIES

When this property is set to 1, or TRUE, the monitor will be set to match the color depth of the movie (hardware configuration permitting). When it is set to 0, or FALSE, the monitor will retain its current setting.

In context:

```
set the switchColorDepth = TRUE
```

Notes: This property can be both tested and set. The default is set in the General Preferences dialog box's Reset Monitor to Movie's Color Depth check box.

This property is ignored on the Windows platform.

systemDate

Elements: the systemDate

Purpose: This property retrieves the current date (as determined by the host computer's system clock) as a date data type. This data type makes it possible to manipulate the date mathematically; use the date independent of international settings; and use the day, month, and year properties to extract those elements.

In context: These statements display the current date in the Message window and then extract the day, month, and year as separate elements:

```
put the systemDate
-- date( 1999, 5, 16 )
put (the systemDate).day
-- 16
put (the systemDate).month
-- 5
put (the systemDate).year
-- 1999
```

Notes: This property can be tested but not set.

See also: The date functions.

tabCount

Elements: [chunkExpression].tabCount

Purpose: This Text cast member property returns the number of tab stops in the specified chunk expression. Tab stops can be set in the Text Editor window or with the tabs property.

In context: This statement uses the Message window to determine that three tab stops are used in the first paragraph of text cast member 4:

```
put member(4).paragraph[1].tabCount
-- 3
```

Notes: This property can be tested but not set.

See also: The tabs property.

tabs

Elements: [*chunkExpression*].tabs

Purpose: This text cast member property returns a list containing information about all of the tab stops in a chunk expression. Each element of the list is a property list containing a #type property and a #position property. The #type property indicates the type of the tab stop and can have the following values: #left, #right, #center, and #decimal. The #position property is an integer specifying the position of the tab stop (in points).

In context: This statement uses the Message window to display all the tab stops for the third paragraph of the text cast member Resume:

```
put member("Resume").paragraph[3].tabs
-- [[#type: #left, #position: 19], [#type: #center, #position: 37]]
```

Notes: This property can be both tested and set.

See also: The tabCount property.

text

Elements: member([*memberRef*]).text
              the text of member [*memberRef*]

Purpose: This property can retrieve or modify the text contained in a given text or field cast member. The cast member can be referred to by name or slot number.

In context: In these Message window statements, the first usage retrieves the text string in cast member Intro. The second changes that string to a new string.

```
put member("Intro").text
-- " Hello, welcome to my movie!"
member("Intro").text = "Whassup?"
put the text of member "Intro"
-- "Whassup?"
```

Chunk expressions can also be retrieved, though not set, using the text property:

```
put member("Secret").paragraph[4].text
```

Notes: This property can be both tested and set. There is an older and rarely used syntax that uses the text of field property.

textAlign

See: This property is obsolete; use the alignment property instead.

textFont

See: This property is obsolete; use the font property instead.

PROPERTIES

textHeight

See: This property is obsolete; use the lineHeight property instead.

textSize

See: This property is obsolete; use the fontSize property instead.

textStyle

See: This property is obsolete; use the fontStyle property instead.

thumbnail

Elements: member([*memberRef*]).thumbnail
         the thumbnail of member *[memberRef]*

Purpose: This cast member property retrieves the thumbnail image of a cast member. This is the same image used to show a thumbnail of a cast member in the Cast. You can use this property to set a new thumbnail image for a cast member or to set the picture of a cast member to the thumbnail image.

In context: The first statement uses a thumbnail image to change the graphic of a placeholder cast member, holder1. The second statement changes the thumbnail image that will appear in the Cast for a cast member.

```
member("holder1").picture = member("choice1").thumbnail
member(3).thumbnail = member(12).picture
```

Notes: This property can be both tested and set.

See also: The picture (cast member) property.

tilt

Elements: sprite([*QTVRRef*]).tilt
         tilt of sprite *[QTVRRef]*

Purpose: This property determines the tilt of a QTVR sprite. The value is given in degrees.

In context: This statement sets a new tilt for the QTVR sprite in channel 5:

```
sprite(5).tilt = sprite(5).tilt + 5
```

Notes: This property can be both tested and set.

See also: The swing function and the pan and fieldOfView properties.

the timeoutKeyDown

Elements: the timeoutKeyDown

Purpose: This property determines whether any keystroke (the keyDown) resets the timeout countdown (the timeoutLapsed property) to zero. If this property is set to 1 (TRUE), the keystroke will cause a reset; if it is set to 0 (FALSE), it won't.

In context: This statements specifies that a key press will not reset the `timeoutLapsed` timer to 0. This setting is useful when you are expecting only mouse events.

```
the timeoutKeyDown = FALSE
```

Notes: This property can be both tested and set, with the default being 1 (TRUE).

See also: The `timeoutLapsed`, `timeoutLength`, `timeoutMouse`, `timeoutPlay`, and `timeoutScript` properties.

the timeoutLapsed

Elements: the timeoutLapsed

Purpose: This property returns the amount of time passed since the last `timeout` event occurred or the last time the `timeoutLength` property was zeroed. This duration is expressed in ticks (1/60 of a second).

In context:

```
put the timeoutLapsed
-- 76190
```

Notes: This property can be tested but not set.

See also: The `timeoutKeyDown`, `timeoutLength`, `timeoutMouse`, `timeoutPlay`, and `timeoutScript` properties.

the timeoutLength

Elements: the timeoutLength

Purpose: This property sets or retrieves the amount of time that must pass without a user action before a `timeout` event is declared. This duration is expressed in ticks (1/60 of a second). This property is useful when you want to perform some action when the user doesn't seem to be doing anything. For example, you can set a time limit before giving the user hints on what to do. A `timeout` event occurs when the `timeoutLapsed` value reaches the `timeoutLength` value. The `timeoutLapsed` value may be reset to 0 by a user's pressing a key or clicking the mouse or by a movie's being played, depending on the value of the `timeoutKeyDown`, `timeoutMouseDown`, and `timeoutPlay` properties, respectively.

In context: This setting for the `timeoutLength` property specifies that a `timeout` event will not occur for at least 30 seconds:

```
the timeoutLength = 30 * 60
```

Notes: This property can be both tested and set. Its default value, 10,800 ticks, is equal to 3 minutes.

See also: The `timeoutKeyDown`, `timeoutLapsed`, `timeoutMouse`, `timeoutPlay`, and `timeoutScript` properties.

the timeoutMouse

Elements: the timeoutMouse

Purpose: This property determines whether clicking the mouse has the effect of resetting the timeout countdown (the timeoutLapsed property) to zero. If this property is set to 1 (TRUE), a mouseDown event will reset the countdown; if it is set to 0 (FALSE), it won't.

In context: This statements specifies that a mouseDown event will not reset the timeoutLapsed timer to 0. This setting is useful when you are expecting only keyboard events.

the timeoutMouse = FALSE

Notes: This property can be both tested and set, with the default being 1 (TRUE).

See also: The timeoutKeyDown, timeoutLapsed, timeoutLength, timeoutPlay, and timeoutScript properties.

the timeoutPlay

Elements: the timeoutPlay

Purpose: This property determines whether the action of playing a movie resets the timeout countdown (the timeoutLapsed property) to zero. If this property is set to 1 (TRUE), playing a movie will reset the countdown; if it is set to 0 (FALSE), it won't.

In context: This statements specifies that the action of playing a movie will not reset the timeoutLapsed timer to 0:

the timeoutPlay = FALSE

Notes: This property can be both tested and set, with the default being 1 (TRUE).

See also: The timeoutKeyDown, timeoutLapsed, timeoutLength, timeoutMouse, and timeoutScript properties.

the timeoutScript

Elements: the timeoutScript

Purpose: This property designates which statement or handler is to be executed as a primary event handler when a timeout event occurs. The value is a string (surrounded by quotation marks) that can be either a Lingo statement or the name of the handler to be called. When a timeoutScript handler is no longer required, set the property's value to EMPTY. Since the timeoutScript defines a primary event handler, the timeout message is automatically passed on, and an on timeout handler will also be called, if one is found.

In context: This statement specifies that the handler userAlert should be called when a timeout event occurs:

the timeoutScript = "userAlert"

This statement specifies that there is no timeout handler:

the timeoutScript = EMPTY

Notes: This property can be both tested and set, with the default being EMPTY.

See also: The timeoutKeyDown, timeoutLapsed, timeoutLength, timeoutMouse, and timeoutPlay properties.

PROPERTIES

the timer

Elements: the timer

Purpose: Think of this property as a sort of temporal variable. You can use it in scripts to set and track duration in ticks ($\frac{1}{60}$ of a second). When the property is set to zero with the startTimer command, it begins counting, and it will continue counting until another startTimer command is executed or until the property is set to a new value.

In context: These handlers set the timer to zero as the answer field appears on the Stage and then check to see if the end user has entered a sufficient number of characters in a text field. If the user hasn't done so after 20 seconds (1200 ticks) have passed, a prompting alert message is posted. Finally, the timer is reset to begin counting again.

```
on beginSprite  -- the answer field
   startTimer
end
on exitFrame
   if the number of items in field "Name" < 3 and the timer > 1200 then
      alert "Please enter your information"
      set the timer = 0
   end if
   go to the frame
end
```

Notes: This property can be both tested and set. It can be addressed in any script; it is not connected to the timeout event.

See also: The startTimer command.

timeScale

Elements: member([*memberRef*]).timeScale
               the timeScale of member *[memberRef]*

Purpose: This property, limited to digital video cast members, provides the timebase of a given cast member, expressed as a whole number. If you're not a video professional, you may not know that a timebase is the smallest unit of time measured by a given image technology—the unit of maximum accuracy. QuickTime, for instance, has a timebase of 600, which means that it can't deal in intervals shorter than $\frac{1}{600}$ of a second.

In context:

```
put member("TestQT").timeScale
-- 600
```

Notes: This property can be tested but not set. Don't confuse it with the playback rate of a video or the frame rate of a Director movie.

See also: The digitalVideoTimeScale property.

title

Elements: window(*[windowRef]*).title
              the title of window *[windowRef]*

Purpose: This property can be used to determine the name displayed in the title bar of a window created by Director. It can be applied to all windows, but is practical only for those whose windowType of window property includes a name display. For Movies in a Window (MIAWs), the default value of this property is the name of the movie that is running in the window.

In context:

```
window("Hamster").title = "Pets!"
(the stage).title = "Programmer's Nightmare"
```

Notes: This property can be both tested and set.

titleVisible

Elements: window(*[windowRef]*).titleVisible
              the titleVisible of window *[windowRef]*

Purpose: This property can determine whether the title of a window is currently displayed in that window's title bar. It is a binary property, with 1 or (TRUE) indicating that the title is visible, and 0 (or FALSE) indicating that it is not. This property has no effect on the Stage title.

In context: This statement hides the title of a Movie in a Window:

```
window("Pets").titleVisible = 0
```

Notes: This property can be both tested and set. Changing it is not the same as changing the property the windowType of window.

See also: The title property.

top

Elements: sprite(*[spriteRef]*).top
              the top of sprite *[spriteRef]*

Purpose: This property retrieves the location of the top of the bounding box of a sprite in the given channel number. This location is expressed as the distance, in pixels, from the top of the Stage.

In context:

```
put sprite(4).top
-- 369
```

Notes: This property can be both tested and set. Changing the top coordinate of a sprite does not change the location of a sprite, only the location of the top edge. Thus, changing the top property without changing the bottom property will result in a resizing of the sprite's bounding rectangle.

See also: The bottom, height, left, locH, locV, right, rect, and width properties.

topSpacing

Elements: *[chunkExpression]*.topSpacing

Purpose: This property sets the spacing applied to the top of paragraphs in a chunk portion of a text cast member. Note that the actual spacing between two paragraphs is the total of the bottom spacing of the first paragraph, the top spacing of the second paragraph, plus the default spacing. The default value is 0. Setting the value to an integer greater that 0 increases the spacing. A value less than 0 decreases the spacing.

In context: This statement closes the gap between paragraphs two and three of the cast member:

```
member(6).paragraph[2..3].topSpacing = -3
```

Notes: The default value (0) results in default spacing between paragraphs.

See also: The bottomSpacing property.

the trace

Elements: the trace

Purpose: This property establishes whether Director's trace function is enabled (TRUE) or not (FALSE). If this property is set to TRUE, the trace information is written in the Message window or in the location set by the traceLogFile property (if set). The trace information consists of a running display of all scripting actions while the movie is running.

In context:

```
the trace = TRUE
```

Notes: This is equivalent to selecting the Trace button in the Message window.

See also: The traceLoad and traceLogFile properties.

the traceLoad

Elements: the traceLoad

Purpose: This property determines the format used in the Message window for information about cast members when they are loaded into RAM. This information is displayed even when the Trace option is not enabled. It can be set to one of three values:

0	No information
1	Cast member names
2	Cast member names, cast slot number, number of the current frame, movie name, file seek offset

In context:

```
the traceLoad = 2
```

Notes: This property can be both tested and set, with the default being 0 (no information).

the traceLogFile

Elements: the traceLogFile

Purpose: This property names the file to which trace information (the display shown when the Trace option is enabled in the Message window or by the `trace` property) is written. If no such file exists, one will be created as a plain text file. This leaves a paper trail (for later perusal) of your scripts in the midst of execution.

In context:

the traceLogFile = "Diagnostic"

Notes: This property can be both tested and set. It's a good tool for analyzing and debugging Lingo code when keeping the Message window open would negatively affect playback. You can use it even when the Trace check box is turned off in the Message window (it also seems to have considerably less impact on playback speed than the on-the-fly Trace option).

See also: The `trace` and `traceLoad` properties.

trackCount

Elements: trackCount (member *[memberRef]*)
              trackCount (sprite *[spriteRef]*)

Purpose: This property returns the number of tracks used in the specified digital video cast member or sprite.

In context:

put trackCount (member "TestQT2")
-- 2

Notes: This property can be tested but not set. You should use it to determine whether a digital video track exists before using other track properties.

trackEnabled

Elements: trackEnabled (sprite*[spriteRef]*, *[track number]*)

Purpose: This property indicates whether the specified track of a digital video is enabled (that is, not turned off by Director for playback purposes). When this property is set to 1 (or TRUE), the specified track is enabled. When it is set to 0 (or FALSE), the specified track is disabled.

In context: This script plays another sound file only when the audio track (track 2) of the QuickTime file in channel 3 has been disabled:

```
on substituteSound
    if trackEnabled (sprite(3), 2) = FALSE then
        puppetsound 2, "JetSound"
    end if
end
```

Notes: This property is limited to digital video files. It can be tested but not set; to disable and enable specific tracks, use the `setTrackEnabled` property.

trackNextKeyTime

Elements: trackNextKeyTime(sprite *[spriteRef]*, *[trackNumber]*)

Purpose: This digital video sprite property returns the time of the next keyframe in the specified digital video track.

In context: This statement sets the variable nextKey to the time of the next keyframe in track 3 of sprite 12:

nextKey = trackNextKeyTime(sprite 12, 3)

Notes: This property can be tested but not set. This property generates a script error if the specified track does not exist.

See also: The digitalVideoTimeScale, trackCount, timeScale, trackPreviousKeyTime, trackStartTime, and trackStopTime properties.

trackNextSampleTime

Elements: trackNextSampleTime(sprite *[spriteRef]*, *[trackNumber]*)

Purpose: This digital video sprite property returns the time of the next sample in the specified digital video track. This property is useful for locating text tracks in a digital video.

In context: This statement assigns to the variable nextSample the time of the next sample in track 3 of sprite 12:

nextSample = trackNextSampleTime(sprite 12, 3)

Notes: This property can be tested but not set. This property generates a script error if the specified track does not exist.

See also: The digitalVideoTimeScale, trackCount, timeScale, trackPreviousSampleTime, trackStartTime, and trackStopTime properties.

trackPreviousKeyTime

Elements: trackPreviousKeyTime(sprite *[spriteRef]*, *[trackNumber]*)

Purpose: This digital video sprite property returns the time of the previous keyframe in the specified digital video track.

In context: This statement sets the variable prevKey to time of the previous keyframe in track 3 of sprite 12:

prevKey = trackPreviousKeyTime(sprite 12, 3)

Notes: This property can be tested but not set. This property generates a script error if the specified track does not exist.

See also: The digitalVideoTimeScale, trackCount, timeScale, trackNextKeyTime, trackStartTime, and trackStopTime properties.

trackPreviousSampleTime

Elements: trackPreviousSampleTime(sprite *[spriteRef]*, *[trackNumber]*)

Purpose: This digital video sprite property returns the time of the previous sample in the specified digital video track. This property is useful for locating text tracks in a digital video.

PROPERTIES

In context: This statement assigns to the variable prevSample the time of the previous sample in track 3 of sprite 12:

prevSample = trackPreviousSampleTime(sprite 12, 3)

Notes: This property can be tested but not set. This property generates a script error if the specified track does not exist.

See also: The digitalVideoTimeScale, trackCount, timeScale, trackNextSampleTime, trackStartTime, and trackStopTime properties.

trackStartTime

Elements: trackStartTime(member *[memberRef]*, *[trackNumber]*)
            trackStartTime(sprite *[spriteRef]*, *[trackNumber]*)

Purpose: This digital video property retrieves the start time of a track in a digital video sprite or cast member.

In context: This statement assigns to the variable dvStart the start time of track 3 in the digital video QTsurf:

dvStart = trackStartTime(member "QTsurf", 3)

Notes: This property can be tested but not set. This property generates a script error if the specified track does not exist.

See also: The digitalVideoTimeScale, movieTime, startTime, trackCount, timeScale, and trackStopTime properties.

trackStopTime

Elements: trackStopTime(member *[memberRef]*, *[trackNumber]*)
            trackStopTime(sprite, *[spriteRef]*, *[trackNumber]*)

Purpose: This digital video property determines the end time of a track in a digital video sprite or cast member.

In context: This statement assigns to the variable dvStop the stop time of track 3 in the digital video QTsurf:

dvStop = trackStopTime(member "QTsurf", 3)

Notes: This property can be tested but not set. This property generates a script error if the specified track does not exist.

See also: The digitalVideoTimeScale, duration, movieTime, stopTime, timeScale, trackCount, and trackStartTime properties.

trackText

Elements: trackText(sprite, *[spriteRef]*, *[trackNumber]*)

Purpose: This digital video sprite property retrieves the text contained in the specified track (which must be a text track) of a digital video. The value returned is a text string with a maximum length of 32K.

In context: This statement places the text content of track 4 of the digital video into the text cast member Lesson:

member("Lesson").text = trackText(sprite 12, 4)

Notes: This property can be tested but not set. This property generates a script error if the specified track does not exist.

See also: The trackType and trackCount properties.

trackType

Elements: trackType(member *[memberRef]*, *[trackNumber]*)
trackType(sprite, *[spriteRef]*, *[trackNumber]*)

Purpose: This digital video property determines the type of data in a track of a digital video sprite or cast member. The possible values returned are #video, #sound, #text, #music, #sprite, #chapter, and #unknown.

In context: This statement uses the Message window to display the track type of track 3 of the digital video QTSurf:

```
put trackType(member "QTSurf", 3)
-- #sound
```

Notes: This property can be tested but not set. This property generates a script error if the specified track does not exist.

See also: The trackCount property.

trails

Elements: sprite(*[spriteRef]*).trails
the trails of sprite *[spriteRef]*

Purpose: This property determines whether the Trails (Score-level) effects option is enabled for the sprite in the given Score channel. It is a binary property, returning 1 (or TRUE) if the option is enabled, and 0 (or FALSE) if it isn't.

In context: This statement turns trails on for sprite 3:

```
sprite(3).trails = TRUE
```

Notes: This property can be both tested and set.

See also: The directToStage property.

transitionType

Elements: member(*[memberRef]*).transitionType
the transitionType of member *[memberRef]*

Purpose: This property, limited to transition cast members, determines the type of transition (expressed as a code).

Here are the codes for built-in transitions:

01	Wipe Right	08	Edges In, Vertical
02	Wipe Left	09	Center Out, Square
03	Wipe Down	10	Edges In, Square
04	Wipe Up	11	Push Left
05	Center Out, Horizontal	12	Push Right
06	Edges In, Horizontal	13	Push Down
07	Center Out, Vertical	14	Push Up

PROPERTIES

15	Reveal Up	35	Cover Up, Left
16	Reveal Up, Right	36	Cover Up, Right
17	Reveal Right	37	Venetian Blinds
18	Reveal Down, Right	38	Checkerboard
19	Reveal Down	39	Strips on Bottom, Build Left
20	Reveal Down, Left	40	Strips on Bottom, Build Right
21	Reveal Left	41	Strips on Left, Build Down
22	Reveal Up, Left	42	Strips on Left, Build Up
23	Dissolve, Pixels Fast (not for monitors set to 32-bit color)	43	Strips on Right, Build Down
		44	Strips on Right, Build Up
24	Dissolve, Boxy Rectangles	45	Strips on Top, Build Left
25	Dissolve, Boxy Squares	46	Strips on Top, Build Right
26	Dissolve, Patterns	47	Zoom Open
27	Random Rows	48	Zoom Close
28	Random Columns	49	Vertical Blinds
29	Cover Down	50	Dissolve, Bits Fast (not for monitors set to 32-bit color)
30	Cover Down, Left		
31	Cover Down, Right	51	Dissolve, Pixels (not for monitors set to 32-bit color)
32	Cover Left		
33	Cover Right	52	Dissolve, Bits (not for monitors set to 32-bit color)
34	Cover Up		

In context: This statement sets a transition cast member to the effect of Cover Down, Right:

```
member ("Scratchy").transitionType = 31
```

Notes: This property can be both tested and set.

See also: The puppetTransition command.

translation

Elements:
```
member([QTmemberRef]).translation
the translation of member [QTmemberRef]
sprite([QTspriteRef]).translation
the translation of sprite [QTspriteRef]
```

Purpose: This QuickTime property determines the offset of a QuickTime sprite's image within the bounding rectangle of the sprite. It can be used to display different portions of a QuickTime image by using the bounding box as a window through which to view the image. The QuickTime cast member's crop property must be set to TRUE, or this property is ignored.

The value of the translation property is a list: [horzOffset, vertOffset]. Each offset is given in pixels and can be either a positive or negative floating-point number.

In context: This statement shifts the digital video image up 20 pixels and 30 pixels to the right:

```
member("QTcar").translation = [30, -20]
```

Notes: This property can be both tested and set.

See also: The crop and center properties.

triggerCallback

Elements: sprite(*[QTmemberRef]*).triggerCallback
triggerCallback of sprite *[QTmemberRef]*

Purpose: This QTVR sprite property determines the handler that is called when a hotspot is activated by the user's clicking it. Setting this property to 0 clears the callback.

The handler named in this property will receive two parameters: the me parameter and the ID of the hotspot that triggered the callback. The handler should return either #continue or #cancel to indicate how the hotspot should be processed. Returning #continue allows the QTVR sprite to continue processing the hotspot as normal. Returning #cancel cancels the default processing of the hotspot.

In context: This statement sets the handler called when a hotspot is triggered to HotCall:

sprite(12).triggerCallback = "HotCall"

This script is an example of a hotspot handler:

```
on HotCall me, hotSpotID
   -- take some actions
   return #continue  -- continue processing
end HotCall
```

Notes: This property can be both tested and set. For hotspots to be triggered, the mouseLevel property must be set to #all or #share.

See also: The mouseLevel property.

tweened

Elements: sprite(*[spriteRef]*).tweened
the tweened of sprite *[spriteRef]*

Purpose: This property is used during Score recording and handles the issue of whether all of a sprite's cells are created as keyframes (that is, points from which in-betweened movements can be automatically extrapolated) upon creation. If this property is set to 1 (or TRUE), only the first frame in the new sprite is the keyframe. If it is set to 2 (or FALSE), all frames in the sprite segment become keyframes. For more information about tweening and keyframes, see Chapter 2.

In context:

set the tweened of sprite 7 = TRUE

Notes: This property can be both tested and set.

type (cast member property)

Elements: member(*[memberRef]*).type
the type of member *[memberRef]*
member *[memberRef]* of castLib *[castRef]*.type
the type of member *[memberRef]* of castLib *[castRef]*

Purpose: This property returns a symbol (indicated by the # character) designating the cast member type of a given cast member. If you're using multiple casts, you can specify the cast as well as the member.

Here are the codes for cast types built into Director or that are created with Xtras that come with Director:

#animgif	#palette
#bitmap	#picture
#button	#QuickTimeMedia
#digitalVideo	#script
#empty (The Cast slot is empty.)	#shape
#field	#sound
#filmLoop	#swa
#flash	#text (#richText is no longer
#font	used.)
#movie	#transition
#ole	#vectorShape

In context: In this example, cast slot 15 is empty, and cast slot 16 contains a bitmap:

```
put the type of member 15
-- #empty
put the type of member 16
-- #bitmap
```

Notes: This property can be tested but not set. It replaces the now-obsolete property the castType of cast.

type (sprite property)

Elements: sprite(*[spriteRef]*).type
             the type of sprite *[spriteRef]*

Purpose: This property is used in Score recording to clear a channel by setting the type of the sprite in that channel to 0.

In context: This handler clears the first five visual channels of sprites for the current frame:

```
on clearFive
  beginRecording
  repeat with x = 1 to 5
    sprite (x).type = 0
  end repeat
  end Recording
end clearFive
```

Notes: This property can be both tested and set; it always returns 16 when tested on a channel containing a sprite, or 0 if the channel is empty.

the updateLock

Elements: the updateLock

Purpose: This property is used to determine whether the Stage of the active movie is updated when the playback head moves or the updateStage command is executed. Generally, it is used while Score-generating Lingo is making changes to the Stage. If you want the end user to see the changes as they're taking place, set this property to 0, or FALSE. If you want the user to see the changes only after your modifications are complete, set it to 1, or TRUE.

You can also use the updateLock property to prevent unintentional score updating when you leave a frame temporarily to examine properties in another frame.

In context: This statement prevents the Stage from being updated.

```
the updateLock = TRUE
```

Notes: This property can be both tested and set.

the updateMovieEnabled

Elements: the updateMovieEnabled

Purpose: You can use this property to ensure that changes made to a movie are (or aren't) saved before playback branches to another root movie. When this property is set to 1 (or TRUE), changes will be saved; when it is set to 0 (or FALSE), they won't be.

In context: This statement tells Director to save changes to the current movie before branching to another movie:

```
the updateMovieEnabled = TRUE
```

Notes: This property can be both tested and set, with the default value being 0 (FALSE). It applies to the root movie, not to MIAW movies playing in the foreground.

URL

Elements: member(*[memberRef]*).URL
              the URL of member *[memberRef]*

Purpose: This property determines the universal resource locator (URL) address of a Shockwave Audio (SWA) or Flash movie cast member.

For SWA cast members, this property can be set only if the cast member is stopped.

For Flash movie cast members, this property is the same as the pathName property.

In context: This statement checks the URL of the cast member NetSound1:

```
put member("NetSound1").URL
-- "http://www.demystified.com/audio/ns1.swa"
```

Notes: This property can be both tested and set. You can use its settability to essentially switch the media of the cast member, by changing the file from which the cast member is derived. Note that the name of the cast member does not have to be the same as the name of the file.

See also: The pathName property.

useAlpha

Elements: member(*[memberRef]*).useAlpha

Purpose: This bitmap cast member property specifies whether a bitmap's alpha channel information is used when the bitmap image is drawn on the Stage. The alpha channel information is an 8-bit layer within a 32-bit graphic that can be used to determine the transparency of any given pixel of the image—sort of a multivalued mask. The alpha channel information is used when the useAlpha property is TRUE, and it is ignored when the value is FALSE (the default). Alpha channels are supported only for sprites using the Matte ink.

In context: This statement enables the LondonFog cast member to be composed on the Stage using the information in its alpha channel:

```
member("LondonFog").useAlpha = TRUE
```

Notes: This property can be both tested and set. Setting useAlpha to TRUE when not required can significantly slow down animation.

See also: The alphaThreshold and ink properties

useHypertextStyles

Elements: member([*memberRef*]).useHypertextStyles

Purpose: This text cast member property determines whether the text of a hyperlink is displayed any differently than other text. When this property is set to TRUE (the default), the hypertext is displayed as blue underlined text, and the cursor changes to a hand as it passes over the hypertext. When it is set to FALSE, there is no text difference or cursor change.

In context: This statement prevents any visible evidence of hyperlinks in the display of cast member GuessWhere:

```
member("GuessWhere").useHypertextStyles = FALSE
```

Notes: This property can be both tested and set. This property cannot be set for individual hyperlinks, only for the entire cast member.

The spelling is different than you might expect (or remember): The property name contains *Hypertext*, not *Hyperlink* as used by all other hyperlink properties.

See also: The hyperLinkClicked handler, the pointInHyperlink function, and the hyperlink, hyperlinkRange, hyperlinks, and hyperlinkState properties.

the useFastQuads

Elements: the useFastQuads

Purpose: Warning: This system property is undocumented. This property determines the quality (and speed of rendering) for sprites that are modified using the new quad sprite property. Setting this property to TRUE increases the display speed but decreases the quality of the image. Setting this property to TRUE also has the side effect of eliminating some of the quad problems in Director 7.0. Setting this property to FALSE (the default) displays the image with normal quality and speed.

In context: This statement specifies that sprites distorted using their quad property will be displayed at the faster rate rather than the higher quality:

```
the useFastQuads = TRUE
```

Notes: This property can be both tested and set.

See also: The quad property.

userName

Elements: the userName

Purpose: This property contains the name of the user entered during your installation of Director. For some reason, this property is valid only while authoring and will generate a script error in a projector. Supposedly, it can be used to customize authoring tools.

In context: This script displays the name of the user that was entered, along with the company name, at the start of the Director 7 installation process:

```
put the userName
-- "Phillip Gross"
```

Notes: This property can be tested but not set. Using this property will generate an error outside of the authoring environment.

See also: The organizationName and serialNumber properties.

vertex

See: The vertex keyword.

vertexList

Elements: member([*memberRef*]).vertexList
the vertexList of member([*memberRef*])

Purpose: This property determines the vertexes of a vector shape cast member. The value of the property is a list, each element of the list being a property list specifying a particular vertex's location and the location of the vertex's control handles (if any). The location points of a vertex are defined relative to the origin of the shape, which is different than the registration point and which can be defined using the originH and originV properties.

The control handles of a vertex define the curve of the line between the adjacent vertices (a Bezier curve). The points for the handles are defined relative to the point of the vertex, so that if the vertex is moved, the handles move with it. Increasing the distance of a handle point from the vertex point increases the length of the curve. Changing the location of the handle relative to the vertex changes the direction of the curve.

In context: This statement displays the vertex list for a vector shape with two vertices:

```
put member(16).vertexList
-- [[#vertex: point(-24.0000, -21.0000),
#handle1: point(72.0000, 35.0000),
#handle2: point(-4.0221, -1.9552)],
[#vertex: point(13.0000, 21.0000)]]
```

Notes: this property can be both tested and set, though Director provides easier methods for modifying vertices.

See also: The addVertex and deleteVertex commands; the count, moveVertex, and moveVertexHandle functions; the originMode, originH, and originV properties; and the vertex keyword.

PROPERTIES

video

Elements: member([*memberRef*]).video
         the video of member *[memberRef]*

Purpose: This property is limited to digital video cast members. When it is set to 1 (or TRUE), the visual portion of the video will be displayed on the Stage; when it is set to 0 (or FALSE), it won't be (although audio portions will still play).

In context: This statement turns off the image display of the digital video Alex on the Boat:

```
member("Alex on the Boat").video = 0
```

Notes: This property can be both tested and set, with the default being TRUE. It is equivalent to selecting the Video check box in the cast member's Properties dialog box.

the videoForWindowsPresent

Elements: the videoForWindowsPresent

Purpose: Use this property to determine whether the end user's computer has Video for Windows installed.

In context: This script branches to the Play Video frame if Video for Windows is present; otherwise, the movie branches to the Special Show frame:

```
if the videoForWindowsPresent = TRUE then
    go to frame "Play Video"
else
    go to frame "Special Show"
end if
```

Notes: This property can be tested but not set.

See also: The quickTimeVersion function.

viewH

Elements: sprite([*spriteRef*]).viewH
         the viewH of sprite *[spriteRef]*
         member([*memberRef*]).viewH
         the viewH of member *[memberRef]*

Purpose: This property determines what part of a Flash movie or vector shape image appears within a sprite's bounding box by determining the horizontal component of the element's viewpoint. The default value is 0. Assigning a positive value shifts the image to the left; assigned a negative value shifts the image to the right. Unlike the viewPoint property, which accepts only integers, the viewH and viewV properties accept floating-point numbers for greater precision.

In context: This script checks to see whether the image in sprite 5 is currently shifted to the left. If it is, the repeat loop pans the image back to the center.

```
if sprite(5).viewH > 1 then
    repeat while sprite(5).viewH > 1
```

```
        sprite(5).viewH = sprite(5).viewH -1
        updateStage
    end repeat
    sprite(5).viewH = 0
end if
```

Notes: This property can be both tested and set. If the scaleMode property is set to #autoSize (the Director 7 default), you must also set the viewH (or viewPoint) property to its default. Otherwise, the image may not be displayed correctly.

See also: The scaleMode, viewV, viewPoint, and viewScale properties.

viewPoint

Elements: sprite([*spriteRef*]).viewPoint
             the viewPoint of sprite [*spriteRef*]
             member([*memberRef*]).viewPoint
             the viewPoint of member [*memberRef*]

Purpose: This property determines what part of a Flash movie or vector shape image appears within a sprite's bounding box by determining the horizontal and vertical components of the element's viewpoint. The value is a Director point: point(horiz, vert). The horizontal and vertical components are integer values, and the default value is point(0,0). The horizontal and vertical components can also be set using the viewH and viewV properties, which allow floating-point values if greater precision is needed.

In context: These statements first check a sprite's viewpoint and then move the viewpoint down and to the left (moving the image up and to the right):

```
put sprite(5).viewPoint
-- point(40, 0)
sprite(5).viewPoint = point(60, -35)
```

Notes: This property can be both tested and set. If you set the scaleMode property to #autoSize, you must also set the viewPoint property to its default. Otherwise, the image may not be displayed correctly.

See also: The scaleMode, viewV, viewH, and viewScale properties.

viewScale

Elements: sprite([*spriteRef*]).viewScale
             the viewScale of sprite [*spriteRef*]
             member([*memberRef*]).viewScale
             the viewScale of member [*memberRef*]

Purpose: This property sets the scale of a Flash movie or vector shape image as it appears in the sprite's bounding rectangle. The value is a floating-point number that indicates a percent; the default value is 100. Setting the value to a lower number will magnify the image, and less of the image will be visible within the sprite. Setting the value to a larger number makes the image shrink. The size of the bounding rectangle is not affected by this property; only the image is affected.

The image is scaled from the center of the sprite's bounding box, so the point of the image in the center will remain in the center after scaling. Compare this behavior with that of the scale property, which scales an image based on a point determined by the originMode property.

In context: This handler implements a Zoom button for the Flash movie sprite in channel 5. Each time the button is clicked, the image magnification increases by 2.

```
on mouseUp
    cv = sprite(5).viewScale
    repeat with i = cv down to cv/2
        sprite(5).viewScale = i
        updateStage
    end repeat
end
```

Notes: This property can be both tested and set. If the scaleMode property is set to #autoSize (the Director 7 default), you must also set the viewScale property to its default. Otherwise, the image may not be displayed correctly.

See also: The scale, scaleMode, viewV, viewPoint, and viewH properties.

viewV

Elements: sprite([*spriteRef*]).viewV
the viewV of sprite *[spriteRef]*
member([*memberRef*]).viewV
the viewV of member *[memberRef]*

Purpose: This property determines what part of a Flash movie or vector shape image appears within a sprite's bounding box by determining the vertical component of the element's viewpoint. The default value is 0. Assigning a positive value shifts the image upward; assigning a negative value shifts the image down. Unlike the viewPoint property, which accepts only integers, the viewH and viewV properties accept floating-point numbers for greater precision.

In context: This script checks to see whether the image in sprite 5 is currently shifted upward. If it is, the repeat loop pans the image back to the center.

```
if sprite(5).viewV > 1 then
    repeat while sprite(5).viewV > 1
        sprite(5).viewV = sprite(5).viewV -1
        updateStage
    end repeat
    sprite(5).viewV = 0
end if
```

Notes: This property can be both tested and set. If the scaleMode property is set to #autoSize (the Director 7 default), you must also set the viewV (or viewPoint) property to its default. Otherwise, the image may not be displayed correctly.

See also: The scaleMode, viewH, viewPoint, and viewScale properties.

visible (of sprite)

Elements: sprite(*[spriteRef]*).visible
the visible of sprite *[spriteRef]*

Purpose: This property can establish whether a sprite occupying the given Score channel is currently displayed on the Stage. When this property is set to 1 (or TRUE), it is displayed according to preset parameters; when it is set to 0 (or FALSE), the image is suppressed.

This property applies to the channel, not a specific sprite, and you must explicitly set the property to change it. When the current sprite in the channel disappears from the Score, the property remains in effect. Subsequent sprites in the channel will also be invisible if the visible property is set to FALSE.

While a sprite is invisible, the sprite does not receive mouse events. Other events (such as beginSprite) will still be sent. This makes using the visible property different from selecting the Mute button for a channel in the Score, which prevents all event messages from being sent to that channel.

In context: This statement toggles the visible property for channel 4:

```
sprite(4).visible = not(sprite(4).visible )
```

Notes: This property can be both tested and set. If the sprite is invisible because of other factors (Transparent ink applied, placement off Stage, and so on), setting this property to TRUE will not render the sprite visible.

visible (of window)

Elements: window(*[windowRef]*).visible
the visible of window *[windowRef]*

Purpose: This property can establish whether a currently open window (as in a Movie in a Window) is displayed on the end user's monitor screen. When this property is set to 1 (or TRUE), the window is shown; when it is set to 0 (or FALSE), the window remains in RAM, but its display is suppressed.

In context: This statement hides the window Pets:

```
window("Pets").visible = FALSE
```

Notes: This property can be both tested and set.

See also: The close window command.

volume (of member)

Elements: member(*[memberRef]*).volume
the volume of member *[memberRef]*

Purpose: This property specifies the volume of a Shockwave Audio (SWA) streaming cast member. The value can range from 0 (no sound) to 255 (full sound, the default).

In context: This statement sets the volume of the SWA streaming cast member SWA file to full volume:

```
member("SWAfile").volume = 255
```

Notes: This property can be both tested and set.

See also: The soundLevel property.

volume (of sound)

Elements: the volume of sound *[whichChannel]*

Purpose: This system property returns or establishes the volume level of sound in a sound channel. This value is expressed as a number ranging from 0 (no sound) to 255 (maximum sound). Note that this property is one of the few for which the dot syntax was never implemented.

In context: This statement sets the volume of sound channel 1 to a median level:

```
the volume of sound 1 = 135
```

Notes: The Score contains only two "official" sound channels (sound channels 1 and 2), but this property can also be used to set levels in virtual sound channels. It can be both tested and set.

volume (of sprite)

Elements: sprite(*[spriteRef]*).volume
            the volume of sprite *[spriteRef]*

Purpose: This property is limited to sprites derived from digital video cast members. It can be used to determine the volume of the video during playback. Volume is expressed as a number ranging from 0 (silent) to 255 (the maximum you should use). Negative numbers can be used, but they will produce the equivalent of 0. Values greater than 255 generally result in unacceptable distortion.

In context:

```
sprite(48).volume = 55
```

warpMode

Elements: sprite(*[QTVRRef]*).warpMode
            the warpMode of sprite *[QTVRRef]*

Purpose: This property specifies the type of warping performed on the panorama of a QTVR sprite. The value is a symbol; allowable values are #full, #partial, and #none.

In context: This statement sets the warpMode property of sprite 4 to #full:

```
sprite(4).warpMode = #full
```

Notes: This property can be both tested and set.

width (of member)

Elements: member(*[memberRef]*).width
              the width of member *[memberRef]*

Purpose: This property returns the width of a specified cast member, expressed in pixels.

In context: This statement uses the Message window to display the width of cast member Scary Clown:

```
put member ("Scary Clown").width
-- 423
```

Notes: This property can be tested but not set.

width (of sprite)

Elements: sprite(*[spriteRef]*).width
              the width of sprite *[spriteRef]*

Purpose: This sprite property determines the width of a specified sprite in the current frame, expressed in pixels. It can be applied to bitmap, animated GIF, Flash movie, vector shape, and shape sprites. Setting a sprite's width property also automatically sets the sprite's stretch property to TRUE.

In context: These statements check and set the width of sprites:

```
put sprite (1).width
-- 209
sprite(3).width = 200
```

Notes: This property can be tested for all cast types, but it cannot be used to set button and field text cast members.

As a result of some of the changes in Director, the width and height properties are not always accurate. Using the height and width properties in conjunction with the rect property should give an accurate indication of a sprite's size when it's drawn on the stage:

```
sprite ([spriteRef]).rect.width
sprite ([spriteRef]).rect.height
```

See also: The height and rect properties.

the windowList

Elements: the windowList

Purpose: This property returns a tally of all windows currently open in the root movie. The root movie itself is not included in the list.

In context: This statement uses the Message window to display a list of all of the movie's windows:

```
put the windowList
-- [(window "Countdown"), (window "Jumping"), (window "Somersault"),
(window "Running")]
```

PROPERTIES

Notes: This property can be tested, but it can be set only in a limited fashion. Windows can be cleared from display by deleting their entries in the windowList, but adding a window name to the list will not make that window appear. All windows can be cleared by setting the windowList to an empty field (that is, to []).

See also: The windowPresent function, the activeWindow and frontWindow properties, and the forget (window) command.

windowType

Elements: window ([*windowRef*]).windowType
              the windowType of window [*windowRef*]

Purpose: This property can be used to determine the physical type of a window during playback. This type is expressed as one of the following codes:

0	Standard (moveable and sizable but no zoom box)
1	Alert box style
2	Plain (no title bar)
3	Plain, with shadow (no title bar)
4	Standard (moveable, but no size box or zoom box)
5	Moveable, modal dialog box
8	Standard document window
12	Zoomable, but not resizable
16	Rounded window (curved border, black title bar)

In context:

```
window ("Pets").windowType = 2
```

Notes: The property can be both tested and set. Generally, you should set this property when the window is not open to avoid display artifacts. The default value is 0.

wordWrap

Elements: member([*memberRef*]).wordWrap
              the wordWrap of member [*memberRef*]

Purpose: This property, limited to field cast members, indicates whether the text is wrapped. If it is set to TRUE (or 1), text will be reflowed to remain within the visible boundaries of the field; if it is set to FALSE (or 0), the field may be resized without changing the text flow (which means that some words may become obscured). It is the Lingo equivalent of setting the Word Wrap option in the cast member's Properties dialog box.

In context:

```
put the wordWrap of member "Answer field"
-- 1
```

Notes: This property can be both tested and set.

xtraList

Elements: the xtraList

Purpose: This property returns a linear list of all Xtras available to the movie. Each list element is a property list containing the properties #name and #version. You can use this property to determine whether a required version of an Xtra is available.

In context: This statement uses the Message window to display the first Xtra in the xtraList list:

```
put (the xtraList)[1]
-- [#name: "photocaster 2.x32", #version: "2, 0, 3, 0"]
```

Notes: This property can be tested but not set. The Director Help listing for xtraList contains an excellent example of a handler that retrieves the version number of an Xtra.

See also: The movieXtraList property.

year

Elements: (the systemDate).year
           [dateVariable].year

Purpose: This property retrieves the number of the year from the systemDate property or other element using the date data type.

In context: This command returns the current year:

```
put the systemDate
-- date( 1999, 5, 16 )
put (the systemDate).year
-- 1999
```

Notes: This property can be both tested and set for variables containing a date data type. It cannot set the systemDate property. It works only with the systemDate property, not the date function.

See also: The day, month, and systemDate properties.

PROPERTIES

Operators

. (dot operator)

Elements: *object.property*

Purpose: This operator is used to set or test properties, to issue commands, or to execute functions relating to objects. Objects can be virtually anything you can come up with in Director, including cast members, sprites, lists, behaviors, and the like.

In context: The following statement sets the `moveableSprite` property of sprite 10:

```
sprite(10).moveableSprite = FALSE
```

@ (pathname)

Elements: "@:*pathReference*"

Purpose: This operator defines the path to the current movie's folder and is system independent (that is, it is valid on both Windows and Macintosh computers). When used to specify a path, the @ operator is replaced by the path to the current folder. Any path separators (colons, slashes, and backslashes) are converted to the correct separator for the system that is running the movie. This path separator conversion takes place for the entire path specified, not just the @ portion. The path separator may be :, \, or /.

In context: This statement branches to the movie Part3 in the folder OtherParts contained within the folder from which the movie is currently running. Notice that the @ operator is within the quotation marks and is followed by a path separator.

```
go to movie "@:OtherParts:Part3.dir"
```

Using two (or more) path separators together specifies a folder up one (or more) level. Thus, the following statement branches to the movie Part8 in the folder that contains the folder containing the currently running movie:

```
go to movie "@//Part8"
```

Both of the preceding statements will be executed equally well on Macintosh and Windows systems.

Notes: Not all commands support the @ operator (for example, the FileIO Xtra command doesn't).

See also: The `moviePath`, `searchPaths`, and `filename` properties.

– [minus sign] (subtraction)

Elements: - *[expression]*

              [expression] - *[expression]*

Purpose: When placed between two numerical expressions, this operator subtracts the second from the first. Unless both expressions are integers, the result is a floating-point number.

When placed before a single numerical expression, this operator reverses the sign of the evaluated expression.

In context:

```
bankBalance = -(4*100)
put bankBalance
-- -400
put 100 - 4
-- 96
```

& [ampersand] (concatenation)

Elements: *[expression]* & *[expression]*

Purpose: This operator *concatenates*, or joins together, two expressions and places the result in a text string. If either of the expressions is a number, the number will be converted to a text string before the concatenation is performed.

In context: The following statement concatenates two strings and places them in a field cast member:

```
member("Word Type").text = "pre" & "fix"
```

The Word Type field would display the string *"prefix"*.

These statements show how a number is converted to a string and how variables can be used as expressions:

```
userLevel = 2
currStatus = "Level" & userLevel
put currStatus
-- "Level2"
```

Notes: A single ampersand concatenates the expressions without leaving any space between them. To introduce a space, use two ampersands (&&).

&& [two ampersands] (concatenation)

Elements: *[expression]* && *[expression]*

Purpose: Like the single ampersand, this operator *concatenates*, or joins together, two expressions and places the result in a text string. If either of the expressions is a number, the number will be converted in a text string before the concatenation is performed.

Unlike the single ampersand, && introduces a space between the two elements as part of the concatenation process.

In context: The following two statements result in exactly the same string:

```
put "1234" && "5678"
-- "1234 5678"
put "1234" & " 5678"
-- "1234 5678"
```

The use of the double ampersand makes keeping track of spaces easier and makes it obvious to anyone reading the code that the space is intended rather than a mistake:

```
nameVar = firstVar && lastVar
put nameVar
-- "Alex Gross"
```

OPERATORS

Notes: To join two expressions together without a space, use a single ampersand (&).

() [parentheses]   (grouping)

Elements: *([expression])*

Purpose: These grouping operators identify multiple elements of a numerical or string expression as a single expression. When enclosed in parentheses, an expression is evaluated before expressions outside the parentheses.

In context: The statement

put 2+3*4+5

returns 19, whereas the statement

put (2+3)*(4+5)

returns 45.

Of the following two statements, the first will successfully concatenate two strings to create a reference to a member, and the second will generate a script error:

sprite(2).member = member(currVar & "Bold")
sprite(2).member = member currVar & "Bold"

Notes: You can use multiple sets of nested parentheses to further prioritize numerical calculations. The most deeply nested ones are calculated first; for example, in the following expression, 4+8 is the first operation performed: ((3*12)+3)*(((4+8)*2)+5).

*   [asterisk]   (multiplication)

Elements: *[expression]* * *[expression]*

Purpose: This operator multiplies the first numerical expression by the second and returns the result. If the expressions consist of integers, the result will be expressed as an integer. Unless both expressions evaluate to integers, the result is a floating-point number.

In context: The statement

put 11 * 3

returns 33, and the statement

put 2 * 3.908023218923823983

returns 7.8160.

Notes: In the case of floating-point numbers (those with decimal points), the number of decimal points displayed is determined by the floatPrecision movie property.

+   [plus symbol]   (addition)

Elements: *[expression]* + *[expression]*

Purpose: This operator adds the first numerical expression to the second and returns the result. If the expressions consist of integers, the result will be expressed as an integer. If one or both of the expressions are floating-point numbers, the result will be expressed as a floating-point number.

In context: The statement

put 2 + 3.908023218923823983

returns 5.9080, and the statement

put var1 + var2

returns the tally of whatever numerical values are in the variables var1 and var2.

Notes: In the case of floating-point numbers (those with decimal points), the number of decimal points displayed is determined by the floatPrecision movie property.

/ [slash] (division)

Elements: *[expression] / [expression]*

Purpose: This operator divides the first numerical expression by the second and returns the result. If one or both of the expressions are floating-point numbers, the result will be expressed as a floating-point number. If the expressions both consist of integers, Director rounds the resultant value to the nearest integer.

In context: The statement

put 11 / 3

returns 3 (as opposed to the more accurate 3.66666), and the statement

put 11.0 / 3

returns 3.6666.

Notes: In the case of floating-point numbers (those with decimal points), the number of decimal points displayed is determined by the floatPrecision movie property.

< (less than)

Elements: *[expression1] < [expression2]*

Purpose: This comparison operator compares the value of the first expression to that of the second and returns a judgment as to whether the first is less than the second. If *expression1* is less than *expression2*, the value is TRUE (or 1). Otherwise, the value is FALSE (or 0).

In context: The statement

put 11 < 3

returns 0, which is another way of stating FALSE. In contrast, the statement

put 3 < 11

returns 1, or TRUE. The statement

```
if score1 < score2 then
        alert "You lose!"
end if
```

compares the variables score1 and score2 and displays an alert message only when score2 is greater than score1. The following statement compares two lists and returns 1 (TRUE):

put [1,2,3] < [1,2,4]

OPERATORS

Notes: The comparison operators can compare numbers, strings, lists, points, and rects. Strings are compared alphanumerically, and the equal (=) and not-equal (<>) operators are not case sensitive. The other comparison operators (greater than and so on) are case sensitive. Lists are compared element by element until an element in one list does not match an element in the other list, at which time the comparison result is determined by the two dissimilar elements. Points and rects are treated as lists for comparison purposes.

<= (less than or equal to)

Elements: *[expression]* <= *[expression]*

Purpose: This comparison operator compares the value of the first expression to that of the second and returns a judgment as to whether the first is less than or equal to the second. If *expression1* is less than or equal to *expression2*, the value is TRUE (or 1). Otherwise, the value is FALSE (or 0).

In context: The statement

```
put 11 <= 3
```

returns 0, which is another way of stating FALSE. In contrast, the statement

```
put 3 <= 11
```

or

```
put (10+1) <= 11
```

returns 1, or TRUE. The statement

```
if score1 <= score2 then
    alert "You didn't beat the best score!"
end if
```

compares the variables score1 and score2 and displays an accurate alert message even if the current score (the first variable) exactly matches the best score (second variable). The following statement compares two points and returns 1 (TRUE):

```
put point(100,120) <= point(100,140)
```

Notes: The comparison operators can compare numbers, strings, lists, points, and rects. Strings are compared alphanumerically, and the equal (=) and not-equal (<>) operators are not case sensitive. The other comparison operators (greater than and so on) are case sensitive. Lists are compared element by element until an element in one list does not match an element in the other list, at which time the comparison result is determined by the two dissimilar elements. Points and rects are treated as lists for comparison purposes.

<> (not equal to)

Elements: *[expression]* <> *[expression]*

Purpose: This comparison operator compares the value of the first expression to that of the second and returns a judgment as to whether the two are equal.

In context: The following statement returns 1, or TRUE:

```
put 11 <> 3
```

In contrast, the statement

```
put (10+1) <> 11
```

returns 0, or FALSE. The statement

```
if answerNum <> correct then
        alert "Sorry, try again."
end if
```

compares the variables answerNum and correct and displays an alert message unless they are equivalent.

Notes: This operator is the opposite of the = (equal) operator.

The comparison operators can compare numbers, strings, lists, points, and rects. Strings are compared alphanumerically, and the equal (=) and not-equal (<>) operators are not case sensitive. The other comparison operators (greater than and so on) are case sensitive. Lists are compared element by element until an element in one list does not match an element in the other list, at which time the comparison result is determined by the two dissimilar elements. Points and rects are treated as lists for comparison purposes.

=   [equals sign]   (comparison)

Elements: *[expression]* = *[expression]*

Purpose: This comparison operator compares the value of the first expression to that of the second and returns a judgment as to whether the two are equal.

In context: The statement

```
put 11 = 3
```

returns 0, or FALSE. In contrast, the statement

```
put (10+1) = 11
```

returns 1, or TRUE, and the statement

```
if score1 = score2 then
   alert "You've matched the high score!"
end if
```

compares the variables score1 and score2 and displays an alert message only when they are equivalent. The following statement compares two strings and returns TRUE, because the equals operator is not case sensitive:

```
put "Alex" = "alex"
```

Notes: This operator is the opposite of the <> (not equal) operator.

The comparison operators can compare numbers, strings, lists, points, and rects. Strings are compared alphanumerically, and the equal (=) and not-equal (<>) operators are not case sensitive. The other comparison operators (greater than and so on) are case sensitive. Lists are compared element by element until an element in one list does not match an element in the other list, at which time the comparison result is determined by the two dissimilar elements. Points and rects are treated as lists for comparison purposes.

OPERATORS

=   [equals sign]   (assignment)

Elements: [container] = [expression]

Purpose: This use of the equal operator assigns the value of *expression* to *container*, which may be a variable or another element that can contain a value. The equal operator enables more concise programming syntax but provides the same functionality as the older set...to command. For setting some properties using dot syntax, the use of =, rather than to, is required.

If *container* is a variable, the variable will be created if it does not already exist.

In context: These statements are all functionally equivalent. The method you choose is up to you.

```
myVar = var1 * var2
set myVar = var1 * var2
set meyVar to var1 * var2
```

The first three of the following four statements are functionally equivalent. The fourth statement will generate a script error.

```
member(1).text = "Hello!"
set member(1).text = "Hello!"
set the text of member 1 to "Hello!"
set member(1).text to "Hello!"  --ERROR!!!
```

See also: The set...to command.

>   (greater than)

Elements: [expression] > [expression]

Purpose: This comparison operator compares the value of the first expression to that of the second and returns a judgment as to whether the first is greater than the second.

In context: The statement

```
put 11 > 3
```

returns 1, or TRUE. In contrast, the statement

```
put 3 > 11
```

returns 0, or FALSE. The statement

```
if score1 > score2 then alert "You win!"
```

compares the variables score1 and score2 and displays an alert message only when the first expression is greater than the second. The following statement compares two strings and returns TRUE because this comparison operator is case sensitive:

```
put "Alex" > "alex"
```

Notes: The comparison operators can compare numbers, strings, lists, points, and rects. Strings are compared alphanumerically, and the equal (=) and not-equal (<>) operators are not case sensitive. The other comparison operators (greater than and so on) are case sensitive. Lists are compared element by element until an element in one list does not match an element in the other list, at which time the comparison result is determined by the two dissimilar elements. Points and rects are treated as lists for comparison purposes.

>= (greater than or equal to)

Elements: *[expression] >= [expression]*

Purpose: This comparison operator compares the value of the first expression to that of the second and returns a judgment as to whether the first expression is greater than or equal to the second.

In context: The statement

```
put 11 >= 3
```

or

```
put (10+1) >= 11
```

returns 1, or TRUE. In contrast, the statement

```
put 3 >= 11
```

returns 0, or FALSE. The statement

```
if score1 >= score2 then
    alert "Hey, you're a pretty good player!"
end if
```

compares the variables score1 and score2 and displays an encouraging message when the current score (the first variable) matches or exceeds the best score (the second variable).

Notes: The comparison operators can compare numbers, strings, lists, points, and rects. Strings are compared alphanumerically, and the equal (=) and not-equal (<>) operators are not case sensitive. The other comparison operators (greater than and so on) are case sensitive. Lists are compared element by element until an element in one list does not match an element in the other list, at which time the comparison result is determined by the two dissimilar elements. Points and rects are treated as lists for comparison purposes.

[ ] [square brackets]   (lists)

Elements: *[list entry1, list entry2, etc.]*

Purpose: When strings, numbers, variables, or symbols are enclosed by square brackets and separated by commas, Lingo will interpret them as entries in a list. This list can then be accessed and manipulated by other commands. Lists can be either linear lists or property lists.

In context: This statement creates a linear list called ballStats and places three numerical entries in that list:

```
ballStats = [2, 8, 7]
```

This statement creates a similar list but assigns symbols as properties to each value:

```
set ballStats = [#runs:2, #hits:8, #errors:7]
```

OPERATORS

Notes: To empty a list (or to create a list before creating any entries), set the list's values to null using an empty bracket statement, such as set ballStats = []. To empty a property list, use a colon as the sole text: set ballStats = [:].

List variables behave differently than other variables. Assigning a list variable to another variable does not create a separate instance of the list—both variables refer to the same list, and making changes to one will also change the other. For example, the following statements actually create only a single list:

```
X1 = ["A", "B", "C"]
X2 = X1
put X2
-- ["A", "B", "C"]
X2[2] = "NEW"
put X2
-- ["A", "NEW", "C"]
put X1
-- ["A", "NEW", "C"]
```

To create a separate copy of a list, use the duplicate function:

```
X3 = duplicate(X1)
X3[2] = "Different"
put X3
-- ["A", "Different", "C"]
put X1
-- ["A", "NEW", "C"]
```

See also: The list count, duplicate, getLast, getOne, getPos, getPref, getProp, max, and min functions and the add, addAt, append, deleteAt, deleteAll, findPos, findPosNear, getAt, setaProp, setAt, and sort commands.

[ ] [square brackets]   (chunk expressions)

Elements: *text.specifier[number]*

   text.specifier[firstNumber..lastNumber]

Purpose: This operator allows you to specify particular elements in a chunk of text. You can retrieve text chunks by characters, words, lines, items, and paragraphs,

In context: This statement retrieves words 1 through 3 of the second line of text cast member Walt Kelly:

```
put member("Walt Kelly").line[2].word[1..3]
-- "Pogo and Albert"
```

These statements address characters of a text string contained in the variable myString:

```
put myString.char[45..47]
-- "del"
```

See also: The char, item, line, paragraph, and word keywords.

and

Elements: *[expression1]* and *[expression2]*

Purpose: Use this operator to determine whether *expression1* and *expression2* are both true. If both expressions are true, the value returned is 1 (TRUE). If 0 is returned, one or both expressions are false.

In context: These statements set a value for X and then check to see if the value is 1 or 2. The value returned is FALSE (or 0) because one of the expressions (X = 1) is FALSE.

```
X = 2
put (X = 1) and (X = 2)
-- 0
```

This script checks to see if it's past noon on a Friday and tries to send the user of the movie home if it is:

```
on startMovie
    if (the long date contains "Friday") and (the time contains "PM") then
        alert "Time to sneak off."
    end if
end
```

See also: The not and or operators.

contains

Elements: *[expression]* contains *[expression]*

Purpose: This operator compares two text strings and returns a judgment as to whether the first contains the second. If it does, the operator returns 1 (TRUE); if it doesn't, the operator returns 0 (FALSE).

In context: This button script checks the text entered by the user (in cast member 3) against a list of misspelled words (stored in the cast member Spelling):

```
on mouseUp
    userText = member(3).text
    if member("Spelling").text contains userText then
        alert "You misspelled a word."
    end if
end
```

Notes: The comparison made by contains ignores diacritical marks and case; uppercase and lowercase letters are treated as identical.

See also: The starts operator.

mod

Elements: *integerExpression1* mod *integerExpression2*

Purpose: This mathematical operation determines the remainder that would be the result of dividing *integerExpression1* by *integerExpression2*. The expressions must be integers, and the result is an integer with the same positive or negative sign as *integerExpression1*. This operation is useful for converting an expression that continually increases, such as a counter, into a number within a limited range.

In context: This sprite behavior rotates sprite 1 so long as the mouse is over the sprite with the behavior. The global variable theDegrees contains the number of degrees of rotation (between 0 and 359) for the rotated sprite, even though the sprite's rotation property may indicate that the sprite has rotated any number of full revolutions.

```
on mouseWithin
   global theDegrees
   sprite(1).rotation = sprite(1).rotation + 5
   theDegrees = sprite(1).rotation mod 360
end
```

The following sprite behavior cycles the cast member of the sprite through the starting member and the following three cast members (four total; hence, the mod 4 statement). The handler is independent of the cast member's location in the Cast, so long as the cast members are contiguous. The sprite always ends up with the original cast member displayed.

```
property spriteNum
on mouseDown
   counter = 0
   memNum = sprite(spriteNum).memberNum
   repeat while the mouseDown
      counter = counter + 1
      sprite(spriteNum).memberNum = memNum + (counter mod 4)
      updateStage
   end repeat
   sprite(spriteNum).memberNum = memNum
end
```

not

Elements: not *logicalExpression*

Purpose: This operator converts a TRUE statement (or expression) to a FALSE statement, and vice versa. In its simplest form, not 1 (or not TRUE) is 0 (or FALSE), and not 0 is 1 (or TRUE). This operator is useful when the expression being tested is the opposite of what you want, or when statements are more easily formatted in one form and tested for the opposite.

In context: This statement checks whether 1 + 1 is not equal to 2:

```
if not (1 + 1 = 2) then
   alert "Something is wrong!"
end if
```

This script performs a set of actions only if the day of the week is not Sunday:

```
if not (the long date contains "Sunday") then
   -- do something
end if
```

This statement turns sound on if it is off and turns it off if it is on:

the soundEnabled = not(the soundEnabled)

or

Elements: *[expression]* or *[expression]*

Purpose: Use this operator to determine whether expressions are at least partially true or partially false. If one or both expressions are true, the value returned is 1 (TRUE). If 0 is returned, both expressions are false.

In context: These statements set a value for X and then check to see if the value is 1 or 2. The value returned is TRUE (or 1) because one of the expressions (X = 2) is TRUE.

X = 2
put (X = 1) or (X = 2)
-- 1

This statement checks to see if the day of the week is a Saturday or Sunday and tries to send the user of the movie home if it is:

on startMovie
    if (the long date contains "Saturday") or¬
    (the long date contains "Sunday") then
        alert "Go home, it's the weekend."
    end if
end

See also: The and and not operators.

starts

Elements: *[expression]* starts *[expression]*

Purpose: This operator compares two text strings and returns a judgment as to whether the first begins with the second. If it does, the operator returns 1 (TRUE); if it doesn't, the operator returns 0 (FALSE).

In context: This statement checks to see if the text entered by the user (the variable lastName) begins with a particular text string:

on mouseUp
    lastName = member(3).text
    if "O'" starts lastName then
        alert "Is that an Irish name?"
    end if
end

Notes: The comparison made by starts ignores diacritical marks and case; uppercase and lowercase letters are treated as identical.

See also: The contains operator.

OPERATORS

KEYWORDS AND CONSTANTS

" [double quotation mark] (strings)

Elements: `"string content"`

Purpose: This string constant, when used before and after a string, indicates that the string is a literal—not a variable, numerical value, or Lingo element that Director should interpret. Literal names of cast members, casts, windows, and external files must always be enclosed in double quotation marks.

In context: This statement uses quotation marks to indicate that the string "Martha's House" is a literal string, the name of a cast member:

```
put member("Martha's House").rect
```

Notes: Certain characters (such as double quotation marks) are difficult to include in strings in some circumstances. Director includes a number of constants that can be used for this purpose. The following string includes quotation mark characters around the word *Mike*:

```
put "My name is" && QUOTE & "Mike" & QUOTE && "Gross."
-- "My name is "Mike" Gross."
```

This string includes a Return character, causing the display to appear on two lines:

```
put "1" & RETURN & "2"
-- "1
2"
```

See also: The & and && concatenation operators and the BACKSPACE, EMPTY, ENTER, QUOTE, RETURN, SPACE, and TAB constants.

[pound sign] (symbols)

Elements: `#nameofSymbol`

Purpose: Director will handle any unit of letters and/or numerals preceded by the # sign as a single symbol.

To understand *symbol* in this context, imagine that you had the ability to add a twenty-seventh letter to the alphabet or a new integer to the series 0 through 9: that would be a new symbol, one manipulated by the computer just like the letters and numbers it presently handles. A symbol is similar to a text or numerical string, but it occupies less memory and processing time. Many of Director's properties are now stored as symbols.

In context: This script examines the global variable guserStatus to see if the user has won a set number of previous consecutive games:

```
on enterFrame
    global guserStatus
    if guserStatus = #WonSeven then
    alert "Sheesh! Give someone else a chance!"
end
```

Notes: Symbols must begin with a letter and can contain only letters, numbers, and the underscore character. They cannot contain other punctuation or special characters. Symbols declared with # can be converted to strings using the string function.

See also: The ilk, string, symbol, and symbolP functions.

-- [two hyphens] (comments)

Elements: -- *[text]*

Purpose: Two hyphens are used to indicate comments in Lingo script. If at any point Lingo encounters this symbol, it doesn't attempt to execute the following text on that line. This symbol is handy for including notes directly in a script.

In context:

```
on mouseDown
    -- the buttonSound handler supplies the sound
    buttonSound
    -- use a different cursor until
    -- the mouse is released
    cursor(member "Butterfly")
end
```

Notes: When writing multiple lines of commentary, remember that each line of comment text must begin with its own pair of hyphens.

: [colon] (property lists)

Elements: [*[propertyName]* : *[value]*]

Purpose: This special character is used to associate a property with a value in a property list. When placed in a list, these units can then be manipulated using a number of commands.

In context: These statements create and then manipulate a property list named myPets:

```
myPets = [#dog: 7, #cat: 4, #fish: 9]
sort myPets
put myPets
-- [#cat: 4, #dog: 7, #fish: 9]
```

Notice that the sort command has placed the symbols in alphabetical order.

Notes: To empty a property list, use a colon as the sole text:

```
myPets = [:]
```

See also: The list function.

¬ (continuation)

Elements: *Lingo statement starts on this line* ¬
          and continues on this one, and ¬
          continues on this one

Purpose: When a statement line is long and cumbersome, you can use this special continuation character to break it into more readable chunks. Lingo will interpret the lines created by such breaks as a single statement.

In context:

```
on mouseDown
   put the clickOn into currSprite
   put the memberNum of sprite currSprite ¬
into thisOne
   set the memberNum of sprite currSprite ¬
= thisOne +1
   puppetSound "Switch"
   updateStage
end mouseDown
```

Notes: This character must fall at the end of a line. You cannot use the continuation character in the Message window (and you don't need to) because lines will wrap automatically.

BACKSPACE

Elements: BACKSPACE

Purpose: This constant represents the Backspace key (on Windows machines) or the Delete key (on MacOS systems).

In context: These statements clear the text of a field when the user presses the Backspace key:

```
if the key = BACKSPACE then
   member("my field").text = EMPTY
end if
```

beginRecording

Elements: beginRecording

Purpose: This keyword is used to commence Score modification in a script. To use Lingo to modify the Score, you must incorporate this keyword and its companion, endRecording.

In context: This handler inserts 99 new copies of the first frame in a Director movie:

```
on makeABunch
   beginRecording
      repeat with x = 1 to 99
         go to frame x
         insertFrame
      end repeat
   endRecording
end makeABunch
```

case

Elements: case *[expression]* of
        [value1]: *[statement]*
        [value2]:
           [multiple statements]
           [multiple statements]
        [value3], *[value4]*:
           [statements]
     otherwise:
        [statements]
     end case

Purpose: This keyword starts a case statement, which is a compact alternative to if...then statements of conditionality. The *expression* argument is evaluated and then compared to the *value* arguments looking for a match. When a match is found, the statement(s) following it are executed. If no match is found, the statements following the optional otherwise keyword will be executed if any are included. Once a match is found, Director no longer searches for additional matches.

Multiple *value* arguments can appear on the same line (if the same statements should be executed), separated by commas.

Each case statement must be followed by a matching end case statement.

In context: This case statement compares the value in the myTime variable to a set of integers. A different text string is displayed in the Countdown field, depending on the value of the variable:

```
on idle
   myTime = the timeoutLapsed / 60
   case (myTime) of
      5 : member("Countdown").text = "1"
      4 : member("Countdown").text = "2"
      3 : member("Countdown").text = "3"
      2 : member("Countdown").text = "4"
      1 : member("Countdown").text = "5"
      otherwise member("Countdown").text = " "
   end case
end idle
```

See also: The end case keyword, and Chapter 11.

castLib

Elements: castLib

Purpose: This keyword helps to identify a particular cast when multiple casts are used in a movie. Each new cast (either internal or external) is given a name and number that can be used to identify it. Numbers are usually assigned in the order in which the Casts are created. The default internal Cast database has the number 1.

In context: This statement assigns a new cast member to sprite 15. The new cast member is in slot 43 of the Images castLib.

```
sprite(15).member = member(43) of castLib("Images")
```

This statement determines the number of the Images castLib:

```
put castLib("Images").number
-- 3
```

Notes: The following statement will generate an error as shown. Notice the use of parentheses around the member, but not around the castLib.

```
member(x) of castLib y
```

Instead, use one of the alternative syntaxes:

```
member(x) of castLib(y)
member x of castLib y
member(x,y)
```

char...of

Elements: *expression*.char[*number*]
              char *number* of *expression*
              expression.char[*number1*..*number2*]
              char *number1* to *number2* of *expression*

Purpose: Use this keyword to retrieve characters from a text chunk. The text chunk can be any element that contains a string. Note that to specify a range of characters using dot syntax, you need to separate the first and last character specifiers with two periods.

To modify a string expression, you must use the put...into (or after or before) command. You cannot use the set command for this purpose.

In context: The following two statements both access the second character in the text of field cast member Explosion:

```
put char 2 of member("Explosion").text
put member("Explosion").char[2]
```

The following statements show some examples of how the char keyword can be used to retrieve or modify a text string in the variable myString. Note how the put command is used to modify the string; also note that the number of characters "put into" do not need to match the number of characters being replaced.

```
myString = "12345"
put myString.char[1..3]
-- "123"
put "abc" into myString.char[1..4]
put myString
-- "abc5"
```

Notes: You must always use the put command to change the characters in an expression, except for field and text cast members (and then only when you use the dot-syntax versions). The following statement is allowed:

```
member("myField").char[1..4] = "Martha"
```

The following statements will generate script errors:

```
myString.char[1] = "A"
char 1 of myString = "A"
```

See also: The put...after, put...before, and put...into commands and the number of chars function.

EMPTY

Elements: EMPTY

Purpose: Use this constant to refer to a blank text string.

In context: These statements clear the text of a field when the user presses the Backspace key:

```
if the key = BACKSPACE then
   member("my field").text = EMPTY
end if
```

end

Elements: end

Purpose: This keyword is used to close a handler script. It can be used either alone or with an optional recapitulation of the name of the handler (for example, end myHandler).

In context:

```
on mouseUp
   buttonClick
   changeCursor
end
```

end case

Elements: end case

Purpose: This keyword closes a case statement, which is a compact alternative to if...then statements of conditionality.

In context:

```
on idle
   put the timeoutLapsed / 60 into myTime
   case (myTime) of
       5 : set the text of member "Count" to "1"
       4 : set the text of member "Count" to "2"
       3 : set the text of member "Count" to "3"
       2 : set the text of member "Count" to "4"
       1 : set the text of member "Count" to "5"
       otherwise set the text of member "Count" to " "
   end case
end idle
```

See also: The case keyword.

endRecording

Elements: endRecording

Purpose: This keyword is used to end Score modification in a script. To use Lingo to modify the Score, you must incorporate this keyword and its companion, beginRecording.

In context: This handler inserts 99 new copies of the first frame in a Director movie:

```
on makeABunch
   go to frame 1
   beginRecording
     repeat with x = 1 to 99
        insertFrame
     end repeat
   endRecording
end makeABunch
```

See also: The beginRecording keyword.

ENTER

Elements: ENTER

Purpose: Use this constant to refer to the Enter key on a MacOS keyboard or to the Enter key on the numeric keypad of a Windows keyboard. It does *not* refer to the key labeled "Enter" on the main portion of many Windows keyboards (that one is represented by the constant RETURN).

In context: These statements check to see whether the Enter key was pressed:

```
on keyDown
   if the key = ENTER then updateStage
end
```

See also: The RETURN keyword.

exit

Elements: exit

Purpose: This keyword directs Director to leave the current handler script without executing any of the remaining statements in the handler. If the handler being exited was called from another handler, execution proceeds from the following statement in the calling handler (that is, the exit statement does not affect the calling handler). The exit statement can provide a convenient escape hatch if it's not necessary to execute an entire script.

In context: This handler performs (supposedly) a number of actions that are specific to Macintosh systems. By first checking whether the system is really a Macintosh and exiting the handler if it is not, the handler avoids performing the actions on the wrong system.

```
on myPowerMacSpecificHandler
   if not (the platform contains "Macintosh") then
     exit
   end if
```

```
   -- do other stuff
   -- many more statements
end
```

See also: The return keyword.

exit repeat

Elements: exit repeat

Purpose: Upon execution, this keyword will cause Director to jump entirely out of a repeat looping script. It's not to be confused with next repeat, which remains with the loop but skips a single operation.

In context: This repeat loop rotates a sprite continuously until the user presses the Return key. Notice that the repeat declaration uses an expression that will always be evaluated as TRUE, so the repeat loop would execute forever except for the escape offered by the exit repeat statement.

```
repeat while TRUE
   if the keyPressed = RETURN then
      exit repeat
   end if
   sprite(4).rotation = sprite(4).rotation + 3
   updateStage
end repeat
```

Notes: Be careful when using repeat loops in this fashion, especially for Shockwave. The continuous execution of the Lingo statements in the loop may prevent system operations from taking place, resulting in a system that appears unresponsive to the user.

See also: The repeat and next repeat keyword.

exit tell

Elements: exit tell

Warning: This is an undocumented keyword.

Purpose: Upon execution, this keyword causes Director to exit a tell...end tell construct without executing any of the following statements.

In context: This script checks to see whether the user has pressed the Return key before instructing the running MIAW to perform certain actions:

```
tell window("running")
   moveSprites
   if the key = RETURN then
      exit tell
   end if
   -- do more stuff
end tell
```

See also: The tell command.

FALSE

Elements: FALSE

Purpose: This constant, along with its counterpart TRUE, provides a means of making scripts using binary values (0 or 1) more readable. FALSE translates to 0, and TRUE translates to 1.

In context: The first two of the following statements set the `pausedAtStart` property of a QuickTime cast member to FALSE, indicating that the video should begin playing as soon as the sprite appears on the Stage. The first statement uses 0 instead of FALSE, but the result is the same. The third statement shows that the value returned in the Message window is 0 instead of the keyword FALSE, although testing for FALSE will work just as well as testing for 0.

```
member("QT4").pausedAtStart = 0
member("QT4").pausedAtStart = FALSE
put member("QT4").pausedAtStart
-- 0
```

Notes: You should be aware that while FALSE is always 0, in most instances binary properties accept any value that is not 0 (FALSE) as TRUE.

See also: The TRUE constant.

field

Elements: field *[name or number]*

Purpose: Use this keyword to specify a field-type text cast member.

In context: These two statements provide the same functionality, the first using the `field` keyword and the second using the `member` keyword:

```
member("News").text = "This just in!!!"
set the text of field "News" to "This just in!!!"
```

Notes: This keyword is retained for backward compatibility with earlier versions of Director. For new movies, you should use the `member` keyword instead. The `field` keyword is not supported in dot syntax.

if...then

Elements: if *expression* then *statement*

if *expression* then
   statement(s)
end if

if *expression* then
   statement(s)
else
   statement(s)
end if

Purpose: The `if...then...end if` construct allows you to use the value of a logical expression to determine whether a statement or block of statements is executed. If *expression* evaluates to TRUE, or to any nonzero value, the statements following the `if` keyword are executed. If *expression* evaluates to FALSE, any statements following the optional else keyword are executed.

Since if constructs can be quite complex, such as when if statements are nested within other if statements, it's a good idea to keep an eye on the indentation provided by Director in the Script window. The indentation should show you which if, else, and end if statements are associated. If the indentation doesn't look correct, first press the Tab key to force Director to check the script and redo the indentation. If that doesn't fix the problem, look for errors in your syntax or in your logic.

In context: In these examples, only a single statement is executed. These show the only times you don't need a matching end if statement.

```
if the key = RETURN then go frame "AnswerDone"
```

```
if the key = RETURN then go frame "AnswerDone"
else go to frame "Retry"
```

In this example, multiple statements are executed. The else statement is optional.

```
if var = 2 then
   -- do some stuff
else
   -- do other stuff
end if
```

This example checks for multiple values using else if statements:

```
if var = 2 then
   -- do some 2 stuff
else if var = 3 then
   -- do some 3 stuff
else if var = 4 then
   -- do some 4 stuff
else
   -- not 2, 3 or 4 stuff
end if
```

This example uses nested if...else...end if statements. Notice how the first end if statement (line 6) lines up with the if statement of line 2. To avoid confusion when nesting if statements, always use the if...end if version rather than the single-line version.

```
if var1 = "red" then
   if var2 > 10 then
      -- do some big red stuff
   else
      -- do some small red stuff
   end if
else
   -- do some blue stuff
end if
```

KEYWORDS

The conditional expression can be a compound expression using logical operators, as shown in the following script. The statements will be executed only if var1 is equal to the string "red" *and* var2 is greater than 10.

```
if (var1 = "red") and (var2 > 10) then
    -- do some statements
end if
```

Notes: When compound logical expressions are used, Director always evaluates all elements of the expressions before deciding if the total is TRUE, even if the value of one expression would prevent the total from ever being TRUE. This can lead to situations in which execution will be faster if you use nested `if` statements rather than compound expressions. The following two `repeat` constructs use `if` statements to find all the numbers that are divisible by 3 but not by 2. Although the code for the first `repeat` construct looks more compact, both mod checks will need to be performed 3 gazillion times. In the second repeat construct, the (i mod 2) expression is checked only one out of three times—a savings of some 2 gazillion operations.

```
repeat with i = 1 to threeGazillion
    if (not (i mod 3)) and (i mod 2) then
        put i
    end if
end repeat
repeat with i = 1 to threeGazillion
    if not (i mod 3) then
        if (i mod 2) then
            put i
        end if
    end if
end repeat
```

See also: The case keyword.

global

Elements: global [*variableName1, variableName2, …*]

Purpose: Use this keyword to declare global variables or to indicate that you're using the globals named. Once a global variable has been declared, that global variable can be used, and its value accessed, in any handler or script that also declares the variable as global.

Placing the global statement in a handler makes the variable available throughout the remainder of the handler. Placing the global statement in a script (outside of any handler) makes the variable accessible through all handlers that follow the declaration in the script. The recommended use is to place global declarations at the start of any handler that uses the variables. This enables handlers to be independent units that don't rely on their location in a particular script.

Once a global variable is declared, it is accessible throughout the movie as well as in any windows (MIAWs) and any other movies that are branched to.

In context: This statement declares three variables to be global:

```
global catsPaw, hammer, hacksaw
```

Notes: When using global variables, don't forget that you have to declare them as global in each script. Otherwise, Director will assume you're working with local variables that simply happen to have the same names as global ones.

Variables used in the Message window are automatically global variables, even though they are not declared as such using a global statement.

It is considered good programming practice to declare and initialize all global variables in a prepareMovie handler. This, however, can lead to complications when your movie branches to another movie and then back again. To prevent your movie from reinitializing the global variables (and losing their current states), use the voidP function as a test in the prepareMovie handler to see if the values are already set:

```
on prepareMovie
   global var1, var2, initialized
   if voidP(initialized) then
     -- only set these once
     initialized = 1
     var1 = "Hello"
   end if
   -- always initialize these
   var2 = 45
end
```

See also: The voidP function; the clearGlobals, showGlobals, and showLocals commands; and the globals property.

handle1 *or* handle2

Elements: vertex[[*VertexNumber*]].handle1
               vertex[[*VertexNumber*]].handle2

Purpose: This keyword allows you to easily determine the point of a vertex handle in a vector shape. Handles are points associated with a vertex that determine how the connection line between two vertices curves. Each vector shape has associated with it a vertexList property containing a point for each vertex. If the vertex also has handles, the handles are also contained in the vertexList list. Rather than having to go to the trouble to parse the list, you can use the vertex and handle keywords to specify a particular handle.

In context: This statement shows how to determine the number of vertices in a vector shape:

```
put member(5).vertex.count
-- 4
```

These statement show how to access and set a vertex point:

```
put member("Seth").vertex[2]
-- point(45.0000, 6.0000)
member("Seth").vertex[2] = point(40, -6)
```

You can also use the handle1 and handle2 keywords to test or modify the handles of a vector shape's vertex:

```
put member("Seth").vertex[2].handle1
-- point(11.0000, 14.0000)
member("Seth").vertex[2].handle1 = ¬
member("Seth").vertex[2].handle1 + point(20, 40)
```

Notes: If a vertex does not currently have a handle (as given in the vertexList property), accessing the handle will return point(0, 0). Setting the handle of a vertex that did not previously contain a handle will create the handle.

See also: The vertexList property and the vertex keyword.

item...of

Elements: *expression*.item[*number*]
item *number* of *expression*
expression.item[*number1*..*number2*]
item *number1* to *number2* of *expression*

Purpose: This keyword refers to an item in a chunk expression. By default, items are text units separated by commas, but other characters can also be used (see the itemDelimiter property). Note that to specify a range of items using dot syntax, you must separate the first and last item specifiers by two periods.

To modify a string expression, you must use the put...into (or after or before) command. You cannot use the set command for this purpose.

In context: The following two statements both access the second item in the text of field cast member Explosion:

```
put item 2 of member("Explosion").text
put member("Explosion").item[2]
```

The following statements show some examples of how the item keyword can be used to retrieve or modify a text string in the variable myString. Note how the put command is used to modify the string; also note that Director automatically adds commas (the item delimiter) when necessary.

```
myString = "1,2,3,4"
put myString.item[3]
-- "3"
put "8" into item 8 of myString
put myString
-- "1,2,3,4,,,,8"
```

Notes: You must always use the put command to change the characters in an expression, except for field and text cast members (and then only when you use the dot-syntax versions). The following statement is allowed:

```
member("myField").item[1] = "Martha"
```

The following statements will generate script errors:

```
myString.item[1] = "A"
item 1 of myString = "A"
```

See also: The put...after, put...before, and put...into commands, the number of items function, and the itemDelimiter property.

line...of

Elements: *expression*.line[*number*]
line *number* of *expression*
expression. line[*number1..number2*]
line *number1* to *number2* of *expression*

Purpose: Use this keyword to refer to a line or lines in a chunk expression. Lines are defined not by the display of text in a text field (which may be word wrapped), but by the number of carriage returns (each one defines a line).

Note that to specify a range of lines using dot syntax, you must separate the first and last line specifiers by two periods.

To modify a string expression, you must use the put...into (or after or before) command. You cannot use the set command for this purpose.

In context: The following two statements both access the second line in the text of field cast member Explosion:

```
put line 2 of member("Explosion").text
put member("Explosion").line[2]
```

The following statement uses put...into to replace line 3 with a new string:

```
put "Hello there!" into line 3 of myString
```

Notes: You must always use the put command to change the lines in an expression, except for field and text cast members (and then only when you use the dot-syntax versions). The following statement is allowed:

```
member("myField").line[1] = "Martha is here."
```

The following statements will generate script errors:

```
myString.line[1] = "Martha is here."
line 1 of myString = "Martha is here."
```

See also: The put...after, put...before, and put...into commands and the number of lines function.

loop

Elements: go loop

Purpose: This keyword refers to the previous marker in the Score. The statement go loop will move the playback head to the previous marker, if it exists, or to the next marker if there is no previous marker.

In context: This handler branches the movie from the current frame to the frame containing the previous marker:

```
on exitFrame
    go loop
end exitFrame
```

See also: The `marker` function.

me

Elements: me

Purpose: This all-important self-referential keyword is a key component in behavior and parent-child scripting. It is best considered as a means by which objects can refer to themselves without having to be given specific identities. For a more in-depth explanation of the use of me in parent-child scripting, see Chapter 18.

Although commonly omitted in a handler declaration, handlers that are used as behaviors receive the me parameter when they are called. For sprite behaviors, this provides a means of determining which sprite the behavior is attached to, without hard coding the information into the behavior.

In context: This `mouseUp` behavior uses me to determine properties of the sprite that was clicked:

```
on mouseUp me
    num = me.spriteNum
    -- or
    num = the spriteNum of me
    put sprite(num).member
end
```

An alternative method is to declare `spriteNum` as a property:

```
property spriteNum
on mouseUp me
    put sprite(spriteNum).member
end
```

Notes: The me keyword is used by convention, not because it has a predefined meaning in Lingo. You could use another name to achieve the same effect.

See also: The `new` function and the `currentSpriteNum` and `spriteNum` properties.

member

Elements: member([*memberRef*])
              member([*memberRef*]) of castLib([*castRef*])
              member([*memberRef*], [*castRef*])

Purpose: This keyword identifies a cast member occupying any Cast (internal or external) linked to the currently open movie. The cast member can be specified as a string (the name) or the number of a cast slot. The member keyword is required to access the properties of a cast member.

In context: This statement identifies a cast member by its name:

```
member("Response").text = "Correct!"
```

This statement determines the cast number of a cast member:

```
put member("Response").number
```

Notes: This keyword replaces the keyword `cast` that was used in versions of Director prior to 5.0.

See also: The `memberNum` and `number` (cast member) properties.

menu:

Elements: `menu:` *[name of menu]*

Purpose: When placed in a field cast member, this keyword makes the remainder of the text line the title of a custom menu. Note the use of the colon (:). The menu is placed in action using the `installMenu` command. For a complete discussion on the installation of menus, see Chapter 11.

In context: These statements create a menu named Swifty Choices. The menu contains four menu items.

```
Menu: Swifty Choices
Change Color | changeColor
Fall Down | fallDown
Beam Up | beamUp
Reset | cleanUp
```

See also: The `installMenu` command.

next

Elements: `next`

Purpose: This keyword is a synonym for "the next marker in the currently active movie." The statement go `next` is equivalent to the statement go `marker(+1)`.

In context: This button script moves the playback head to the next marker:

```
on mouseUp
    go next
end
```

See also: The `loop` keyword and the go `next` and go `previous` commands.

next repeat

Elements: `next repeat`

Purpose: Upon execution, this keyword causes Director to go to the next step in a `repeat` looping script. It's not to be confused with `exit repeat`, which leaves the loop entirely. Use it when you want to skip one or more steps in a sequence, rather than modify that sequence.

In context: The following script executes all but the sixteenth operation in a `repeat` loop that moves sprites across the Stage.

KEYWORDS

```
repeat with count = 5 to 20
   if count = 16 then next repeat
   sprite(count).locH = sprite(count).locH + 3
end
```

on

Elements: on handlerName *[argument1]* [, *arg2*] [, *arg3*] ...
                        statement(s)
                  end handlerName

Purpose: This keyword declares the beginning of a handler definition. The handler definition is terminated by a matching end statement.

otherwise

Elements: otherwise

Purpose: When used in the context of a case statement (a compact alternative to if...then statements), this keyword points to the instruction to be followed when none of the listed conditions can be met. It's roughly analogous to the else in if...then statements.

In context: This case construct uses the otherwise keyword to clear a text cast member when none of the test values is matched:

```
on idle
   myTime = the timeoutLapsed / 60
   case (myTime) of
      5 : member("Countdown").text = "1"
      4 : member("Countdown").text = "2"
      3 : member("Countdown").text = "3"
      2 : member("Countdown").text = "4"
      1 : member("Countdown").text = "5"
      otherwise member("Countdown").text = " "
   end case
end idle
```

See also: The case and end case keywords; and Chapter 11.

paragraph

Elements: *expression*.paragraph[*number*]
                  expression.paragraph[*number1..number2*]

Purpose: Use this keyword to refer to a paragraph, or sequence of paragraphs, in a chunk expression. Paragraphs are delimited by Return characters in the text.

Note that to specify a range of paragraphs, you must separate the first and last paragraph specifiers by two periods.

You can set paragraphs only for text and field cast members, not for other strings.

In context: The following statement displays the second, third, and fourth paragraphs of the text cast member Explosion:

```
put member("Explosion").paragraph[2..4]
```

The following statement replaces paragraph 3 of cast member 14 with a new string:

```
member(14).paragraph[3] = "Deck us all with Boston Charlie."
```

See also: The `line...of` keyword.

PI

Elements: `PI`

           `the PI`

Purpose: This mathematical constant contains the value of pi (π), the ratio of a circle's circumference to its diameter. The value is a floating-point number. The number of decimal places displayed is determined by the property the `floatPrecision`.

In context:

```
put PI
-- 3.1416
areaCalc = PI * power(12,2)
put areaCalc
-- 452.3893
```

See also: The `floatPrecision` property.

previous

Elements: `go previous`

Purpose: This keyword is a synonym for "the previous marker in the currently active movie."

In context: This button script moves the playback head to the previous marker in the Score:

```
on mouseUp
    go previous
end
```

See also: The `loop` keyword and the `go next` and `go previous` commands.

property

Elements: `property` *[property variable]*

Purpose: This keyword is used to declare one or more variables as property variables. Property variables can be used in parent scripts and behaviors. In the case of parent scripts, these properties can be points of individuation for child objects derived from those scripts, and they can be accessed from outside of the parent script. In the case of behaviors, properties declared in one behavior are also accessible to other behaviors attached to the same sprite.

Properties can be accessed from outside the parent script or behavior using the the keyword or using dot syntax:

```
the boxNumber of myPostObject
myPostObject.boxNumber
```

Within parent scripts and behaviors, you can access a property by name or by using the optional syntax `me.property`. To access a property in an ancestor script, the syntax `me.property` (or the *property* of me) is required.

In context: This parent script declares three properties and uses parameters to set their values in the on new handler:

```
property sign, color, haircut
on new me, mySign, myColor, myHaircut
   set sign = mySign
   set color = myColor
   set haircut = myHaircut
   return me
end new
```

Notes: Properties can be added to child objects using the setaProp command.

The spriteNum property is automatically set for any behavior that declares it.

See also: The me keyword, the new and setaProp commands, and the spriteNum property.

QUOTE

Elements: QUOTE

Purpose: This character constant represents quotation marks. It's necessary because Director uses quotation marks to define the limits of text strings—so therefore, a way is needed to discern text strings that actually contain quotation marks.

In context: This statement uses concatenation and the QUOTE constant to create a string that contains quotation marks:

```
put "Isn't it" && QUOTE &"Ironic"& QUOTE & "?"
-- "Isn't it "Ironic"?"
```

repeat while

Elements: repeat while *[condition]*

Purpose: When this keyword is used, all the script lines in the subsequent repeat statement will be executed so long as the designated condition persists. The condition is considered to be TRUE so long as *condition* does not evaluate to zero.

In context: This button script uses repeat while in conjunction with the stillDown function to "flutter" a sprite (swapping cast members) so long as the mouse button is down:

```
on mouseDown
   puppetSound "Quick move"
   updateStage
   repeat while the mouseDown = TRUE
      if sprite(15).member = member("Oval1") then
         sprite(15).member = member("Oval2")
      else
         sprite(15).member = member("Oval1")
      end if
      updateStage
   end repeat
   sprite(15).member = member("Oval1")
end
```

KEYWORDS

Note that in this repeat statement, the condition the mouseDown = TRUE, while possibly more understandable, could also be written without the = TRUE portion since the mouseDown function returns TRUE so long as the mouse button is down.

Notes: Use repeat loops with care because most events are not processed while the loop persists. This can make the system appear unresponsive if the loop does not test for user interaction. Also, some properties and functions will not update correctly while a repeat loop is in effect, instead giving information that was current when the repeat loop began. To test for user interaction within a repeat loop, you should use the mouseDown function (rather than the stillDown property) or the keyPressed function (rather than the key function), because both of these are guaranteed to be updated within repeat loops.

See also: The exit repeat, next repeat, repeat with, and repeat with...down to keywords.

repeat with

Elements: repeat with [counter] = [value1] to [value2]

Purpose: You can use this keyword to automate repetitious operations, rather than write a script line for each operation. When the repeat statement is first encountered, *counter* is set to *value1*. The *counter* value is then incremented by 1 for each iteration of the loop until (and including) *value2* is reached. The statements within the repeat...end repeat construct are executed for each iteration of the loop.

In context: This handler moves sprites 5 through 10 a random amount each time the handler is called:

```
on moveHorses
   repeat with n = 5 to 10
      sprite(n).locH = sprite(n).locH + random(5)
      updateStage
   end repeat
end
```

Notes: Use repeat loops with care because most events are not processed while the loop persists. This can make the system appear unresponsive if the loop does not test for user interaction. Also, some properties and functions will not update correctly while a repeat loop is in effect, instead giving information that was current when the repeat loop began. To test for user interaction within a repeat loop, you should use the mouseDown function (rather than the stillDown property) or the keyPressed function (rather than the key function), because both of these are guaranteed to be updated within repeat loops.

See also: The exit repeat, next repeat, repeat while, and repeat with...down to keywords.

repeat with...down to

Elements: repeat with [counter] = [value1] down to [value2]

Purpose: You can use this keyword to automate repetitious operations, rather than writing a script line for each operation. When the repeat statement is first encountered, the counter is set to *value1*. The counter is then decremented by 1 for each iteration of the loop until (and including) *value2* is reached. The statements within the repeat...end repeat construct are executed for each iteration of the loop.

In context: This handler spins a sprite counter clockwise:

```
on spinSprite
   repeat with n = 360 down to 0
     sprite(12).rotation = n
     updateStage
   end repeat
end
```

Notes: Use repeat loops with care because most events are not processed while the loop persists. This can make the system appear unresponsive if the loop does not test for user interaction. Also, some properties and functions will not update correctly while a repeat loop is in effect, instead giving information that was current when the repeat loop began. To test for user interaction within a repeat loop, you should use the mouseDown function (rather than the stillDown property) or the keyPressed function (rather than the key function), because both of these are guaranteed to be updated within repeat loops.

See also: The exit repeat, next repeat, repeat while, repeat with...in list, and repeat with...down to keywords.

repeat with...in list

Elements: repeat with *[variable]* in *[listRef]*

Purpose: This repeat loop is executed once for each element in a list. When the repeat statement is first encountered, the variable is set to the value of the first element in the list. On each subsequent iteration of the loop, the variable is set to the following list element until (and including) the last element in the list is reached.

In context: This handler adds all of the elements (monthly salaries) in a list to return the total (total monthly salaries for the company):

```
on getMonthly
   total = 0
   repeat with current in monthlyList
     total = total + current
   end repeat
   return total
end getMonthly
```

Notes: Use repeat loops with care because most events are not processed while the loop persists. This can make the system appear unresponsive if the loop does not test for user interaction. Also, some properties and functions will not update correctly while a repeat loop is in effect, instead giving information that was current when the repeat loop began. To test for user interaction within a repeat loop, you should use the mouseDown function (rather than the stillDown property) or the keyPressed function (rather than the key function), because both of these are guaranteed to be updated within repeat loops.

See also: The exit repeat, next repeat, repeat while, and repeat with...down to keywords.

KEYWORDS

return

Elements: return *[expression]*

Purpose: Not to be confused with the constant also called return (usually spelled RETURN), this keyword has another purpose: It exits a handler and returns a value (specified by *expression*) to the handler that called the current handler. In other words, return turns a custom handler into a do-it-yourself function, as it specifies what will be given when the handler is invoked.

The return keyword also is a vital component of any parent scripts that contain an on new handler. Each on new handler must return the keyword me to provide a reference to the child object being created.

The syntax of a statement calling a handler that returns a value must include parentheses, even if there are no parameters. This identifies the called handler as a function that returns a value.

In context: This handler returns a numerical result (a simple calculation) whenever it is invoked:

```
on addTip
    global gCheckAmount
    set newTotal = gCheckAmount + (gCheckAmount / 0.15)
    return newTotal
end
```

This statement calls the addTip handler and assigns the result to the payment variable. Note that the parentheses are required.

```
payment = addTip()
```

See also: The result function and the exit keyword.

RETURN

Elements: RETURN

Purpose: This keyword represents the Return key on the Macintosh and the Enter key on Windows systems. This is the key on the main section of the keyboard, not the key on the numeric keypad. This keyword serves the dual purpose of enabling you to test whether the user has pressed the Return key and enabling you to insert a Return character into a string.

In context: This script checks to see whether the user has pressed the Return key:

```
if (the key = RETURN) then
    go to frame "checkAnswer"
end if
```

This string includes a Return character, causing the display to appear on two lines:

```
put "1" & RETURN & "2"
-- "1
2"
```

See also: The & and && concatenation operators and the BACKSPACE, EMPTY, ENTER, QUOTE, SPACE, and TAB constants.

SPACE

Elements: SPACE

Purpose: The final frontier. Actually, this constant (usually spelled in all capital letters) simply refers to the invisible character created by pressing the Spacebar. You can, of course, use a space rather than SPACE, but spaces are often easier to keep track of when the character name is spelled out. When concatenating text strings, you can also use the && operator to introduce a space.

In context: The following three script lines are functionally identical:

```
put "the"&&"happy"&&"hamster"
put "the"&SPACE&"happy"&SPACE&"hamster"
put "the happy hamster"
```

This script checks to see whether the Spacebar has been pressed:

```
if (the key = SPACE) then
    fireLaser
end if
```

See also: The & and && concatenation operators and the BACKSPACE, EMPTY, ENTER, QUOTE, RETURN, and TAB constants.

sprite

Elements: sprite([*spriteRef*]).[*property*]
             the [*property*] of sprite [*spriteRef*]

Purpose: This keyword identifies a sprite specified by the sprite's channel number as given by *spriteRef*. The sprite keyword is required to access a sprite's properties.

In context: These two statements save the current height of a sprite and set the height to a new value:

```
curHeight = sprite(12).height
sprite(12).height = curHeight + 5
```

See also: The spriteNum property.

sprite...intersects

Elements: sprite([*sprite1Ref*]).intersects([*sprite2Ref*])
             sprite [*sprite1Ref*] intersects [*sprite2Ref*]

Purpose: You can use this operator to determine whether two sprites intersect on the Stage. The operator returns TRUE if the sprites intersect or FALSE if they do not. For sprites using Matte ink, the area of the sprite is determined by the actual outline of the sprite. For other inks, the sprite is considered to be the entire bounding rectangle.

In context: These statements provide the same test (using different syntax) to determine whether sprites 1 and 2 intersect:

```
put sprite 1 intersects 2
put sprite 1 intersects sprite 2
put sprite(1).intersects(2)
put sprite(1).intersects(sprite(2))
```

Notes: If *sprite1Ref* is not an integer, the dot syntax version must be used.

See also: The `sprite...within` keyword.

sprite...within

Elements: `sprite([sprite1Ref]).within([sprite2Ref])`
`sprite [sprite1Ref] within [sprite2Ref]`

Purpose: You can use this operator to determine whether the sprite *sprite1Ref* is contained within the sprite specified by *sprite2Ref*. The operator returns TRUE if the first sprite is contained entirely within the second sprite or FALSE if it is not. For sprites using Matte ink, the area of the sprite is determined by the actual outline of the sprite. For other inks, the sprite is considered to be the entire bounding rectangle.

In context: These statements provide the same test (using different syntax) to see if sprite 1 is entirely hidden by sprite 2:

```
put sprite 1 within 2
put sprite 1 within sprite 2
put sprite(1).within(2)
put sprite(1).within(sprite(2))
```

See also: The `sprite...intersects` keyword.

TAB

Elements: `TAB`

Purpose: This keyword constant represents the Tab key on the keyboard. This keyword serves the dual purpose of enabling you to test whether the user has pressed the Tab key and enabling you to insert a Tab character into a string. Although it is possible to manually insert a Tab character into a string (unlike a Return character, for example), Tab characters look similar to spaces, so using the TAB constant makes it obvious that a Tab character is intended.

In context: This construct checks to see whether the user has pressed the Tab key:

```
if (the key = TAB) then
    go to frame "checkAnswer"
end if
```

This string includes a Tab character. Notice that when the string is displayed in the Message window, it is not obvious whether the character between 1 and 2 is several spaces or a Tab.

```
put "1" & TAB & "2"
-- "1       2"
```

See also: The & and && concatenation operators and the BACKSPACE, EMPTY, ENTER, QUOTE, RETURN, and SPACE constants.

the

Elements: `the` *property*

Purpose: This keyword can be used to precede a property name, as well as many functions, to distinguish the property or function name from the name of a variable or object. It is not required when using the dot syntax.

In context: These two statements both access the height property of a sprite. The first uses the the keyword; the second uses the newer dot syntax. Both statements are functionally equal.

```
h = the height of sprite 12
h = sprite(12).height
```

See also: The dot (.) operator.

TRUE

Elements: TRUE

Purpose: This constant, along with its counterpart FALSE, provides a means of making scripts using binary values (0 or 1) more readable. FALSE translates into 0, and TRUE is any nonzero number, though by tradition it is usually 1.

In context: The first two of the following statements set the pausedAtStart property of a QuickTime cast member to TRUE, indicating that the video will not automatically begin playing when it appears on the Stage. The first statement uses 1, instead of TRUE, but the result is the same. The third statement shows that the value returned in the Message window is 1 instead of the keyword TRUE, although testing for TRUE will work just as well as testing for 1.

```
member("QT4").pausedAtStart = 1
member("QT4").pausedAtStart = TRUE
put member("QT4").pausedAtStart
-- 1
```

Notes: You should be aware that although FALSE is always 0, in many instances binary properties accept any value that is not 0 (FALSE) as TRUE.

See also: The FALSE constant.

version

Elements: version

Purpose: When called, this keyword returns the version number of Director currently running. This is the same information that appears in the Get Info dialog box on the Macintosh or in the Properties dialog box in Windows.

In context:

```
put version
-- "7.0"
```

vertex

Elements: vertex[*[VertexNumber]*]

Purpose: This keyword allows you to easily retrieve a vertex point of a vector shape. Each vector shape has associated with it a vertexList property containing, among other elements, a point for each vertex. Rather than having to parse the list, you can use the vertex keyword to specify a vertex by number and then retrieve (or set) the point for that vertex.

In context: This statement shows how to determine the number of vertices in a vector shape:

```
put member(5).vertex.count
-- 4
```

These statements show first how to test a vertex point and then set the point in two different ways:

```
put member("Seth").vertex[2]
-- point(45.0000, 6.0000)
member("Seth").vertex[2] = point(40, -6)
member("Seth").vertex[2] = member("Seth").vertex[2] - point(5, 12)
```

You can also use the `handle1` and `handle2` keywords to test or modify the handles of a vector shape's vertex:

```
put member("Seth").vertex[2].handle1
-- point(11.0000, 14.0000)
```

See also: The `vertexList` property and the `handle1` and `handle2` keywords.

VOID

Elements: VOID

Purpose: This constant represents an indeterminate value. It specifically applies to global variables and properties that have been declared but have not been initialized. You can also use VOID to clear variables that contain lists or objects when you want to free up the memory used to store the element.

In context: This statement removes a reference to a child object `myObject`. If `myObject` is the only reference to that particular child object, the object will be removed from memory.

```
myObject = VOID
```

This statement shows the value returned in the Message window when an uninitialized variable is accessed:

```
put asdf
-- <Void>
```

Notes: Accessing an uninitialized variable will result in a script error. You should be careful to always initialize variables before using them. If you are unsure about the state of a variable, use the `voidP` function to test whether a value has been set.

See also: The `voidP` function.

window

Elements: window *[windowRef]*

Purpose: This keyword allows you to identify a window containing a Director movie and access its properties.

In context: This statement defines the size of the window Brothers:

```
window("Brothers").drawRect = rect(0, 0, 40, 80)
```

This statement opens the window named Brothers:

```
open window "Brothers"
```

See also: The `close window`, `forget window`, `moveToBack`, `moveToFront`, and `open window` commands and the `activeWindow` and `windowList` properties.

word...of

Elements: *expression.*char[*number*]
  char *number* of *expression*
  *expression.*char[*number1*..*number2*]
  char *number1* to *number2* of *expression*

Purpose: Use this keyword to retrieve words from a text chunk. The text chunk can be any element that contains a string. Note that to specify a range of words using dot syntax, you must separate the first and last word specifiers by two periods.

To modify a string expression, you must use the put...into (or after or before) command. You cannot use the set command for this purpose.

In context: The following two statements both access the second word in the text of field cast member Explosion:

```
put word 2 of member("Explosion").text
put member("Explosion").word[2]
```

The following statements show some examples of how the word keyword can be used to retrieve or modify a text string in the variable myString. Note that the put command is used to modify the string; also note that the number of words "put into" do not need to match the number of words being replaced.

```
myString = "Now is the time"
put myString.word[1..3]
-- "Now is the"
put "Don't bother me just now." into myString.word[1..4]
put myString
-- "Don't bother me just now."
```

Notes: If the word number of the word being retrieved is larger than the number of words in the expression (for example, word 300 in a 225-word expression), the value returned will be two quotation marks (""), which indicate an empty string.

You must always use the put command to change the characters in an expression, except for field and text cast members (and then only when you use the dot-syntax versions). The following statement is allowed:

```
member("myField").word[1..3] = "Martha and I"
```

The following statements will generate script errors:

```
myString.word[1] = "Alex"
word 1 of myString = "Alex"
```

See also: The put...after, put...before, and put...into commands and the number of words function.

KEYWORDS

APPENDIX D

LINGO CODE REFERENCE

The following is an easy-to-access compilation of identifying codes and symbols you'll probably use repeatedly in your Lingo scripting adventures. For more in-depth discussion of Lingo terms, check their entries in Appendix C: *A Lingo Lexicon*.

buttonType symbols

These are the identifying symbols returned by the buttonType property:

#checkBox	Check-box-type button
#pushButton	Pushbutton
#radioButton	Radio button

checkBoxAccess

The following values can be set to determine the result of the end user's clicking radio buttons or check boxes:

0	Lets user click buttons off and on (default)
1	Lets user click buttons on but not off
2	Prevents user from modifying buttons (buttons are controlled only by script)

checkBoxType

These values represent styles used by check boxes to indicate they've been selected by the end user:

0	Standard check box containing an "x" when selected (default)
1	Check box containing unfilled black rectangle when selected
2	Check box containing filled black rectangle when selected

Color depth codes

Use these codes to determine or set (Macintosh only) the monitor color on host computers:

1	1-bit color: black and white
2	2-bit color: 4 colors
4	4-bit color: 16 colors
8	8-bit color: 256 colors
16	16-bit color: 32,768 colors
32	32-bit color: 16,777,216 colors

Color palette codes

These are the built-in palettes used by Director. You can check the current palette using the `framePalette` property or set it using the `puppetPalette` command.

`-1`	System palette (System-Mac)		`-4`	Pastels
`-102`	System palette (System-Win)		`-5`	Vivid
`-101`	System palette (System-Win Director 4)		`-6`	NTSC
`-2`	Rainbow		`-7`	Metallic
`-3`	Grayscale		`-8`	Web 216

Cursor codes

These are the cursor designation codes used with the `cursor` command:

`0`	No custom cursor (returns cursor choice to computer)
`-1`	Arrow cursor
`1`	Insertion (I-beam) cursor
`2`	Crosshair cursor
`3`	Thick cross (crossbar) cursor
`4`	Wristwatch cursor (Macintosh)
`4`	Hourglass cursor (Windows)
`200`	Blank cursor (no cursor is displayed)

getError and getErrorString codes

The following error codes pertain to Shockwave Audio cast members retrieved through either the `getError` or `getErrorString` function:

`0`	OK (no error has occurred)
`1`	Memory (insufficient RAM or memory malfunction)
`2`	Network (connection or data transfer problem)
`3`	Playback device (system sound capabilities failure)
`99`	Other

ilk type symbols

These are the symbols used with the `ilk` function to identify the list type (linear list, property list, points, or rect coordinates). Remember: The symbol is not returned—rather, you must use it in a construction like

`put ilk(ListName, #proplist)`

which will return 1 if the list in question is a property list and 0 if it is not.

`#color`	Color
`#date`	Date
`#linearlist`	Linear list
`#proplist`	Property list
`#point`	Point
`#rect`	Rect

Note: All types will also return 1 if the symbol `#list` is used.

transition type p1071

P. 401 sprite (which sprite). ink = effect code
sprite num.

Ink effect codes

These are the code equivalents of the standard suite of Score-level ink effects, settable with the ink property:

0	Copy	32	Blend
1	Transparent	33	Add Pin
2	Reverse	34	Add
3	Ghost	35	Subtract Pin
4	Not Copy	36	Background Transparent
5	Not Transparent	37	Lightest
6	Not Reverse	38	Subtract
7	Not Ghost	39	Darkest
8	Matte	40	Lighten
9	Mask	41	Darken

transparent
sprite(spriteNum). blend = 0
sets it transparent

platform codes

Instead of the many codes that were returned by the obsolete machineType property, the platform property (currently) returns only two values:

"Macintosh,PowerPC"	PPC Macintosh
"Windows,32"	Windows 95, 98, or NT

state codes

These codes return the current condition of a Shockwave Audio cast member when the state property is checked:

0	Stopped
1	Preloading
2	Preloading completed successfully
3	Playing
4	Paused
5	Done
9	Generic error
10	Insufficient memory

For Flash movies, the codes are valid only while Director is running. Possible values are as follows:

0	Not in memory
1	Loading header
2	Header successfully loaded
3	Media is currently loading
4	Media is loaded
-1	Error

traceLoad codes

When monitoring the loading and unloading of cast members in the Message window, these codes can be used in conjunction with the traceLoad property to set the level of detail in the display:

0	No information displayed
1	Cast member names displayed
2	Cast member names, number of current frame, movie name, and file seek offset are all displayed

Transition codes

For use with the transitionType property and puppetTransition command. Note that the codes are limited to the built-in suite of transitions; transition Xtras may provide their own means of referencing Lingo.

01	Wipe Right		28	Random Columns
02	Wipe Left		29	Cover Down
03	Wipe Down		30	Cover Down, Left
04	Wipe Up		31	Cover Down, Right
05	Center Out, Horizontal		32	Cover Left
06	Edges In, Horizontal		33	Cover Right
07	Center Out, Vertical		34	Cover Up
08	Edges In, Vertical		35	Cover Up, Left
09	Center Out, Square		36	Cover Up, Right
10	Edges In, Square		37	Venetian Blinds
11	Push Left		38	Checkerboard
12	Push Right		39	Strips on Bottom, Build Left
13	Push Down		40	Strips on Bottom, Build Right
14	Push Up		41	Strips on Left, Build Down
15	Reveal Up		42	Strips on Left, Build Up
16	Reveal Up, Right		43	Strips on Right, Build Down
17	Reveal Right		44	Strips on Right, Build Up
18	Reveal Down, Right		45	Strips on Top, Build Left
19	Reveal Down		46	Strips on Top, Build Right
20	Reveal Down, Left		47	Zoom Open
21	Reveal Left		48	Zoom Close
22	Reveal Up, Left		49	Vertical Blinds
23	Dissolve, Pixels Fast (not for monitors set to 32-bit color)		50	Dissolve, Bits Fast (not for monitors set to 32-bit color)
24	Dissolve, Boxy Rectangles		51	Dissolve, Pixels (not for monitors set to 32-bit color)
25	Dissolve, Boxy Squares			
26	Dissolve, Patterns		52	Dissolve, Bits (not for monitors set to 32-bit color)
27	Random Rows			

type of member symbols

The type member property identifies the cast member type by returning one of the following values:

#animgif	Animated GIF file
#bitmap	Graphic (opens in Paint)
#button	Radio button, check box, or pushbutton
#digitalVideo	QuickTime or AVI file
#empty	Vacant cast slot
#field	Field (as opposed to text) text
#filmloop	Film loop
#flash	Flash movie
#font	Font
#movie	Other Director movie imported into Cast
#ole	Object Linking and Embedding (OLE) item
#palette	Color palette in Cast
#picture	PICT file
#flash	Flash movie
#QuickTimeMedia	QuickTime file
#script	Lingo script
#shape	QuickDraw shape, vector shape, or line
#sound	Digital audio file
#swa	Shockwave audio file
#text	Text
#transition	Transition cast member
#vectorShape	Vector shape

Window type codes

You'll use these codes with the windowType property:

0	Standard document window (no zoom box)
1	Alert box style
2	Plain box style (no title bar)
3	Plain box shadow style
4	Document window without size box or zoom box
5	Sizable modal document box
8	Document window with zoom and variable resize box
12	Document with variable resizing disabled
16	Curved border
49	Windoid, or palette-type style in authoring

Note the following:

- The value 49 may convert to a fixed-window type (similar to the Stage) when used in MacOS projectors.
- On the Windows side, experimenting with different values may produce other window types. But proceed with caution—you can invoke windows that can't be closed without rebooting the computer.

APPENDIX E

KEYBOARD SHORTCUTS IN DIRECTOR

The following is a compilation of the keyboard shortcuts for Director 7.

TOGGLING WINDOWS

These commands open and close specific windows in the Director 7 interface.

	Macintosh	Windows
Open/close Stage:	Command-1	Control-1
Open/close Control Panel:	Command-2	Control-2
Open/close Cast:	Command-3	Control-3
Open/close Score:	Command-4	Control-4
Open/close Paint window:	Command-5	Control-5
Open/close Text window:	Command-6	Control-6
Open/close tool palette:	Command-7	Control-7
Open/close color palette:	Command-Option-7	Control-Alt-7
Open/close Field window:	Command-8	Control-8
Open/close Digital Video window:	Command-9	Control-9
Open/close Script window:	Command-0	Control-0
Open/close Message window:	Command-M	Control-M
Open/close Markers window:	Command-Shift-M	Control-Shift-M
Open/close Tweak window:	Command-Shift-K	Control-Shift-K
Open/close Align window:	Command-K	Control-K
Open/close toolbar:	Command-Shift-Option-B	Control-Shift-Alt-B
Open/close Debugger window:	Command-'	Control-'
Open/close Watcher window:	Shift-Command-'	Shift-Control-'
Open Font window while Text open:	Command-Shift-T	Control-Shift-T
Open/close Behavior Inspector:	Command-Option-;	Control-Alt-;
Open/close Text Inspector:	Command-T	Control-T
Open/close Sprite Inspector:	Command-Option-S	Control-Alt-S
Open/close Vector Shape window:	Command-Shift-V	Control-Shift-V

PLAYBACK OPERATIONS

These shortcuts can be substituted for selections in the Control Panel. For numeric keypad entries, NumLock must be off.

	Macintosh	Windows
Play:	Command-Option-P	Control-Alt-P
Play and close all but Stage:	Shift-keypad Enter	Shift-keypad Enter
Stop:	Command-. (period) *or* keypad period	Control-. (period) *or* keypad period
Toggle between play and stop:	Keypad Enter	Keypad Enter
Rewind:	Command-Option-R *or* keypad 0	Control-Alt-R *or* keypad 0
Step forward one frame:	Command-Option-right arrow *or* keypad 3	Control-Alt-right arrow *or* keypad 3
Step backward one frame:	Command-Option-left arrow *or* keypad 1	Control-Alt-left arrow *or* keypad 1
Toggle looping on/off:	Command-Option-L *or* keypad 8	Control-Alt-L *or* keypad 8
Toggle sound on/off:	Command-Option-M *or* keypad 7	Control-Alt-M *or* keypad 7
Move to end of movie:	Tab	Tab

KEYPAD SHORTCUTS

These shortcuts can be used from the numeric keypad. For numeric entries, NumLock must be off.

	Macintosh keypad	Windows keypad
Toggle play/stop:	Enter	Enter
Play and close all but Stage:	Shift-Enter	Shift-Enter
Stop:	. (period)	. (period)
Rewind:	0	0
Step forward one frame:	3	3
Step backward one frame:	1	1
Toggle looping on/off:	8	8
Toggle sound on/off:	7	7
Move to previous marker:	4	4
Move to next marker:	6	6
Center playback head in Score:	5	5

MOVIE SHORTCUTS

These shortcuts apply to general housekeeping commands.

	Macintosh	Windows
Create new movie:	Command-N	Control-N
Create new Cast:	Command-Option-N	Control-Alt-N
Open files:	Command-O	Control-O
Close foreground window:	Command-W	Control-W
Save:	Command-S	Control-S
Export:	Command-Shift-R	Control-Shift-R
Import:	Command-R	Control-R
Open sprite scripts:	Command-Shift-' (apostrophe)	Control-Shift-' (apostrophe)
View cast member properties:	Command-I	Control-I
View sprite properties:	Command-Shift-I	Control-Shift-I
View movie properties:	Command-Shift-D	Control-Shift-D
Find text:	Command-F	Control-F
Find handler:	Command-Shift-; (semicolon)	Control-Shift-; (semicolon)

SPRITE SHORTCUTS

These shortcuts perform actions when one or more sprites are selected on the Stage or in their Score cells. When the term *click* is used, it means "click a specific sprite."

	Macintosh	Windows
Move 1 pixel in a direction:	Use arrow keys *(Will not work on sprites with internal cursors, such as text and buttons)*	Use arrow keys
Move sprite 10 pixels:	Shift-arrow keys	Shift-arrow keys
Open the source cast member:	Double-click *(With text boxes and buttons, click the selection border)*	Double-click
Access the Inks pop-up menu:	Command-click	Control-click
Display shortcut menu:	Control-click	Right-click
Record in real time:		Control-spacebar *(hold down while dragging sprite)*
Replace sprite with one from another cast member (selected):	Command-E	Control-E
Delete a sprite:	Delete	Backspace
Find selected cast member in Score:	Command-H	Control-H
Step through script:	Command-Shift-Option-down arrow	F10
Step into script:	Command-Shift-Option-right arrow	F8
Attach a score script to a sprite:	Click area above markers in the Score	Click area above markers in the Score

Sprite shortcuts (continued)	Macintosh	Windows
Apply Extend Sprite: *(Apply to selected range of cells)*	Command-B	Control-B
Apply sprite tweening: *(Apply to selected range of cells)*	Command-Shift-B	Control-Shift-B
Join sprites:	Command-J	Control-J
Edit sprite:	Command-Option-[(open bracket)	Control-Alt-[(open bracket)
Run script:	Command-Shift-Option-up arrow	F5
Move playback head to beginning of Score:	Shift-Tab	Shift-Tab
Move playback head to end of Score:	Tab	Tab
Center playback head in Score:	Keypad 5	Keypad 5 *(with NumLock off)*
Move playback head to next marker:	Keypad 6	Keypad 6 *(with NumLock off)*
Move playback to previous marker:	Keypad 4	Keypad 4 *(with NumLock off)*
Jump to next marker comment:	Command-right arrow	Control-right arrow
Jump to previous marker comment:	Command-left arrow	Control-left arrow
Shuffle back:	Command-up arrow	Control-up arrow
Shuffle forward:	Command-down arrow *or* keypad 3	Control-down arrow

STAGE SHORTCUTS

These key combinations affect the way items are displayed on the screen.

	Macintosh	Windows
Invert all colors on Stage:	Keypad / (slash)	
Black out Stage and its contents:	Keypad – (minus)	Keypad – (minus)
Hide cursor until mouse moves:	Keypad = (equal)	
Cut:	Command-X	Control-X
Copy:	Command-C	Control-C
Paste:	Command-V	Control-V
Select all:	Command-A	Control-A
Exchange cast members:	Command-E	Control-E
Open cast member scripts:	Command-' (apostrophe)	Control-' (apostrophe)
Open script in new window:	Option-script button	Alt-script button
Scroll to last occupied cast member:	End	End
Open source cast member information:	Control-click	Control-I
Ignore breakpoints:	Command-Shift-Option	Alt-F9
Toggle breakpoint on/off:	Command-Shift-Option-K	F9

Paint window shortcuts

You can use these shortcuts when the Paint window of a graphic cast member is open.

	Macintosh	Windows
Undo last action:	Command-Z or ~ (tilde)	Control-Z or ~ (tilde)
Go to next graphic cast slot:	Right arrow	Right arrow
Go to previous graphic cast slot:	Left arrow	Left arrow
Move selected item by one pixel:	Any direction arrow	Any direction arrow
Duplicate selected area:	Option-drag	Alt-drag
Copy selected area:	Command-C	Control-C
Clear selected area:	Command-X	
Paste selected area:	Command-V	Control-V
Stretch selected area:	Command-drag	Control-drag
Clear canvas area:	Double-click eraser tool	Double-click eraser tool
Turn current tool into hand:	Hold down spacebar	Hold down spacebar
Sample new destination color:	Option-eyedropper	Alt-eyedropper
Sample new background color:	Shift-eyedropper	
Sample new foreground color: *(When another tool is selected)*	Control	
Draw with background color:	Option-pencil	Alt-pencil
Zoom In/Zoom Out:	Command-click *or* double-click pencil	Control-click
Create shape with current pattern:	Option-shape/line tools	Alt-shape/line tools
Turn selected tool into foreground eyedropper:	D	D
Turn selected tool into background eyedropper:	Shift-D	Shift-D
Turn selected tool into destination eyedropper:	Option-D	Alt-D
Polygon lasso:	Option-lasso	Alt-lasso

APPENDIX F

THIRD-PARTY XTRA COMPANY DIRECTORY

The following is a listing of companies that produce and/or distribute third-party Xtras. To find out more about specific products, contact the companies directly.

Ballard Davies, Ltd.

4 High Street
Dorking, Surrey, UK RH4 1AT
+44 1306 884411
xtras@ballard.co.uk
http://www.ballard.co.uk/xtras/

Products include: Behaviors (a custom behavior creator) and Speller (for checking spelling in your Director cast members).

Digital Dreams

4308 Harbor Dr.
Oakland, CA 94618
(510) 547-6929
http://www.surftalk.com

Products include: Speech Xtra and XObject (allow speech recognition) and ShockTalk (plug-in for Shockwave). MacOS only; demos are available at the Web site.

DirectXtras, Inc.

P.O. Box 423417
San Francisco, CA 94142-3417
(415) 505-8249
http://www.directxtras.com/
info@directxtras.com

Products include: DirectEmail (lets you compose and send e-mail from Director), DirectControl (controls joysticks or other input devices), DirectSound (uses Microsoft's DirectSound API in Director), and DirectOS for Windows (accesses the Windows operating system via Lingo). Demo or full versions are available for downloading.

Dirigo Multimedia

http://www.maine.com/shops/gpicher
gpicher@maine.com

Products include: Numerous helpful development tools (both Xtras and XObjects) from this prolific freelance programmer, including Progress Copy (enables speedy file manipulation), MasterApp (enables multiple-application control), DisplayRes (enables graphics mode manipulation), AutoRun/AutoStart. Many individual products are distributed by updateStage.

FileFlex Software

http://www.fileflex.com

Products include: FileFlex (a powerful file and database management tool). Free demo and Software Developers' Kit at the Web site.

Media Lab, Inc.

400 S. McCaslin Blvd., Suite 211
Louisville, CO 80027
(303) 499-5411 (800) 282-5361
http://www.medialab.com

Products include: AlphaMania and PhotoCaster (both provide special import features for PhotoShop files) and Effector Set (provides special effects). You can order these from the Web site and download demonstration versions.

Paul Farry

http://www.magna.com.au/~farryp/
    director/xtras/

Products include: OSUtil Xtra (a "Swiss Army Knife" Xtra providing no less than 66 unique functions), CastControl (provides dynamic linking and unlinking with external castLibs), and Style Util (text formatting manager). All products are available for downloading.

Penworks Corporation

PO Box 531, Holderness, NH 03245-0531
(800) PENWORK
http://www.penworks.com

Products include: Precision Xtra (provides pixel-level control over mouse events), Rollover Toolkit Xtra (simplifies rollover creation), Blinker Xtra (creates blinking sprites), DateMaster! (provides calendar calculations and date manipulation), CastEffects! (manipulates bitmap images automatically). Downloadable versions and online ordering are available.

Sight & Sound Software, Inc.

1200 NW Front Ave. Suite 200
Portland, OR 97209
(503) 274-0938, fax (503) 274-0939.
http://www.datagrip.com/

Products include: DataGrip Xtras for accessing Microsoft Access databases.

Tabuleiro da Baiana Multimedia

Rua Conego Eugenio Leite, 1089
Sao Paulo-SP Brazil 05414-012
55–11–2636704
http://www.tbaiana.com/

Products include: DirectMedia (controls video and sound files, including adding cue points), Mpeg Xtra Pro (lets you easily bring MPEG videos into Director movies). You can download products from the Web site.

updateStage

1341 Massachusetts Ave, Mailstop 124
Arlington, MA 02476
(781) 641-6043
http://www.updatestage.com

Products include: MUI Maker (dialog box creation tool with a GUI), MasterApp (for running other applications, including Adobe Acrobat, from Director), PopUp (for creating customizable pop-up menus), and many more. Demo versions are downloadable; online ordering is available.

Xtra Media

3450 Sacramento St., Suite 502
San Francisco, CA 94118
info@xtramedia.com
http://www.xtramedia.com

Products include: ChartsInMotion (converts charts to animated members), Tablemaker (creates a data display window), and AcroViewer (controls and manipulates Adobe Acrobat viewers). You can order through the Web site.

GLOSSARY

AIFF file

A sound file saved in Audio Interchange File Format, which is the preferred format for Director. Usually, the file extension is .aiff or .aif.

active frame

The frame in which the playback head currently resides; the frame displayed on the Stage at a given moment. Also known as the *current frame*.

Afterburner

The now-obsolete application used to convert Director movies into Shockwave-compatible files prior to the integration of the technology into Director itself. Movies converted with Afterburner display the .dcr file extension.

AfterShock

A utility included with Director 7 that generates HTML code compatible with various browser configurations.

alert, alert box

A dialog box that appears on the screen. It usually has only one button for response: for example, an OK button.

animated color cursor

A custom cursor created from a number of graphic cast members that can be animated by cycling through the images.

anti-alias

The process of smoothing the borders of a graphic item by modifying its edge pixels. Anti-aliasing is an option in the Cast Member Properties dialog box.

argument

An item of data passed to a handler as part of the handler call. The handler declaration contains a list of parameters that correspond to the arguments being passed. In Director, as in other languages, arguments and parameters are often used synonymously without any ill effects.

authoring, authoring environment

Running Director while developing a movie, as opposed to playing a movie as a projector or using Shockwave.

AVI

Audio-Visual Interchange, a digital video format supported by Director on the Windows platform.

background

A sprite whose layer on the Stage is behind the layer of another sprite. Since layering generally follows the numerical order of visual channels in the Score, a sprite in channel 1 would remain in the background of all other channels. Do not confuse the background with the Stage itself (which can be colorized).

background color

In the Paint window, this refers to the color that is used to fill selected areas, which is changed via the background paint chip. In the Stage window, it refers to the color of the Stage. For sprites, it is the color that is transparent when the ink is set to Background Transparent.

behavior

An encapsulated Lingo script, which can be applied to a sprite or frame via dragging and dropping.

Behavior Inspector

A window that enables you to monitor the behaviors attached to a sprite. You can also use it to remove such attachments and to change the order in which behavior scripting is executed.

bit depth

A measure of the number of colors that an image can contain; 8-bit color yields 256 colors, 16-bit color yields 32,768 colors, 32-bit color yields 16.7 million colors. By default, color images are imported into Director at the bit depth of the current monitor setting, independent of the true bit depth of the image.

bitmapped type

Type that has been created as (or converted to) artwork rather than editable type.

Boolean

Indicates that a value can be one of two states: 1 or 0, TRUE or FALSE, on or off.

bounding box

The rectangular area that appears around a sprite when that sprite is selected on the Stage. All sprites, even irregularly shaped ones, are contained within such an area. Ink effects relate to the entire bounding box when applied. A sprite with the Copy effect may display the box permanently if the sprite is placed against a colored background.

button

Any cast member or sprite that performs a function when selected (that is, when clicked) by the user. There are specific tools for creating buttons, but any graphic cast member (an image, shape, or line) can be turned into a button.

button tools

The tool palette offers button tools so you can create three different types of custom buttons. See also *check-box button, pushbutton,* and *radio button.*

call

To invoke during performance. A Lingo script line that triggers a handler is said to call that handler. A handler that calls another handler is referred to as the calling handler or calling routine.

case statement

An alternative to *if...then* conditional scripting, which avoids the often unwieldy nested `if...then` statement lines.

Cast, Cast file, Cast library, castLib

A database in which the elements of a movie are stored. Graphics, sounds, text fields, digital video, animations, color palettes, and Lingo scripts can all be placed in a Cast file. Casts can be internal to a movie or stored externally and linked to the movie.

cast member

Any multimedia element residing in its own slot in a Cast window database.

cast member name

Imported cast members are automatically given the names of the files from which they were imported. Names can be added or modified by typing in the Name fields of the Paint, Text, Script, Info, and Cast windows. Naming cast members is optional, but it is good programming practice.

cast member number

This number reflects a cast member's position in a Cast window database and is assigned automatically by the Cast in the order of a cast member's creation or importation. Cast member numbers can be changed only by rearranging the order of cast members in the Cast.

cast member script

A Lingo script attached to a cast member and, by extension, to all sprites derived from that cast member. When a cast member contains a script, its icon in the Cast displays a distinctive icon in the lower-left corner.

cast slot

An individual unit in a Cast database, each a potential address for a cast member. Cast slots are listed and displayed in numerical order in a Cast window.

cast type

The category of multimedia element to which a cast member belongs (graphic, script, text, sound, and so on). Each cast type is indicated in a Cast window by a distinctive icon, or *picon*. See the type cast member property in Appendix C, *A Lingo Lexicon,* for a list of the 20 current cast types.

Cast window

The window in which a Cast file is displayed. A Cast window can have a different name than the Cast file it displays, and the Cast shown within the window can be switched via Lingo.

cell

The box in the Score in which an individual sprite, script, or command is placed; the area created by the intersection of the *frame* and *channel*.

channel

A horizontal row of cells in the Score window. There can be up to 1000 *visual channels*, plus the two *sound channels*, a *script channel*, a *transition channel*, a *palette channel*, and a *tempo channel*.

check-box button

A button in which users toggle an "X" or check mark on and off in a standard box. It is created with a custom button tool in the tool palette or through the use of third-party Xtras.

child object

An entity residing in RAM that was created with reference to a *parent script*. A child object may control physical objects on the stage as part of its scripting, but is not a physical object itself.

color cycling

A special color palette effect. It changes the appearance of a display by rapidly showing each of a range of colors in a sequence. The sequence, and the order of cycling, can be set by the user.

color depth

See *bit depth*.

columns

A vertical row in the Score window, formed by a stack of cells in an individual frame.

command

A Lingo element that refers to a specific action. Some examples of commands are add, beep, and duplicate cast. Also commonly used to refer to any Lingo statement.

comment

A line in a Lingo script that is used to make scripts more readable and understandable. Any text following a double dash (--) will be ignored by Director when the script executes.

commenting out

The process of temporarily disabling Lingo script lines by adding a double dash (--) to the beginning of each line. Director interprets such lines as text comments, not Lingo.

concatenate

The combining of one or more strings of text. It typically is achieved with one of the concatenation characters: & and &&.

constant

A value that is fixed and doesn't change. Director supplies a number of constants, including RETURN and TRUE. Numbers, such as the number 4, and strings, such as "Mike", are also considered constants or literals.

continuation character

A character (¬) used in scripts to allow a long or unwieldy line to be continued on the following line. If the continuation character is the last character on a line, the two lines thus separated will be treated as a single line.

Control Panel

The window that contains Director's playback controls.

crosshairs

See *registration point*.

cue point

A named marker in a sound, QuickTime video, or SWA sound file that can be used to synchronize the file with other actions, such as animation. Cue points are placed in the file by external applications (such as SoundEdit 16) but can be read and tracked by Director.

current frame
See *active frame*.

current palette
The color palette that is currently being used to determine the colors displayed on the Stage if the system is running in 8-bit color depth. The default palette is the standard Macintosh or Windows system palette.

custom cursor
A cursor derived from a graphic cast member (and optional mask), as opposed to the cursors built into the operating system. See also *animated color cursor*.

declare
To define a variable or handler. A global or property variable is declared using the global or property keyword. Local variables (and global variables in the Message window) are automatically declared when they are assigned a value. Handlers are declared using the on keyword.

delimiter, item delimiter
A character that separates elements. In Director this typically means the character that separates items in text (item delimiter). This is the comma by default, but can be changed using the itemDelimiter property. Technically, characters that separate list elements and parameters (commas) and properties from property values in a property list (colons) are also delimiters.

digital video
A cast member category. On the Macintosh platform, digital video consists primarily of QuickTime files. In Windows, it can be QuickTime for Windows or AVI-formatted files.

dithering
A process by which a range of colors or grays are simulated on the screen. Dithering creates the impression of a third color by adjusting the colors of two adjacent pixels; the eye sees the two actual colors as a blend. Dithering is often used when a high-quality image (such as a 16-bit photo) is converted to a lower-quality one.

editable text
A text cast member in which the end user can enter or delete content. Sprites derived from such cast members display a text insertion cursor.

embedded cast member
A cast member that resides entirely in the file space of the current Director movie (as opposed to a *linked cast member*, which appears in a Cast but is actually an external file).

end user
The hypothetical person or persons who will be using your multimedia production. When developing, it's important to make the distinction between options available to you (the creator) and the end user. For example, you can stop a Director movie at any time by clicking Stop on the Control Panel—but unless you add a Stop button to the Stage, the end user of a projector file made from that movie will not be able to stop it.

event
In Lingo, an action that will automatically trigger a script known as an *event handler*. Typical examples of events are mouseUp, exitFrame, and keyDown.

event handler
A script that is intended for execution when a Lingo event occurs. Each begins with the word on (on mouseUp, on enterFrame, and so on). Event handlers are called automatically by Director in response to the appropriate event.

event hierarchy
The order in which event messages are passed to Lingo scripts. For example, news of the event mouseUp is sent first to any primary event handlers, then to scripts attached to sprites, then to scripts attached to cast members, then to handlers in the script cell of the current frame, and finally to movie scripts. The primary event handler will pass on the event message, but when an appropriate script is encountered at any other location, the flow down the hierarchy will end there (unless the message is specifically passed on with the pass command).

execute

Lingo executes a script (or statement) when it interprets and attempts to carry out the script's (or statement's) instructions. Therefore, to execute is to trigger a Lingo script.

external Cast

A Cast database that is saved as a file separate from the Director movie in which it is used (allowing it to be used in multiple movies). External Casts are saved with the .cst file extension. (See also *internal Cast*.)

field

One of two types of text cast members and sprites available in Director. Text saved as a field can be changed either on the fly—that is, modified in the end product by the end user—or by Lingo. Text cast members enable better text display under certain conditions, but they also require more memory.

file extension

The three-character suffix used to identify file types under the DOS and Windows operating systems, separated from the rest of the file name by a period. The standard file extension .dir is used for editable Director movies.

film loop

A cast member produced from a sequence of other cast members. An animation created by a succession of sprites can be encapsulated in a film loop, which, when placed on the Stage, will perform as the original sequence did, but in a continuous loop. For a film loop to function correctly, the cast members from which it was derived must remain in the Cast database.

Flash, Flash movie

A multiframe vector-based animation created with Macromedia's Flash application.

float, floating-point number

A number that includes decimal places, as opposed to an integer. The number of decimal places displayed in a floating-point number is determined by the `floatPrecision` property.

flow chart

A diagram sketching out the structure of an interactive production, documenting the relationship among screens, scenes, and other discrete units.

foreground

A sprite whose layer on the Stage is in front of the layer of another sprite. Since layering follows the numerical order of visual channels in the Score, a sprite in channel 1 would remain in the background; other channels would be in the foreground relative to that sprite.

foreground color

The color designated in the leftmost color chip in the color section of the Paint window's or tool palette's toolbar. Click and hold this color chip to access a pop-up menu from which a new color can be selected.

frame

An individual column in the Score. A frame can be referred to by number (frame 15) or by the name attached to it with a marker (the frame "Central").

frame behavior, frame script

A Lingo script attached to an individual frame by placement in the behavior channel cell for that frame.

function

A Lingo element that provides information on a particular state or condition. For example, the `time` function will return the current time, and the function `the name of member [castmember]` will return the name of the cast member residing at the given cast slot number. Lingo provides a number of functions that can be invoked from any script; you can also design and program custom functions by writing handlers that return values.

global variable

A variable designed to be accessible by Lingo throughout the movie (or movies), not just in the context of a single script. All global variables must be declared with the `global` keyword. Global variables are accessible within the root movie, within any subsequent movies branched to, and within any movies playing in a window (MIAW). (See also *local variable*.)

gradient

A type of fill found in the Paint and Vector Shape windows. The fill does not consist of a single color, but makes a gradual transition from one color (the foreground color) to another (the background color). The shape of the gradient and the proportion of the two colors can be varied.

handler

A grouping of Lingo elements intended for execution as a unit, beginning with the keyword on. A handler can be triggered by events (on mouseUp, and so on) or—if it cites a custom event (such as on getHappy)—by another handler invoking the name of that event as a command (for example, getHappy).

hierarchy

See *object hierarchy*.

highlight

A feature of all bitmap cast members, accessed via the cast member's Properties dialog box. When the Highlight When Clicked check box is selected, sprites derived from that cast member will reverse color when clicked if a script is attached to the sprite or cast member. This feature is often used when the cast member is intended as a button.

host computer

The hypothetical computer (or computers) on which your multimedia production will run. The host computer may be configured differently than those you use for creation or troubleshooting.

HTML

Hypertext markup language; the tags placed in a text file that provide directions to a browser that reads it.

if...then statement

An element of Lingo scripting that specifies actions to be undertaken when certain conditions exist.

in-betweening

See *tweening*.

index

An integer or integer expression that can reference a particular element of a list.

ink effect

Any one of a series of effects that do not modify artwork so much as change the rules by which the artwork is displayed. They can be applied in both the Score and Paint windows.

inks

The group of choices that modify an element's appearance and/or its display relative to other elements. In the Paint window, inks can be used for a variety of artistic effects. In the Score, inks dictate the sprite's appearance on the Stage. Paint window inks are permanent, whereas Score inks can be changed at will.

instance

A RAM-resident object created by a Lingo script. *Instance* usually is used to refer to a child object derived from a parent script, but the term can also be applied to behaviors. For child objects, each instance is a combination of two scripts: the master script (the parent script) and the "birthing" script (the script used to create an individual entity adapted to a specific task).

instance variable

A variable that contains a reference to a child object instance. Such variables are necessary to apply additional operations to the instance.

integer

A whole number; a number without any decimal components. Integers can be positive, negative, or zero.

internal Cast

A Cast database that is saved as part of a Director movie's file (as opposed to an *external Cast*, which is a separate file). Director supports multiple Casts within a single movie. (See also *external cast*.)

keyframe

An individual cell in a sprite's sequence of animation, from which other frames are extrapolated.

For instance, a sprite's linear movement can be extrapolated from two keyframes: one at the beginning and one at the end of the movement.

keyword

A Lingo term used to clarify or further define aspects of scripting. Terms such as the, of, cast, field, and end are all keywords.

kiosk

A software and hardware unit, usually designed for public placement and general use.

lasso

One of the selection tools in the Paint window. It is used to make nonrectangular selections of artwork.

Lingo

Director's custom control language. In this book, this typeface designates the use of Lingo.

linked cast member

A cast member that appears in a Cast database, but is not physically resident in the file space of the current Director movie; instead, it occupies an external file of its own. See also *embedded cast member*.

list

A type of variable that can contain several discrete units of data at once. Each unit (known as elements or entries) can be manipulated without affecting the others. Director supports two types of lists: linear lists and property lists.

literal

A fixed number, such as 4, or a text string enclosed in quotation marks, such as "John Kuhl". Literals are also considered constants.

loaded

A cast member is loaded when it has been brought into RAM. Because the size of a movie may exceed the amount of available RAM, not all cast members are loaded at all times.

local variable

Unlike a *global variable*, a local variable is a data container that persists only while the handler that contains it is being executed. Unlike global variables (or property variables), local variables are created automatically when used and do not need to be explicitly declared.

looped sound

A sound file with the loop property set to TRUE, either by having the Loop option checked in its Properties dialog box or by having the property set through Lingo. Unless overridden by the Score or scripting, a looped sound will play again and again.

looping

The process of continuously returning the playback head to a location in the Score until another action occurs, such as the movement of the mouse or the clicking of a button. Looping is the processing of cycling through a sequence of statements with a repeat construct.

MacOS

Macintosh operating system. This abbreviation is used in this book to refer to all Macintosh and Macintosh-compatible computer systems.

marker

The tabs that can be placed in the Marker area (above the channels in the Score), used to indicate individual frames. Once placed, markers can have names assigned to them as well. Markers can be relocated, renamed, and removed.

marquee

The blinking lines indicating the area selected with the lasso or selection rectangle in the Paint window.

mask

A cast member used in conjunction with a custom cursor (usually a negative or filled version of the cursor) or QuickTime cast member. When the cursor is moved over areas on the Stage, the mask is used to create a solid cursor image. For QuickTime cast members, the mask defines which areas of the image are seen. Do not confuse mask with the Mask ink effect.

Memory Inspector

The window used to display information about Director's current RAM use.

Message window

A diagnostic and "behind-the-scenes" window used in Lingo programming and debugging. Script lines entered in this window will be executed immediately (no need to place a script in the Score). If the Trace option is enabled, the Message window will keep a running text display of actions during movie playback.

method

An object-oriented term for describing handlers within a parent script or behavior.

MIAW

See *Movie in a Window*.

modal

A modal scene is a sequence in a movie that presents opportunities for user interaction. A modal dialog box requires the user to respond before the user can continue interaction with the application. The alert box in Director is an example of a modal dialog box. A typical "Now printing" dialog box is *nonmodal* because it displays information, but the user has no means of interacting with it.

moveable sprite

A sprite that can be moved by the end user. This option is enabled by selecting the sprite's Moveable check box in the Score window or by setting the sprite's moveableSprite property.

movie

A Director file; also used to refer to digital video (such as QuickTime) files.

Movie in a Window (MIAW)

A Director movie running in a window of its own, separate from the Stage of the root movie running underneath. MIAWs can be fully interactive and even pass information (such as commands) to other open movies.

movie script

When a script cast member is designated a movie script via its Properties dialog box, the handlers it contains can be accessed during playback of the movie. Movie-level operations (such as those in on startMovie and on stopMovie handlers) should be placed in a movie script along with handlers called by a number of unrelated other handlers.

NetLingo

Additions to the Lingo language designed especially for scripting in the platform-independent realm of the Internet (and intranets). Because such scripts must interface with a variety of operating systems and other scripting languages, their syntax may vary somewhat from conventional Lingo.

nonmodal

A nonmodal scene is a sequence in a movie that is not interactive, but is intended to be passively experienced. A logo animation and a "Please wait" message are examples of nonmodality. A nonmodal movie or window is one that displays information but cannot receive user interaction. Nonmodal is the opposite of *modal*.

object

Any unit of Lingo scripting that is designed to both receive input and produce a result. Every event handler is an object, since it takes input (the news of an event) and produces something (whatever scripted actions it contains).

object hierarchy

See *event hierarchy*.

object-oriented programming (OOP)

A programming approach that combines data and scripting into objects, which are then used as the primary logical units for constructing software. Lingo is an OOP language.

operator

A symbol or term in Lingo used to perform a specific operation. For example, the asterisk (*) will multiply two values; the greater-than symbol (>) will compare the first value against the second and decide which one is larger.

palette

A collection of colors for displaying artwork on the Stage when a movie is playing on a system running at an 8-bit color depth. Director provides several built-in palettes to choose from, and you can create custom palettes as well. A palette is applied not to an individual piece of artwork, but to all graphic elements on the Stage in a given frame of the Score.

palette channel

The channel in the Score in which palettes can be applied. This channel is also used for embedding palette-related special effects such as color cycling.

Palette window

The window in which color palettes can be copied and modified.

parameter

The elements in a handler declaration that specify the arguments to be passed in when the function is called. Arguments are items of data passed to a handler as part of the handler *call*. The handler declaration contains a list of parameters that correspond to the arguments being passed. In Director, as in other languages, arguments and parameters are often used synonymously without any ill effect.

parent script

A script from which child objects are derived. A parent script contains *handlers* (also called *methods*) common to all objects derived from that script. When each *child object* is created, additional instructions can be given concerning the behavior of that individual object. Ancestor scripts are also parent scripts. A script is made a parent script by changing its type in the script cast member's Properties dialog box.

parse

The process of breaking up a compound object into its individual components. For example, a field cast member may contain text that is actually a list of all the names and addresses of employees of a company. To parse the text would be to extract individual names and addresses.

Paste Relative

A command that copies a selected segment of sprites—but rather than repeat the sprite positioning exactly, it uses the last sprite of the selection as a *keyframe* for the new sprites. Thus, the animation is repeated at a point relative to where it last ended.

picon

The graphic representation of a cast member's presence in the Cast. Usually, a picon is a thumbnail image of the cast member plus a subicon indicating the member's cast type. To this information is added the cast member number and name (if any).

pixel

The individual units of display, each corresponding to a color, black or white, or grayscale dot on your monitor. Typical Stage dimensions for a 13-inch monitor are 640 pixels by 480 pixels, but monitor sizes vary, as do the screen resolution settings.

playback

The process of running a Director movie. For the movie to operate, it must be played, even if the display on the Stage is static.

playback head

The "cursor" in the area between the effects channels and the visual channels in the Score window, which travels through the Score during playback to indicate the currently active *frame*. In Director 7's interface, the playback head is made easier to trace by the addition of a thin line extending from it to the bottom of the score channels. Even when the Score is not visible (or doesn't exist, such as in projectors), movement through the movie is described as "the playback head moves to the next frame," for example.

plug-in

A standard software architecture used to extend the functionality of Director or other applications. *Xtras* are generally implemented as plug-ins in Director. Director can also incorporate plug-ins written to other standards, such as Photoshop standards; they'll appear as menu options in the Paint window.

primary event handler

Primary event handlers are written like other handlers, but are declared to Director in a manner that gives them the first opportunity to react to specific events. There are six events for which primary event handlers can be assigned: `alert`, `keyDown`, `keyUp`, `mouseDown`, `mouseUp`, and `timeOut`. For all but the alert event, primary event handlers are specified by setting the following properties: `keyDownScript`, `keyUpScript`, `mouseDownScript`, `mouseUpScript`, and `timeOutScript`. The `alertHook` property specifies a parent script that contains the on `alertHook` handler. When you set each of these properties to a specific handler, that handler will then be executed whenever the event occurs. Unlike with other stops in the event hierarchy, primary event handlers will automatically pass on the event message unless directed not to with the `stopEvent` command.

projector

A self-contained, self-running version of a Director movie. Once created, a projector file can run on host systems that do not have a copy of Director installed. Unfortunately, although Director movies are pretty much cross platform, a Windows projector must be created with Director running under Windows, and a Macintosh projector must be created with Director running under Macintosh. The new Shockwave player (also known as System Player or Slim Projector, and by other names) should eliminate this requirement for systems that have Shockwave 7 installed.

Properties dialog box

The dialog box in which information about an individual cast member is stored. It is accessed by selecting the cast member and then clicking the "i" button. It is also referred to as *Info window*.

property

An aspect or quality of an element controllable by Lingo. For example, the ink of sprite, the height of sprite, and the foreColor of sprite are all properties of a given sprite. Behaviors and child objects can also declare properties using the property keyword. These properties become available to the movie in a manner similar to that used for Director's built-in properties.

property variable

A variable declared using the property keyword in a behavior or parent script. Once declared, the variable can be used as a custom property. The variable exists so long as the behavior or child object using the property variable exists.

protected movie

A Director movie with the Protect Movies option enabled. A protected movie can be played via projectors and other movies, but it can no longer be opened directly. Since no changes can be made to a protected movie, always make a copy of your movie before using this option.

prototype

An early version of a multimedia production designed to demonstrate the structure and design projected for the final product. In Director, prototypes are often used as structures upon which the final product is superimposed.

puppet, puppet status

When a Director element is puppeted, it is controlled by Lingo rather than by instructions embedded in the Score. For example, a sprite may be derived from one cast member, but when puppeted, another cast member may be substituted. Puppeting is a condition applied to the channel the sprite occupies—not to the sprite itself. Director has implemented autopuppeting, which eliminates the need for explicitly puppeting a channel unless the puppeting needs to continue past the point in the Score where a sprite no longer exists (or to create a sprite in a channel where there is no current sprite). Puppet commands are still used for the special effects channels (puppetSound, for example).

purge

The removal of a movie's cast members from RAM. Because the file size of a movie can be larger than the available memory, cast members may need to be removed from memory (purged) to make room for other cast members that are required. Director always tries to do this in an intelligent manner, removing members not used for some time, but it also uses the cast member's Unload property (as set in the Cast Member Property dialog box) as a guideline. A cast member that has been purged is said to have been unloaded.

pushbutton

A button created with the Tool Palette. It is highlighted when selected, and it is selected by being clicked.

QuickDraw shape

A rectangle, oval, or line drawn with the tool palette tools.

QuickTime

A standard for digital video. To operate QuickTime videos in conjunction with Director, a copy of QuickTime (or QuickTime for Windows) must be installed. Director 7 supports only QuickTime version 3.0 or later.

radio button

A style of button created with the Tool Palette or a third-party Xtra.

real-time recording

A method of recording animation when exporting a segment of a movie to QuickTime. When recorded in real time, any movements of sprites on the Stage will be played back with the same speed and sequence as when they were recorded. (See also *step recording*.)

registration point

The location that Director considers to be the physical center of sprites derived from a cast member. The registration point can be moved in the Paint window and through Lingo; it does not have to be the actual center of the artwork. The registra-tion point enables you to align sprites as they are placed on the Stage.

returns

The response of an element of Lingo scripting. When a function or property is called, it returns a result. For example, the function the `frameLabel` returns the name applied to the marker (if any) of the currently active frame.

Rich Text Format (RTF)

One of two types of text available in Director. Text saved in this format (text cast members) can be automatically anti-aliased and subjected to a number of typographical controls (such as kerning and leading). *Field* text (the other kind of text) does not have as many display options, and its display depends on the fonts installed in the host computer.

rollover

The act of rolling the cursor over a given element on the screen. It's possible to write Lingo scripts that perform certain actions when the cursor rolls over individual sprites.

root movie

The movie playing on the Stage, as opposed to movies playing in windows created by scripting in the root movie (such as Movies in a Window).

runtime

Runtime mode is the opposite of authoring mode. It indicates that the movie is being played outside of the development environment of Director.

scene

A particular unit of animation or scripting that has a discrete identity in the context of a Director movie. For example, "Opening Screen" might be a scene, as would "Help File." A scene may contain a single frame or a multitude of frames. The concept of a scene is useful for mapping out a prototype of a movie.

script channel

A channel in the Score where frame behaviors or frame scripts can be placed.

Score, Score window

The spreadsheet-like database in which instructions and information about a Director movie are placed. To appear on the Stage during playback, a cast member must first be placed in a location in the Score.

Score display mode

Any of several formats for viewing information in the Score window. For instance, the Extended mode displays detailed information about individual sprites, and the Behavior mode displays information about behaviors attached to sprites.

Score-modification script

A Lingo script that assumes author-level control of the Score. Director features Lingo that can add and delete frames from the Score and add, remove, and arrange sprites within those frames.

script

A cast member containing Lingo statements, or Lingo statements attached to a cast member. A script can contain one or more handlers and can be classified as a movie script, parent script, cast script, or behavior.

Script window

The window in which script cast members (and scripts attached to cast members) can be viewed and edited.

segment

See *sprite segment*.

session

A single instance of the end user's running of the Director production. A session extends from the moment the production is launched to the moment it is quit.

Shockwave

The technology used to compress, encapsulate, and embed Director movies in HTML (hypertext markup language) documents, the sort used on the World Wide Web; also used to refer to the plug-in necessary to view such movies in online browsers such as Netscape Navigator.

Shockwave Audio (SWA)

The sound-compression format used by both Director and Macromedia SoundEdit 16. It can be used independent of the Shockwave playback technology

Shockwave player, Shockwave projector

See *System Player*.

Slim Projector

See *System Player*.

slot

See *cast slot*.

sound channel

Either of the two channels in the Score devoted to sound playback. This term can also be applied to virtual sound channels, which can be directed by Lingo to play additional sounds.

sound file

A cast member containing either a digital sound or a link to a digital sound file.

source cast member

The cast member from which a given sprite (in the Score) was derived.

Space to Time

A Director command that takes a selected range of sprites in a single frame and spreads them across multiple frames, using their placement as a cue to their sequence.

sprite

An individual instance of a cast member on the Stage, as documented by the placement of that cast member in the Score. Sprites can display several qualities not shared by the source cast member, but changes to the cast member are immediately reflected in all sprites derived from that cast member. The term *sprite* is used to refer to an individual Score cell containing a cast member as well as to a contiguous group of cells containing the same cast member in the Score. In this book, such a grouping is referred to as a *sprite segment*.

sprite options

Sprite properties in the Score that can be set using the check boxes and pull-down menus in the upper portion of the Score window or in the Sprite Inspector. They include such options as Ink Effects, Blend, Trails, Moveable, and Editable. Most properties that can be set in the Score can also be set using Lingo.

sprite script, sprite behavior

A Lingo script (behavior) that is attached to an individual sprite in the Score. This is done by selecting the sprite and then selecting a script in the Score's pop-up Script menu, or by dragging a behavior from the Cast or library palette onto the sprite.

sprite segment

A group of sprites from the same cast member occupying contiguous cells in a single channel, intended to collectively represent an element on the Stage during playback. Sprites in the sprite segment can vary in position and other properties and still be considered part of the same sprite segment.

stacking order

See *Z-order*.

Stage color

The color of the Stage window, which can vary from movie to movie. It is set in the Movie Properties dialog box and can be modified with Lingo using the stageColor and bgColor properties.

Stage window

The primary window of a movie in Director that represents the action transpiring during playback. The root movie of a production has a Stage, as do any Movies in a Window (MIAWs).

step recording

The process of recording animation (Stage movement) on a frame-by-frame basis, as opposed to *real-time recording*.

streaming Shockwave

The compression technology that allows playback of Shockwave movies to begin quickly in Internet browsers. Playback can begin as soon as a portion of the movie has been downloaded and continues while the remainder of the movie loads. Previously, the end user had to wait until the entire movie was downloaded before playback could begin.

stub projector

A projector containing little content for playback, serving instead to launch movie files immediately after being launched itself. Stub projectors are typically only a single frame long, containing only Lingo scripting to test for certain conditions (such as the end user's monitor configuration) before launching the appropriate movie. Providing one stub projector for Windows and another for Macintosh enables the movies in a project to be system independent.

SWA

Shockwave Audio; sound compressed with the Shockwave technology that can be streamed from disk or the Internet.

synchronization

The process of making multiple elements, such as sound and animation, perform at the appropriate point in relation to each other. Synchronization typically is accomplished through the use of cue points.

System Player

Also called a Slim Projector, Shockwave projector, or Lite Projector. This new standard for projectors enables a projector to use system components (including Xtras) installed with Shockwave 7 on the end user's system. This enables projectors using the System Player option to be much smaller than otherwise, but this feature works only if Shockwave 7 is installed.

tempo

The rate at which the playback head moves from frame to frame in the movie. It can be set from a minimum of 1 frame per second to a maximum of 999 frames per second.

tempo channel

The Score channel where time-related controls are placed. This is where you set the tempo, but you can also use it to introduce pauses (from 1 to 60 seconds long), wait for user interaction, and synchronize frame movement with sound and digital video.

text effects

The means used to modify the display of non-bitmapped text, such as boldfacing, underlining, and italicizing.

Text window

The window in which nonbitmapped text cast members are stored, displayed, and edited.

tick, ticks

The primary unit of time measurement in Director. One tick equals 1/60 of a second.

tile

A design (or portion of a cast member) that is indefinitely extensible in the context of a piece of Paint window artwork.

timeout

The only variable event in Director. A `timeout` event occurs when a given period of time has passed without user input. Both the length of time and the type of user interaction that is considered input can be set with Lingo (see properties beginning with `timeout` in the "Lingo Lexicon"). When a timeout occurs, the scripting encapsulated in the `timeoutscript` primary event handler or an on `timeOut` handler is executed.

toggling

The process of switching from one state (for example, ON or TRUE) to the opposite state (for example, OFF or FALSE).

toggling button

A button that has two conditions: on or off, enabled or disabled. Radio buttons and check boxes are toggling buttons; pushbuttons are not.

Tool Palette

The palette from which certain tools (pertaining to buttons, fields, text, shapes, and lines) are selected in Director. It is called a *windoid* because it is not resizable by the user.

trailing sprites

Sprites in the Score that have the Trails option enabled. With Trails on, the images of earlier sprites are retained on the Stage, creating the sense of a chain of sprites or of motion, rather than simple movement over time.

trails

The evidence of earlier sprites, retained on the Stage even though other sprites currently occupy the channels in the Score.

transition

A special effect triggered when playback moves from one frame to the next in the Score. Transitions can be used to blend a new scene into the previous scene.

transition channel

The channel dedicated to transition effects in the Score. Transitions can also be implemented through Lingo.

Tweak window

The window in which individual sprites on the Stage can be moved a small distance (corresponding to a mouse movement or pixel value).

tweening

Also known as *in-betweening*. The process of automatically filling in the gaps in a sequence. Director extrapolates the motion and position implied by the difference between two or more *keyframes* and creates the appropriate intermediate sprites.

unloaded

See *purge*.

user

See *end user*.

variable

A container in RAM for data generated within a Director movie. For example, the statement `myVar = 2 + 2` would create a variable named `myVar` containing the value 4. Variables can be either local (existing only in the context of a script) or global (containing values that can be accessed by other scripts throughout the movie).

visual channels

The channels in the Score designed to contain graphic cast members, such as bitmapped artwork, text fields, digital video, buttons, and shapes. These channels are numbered, beginning with 1 and continuing on up to 1000 (depending on the Score Channels setting in the Movie Properties dialog box).

XObject

The now obsolete predecessor to Xtras. XObjects are no longer supported in Director 7.

Xtra

A software module that adds enhanced capabilities to Director. A number of these are supplied with Director, and additional Xtras can be purchased separately from a variety of vendors and integrated into the Director authoring environment by placing them in the Xtras folder in the same folder with the Director application.

Z-order

The order that determines the layering of sprites on the Stage. By default, sprites in higher-numbered channels will be displayed overlaying sprites in lower-numbered channels. The Z-order of a sprite can be changed by setting the sprite's `locZ` property.

INDEX